# Check Out RMC's Other PMP® Exam Prep Options

## The PMP Exam Doesn't Stand a Chance

## Additional Self-Study Tools — Flashcards and Exam Simulator

### PM FASTRACK® Cloud Exam Simulator

Designed to simulate the exam in every detail. A database of 1,600+ questions allows exams by Knowledge Area, Process Group, Keyword, PMP, and SuperPMP Simulation. Find your gaps before they find you!

### *Hot Topics* Flashcards

More than 350 of the most important and difficult-to-recall exam terms and concepts are now available in a convenient flipbook—compact and easy to take with you while on the go! Also available in an audio CD format.

## PMP® Exam Prep eLearning Course — Interactive PMP Exam Training

- Dozens of exercises and games
- 1,600+ practice exam questions
- Engaging narrated audio
- Rita's Process Chart™ in an interactive format
- Pre- and post-testing
- Unlimited 24/7 access

**Full Registration $988** per student (180 days)

Study on your own time—you control the schedule!
Satisfies PMI's requirements of 35 contact hours.

**Refresher Course $288** per student (3 days)

Perfect as a supplement to classroom-based prep courses or self-study. Fill your gaps! Earn 12 contact hours.

## Virtual Classroom Training — Project Management Fundamentals

### PM Fundamentals and Tricks

Translate the international PM standards into real-world understanding and applications. Add 3 valuable days to your PMP exam preparation. Attend from anywhere in the world! Earn 18 contact hours.

**RMC** PUBLICATIONS™

web: rmcls.com
phone: 952.846.4484
email: info@rmcls.com

All eLearning courses are offered in English only.

Tricks of the Trade and PM FASTrack are registered trademarks of RMC Project Management, Inc.

This publication uses the following terms copyrighted by the Project Management Institute, Inc.:
Project Management Institute (PMI)® and Project Management Professional (PMP)®.

**PMI** Project Management Institute
Registered Education Provider

PMP, PMI, and the PMI R.E.P. logo are registered trademarks of the Project Management Institute, Inc.

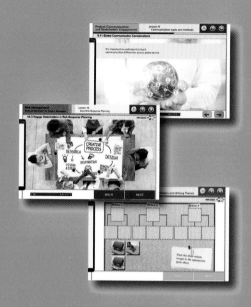

# PMP® Exam Prep

## Accelerated Learning to Pass the
## Project Management Professional (PMP)® Exam

By Rita Mulcahy, PMP, et. al

 RMC PUBLICATIONS™

Minnetonka, Minnesota

Printed in the United States of America
Third Printing


ISBN 978-1-943704-04-0

Library of Congress Control Number: 2017957473

Tricks of the Trade and PM FASTrack are registered trademarks of RMC Project Management, Inc. Rita's Process Chart, Rita's Process Game, RMC Learning Solutions, and RMC Publications, Inc. are trademarks of RMC Project Management, Inc.

PMI, PMP, PMBOK, CAPM, and OPM3 are registered marks of the Project Management Institute, Inc.

This publication contains material from *A Guide to the Project Management Body of Knowledge (PMBOK® Guide)—Sixth Edition*, which is copyrighted material of, and owned by, Project Management Institute, Inc. (PMI), copyright 2017. This publication has been developed and reproduced with the permission of PMI. Unauthorized reproduction of this material is strictly prohibited.

This publication uses the following terms trademarked by the Project Management Institute, Inc.: Project Management Institute (PMI)®, Project Management Professional (PMP)®, *A Guide to the Project Management Body of Knowledge (PMBOK® Guide)*, Certified Associate in Project Management (CAPM)®, and Organizational Project Management Maturity Model (OPM3)®.

IIBA® and the IIBA® logo are registered trademarks owned by International Institute of Business Analysis.

Phone: 952.846.4484
Fax: 952.846.4844
Email: info@rmcls.com
Web: www.rmcls.com

This and all editions of this book are dedicated to Rita Mulcahy.

Her vision made RMC the company it is today. She had a profound influence on so many people—her readers, her students, and, not least, her employees. May we all apply what we learned from her and embody her passion for improving our organizations, our communities, and our world through effective project management.

# Contents

© 2018 RMC Publications, Inc.™ • 952.846.4484 • info@rmcls.com • www.rmcls.com

# Contents

© 2018 RMC Publications, Inc.™ • 952.846.4484 • info@rmcls.com • www.rmcls.com

# Contents

© 2018 RMC Publications, Inc.™ • 952.846.4484 • info@rmcls.com • www.rmcls.com

# Contents

# Acknowledgments

*The following people made invaluable contributions to this book:*

## Subject Matter Experts

Sonja Almlie, PMP, CCBA, PMI-ACP, CSM
Mary Jeffery, PMP

## Project Manager/Content Editor

Tori Turnquist

## Copy Editor

Mary Pat Shaffer

## Production Editors

Rose Brandt
Patti Frazee

## Content Reviewers/Contributors

Barbara A. Carkenord, CBAP, PMP, PMI-PBA, PMI-ACP, MBA
Patricia Henao, PMP, CPF, CSM
Margo Kirwin, CPLP, PMP, PMI-ACP, PMI-PBA
Ursula Kusay, PMP, PMI-ACP
Jean McKay, PMP, MSCIS, PMI-ACP, PMI-RMP
Nah Wee Yang, PMP, PMI-ACP, SCPM

## Additional Contributors

Richard Conniff
Cynthia Holeman
Becca O'Brien Moser
Tim Mulcahy
Tia Picard
Levi Satterlee
Samuel Thulin

# History of This Book

The first edition of Rita Mulcahy's *PMP® Exam Prep* was published in 1998, and at the time, it was the first and only comprehensive resource dedicated to PMP exam preparation.

As a project manager in the late 1990s—as well as one of the world's first certified PMPs—Rita was frustrated by the lack of quality PMP preparation materials available to her and her colleagues. So, combining her knowledge of accelerated learning with her extensive project management experience, Rita wrote the first draft of *PMP® Exam Prep*. Since then, the popularity of the book has grown immensely, through nine wildly successful editions. Today, the book is by far the best-selling PMP exam preparation guide in the world, with thousands of copies in circulation in multiple languages.

Tragically, Rita passed away on May 15, 2010. RMC continues her mission today with the ninth edition of the *PMP® Exam Prep* book, and with a growing line of other project-management-related courses and products that promote her vision of improving the world through effective project management. Available in English, Spanish, and Portuguese, *PMP® Exam Prep* and its related products are used as study tools by many project managers across the globe, and in hundreds of classroom-based prep classes at universities, training companies, and corporations.

© 2018 RMC Publications, Inc.™ • 952.846.4484 • info@rmcls.com • www.rmcls.com

## Free Updates

The purchase of this book includes access to updates regarding the PMP exam, as well as additional tricks, tips, and information to help you prepare for the exam. Access this information at rmcls.com. Have this book with you when you go to the website as you'll need to verify your product purchase.

## We Need You to Help Us Stop Copyright Infringement

As the publisher of the best-selling PMP exam prep book on the market, RMC is also, unfortunately, the most illegally copied. It is true that many people use our materials legally and with our permission to teach PMP exam preparation.

However, from time to time, we are made aware of others who copy our exam questions, Tricks of the Trade®, and other content illegally and use them for their own financial gain.

If you recognize any of RMC's proprietary content being used in other PMP exam prep materials or courses, please notify us at copyright@rmcls.com. Please also contact us for clarification on how to use our materials in your class or study group without violating any laws.

## Contact Us

We love to hear your feedback. Is there anything in this book that you wish was expanded? Is there anything that we focus on too much, or is there anything not covered that you think should be here? We would love to hear from you. Send us an email at info@rmcls.com.

# Introduction to the Ninth Edition

Welcome to the ninth edition of *PMP® Exam Prep*. It's been 20 years since Rita published the first edition of this book. RMC has come far since the publication of the first edition back in 1998, as has the project management profession.

Back when the first edition was published, most project managers were in the United States. Now there are more international project managers than ever before. As a result of this industry growth, RMC's best-selling materials are now sold in three different languages all over the world.

Project management is also a more complex profession than it used to be. Processes have been added, concepts have been expanded, and new techniques have been included. All of these updates have resulted in changes to the exam. There is more to learn today than ever, and this increased complexity is reflected in the ninth edition.

First, the process of managing project knowledge is now covered in the *PMBOK® Guide*. This process includes the management of knowledge and information, and results in the creation of a lessons learned register. We've updated our Integration Management chapter to include this process and to emphasize the concept that any previous organizational knowledge can be leveraged to help produce or improve the outcomes of a project.

Another big change within the *PMBOK® Guide* is the addition of Implement Risk Responses as its own process and the expansion of risk management. As part of that expansion, the Control Risks process was renamed Monitor Risks. We've updated our Risk Management chapter to reflect these changes.

We have also improved our Quality Management chapter by adding updated content, including a discussion of the Manage Quality process, which replaced the Perform Quality Assurance process. The "Manage Quality" section explains all the tools and techniques needed to perform quality management based on a project's quality management plan.

We updated our Resource Management chapter, which now includes both team members and physical resources as well as the Estimate Activity Resources process. Lastly, our Time Management chapter has been revised and renamed Schedule Management.

While these are significant changes, important aspects of our book remain the same. First, and most importantly, is the conversational tone of the book. The ninth edition maintains its down-to-earth conversational style—explaining things simply and clearly. Students say that when they read this book, it feels like Rita is talking to them. In many ways, she still is.

Another thing that remains the same is our continued commitment to helping our students not only pass the exam but also become better project managers. That is what the book, and, in fact, our company, is all about.

As you read this book, know that our plan is not to have you memorize a bunch of rules and formulas just to pass the exam and then promptly forget them. For one thing, given the situational nature of most questions on the exam these days, we believe that such an approach would be unsuccessful. For another, it's not what we're about. This book is not just a prep guide—it's a learning tool. If you master the contents of our book, you will pass the exam, but it's more than that. After you learn what we have to teach, you'll be a better project manager. At the end of the day, that's what the world needs. Still, our goal with this book is to get you to pass the exam on the first try.

I couldn't allow this book to go out the door without acknowledging the efforts of the team at RMC that made this happen. In particular, I'd like to thank Sonja Almlie, Mary Jeffery, and Tori Turnquist for their dedication and hard work on this edition.

Sonja is our leading subject matter expert and Practice Director for Project Management at RMC. She was hired and trained to teach by Rita. Sonja's extensive knowledge base combined with her unique experience of working directly with Rita has allowed RMC to continue updating this book while keeping Rita's voice alive.

Mary was one of the first employees at RMC and worked closely with Rita to create many editions of *PMP® Exam Prep*. Mary's overwhelming dedication to thoroughness and quality—along with her deep understanding of project management—was an invaluable contribution to this edition.

Finally, there is Tori, who served as the project manager and content editor for this update. In addition to being a fantastic writer, Tori brought an incomparable set of skills that allowed her to help develop and edit content with our subject matter experts while also managing the constantly moving pieces of the project. Without her, this book would not have been published on time, if at all.

When Rita created RMC, she did so to help people. That is still our goal and one of the driving values of this company. So enjoy the book, learn, and have fun.

What are you waiting for? Go get 'em.

*Tim Mulcahy*
President and CEO
RMC Learning Solutions and RMC Publications

# Tricks of the Trade® for Studying for This Exam

ONE

## Why Take the PMP Exam?

Preparing to take the PMP exam is a journey. If you let it, this journey can help you expand yourself and your abilities. In preparing for the exam, you have an opportunity to become a better project manager—not just pass the exam. This opportunity to learn is one of the best reasons to get your PMP certification.

To pass the PMP exam, you cannot simply cram a lot of information into your brain and try to retain it just long enough to get through the four-hour testing period. Instead, you need to take your knowledge to the next level. You need to truly understand the process of project management and what value that process can bring to your daily work on projects. The PMP exam is an international exam designed to prove your knowledge and experience in applying the art and science of project management. The exam focuses on situations you might encounter in the real world, rather than just asking you to repeat data you have learned. Achieving the PMP certification is a way to set yourself apart.

In addition to the opportunity to improve yourself and your abilities, there can be financial incentives for passing the exam. A 2015 salary survey conducted by the Project Management Institute (PMI®) found that PMP-certified project managers, across all countries, are paid on average 20 percent more than those without this certification. RMC has had students who received a bonus, a raise, or both when they passed the exam. Other students have reported they were offered a job when hundreds of other qualified candidates had applied, simply because they were PMP certified. Having a PMP certification can be the reason you get a job, keep your job, or are promoted.

## Qualifying to Take the Exam

To take the PMP exam, you must meet the requirements outlined by PMI. The current requirements are described in the following table.

| Category | General Education | Project Management Education | Project Management Experience | | Number of Questions |
|----------|-------------------|----------------------------|-------------------------------|--|---------------------|
| One | Bachelor's degree | 35 contact hours | 4,500 hours | Three years | 200 |
| Two | High school diploma | 35 contact hours | 7,500 hours | Five years | |

RMC offers CAPM exam prep courses (classroom or online training) and a CAPM Exam Prep System of products to use in preparing for the CAPM exam. Visit rmcls.com for more information about this series of products and courses.

Keep in mind that just because you qualify on paper to take the exam does not mean you will be able to pass it. You must know project management and have experience applying it—this includes both managing and leading. Consider taking PMI's CAPM® exam if you do not meet the requirements in the previous table. You can find the requirements for the CAPM exam at pmi.org. At the time this book was published, CAPM test takers were required to have a high school diploma as well as 1,500 hours of experience working on projects or 23 hours of project management education to qualify for the CAPM exam.

## Are You Ready for the PMP Exam?

In RMC's experience, 50 percent of those who fail the exam do so because they have not had project management training that uses PMI terminology and concepts. This is a serious factor to consider in determining whether you are ready to take the exam. Understanding PMI's approach to managing projects is not as simple as reading the *PMBOK® Guide*. Although reading the *PMBOK® Guide* will help you improve your knowledge, it will not teach you project management. This exam prep book will explain the project management process and help you understand it from PMI's perspective; however, if you find that many of the concepts and terms presented in this book are new to you—or you do not use important tools discussed in this book (such as a charter, WBS, network diagram, and management plans)—you probably need additional project management training before continuing to study.

Another large percentage of people who fail the exam do not have real-world experience working on large projects. Instead, they may be managing a help desk or small projects; some might not even be working as a project manager. The PMP exam is designed to identify those who have not had project management training and who do not have experience. It is not an exam for a beginning project manager or for one who hopes to become a project manager. On the exam, it is helpful to answer questions from the perspective of a project manager who is managing large projects. Therefore, the more experience you have had working on large projects with the tools and techniques as well as the inputs and outputs described in the *PMBOK® Guide*, the better prepared you will be for the exam.

The following are examples of large projects:

- Designing a new call center (versus handling small call center projects)
- Designing a new manufacturing process (versus manufacturing a standard product for a customer)
- Installing commercial software across a company (versus installing a PC desktop operating system and associated software updates)
- Designing and constructing a new building (versus getting an existing building repainted)

What is the depth of your knowledge and understanding of project management? Review the following list. Do you routinely experience two or more of the following problems on projects? If so, you may benefit from learning more about project management prior to taking the exam.

- Cost or schedule overruns
- Unrealistic schedules
- Excessive changes to the scope or schedule
- Communication problems and increased conflict
- Running out of time near the end of the project
- Unsatisfactory quality
- Low morale
- Team member uncertainty about what needs to be done
- Excessive rework and overtime
- Too many project meetings

Now think about your project management experience, particularly your experience working on large projects. Review the following list of topics covered on the exam. Do you understand these topics, and do you currently apply the tools and techniques included in this list when working on your projects?

- The step-by-step process for managing projects, including why each step is necessary
- The roles of the project manager, sponsor, team, and stakeholders
- The use of historical information from previous projects
- The use of lessons learned from previous projects as well as the creation of lessons learned for current projects
- What a project charter is and how to create it
- What a work breakdown structure (WBS) is (not a list or bar chart) and how to create it
- How to manually create a network diagram
- What the critical path is, how to find it, and what benefits it provides the project manager
- Three-point estimating
- Monte Carlo analysis
- Earned value analysis
- Schedule compression (crashing and fast tracking)
- Managing float
- How to create a realistic schedule
- Managing the quality of both the project and the resulting product(s) or deliverables
- Developing relationships with stakeholders, and keeping them interested and involved in the project
- What is included in the process of risk management
- Calculating reserves and understanding their relationship to risk management
- Creating a realistic and approved project management plan that you are willing to be held accountable to achieving
- Monitoring and controlling the project according to the project management plan
- Managing change requests, and controlling change
- Considering the professional and social responsibilities expected of a project manager when managing a project

> If you are unfamiliar with any of the items in this list, we suggest you take our three-day PM Tricks of the Trade® in-person or Live Online class. This course will assist you in dealing with situational questions on the exam, and will also give you over half of the contact hours required to sit for the PMP exam. Please visit rmcls.com or call (952) 846-4484 for more information.

On large projects, a project manager does not have time for incorrect project management activities. A project can easily get out of control if the project manager spends too much time solving problems rather than preventing them, or micromanaging people instead of making sure they know what they need to do before the project starts. When preparing for the exam, think about the concepts presented in this book (and those you've learned through your training) in terms of what a project manager of a large, plan-driven project should be doing. This will help you identify gaps between your own project management experience and PMI's approach to managing projects, and will therefore better prepare you to answer questions on the exam.

## Applying to Take the Exam

You must submit an application to PMI to take the exam. Applications may be submitted online or by mail. Submit online if at all possible, since PMI's response time is faster for electronic submissions. In addition, the online application process makes it easier for you to document your project management hours and experience while adhering to the application guidelines. (Numerous spreadsheets for documenting your project management experience are available online, but using one not created by PMI often means you'll end up duplicating your application efforts.) After submitting your application, you'll receive a notice that will confirm your application has been accepted; you will then be prompted to pay for your exam appointment. Once payment is received, you'll receive an email authorizing you to make an appointment to take the exam. You may be subject to an audit of your application before it is approved. Be aware that an audit will delay your authorization to take the exam.

The exam is usually offered on a computer at designated testing sites, but it might be different depending on the country you are in. Your authorization notice will give you specific instructions. The PMI website has information about testing locations and languages available for the exam; visit pmi.org for details.

Once you receive your authorization notice, you must pass the exam within one year. (You can take the exam up to three times within that year; if you fail all three times, you must wait one year to reapply for the exam.) In some instances, testing centers may not have openings for several weeks.

## How to Use This Book

### Be Sure You Have Current Materials for the Exam
Before you begin using this book, you should make sure it's the correct edition. RMC products are updated to give you the most current information available, and take into account the latest changes to the exam. Previous editions of this book are out of date and should not be used to try to pass the exam. This edition of the *PMP® Exam Prep* book is in alignment with the *PMBOK® Guide, Sixth Edition* that was published September 6, 2017, and is meant to be used to study for exams taken after March 26, 2018. This edition also reflects the information in the Exam Content Outline dated June 2015.

### How This Book Is Organized
Most of the chapters in this book have been organized the same way: an introductory discussion, a list of Quicktest topics (generally listed in order of importance), Rita's Process Chart™, review materials, and a practice exam. All page references in this book refer to the *PMBOK® Guide, Sixth Edition*, unless otherwise stated. This *PMP® Exam Prep* book can be used alone, but it is also part of our PMP Exam Prep System that includes our PM FASTrack® Cloud exam simulator as well as our *Hot Topics* flashcards.

### Introduction to Each Chapter
The introductory discussion provides an overview of the chapter and key information for understanding the material covered in the chapter.

### Quicktest
The list at the beginning of each chapter indicates the topics covered in the chapter and our impression as to their general order of importance. To test your knowledge of the chapter contents and to review what is most important, refer back to this list when you are finished with each chapter.

### Rita's Process Chart™
Created in 1998 for the first edition of this book, Rita's Process Chart™ has been greatly expanded to help you understand the process of managing a project. It is a key trick for passing the exam with less study. You will first see this chart in chapter 3, Project Management Processes. It then appears in most of the remaining chapters in the book, with the relevant processes highlighted for each chapter. Use the chart at the beginning of each chapter to understand how the different knowledge areas relate to the efforts involved in the project management process.

**Tricks of the Trade® for Studying for This Exam**

**Review Materials and Exercises**    This book contains extensive review materials and many exercises. These materials, which can be found within each chapter, have been developed based on accelerated learning theory and an understanding of the difficult topics on the exam. Make sure you do the exercises, rather than jumping right to the answers. Do not skip the exercises, even if their value does not seem evident to you. The exercises and activities are key benefits of this book. They will help you pass the exam.

The answers are listed immediately following the exercises. We have found that it is most effective to place the answers right after the exercises rather than later in the book. If you want to keep yourself from seeing the answers, here is a trick: keep a blank piece of paper handy to cover the answers until you have completed each exercise and are ready to review them.

**TRICKS OF THE TRADE®**    Also included in the review material are tricks to passing the exam called Tricks of the Trade® (a registered trademark of RMC). The tricks are designated by the image shown here to the left and will give you some extra insight about what you need to know about project management and how to study for the exam. Many of the Tricks of the Trade® first described or presented in this book have since become industry standards.

    Our method of helping you prepare for the exam does not focus on rote memorization. It focuses on understanding the actions and tools of project management. The few things you should memorize are designated by this image.

**Practice Exam**    The practice exam at the end of each chapter allows you to review the material and test your understanding. Please refer to the "How to Study for the PMP Exam" section on page 14 to understand how and when to use these practice exams as part of your overall study plan. On the following pages, you will find a score sheet to use as you take the practice exams. Make a copy of it for each practice exam.

Note that the practice exam questions are representative of the knowledge and principles tested on the exam. However, in many cases, the exam questions are much longer than those presented in this book. To gain valuable experience answering longer questions, consider purchasing PM FASTrack® Cloud exam simulator, described below.

Please also keep in mind that you cannot simply practice answering questions to prepare for the exam. The questions in this book and in PM FASTrack® are provided to help you assess your knowledge and become familiar with the types of questions on the exam. Make sure you focus your study efforts on reading this book, doing the exercises and review activities, and filling gaps in your project management knowledge.

> The questions in this book are representative of what you may see on the exam, but do not simulate the complete range and depth of all PMP exam questions.
>
> Please see the "Practice Exam" section on this page for more information.

**Endnotes**    Throughout this book, you will see superscripted note references when many project management terms are first introduced. These notes provide the historical origin of the terms or concepts and are explained in the back of this book. Historical origin is not tested on the exam. These notes are provided for your interest and reference. For some, understanding the development of a concept helps them remember it better. For others, such information is a distraction. If you find these notes distracting, do not continue to read them. Instead, focus your study efforts on the primary content of this book.

**Using This Book with PM FASTrack® Cloud Exam Simulator**    This book may be used on its own or in conjunction with the PM FASTrack® Cloud exam simulator. For information about using PM FASTrack® in conjunction with this book, see Plan A under "How to Study for the PMP Exam" on page 14. To access a free demo of the exam simulator, visit exams.rmcls.com.

## Score Sheet

Use this score sheet to test your understanding. Make a copy of it for each chapter's practice exam. (NOTE: If you are using RMC's PMP Exam Prep System, please see the study plan on page 14.)

| Question Number | First Time | Why I Got the Question Wrong | Second Time | Why I Got the Question Wrong |
|---|---|---|---|---|
| 1 | | | | |
| 2 | | | | |
| 3 | | | | |
| 4 | | | | |
| 5 | | | | |
| 6 | | | | |
| 7 | | | | |
| 8 | | | | |
| 9 | | | | |
| 10 | | | | |
| 11 | | | | |
| 12 | | | | |
| 13 | | | | |
| 14 | | | | |
| 15 | | | | |
| 16 | | | | |
| 17 | | | | |
| 18 | | | | |
| 19 | | | | |
| 20 | | | | |
| 21 | | | | |
| 22 | | | | |
| 23 | | | | |

© 2018 RMC Publications, Inc.™ • 952.846.4484 • info@rmcls.com • www.rmcls.com

| Question Number | First Time | Why I Got the Question Wrong | Second Time | Why I Got the Question Wrong |
|---|---|---|---|---|
| 24 | | | | |
| 25 | | | | |
| 26 | | | | |
| 27 | | | | |
| 28 | | | | |
| 29 | | | | |
| 30 | | | | |
| 31 | | | | |
| 32 | | | | |
| 33 | | | | |
| 34 | | | | |
| 35 | | | | |
| 36 | | | | |
| 37 | | | | |
| 38 | | | | |
| 39 | | | | |
| 40 | | | | |
| 41 | | | | |
| 42 | | | | |
| 43 | | | | |
| 44 | | | | |
| 45 | | | | |
| Total Score | First Time | | Second Time | |

How will I improve how I take the exam next time?

© 2018 RMC Publications, Inc.™ • 952.846.4484 • info@rmcls.com • www.rmcls.com

## Other Materials to Use to Study for the PMP Exam

You can use this book as a stand-alone prep tool or combine it with the following products for a comprehensive exam prep experience. Do not risk overstudying or confusing yourself by using other prep books or products beyond the following resources.

### Rita Mulcahy's™ PM FASTrack® Cloud Exam Simulator

Our PM FASTrack® Cloud exam simulator offers over 1,600 questions—including tricky situational questions with more than one "right" answer. In addition to this book, PM FASTrack® is the most important tool for passing the exam. The online subscription allows you to create sample exams by knowledge area, process group, keyword, PMP simulation, and even super PMP simulation. It also saves you a huge amount of time by automatically scoring and keeping records of exams, and it includes comprehensive grading and reporting capabilities. All questions are cross-referenced with this book or the *PMBOK® Guide*, making it easy to go back to the topics on which you need more studying.

### Rita Mulcahy's™ *Hot Topics* Flashcards (Hard Copy or Audio CD)

Are you looking for a way to prepare for the PMP exam that fits into your busy schedule? Now you can study at the office, on a plane, or even in your car with RMC's portable and extremely valuable *Hot Topics* flashcards—in hard copy or audio CD format. Over 300 of the most important and difficult-to-recall PMP exam–related terms and concepts are now available for study as you drive, fly, or take your lunch break. Add instant mobility to your study routine.

### PMP® Exam Prep eLearning Course

This self-directed eLearning course for the PMP exam offers bite-size mobile-friendly interactive lessons, hundreds of audio clips, dozens of exercises and games, digital *Hot Topics* flashcards, unlimited timed and scored practice exams with the PM FASTrack® exam simulator, and all 35 contact hours necessary to apply to sit for the PMP exam. It also includes a comprehensive document library along with an abridged digital copy of this exam prep book.

## Instructor-Led PMP® Exam Prep Courses

For those who learn more easily in a person-to-person interactive environment, RMC regularly schedules a variety of instructor-led exam prep classes as well as live virtual courses. All courses were originally designed by Rita Mulcahy to prepare you for the PMP exam in a fun and effective way—with minimal studying after class. For more information or to find a class near you, go to rmcls.com.

## *PMBOK® Guide, Sixth Edition*

The *PMBOK® Guide, Sixth Edition* (2017), is the international standard for project management from PMI.

## What Is the PMP Exam Like?

Keep in mind three important things about the PMP exam. First, the exam is not a test of the information in the *PMBOK® Guide*. Second, you cannot rely only on real-world experience. Third, training in professional project management that is aligned with the *PMBOK® Guide* is critical.

The exam includes 200 multiple-choice questions with four answer choices per question. The exam must be completed in four hours. Twenty-five (25) of the 200 exam questions are experimental questions, meaning they are not included in your score for the exam. These questions will be randomly placed throughout the exam. You will not know which ones are which. The experimental questions are included by PMI to validate questions for future inclusion in their master database. Your score will be calculated based on your response to the remaining 175 questions. PMI has not published what it considers to be a passing score. Based on the exam history, however, we estimate that it is somewhere between 65 and 69 percent (about 114 to 121 questions out of 175 answered correctly).

The questions are randomly generated from a database containing hundreds of questions. The questions may jump from topic to topic, and a single question may integrate multiple concepts. You get one point for each correct answer. There is no penalty for wrong answers.

The following table breaks out the percentage of scored questions currently on the exam in each process group.

| Project Management Process Group | Percentage of Questions |
| --- | --- |
| Project initiating | 13% |
| Project planning | 24% |
| Project executing | 31% |
| Project monitoring and controlling | 25% |
| Project closing | 7% |

PMI occasionally makes changes to aspects of the exam, including the qualification requirements, the application process, the passing score, and the breakdown of questions in each process group. For the latest information, please visit pmi.org and read your authorization notice carefully. Any differences between what is listed here and what is communicated by PMI should be resolved in favor of PMI's information.

The following diagram indicates the topics tested on the exam along with their level of difficulty. For many people, the most difficult areas are project management processes, procurement management, risk management, quality management, and integration management. This information is based on our own research, in which we asked students preparing to take the exam to identify which knowledge areas they find to be the most difficult.

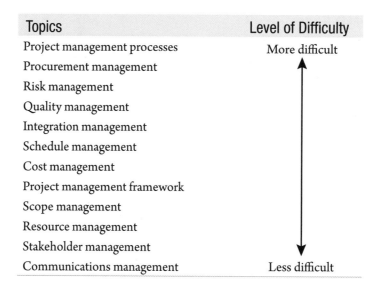

| Topics | Level of Difficulty |
|---|---|
| Project management processes | More difficult |
| Procurement management | |
| Risk management | |
| Quality management | |
| Integration management | |
| Schedule management | |
| Cost management | |
| Project management framework | |
| Scope management | |
| Resource management | |
| Stakeholder management | |
| Communications management | Less difficult |

This next diagram indicates the level of difficulty of the process groups. Many people find project monitoring and controlling, executing, and initiating to be the most difficult. Make sure you study these carefully.

| Project Management Process Group | Level of Difficulty |
|---|---|
| Project monitoring and controlling | More difficult |
| Project executing | |
| Project planning | |
| Project initiating | |
| Project closing | Less difficult |

Be aware of the following for the PMP exam:

- The exam tests knowledge, application, and analysis. This makes the exam more than a test of memory. You must know how to apply the information in this book and be able to analyze situations involving this information. Do not expect the exam to have all straightforward, definition-type questions.

- It is important to realize that the exam deals with real-world use of project management. The majority of the questions are situational. For those who have not used project management tools in the real world—or whose project management efforts include common errors—these questions can be extremely difficult.

- There may be instances on the exam where the same data is used for multiple questions, such as with network diagram questions.

- Although it often feels like more for the test taker, historically there have been only 10 to 12 questions requiring you to identify inputs or outputs from the *PMBOK® Guide*. To answer these questions correctly, however, you need to know more than just the input and output names: you need to understand the processes involved and how the inputs feed into and the outputs result from the processes. (Inputs and outputs are discussed in later chapters.)

- Expect 15 to 20 formula-related calculations on the exam.

- Expect 10 to 15 earned-value questions on the exam. Not all of these require calculations using the formulas.

- Most acronyms will be spelled out (for example, the exam typically uses the full term "work breakdown structure" rather than "WBS"), but you should know both the acronym and the full term.
- The correct answers should not include direct quotations from the *PMBOK® Guide*.
- Most people feel uncertain about only 40 or fewer of the 200 questions on the exam.
- Many people need about three hours to finish the first pass through the exam; they then spend the rest of the time reviewing their answers.

The questions on the exam are mostly situational, many are ambiguous and wordy, and some even seem like they have two or more right answers. Be prepared for the following types of questions so you will not waste time or be caught off guard when you are taking the exam.

1. **Situational questions** These questions demonstrate why having project management experience is critical to passing this exam. Such questions require you to integrate your real-world experience and your knowledge of the exam concepts. For example:

   *Question*   You receive notification that a major item you are purchasing for a project will be delayed. What is the best thing to do?

       A. Replan your project to accommodate this delay.
       B. Notify your manager.
       C. Let the customer know about it, and talk over options.
       D. Meet with the team, and identify alternatives.

   *Answer*   D

2. **Questions with two or more right answers** Questions that appear to have two, three, or even four right answers are a major complaint from many test takers. Many questions will list several choices that could reasonably be done, or that less-experienced or less-qualified project managers would be likely to choose.

   As you go through questions and review the answers in this book (or in PM FASTrack® for PMP Exam Prep System users), look for questions you think have more than one right answer and try to figure out why you think multiple choices are correct. We have intentionally included such questions in our products to give you exposure to the types of questions you will see on the exam; we provide explanations to help you understand why your right answer may not be the best choice.

   Let's look again at the previous situational question. Couldn't we really do all of the choices? The right answer is certainly D, but isn't it also correct to tell the customer? Yes, but that is not the first thing to do. Essentially this question is really saying, "What is the best thing to do next?" As you answer practice questions, keep in mind the concept of the "best thing to do next" to help you decide which answer identifies the next step in proper project management.

3. **Questions with extraneous information** It is important to realize that not all information included in a question will be relevant. For example, the numbers in the following question are extraneous data.

   *Question*   Experience shows that each time you double the production of doors, unit costs decrease by 10 percent. Based on this, the company determines that production of 3,000 doors should cost $21,000. This case illustrates:

       A. Learning cycle
       B. Law of diminishing returns
       C. 80/20 rule
       D. Parametric cost estimating

   *Answer*   D

Many questions will be much longer than the previous example. But again, you may not need all the information presented to answer the question. For example, imagine we changed the previous question to include even more information.

> *"Your company is a major manufacturer of doors and has received numerous awards for quality. As the head of the manufacturing department, you have 230 people reporting to you on 23 different projects. Experience shows that each time you double the production of doors, unit costs decrease by 10 percent. Based on this, the company determines that production of 3,000 doors should cost $21,000. This case illustrates . . ."*

Can you see how the additional data does not change the intent of what is being presented in the question? The data is a distractor. On the exam, you will see data that is not needed to answer the question. The trick is to look at each question to determine what the question is asking—rather than getting lost in all the information provided. Then, you can determine what information to focus on to select the best answer to the question. Do not get upset if you have difficulty with these long questions. For computer-based exams, PMI has added strikethrough and highlight features so you can highlight relevant information and strike through unneeded data. Pay attention to how many times you read questions and answers. A Trick of the Trade® is to read a question once and then organize the data using the strikethrough and highlight tools in order to answer the question during your first read-through. If you are not sure of the answer, mark the question and come back to it later; note that your highlight and strikethrough notations will still be there. If you know you will not answer all questions during your first read-through, you know what to expect. You will stay calm and not lose confidence when you see such questions.

4. **Questions using made-up terms** Many people taking the exam expect that all the terms used as choices should mean something. But that's not the case. The exam often includes made-up terms. If you consider yourself well trained and see a term on the exam that you do not know, chances are it is not the right answer. For example:

   *Question*  The ongoing definition of a project as more information becomes available to the team is called:

   A. Scope validation
   B. Strategic planning
   C. Progressive elaboration
   D. Quantitative elaboration

   *Answer*  C

In this question, "quantitative elaboration" (choice D) is not a real project management term.

5. **Questions where understanding is important** Let's look at the following question:

   *Question*  The process of decomposing deliverables into smaller, more manageable components is complete when:

   A. Project justification has been established.
   B. Change requests have occurred.
   C. Cost estimates can be developed for each work element.
   D. Each work element is found in the WBS dictionary.

   *Answer*  C

In order to answer this question, you must understand the terms used, including the concept of decomposition and what value this technique has in the project management process.

6. **Questions with a new approach to a known topic** There will be many instances where you understand the topic, but have never thought about it in the way the question describes. For example:

*Question* In a matrix organization, information dissemination is most likely to be effective when:

  A. Information flows both horizontally and vertically.
  B. The communication flows are kept simple.
  C. There is an inherent logic in the type of matrix chosen.
  D. Project managers and functional managers socialize.

*Answer* A

Many people know what a matrix organization is but have not taken the time to consider how this organizational structure affects the directions in which information is shared.

7. **Questions with more than one item in each choice** Let's look at the following example:

*Question* The seller on the project has presented the project manager with a formal notification that the seller has been damaged by the buyer's activities. The seller claims that the buyer's slow response to requested approvals has delayed the project and has caused the seller unexpected expense. The first things the project manager should do are:

  A. Collect all relevant data, send the data to the company attorney, and consult with the attorney about legal actions.
  B. Review the contract for specific agreed-upon terms that relate to the issue, see if there is a clear response, and consult an attorney if needed.
  C. Review the procurement statement of work for requirements, send a receipt of claim response, and meet to resolve the issue without resorting to legal action if possible.
  D. Hold a meeting with the team to review why the acceptances have been late, make a list of the specific reasons, and correct those reasons.

*Answer* B

These questions can seem hard until you apply this little trick: use the process of elimination, one item at a time. Consider the first item listed in each choice and eliminate the choices that contain an implausible first item. Then look at the second item in each remaining choice and eliminate any implausible choices. Keep going until you have only one choice remaining.

Watch out; sometimes the items in each choice show a flow or process. See the following example:

*Question* When managing a project, which of the following is the best order to deal with problems that arise?

  A. Go to the team, go to management, go to resource managers
  B. Go to resource managers, go to management, go to the customer
  C. Handle it yourself, go to the customer, go to management
  D. Resolve problems with resources you control, go to resource managers, go to the customer

*Answer* D

In this case, you need to look at each choice independently to see if the process listed is correct.

13

8. **Excessively wordy questions**  Instead of saying, "The project is behind schedule," the exam might use wordier phrasing, such as, "The project float was zero and has recently gone to negative 2." Instead of saying, "The team is not reporting properly," the exam could say, "The team has lost sight of the communications management plan." The first step in answering many questions is to determine what the question is asking, and then to translate the wordy phrasing. If you are not a native English speaker, this can be an especially big problem, but it is also difficult for native English speakers. Just take your time, and practice reading wordy questions before you take the exam.

See chapter 15 of this book for more information on the exam and additional help in assimilating the information provided throughout this book.

## How to Study for the PMP Exam

Some people believe you need to read every resource available and spend as much time as possible preparing for the PMP exam. Do not make that mistake. You should not read every book you can find, and there is a risk in overstudying. Instead, we recommend the approach outlined in the following sections.

### The Magic Three
Studies have shown that if you visit a topic three times, you will remember it. Therefore, you should read this book once and then skim through it two more times, focusing most on the activities you do not do in the real world and on the concepts you have trouble understanding.

### Be in Test-Taking Mode
The actual exam will not present questions in order based on process groups. Get used to jumping from one topic to another. You'll also need to practice answering questions for four hours. You can do this by skipping all practice exams until you feel ready to answer the questions. Then take all practice exams in one sitting (see step 4 in plan B later in this chapter). Do not underestimate the physical, mental, and emotional aspects of taking an exam lasting that long. You can also get into test-taking mode using our PM FASTrack® exam simulator.

### Your Step-by-Step Study Plan
We recommend that you use one of the following study plans. Follow Plan A if you own RMC's complete PMP Exam Prep System. Follow Plan B if you do not own the entire system.

### Plan A: Using This Book with the PMP Exam Prep System *(PMP® Exam Prep* book, PM FASTrack® Cloud Exam Simulator, and *Hot Topics* Flashcards)

One common mistake made by people who purchase the PMP Exam Prep System is to spend most of their time answering question after question in PM FASTrack®, thinking that will prepare them to pass the exam. This approach won't work. As we mentioned earlier, you need to focus your study efforts on reading this book, completing the exercises and review activities, and filling the gaps in your project management experience. To do this, follow the steps listed here to study this book in conjunction with using PM FASTrack® and the *Hot Topics* flashcards:

1. Read this book for the first time and complete all the exercises, but don't do the practice exams at the end of each chapter. Spend more time on the areas where you have the most gaps in your knowledge or real-life project management experience, and on items you did not know or did not do prior to beginning this course of study. Refer to Rita's Process Chart™ for each chapter, and be sure you

© 2018 RMC Publications, Inc.™ • 952.846.4484 • info@rmcls.com • www.rmcls.com

understand all the efforts involved in the knowledge areas you are working on. At the same time, skim through the corresponding chapter in the *PMBOK® Guide* to get an understanding of the flow of the processes.

2. As you finish each chapter, review the Quicktest terms listed on the first page of the chapter to make sure you know the meaning of each term or concept. Use the *Hot Topics* flashcards to improve recall and test your understanding of that chapter.

3. If it is at all possible, form a study group after you have read the book for the first time on your own. This will actually make your study time shorter and more effective. You will be able to ask someone questions, and the studying (and celebrating afterward) will be more fun. A study group should consist of only three or four people. (See the "How to Use This Book in a Study Group" section later in this chapter.)

4. Skim through this book again.

5. Make sure you really know the material, and then take a full exam simulation on PM FASTrack®. This step will give you a baseline against which to track your progress as you continue to study.

   WARNING: You should limit yourself to no more than two full exam simulations before you take the actual exam. Otherwise, you diminish the value of PM FASTrack® by memorizing questions and answers that will not be presented in the exact same way on the exam.

   WARNING: If you do not score over 70 percent the first time you take a full exam simulation (not just an individual knowledge area or process group exam), you may need a refresher in core project management concepts. If you have taken a basic project management class, review the materials you received from that class. If you have not had such a class, consider taking one.

6. Review each question you got wrong in PM FASTrack®, writing down the specific reasons for each wrong answer. Assess why the correct choice is correct and why the other answers are wrong.

7. Use your list of why you got each question wrong (from step 6) to determine which material to study further. This will help you determine how much more study time you need and which chapters to read more carefully. Continue to study this book, focusing on the areas in which you have gaps in your knowledge and skimming the sections or chapters on which you did well. Correct any errors in your understanding of the concepts discussed in this book. Review the *PMBOK® Guide* to focus on these gaps. And remember, think large project and how proper project management should be done, regardless of how you manage your projects in the real world.

8. If you had difficulty with certain knowledge areas, process groups, or concepts and you have studied your gap areas, you may want to answer a small sample of questions (no more than 20) using the Knowledge Area, Process Group, or Keyword function in PM FASTrack®. Analyze why you answered any questions wrong, and continue to study your gap areas.

   WARNING: You might be tempted to answer more than 20 questions, but that number should be sufficient to help you assess whether you have progressed in the particular knowledge area, process group, or concept—or whether you need to study more. Answering more than 20 questions in a particular area can diminish the value of PM FASTrack® and will not prepare you properly for the breadth of the exam experience.

9. Take your final PMP simulation exam. You should score over 75 percent before you take the real exam. You are overusing PM FASTrack® if you see many of the questions repeated.

10. Use the *Hot Topics* flashcards and other materials to retain the information you have learned until you take the exam.

11. PASS THE EXAM!

### Plan B: Using This Book as a Stand-Alone

1. Read this book for the first time and complete all exercises, but don't do the practice exams at the end of each chapter. Spend more time on the areas where you have the most gaps in your knowledge or your real-life project management experience, and on items you did not know or did not do prior to beginning this course of study. Refer to Rita's Process Chart™ for each chapter, and be sure you understand all the efforts involved in the knowledge areas you are working on. At the same time, skim through the corresponding chapter in the *PMBOK® Guide* to get an understanding of the flow of the processes.

2. As you finish each chapter, review the Quicktest terms listed on the first page of the chapter to make sure you know the meaning of each term or concept.

3. If it is at all possible, form a study group after you have read the book for the first time on your own. This will actually make your study time shorter and more effective. You will be able to ask someone questions, and the studying (and celebrating afterward) will be more fun. A study group should consist of only three or four people. (See the "How to Use This Book in a Study Group" section later in this chapter.)

4. Once you feel confident about the material, take the practice exams at the end of each chapter in one sitting. This will give you a baseline to tell you how much you have learned. It will also help you determine how much additional study time you need and which chapters to read more carefully.

5. Review each question you got wrong in the chapter practice exams, writing down the specific reasons for each wrong answer on the Score Sheet that is provided in this chapter. Assess why the correct choice is correct and why the other answers are wrong. Continue to study this book, focusing on the areas in which you have gaps in your knowledge and skimming the sections or chapters on which you did well. Correct any errors in your understanding of the concepts discussed in this book. Review the *PMBOK® Guide* to focus on these gaps.

   WARNING: If you do not score 70 percent or higher overall on the chapter practice exams, you may need a refresher in core project management concepts. If you have taken a basic project management class, review the materials you received from that class. If you have not had such a class, consider taking one. You cannot rely on these practice questions alone to prepare you for the exam.

6. Make sure you really know the material, and then retake the practice exams in the book. As with step 5, use the Score Sheet to identify in writing the specific, not general, reason you got each question wrong.

7. Use your list of why you got each question wrong (from step 6) to determine which material to study further, and then study this material. Remember, think large project and how proper project management should be done, regardless of how you manage your projects in the real world. Make sure you are confident you have filled your gaps before taking the exam.

8. PASS THE EXAM!

## How to Use This Book in a Study Group

To get started, pick someone to lead the discussion of each chapter (preferably someone who is not comfortable with the chapter, because the presenter often learns and retains the most in the group). Each time you meet, go over questions about topics you do not understand and review the hot topics on the exam using the *Hot Topics* flashcards, if you have them. Most groups meet for one hour per chapter. Either independently or with your study group, do further research on questions you do not understand or answered incorrectly.

Each member of the study group should have their own copy of this book, which provides exercises, homework, and even class activities. (Please note that it is a violation of international copyright laws to make copies of the material in this book or to create derivative works from this copyrighted book.)

## Recurring Themes—PMI-isms to Know for the PMP Exam

RMC has been helping people pass the PMP exam and become better project managers for more than 20 years. During that time, we have developed the following list of things that the exam emphasizes but that many project managers do not know. We suggest you read it now and then remember to reread it before you take the actual exam. Rita coined the term "PMI-isms" to refer to the things uniquely emphasized on the exam. Understanding PMI-isms will help you pick the best answer from what seems like more than one correct answer. Some of the topics are listed only here, and others are summarized here and described in more detail later in this book. For the exam, assume that you have (or do) all the following and that these items are true for your projects. As you review the list of PMI-isms here, place a check mark next to the ones that are true for your projects.

| General PMI-isms | Place ✓ Here If It's True of Your Projects |
| --- | --- |
| Project managers are the center of the project universe. Without a skilled project manager, a project is destined to fail. With a person educated in the skills of project management, regardless of title (whether they carry the title of project manager or not), a project will succeed. | |
| The project manager puts the best interests of the project first—not their own interests. | |
| The exam generally tests from the perspective of a project manager who understands the value of the tools and techniques of project management and knows how to adapt them to a large project. So, it's helpful to assume, unless stated otherwise, that the project manager is working on a large project that involves more than 200 people from many countries, will take at least one year to complete, has never been done before in the organization, and has a budget of $10 million or more. | |
| Project managers have all the power described in the *PMBOK® Guide* and perform all the stated activities in the real world. | |
| The project manager is assigned during project initiating, not later in the life of the project. | |
| The project manager understands the process of project management (i.e., what to do first, second, etc., and why). (For more on this, see Rita's Process Chart™ and Rita's Process Game™ in the Project Management Processes chapter.) | |
| Organizations have a formal project selection process, and they always choose projects based on how well those projects meet the organization's strategic goals. | |
| The project manager always knows why their project was selected by management, and they make sure those objectives and the business case are met while planning and managing the project. | |
| Team members are motivated, empowered, and engaged, and come prepared with suggestions; they don't require micromanagement from the project manager. | |

|  | Place ✓ Here If It's True of Your Projects |
|---|---|
| **General PMI-isms** | |
| The project manager spends time planning, managing, assessing, and monitoring and controlling scope, schedule, cost, quality, risk, resources, and customer satisfaction. | |
| Organizations have a project management office (PMO), and that office has important, clearly defined responsibilities regarding projects across the organization. | |
| Organizations have project management policies, which the project manager adapts for use on their project. These policies may include project management methodologies, risk procedures, and quality procedures. | |
| A project may be part of a program or portfolio, and the project's relationship to other projects could significantly influence how the project manager does their work. | |
| Organizations have records (historical information and lessons learned) for all previous projects that include what the work packages were, how much each work package cost, and what risks were uncovered (referred to in the *PMBOK® Guide* as part of organizational process assets). The project manager uses this history from other projects to plan the current project. As the project progresses, the project manager feeds historical records and lessons learned from the current project back into the organization's knowledge base. | |
| The project manager works within the existing systems and culture of a company (enterprise environmental factors), and one of a project's results is to provide input to improve those systems. | |
| Every project has a project charter, which authorizes the project and the role of the project manager. | |
| A work breakdown structure (WBS) and WBS dictionary are used on every project. | |
| A project management plan is not a bar chart, but rather a series of management plans. The project manager knows what is involved in creating a project management plan. | |
| The project manager creates and keeps current other documents (project documents) in addition to the project management plan to help plan, manage, and monitor and control a project. | |
| Stakeholders are involved throughout the project. Their needs are taken into account while planning the project and creating the communications management plan and the stakeholder engagement plan. They may also help identify and manage risks. | |
| People must be compensated for their work and deserve a fair and positive environment in which they can contribute their best work. | |
| Gold plating (adding extra functionality) is not in the best interests of the project and should be prevented. | |

| General PMI-isms | Place ✓ Here If It's True of Your Projects |
|---|---|
| Since most projects are managed in a matrix environment, seemingly easy topics, such as motivation theories or conflict resolution, can be complicated on the exam. | |
| The project manager has a professional responsibility to properly use the tools and processes of project management. | |

| Planning the Project | Place ✓ Here If It's True of Your Projects |
|---|---|
| Planning is important, and all projects must be planned. | |
| The project manager plans the project with input from the team and stakeholders, not on their own. | |
| Part of planning involves deciding which processes in the *PMBOK® Guide* should be used on each project and how to tailor those processes to the project. The approach (plan-driven or change-driven) to the project should also be determined. | |
| There are plans for how the knowledge areas of scope, schedule, cost, quality, resources, communications, risk, procurement, and stakeholder management will be planned, managed, and monitored and controlled. These are called management plans, and every project has one for every knowledge area (note that the length and detail of these plans may vary by size and importance to the project). | |
| If at all possible, all the required work and all the stakeholders are identified before the project work actually begins. | |
| The project manager determines metrics to be used to measure quality. | |
| The project manager plans to improve project processes. | |
| The project manager creates a system to reward team members and stakeholders. | |
| All roles and responsibilities are clearly documented and assigned to specific individuals on the project. These may include things such as reporting responsibilities, risk management assignments, and meeting attendance, as well as project work. | |
| The project manager focuses extensively on identifying risks. | |
| The stakeholders, as well as team members, are assigned risk identification and risk management duties. | |
| The project manager realizes that managing risks saves the project time and money. | |
| Project cost and schedule cannot be finalized without completing risk management. | |

19

| Planning the Project | Place ✓ Here If It's True of Your Projects |
|---|---|
| The project manager creates realistic estimates for the overall project schedule and its associated costs. | |
| The project manager assesses whether the project can meet the end date and other project constraints and objectives. They then meet with management to resolve any differences before the project work starts. The project manager knows unrealistic schedules are their fault because they have tools and skills to help solve them. | |
| The project manager plans when and how to measure performance against the performance measurement baseline, as documented in the project management plan, but also has other measurements to use to determine how the project is performing while the work is being done. | |
| The project management plan is realistic, and everyone believes it can be achieved. | |
| The exam defines a kickoff meeting in a way that may be different from your understanding of a kickoff meeting (see the Integration Management chapter). | |

| While the Project Work Is Being Done | Place ✓ Here If It's True of Your Projects |
|---|---|
| The project is managed to the project management plan, which is realistic and complete. | |
| The project manager is responsible for documenting and sharing knowledge acquired during the project. | |
| The project manager measures against the project management plan to help determine project status throughout the life of the project. | |
| Projects are reestimated throughout the life of the project to make sure the end date and cost objectives will be met. Therefore, the project manager almost always knows if the project can meet the agreed-upon end date and budget. | |
| Delays must be made up by adjusting future work, rather than by asking for more time. | |
| The project manager has authority and power. They can say no and work to control the project for the benefit of the customer. | |
| The project manager lets others know they cannot get something for nothing. A change in scope must be evaluated for its impacts to the project's schedule, cost, quality, risk, resources, and customer satisfaction. The project manager has enough data about the project to do this analysis. | |

| While the Project Work Is Being Done | Place ✓ Here If It's True of Your Projects |
|---|---|
| The project manager realizes that, over time, not everyone associated with the project will have the same understanding of what the project is and what could occur during the life of the project. Therefore, the project manager is continually looking to ensure everyone knows what is going on and has appropriate expectations. | |
| The project manager understands, and takes seriously, resource responsibilities on a project. | |
| The project manager spends time on such activities as team building and ensuring high team performance. | |
| The project manager is proactive, and finds problems early, looks for changes, and prevents problems. | |
| The project manager spends more time focusing on preventing problems than on dealing with problems. | |
| Most problems that occur have a risk response plan already created to deal with them. | |
| Risks are a major topic at every team meeting. | |
| Team meetings do not focus on status. That can be collected by other means. | |
| All changes to the project management plan flow through the change management process and integrated change control. | |
| The project manager ensures that organizational policies are followed on the project. | |
| The project manager recommends improvements to the performing organization's standards, policies, and processes. Such recommendations are expected and welcomed by management. | |
| Quality should be considered whenever there is a change to any component of the project. | |
| Quality should be checked before an activity or work package is completed. | |
| The project manager works closely with the quality department in performing some of the quality activities discussed in the *PMBOK® Guide*. | |
| The project manager is actively involved with the procurement process and assists in managing procurements. | |
| The project manager understands contract language. | |
| The project manager makes sure all the terms of the contract are met, including those that do not seem important. | |

© 2018 RMC Publications, Inc.™ • 952.846.4484 • info@rmcls.com • www.rmcls.com

| Closing the Project | Place ✓ Here If It's True of Your Projects |
|---|---|
| The project manager archives all project records. | |
| No project is complete unless there has been final acceptance from the customer. | |
| All projects produce a final report that gives the project team a chance to announce the project objectives have been met. | |

Which items in this list seem different from the way you manage your projects? Which of these items do you not understand? Reread this list when you think you are finished studying, and pay particular attention to those items you left unchecked. Are there any items you need to think about more to make sure you will remember them when you take the exam? Knowing these PMI-isms can make a significant difference on the exam.

# Project Management
# Framework

This is a very important chapter. Yes, we could say that about every chapter in this book, as they all will add to your understanding of project management and get you closer to passing the PMP exam. But this chapter is especially important.

This chapter includes an overview of terms and concepts used throughout this book. Understanding what is presented here will make the rest of your studying easier. Look for gaps in your knowledge as you read on.

## Definition of a Project  PAGE 4*

Because the art and science of project management revolves around projects, knowing the definition of a project—as the term is used on the exam—has helped many test takers get up to four questions right on the exam. Many people call their work a project when it is not.

On the exam, a project is assumed to have the following characteristics:

- It is a temporary endeavor—with a beginning and an end.
- It creates a unique product, service, or result.

**QUICKTEST**

- Project management
- Definition of a project
- Project team
- Project management team
- Stakeholder
- Stakeholder management
- Governance
- Project management office (PMO)
  - Supportive
  - Controlling
  - Directive
- Organizational project management (OPM)
- Organizational structure
  - Matrix
    » Strong
    » Weak
    » Balanced
  - Functional
  - Project-oriented
- Project expediter
- Project coordinator
- Enterprise environmental factors
- Organizational process assets
  - Processes, procedures, and policies
  - Historical information
  - Lessons learned
- Assumption log
- Assumptions
- Constraints
- Work performance data, information, and reports
- Operational work
- Program management
- Portfolio management
- Expert judgment
- Meetings

Does the exam ask, "What is a project?" No, but it will describe situations, and in your analysis of those situations, you will need to ask questions such as, "Is this a project being described?"

So, what is a project? If your manager walked into your office today and said, "The system is broken. Can you figure out what is wrong with it and fix it?" Would this be a project?

---

* All page number references are to the *PMBOK® Guide, Sixth Edition.*

23

Are you reading on before you have thought through the question? If so, read it again, and think about your answer. This is an important concept, both for the exam and in the real world.

Of the thousands of students RMC has taught, very few came into our classes understanding that you must first take what you are given and organize the work into appropriate projects, phases, and a life cycle. The project planning process will produce schedules and budgets. Can you schedule "fix it" if you do not know what is wrong? You can't; in fact, there are at least two projects in the previous scenario. The Project Management Processes chapter goes into more detail about dividing work into projects and life cycle phases.

Are you really working on projects? If you work at a help desk and someone contacts you about a problem they are having, you may be able to use a WBS, but do you need a network diagram? Do you need to use earned value management? How about management plans for scope, schedule, and cost? Probably not. Some activities are simply part of the company's normal operations, rather than a project.

 In preparing for the exam, make sure your definition of a project is in alignment with the *PMBOK® Guide*. You should have a large, plan-driven project in mind when you are studying for the exam, and when answering exam questions. Think of a project that is new to an organization (it has not been done before), utilizes resources from many countries, has more than 200 people on the team, lasts longer than one year, and has a budget of over $10 million. Such an initiative would require you to use many of the tools of project management.

Regardless of whether you currently work on large projects, you will need to answer questions on the exam as if you do. There is a big difference between managing small and large projects. A large project requires using the full breadth of project management processes and tools.

On a small project, you walk over to the person you need to speak to when you have an issue to resolve. On a large project, you may have spent weeks planning communications. When there is an issue, you have to figure out who is involved and where they are located, look up their contact information and their preferred method of communication, and then communicate with them in that way. If you keep this large-project focus in mind as you read this book, you will see that the many different elements being described here as part of project management make sense, are necessary, and add value. And if the concepts make sense to you, you do not have to memorize them—you can use logic to answer questions on the exam.

Another thing to keep in mind for the exam is that you should assume project proposals are formally reviewed and approved by management in your organization after a comparison of all proposed projects. Projects are not selected arbitrarily or informally. (See the discussion of business documents as an input to Develop Project Charter in the Integration Management chapter.)

## Why Projects Exist

Projects are created to provide business value and to deliver benefits defined in the business case[1] and the benefits management plan.[2] Projects are designed to bring a positive change to the organization, usually to add or improve products or services, and, in some cases, to satisfy legal or other regulatory requirements.

## Operations and Projects   PAGE 16

Most work done in organizations can be described as either operational or project work. Operational work is ongoing work to support the business and systems of the organization, whereas project work ends when the project is closed. It is important to understand the difference for the exam. You may see instances where the real problem in the question is that someone is attempting to manage ongoing (operational) work, such as manufacturing, as a project.

Although these are two distinct areas of work, they are closely connected. When a project is finished, the deliverables are transitioned to ongoing business operations so the benefits of the project work can be incorporated into the organization. A successful transition may require employee training or adjustments to operational processes. For example, when an insurance company's internal project to develop a new caseload tracking system is completed, employees will need to learn how to use the system and adjust their processes to incorporate it into their daily work so the benefits can be realized.

And this relationship goes both ways. While a project may develop a product or service to be used in operational work, the need to change or improve operational work may prompt the initiation of a project. For example, the need to develop a new caseload tracking system may have arisen from problems occurring in the organization's business operations. As another example, imagine the caseload tracking system has moved into operations and users have started working with it, but some bugs have been identified. Fixing these bugs would likely be addressed as the operational work of maintaining business systems rather than as a new project. If the organization decides new features or functions must be added to the caseload tracking system after it is in operation, however, this may prompt a new project.

## Governance   PAGE 16

Organizational governance refers to the overall structure of an organization, and it involves setting the policies and procedures for how work will be performed to meet high-level strategic goals. Also note that there are multiple levels of governance within an organization. Generally, a board of directors is responsible to ensure that work throughout the organization conforms to external (government or regulatory) and internal standards and requirements. Internal requirements include policies and procedures regarding portfolio, program, and project work, which help to ensure that these endeavors are within the strategic plan of the organization and that they contribute to the delivery of specific benefits or value. Every organization is different, and governance is designed to support the specific culture and attributes of the organization.

Project governance includes the framework within which project work is performed across the organization. It may involve the creation or enforcement of processes and policies regarding areas such as risk, resources, communications, and change management. Project governance can be established and administered by a project management office (PMO).[3] We will discuss the various types of PMOs later in this chapter.

## What Is Portfolio Management? PAGE 15

A portfolio includes programs, individual projects, and other related operational work that are prioritized and implemented to achieve a specific strategic business goal (see fig. 2.1). Combining programs, projects, and operations into one or more portfolios helps optimize the use of resources, enhances the benefits to the organization, and reduces risk. The programs and projects that make up a portfolio may not be related, other than by the fact that they are helping to achieve a common strategic goal. The work of an organization can comprise one or multiple portfolios. A project is included in a portfolio based on potential return on investment, strategic benefits, alignment with corporate strategy, and other factors critical to organizational success.

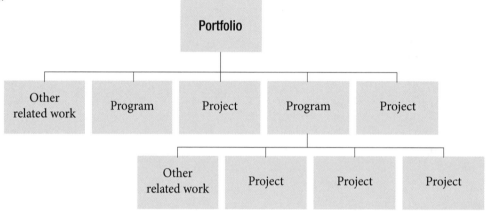

FIGURE 2.1   *Portfolio management*

## What Is Program Management? PAGE 14

If you want to learn more about program management, visit RMC's website at rmcls.com for information about courses on this topic.

By grouping related projects into a program, an organization can coordinate the management of those projects (see fig. 2.2). The program approach focuses on the interdependencies between the projects and may help decrease risk, achieve economies of scale, and improve management. In addition to the work required to complete each individual project, the program also includes efforts such as the program manager's coordination and management activities. So, when you discover that your work encompasses more than one project, you can manage all the projects as a program if there is a benefit to doing so. However, this should be done only when the program approach adds value. Projects are combined into programs to provide coordinated control, support, and guidance. The program manager works to ensure projects and programs achieve the benefits for which they were initiated.

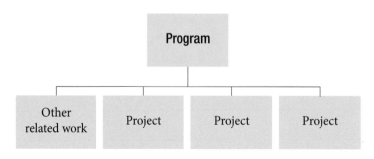

FIGURE 2.2   *Program management*

26

## What Is Project Management? Why Is It Important? PAGE 10

Project management is both a science and an art. The science is the systematic process of managing work efficiently and effectively to deliver planned results. This includes tailoring efforts to meet the needs of the project and using the appropriate processes and tools to accomplish the work. The art of project management relates to how a project manager uses skills such as influencing, organizing, and strategizing, in addition to other interpersonal and team skills.

The *PMBOK® Guide* breaks project management into process groups and knowledge areas. The project management process groups are initiating, planning, executing, monitoring and controlling, and closing. Each of these process groups is discussed more fully in the Project Management Processes chapter. The knowledge areas are integration, scope, schedule, cost, quality, resource, communications, risk, procurement, and stakeholder management. The work of these process groups and the knowledge areas within them can occur simultaneously, and is iterated as the project progresses.

Chances are, there are some key aspects of project management you do not know. The answer to the question, "What is project management?" is described throughout this book. It can involve technical terms and processes, but it also involves roles and responsibilities and authority levels. Applying the practices, tools and techniques, and knowledge and skills of project management increases the likelihood of project success. As you read this book, you may find that project management involves more than you thought.

Effective use of project management ensures that the organization is focused on the most important work and, because of appropriately tailored planning efforts, the work is done correctly and in the most time- and cost-effective manner. Risks are identified and planned for before they occur, communication is managed effectively, and quality is achieved. These efforts result in satisfied stakeholders and achievement of business objectives.

## What Is Organizational Project Management (OPM)?[4] PAGE 16

Organizational Project Management (OPM) serves as a guide or driver for project, program, and portfolio management as well as other organizational practices. It is a framework for keeping the organization as a whole focused on overall strategy. OPM provides direction for how portfolios, programs, projects, and other organizational work should be prioritized, managed, executed, and measured to best achieve strategic goals and desired benefits. Figure 2.3 shows how organizational project management drives an organization with project, program, and portfolio management in place to achieve strategic goals. Understanding how these pieces interrelate, as depicted in this illustration, can help you answer questions correctly on the exam. Unless you are told otherwise, assume this organizational framework is in place when answering exam questions.

27

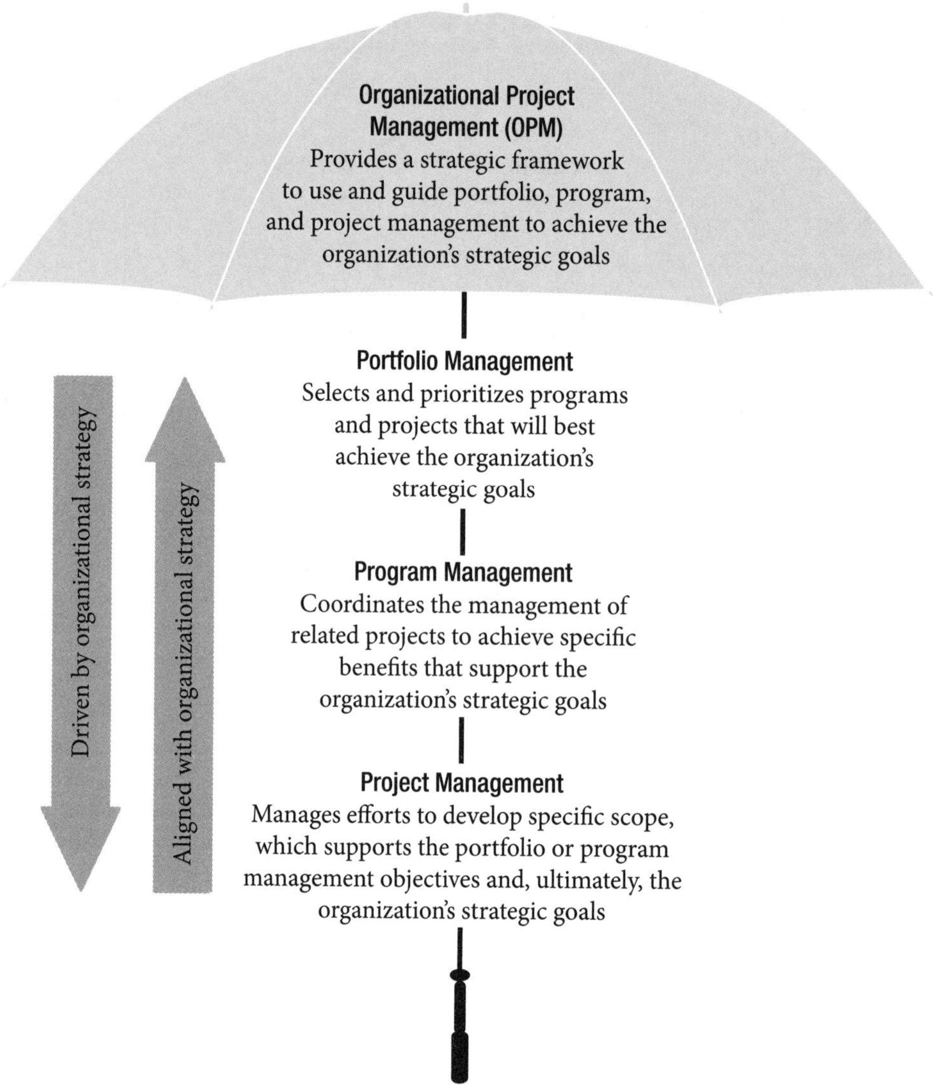

**Organizational Project Management (OPM)**
Provides a strategic framework to use and guide portfolio, program, and project management to achieve the organization's strategic goals

**Portfolio Management**
Selects and prioritizes programs and projects that will best achieve the organization's strategic goals

**Program Management**
Coordinates the management of related projects to achieve specific benefits that support the organization's strategic goals

**Project Management**
Manages efforts to develop specific scope, which supports the portfolio or program management objectives and, ultimately, the organization's strategic goals

Driven by organizational strategy

Aligned with organizational strategy

FIGURE 2.3  *Organizational project management*

A key point to understand is that all efforts in the organization—whether they are part of project, program, portfolio, or operational work—should be guided by the organization and support its strategic goals. This means that any changes to the organizational strategy will necessitate changes to the organization's portfolios, programs, projects, and operational work—both ongoing efforts and future initiatives. For example, if a project no longer aligns with the organizational strategy, the project may be changed midcourse to bring it into alignment, or it may be terminated.

## Project Management Office (PMO)   PAGE 48

The project management office (PMO) is a departmental unit within an organization that provides or ensures compliance with project governance. The office oversees and standardizes the management of projects. A PMO can take one of several different forms, including the following:

- **Supportive**  A supportive PMO provides the policies, methodologies, templates, and lessons learned for managing projects within the organization. It typically exercises a low level of control over projects.

- **Controlling**  A controlling PMO provides support and guidance on how to manage projects, trains others in project management and project management software, assists with specific project management tools, and ensures compliance with organizational policies. It typically has a moderate level of control over projects.

- **Directive**  A directive PMO provides project managers for different projects, and is responsible for the results of those projects; all projects, or projects of a certain size, type, or influence, are managed by this office. A directive PMO has a high level of control over projects.

The PMO may:

- Manage the interdependencies among projects, programs, and portfolios.
- Integrate information from all projects to assess whether the organization is achieving its strategic objectives.
- Help provide resources.
- Recommend the termination of projects when appropriate.
- Monitor compliance with organizational processes.
- Help gather lessons learned into a repository and make them available to other projects.
- Provide templates for documents such as work breakdown structures or communications management plans.
- Provide guidance and project governance.
- Provide centralized communication about the projects.
- Be more heavily involved during project initiating than later in the project.
- Have representation on the change control board.
- Be a stakeholder.
- Prioritize projects.

**Exercise**  Test yourself! Read the description of the PMO, and determine whether it is likely to be supportive, controlling, or directive, or a combination of the three.

| | Description | Type of PMO |
|---|---|---|
| 1 | Manages all projects throughout the organization | |
| 2 | Provides support and guidance; requires all projects within the organization to use designated project management software and templates, but doesn't otherwise exert control over the project | |

29

| | Description | Type of PMO |
|---|---|---|
| 3 | Coordinates all projects within the organization | |
| 4 | Recommends common terminology, templates, reporting, and procedures to be used on projects throughout the organization to promote consistency and streamline efforts | |
| 5 | Appoints project manager | |
| 6 | Prioritizes projects | |
| 7 | Has the highest level of control over projects | |

NOTE: You may prefer that the answers to the exercises were not listed right after the questions. If this is distracting for you, we recommend you keep a blank piece of paper available to cover the answers until you have completed each exercise and are ready to review it. Our analysis shows that having the answers right after the questions helps you more than it hurts.

## Answer

| | Description | Type of PMO |
|---|---|---|
| 1 | Manages all projects throughout the organization | Directive |
| 2 | Provides support and guidance; requires all projects within the organization to use designated project management software and templates, but doesn't otherwise exert control over the project | Controlling |
| 3 | Coordinates all projects within the organization | Controlling or Directive |
| 4 | Recommends common terminology, templates, reporting, and procedures to be used on projects throughout the organization to promote consistency and streamline efforts | Supportive |
| 5 | Appoints project manager | Directive |
| 6 | Prioritizes projects | Controlling or Directive |
| 7 | Has the highest level of control over projects | Directive |

 **TRICKS OF THE TRADE®** When answering exam questions, assume there is a PMO in the organization, unless the question states otherwise. Read situational questions carefully to determine if the PMO is supportive, controlling, or directive.

## Organizational Structure  PAGE 45

A project does not operate in a vacuum. Projects are impacted by, and have an impact on, the cultural norms, management policies, and procedures of the organizations of which they are a part. These factors are increasingly important in global organizations in which team members are often located in different offices and in multiple countries. The best project managers look for these influences and manage them for the benefit of the project and the organization.

One of the primary forms of influence is how the company is organized. The organizational structure will dictate who the project manager goes to for help with resources, how communications must be handled, and many other aspects of project management. This influence is so important that an answer to a question on the exam can change depending on the structure of the organization being discussed.

Questions on the exam are often phrased in terms of the project manager's level of authority and how the form of organization impacts their management of projects. For example, exam questions may deal with who has the power in each type of organization (the project manager or the functional manager), or they may require you to understand the advantages and disadvantages to the project manager in each type of organization.

As you read through the following sections defining the different organizational structures, take the time to think about how each form would impact your work as a project manager and how you would solve problems in different situations within each structure.

### Functional
This is a common organizational structure. Functional organizations are grouped by areas of specialization within functional areas, such as accounting, marketing, or manufacturing. When you see "functional" on the exam, think "silo." Projects generally occur within a single department. If information or project work is needed from another department, employees transmit the request to the head of the department who communicates the request to the other department head. Otherwise, communication stays within the project. Team members complete project work in addition to normal departmental work.

### Project-Oriented
In a project-oriented, or projectized, organization, the entire company is organized by projects, and the project manager has control of the project. Personnel are assigned and report to a project manager. When you see "project-oriented" on the exam, think "no home." Team members complete only project work, and when the project is over, they do not have a department to go back to. They need to be assigned to another project or get a job with a different employer. Communication primarily occurs within the project. This type of organization can also be referred to as composite or hybrid.

### Matrix[5]
This form is an attempt to maximize the strengths of both the functional and project-oriented structures. When you see "matrix" on the exam, think "two managers." The team members report to two managers: the project manager and the functional manager (for example, the engineering manager). Communication goes from team members to both managers. Team members do project work in addition to normal departmental work.

In a strong matrix, power rests with the project manager. In a weak matrix, power rests with the functional manager, and the power of the project manager is comparable to that of a coordinator or expediter. In a balanced matrix, the power is shared between the functional manager and the project manager.

As stated in the previous paragraph, the project manager's role in a weak matrix or in a functional organization might be one of the following:

© 2018 RMC Publications, Inc.™ • 952.846.4484 • info@rmcls.com • www.rmcls.com

- **Project expediter**[6] The project expediter acts primarily as a staff assistant and communications coordinator. The expediter cannot personally make or enforce decisions.
- **Project coordinator** This position is similar to the project expediter, except the coordinator has some authority and power to make decisions, and reports to a higher-level manager.

 The exam typically does not identify the form of organization being discussed. When it does not specify a form, assume matrix. If you remember this, you should get a few more questions right.

 A tight matrix has nothing to do with a matrix organization. It simply refers to colocation—the practice of locating the work spaces for the project team in the same room. Because it sounds similar to the other forms of organization, it has often been used as a fourth choice for these questions on the exam.

## Exercise
Test yourself! You can expect questions on the exam that will test your understanding of the advantages and disadvantages of the functional, project-oriented, and matrix organizational structures. Understanding the advantages and disadvantages of each will help you evaluate situations presented and choose the right answer within the identified constraints. Practice by listing your answers in the spaces below.

### Functional

| Advantages | Disadvantages |
|---|---|
| | |
| | |
| | |

### Project-Oriented

| Advantages | Disadvantages |
|---|---|
| | |
| | |

### Matrix

| Advantages | Disadvantages |
|---|---|
| | |
| | |
| | |

## Answer

### Functional

| Advantages | Disadvantages |
|---|---|
| Easier management of specialists | People place more emphasis on their functional specialty to the detriment of the project |
| Team members report to only one supervisor | No career path in project management |
| Similar resources are centralized, as the company is grouped by specialties | The project manager has little or no authority |
| Clearly defined career paths in areas of work specialization | |

### Project-Oriented

| Advantages | Disadvantages |
|---|---|
| Efficient project organization | No "home" for team members when project is completed |
| Team loyalty to the project | Lack of specialization in disciplines |
| More effective communications than functional | Duplication of facilities and job functions |
| Project manager has more power to make decisions | May result in less efficient use of resources |

### Matrix

| Advantages | Disadvantages |
|---|---|
| Highly visible project objectives | Extra administration is required |
| Improved project manager control over resources (as compared to functional) | Project team members have more than one manager |
| More support from functional areas | More complex to monitor and control |
| Maximum utilization of scarce resources | Resource allocation is more complex |
| Better coordination | Extensive policies and procedures are needed |
| Better horizontal and vertical dissemination of information | Functional managers may have different priorities than project managers |
| Team members maintain a "home" | Higher potential for conflict |

Now that we have discussed the organizational structure, let's look at specific roles within projects.

33

## Project Roles

For the exam, it is important to understand who is involved in the project and what they should be doing. Some people actually fail the exam because they are not clear about roles within a project and do not really know what a project manager does, or at least do not understand how the exam expects the role to be performed. They may also have problems differentiating between what the team, project manager, and management should be doing.

This exercise will help you focus on roles and responsibilities within the context of the exam. The answers may provide you with new information or simply refresh your memory. You will see many of the items listed in the answers to these exercises as you read the rest of this book.

**Exercise**  **The Role of the Project Sponsor/Initiator**  Test yourself! Describe the role of the project sponsor/initiator.

**Answer** The Role of the Project Sponsor/Initiator  A basic definition of a sponsor is one who provides the financial resources for the project; however, the exam has attributed additional duties to the sponsor—including providing support for the project and protecting the project from unnecessary changes. The role of the sponsor may be filled by two or more individuals, working together.

In procurement situations, the customer (buyer) may also be the sponsor. In such cases, the selling organization should also have a sponsor.

Think about your company's management as you read this. Do they know what their role is on projects? Do you? How can you help them better understand their role? Without having the sponsor or someone in management performing the functions detailed in the lists that follow, the project will suffer, wasting time and resources. Management must serve as a protector of the project (so long as the project continues to meet the organization's strategic goals). Management is anyone senior to the project manager in the organization, including program or portfolio managers.

Read the following list carefully to understand the role of the sponsor and/or senior management in an organization. Since the list is so long—and since many project managers have gaps in their knowledge here—we have organized this section by process group.

During or prior to project initiating, the sponsor:
- Has requirements that must be met
- Is a project stakeholder
- Participates in developing the business case for the project
- Helps to define the measurable project objectives
- Advocates for or champions the project, especially while the project concept is being put together
- Serves as a voice of the project or spokesperson to those who do not know about the project, including upper management
- Gathers the appropriate support for the project
- Ensures buy-in throughout the organization
- Provides funding
- Provides high-level requirements
- Provides information regarding the initial scope of the project
- May dictate milestones, key events, or the project end date (along with the customer)
- Determines the priorities between the constraints (if not done by the customer)
- Provides information that helps develop the project charter
- Gives the project manager authority as outlined in the project charter
- Sets priorities between projects
- Encourages the finalization of high-level requirements and scope by the stakeholders
- Guides the process to get the project approved and formalized, assisted by the project manager as necessary

During project planning, the sponsor:
- Provides the project team with time to plan
- May review the WBS
- Identifies risks

- Determines the reports needed by management to oversee the project
- Provides expert judgment
- Helps evaluate trade-offs during crashing, fast tracking, and reestimating
- Approves the final project management plan

During project executing and project monitoring and controlling, the sponsor:
- Supports the efforts of the project manager
- Protects the project from outside influences and changes
- Enforces quality policies
- Provides expert judgment
- Helps evaluate trade-offs during crashing, fast tracking, and reestimating
- Resolves conflicts that extend beyond the project manager's control
- Approves, rejects, or defers changes, or authorizes a change control board to do so
- May direct that a quality review be performed
- Clarifies scope questions
- Works with the project manager to monitor progress

During project closing, the sponsor:
- Provides formal acceptance of the deliverables (if they are the customer)
- Enables an efficient and integrated transfer of deliverables to the customer
- Supports the collection of historical records from the project

## Exercise  The Role of the Project Team  Test yourself! Describe the role of the team.

_____
_____
_____
_____
_____

**Answer** **The Role of the Project Team** The project team is a group of people, including the project manager, who will complete the work of the project. The team members can change throughout the project as people are added to and released from the project.

Generally, it is the team's role to help plan what needs to be done by creating the WBS and schedule estimates for their work packages or activities. During project executing and monitoring and controlling, the team members complete activities to produce the deliverables represented in work packages and help look for deviations from the project management plan. More specifically, the team may help:

- Identify and involve stakeholders.
- Identify requirements.
- Identify constraints and assumptions.
- Create the WBS.
- Decompose the work packages for which they are responsible into schedule activities.
- Identify dependencies between activities.
- Provide schedule and cost estimates.
- Participate in the risk management process.
- Comply with quality and communications plans.
- Enforce ground rules.
- Execute the project management plan to accomplish the work defined in the project scope statement.
- Attend project team meetings.
- Recommend changes to the project, including corrective actions.
- Implement approved changes.
- Share new knowledge.
- Contribute to the lessons learned knowledge base.

In agile environments, team members are responsible for clarifying user stories with the customer so that they can estimate and plan the releases and iterations, hold reviews and retrospectives, and update the project information using tools such as Kanban boards and burndown charts.

On large projects, there may be too much project management work for one person to perform. Therefore, the project manager may select some project team members to help perform the project management activities. The *PMBOK® Guide* refers to these people as the project management team. Members of this team must have project management training. Keep all this information in mind when the exam uses the term "project management team" versus "project team" or "team."

37

**Exercise**  **The Role of the Stakeholders**  Test yourself! Describe the role of the stakeholders as a group.

_____
_____
_____
_____
_____
_____
_____
_____
_____
_____
_____
_____
_____
_____
_____
_____

**Answer**  **The Role of the Stakeholders**  A stakeholder is anyone who will be impacted by the project or can positively or negatively influence the project. This includes the customer or end user, the project manager and team, the project's sponsor, program and portfolio managers, the project management office, functional or operational managers within the organization, other departments or groups within the organization (such as business analysis, marketing procurement, quality, or legal), and external sellers that provide services or materials for the project. Questions about the role of stakeholders and how they should be managed appear throughout the exam.

The stakeholders' role on a project is determined by the project manager and the stakeholders themselves. Stakeholders should be involved in planning the project and managing it more extensively than many people are used to on their real-world projects. For example, stakeholders may be involved in:

- Creating the project charter and the project scope statement
- Developing the project management plan
- Approving project changes and being on the change control board
- Identifying constraints and assumptions

- Identifying requirements
- Managing risk

In an agile environment, the project owner role can be filled by someone from the business who is responsible for working with the agile team to prioritize features and functions. This person may also:

- Attend reviews and accept the deliverables presented.
- Be a risk owner.
- Participate in phase gate reviews.
- Be involved with governance.
- Identify issues.
- Document lessons learned.
- Provide expert judgment.

**Exercise**  **The Role of the Functional or Resource Manager** Test yourself! Describe the role of the functional or resource manager.

_____

_____

_____

_____

_____

_____

_____

_____

_____

_____

_____

_____

_____

39

### Answer The Role of the Functional or Resource Manager

A functional or resource manager manages and is responsible for the human and physical resources in a specific department, such as IT, engineering, public relations, marketing, etc. They are responsible for working with the project manager to meet the needs of the project. As managers of people, facilities, or equipment, functional or resource managers maintain a calendar indicating availability of these resources for projects and other organizational work, and they coordinate with project managers who need the resources. This might involve negotiation if people, facilities, or equipment are needed by more than one project at the same time. If the project manager has issues with resources provided by the functional manager, the managers collaborate to resolve the issues.

The degree to which functional managers are involved in a project depends on the organizational structure. In a matrix organization, the functional managers and project manager share responsibility for directing the work of individuals and managing physical resources needed on the project. In a project-oriented organization, the project manager does all the directing of team resources. In contrast, the project manager does little directing in a functional organization, where that responsibility falls to functional managers. To avoid conflict, the project manager and functional managers must balance their respective needs regarding the use of resources to complete project and functional work. It is generally the responsibility of the project manager to manage this relationship by using clear communication and interpersonal and team skills, such as conflict management and emotional intelligence.

The specific activities performed by functional managers on a project vary greatly based on the type of organizational structure, as well as the type of project, but may include the following:

- Assigning specific individuals to the team and negotiating with the project manager regarding team and physical resources
- Letting the project manager know of other projects or departmental work demands that may impact the project
- Participating in the initial planning until work packages or activities are assigned
- Providing subject matter expertise
- Approving the final schedule during schedule development when it involves team or physical resources under their control
- Approving the final project management plan during project management plan development when it involves team or physical resources under their control
- Recommending changes to the project, including corrective actions
- Managing activities within their functional area
- Assisting with problems related to team or physical resources under their control
- Improving resource utilization
- Participating in rewards and recognition of team members
- Participating in risk identification
- Participating in quality management
- Sitting on the change control board

**Exercise** The Role of the Project Manager Test yourself! Describe the role of the project manager.

_____

_____

_____

_____

_____

_____

_____

_____

_____

_____

_____

_____

_____

_____

**Answer** The Role of the Project Manager To put it simply, the project manager is responsible for managing the project to meet project objectives and deliver value and benefits to the organization. Think about your role on projects. Do you have the knowledge, abilities, and authority described in this book? Do you fully plan and control your projects? Are you leading and managing your projects effectively?

Remember that as a project manager, you must come up with a project management plan that people agree to and believe is realistic, and, even more importantly, that you can stake your reputation on. A project manager is responsible for ensuring that a project is completed according to the project schedule and budget, including approved changes, and that it meets other objectives. The project manager is held accountable for delivering project benefits.

In today's project environments, people managing projects may not realize they lack knowledge of what proper project management involves, and many companies do not understand why project management is so important in delivering the benefits they want to realize. People with the title of project manager are often not really project managers at all; instead, their role is more of a project coordinator. Before taking the exam, it is important that you understand not only the project manager's role but also all the roles of other people involved in projects.

41

Remember that the work of the project manager may be shared by members of the project team, referred to as the project management team. This is described in the "Role of the Project Team" exercise.

The project manager's level of authority can vary depending on the structure of the organization and other factors, such as whether they are assigned part-time or under contract. On the exam, however, the authority of the project manager has generally been interpreted to mean that the project manager:

- Is assigned to the project no later than project initiating
- Helps write the project charter
- Is in charge of the project, but not necessarily the resources
- Does not have to be a technical expert
- Identifies and analyzes constraints and assumptions
- Leads and directs the project planning efforts
- Selects appropriate processes for the project
- Identifies dependencies between activities
- Analyzes unrealistic schedule requirements, and takes action to produce a realistic schedule
- Develops time and cost reserves for the project
- Has the authority and accountability necessary to accomplish the project management work
- Says no when necessary
- Integrates the project components into a cohesive whole that meets the customer's needs
- Finalizes and gains approval of the project management plan
- Influences the project team and the atmosphere in which the team works by promoting good communication, insulating the team from politics (both internal and external to the project), enhancing the positive aspects of cultural differences, and resolving team issues
- Spends more time being proactive than dealing with problems (being reactive)
- Understands how cultural differences may impact the project, particularly in the case of global teams, virtual teams, or projects involving multiple organizations
- Ensures professional interactions between the project team and other stakeholders
- Coordinates interactions between the project team and key stakeholders
- Understands and enforces professional and social responsibility
- Assists the team and other stakeholders during project executing
- Communicates
- Develops the team
- Uses rewards and recognition
- Identifies and delivers required levels of quality
- Identifies stakeholders, supports stakeholder engagement, and manages stakeholder expectations throughout the project
- Manages project knowledge, including sharing lessons learned
- Solves problems
- Makes decisions
- Demonstrates ethics and leadership
- Manages and controls resources

42

- Maintains control over the project by measuring performance and determining variances from the plan
- Monitors risk, communications, and stakeholder engagement to ensure they are in conformance with expectations
- Determines the need for change requests, including recommended corrective and preventive actions and defect repair
- Approves or rejects changes as authorized, manages the change control board, and frequently sits on the change control board
- Uses metrics to identify variances and trends in project work, and is responsible for analyzing the impact of these variances and trends
- Works with team members to resolve variances from the project management plan
- Keeps the team members focused on risk management and possible responses to the risks
- Performs project closing at the end of each phase and for the project as a whole
- Performs or delegates most of the activities outlined in this book
- Applies project management knowledge and uses personal and leadership skills to achieve project success
- Is accountable for project success or failure

Other roles you may see referenced in scenario questions on the exam include the portfolio manager and the program manager, both of which are described in the following sections.

## The Role of the Portfolio Manager

The portfolio manager is responsible for governance at an executive level of the projects or programs that make up a portfolio. A project is included in a portfolio based on the value of the project, the potential return on investment, whether it aligns with corporate strategy, whether the level of risk associated with the project is acceptable, and other factors critical to organizational success.

The work of the portfolio manager may include the following:

- Managing various projects or programs that may be largely unrelated to each other
- Ensuring selected projects provide value to the organization
- Working with senior executives to gather support for individual projects
- Getting the best return from resources invested

## The Role of the Program Manager

The program manager is responsible for managing a group of related projects. Projects are combined into programs to provide coordinated control, support, and guidance. The program manager works to meet project and program goals.

The work of the program manager may include the following:

- Managing related projects to achieve results not obtainable by managing each project separately
- Ensuring projects selected support the strategic goals of the organization
- Providing oversight to adjust projects for the program's benefit
- Guiding and supporting individual project manager's efforts

In addition to understanding the basics we have just discussed, it is also important to become familiar with many terms you will see used throughout the rest of this book. Many of them are used in multiple processes and for different purposes throughout a project.

## Organizational Process Assets (OPAs)   PAGE 39

Most organizations maintain two types of OPAs: processes, procedures, and policies and organizational knowledge repositories.

### Processes, Procedures, and Policies
Over time, organizations develop or adopt processes, procedures, and policies for projects. Collectively, these processes, procedures, and policies are referred to as organizational process assets, and they apply to aspects of the project such as quality, procurement, and resource management, as well as change control, safety, compliance, and more. Projects may recommend changes or ways to increase the efficiency of these processes and procedures, but they are generally owned by the project management office or other departments responsible for organizational governance.

### Organizational Knowledge Repositories[7]
The other type of organizational process asset is organizational knowledge repositories, which include information on many facets of projects.

Historical knowledge bases are maintained and updated by every project, and made accessible to the rest of the organization as part of the historical information repository. It can be used to plan and manage future projects, thereby improving the process of project management and avoiding challenges experienced by past projects.

Historical information can include:

- Activities
- WBSs
- Benchmarks
- Reports
- Risks and risk response plans
- Estimates
- Resources used
- Project management plans
- Project documents
- Baselines
- Correspondence

Another part of historical information is lessons learned. We will discuss lessons learned in more detail in the Integration Management chapter. For now, you need to know that lessons learned, which are created throughout projects, document what went right, what went wrong, and what the team would do differently if they had the opportunity to start the project over again. The lessons learned register from each project becomes part of the lessons learned repository[8] after project closure.

Other organizational knowledge repositories include:

- Configuration management, including file structure, file-naming conventions, baselines of organizational standards, and templates of project documents
- Financial data, including budgets and actual costs of completed projects
- Issue logs and documentation regarding defects on projects

- Metrics that may be useful for other projects
- Project management plans and baselines, as well as project documents, such as network diagrams, risk registers, and stakeholder registers

When answering questions on the exam, assume the organization has information such as historical records and lessons learned from previous projects and that the company has incorporated these records into an indexed organizational knowledge repository available to all.

## Enterprise Environmental Factors   PAGE 38

Enterprise environmental factors (EEFs) are similar to organizational process assets in that they provide context within which to plan the project. However, enterprise environmental factors are generally outside the control of the project team.

Enterprise environmental factors external to the organization include governmental or other rules and regulations that apply to the performing organization.

Internal enterprise environmental factors include the structure, culture, systems, and geographic location(s) of the organization. Resource-related EEFs include the technology and resources available for assignment to projects, such as documentation of the skills and abilities of internal and preapproved external resources that are available through approved agreements. EEFs related to project management may include a resource management system, a procurement system, and a quality management system.

When answering questions on the exam, assume that the impacts and limitations imposed by enterprise environmental factors are taken into consideration during planning and as the work is carried out.

EEFs are inputs to many planning, executing, and monitoring and controlling processes. The project may suggest improvements to the EEFs, particularly in the area of resource management.

## Assumption Log

The assumption log is a repository of both assumptions and constraints. It is started at the time the project charter is developed. Assumptions and constraints are first identified at a high level in the business case and project charter. They will receive further attention as the project progresses. The assumption log is an input to many project processes, and assumption log updates are a frequent output.

### Assumptions
It is an important part of communication to understand what your management and stakeholders believe to be true about the project—these are assumptions. Assumptions are comparable to expectations, as they may not be entirely based on fact. Stakeholders may not realize they are making assumptions, and therefore may not articulate them when communicating their requirements. Incorrect assumptions introduce risk to the project, so they must be identified and managed by the project manager. The assumption log is a frequent input to planning processes, and updates to the log are outputs of many planning and control processes.

### Constraints[9]
Constraints are easier to identify than assumptions, as they are usually clearly imposed by management or the sponsor. Constraints limit options during planning and beyond. A project manager must juggle many things on a project, including project constraints such as schedule, cost, risk,

45

scope, quality, resources, customer satisfaction, and any other factors that limit options (see fig. 2.4). For example, the date a milestone deliverable is due, the date by which the project must be completed, and the maximum allowable risk a project is allowed to have are all constraints. Constraints can be a challenge to manage.

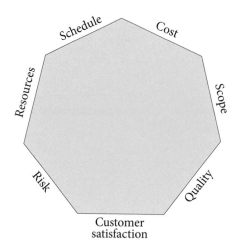

FIGURE 2.4    *Project constraints*

Management directly or indirectly sets the priority of each constraint. This prioritization is then used to plan the project, evaluate the impact of changes, and prove successful project completion. It is important to evaluate the effect a change to one constraint has on another. In other words, you probably cannot shorten the schedule without causing a negative impact on cost, risk, etc. This comes into play in planning, and as the project manager deals with change requests. For example, an additional activity may only take one day, but the cost of adding the activity must be evaluated, along with the impact to the critical path. The risk of adding or rejecting the requested activity must also be evaluated. Changes to the project plan generally impact multiple constraints. The project manager and team can assess them, but change requests that impact approved parts of the plan must go through integrated change control.

Constraints are discussed in many areas of this book. Take time to really understand the discussion of integrated change control in the Integration Management chapter, including how it relates to constraints. Understanding the relationship between the constraints and how they impact a project can help you get several questions right on the exam.

## Stakeholders[10] and Stakeholder Management[11]

Stakeholders include more than the project manager, customer, sponsor, and team; stakeholders are any people or organizations whose interests may be positively or negatively impacted by the project or the product of the project. They can include individuals and groups you may not have thought about before, such as the project management team, the project management office, portfolio managers, program managers, other departments or groups within the organization (marketing, legal, or customer service, for example), functional or operational managers, and business analysts. Stakeholders may be actively involved in the project work or may fill an advisory role. Stakeholders may also be external to the organization, including government regulators, consultants, sellers, end users, customers, taxpayers, banks, and other financial institutions. People or groups who could exert positive or negative influence over the project but would not otherwise be considered part of the project are also considered stakeholders.

Think about how you involve stakeholders on your projects. Proper stakeholder management means you keep them informed, solicit their input, and work to satisfy their needs and expectations. Without this effort, the project may fail.

The topic of stakeholders is discussed throughout this book because a project manager should analyze and manage the needs and levels of influence of stakeholders throughout a project. The Stakeholder Management chapter includes an in-depth discussion of the concept of stakeholder management. Also note that the Resource Management and Communications Management chapters give a special focus to this topic.

## Work Performance Data, Information, and Reports   PAGE 26

A great deal of data and information is generated, considered, and communicated throughout the life of a project, from initial observations and measurements to analyzed content and reports. The *PMBOK® Guide* uses three different terms to identify the stages through which this data and information move. Work performance data includes the initial measurements and details about activities gathered during the Direct and Manage Project Work process in executing. When monitoring and controlling a project, work performance data is analyzed to make sure it conforms to the project management plan. It is also assessed to determine what the data means for the project as a whole. The result is known as work performance information. Work performance information can then be organized into work performance reports, which are distributed to the various stakeholders who need to receive and possibly act on the information.

For example, let's say a project team performs their assigned work according to the project management plan. They provide information and data on their progress: a certain activity took 10 hours and was completed on July 21st. This is work performance data. The next step is to look at how this data compares to the project management plan (in this case, the project schedule). The activity in this example was estimated to take 12 hours, with an estimated completion date of July 22nd. You need to analyze why this activity took less time than planned and what this will mean for the rest of the project. Why was the work completed early? Will this mean improved performance for the rest of the project? Did the team follow the communications management plan and notify resources assigned to successor activities about the anticipated early completion so they could start their work early? Should future activities be reestimated if similar resources will be performing similar work? The result of this analysis is work performance information. This information can then be organized into work performance reports that are distributed through the Manage Communications process. If the activity was on the critical path and had taken longer than scheduled, a formal change request might have been required to adjust the rest of the schedule.

## Frequently Used Tools and Techniques

There are over 100 tools and techniques in the *PMBOK® Guide*, and there are many more that we discuss in this book. The key is to use the right ones for the right purpose under the right conditions. It is also important to realize tools and techniques can have multiple applications throughout the project management process.

You will see tools and techniques described throughout this book, in the knowledge area chapter(s) where they are primarily used. You don't have to be an expert at using all of them, but you do need to understand the purpose of each. The following tools and techniques are categorized by their function.

47

### Data Gathering
If you need to collect input from stakeholders, you can use one or more of the following data-gathering tools and techniques:

- Benchmarking
- Brainstorming
- Prompt lists
- Checklists
- Interviews
- Market research
- Questionnaires and surveys

### Data Analysis
Depending on the type of data you are working with and the depth of analysis you need to do, you can choose from many data analysis tools and techniques, including the following:

- Alternatives analysis
- Assumptions and constraints
- Cost-benefit analysis
- Document analysis
- Earned value analysis
- Performance reviews
- Reserve analysis
- Root cause analysis
- Simulation
- SWOT
- Trend analysis
- Variance analysis
- What-if analysis

### Data Representation
Throughout the project, you will gather and generate data from various sources for a number of purposes. You will likely need to communicate that information to others. This category includes options for representing, or communicating, data. Some tools and techniques are designed for a specific purpose. You will need to choose which ones to use based on the type and amount of data you are working with, the audience with whom you will be communicating, and, possibly, other considerations, such as the knowledge area you are working in. Data representation tools and techniques include the following:

- Affinity diagrams
- Cause-and-effect diagrams
- Control charts
- Flow charts
- Hierarchical charts
- Histograms
- Logical data models
- Matrix diagrams/charts
- Mind mapping

- Probability and impact matrices
- Scatter diagrams
- Stakeholder engagement assessment matrices
- Stakeholder mapping/representation
- Text-oriented formats

## Decision-Making
Throughout the project, you will have to make countless decisions, often with the input of the project team. There are many approaches to decision-making, including the following techniques, which are used in many project management processes:

- Multicriteria decision analysis
- Voting

## Communication
As you will read later in this book, a great deal of a project manager's time is spent communicating with management, the team, the customer, and other stakeholders. The following are several important communication techniques and concepts you will use throughout the project:

- Active listening
- Feedback
- Presentations
- Meeting management
- Communication methods
- Communications technology

## Interpersonal and Team Skills
Interpersonal and team skills are elements of the art of project management. Closely related to the communication techniques and concepts listed above, the following skills are essential for project success:

- Conflict management
- Cultural awareness
- Decision-making
- Emotional intelligence
- Facilitation
- Influencing
- Leadership
- Meeting management
- Motivation
- Negotiation
- Networking
- Observation/conversation
- Political awareness
- Team building

49

### Estimating
The project manager is responsible for leading estimating efforts for many aspects of the project, including schedule, cost, and resources. The following are common estimating techniques you will learn about in this book:

- Estimating
- Analogous
- Bottom-up
- Top-down
- Expert judgment

### Project Management Information System (PMIS)
An organization's project management information system is part of its enterprise environmental factors. The PMIS includes automated tools, such as scheduling software, a configuration management system, shared workspaces for file storage or distribution, work authorization software, time-tracking software, and procurement management software, as well as repositories for historical information. The PMIS is used in many planning, executing, and monitoring and controlling processes.

### Expert Judgment
Sometimes, the easiest way to get information is to consult experts. Often, those with expertise needed by the project are working on the team, or at least within the organization. Expert judgment is a common tool of the project management planning processes, although it is not frequently discussed in this book.

### Meetings
Meetings are often used in the planning processes of a project, although you will not always see meetings discussed in this book as a planning tool. Meetings can be an effective way to get input or feedback from groups of people, but they can be overused. The project manager is responsible for determining whether a meeting is worth the time of those who would attend it, or if there is a more efficient way to achieve an objective. The value of meetings, as well as some suggested ground rules for meetings, is discussed in the Resource Management chapter.

Make sure you are comfortable with all the concepts in this chapter before reading further; these concepts provide a basis for understanding much of the material presented in the remainder of this book.

## Practice Exam

1. Understanding the culture, policies, and procedures of the organization in which the project is being performed is most challenging in:
   A. Global organizations
   B. Manufacturing organizations
   C. Small organizations
   D. Agile organizations

2. A project team is discussing the benefits and drawbacks of working on projects within their organization now that it has become project oriented. They can agree on many advantages for the team and for the organization, but also agree there are some drawbacks relative to the strong matrix structure the organization used to have. In a project-oriented organization, the project team:
   A. Reports to many managers
   B. Has no loyalty to the project
   C. Reports to the functional manager
   D. Will not always have a "home"

3. A project manager is trying to complete a software development project, but cannot get enough attention for the project. Resources are focused on completing process-related work, and the project manager has little authority to assign resources. What form of organization must the project manager be working in?
   A. Functional
   B. Matrix
   C. Expediter
   D. Coordinator

4. A project manager has little project experience, but she has been assigned as the project manager of a new project. Because she will be working in a matrix organization to complete her project, she can expect communications to be:
   A. Simple
   B. Open and accurate
   C. Complex
   D. Hard to automate

5. A project team member is talking to another team member and complaining that many people are asking him to do things. If he works in a functional organization, who has the power to give direction to the team member?
   A. The project manager
   B. The functional manager
   C. The team
   D. The PMO

51

6. Two project managers have just realized that they are in a weak matrix organization and that their power as project managers is quite limited. One figures out that he is really a project expediter, and the other realizes she is really a project coordinator. How is a project expediter different from a project coordinator?

   A. The project expediter cannot make decisions.
   B. The project expediter can make more decisions.
   C. The project expediter reports to a higher-level manager.
   D. The project expediter has some authority.

7. Who has the most power in a project-oriented organization?

   A. The project manager
   B. The functional manager
   C. The team
   D. They all share power

8. All the following are characteristics of a project except:

   A. It is temporary.
   B. It has a definite beginning and end.
   C. It has interrelated activities.
   D. It repeats itself every month.

9. A framework for keeping an organization focused on its overall strategy is:

   A. Organizational project management
   B. The PMBOK® Guide
   C. Project governance
   D. Portfolio management

10. A project manager's primary responsibility is to deliver the product of the project within project constraints. Actions taken and changes made to the benefit of one constraint could negatively affect another. Which of the following best describes the major constraints on a project?

   A. Scope, number of resources, and cost
   B. Scope, cost, and schedule
   C. Scope, schedule, cost, quality, risk, resources, and customer satisfaction
   D. Schedule, cost, and number of changes

11. If a project manager is concerned with gathering, integrating, and disseminating the outputs of all project management processes, she should concentrate on improving the:

   A. Work breakdown structure (WBS)
   B. Communications management plan
   C. Project management information system (PMIS)
   D. Scope management plan

12. A project manager is managing his second project. It started one month after the first one did, and both projects are still in process. Though his first project is small, the new project seems to be quickly growing in size. As each day passes, the project manager is feeling more and more in need of help. The project manager has recently heard that there was another project in the company last year that was similar to his second project. What should he do?

   A. Contact the project manager for the other project, and ask for assistance.
   B. Obtain historical records and guidance from the project management office (PMO).
   C. Wait to see if the project is impacted by the growth in scope.
   D. Make sure the scope of the project is agreed to by all the stakeholders.

13. To obtain support for the project throughout the performing organization, it's best if the project manager:

   A. Ensures there is a communications management plan
   B. Correlates the need for the project to the organization's strategic plan
   C. Connects the project to the personal objectives of the sponsor
   D. Confirms that the management plan includes the management of team members

14. Your management team has decided that all orders will be treated as projects and that project managers will be used to update orders daily, to resolve issues, and to ensure the customer formally accepts the product within 30 days of completion. Revenue from the individual orders can vary from $100 to $150,000. The project manager will not be required to perform planning or provide documentation other than daily status. How would you define this situation?

   A. Because each individual order is a "temporary endeavor," each order is a project.
   B. This is program management since there are multiple projects involved.
   C. This is a recurring process.
   D. Orders incurring revenue over $100,000 would be considered projects and would involve project management.

15. As a project manager, you have had to develop skills to help plan and manage projects successfully. Which skills would best help you encourage project teams to reach levels of high cooperation and achievement, promote a positive relationship with sellers on a project, and involve stakeholders appropriately through all aspects of the project?

   A. Active listening, negotiating, and political awareness
   B. Networking, communication models, and SWOT
   C. Sensitivity analysis, active listening, and leadership
   D. Communication methods, team building, and claims administration

16. A project team is working on manufacturing a new product, but they are having difficulty creating a project charter. What is the best description of the real problem?

   A. They have not identified the project objectives.
   B. They are working on a process and not a project.
   C. The end date has not been set.
   D. They have not identified the product of the project.

17. One of your team members informs you that he does not know which of the many projects he is working on is the most important. Who should determine the priorities between projects in a company?

    A. The project manager
    B. The project management team
    C. The project management office (PMO)
    D. The project team

18. The difference between a project, program, and portfolio is:

    A. A project is a temporary endeavor with a beginning and an end, a program may include other nonproject work, and a portfolio is all the projects in a given department or division.
    B. A project is a lengthy endeavor with a beginning and an end, a program combines two or more unrelated projects, and a portfolio combines two or more programs.
    C. A project is a temporary endeavor with a beginning and an end, a program is a group of related projects, and a portfolio is a group of projects and programs related to a specific strategic organizational objective.
    D. A project is a contracted endeavor with a beginning and an end, a portfolio is a group of projects with more open-ended completion dates, and a program combines two or more portfolios.

19. Operational work is different from project work in that operational work is:

    A. Unique
    B. Temporary
    C. Ongoing and repetitive
    D. A part of every project activity

20. Company procedures require the creation of a lessons learned register. Which of the following is the best use of lessons learned?

    A. Historical records for future projects
    B. Planning record for the current project
    C. Informing the team about what the project manager has done
    D. Informing the team about the project management plan

21. A complex aerospace engineering project is nearing completion. Because the work was highly technical and new to the organization, the product of the project was released two months later than planned. Despite the late delivery, management is appreciative of the effort expended and believes that this product will generate additional opportunities for the organization. Management also thinks that the experience of this team will provide great value for teams working on similar projects in the future. The sponsor requests that lessons learned be thoroughly documented. Lessons learned are best completed by:

    A. The project manager
    B. The team
    C. The sponsor
    D. The stakeholders

22. Consideration of ongoing operations and maintenance is crucially important to products of projects. Ongoing operations and maintenance should:

    A. Be included as activities to be performed during project closure
    B. Be a separate phase in the project life cycle because a large portion of life cycle costs is devoted to maintenance and operations
    C. Not be viewed as part of a project
    D. Be viewed as a separate project

23. What is a program?

    A. An initiative set up by management
    B. A means to gain benefits and control of related projects
    C. A group of unrelated projects managed in a coordinated way
    D. A government regulation

24. A company is making an effort to improve its project performance and create historical records of past projects. What is the best way to accomplish this?

    A. Create project management plans.
    B. Create lessons learned.
    C. Create network diagrams.
    D. Create status reports.

## Answers

1. **Answer** A

   **Explanation** Understanding the culture, policies, and procedures of the organization in which the project is being performed is especially challenging in global organizations. The culture, policies, and procedures of the performing office may be different from those of the office from which the project is managed, and may also vary between international offices of the same organization.

   This will influence how the project is managed.

2. **Answer** D

   **Explanation** The main drawback of a project-oriented organization is that at the end of the project when the team is dispersed, they do not have a functional department ("home") to which to return. They need to be assigned to another project or get a job with a different employer.

3. **Answer** A

   **Explanation** In a functional organization, the project manager has the least support for the project and has little authority to assign resources. Project expediter and project coordinator are roles in a weak matrix organization.

4. **Answer** C

   **Explanation** Because a project done in a matrix organization involves people from across the organization, communications are more complex.

5. **Answer** B

   **Explanation** In a functional organization, the team members report to the functional manager. The project manager probably reports to the functional manager as well.

6. **Answer** A

   **Explanation** The project coordinator reports to a higher-level manager and has authority to make some decisions. The project expediter has no authority to make decisions.

7. **Answer** A

   **Explanation** In a project-oriented organization, the entire company is organized by projects, giving the project manager the most power.

8. **Answer** D

   **Explanation** "It repeats itself every month" implies that the whole project repeats every month. Generally, the only things that might repeat in a project are some activities. The whole project does not repeat. This is more likely a characteristic of ongoing business operations.

9. **Answer** A

   **Explanation** Organizational project management (OPM) provides a framework and direction for how projects, programs, portfolios, and organizational work should be done to meet the organization's strategic goals.

10. **Answer** C

    **Explanation** "Scope, schedule, cost, quality, risk, resources, and customer satisfaction" is the most accurate list of constraints, or competing demands, that a project manager must deal with.

11. **Answer**  C

    **Explanation**  The scope management plan and the WBS focus on project scope. The communications management plan addresses who will be communicated with, when, and in what format. The only choice that addresses gathering, integrating, and disseminating information is the PMIS.

12. **Answer**  B

    **Explanation**  There are many things the project manager could do. Asking the other project manager for assistance is not the best choice, as the other project manager might not be an experienced mentor. Her advice might not be adequate to help this project manager. Waiting to assess the impact on the project is reactive; a project manager should be proactive. Gaining agreement of all the stakeholders on the project scope is also not the best choice. It would be helpful, but does not specifically address the issue in this situation. By contacting the PMO, the project manager can access the knowledge of many project managers, historical information from many projects, and the assistance of someone whose job it is to help.

13. **Answer**  B

    **Explanation**  Connecting the project to the sponsor's objectives might be a good idea, but it does not address the issue of obtaining support throughout the performing organization. Neither ensuring there is a communications management plan nor confirming that the management plan includes the management of team members directly addresses the need to obtain support for the project. Correlating the need for the project to the organization's strategic plan is the best way to gain support for the project.

14. **Answer**  C

    **Explanation**  Because orders are numerous and of short duration, this situation is a recurring process, not a project.

15. **Answer**  A

    **Explanation**  Active listening, negotiating, and political awareness are all important interpersonal and team skills a project manager should strive to develop.

16. **Answer**  B

    **Explanation**  Manufacturing a product is an ongoing process; it is operational work, not project work. Therefore, the manufacturing team would have no reason to create a project charter and would have difficulty doing so if they tried, because of the ongoing nature of the work. If the question referred to a team developing a new product, however, that would qualify as a project.

17. **Answer**  C

    **Explanation**  Because the question talks about priorities between projects, this cannot be the role of the project manager, the project management team, or the project team. Determining priorities between projects is a role of the PMO.

18. **Answer**  C

    **Explanation**  A project is a temporary endeavor with a beginning and an end, a program is a group of related projects, and a portfolio is a group of projects and programs related to a specific strategic organizational objective. Remember to use the process of elimination, ruling out any answer that is not completely correct.

19. **Answer**  C

    **Explanation**  Operational work is that which is ongoing and frequently requires performing job functions repeatedly to sustain an organization.

20. **Answer** A

    **Explanation** Notice that this question asks about the use of a tool of project management. Many people can learn from a book what a lessons learned register is, but questions like this can more readily be answered if you actually use the tool and know from experience its value. Ask yourself about the other tools of project management. Why are they beneficial? The best uses of lessons learned are as continuous improvement within the current project, historical records for future projects, and improving the organization's processes and systems. There are other tools that are better for accomplishing the things listed in the other choices.

21. **Answer** D

    **Explanation** The best answer is stakeholders, as their input is critical for collecting all the lessons learned on each project. The term "stakeholders" includes all the groups mentioned in the other answer options.

22. **Answer** C

    **Explanation** Remember the definition of a project: temporary and unique. Operations and maintenance are considered ongoing activities, not temporary. Therefore, such work is not considered a project or part of a project.

23. **Answer** B

    **Explanation** Did you select "a group of unrelated projects managed in a coordinated way"? If so, you missed the word "unrelated." Programs are groups of related projects.

24. **Answer** B

    **Explanation** Lessons learned help to avoid future pitfalls and use the good ideas of past projects. This leads to improvements in future projects. The organization benefits from creating a lessons learned repository.

# Project Management Processes

Before we discuss the actions that take place in each of the project management process groups, let's go through the definition of a project life cycle and the project management process.

## Project Life Cycles and the Project Management Process

For the exam, you should understand the difference between the project life cycle and the project management process. Both are necessary to complete a project. The project life cycle is what you need to do to *do* the work, and the project management process is what you need to do to *manage* the work.

**Project Life Cycle**[1]   PAGE 19   A life cycle is a progression of phases through a series of developmental stages. The project life cycle is the performing organization's or department's methodology for managing a project. It is the logical breakdown of what you need to do to produce the deliverables of the project. The project life cycle for a particular project is selected based on factors such as the type of product being developed, the industry, and the organization's preferences.

Project life cycles can be either plan driven or change driven. Within a project life cycle, there are generally one or more phases. These phases are collectively referred to as the development life cycle of a project. The development life cycle[2] is used to ensure that the expected or planned result of each phase is achieved. An example of a development life cycle for a software project might include the following life cycle phases: research, design, code, test, and implement.

**Plan-Driven Project Life Cycle**   Plan-driven projects have predictive development life cycles (sometimes referred to as waterfall or traditional life cycles) that require scope, schedule, and cost to be determined in detail early in the life of a project—before the work begins to produce the project deliverables. For example, a construction project would typically be managed using a predictive life cycle.

### Change-Driven Project Life Cycle   Change-driven projects use iterative, incremental, or adaptive (agile) development life cycles, and have varying levels of early planning for scope, schedule, and cost.

Incremental and iterative life cycles involve early planning of high-level scope sufficient enough to allow for preliminary estimates of time and cost; scope is developed a little more with each iteration.

An incremental development life cycle delivers a complete, usable portion of the product for each iteration. For example, a project to build a website using an incremental life cycle would involve prioritizing requirements into iterations that deliver a fully functioning portion of the website at the end of each iteration.

With an iterative development life cycle, the complete concept is built in successive levels of detail to create the end result. To build the website mentioned in the previous paragraph using an iterative life cycle, planning for the first iteration would focus on planning to create a prototype of the entire website. After the basic skeleton of the site is built, each successive iteration would be planned to add more detail until a complete and fully functioning site is achieved.

Note that a project may use a combination of incremental and iterative life cycles throughout the project or for phases of the project.

Adaptive development life cycles involve a fixed schedule as well as fixed costs. Scope is broadly defined with the understanding that it will be refined throughout the life of the project. The customer's requirements are documented and prioritized in a backlog, which can be adjusted as the project progresses. Work is planned in short increments to allow the customer to change and reprioritize requirements within the time and cost constraints. A new software development project may follow an adaptive approach, using phases that might include high-level feasibility, design, and planning followed by short, iterative phases of detailed design, coding, testing, and release.

### Hybrid Development Life Cycle   A hybrid life cycle is a combination of a predictive and an adaptive development life cycle. With such an approach, a predictive life cycle is used to manage the project require-ments that are well defined, while an adaptive life cycle is used to manage the requirements that are less clear.

 The processes, tools and techniques, and concepts discussed in this book can be modified based on the nature of the project, the characteristics of the organization, and other factors, including the project and development life cycle. As you read through this book and prepare for the exam, think in terms of a plan-driven project life cycle. Just remember that many of the same processes, tools, and techniques can be used on change-driven projects as well. Tailoring project management practices to fit the needs of the project and the organization is your responsibility as a project manager.

### Project Management Process   As noted earlier, the project management process is what you need to do to *manage* the work throughout the project life cycle. It includes managing the efforts related to initiating, planning, executing, monitoring and controlling, and closing the project.

Figure 3.1 shows how the project management process groups interact.

60

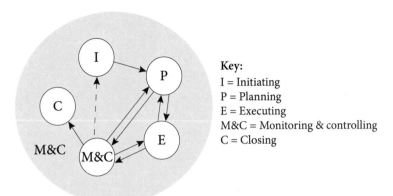

FIGURE 3.1    *Project management process*

The process groups are described in detail later in this chapter, but let's take some time now to discuss the difference between the project management process and the project life cycle—including how the overall project management process interacts with the project life cycle. For small projects following a plan-driven (or predictive) life cycle, you may go through the overall project management process (initiating through closing) once for the entire project, although portions of the process may be iterated or repeated throughout the project life cycle (see fig. 3.2).

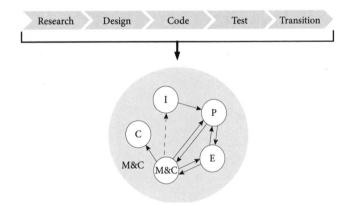

FIGURE 3.2    *Small project with a predictive life cycle*

Large projects often require each life cycle phase to be managed through the project management process groups. The example illustrated in figure 3.3 is for a large construction project. In this project, the development life cycle phases of feasibility, planning, design, production, turnover, and start-up are all extensive, requiring separate planning and management of each phase. This means there would be an overall initiating effort in which the project manager would help create a charter and do high-level planning for the entire project to get charter approval. Then, a separate initiating process for the feasibility phase would take place, followed by a planning effort for the work that will be done in the feasibility phase, the execution and control of that work, and, finally, a closeout of the phase, which typically includes a handoff of deliverables (in this example, the results of the feasibility analysis). This would then be repeated for each of the life cycle phases.

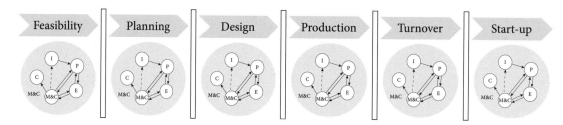

FIGURE 3.3    *Large project with a predictive life cycle with phase gates (indicated by the vertical bars)*

At the end of each phase, an event called a phase gate may take place.[3] A phase gate involves analyzing the results of the completed phase by comparing the results of the phase with the business documents, the project charter, and the project management plan. Based on that analysis, a decision is made. Options include redoing the same phase, moving forward with the next phase, or choosing not to continue with the project. If the decision is made to move forward, the project would begin initiating work on the next phase and progress through the project management process groups for that phase.

Large change-driven projects may also be broken into phases and then into smaller releases and iterations within those phases. The project management processes of initiating, planning, executing, monitoring and controlling, and closing are done for each phase. This process is typically done within each release and iteration as well. The level of detail and the time spent on each of the project management process groups may vary based on the phase of the project you are working on, but the entire project management process is typically followed, as indicated in figure 3.4, which depicts an adaptive life cycle.

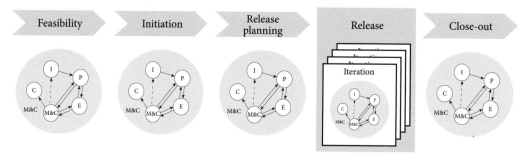

FIGURE 3.4    *Large project with an adaptive life cycle*

This may all seem fairly complicated. Don't worry! For the exam, understand that there is a project life cycle and a project management process. Read exam questions carefully to determine whether the project life cycle or project management process is being discussed.

The project life cycle varies depending on the industry, the organization, and the type of product, service, or result being developed. As the project manager, you work with the project management team and project governance to select the right approach for the project.

Some people think they need to understand a variety of industries to pass this exam. Although some questions may refer to specific types of projects and industries (for example, "You are building a bridge" or "You are creating a new system for your company"), that type of information is mostly background data. The exam will not ask you to select the "correct" project life cycle for a specific type of project, nor will it ask how to do work on a certain type of IT, construction, or engineering project. Instead, the exam will ask you about managing projects. The questions are general and can be answered without an understanding of the industry—if you know project management.

You may, however, see questions that require you to understand how the project life cycle (plan-driven versus change-driven) influences both how a project is planned and the flow of the work itself. Also remember that the project management process is the same, regardless of the development life cycle used. The process groups of initiating, planning, executing, monitoring and controlling, and closing do not change, although there are variations in the level of attention and formality given to each of the process groups depending on the life cycle used.

The rest of this chapter examines the project management process, both at a high level and in more detail with Rita's Process Chart™. Carefully review the information in the chapter, especially the process chart, and complete all the exercises. These are valuable tools for helping you identify the gaps in your knowledge and will significantly cut down your study time. Understanding the process of managing a project and knowing what should be done and when provides a framework for understanding all the inputs, tools and techniques, and outputs involved in project management. If you understand the process, you can use logic on the exam, rather than having to rely on memorization. So are you ready? Read on!

The illustration that appeared in figure 3.1 is shown again here in figure 3.5 for your reference as you read the following section.

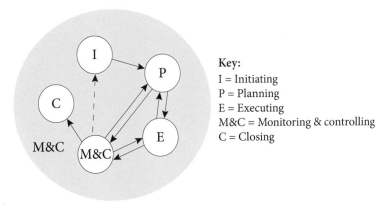

**FIGURE 3.5**   *Project management process*

In initiating, the project manager determines whether the business case and the benefits management plan can be achieved and does some high-level planning to verify that it is likely the project can be completed within the given constraints of scope, schedule, cost, etc. Stakeholders are identified, and stakeholder analysis is performed to assess each stakeholder's potential involvement and influence on the project.

The project is formally authorized in project initiating when the sponsor signs the project charter. After the project charter has been approved, the project moves from initiating into detailed planning, where a project management plan (including plans for how to plan, execute, monitor and control, and close the project) is developed. When the project management plan includes the appropriate amount of detail for the project life cycle and development approach, it is approved by the sponsor.

The project then moves into executing, where the team completes the work according to the processes and procedures detailed in the project management plan.

While the work is being done, the work results (or work performance data) are fed into monitoring and controlling, to make sure the project is progressing according to the baselines established in the project management plan.

© 2018 RMC Publications, Inc.™ • 952.846.4484 • info@rmcls.com • www.rmcls.com

If variances from the plan require changes, the change requests are evaluated in the Perform Integrated Change Control process (part of monitoring and controlling) to determine their impact on the project, identify the best options for dealing with them, and decide whether they should be approved, rejected, or deferred.

For approved changes that require adjustments to the baselines and project management plan, a replanning effort must be completed before the team can start working from the updated version of the plan and baselines in executing. This replanning effort is done as part of the Perform Integrated Change Control process in monitoring and controlling. After the plan and baselines are modified, the revised plan is provided to the team in executing, and the project is executed according to the updated plan, and monitored and controlled to the revised baselines. If the project gets so far off the baselines that it requires an analysis of whether the project should continue at all, or if significant changes are suggested that are outside the project charter, it may move back into initiating while that decision is made (since the charter, which is created in initiating, would have to change in such a situation). Ultimately, when the work is done (or the project is terminated), the project moves into closing.

Throughout the project, it may be necessary to revisit project planning. For example, if a stakeholder is identified and their requirements need to be analyzed after work has begun or if a new risk that needs to be analyzed using qualitative risk analysis is identified in a risk review, the project will need to return to planning. The project also returns to planning to do rolling wave planning. Another instance when the project returns to planning is when new information becomes available through progressive elaboration (for example, more accurate estimates are generated that could impact the project schedule and budget).

There's one last point to keep in mind about the illustration shown in figure 3.1 and figure 3.5. Did you notice the large monitoring and controlling circle encompassing all the project management processes? It's there to illustrate that all the work of the project and project management must be monitored and controlled. This is an important concept to remember for the exam: throughout the life of the project, you'll be monitoring and measuring the outcomes of the project and any project management efforts, and analyzing them to help identify variances from the plan so that you can make proactive decisions to keep the project on track.

This process might be exactly what you need to use to manage small projects. For large projects that are broken into phases, this process may be repeated multiple times. For example, on a project with a research phase, you complete initiating through closing for that phase, and then repeat the process from initiating to closing for the next phase. When answering situational questions on the exam, remember that the level of detail to which the project management processes are performed will be adjusted or tailored to the type and strategic importance of the project and the chosen life cycle.

Now let's look at the project management process in more detail, using Rita's Process Chart™.

 **Rita's Process Chart™**    In the past, there have been more than 70 exam questions that require knowledge of the project management process. Therefore, to pass the exam, you must understand this process. It can seem like a lot to learn. This chapter, and the remaining chapters in this book, will help you understand it with little or no memorization.

Since the first edition of this book, people all over the world have used the following chart as a trick to learn the project management process quickly and effectively. It helps you understand what should be done when. This chart was created by Rita Mulcahy and is unique to RMC's books and products.

It is not intended to map to other project management resources; instead, its function is to state, simply and directly, the efforts that are involved in managing a project. Understanding these efforts will provide the context you need to clearly understand the project management process for the exam.

# Project Management Processes

| INITIATING | PLANNING (This is the only process group with a set order.) | EXECUTING | MONITORING & CONTROLLING | CLOSING |
|---|---|---|---|---|
| Select project manager | Determine development approach, life cycle, and how you will plan for each knowledge area | Execute work according to the project management plan | Take action to monitor and control the project | Confirm work is done to requirements |
| Determine company culture and existing systems | Define and prioritize requirements | Produce product deliverables (product scope) | Measure performance against performance measurement baseline | Complete final procurement closure |
| Collect processes, procedures, and historical information | Create project scope statement | Gather work performance data | Measure performance against other metrics in the project management plan | Gain final acceptance of product |
| Divide large projects into phases or smaller projects | Assess what to purchase and create procurement documents | Request changes | Analyze and evaluate data and performance | Complete financial closure |
| Understand business case and benefits management plan | Determine planning team | Implement only approved changes | Determine if variances warrant a corrective action or other change request(s) | Hand off completed product |
| Uncover initial requirements, assumptions, risks, constraints, and existing agreements | Create WBS and WBS dictionary | Continuously improve; perform progressive elaboration | Influence factors that cause change | Solicit customer's feedback about the project |
| Assess project and product feasibility within the given constraints | Create activity list | Follow processes | Request changes | Complete final performance reporting |
| Create measurable objectives and success criteria | Create network diagram | Determine whether quality plan and processes are correct and effective | Perform integrated change control | Index and archive records |
| Develop project charter | Estimate resource requirements | Perform quality audits and issue quality reports | Approve or reject changes | Gather final lessons learned and update knowledge bases |
| Identify stakeholders and determine their expectations, interest, influence, and impact | Estimate activity durations and costs | Acquire final team and physical resources | Update project management plan and project documents | |
| Request changes | Determine critical path | Manage people | Inform stakeholders of all change request results | |
| Develop assumption log | Develop schedule | Evaluate team and individual performance; provide training | Monitor stakeholder engagement | |
| Develop stakeholder register | Develop budget | Hold team-building activities | Confirm configuration compliance | |
| | Determine quality standards, processes, and metrics | Give recognition and rewards | Create forecasts | |
| | Determine team charter and all roles and responsibilities | Use issue logs | Gain customer's acceptance of interim deliverables | |
| | Plan communications and stakeholder engagement | Facilitate conflict resolution | Perform quality control | |
| | Perform risk identification, qualitative and quantitative risk analysis, and risk response planning | Release resources as work is completed | Perform risk reviews, reassessments, and audits | |
| | Go back—iterations | Send and receive information, and solicit feedback | Manage reserves | |
| | Finalize procurement strategy and documents | Report on project performance | Manage, evaluate, and close procurements | |
| | Create change and configuration management plans | Facilitate stakeholder engagement and manage expectations | Evaluate use of physical resources | |
| | Finalize all management plans | Hold meetings | | |
| | Develop realistic and sufficient project management plan and baselines | Evaluate sellers; negotiate and contract with sellers | | |
| | Gain formal approval of the plan | Use and share project knowledge | | |
| | Hold kickoff meeting | Execute contingency plans | | |
| | Request changes | Update project management plan and project documents | | |

## Rita's Process Chart™
Where are we in the project management process?

65

### How to Use Rita's Process Chart™    As you review Rita's Process Chart™, make sure you:

- Understand the overall project management process (a PMI-ism).
- Find terms you do not know, and learn what they are by looking them up in this book.
- Understand why each item is in the column (process group) it falls into.
- Are able to replicate the specific order of the planning process by understanding what happens when, how previous work supports what comes next, and why; knowing the Planning column in this order can help you get a large number of questions right on the exam because the exam often asks what should be done next. The work in the other process groups does not have a set order.
- Understand the project management process groups of initiating through closing, including when each effort should be done on projects. The exam asks questions that present a situation and require you to know which process group the project is in.
- Understand that project planning is an iterative process. Consider how you might go back and redo (iterate) some of the items in the Planning column to refine the plan for a large project. Or think about how rolling wave planning would be used on a large project to refine and detail plans for each phase as you move through the life cycle of a project.
- Complete Rita's Process Game™ (which follows the chart) at least three times. Going through the game will solidify your understanding of the overall project management process and help you find gaps in your knowledge. Focus your study on those gap areas so you understand the processes before taking the exam.

### Notes on the Chart

- Notice the phrase "Understand business case and benefits management plan" in the Initiating column. This could be read as, "Understand the reason the project is being done and what benefits the organization expects to gain as a result of the project." These business documents will guide all project management activities to ensure the project is worth the required investment and that it will return the anticipated or expected benefits to the organization. This is a major concept on the exam that many project managers miss.

  A project is initiated for specific reasons, and the project results must support those reasons. It seems easy, but many projects do not satisfy the business need or deliver the benefits for which they were intended. Project managers may create the project they want, rather than what was asked of them, or they may complete the project to the technical requirements and forget the reasons (stated or otherwise) the project was initiated. The problem is that many project managers do not appreciate the importance of the effort that takes place before the project has a charter and is therefore authorized.

  Here is what should be happening in your organization: the company should know what its strategic objectives are, and all projects should help meet those objectives. This is not what happens in many real-world organizations, however—to the detriment of those organizations. A company that manages itself well has strategic objectives, and it evaluates various options for achieving those objectives. Many project ideas are proposed, and the company performs analysis to see which proposed projects meet the objectives for the least cost, time, resources, and, if it is a well-run company, risk. The organization then authorizes one or more projects by issuing project charters. This is the project selection process you need to understand for the exam, and you need to know how that process affects project management activities.

- As the project manager, you should understand why the project you are assigned to was selected and what benefits the project is expected to deliver. Is the project being done so the organization can enter a new market? Is it intended to meet a regulatory requirement? Is it the result of a customer request?

Is it just a priority project for a company executive? Is it expected to dramatically improve the future of the company? If you lose sight of the objectives, the project may finish on schedule and on budget but still fail because it does not achieve those objectives or does not deliver the benefits expected.

- Team building, risk identification, stakeholder identification, risk response planning, and many other activities primarily occur in the process groups in which they are placed on the chart, but these activities can start in initiating and continue until closing.

- In the Planning column, note the first box: "Determine development approach, life cycle, and how you will plan for each knowledge area." Each knowledge area (scope, schedule, cost, etc.) requires management plans as well as additional plans for configuration, change, and requirements management. The first thing you need to do as you start planning is figure out how you are going to plan, execute, and control for each knowledge area. This will help guide the rest of your planning efforts.

- Notice the phrase "Determine team charter and all roles and responsibilities" in the Planning column. You should be aware that determining roles and responsibilities involves more than determining who is going to do which product-related work activities. It also includes who will be required to provide reports, who will attend meetings, who will help with risk identification, who will work with the quality department, etc. All roles and responsibilities on a project should be defined. They may be documented as part of the resource management plan, in project job descriptions, and in the management plans for each knowledge area. This item also includes developing a responsibility assignment matrix and a rewards and recognition system. If all this effort seems unnecessary to you, you may be thinking about it in the context of a small project that uses the same handful of team members as the last project. Remember to think in terms of large projects that have hundreds of team members.

- Look at the phrase "Go back—iterations" in the Planning column. This is an important concept. When planning a project, the project manager and the team complete each item listed in the Planning column above this point to the best of their ability. But a project will evolve as each item is planned, and much of the earlier planning work will need to be modified or added to. For example, it is only after completing the risk management planning efforts that the WBS and the other items can be finalized. A risk response strategy (see the Risk Management chapter) may be used to avoid a portion or all of a threat by planning to perform additional testing as part of the project. This testing will require adjusting the WBS for added scope, the network diagram to determine the order of the work, the budget for added cost, etc. The project manager might also work with discretionary dependencies (see the Schedule Management chapter) to decrease some risk and thereby change the network diagram. The important thing to remember is that planning should lead to a realistic, bought-into, approved, and formal project management plan that is updated throughout the project to reflect approved changes. Iterations help you create and maintain such a plan.

- On a related note, the Planning column includes a reminder that planning is the only process group with a set order. Occasionally, however, a planning process will require an input that, according to this column, won't be available yet. The risk register, for example, is an input to several processes leading to the creation of the schedule. The schedule is developed before we get to risk management activities in the Planning column, so how can the risk register be an input? In such situations, you'll start off using a preliminary version of the input. Initial risks are uncovered during initiating, so although the risk register will by no means be complete by the time you're creating the schedule, the known risks can be factored into your planning. Then, after performing risk management activities, you'll have a more complete risk register that you can use to refine your schedule through iterations.

- Notice the term "procurement strategy and documents" in the Planning column. This phrase refers to documents such as the procurement statement of work (a description of the work to be done), contract provisions, source selection criteria, and bid documents such as the request for proposal (RFP), request for quotation (RFQ), and request for information (RFI). It encompasses the breadth of preparation required in planning for procurements. Note also the placement of "Finalize procurement strategy and documents" after "Go back—iterations." It's likely the risk management process will generate risk response strategies involving contracts; through iterations the procurement documents can be created, refined, and finalized.

- Team members can be released at any time during the project, once their work is approved and accepted and they have completed any documentation or other activities that pertain to their work. For example, the electricians on a project to build a house may test their work, get acceptance of their work, document lessons learned, suggest process improvements, and turn the work over. They can then be released from the project while other team members doing drywall are still working (executing their part of the plan). Keep in mind that some team members remain on the project to its end to assist the project manager in creating the final lessons learned, archiving final records, and producing the final report.

- As project executing progresses, the project manager may determine that a change to the project is needed. The same could happen while the project manager is monitoring and controlling the work. That is why changes can be requested in both the executing and monitoring and controlling process groups. Change requests may also be generated in planning as a result of rolling wave planning that occurs after the plan has been approved and work has started. Change requests are evaluated and approved or rejected as part of the Perform Integrated Change Control process (see the Integration Management chapter).

- Do the project management process groups occur sequentially? No; they all overlap. For example, you could be using monitoring and controlling processes to control the identification of stakeholders, the adherence to organizational requirements for project planning, or the creation of baselines and project documents. Defects could be identified in executing that will require work in executing to fix them, as well as work in monitoring and controlling to decide if the defects require a change to the plan to prevent future rework and delays. Controlling procurements and the final closure of procurements can occur simultaneously on projects because some sellers will complete their contractual obligations to the project while others are still producing deliverables. Look again at Rita's Process Chart™, and think about the overall focus of each process group.

- Make sure you understand the difference between executing and monitoring and controlling actions, because they continually overlap while the work of the project is going on. The focus of executing is managing people, physical resources, and work to accomplish the project as planned. The focus of monitoring and controlling is ensuring the project is progressing according to plan, and approving necessary changes to the plan to meet the organization's strategic objectives and deliver the expected benefits.

**TRICKS OF THE TRADE®** **Rita's Process Game™**   The following pages contain the pieces for Rita's Process Game™. Cut them out, and practice putting each item into the correct process group, on your own or in a group. When you think the cards are sorted into the correct process groups, put the planning efforts in order. Check your answers using Rita's Process Chart™. Play this game at least three times to ensure you understand the efforts involved in the project management process that are discussed throughout this chapter.

INITIATING

PLANNING

EXECUTING

MONITORING
& CONTROLLING

CLOSING

Evaluate sellers; negotiate
and contract with sellers

Release resources as
work is completed

Evaluate team and
individual performance;
provide training

Create measurable
objectives and
success criteria

Gather work
performance data

Manage reserves

Manage, evaluate, and
close procurements

Analyze and evaluate data
and performance

Develop
stakeholder register

Finalize all
management plans

69

Create project
scope statement

Create change and
configuration management
plans

Facilitate conflict resolution

Solicit customer's feedback
about the project

Confirm
configuration compliance

Perform quality control

Use issue logs

Determine whether quality
plan and processes are
correct and effective

Determine development
approach, life cycle, and
how you will plan for each
knowledge area

Request changes

Evaluate use of
physical resources

Determine if variances
warrant a corrective action
or other change request(s)

Divide large projects into
phases or smaller projects

Collect processes,
procedures, and
historical information

Go back—iterations

Hold team-building activities

Select project manager

Execute work according to the project management plan

Perform risk reviews, reassessments, and audits

Influence factors that cause change

Facilitate stakeholder engagement and manage expectations

Determine team charter and all roles and responsibilities

Approve or reject changes

Request changes

Complete financial closure

Assess what to purchase and create procurement documents

Give recognition and rewards

Develop assumption log

Execute contingency plans

Create activity list

Perform quality audits
and issue quality reports

Gain formal approval
of the plan

Understand business
case and benefits
management plan

Perform risk identification,
qualitative and quantitative
risk analysis, and risk
response planning

Confirm work is done
to requirements

Update project management
plan and project documents

Use and share
project knowledge

Follow processes

Hold kickoff meeting

Complete final
procurement closure

Identify stakeholders
and determine their
expectations, interest,
influence, and impact

Update project management
plan and project documents

Uncover initial
requirements, assumptions,
risks, constraints, and
existing agreements

Report on
project performance

Measure performance
against other metrics in the
project management plan

Hold meetings

Hand off completed product

Estimate activity durations and costs

Measure performance against performance measurement baseline

Estimate resource requirements

Manage people

Develop schedule

Determine critical path

Gain final acceptance of product

Determine company culture and existing systems

Acquire final team and physical resources

Finalize procurement strategy and documents

Monitor stakeholder engagement

Take action to monitor and control the project

Develop realistic and sufficient project management plan and baselines

Define and
prioritize requirements

Assess project and
product feasibility within
the given constraints

Inform stakeholders of all
change request results

Continuously improve;
perform
progressive elaboration

Complete final
performance reporting

Determine quality standards,
processes, and metrics

Index and archive records

Develop budget

Gather final lessons
learned and update
knowledge bases

Develop project charter

Request changes

Plan communications
and stakeholder
engagement

Create WBS and
WBS dictionary

Gain customer's acceptance
of interim deliverables

Produce
product deliverables
(product scope)

Send and receive
information, and
solicit feedback

Determine planning team

Create forecasts

Request changes

Perform integrated
change control

Implement only
approved changes

Create network diagram

**The What-Comes-Before Game**    Here is another game to help you understand the overall project management process. Playing this game after you have completed Rita's Process Game™ at least three times will really help solidify your understanding of these concepts.

Name the project planning effort that comes before each of the following items on Rita's Process Chart™.

| | Planning | What Comes Before? |
|---|---|---|
| 1 | Create network diagram | |
| 2 | Finalize procurement strategy and documents | |
| 3 | Create project scope statement | |
| 4 | Create WBS and WBS dictionary | |
| 5 | Determine critical path | |
| 6 | Develop budget | |
| 7 | Estimate activity durations and costs | |
| 8 | Gain formal approval of the plan | |
| 9 | Hold kickoff meeting | |
| 10 | Determine quality standards, processes, and metrics | |
| 11 | Assess what to purchase and create procurement documents | |
| 12 | Plan communications and stakeholder engagement | |
| 13 | Go back—iterations | |
| 14 | Determine team charter and all roles and responsibilities | |
| 15 | Develop realistic and sufficient project management plan and baselines | |
| 16 | Perform risk identification, qualitative and quantitative risk analysis, and risk response planning | |
| 17 | Estimate resource requirements | |
| 18 | Create activity list | |

© 2018 RMC Publications, Inc.™ • 952.846.4484 • info@rmcls.com • www.rmcls.com

## Answer   The What-Comes-Before Game

| | Planning | What Comes Before? |
|---|---|---|
| 1 | Create network diagram | Create activity list |
| 2 | Finalize procurement strategy and documents | Go back—iterations |
| 3 | Create project scope statement | Define and prioritize requirements |
| 4 | Create WBS and WBS dictionary | Determine planning team |
| 5 | Determine critical path | Estimate activity durations and costs |
| 6 | Develop budget | Develop schedule |
| 7 | Estimate activity durations and costs | Estimate resource requirements |
| 8 | Gain formal approval of the plan | Develop realistic and sufficient project management plan and baselines |
| 9 | Hold kickoff meeting | Gain formal approval of the plan |
| 10 | Determine quality standards, processes, and metrics | Develop budget |
| 11 | Assess what to purchase and create procurement documents | Create project scope statement |
| 12 | Plan communications and stakeholder engagement | Determine team charter and all roles and responsibilities |
| 13 | Go back—iterations | Perform risk identification, qualitative and quantitative risk analysis, and risk response planning |
| 14 | Determine team charter and all roles and responsibilities | Determine quality standards, processes, and metrics |
| 15 | Develop realistic and sufficient project management plan and baselines | Finalize all management plans |
| 16 | Perform risk identification, qualitative and quantitative risk analysis, and risk response planning | Plan communications and stakeholder management |
| 17 | Estimate resource requirements | Create network diagram |
| 18 | Create activity list | Create WBS and WBS dictionary |

## How to Use the Rest of This Chapter

For many people, this is the hardest chapter in this book, and it uncovers the most gaps in their knowledge. If this chapter is difficult for you, trust us to help you; carefully follow along and try to complete each exercise. Then look for gaps in your knowledge. Do not simply skip to the answers.

The exercises in this chapter are extensive and are designed to help you explore what a project manager needs to do during each of the project management process groups. Take your time completing each exercise and reviewing the answers. Note your gaps on a separate sheet. Then spend some time making sure you research each knowledge gap as you read the rest of the book and clear it from your list.

Again, we encourage you to complete all exercises as they are intended to be completed. The exam includes common project management errors as choices and will focus on things most people do not know they should be doing. RMC has helped people all over the world find their knowledge gaps, and we have determined which gaps are most common. We then created exercises to fill those gaps. So, approach these exercises with the intent of discovering your personal gaps, and make sure you are thinking of a large, plan-driven project when you complete each exercise.

Also remember that you should read each chapter in this book more than once. When you go through this chapter the second time, focus on filling the gaps you discovered in the first pass through the chapter, rather than recreating the complete list for each exercise.

## Initiating Process Group

The processes in the initiating process group formally start a new project or project phase. The initiating process group involves identifying and analyzing stakeholders to align their expectations about the project. It also provides a guiding vision for the project in terms of the organization's strategic objectives, the benefits the project will help achieve, the project's high-level scope, and any known constraints. The project is officially authorized through project initiating, and this process group provides the project manager with the authority and information necessary to begin the project. The project charter and the stakeholder register are the outputs of this process group.

### Inputs to Project Initiating
You do not have to memorize inputs to pass this exam. It is much better to use logic and rely on your understanding of the project management process. Try this exercise.

**Exercise** What does a project manager need to know or have before initiating a project?

**Answer** If you know what efforts are involved in project initiating (such as drafting the project charter and identifying and analyzing stakeholders), the inputs are easier to logically identify. To initiate a project, you need to know or have the following:

- The business case and the benefits management plan for the project
- The product description and requirements as they are known up to this point; in other words, what is the project supposed to do?

85

© 2018 RMC Publications, Inc.™ • 952.846.4484 • info@rmcls.com • www.rmcls.com

- How the project fits into or supports the company's strategic plan
- A list of likely stakeholders
- Any known constraints (such as imposed schedule, budget, or resources), risks, and assumptions
- Any relevant agreements, including contracts, if any of the work will be done under contract
- Industry standards
- Marketplace trends and legal, regulatory, or compliance factors
- The company's change control system
- Defined processes and procedures for how the company operates
- Relationships with the sponsor of the project, likely stakeholders, and possible team members
- Templates from past projects
- Historical WBSs
- Historical estimates
- Lessons learned from previous projects
- What is going on in the company today, including major projects and the potential impact that current and planned initiatives could have on this project
- An understanding of the company's culture
- A list of people who may be good team members
- Information on organizational and project governance

Make sure you identify anything from the previous list that you did not think of, and add it to your gaps list.

**TRICKS OF THE TRADE®** Remember, many questions on the exam will include common errors in project management. You will be required to know the activities that should be done during each part of the project management process. The only way to check your knowledge is to first determine what your knowledge is and then compare it to what it should be. The following exercises are designed to help you do just that.

**Exercise** Let's go beyond inputs. What are the specific actions required to complete project initiating?

**Answer** If you are thinking only in terms of high-level processes, you probably came up with the following:

- Develop Project Charter (Integration Management chapter)
- Identify Stakeholders (Stakeholder Management chapter)

Knowing the names of these two processes will not be enough to pass the exam, however. You need to have a more detailed understanding of what really should be done (the actions) in project initiating.

The following table provides a list of the actions involved in project initiating—from the time the project manager is assigned. Remember that what needs to be done on a project varies based on the specific project, its life cycle, development approach, and the industry, so it may not be practical to do all these actions on every project.

As you review the list, place a check mark next to the actions you have done on your real-world projects and leave any actions you do not know or have never done unchecked. Then make sure you study the areas that are unchecked. The items in the list are not in any particular order.

| Actions Involved in Project Initiating | Place ✓ Here If You Do It; Study Areas Unchecked |
|---|---|
| 1 Sponsor(s) selects the project manager. | |
| 2 Sponsor(s) determines the authority of the project manager. | |
| 3 Collect historical information. | |
| 4 Divide large projects into phases. Use project governance rules and apply them to the project. | |
| 5 Identify stakeholders, and determine their influence, expectations, and impact. Document that information in a stakeholder register. | |
| 6 Determine high-level requirements, constraints, assumptions, and risks. | |
| 7 Turn high-level stakeholder needs, wants, and expectations into requirements. | |
| 8 Make sure the business case and the analysis supporting the need for the project are documented and understood. | |
| 9 Use the benefits management plan to understand the benefits that the project is expected to deliver to the business. | |
| 10 Ensure the high-level product scope is documented with as much detail as is practical. | |
| 11 Understand how the project supports the organization's strategic objectives. | |
| 12 Collect and use any relevant, existing agreements (including contracts) that might be generating the project or that will be required during the project. | |
| 13 Determine success criteria and measurable project and product objectives. | |
| 14 Facilitate the resolution of conflicting objectives. | |

87

| | Actions Involved in Project Initiating | Place ✓ Here If You Do It; Study Areas Unchecked |
|---|---|---|
| 15 | Become familiar with the company culture and structure as they relate to the project. | |
| 16 | Find existing processes, standards, and compliance requirements that affect the project. | |
| 17 | Understand how the organization does business (business knowledge) and what governance, procedures, and policies are already in place to use on the project. | |
| 18 | Do planning on a high-level basis. | |
| 19 | Perform high-level estimating for the project schedule and budget. | |
| 20 | Use the high-level planning and estimating data to determine whether the project objectives can be achieved within the given constraints and whether the expected benefits can be realized. | |
| 21 | Determine what form the project charter will take, including its level of detail. | |
| 22 | Coordinate project initiating efforts with stakeholders, including the customer. | |
| 23 | Work with the customer and others to determine high-level acceptance criteria and clarify what is and is not in the project. | |
| 24 | Determine the initial project organization. | |
| 25 | Identify any inherent or required milestones on the project. | |
| 26 | Finalize the project charter. | |
| 27 | Obtain formal approval of the project charter. | |
| 28 | Define the exit criteria for the project (when and why the project or phase should be closed). | |
| 29 | Involve subject matter experts in developing the project charter and identifying stakeholders. | |
| 30 | Develop project documents such as the risk register, the stakeholder register and the assumption log, including data on identified risks and stakeholders. | |
| 31 | Use stakeholder mapping to analyze data on identified stakeholders to understand their power, interest, and influence. | |

The following are some points from the previous list of actions that could use further clarification.

## Progressive Elaboration[4]

You may notice that many of the items in the previous list (including estimates, product scope description, etc.) start in the initiating process group and then are iterated or refined into plans that can be used to manage the project. Although the project management plan is finalized in planning, items such as detailed estimates and project scope and product scope descriptions may be clarified as the work is being done during the executing and monitoring and controlling processes. The process of continually refining estimates and scope definition is called progressive elaboration.

## Rolling Wave Planning[5]

The technique of rolling wave planning is a form of progressive elaboration. The earliest parts of the project are planned in sufficient detail for work to begin. Later phases of project work are planned at a high level. As the project progresses, and more information impacting the work becomes available, plans are elaborated in sufficient detail to accomplish the work.

## Project Manager Assigned

You should notice in the previous list that the project manager is assigned early in the process. This means the project manager is involved in project initiating. Is this true on your projects? For the exam, assume you are involved this early in the project, and make sure you understand what is going on during initiating.

## Business Documents

Do you know why your project was selected? Does it matter? As noted in the discussion of Rita's Process Chart™, the project manager needs to keep in mind throughout the project the reason the project was started. It will influence how the project is planned, what changes are allowed, and how the project scope is defined. The business case and the benefits management plan are inputs to developing the charter. (See the Develop Project Charter discussion in the Integration Management chapter for more about the importance of project business documents.)

## High-Level Planning Is Done during Project Initiating

The other important thing to notice in the previous exercise is that high-level planning is done during project initiating. Such planning may include creating a high-level WBS, performing order of magnitude estimating, and doing high-level risk identification. You use this information to determine whether the product of the project can be delivered by the end date and within the organization's established budget for the project. In other words, you need to assess whether the project has a chance of being successful before the organization commits money and resources to it. This high-level planning effort is part of creating the project charter, which documents measurable project objectives, success criteria, milestone schedules, and an initial budget for the project.

Figure 3.6 shows the reasons why project initiating is begun.

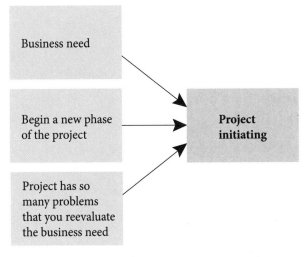

FIGURE 3.6   *Reasons for entering project initiating*

## Planning Process Group

If you could magically do your last project over again, how much better would it be? This is the power of planning. Project planning entails walking through the project using a consistent process, iterating your plans, and getting the project organized in sufficient detail before actually doing the work to produce the product of the project. Planning efforts save resources, time, and money, and encourage increased stakeholder buy-in and commitment to the project.

In project planning, the project manager and the team perform a detailed analysis of whether the objectives in the project charter and the expected business benefits can be achieved. They then decide how the project objectives will be accomplished, addressing all appropriate project management processes and knowledge areas. This means determining what processes are appropriate for the needs of the project and tailoring them to the needs of the project.

**Exercise**   What are the specific actions required to complete project planning?

**Answer**   If you are thinking only in terms of high-level processes, you may have come up with the following:

- Develop Project Management Plan (Integration Management chapter)
- Plan Scope Management (Scope Management chapter)
- Collect Requirements (Scope Management chapter)
- Define Scope (Scope Management chapter)
- Create WBS (Scope Management chapter)
- Plan Schedule Management (Schedule Management chapter)
- Define Activities (Schedule Management chapter)
- Sequence Activities (Schedule Management chapter)
- Estimate Activity Durations (Schedule Management chapter)
- Develop Schedule (Schedule Management chapter)
- Plan Cost Management (Cost Management chapter)
- Estimate Costs (Cost Management chapter)

- Determine Budget (Cost Management chapter)
- Plan Quality Management (Quality Management chapter)
- Plan Resource Management (Resource Management chapter)
- Estimate Activity Resources (Resource Management chapter)
- Plan Communications Management (Communications Management chapter)
- Plan Risk Management (Risk Management chapter)
- Identify Risks (Risk Management chapter)
- Perform Qualitative Risk Analysis (Risk Management chapter)
- Perform Quantitative Risk Analysis (Risk Management chapter)
- Plan Risk Responses (Risk Management chapter)
- Plan Procurement Management (Procurement Management chapter)
- Plan Stakeholder Management (Stakeholder Management chapter)

Again, simply knowing the names of processes will not be enough to pass the exam. You need to have a detailed understanding of what really should be done (the actions) during each part of the project. To be well prepared for the exam, you need to identify and understand any required actions you do not know or have never done.

Complete the following checklist, noting which actions you currently perform when planning your projects. Although all the following actions are done during project planning, the level of detail to which each action is performed will vary based on the particular project.

NOTE: Avoid losing focus when working through these long lists as they contain a lot of information that will help you understand the actions you need to be familiar with when answering exam questions. Spend about 15 minutes thinking through the following list.

| Actions Involved in Project Planning | Place ✓ Here If You Do It; Study Areas Unchecked |
|---|---|
| 1  Determine how you will plan the planning, executing, and monitoring and controlling efforts for stakeholders, requirements, scope, schedule, cost, quality, resources, communications, risk, procurement, changes, and configuration, and put that information into the beginnings of management plans. | |
| 2  Refine the high-level requirements from project initiating so they are more specific and detailed, and look for additional requirements, being sure to consider any internal or external analysis, reports, or regulations; analyze and prioritize requirements. | |
| 3  Expand on the assumptions identified in project initiating, looking for new assumptions and documenting the details of the assumptions. | |
| 4  Refine the high-level constraints (such as resources, schedule, and cost) from project initiating so they are more specific and detailed. | |
| 5  Create a description of the project deliverables, the work required to complete those deliverables, and their acceptance criteria (project scope statement). | |

91

| | Actions Involved in Project Planning | Place ✓ Here If You Do It; Study Areas Unchecked |
|---|---|---|
| 6 | Use the project scope statement to gain approval of the "final" scope from stakeholders before further planning is done. | |
| 7 | Assess what may need to be purchased on the project. Identify any pieces of work that may be outside the organization's abilities to complete, and determine if new equipment or technology is needed to perform the project work. | |
| 8 | Select the procurement strategy for each contract. Create a draft of the procurement documents for necessary contracts, including bid documents, procurement statements of work, source selection criteria, and contract provisions. | |
| 9 | Determine what subject matter experts you will need on the project team to help with project planning. | |
| 10 | Break down the deliverables into smaller, more manageable pieces (WBS). | |
| 11 | Create descriptions of each work package in a WBS dictionary so that the work can be understood and produced without gold plating. | |
| 12 | Break down the work packages from the WBS into lists of activities to produce them. | |
| 13 | Sequence activities and determine predecessors and successors in the network diagram. | |
| 14 | Estimate resource requirements (such as staff, facilities, equipment, and materials). | |
| 15 | Meet with managers to gain resource commitments. | |
| 16 | Decide what level of accuracy is needed for estimates. | |
| 17 | Use historical data to support estimating time and cost. | |
| 18 | Involve experts or those who will work on activities to estimate time and cost. | |
| 19 | Determine how long the project will take without compressing the schedule (determine critical path). | |
| 20 | Develop a schedule model, evaluate it against the schedule constraint in the project charter, and use schedule compression techniques to reconcile the two to come up with a final schedule for the project management plan. | |
| 21 | Develop a preliminary budget and compare it to the budget constraint in the project charter. Then, develop options to reconcile the two to come up with the final budget for the project management plan. | |
| 22 | Determine quality policies, practices, and standards, and then determine metrics to measure quality performance. | |
| 23 | Determine processes to fulfill quality requirements and conform to organizational standards and policies. | |
| 24 | Determine how you will improve the processes in use on the project. | |

© 2018 RMC Publications, Inc.™ • 952.846.4484 • info@rmcls.com • www.rmcls.com

| Actions Involved in Project Planning | Place ✓ Here If You Do It; Study Areas Unchecked |
|---|---|
| 25  Create a system for recognizing and rewarding the efforts of project team members to help keep them motivated and engaged in project efforts. | |
| 26  Plan for acquisition, team building, training, assessment, and release of team members. Plan for physical resources requirements, including acquisition and logistics. | |
| 27  Clearly determine all roles and responsibilities so team members and stakeholders know their roles on the project and what work they will need to do. | |
| 28  Work with the project team to develop a team charter defining their commitments and interactions with each other, including ground rules for meetings, conflict resolution processes, etc. | |
| 29  Determine what information you need from other projects and what information you will share with the organization and other projects. | |
| 30  Plan what will be communicated on the project, to whom, by whom, when, and how. | |
| 31  Plan how to involve stakeholders and manage their expectations during the project. | |
| 32  Complete detailed risk identification, subjectively analyze risks (qualitative risk analysis), perform quantitative risk analysis as necessary, and do risk response planning. | |
| 33  Iterations—go back and update project plans and documents as necessary to work toward a project management plan that is bought into, approved, realistic, and formal. | |
| 34  Finalize the procurement statement of work and other bid documents for each contract. | |
| 35  Look for potential positive and negative interactions with other projects that could affect the project. | |
| 36  Determine the processes that will be used to request, approve, and manage changes on the project. | |
| 37  Develop the configuration management plan, outlining naming conventions and processes for document versioning, storage, and retrieval. | |
| 38  Plan ways to measure project performance, including determining the measurements to be used, when they will be taken, and how the results will be evaluated. | |
| 39  Determine what meetings, reports, and other activities you will use to control the project to the project management plan. | |
| 40  Finalize the "execute" and "monitor and control" aspects of all management plans. Document closing requirements and actions. | |

© 2018 RMC Publications, Inc.™ • 952.846.4484 • info@rmcls.com • www.rmcls.com

| | Place ✓ Here If You Do It; Study Areas Unchecked |
|---|---|
| **Actions Involved in Project Planning** | |
| 41 Develop the final project management plan, project documents, and performance measurement baseline by performing schedule network analysis, looking for options, and confirming that project objectives can be met. | |
| 42 Gain formal approval of the project management plan from the sponsor, team, and managers of resources. | |
| 43 Hold a kickoff meeting with key stakeholders, team members, managers of team members, and the customer to make sure everyone is on the same page and to gain buy-in. | |
| 44 Throughout the project, return to the planning processes to do rolling wave planning (progressive elaboration or iteration) as more information becomes available. Results will likely require change requests and updates to the project management plan and project documents. | |

Project planning is iterative. Each planning process may use the results of the previous processes, and each process may affect or cause changes to the previous processes. The idea, in the real world, is to attempt to complete each planning process as completely as possible. Then, after risk identification, qualitative and quantitative risk analysis, and risk response planning, you go back to finalize all the components of the project management plan and project documents. This approach to planning saves time and is efficient. It is only after risk management planning is completed that the final cost and schedule can be determined. Risk management could also result in iterations to the scope, the deliverables, the project resources (including when they are used), the sequence in which activities are performed, and almost all other parts of the project. The results of the planning effort are the project management plan and project documents that will guide the execution and control of the project.

Notice the references to management plans in the previous table. As described in chapter 1, management plans are a PMI-ism. Too often, project managers jump right into whatever they are doing without analyzing or planning. Such actions lead to inefficiencies, rework, mistakes, conflict, and needless overtime. Project managers are supposed to think about things before they do them. The exam assumes you take a more formal approach that includes considering how you will do the work and documenting that information in a management plan.

There are many components to management plans, but generally they answer the questions such as: "How will we go about planning scope, schedule, cost, etc.?" "How will we manage and monitor and control scope, schedule, cost, etc. now that we have planned what needs to be done?" "How will we perform the closing of project phases and the overall project?" The answers to these questions are determined as part of project planning. For clarity, the previous table groups management plans together instead of listing each management plan separately. It also accounts for the iterations of the management plans by separating them into the planning, executing, and monitoring and controlling parts of each plan. The individual management plans are combined into the overall project management plan. We will further discuss the project management plan and its components in the Integration Management chapter.

Another important concept to understand about planning is that the amount of time the team spends in project planning and the level of detail achieved in the plan should be appropriate to the needs of the project. The appropriate level of detail is dictated by the selected development approach and project governance. If a high-priority project has a tight schedule that does not allow much room for variance, the project will require more planning than a low-priority project with a fairly flexible schedule.

Some projects cannot be fully planned to a detailed degree prior to starting work. Often, such projects are organized by phases (such as test phase, install phase, etc.), or they use an adaptive life cycle approach. Using an adaptive life cycle, only the first part of the project may be fully planned, while the later pieces are planned at a higher level and then progressively elaborated when more is known about the project. Detailed planning for the next phase is done as the previous phase nears completion.

Everyone is involved in the planning processes. The project manager compiles the project management plan and project documents with input from stakeholders. The project manager may also use information gathered from resources such as historical records from previous projects, company policies, governance, regulatory and compliance policies and procedures, and other such sources to plan the project.

Figure 3.7 shows the reasons for entering project planning.

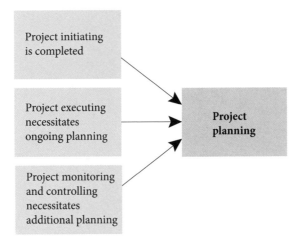

FIGURE 3.7   *Reasons for entering project planning*

For descriptions of each of the individual planning processes, see the rest of this book—particularly the Integration Management chapter, which discusses the development of the project management plan.

## Executing Process Group

The purpose of project executing is to complete the project work as defined in the project management plan to meet the project objectives and achieve the expected business value. In other words, the goal is to produce the project deliverables within the project's planned budget and schedule to deliver the agreed-upon benefits. The focus is on leading and managing the project; that includes engaging stakeholders, working with the team to complete work, following processes, and communicating according to the plan. During executing, the project manager essentially has a guiding, proactive role, and uses the project management plan and project documents as reference points in managing the work.

95

Many project managers do not create management plans that include specific plans (for scope, schedule, cost, etc.), and that are realistic and have the support of management. Without experience in using such a plan, they do not realize the value a project management plan can provide in properly managing and executing a project. They may find exam questions about executing with this type of project management plan to be extremely difficult because it is so different from their daily work practices. For the exam, get your mind around the critical difference planning makes, and assume the project was properly planned before work began, unless the question indicates otherwise.

**Exercise**  Imagine you are about to begin project executing. What type of actions must be taken?

**Answer** If you are thinking only in terms of high-level processes, you may have come up with the following:

- Direct and Manage Project Work (Integration Management chapter)
- Manage Project Knowledge (Integration Management chapter)
- Manage Quality (Quality Management chapter)
- Acquire Resources (Resource Management chapter)
- Develop Team (Resource Management chapter)
- Manage Team (Resource Management chapter)
- Manage Communications (Communications Management chapter)
- Implement Risk Responses (Risk Management chapter)
- Conduct Procurements (Procurement Management chapter)
- Manage Stakeholder Engagement (Stakeholder Management chapter)

Again, you need to know more than the names of processes. Let's look at the actions involved in executing a project. As you check your answers against the following table, note which actions you do on your projects, which actions were not on your list, and which actions that you wrote down are not included here. Note that some of these items, such as "Complete work packages," will be largely undertaken by the project team.

NOTE: This is another long list. Keep focused, and spend 15 minutes thinking through these actions. Remember that the list is not sequential.

| Actions Involved in Project Executing | Place ✓ Here If You Do It; Study Areas Unchecked |
|---|---|
| 1 Communicate your expectations for stakeholders and the project, and manage the involvement and needs of all stakeholders throughout the project to ensure everyone has a common understanding of the work. | |
| 2 Implement the most up-to-date version of the project management plan, including revisions made as a result of control activities. | |
| 3 Complete work packages. | |
| 4 Collect, document, and share lessons learned. | |
| 5 Establish and manage communication channels. | |
| 6 Evaluate how effectively the team members function as a team. | |
| 7 Implement approved changes, including corrective actions, preventive actions, and defect repair. | |
| 8 Confirm that practices and procedures are being followed and are still appropriate for the project. | |
| 9 Produce and distribute reports on project performance. | |
| 10 Hold team-building activities. | |
| 11 Use the team charter for guidance on team interactions. Follow ground rules at team meetings. | |
| 12 Obtain needed training for team members. | |

97

| | Actions Involved in Project Executing | Place ✓ Here If You Do It; Study Areas Unchecked |
|---|---|---|
| 13 | Exchange information about the project according to the plan, and solicit feedback to ensure communication needs are being met. | |
| 14 | Remove roadblocks. | |
| 15 | Achieve work results that meet requirements. | |
| 16 | Meet with managers to reconfirm resource commitments. | |
| 17 | Keep managers apprised of when their resources will be needed on the project. | |
| 18 | Commit, manage, and release physical and team resources in accordance with the project management plan. | |
| 19 | Guide, assist, communicate, lead, negotiate, facilitate, and coach. | |
| 20 | Use your technical knowledge. | |
| 21 | Hold meetings to identify and address issues, assess risks, and keep the project work moving forward. | |
| 22 | Manage stakeholder engagement and expectations, increase project support, and prevent possible problems. | |
| 23 | Focus on preventing problems rather than just dealing with them as they arise. | |
| 24 | Make sure all team members have the skills, information, and equipment needed to complete their work. | |
| 25 | Look for exceptions to the approved project management plan in team members' performance, rather than checking up on every person's work. | |
| 26 | Recommend changes to be evaluated in the Perform Integrated Change Control process. | |
| 27 | Follow organizational policies, processes, and procedures. | |
| 28 | Increase the effectiveness of processes. | |
| 29 | Make updates to the project management plan and project documents to reflect current information about the project. | |
| 30 | Create recommendations for the performing organization to increase its effectiveness. | |
| 31 | Ensure continued agreement from the stakeholders to the project management plan. | |
| 32 | Keep everyone focused on completing the project to the project charter and project management plan. | |
| 33 | Keep the project's business case and benefits management plan in mind while managing the project, especially when problems occur. | |
| 34 | Solve problems. | |
| 35 | Determine where project changes are coming from and what you can do to eliminate the root cause of the need for change. | |
| 36 | Determine final team members and other resources, and bring them on to the project as needed. | |

| | Actions Involved in Project Executing | Place ✓ Here If You Do It; Study Areas Unchecked |
|---|---|---|
| 37 | Recognize and reward the team and individuals for their work and performance on the project. | |
| 38 | Gather initial measurements and details about activities of project work (work performance data). | |
| 39 | Implement approved process improvements. | |
| 40 | Use an issue log to record project issues and details about their resolution, including who is responsible for resolving each issue and the expected timeline. | |
| 41 | Obtain seller responses to bid documents. | |
| 42 | Review proposals, bids, and quotes; negotiate contract terms with prospective sellers; and manage the evaluation and selection of sellers. | |
| 43 | Manage the integration of sellers' work and deliverables into the overall work and deliverables of the project; manage any seller-related conflicts or challenges. | |
| 44 | Expend and manage project funds. | |
| 45 | Facilitate conflict resolution using conflict resolution techniques. | |
| 46 | Assess individual team member performance. | |
| 47 | Update human resource records of team members to reflect new skills acquired while working on the project. | |
| 48 | Carry out contingency plans in response to risk triggers. | |

Did your list include items that were not in the previous table? If so, make sure those items should actually be part of executing a properly managed project. Did you include such things as getting the team to cooperate, discovering added scope, or coordinating unplanned overtime work? Although these things could (and often do) occur on a project, they result from a lack of proper project management.

How about dealing with problems? Notice that "solves problems" is only one of 48 items on the list of actions to be done during project executing. As a project manager, you should be focused on preventing problems so you do not have to deal with them. With proper project management, problems occur less often, and should not have a major impact on the project. Assume risk management efforts have identified and evaluated risks, and that contingency plans are in place to deal with risks that have high probability or impact ratings. Instead of handling risk events, you can spend your time engaging stakeholders and encouraging team members. Again, for the exam, assume proper project management was done unless the questions say otherwise.

Did you list meetings? Meetings are certainly part of executing a project, but many people do not realize that proper planning can decrease the number of meetings they need. If you were thinking about "go around the room and report what you have done" types of meetings, realize that status can also be collected through other means. Effective agile teams have focused daily stand-up meetings to keep the team on track to complete their commitments for the iteration. The occasions when the team gets together are too important to just focus on collecting status. How about reviewing risk triggers and upcoming contingency plans during meetings? Having too many meetings can cause you to lose buy-in from your team if they feel you are wasting their time.

Keep the following in mind as a way to summarize executing activities: work according to the project management plan, be proactive, lead and engage, and guide.

The processes of project management are not always performed in the same sequence. Executing means working with the latest revision of the project management plan. In other words, you are always executing according to the project management plan, but the plan might change over time. Figure 3.8 illustrates the reasons for entering project executing.

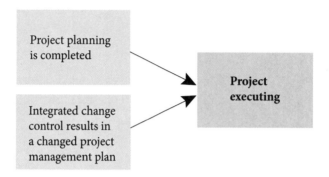

FIGURE 3.8　*Reasons for entering project executing*

## Monitoring and Controlling Process Group

Monitoring and controlling are combined into one process group, but each has a different focus. Monitoring requires the project manager to focus their attention on how the project is progressing. The project manager will need to assess how stakeholders are participating, communicating, and feeling about the project, the work, and the uncertainties that have been identified. Controlling requires evaluating hard data on how the project is conforming to the plan and taking action to address variances that are outside of acceptable limits—by recommending changes to the way the work is being done, or possibly adjusting baselines to reflect more achievable outcomes. In this context, the term "changes" encompasses corrective and preventive actions and defect repair.

Test takers often find project monitoring and controlling to be one of the most challenging process groups on the exam. One reason for this is that you are expected to know how to observe, measure, evaluate, and analyze a project in a more planned and complete way than most project managers do on their real-world projects. The project management plan includes monitoring activities, such as observing, communicating, and evaluating. It also specifies control activities to be used on the project, along with a plan for how variations will be addressed.

Without organizational support for monitoring and controlling the project to the plan, a project manager could spend most of their time asking for percent complete, being unsure if the project will meet its performance measurement baseline.

We saw earlier in this chapter that monitoring and controlling applies to change-driven projects as well as plan-driven ones, but it can be useful to think in terms of plan-driven projects to understand the work of this process group and to answer questions on the exam (unless, of course, a question specifies a change-driven project).

**For the exam, assume:**

- You have a formal project management plan that is realistic and complete to the level appropriate for the project.

- You have plans already in place for how and when you will measure schedule, cost, and scope performance against the performance measurement baseline.

- You are accountable for meeting the performance measurement baseline.

- You also measure against the other metrics included in the project management plan to see how the project is performing.

- You take action to correct any variances that warrant action.

- Any deviations from the plan should be made up, rather than requesting a change to the project to accommodate them. Submitting a change request should be the very last resort and only used if there is no other way to make up the deviation.

The following exercise should help you get your mind around what a project manager should do to monitor and control a project. Again, we encourage you to work through this exercise. Find the gaps in your knowledge and experience, and fill those gaps, rather than relying on memorization for the exam. As a result, you will pass the exam—and be a better project manager!

**Exercise** What are the specific actions required as part of project monitoring and controlling?

_____
_____
_____
_____
_____

**Answer**  If you are thinking only in terms of high-level processes, you may have come up with the following:

- Monitor and Control Project Work (Integration Management chapter)
- Perform Integrated Change Control (Integration Management chapter)
- Validate Scope (Scope Management chapter)
- Control Scope (Scope Management chapter)
- Control Schedule (Schedule Management chapter)
- Control Costs (Cost Management chapter)
- Control Quality (Quality Management chapter)
- Control Resources (Resource Management chapter)
- Monitor Communications (Communications Management chapter)
- Monitor Risks (Risk Management chapter)
- Control Procurements (Procurement Management chapter)
- Monitor Stakeholder Engagement (Stakeholder Management chapter)

The previously listed processes are described in the chapters of this book as referenced. Now let's look at what actions should be done in monitoring and controlling a project. Review the following list, and identify any you do not know or have never done. If you included actions that are not listed here, make sure those actions are part of monitoring and controlling.

NOTE: Because this is one of the most challenging process groups on the exam, you should spend considerable time here. Do not lose focus as you read. Take a break in the middle of the list if you need to, and remember the list is not sequential.

| Actions Involved in Project Monitoring and Controlling | Place ✓ Here If You Do It; Study Areas Unchecked |
| --- | --- |
| 1  Measure project performance according to the planned measures in the management plans. | |
| 2  Measure against the performance measurement baseline. | |
| 3  Analyze and evaluate work performance data. | |
| 4  Determine variances. | |
| 5  Use your judgment to determine what variances are important and if they warrant recommending a change or corrective action. | |
| 6  Recommend changes, including defect repair and preventive and corrective actions. Do not just wait for others to recommend them. | |

| | Actions Involved in Project Monitoring and Controlling | Place ✓ Here If You Do It; Study Areas Unchecked |
|---|---|---|
| 7 | Make or obtain a decision in integrated change control about whether changes should be approved, rejected, or deferred. | |
| 8 | Track and evaluate naming conventions, version control processes, the storage and retrieval system (configuration management), and the use of the PMIS. This ensures everyone knows which version of the project or product documentation is the latest version. | |
| 9 | Control scope, schedule, and cost to their baselines. | |
| 10 | Perform procurement inspections and reviews of seller performance to the contract. | |
| 11 | Refine control limits as needed. | |
| 12 | Identify the root causes of problems with the help of techniques such as process analysis (for example, Lean, Kanban, and Six Sigma). | |
| 13 | Obtain formal acceptance of interim deliverables from the customer. | |
| 14 | Identify the need for replanning. | |
| 15 | Replan and make updates to the project management plan and project documents to reflect approved changes and updates to the project. | |
| 16 | Evaluate stakeholder relationships and involvement to determine if they require improvement. | |
| 17 | Manage the schedule and cost reserves. | |
| 18 | Recalculate how much the project will cost and how long it will take, and create forecasts. | |
| 19 | Obtain additional funding if needed. | |
| 20 | Prepare work performance reports from the analyzed data and measurements. | |
| 21 | Hold periodic quality inspections. | |
| 22 | Make decisions to accept or reject completed deliverables. | |
| 23 | Evaluate the effectiveness of implemented corrective actions. | |
| 24 | Assess the effectiveness of project control systems. | |
| 25 | Spend time trying to improve quality. | |
| 26 | Determine if project controls need to be updated. | |
| 27 | Identify and analyze trends. | |
| 28 | Evaluate the effectiveness of risk responses in a risk review. | |
| 29 | Look for newly arising risks. | |
| 30 | Reanalyze identified risks. | |
| 31 | Use milestones as a project control tool. | |
| 32 | Observe and analyze. | |
| 33 | Use variance reports to help correct small problems before they become serious. | |
| 34 | Calculate estimate to complete. | |

103

| | Actions Involved in Project Monitoring and Controlling | Place ✓ Here If You Do It; Study Areas Unchecked |
|---|---|---|
| 35 | Use and interpret earned value calculations. | |
| 36 | Use quality control tools such as inspections, histograms, performance reviews, and cause-and-effect diagrams. | |
| 37 | Influence any factors that could result in the project's change control and configuration management measures being bypassed. | |
| 38 | Control changes. | |
| 39 | Control to make sure that only approved changes are implemented. | |
| 40 | Work with the change control board. | |
| 41 | Evaluate stakeholder satisfaction. | |
| 42 | Control procurements through actions such as reviewing, approving, and paying invoices, administering claims, and performing inspections and audits. | |
| 43 | Validate defect repair. | |
| 44 | Determine where project changes are coming from and what you can do to eliminate the root cause of the need for change. | |
| 45 | Consider the project's business case and the organization's strategic objectives when analyzing change requests. | |
| 46 | Use active listening, inquiry, and data gathering to confirm that communications and stakeholder engagement efforts are effective and working as planned. Make or recommend needed adjustments. | |
| 47 | Evaluate the use, cost, and other aspects of physical resources. Make appropriate changes and adjustments. | |
| 48 | Close procurements after final deliverables are accepted. | |
| 49 | Update risk report to keep key stakeholders informed about the status of overall project risk and the highest-ranked individual risks. | |

Not all monitoring and controlling efforts result in the discovery of variances that warrant preventive or corrective action, defect repair, or changes to the baselines or plan. When a project has been planned appropriately, most control efforts result in information that proves work is being done according to the plan and that scope is being produced to the agreed-upon standards and metrics. Results of measurements (whether positive or negative) and outcomes of other monitoring and controlling efforts are added to the project management plan and project documents as updates. In fact, project management plan and project documents updates are outputs of every monitoring and controlling process. Records of the work, measurements, and lessons learned are used for reference and comparison throughout the life of the project. In addition to identifying variances, measurements can be useful in trend analysis, forecasting, and estimating the remaining work.

We have included the following information about the processes to help you develop a better overall understanding of project monitoring and controlling. Read the following carefully to expand your understanding of what "monitoring and controlling" is.

## Control Scope

- Follow the change management plan.
- Measure scope performance against the performance measurement baseline.
- Influence the factors that cause changes.
- Control scope changes and the impacts of those changes.
- Analyze work performance data and variances.
- Request changes.
- Update the scope baseline, other parts of the project management plan, and requirements documentation with approved changes.
- Validate changes to make sure they do not over- or undercorrect problems.
- Document lessons learned.

## Control Schedule

- Follow the change management plan.
- Measure schedule performance against the performance measurement baseline.
- Influence the factors that cause changes.
- Control schedule changes and the impacts of those changes.
- Analyze work performance data and variances.
- Request changes.
- Update the schedule baseline, other parts of the project management plan, and schedule-related documentation with approved changes.
- Document lessons learned.
- Manage the schedule reserve.
- Use earned value analysis to create schedule forecasts.
- Validate changes to make sure they do not over- or undercorrect problems.

## Control Costs

- Follow the change management plan.
- Measure cost performance against the performance measurement baseline.
- Influence the factors that cause changes.
- Control cost changes and the impacts of those changes.
- Analyze work performance data and variances.
- Request changes.
- Update the cost baseline, other parts of the project management plan, and cost estimates.
- Document lessons learned.
- Manage the cost reserve.
- Use earned value analysis to recalculate the estimate at completion and other cost forecasts.
- Obtain additional funding when needed.
- Validate changes to make sure they do not over- or undercorrect problems.

## Control Quality

- Hold periodic inspections.
- Ensure the deliverables are meeting the standards.
- Influence the factors that cause changes.
- Request changes or improvements to work and processes.
- Make decisions to accept or reject work.
- Assess the effectiveness of project quality control systems.
- Analyze work performance data and variances.
- Update the quality management plan, as well as quality- and process-related documentation.
- Validate changes to make sure they do not over- or undercorrect problems.
- Document lessons learned.

## Control Resources

- Confirm the type and quantity of resources used are consistent with what was planned.
- Evaluate the effectiveness of the physical resources.
- Analyze work performance data and variances.
- Request changes.
- Validate changes to make sure they do not over- or undercorrect problems.
- Update the resource management plan, as well as resource-related documentation.
- Document lessons learned.

## Monitor Communications

- Ensure information is being communicated to the appropriate people in the right way and at the right time.
- Analyze work performance data and variances.
- Request changes.
- Analyze information about communications to make sure they are meeting stakeholder needs.
- Validate changes to make sure they do not over- or undercorrect problems.
- Document lessons learned.

## Monitor Risks

- Reassess risks, planned risk responses, and risk reserves.
- Identify new risks.
- Watch for the occurrence of risk triggers.
- Create and implement workarounds.
- Perform risk audits to evaluate the effectiveness of risk management processes. Analyze work performance data, work performance reports, and variances.
- Request changes.
- Evaluate the effectiveness of implemented risk response plans.
- Document lessons learned.

## Control Procurements

- Monitor performance to make sure both parties to the contract meet contractual obligations.
- Inspect and verify the contract deliverables.
- Protect your legal rights.
- Follow the defined procurement management procedures, including the contract change control system.
- Analyze work performance data, seller work performance reports, and variances.
- Request and manage changes.
- Authorize contract-related work.
- Issue and review claims.
- Maintain comprehensive records.
- Report on seller performance compared to contract.
- Review invoices and make payments.
- Update the project management plan and procurement documentation.
- Validate contract changes, control contracts to updated versions, and evaluate effectiveness of changes.
- Document lessons learned.
- Close out contracts as final deliverables are completed and accepted.

## Monitor Stakeholder Engagement

- Analyze work performance data and variances.
- Evaluate stakeholder engagement and stakeholder relationships, and look for opportunities for improvement.
- Assess whether stakeholders' expectations are aligned with the project.
- Resolve conflicts.
- Maintain an issue log.
- Request changes.
- Update the stakeholder management plan and the stakeholder register.
- Document lessons learned.
- Validate success of changes to stakeholder engagement strategy.

Project management does not progress sequentially from initiating to planning to executing to monitoring and controlling to closing; the processes overlap. In fact, you are doing some level of monitoring and controlling throughout the project—from initiating to closing. Figure 3.9 illustrates key project outputs that trigger a focus on monitoring and controlling. It also shows that you might go from monitoring and controlling to other process groups depending on the needs of the project.

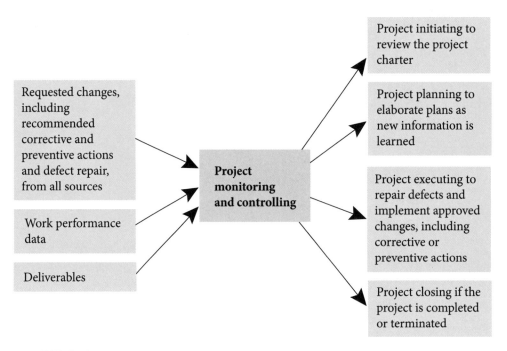

FIGURE 3.9   *Key outputs that trigger project monitoring and controlling, and potential next steps*

## Closing Process Group

The project or phase is not over when the product scope is completed; there is one more process to be done. Project closing, where the project is finished, is one of the most ignored parts of the project management process. However, if you take time now to understand the concepts that we'll discuss in this section, the 12 or so questions about closing on the exam should be easy.

The closing effort includes administrative activities such as collecting and finalizing all the paperwork needed to complete the project, and technical work to confirm that the final product of the project is acceptable. It will also include any work needed to transfer the completed project to those who will use it and to solicit feedback from the customer about the product and the project.

In many real-world situations, projects never seem to officially finish. Sometimes the project manager gets pulled off a project to do other things. Sometimes work on the project just stops. Sometimes the project priority decreases. Because all projects are unique, there is no universal way in which a project officially ends; however, all projects must follow the closing process and complete the required closing activities.

The work done during closure is extremely important to the performing organization and to the customer. The exam asks questions in this area to see if you know what those valuable activities are and when a project is really finished. Try this next exercise to test your knowledge.

**Exercise**   What are the specific actions required to complete the Close Project or Phase process?

_____

_____

_____

_____

_____

_____

_____

_____

_____

_____

_____

_____

_____

**Answer**   Compare the list of closing actions in the following table to what you wrote in the exercise above, and identify any that you do not know or have never done. Look for gaps in your knowledge.

| Actions Involved in Project Closing | Place ✓ Here If You Do It; Study Areas Unchecked |
|---|---|
| 1 Confirm that all project requirements have been met. | |
| 2 Verify and document that the project, or project phase, meets completion or exit criteria set in place during project planning. | |
| 3 Obtain formal (legal) sign-off and final acceptance of the product of the project from the customer. | |
| 4 If any issues prevent final acceptance by the customer, negotiate a settlement or other resolution. | |
| 5 If the project was terminated before completion, document the reasons for termination and the status of the project and deliverables. | |
| 6 Make final payments, and complete cost records. | |
| 7 Gather final lessons learned and share with the organization. | |
| 8 Update project records. | |
| 9 Ensure all the project management processes are complete. | |
| 10 Update corporate processes, procedures, and templates based on lessons learned. | |
| 11 Complete project (or phase) closure. | |
| 12 Analyze and document the success and effectiveness of the project. | |

109

| | Actions Involved in Project Closing | Place ✓ Here If You Do It; Study Areas Unchecked |
|---|---|---|
| 13 | Create and distribute a final report of project (or phase) performance. | |
| 14 | Index and archive project records. | |
| 15 | Evaluate customer satisfaction regarding the project and the deliverables. | |
| 16 | Hand off the completed project deliverables to the appropriate stakeholders (the customer, operations and maintenance, etc.). | |
| 17 | Confirm all contracts have been formally closed; update and archive records. | |
| 18 | Celebrate! | |

Does this list of actions make sense? Take a moment to go back and look again at the previous table. Make sure you understand why each item is important and valuable. Spending some time on the lists of actions in each process group will help you prepare for the exam and give you a solid understanding of the overall project management process.

Because many organizations do not require formal closure procedures, let's take a moment to discuss some of the key actions listed in the previous table that many people miss.

Confirming that all the requirements have been met may seem unimportant; however, most studies show that many requirements are not met on projects, especially on projects with numerous pages of requirements. This confirmation needs to take place and can be done by reviewing the project management plan and accepted deliverables.

What about handing off the completed project deliverables to operations and maintenance? Work involved in completing such a transfer is considered part of the project. The work could include meetings to explain the project nuances, training, documentation for maintenance, and other activities as needed.

Now let's think about formal sign-off and acceptance. These are important because they confirm that the customer considers the project completed and accepts the whole project. Without that acceptance, you cannot be sure the project was finished. Imagine the team never gains formal acceptance on a project for an external customer, but moves on to other projects. Then the customer calls for additional scope to be added to the project. How difficult would it be to regroup the team to perform the work? Gaining formal acceptance helps ensure this won't be necessary.

Measuring customer satisfaction is another important part of project closing. Have you ever had a customer accept your work although they were not happy with the project? It's highly beneficial for the project manager to solicit feedback from the customer about both the project and the product, and to evaluate the customer's satisfaction level during project closing. Just like lessons learned, measuring customer satisfaction should be ongoing throughout the project, but it must occur during project closing. The satisfaction level of stakeholders should also be assessed, and they should be asked for input to improve processes and procedures on future projects.

In the first chapter of this book, we noted that historical records are a PMI-ism. For the exam, make sure you understand the value of these records and the project manager's and team's responsibility for creating them. Historical information is collected throughout the project, but it is during project closing that the final versions of the lessons learned are compiled and archived in the lessons learned repository. In addition, project closing involves a concerted effort to index all files, letters, correspondence, and other records of the project into an organized archive that is stored for use on future projects.

Some project managers consider completing the final project performance report and holding an end-of-the-project celebration to be unimportant. But there is good reason for these activities—both of which recognize the team's efforts. The final report communicates to all stakeholders and the entire organization benefits achieved by the team members' efforts on the project.

After the administrative pieces of project closure are completed and the customer, sponsor, and other stakeholders provide formal sign-off that the product of the project is acceptable, the project is closed. At that point, any team members utilized to close the project or project phase are released.

Figure 3.10 illustrates the reasons a project might enter the closing process group.

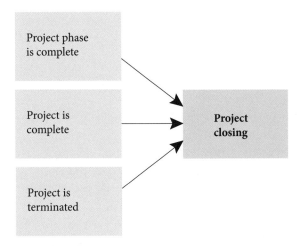

FIGURE 3.10   *Reasons for entering project closing*

**TRICKS OF THE TRADE®** **The Project Management Scramble Game**   The following exercise is an extension of Rita's Process Game™ and should help you assess how well you've understood what you've read. This exercise will look at more specific actions, rather than the generalized ones stated in Rita's Process Chart™. For each item listed in the following table, simply determine if it is done in initiating, planning, executing, monitoring and controlling, or closing.

| | Actions | During Which Process Group Is This Done? |
|---|---|---|
| 1 | Use the project scope statement to gain approval of the "final" scope from the stakeholders before further planning is done. | |
| 2 | Determine high-level requirements, constraints, assumptions, and risks. | |
| 3 | Measure against the performance measurement baseline. | |
| 4 | Implement approved changes, including corrective actions, preventive actions, and defect repair. | |
| 5 | Reanalyze identified risks. | |
| 6 | Use high-level planning and estimating data to determine whether the product can be achieved within the given constraints. | |

111

| | Actions | During Which Process Group Is This Done? |
|---|---|---|
| 7 | Verify and document that the project or project phase meets completion or exit criteria set in place during project planning. | |
| 8 | Conduct team-building activities. | |
| 9 | Evaluate the effectiveness of risk responses in a risk review. | |
| 10 | Determine how you will plan the planning, executing, and monitoring and controlling efforts for stakeholders, requirements, scope, schedule, cost, quality, resources, communications, risk, procurement, changes, and configuration, and put that information into the beginnings of management plans. | |
| 11 | Obtain formal (legal) sign-off and final acceptance of the product of the project from the customer. | |
| 12 | Increase the effectiveness of processes. | |
| 13 | Recalculate how much the project will cost and how long it will take, and create forecasts. | |
| 14 | Plan what will be communicated on the project, to whom, by whom, when, and how. | |
| 15 | Spend time trying to improve quality. | |
| 16 | Make sure the business case and the analysis supporting the need for the project are documented and understood. Also make sure the expected benefits are understood and likely to be realized through the project. | |
| 17 | Evaluate how effectively the team members function as a team. | |
| 18 | Determine how and when you will analyze processes in use on the project. | |
| 19 | Determine measurable project and product objectives. | |
| 20 | Manage schedule and cost reserves. | |
| 21 | Focus on looking for exceptions to the approved project management plan in team members' performance, rather than checking up on every person's work. | |
| 22 | Develop the final project management plan, project documents, and performance measurement baseline by performing schedule network analysis, looking for options, and confirming that project objectives can be met. | |
| 23 | Gather final lessons learned. | |
| 24 | Keep everyone focused on completing the project to the project charter and project management plan. | |
| 25 | Calculate estimate to complete. | |
| 26 | Understand how the project supports the organization's strategic objectives. | |
| 27 | Implement approved improvements to project processes. | |
| 28 | Identify stakeholders, and determine their influence, expectations, and impact. | |
| 29 | Determine variances. | |
| 30 | Meet with managers to gain resource commitments. | |
| 31 | Use and interpret earned value calculations. | |
| 32 | Ensure a high-level product scope is identified through an evaluation of a business need, and then documented in the project charter. | |

| Actions | During Which Process Group Is This Done? |
|---|---|
| 33 | Create and distribute a final report of project or phase performance. | |
| 34 | Use your judgment to determine what variances are important and if they warrant recommending a change or corrective action. | |
| 35 | Finalize the "execute" and "monitor and control" aspects of all management plans. | |
| 36 | Index and archive project records. | |
| 37 | Keep managers apprised of when their resources will be needed on the project. | |
| 38 | Evaluate customer satisfaction regarding the project and the deliverables. | |
| 39 | Determine who will be on the project team to help with project planning. | |
| 40 | During the project, share knowledge and make recommendations to increase project effectiveness throughout the organization. | |
| 41 | Perform procurement inspections. | |
| 42 | Turn high-level stakeholder needs, wants, and expectations into requirements. | |
| 43 | Look for newly arising risks. | |
| 44 | Determine what processes should be followed on the project to reduce the need to supervise work, improve quality, and make use of standards. | |
| 45 | Obtain formal acceptance of interim deliverables from the customer. | |
| 46 | Determine what specifically will constitute project success. | |
| 47 | Assess individual team member performance. | |
| 48 | Make or obtain a decision in integrated change control about whether changes should be approved, rejected, or deferred. | |
| 49 | Manage quality to ensure the defined practices and procedures are being followed and are still appropriate for the project. | |
| 50 | Evaluate the effectiveness of implemented corrective actions. | |
| 51 | Manage stakeholder engagement and expectations, increase project support, and prevent problems. | |
| 52 | Plan ways to measure project performance, including determining the measurements to be used, when they will be taken, and how they will be interpreted. | |
| 53 | Keep the project's business case in focus while managing the project, especially when problems occur. | |
| 54 | Determine the process that will be used to request, approve, and manage changes on the project. | |
| 55 | Obtain seller responses to bid documents. | |
| 56 | Implement planned risk responses as appropriate. | |
| 57 | Evaluate the use, cost, and other aspects of physical resources. Make appropriate changes and adjustments. | |
| 58 | Collect and share project information as it is discovered. | |
| 59 | Negotiate with potential sellers; sign contracts. | |

113

## Answer  The Project Management Scramble Game

| | Actions | During Which Process Group Is This Done? |
|---|---|---|
| 1 | Use the project scope statement to gain approval of the "final" scope from stakeholders before further planning is done. | Planning |
| 2 | Determine high-level requirements, constraints, assumptions, and risks. | Initiating |
| 3 | Measure against the performance measurement baseline. | Monitoring and controlling |
| 4 | Implement approved changes, including corrective actions, preventive actions, and defect repair. | Executing |
| 5 | Reanalyze identified risks. | Monitoring and controlling |
| 6 | Use high-level planning and estimating data to determine whether the product can be achieved within the given constraints. | Initiating |
| 7 | Verify and document that the project, or project phase, meets completion or exit criteria set in place during project planning. | Closing |
| 8 | Conduct team-building activities. | Executing |
| 9 | Evaluate the effectiveness of risk responses in a risk review. | Monitoring and controlling |
| 10 | Determine how you will plan the planning, executing, and monitoring and controlling efforts for stakeholders, requirements, scope, schedule, cost, quality, resources, communications, risk, procurement, changes, and configuration, and put that information into the beginnings of management plans. | Planning |
| 11 | Obtain formal (legal) sign-off and final acceptance of the product of the project from the customer. | Closing |
| 12 | Increase the effectiveness of processes. | Executing |
| 13 | Recalculate how much the project will cost and how long it will take, and create forecasts. | Monitoring and controlling |
| 14 | Plan what will be communicated on the project, to whom, by whom, when, and how. | Planning |
| 15 | Spend time trying to improve quality. | Monitoring and controlling |
| 16 | Make sure the business case and the analysis supporting the need for the project are documented and understood. Also make sure the expected benefits are understood and likely to be realized through the project. | Initiating |
| 17 | Evaluate how effectively the team members function as a team. | Executing |
| 18 | Determine how and when you will analyze processes in use on the project. | Planning |
| 19 | Determine measurable project and product objectives. | Initiating |
| 20 | Manage schedule and cost reserves. | Monitoring and controlling |
| 21 | Focus on looking for exceptions to the approved project management plan in team members' performance, rather than checking up on every person's work. | Executing |

| | Actions | During Which Process Group Is This Done? |
|---|---|---|
| 22 | Develop the final project management plan, project documents, and performance measurement baseline by performing schedule network analysis, looking for options, and confirming that project objectives can be met. | Planning |
| 23 | Gather final lessons learned. | Closing |
| 24 | Keep everyone focused on completing the project to the project charter and project management plan. | Executing |
| 25 | Calculate estimate to complete. | Monitoring and controlling |
| 26 | Understand how the project supports the organization's strategic objectives. | Initiating |
| 27 | Implement approved improvements to project processes. | Executing |
| 28 | Identify stakeholders, and determine their influence, expectations, and impact. | Initiating |
| 29 | Determine variances. | Monitoring and controlling |
| 30 | Meet with managers to gain resource commitments. | Planning |
| 31 | Use and interpret earned value calculations. | Monitoring and controlling |
| 32 | Ensure a high-level product scope is identified through an evaluation of a business need, and then documented in the project charter. | Initiating |
| 33 | Create and distribute a final report of project or phase performance. | Closing |
| 34 | Use your judgment to determine what variances are important and if they warrant recommending a change or corrective action. | Monitoring and controlling |
| 35 | Finalize the "execute" and "monitor and control" aspects of all management plans. | Planning |
| 36 | Index and archive project records. | Closing |
| 37 | Keep managers apprised of when their resources will be needed on the project. | Executing |
| 38 | Evaluate customer satisfaction regarding the project and the deliverables. | Closing |
| 39 | Determine who will be on the project team to help with project planning. | Planning |
| 40 | During the project, share knowledge and make recommendations to increase project effectiveness throughout the organization. | Executing |
| 41 | Perform procurement inspections. | Monitoring and controlling |
| 42 | Turn high-level stakeholder needs, wants, and expectations into requirements. | Initiating |
| 43 | Look for newly arising risks. | Monitoring and controlling |
| 44 | Determine what processes should be followed on the project to reduce the need to supervise work, improve quality, and make use of standards. | Planning |
| 45 | Obtain formal acceptance of interim deliverables from the customer. | Monitoring and controlling |
| 46 | Determine what specifically will constitute project success. | Initiating |
| 47 | Assess individual team member performance. | Executing |

| | Actions | During Which Process Group Is This Done? |
|---|---|---|
| 48 | Make or obtain a decision in integrated change control about whether changes should be approved, rejected, or deferred. | Monitoring and controlling |
| 49 | Manage quality to ensure the defined practices and procedures are being followed and are still appropriate for the project. | Executing |
| 50 | Evaluate the effectiveness of implemented corrective actions. | Monitoring and controlling |
| 51 | Manage stakeholder engagement and expectations, increase project support, and prevent problems. | Executing |
| 52 | Plan ways to measure project performance, including determining the measurements to be used, when they will be taken, and how they will be interpreted. | Planning |
| 53 | Keep the project's business case in focus while managing the project, especially when problems occur. | Executing |
| 54 | Determine the process that will be used to request, approve, and manage changes on the project. | Planning |
| 55 | Obtain seller responses to bid documents. | Executing |
| 56 | Implement planned risk responses as appropriate. | Executing |
| 57 | Evaluate the use, cost, and other aspects of physical resources. Make appropriate changes and adjustments. | Monitoring and controlling |
| 58 | Collect and share project information as it is discovered. | Executing |
| 59 | Negotiate with potential sellers; sign contracts. | Executing |

**Inputs and Outputs**   Inputs and outputs are logical and should not require memorization if you have a good understanding of the actions involved in each of the knowledge area processes. Test your understanding by answering the following question: What is an input to a WBS? Make sure you read the Create WBS discussion carefully in the Scope Management chapter, and pay attention throughout this book to when and how a WBS is used.

 Why worry about inputs and outputs? Here is a trick to help you gain confidence in your understanding of the project management processes

An input means:

*"What do I need before I can. . ."*

An output means:

*"What will I have when I am done with. . ."*

Or, *"What am I trying to achieve when I am doing. . ."*

Do not expect all the inputs tested on the exam to be included or clearly stated in the *PMBOK® Guide*. For example, you know you need the project team (or at least an initial version of the project team) to create a WBS, yet the team is not specifically listed as an input to creating a WBS in the *PMBOK® Guide*. The remaining chapters of this book will help you understand the processes of project management along with their inputs and outputs.

## Practice Exam

1. A project manager has received some help from the team, and she needs help from them again so that she can create a detailed project budget. Which project management process group is she in?

   A. Initiating
   B. Before the project management process
   C. Planning
   D. Executing

2. The project charter is created in which project management process group?

   A. Executing
   B. Planning
   C. Closing
   D. Initiating

3. The project team has just completed the initial project schedule and budget. The next thing to do is to:

   A. Identify risks.
   B. Begin iterations.
   C. Determine communications requirements.
   D. Create a bar (Gantt) chart.

4. A detailed project schedule can be created only after creating the:

   A. Project budget
   B. Work breakdown structure
   C. Project management plan
   D. Detailed risk assessment

5. The person who should be in control of the project during project planning is the:

   A. Project manager
   B. Team member
   C. Functional manager
   D. Sponsor

6. Which of the following is not an input to the initiating process group?

   A. Company processes
   B. Company culture
   C. Historical WBSs
   D. Project scope statement

7. The project sponsor has just signed the project charter. What is the next thing to do?

   A. Begin to complete work packages.
   B. Validate scope.
   C. Start integrated change control.
   D. Start to create management plans.

© 2018 RMC Publications, Inc.™ • 952.846.4484 • info@rmcls.com • www.rmcls.com

8. The high-level project schedule constraints have just been determined. What project management process group are you in?

    A. Initiating

    B. Planning

    C. Executing

    D. Monitoring and controlling

9. The WBS and WBS dictionary have been completed, and the project team has begun working on identifying risks. The sponsor contacts the project manager, requesting that the responsibility assignment matrix be issued. The project has a budget of $100,000 and is taking place in three countries using 14 human resources. There is little risk expected for the project, and the project manager has managed many projects similar to this one. What is the next thing to do?

    A. Understand the experience of the sponsor on similar projects.

    B. Create an activity list.

    C. Make sure the project scope is defined.

    D. Complete risk management and issue the responsibility assignment matrix.

10. A project manager does not have much time to spend on planning before the mandatory start date arrives. He therefore wants to move through planning as effectively as possible. What advice would you offer?

    A. Make sure you have a signed project charter and then start the WBS.

    B. Create an activity list before creating a network diagram.

    C. Document all the known risks before you document the high-level assumptions.

    D. Finalize the quality management plan before you determine quality metrics.

11. The best time to assign a project manager to a project is during:

    A. Integration

    B. Project selection

    C. Initiating

    D. Planning

12. A project manager gets a call from a team member notifying him that there is a variance between the speed of a system on the project and the desired or planned speed. The project manager is surprised because that performance measurement was not identified in planning. If the project manager then evaluates whether the variance warrants a response, he is in which part of the project management process?

    A. Initiating

    B. Executing

    C. Monitoring and controlling

    D. Closing

13. A team member notifies the project manager that the activities comprising a work package are no longer appropriate. It would be best for the project manager to be in what part of the project management process?

    A. Corrective action

    B. Integrated change control

    C. Monitoring and controlling

    D. Project closing

14. During a team meeting, a team member asks about the measurements that will be used on the project to assess performance. The team member feels that some of the measures related to activities assigned to him are not valid measurements. The project is most likely in what part of the project management process?

    A. Closing
    B. Monitoring and controlling
    C. Executing
    D. Initiating

15. Which of the following is the most appropriate thing to do during the initiating process group?

    A. Create a detailed description of the project deliverables.
    B. Get familiar with the company culture and structure as they relate to the project.
    C. Identify the root cause of problems.
    D. Ensure all project management processes are complete.

16. Which of the following is a characteristic of project management processes?

    A. Iterative
    B. Unique
    C. Unnecessary
    D. Standardized

17. Which project management process group generally takes the most project time and resources?

    A. Planning
    B. Design
    C. Integration
    D. Executing

18. You are managing two projects and have been assigned to a third project that has just been approved. You begin the new project, and are able to manage it well along with the others you are managing. During initiating, you are focused on accomplishing a number of activities. Which of the following are you not concerned with at this time?

    A. Identifying and documenting business needs
    B. Creating a project scope statement
    C. Dividing a large project into phases
    D. Accumulating and evaluating historical information

19. The software development project has progressed according to plan. The team is very enthusiastic about the product they have created. Now they are looking ahead to finding new projects to work on. You caution them that the current project cannot be considered complete until after the closing process group. Closure includes all the following except:

    A. Determining performance measures
    B. Turning over the product of the project
    C. Documenting the degree to which each project phase was properly closed after its completion
    D. Updating the company's organizational process assets

119

20. The first phase of your project has come to an end. What is the most important thing to ensure is done before beginning the next phase?
    A. Verify that the resources are available for the next phase.
    B. Check the project's progress compared to its baselines.
    C. Confirm that the phase has reached its objectives, and have its deliverables formally accepted.
    D. Recommend corrective action to bring the project results in line with project expectations.

21. During which process group does the team measure and analyze the work being done on the project?
    A. Initiating
    B. Executing
    C. Monitoring and controlling
    D. Closing

22. Which process groups must be included in every project?
    A. Planning, executing, and closing
    B. Initiating, planning, and executing
    C. Planning, executing, and monitoring and controlling
    D. Initiating, planning, executing, monitoring and controlling, and closing

23. Which of the following is the most appropriate thing to do in project closing?
    A. Work with the customer to determine acceptance criteria.
    B. Confirm all the requirements in the project have been met.
    C. Collect historical information from previous projects.
    D. Gain formal approval of the management plans.

24. Which process group focuses on completing the requirements of the project?
    A. Initiating
    B. Planning
    C. Executing
    D. Closing

25. All the following occur during the planning process group except:
    A. Develop Project Charter
    B. Create WBS
    C. Estimate Costs
    D. Sequence Activities

26. A market demand, a business need, and a legal requirement are examples of:
    A. Reasons to hire a project manager
    B. Reasons projects are initiated
    C. Reasons people or businesses become stakeholders
    D. Reasons to sponsor a project

## Answers

1. **Answer** C

   **Explanation** Notice the use of the word "detailed." Such a budget is created during project planning.

2. **Answer** D

   **Explanation** The project charter is needed before planning and execution of the work can begin. Therefore, it is created and approved in project initiating.

3. **Answer** C

   **Explanation** Communications requirements and quality standards are needed before risks (especially risks related to communications and quality) can be determined. Iterations cannot begin until the risks are identified, qualified, and quantified, and the responses are developed. Through iterations, the WBS and other parts of the project management plan are revised. A bar chart would have been done during the creation of the schedule, so it cannot be the next thing. Of the choices listed, determine communications requirements is the best option.

4. **Answer** B

   **Explanation** In the project management process, the project budget, detailed risk assessment, and project management plan come after the schedule is created. The only answer that could be an input is the work breakdown structure.

5. **Answer** A

   **Explanation** The project manager should be named early in the project, during project initiating if possible. It is then their responsibility to control the project throughout its life.

6. **Answer** D

   **Explanation** Notice the question asks which is not an input to project initiating. Did you read it correctly? Companies should have processes in place for hiring resources, reporting, and managing risks on projects (to name only a few). These are inputs to project initiating, as are company culture and historical WBSs. The project scope statement is an output of project planning.

7. **Answer** D

   **Explanation** To answer this type of question, look for the choice that occurs closest to the process group you are in. The project charter is created during project initiating. Completing work packages is done during project executing. Validating scope and performing integrated change control are done during project monitoring and controlling. Starting to create management plans is the best choice, as it is part of project planning.

8. **Answer** A

   **Explanation** High-level constraints are identified in the project charter, which is created during project initiating.

9. **Answer** B

   **Explanation** Look at the order of planning the project that the team has chosen. Although understanding the experience of the sponsor might sound like a good idea, the sponsor is a stakeholder, and understanding the stakeholders is part of stakeholder analysis. That should have occurred before the creation of a WBS. Project scope must be defined before a WBS can be created. Completing risk management and issuing the responsibility assignment matrix cannot be best, as that work does not come next in the process. Other work must be done before risk management can effectively be completed. Creating an activity list comes next after the WBS and WBS dictionary.

10. **Answer** B

     **Explanation** This question is asking which of the choices is the most effective way to move through project planning. Starting the WBS immediately after obtaining a project charter skips the important steps of defining the scope and other activities. High-level assumptions are determined in project initiating. Quality metrics are determined as part of the quality management plan, not after it. The activity list is created before the network diagram, so that is the best option.

11. **Answer** C

     **Explanation** The project manager should be assigned during project initiating.

12. **Answer** C

     **Explanation** Even though the measurement was not identified in planning, the project manager would still have to investigate the variance and determine if it is important. The project manager is in project monitoring and controlling.

13. **Answer** C

     **Explanation** If you chose another part of the project management process, you probably forgot that the situation needs to be evaluated by the project manager before recommending a change or beginning integrated change control.

14. **Answer** C

     **Explanation** This situation does not describe an actual measurement (a monitoring and controlling activity) but rather a meeting occurring during project executing.

15. **Answer** B

     **Explanation** A detailed description of the project deliverables is created during project planning, as part of creating the project scope statement. Root cause analysis occurs during project monitoring and controlling, not initiating. Ensuring all project management processes are complete occurs during project closing. It is important for a project manager to become familiar with the company culture and structure as they relate to the project as early in the project as possible. This is the most appropriate choice to do in project initiating.

16. **Answer** A

     **Explanation** As the project life cycle progresses, more information becomes available, allowing the team to manage the project to a more detailed level.

17. **Answer** D

     **Explanation** Did you notice that planning and executing are the only process groups offered as choices? Therefore, design and integration can be eliminated as options. Doing the actual work (in executing) will generally take the most project time and resources.

18. **Answer** B

     **Explanation** A project scope statement is created during project planning.

19. **Answer** A

     **Explanation** Performance measures are determined earlier in the project so they can be used to measure progress during the project, making determining performance measures the only correct answer to this question.

20. **Answer** C

     **Explanation** A phase or project must be formally closed and accepted.

21. **Answer** C
    **Explanation** During monitoring and controlling, project performance is measured and needed changes are identified and approved.

22. **Answer** D
    **Explanation** All five process groups are addressed in each project. It is the responsibility of the project manager to determine the level of attention to give to each process group.

23. **Answer** B
    **Explanation** Collecting historical information and determining high-level acceptance criteria are done in project initiating. Gaining approval of management plans is part of project planning. Confirming that project requirements have been met occurs in project closing.

24. **Answer** C
    **Explanation** Project executing is where work is done to produce the product of the project.

25. **Answer** A
    **Explanation** Develop Project Charter occurs in project initiating.

26. **Answer** B
    **Explanation** These are all reasons projects are initiated.

123

# Integration Management

## FOUR

How would you respond if you were asked, "What is a project manager's primary role?" The correct answer is: to perform integration management[1]—to pull all the pieces of a project together into a cohesive whole. This is so much a part of a project manager's job that it is arguably the reason for the project manager's existence in an organization and on a project.

Many people who have trouble with this knowledge area on the exam either do not currently perform integration management on their projects or do not think about integration management from a large-project perspective.

While the work of the project is being done, the team members are concentrating on completing the work packages, and the project sponsor is protecting the project from changes and loss of resources. The project manager is responsible for integration—putting all the pieces of the project together into one cohesive whole that gets the project done faster, cheaper, and with fewer resources, while meeting the project objectives.

 **TRICKS OF THE TRADE®** Think about integration as balancing all the processes in all the knowledge areas (scope, schedule, cost, quality, resources, communications, risk, procurement, and stakeholder management) with each other. Project management processes do not happen independently. To complete a cost estimate, for example, factors such as the number of resources on the project, the scope being estimated, and the risk reserves should be taken into account. As another example, adding a new resource to the project may require cost or schedule changes. In dealing with situations that develop during a project, the project manager is integrating the processes of project management.

## QUICKTEST

- Integration management process
- Integrated change control
- Process for making changes
- Project management plan
  - Knowledge area management plans
  - Baselines
  - Requirements management plan
  - Change management plan
  - Configuration management plan
  - Project life cycle approach
- Project charter
- Business case
- Project selection
  - Benefit measurement methods
  - Constrained optimization methods
- Knowledge management
- Information management
- Types of knowledge
  - Tacit
  - Explicit
- Project documents
- Benefits management plan
- Assumption log
- Change requests
- Corrective action
- Preventive action
- Defect repair
- Constraints and assumptions
- Configuration management system
- Change control system
- Change control board
- Cost-benefit analysis
- Kickoff meeting
- Work authorization system
- Net present value
- Internal rate of return
- Payback period
- Present value
- Economic value added
- Opportunity cost
- Sunk costs
- Law of diminishing returns
- Working capital
- Depreciation

# Integration Management

| INITIATING | PLANNING (This is the only process group with a set order.) | EXECUTING | MONITORING & CONTROLLING | CLOSING |
|---|---|---|---|---|
| Select project manager | Determine development approach, life cycle, and how you will plan for each knowledge area | Execute work according to the project management plan | Take action to monitor and control the project | Confirm work is done to requirements |
| Determine company culture and existing systems | Define and prioritize requirements | Produce product deliverables (product scope) | Measure performance against performance measurement baseline | Complete final procurement closure |
| Collect processes, procedures, and historical information | Create project scope statement | Gather work performance data | Measure performance against other metrics in the project management plan | Gain final acceptance of product |
| Divide large projects into phases or smaller projects | Assess what to purchase and create procurement documents | Request changes | Analyze and evaluate data and performance | Complete financial closure |
| Understand business case and benefits management plan | Determine planning team | Implement only approved changes | Determine if variances warrant a corrective action or other change request(s) | Hand off completed product |
| Uncover initial requirements, assumptions, risks, constraints, and existing agreements | Create WBS and WBS dictionary | Continuously improve; perform progressive elaboration | Influence factors that cause change | Solicit customer's feedback about the project |
| Assess project and product feasibility within the given constraints | Create activity list | Follow processes | Request changes | Complete final performance reporting |
| Create measurable objectives and success criteria | Create network diagram | Determine whether quality plan and processes are correct and effective | Perform integrated change control | Index and archive records |
| Develop project charter | Estimate resource requirements | Perform quality audits and issue quality reports | Approve or reject changes | Gather final lessons learned and update knowledge bases |
| Identify stakeholders and determine their expectations, interest, influence, and impact | Estimate activity durations and costs | Acquire final team and physical resources | Update project management plan and project documents | |
| Request changes | Determine critical path | Manage people | Inform stakeholders of all change request results | |
| Develop assumption log | Develop schedule | Evaluate team and individual performance; provide training | Monitor stakeholder engagement | |
| Develop stakeholder register | Develop budget | Hold team-building activities | Confirm configuration compliance | |
| | Determine quality standards, processes, and metrics | Give recognition and rewards | Create forecasts | |
| | Determine team charter and all roles and responsibilities | Use issue logs | Gain customer's acceptance of interim deliverables | |
| | Plan communications and stakeholder engagement | Facilitate conflict resolution | Perform quality control | |
| | Perform risk identification, qualitative and quantitative risk analysis, and risk response planning | Release resources as work is completed | Perform risk reviews, reassessments, and audits | |
| | Go back—iterations | Send and receive information, and solicit feedback | Manage reserves | |
| | Finalize procurement strategy and documents | Report on project performance | Manage, evaluate, and close procurements | |
| | Create change and configuration management plans | Facilitate stakeholder engagement and manage expectations | Evaluate use of physical resources | |
| | Finalize all management plans | Hold meetings | | |
| | Develop realistic and sufficient project management plan and baselines | Evaluate sellers; negotiate and contract with sellers | | |
| | Gain formal approval of the plan | Use and share project knowledge | | |
| | Hold kickoff meeting | Execute contingency plans | | |
| | Request changes | Update project management plan and project documents | | |

## Rita's Process Chart™
## Integration Management
Where are we in the project management process?

© 2018 RMC Publications, Inc.™ • 952.846.4484 • info@rmcls.com • www.rmcls.com

The other knowledge area chapters in this book explain the detailed work of a project manager. This chapter, however, is about the high-level work a project manager needs to do. Read this chapter carefully. Integration management is a difficult area on the exam.

The following should help you understand how each part of integration management fits into the overall project management process:

| The Integration Management Process | Done During |
| --- | --- |
| Develop Project Charter | Initiating process group |
| Develop Project Management Plan | Planning process group |
| Direct and Manage Project Work | Executing process group |
| Manage Project Knowledge | Executing process group |
| Monitor and Control Project Work | Monitoring and controlling process group |
| Perform Integrated Change Control | Monitoring and controlling process group |
| Close Project or Phase | Closing process group |

Integration management cannot be understood without a solid understanding of the process of project management. Therefore, if you have limited project management training or experience, you might want to do a high-level review of this chapter now, read the rest of this book, and then come back and read this chapter again. It will make more sense the second time. Remember that integration management is the primary role of a project manager. You must understand integration from a real-world, large-project perspective.

Figure 4.1 shows the relationship between knowledge areas and process groups. All knowledge areas include processes that occur in planning and monitoring and controlling. Integration Management is the only knowledge area that has processes occurring in all process groups, throughout the project management process. The project manager is always integrating.

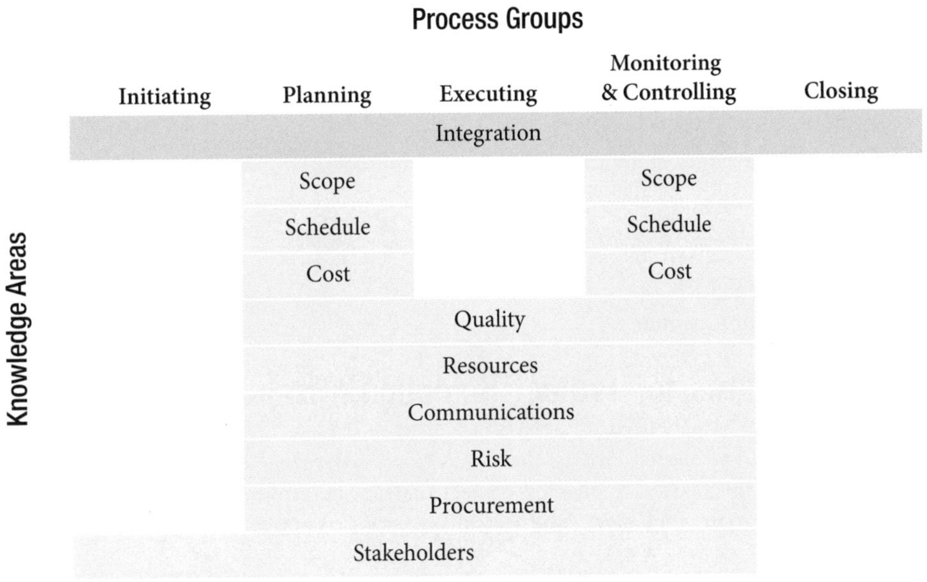

**Process Groups**

| | Initiating | Planning | Executing | Monitoring & Controlling | Closing |
| --- | --- | --- | --- | --- | --- |
| **Knowledge Areas** | Integration | Integration | Integration | Integration | Integration |
| | | Scope | | Scope | |
| | | Schedule | | Schedule | |
| | | Cost | | Cost | |
| | | Quality | Quality | Quality | |
| | | Resources | Resources | Resources | |
| | | Communications | Communications | Communications | |
| | | Risk | Risk | Risk | |
| | | Procurement | Procurement | Procurement | |
| | Stakeholders | Stakeholders | Stakeholders | Stakeholders | |

FIGURE 4.1   *The relationship between the knowledge areas and process groups*

127

## Project Selection

Before we discuss the processes of Integration Management and all the work involved in successfully managing a project, let's take a moment to discuss what happens before a project is chartered. It is important for a project manager to know a project's history in order to manage it effectively and achieve the results for which it was intended.

The departments and individuals within your company present management with requests for many different initiatives (potential projects), all of which would require an investment of corporate resources. When answering questions on the exam, assume that the organization has a formal process to review and analyze these potential projects and select the project that best aligns with the strategic goals of the organization. There might even be a project selection committee in place to evaluate project proposals.

A project manager is not typically involved in project selection. So, you might ask, "Why is this an important topic to understand?" Good question! The reasons a project is selected and the value it is expected to bring to an organization indicate its significance to the company. The project manager needs to know if the project was selected because it will establish a new area of business, if it is being implemented to meet regulatory or compliance requirements, or if it was chosen because it was the least expensive or most feasible solution to a problem. The reasons a project was selected can impact which constraints are most flexible, and knowing this information will influence how the project manager plans and manages the project. A project manager must keep the reasons the project was selected in mind throughout the project to ensure the objectives are achieved.

For the exam, you should be familiar with the project selection methods described next, but understanding these methods is not as important as knowing that such activities occur prior to initiating a project. These activities fall outside the project boundaries (the period from project authorization through closure).

Benefit measurement and constrained optimization are two categories of project selection methods. You may see these terms used in scenarios or as distractors in answer choices. Present value is the only calculation you may be asked to perform. For the exam, you should simply be aware that the following terms relate to project selection:

- Benefit measurement methods[2] (comparative approach); examples of this method include:
  - A murder board[3] (a panel of people who try to shoot down a new project idea)
  - Peer review
  - Scoring models
  - Economic measures (described next)
- Constrained optimization methods[4] (mathematical approach); examples of this method include:
  - Linear programming
  - Integer programming
  - Dynamic programming
  - Multiobjective programming

## Economic Measures for Project Selection

The following sections discuss several economic measures[5] that can be used for selecting a project. It is important to note that some of these measures are also used in processes such as quality, cost, and risk management, and in integrated change control. The measures can be used to develop project metrics, determine when changes to the plan are needed, and evaluate progress, changes, and overall project success. Such economic measures take a comparative approach.

Keep in mind that these measures aren't generally used on their own; that is, an organization would likely consider more than one of these measures (along with other factors) when selecting a project.

### Return on Investment (ROI)
Return on investment determines the potential profitability of an investment by calculating the benefits received in relation to the cost.

### Present Value (PV)
Note that you may encounter a couple of questions on the exam that require you to calculate present value. Present value means the value today of future cash flows, and it can be calculated using the following formula:

$$PV = \frac{FV}{(1 + r)^n}$$

FV = future value
$r$ = interest rate
$n$ = number of time periods

The acronym PV is also used for planned value (described in the Cost Management chapter). You can avoid confusing these terms by considering the context in which they are used. If the question involves project work that has started, and you are evaluating schedule or cost performance, the acronym PV is represents planned value within earned value management. If the question is discussing how the project was evaluated for selection or funding, PV represents present value.

Using a simple example, see if you can answer the following question:

*Question*    Is the present value of $300,000 to be received three years from now, with an expected interest rate of 10 percent, more or less than $300,000?

*Answer*    Less. You can put an amount of money less than $300,000 in the bank and in three years have $300,000.
To perform the calculation: $300,000/(1 + 0.1)^3 = $300,000/1.331 = $225,394$.

### Net Present Value (NPV)
You will not have to calculate NPV; just know that it is the present value of the total benefits (income or revenue) minus the costs over many time periods. Calculating the NPV of each proposed project provides a means for the organization to compare many projects and select the best project to initiate. Generally, if the NPV is positive, the investment is a good choice—unless an even better investment opportunity exists. The project with the greatest NPV is typically selected.

To learn more about calculating NPV, visit rmcls.com.

Do you already have a good understanding of this topic? Test yourself with the following question.

*Question*    An organization has two projects from which to choose. Project A will take three years to complete and has an NPV of $45,000. Project B will take six years to complete and has an NPV of $85,000. Which one is a better investment?

*Answer*    Project B. The number of years is not relevant, as that would have been taken into account in the calculation of the NPV.

### Internal Rate of Return (IRR)
To understand this concept, think of a bank account. You put money in a bank account and expect to get a return—for example, 1 percent. You can think of a project in the same way. If a company has more than one project in which it could invest, the company may look at the returns of the different projects and then select the project with the highest return.

129

IRR does get confusing when you give it a formal definition: the rate ("interest rate") at which the project inflows ("revenues") and project outflows ("costs") are equal. Calculating IRR is complex and requires the aid of a computer. You will not have to perform any IRR calculations on the exam. Simply know that the higher the IRR number, the better.

Question — An organization has two projects from which to choose: Project A with an IRR of 21 percent and Project B with an IRR of 15 percent. Which one is a better option?

Answer — Project A

## Payback Period

This term refers to the length of time it takes for the organization to recover its investment in a project before it starts accumulating profit. For example:

Question — There are two projects from which to choose: Project A with a payback period of six months and Project B with a payback period of 18 months. Which one should the organization select?

Answer — Project A

Based on the information given in this example, the project with the shorter payback period is the best choice, but keep in mind that payback period is likely to be one of only several financial factors, along with other considerations, used in selecting a project. In some cases, the best choice might be a project that has a longer payback period but various other advantages.

## Cost-Benefit Analysis

Cost-benefit analysis compares the expected costs of a project to the potential benefits it could bring the organization. (For project selection purposes, benefits are the same as revenue. Remember that revenue is not the same as profit.) This analysis results in the calculation of a benefit-cost ratio, which can be expressed as a decimal or a ratio. A benefit-cost ratio of greater than 1 means the benefits are greater than the costs. A benefit-cost ratio of less than 1 means the costs are greater than the benefits. A benefit-cost ratio of 1 means the costs and benefits are equal.

Question — What does a benefit-cost ratio of 1.7 mean?

A. The costs are greater than the benefits.
B. Revenue is 1.7 times the costs.
C. Profit is 1.7 times the costs.
D. Costs are 1.7 times the profit.

Answer — B. The benefits, or revenue, the project brings to the organization are 1.7 times the cost of the initiative. Remember, the benefit-cost ratio calculation is looking at revenue, not the smaller figure of profits.

The organization may use the benefit-cost ratio to help choose from many potential projects. A project manager may also perform cost-benefit analysis to determine the best solution approach once a project is selected. The project manager may perform the analysis at a high level during project initiating and at a more detailed level during project planning. This information helps determine things such as what level of quality efforts are appropriate for the project, what equipment or technology should be purchased, and whether it would be best to outsource certain pieces of work.

© 2018 RMC Publications, Inc.™ • 952.846.4484 • info@rmcls.com • www.rmcls.com

**Exercise**   Remember, you do not have to be an accountant to pass the exam. You do not have to use accounting formulas (aside, possibly, from a couple of present value questions). But you do need to have a general understanding of what the terms mean. So, test yourself! For each row in the following chart, enter the letter of the project you would select based on the information provided.

| | Project A | Project B | Which Project Would You Pick? |
|---|---|---|---|
| Net present value | $95,000 | $75,000 | A |
| IRR | 13 percent | 17 percent | B |
| Payback period | 16 months | 21 months | A |
| Benefit-cost ratio | 2.79 | 1.3 | A |

## Answer

| | Project A | Project B | Which Project Would You Pick? |
|---|---|---|---|
| Net present value | $95,000 | $75,000 | A |
| IRR | 13 percent | 17 percent | B |
| Payback period | 16 months | 21 months | A |
| Benefit-cost ratio | 2.79 | 1.3 | A |

The following are some additional accounting terms related to project selection that you should be familiar with for the exam.

**Economic Value Added (EVA)[6]**   In terms of project selection, this concept is concerned with whether the project returns to the company more value than the initiative costs. (Note that this is a different concept than earned value analysis, which can also have the acronym of EVA. Earned value, discussed in the Cost Management chapter, is frequently mentioned on the exam, whereas economic value added should rarely appear in questions or answer choices.)

**Opportunity Cost**   This term refers to the opportunity given up by selecting one project over another. This does not require any calculation. See the following example:

*Question*   An organization has two projects to choose from: Project A with an NPV of $45,000 and Project B with an NPV of $85,000. What is the opportunity cost of selecting Project B?

*Answer*   $45,000

The opportunity cost is the value of the project not selected.

**Sunk Costs**   Sunk costs are expended costs. People unfamiliar with accounting standards might have trouble with the following question:

Question    An organization has a project with an initial budget of $1,000,000. The project is half complete, and it has spent $2,000,000. Should the organization consider the fact that it is already $1,000,000 over budget when determining whether to continue with the project?

Answer    No. The money spent is gone.

Accounting standards say that sunk costs should not be considered when deciding whether to continue with a troubled project.

**Law of Diminishing Returns**[7]   This law states that after a certain point, adding more input (for example, programmers) will not produce a proportional increase in productivity (such as modules of code per hour). A single programmer may produce at a rate of 1 module per hour. With a second programmer, the two may produce at a rate of 1.75 modules per hour (0.75 increase). With a third programmer, the group may produce at a rate of 2.25 modules per hour (0.5 increase). This disparity may be due to many factors. For example, additional coordination is required as more programmers are added to a project.

**Working Capital**   This term refers to an organization's current assets minus its current liabilities. In other words, it is the amount of money the company has available to invest, including investing in projects.

**Depreciation**   Large assets, such as equipment, lose value over time. Accounting standards call this depreciation. Several methods are used to account for depreciation. The exam may ask you what they are. You will not have to perform any calculations. (See, we said we could make this easy for you!) Rather, you should simply understand the following concepts about the two forms of depreciation:

- **Straight-line depreciation**  With straight-line depreciation, the same amount of depreciation is taken each year.

  *Example*: A $1,000 item with a 10-year useful life and no salvage value (the value of an item at the end of its life) would be depreciated at $100 per year.

- **Accelerated depreciation**  For many years, the exam has not asked detailed questions on this topic. Just know the following for the exam:

  - There are two forms of accelerated depreciation:

    » Double declining balance

    » Sum of the years digits

  - Accelerated depreciation depreciates faster than straight-line depreciation.

  *Example*: A $1,000 item with a 10-year useful life and no salvage value (the value of an item at the end of its life) would be depreciated at $180 the first year, $150 the second, $130 the next, and so on.

**TRICKS OF THE TRADE®**   The exam may present information about project selection in the following ways.

First, the exam may ask questions relating to business cases and project selection methods. You need to understand that there is a selection process for a project, know what that process is, and be aware that the project must support the company's strategic goals.

Second, the exam may use project selection concepts, such as internal rate of return, as distractors. Such information may be provided in the question even when you do not need the data to answer the question. Read the questions carefully to pick out which data is relevant.

The project selection process results in the development of a business case. The business case describes the business need, the proposed solution, and the expected value of the change. It includes both tangible and intangible costs and benefits of the proposed solution. The business case will influence how you approach every project management process covered in this book, beginning with the creation of a project charter.[8] Developing the charter is the first of many processes that make up a successful project.

## Develop Project Charter   PAGE 75

> **Process** Develop Project Charter
> **Process Group** Initiating
> **Knowledge Area** Integration Management

The first part of integration management is developing a project charter. The exam could include up to eight questions that reference a charter. You should understand what a project charter is, why it is important, and how it is used throughout the life of the project.

**Exercise**   Test yourself! Answer the following question.

### What Is Included in a Project Charter?

_____

_____

_____

_____

_____

_____

_____

_____

**Answer**   Unfortunately, many companies expect project charters to include information such as a detailed schedule and a full risk analysis. Such information is not available at this point in the project management process, however. A project charter is not a project management plan! Read the rest of this section to learn what is included in a project charter and to see some examples.

Creating the project charter involves planning the project at a high level to assess whether it is feasible within the given constraints, but detailed planning does not happen until after the charter is signed. In project initiating, you may meet with key stakeholders and define the high-level objectives, constraints, requirements, scope, risks, and assumptions in an effort to assess the feasibility of the project. Much of this information will also be used for benefits analysis, in which you and key stakeholders confirm the project aligns with the organization's strategic goals and is likely to deliver the anticipated value. Detailed planning takes time and costs money, and this time and money should not be spent until the project is officially authorized by approval of the project charter.

Business documents—including the business case and the benefits management plan—are key inputs to the development of the project charter. They provide critical information to the project manager and team, such as:

- Why the project was undertaken
- A summary of the relationship between the project objectives and the strategic goals of the organization

Note that these documents do not need to be updated throughout the life of the project, but can be periodically reviewed by the project manager.

## Business Case

A business case is the justification for a project or initiative. Most organizations require a strong business case to fund a project because there are so many competing needs for available resources. Defining a business case requires sophisticated analysis and evaluation, as we discussed in the project selection topic. It will help the organization decide whether or not to move forward with creating the solution.

The exam assumes that every project has a defined business case and that it is unacceptable to select a project based on anything but a sound business case. The business case captures the business need; it explains why the project was selected, how it fits into the organization's strategic goals, and how it will bring business value to the organization. (How each organization defines business value will vary, but such a definition could include quantifiable benefits, such as financial gain, as well as less obvious benefits such as increased name recognition.)

Let's look at an example of how a business case can affect the way a project is managed.

> *A company has selected a particular project because the project will contribute to its strategic plan of entering a new area of business. The project manager has a project management plan that includes an approved schedule and budget. The project manager finds that the approved budget is a constraint that could inhibit the company's successful entrance into the new market. She asks for a change in budget, rather than cutting costs on the project to stay within the project management plan. If the project manager had not asked for the budget increase, the company might have missed its objective of successfully launching itself into the new area of business.*

## Benefits Management Plan

The benefits management plan is a document that captures the organization's desired benefits from a project, whether economic or intangible, and explains how those benefits will be maximized and sustained. It also defines metrics and processes for measuring a project's benefits. As an input to the charter, the benefits management plan is important, as it provides information to be used to determine whether a project's deliverables will help the organization in meeting its strategic goals and objectives.

## Constraints and Assumptions

Identifying and documenting high-level project constraints and assumptions uncovered during project initiating is important. Assumptions and constraints are documented as part of the business case. These are often highlighted in the project charter (as depicted in the charter examples within this chapter) to make sure they are considered and accepted as part of the sponsor's formal approval. Assumptions and constraints are also documented in the assumption log.[9]

Constraints are factors—such as limits on resources, budget, schedule, and scope (for example, management saying the project must be completed with only five resources)—that limit the team's options. Assumptions are things that are assumed to be true but that may not be true (for example, "It is assumed that we will not need engineering department approval before we start the activity."). Constraints and assumptions are inputs to many project management processes. They are identified at a high level in project initiating and are then refined and documented in detail as part of the Define Scope process in project planning.

Once they are identified, constraints and assumptions need to be managed. The sponsor, the team, and other stakeholders may help identify constraints and assumptions and review them for validity throughout the life of the project. If the constraints change or the assumptions are proven wrong, the project management plan[10] may need to change. Assumptions analysis is part of the risk management process.

## Agreements/Contracts

All projects should have charters, whether the project is an internal initiative or is being done for an external customer. The development of a charter often starts with some form of agreement or understanding. In the case of an internal project, the initial agreement may be as informal as an email or a conversation about what the project will entail. It could also take the form of a memorandum of understanding or a letter of agreement. When the work is being done for an outside organization, a formal contract is typically involved. (See the Procurement Management chapter for more information about agreements and contracts.)

Although we often think of the buyer creating a project charter, the organization providing services to the buyer should also create a charter. This means that on a project where there is a buyer and a seller, both organizations would create project charters that have different points of view. The buyer's reason for the project, as stated in their project charter, might be to achieve a particular product scope while meeting project constraints. The seller's reason for working on the project, as stated in their project charter, might be to increase revenue, enhance their reputation, or gain additional work from the buyer.

In addition to these items, any relevant organizational process assets (such as processes, any governance framework, methods for monitoring and reporting, templates, historical information, and lessons learned) or enterprise environmental factors (such as applicable standards, legal requirements, existing infrastructure, and organizational culture) that are present in the organization should be taken into consideration when creating the charter. The project manager works with the sponsor and others who can offer expertise on different aspects of the project to create the charter.

The following is a brief example of a project charter for a small project. It does not represent the scale of projects you should be thinking about for the exam, but it should help you to understand the elements of a project charter. You will see a sample charter for a large project later in this chapter. These charter examples focus on what is done in the real world and what you need to know for the exam. They go beyond what is listed as part of the project charter in the *PMBOK® Guide*.

NOTE: The following project charter example refers to attached documents. These documents are not shown as part of this example.

## Project Charter

### Project Title and Description (*What is the project?*) **Customer Satisfaction Fix-It Project**

Over the last few months, the quality assurance department has discovered that it takes many customers four times longer to place orders for XYZ equipment using our online ordering system than it takes to place similar orders through our competitors' systems. The purpose of this project is to investigate the reasons for the problem and propose a solution. Development and implementation of the solution will be authorized as a subsequent project (Customer Satisfaction Fix-It Project II).

The quality control department has detailed records of their findings, which will contribute to the analysis work on this project.

### Project Manager Assigned and Authority Level (*Who is given authority to lead the project, and can they determine, manage, and approve changes to budget, schedule, and team assignments?*)

Victor Rojas will be the project manager for this project and will have the authority to select team members and determine the final project budget and schedule.

### Business Case (*Why is the project being done? On what financial or other basis can we justify doing this project? Describe the project purpose and justification.*)

Because it takes many customers four times longer to place orders for XYZ equipment using our online ordering system than it takes to place similar orders through our competitors' systems, our company is losing potential revenue. The company has also experienced a measured decrease in customer satisfaction as a result of the problems with the online ordering system. This project is the first of two projects designed to prevent a further erosion of customer satisfaction. We expect that improved customer satisfaction will increase revenue to the company in the first year by at least $200,000 due to a decrease in service calls and incomplete orders. As a side benefit, we hope the project will generate ideas on improving customer satisfaction while determining how to address the problem with our online ordering system.

### Resources Preassigned (*How many or which resources will be provided?*)

Two IT analysts have been assigned and dedicated to the project because of their expertise in computer systems of this type. Other resources will be determined by the project manager during planning.

### Key Stakeholder List (*Who will affect or be affected by the project [influence the project], as known to date?*)

Key stakeholders include Vihaan Gupta representing Quality Control, Benjamin Lang in Customer Service, and Shirley Price in Marketing. These stakeholders will be available as needed.

### Stakeholder Requirements as Known (*Requirements related to both project and product scope.*)

Attached to this document are the detailed specifications for the existing system along with the requirements the existing system was designed to meet. It is expected that this project will not change the existing system, but rather make a recommendation for improving it.

The project includes utilizing the data available from Quality Control.

### High-Level Product Description/Key Deliverables (*What are the key product deliverables that are wanted, and what will be the end result of the project?*)

Interim deliverables will include:

- Detailed customer ordering process flow
- Analysis of the time it takes to complete each step of the ordering process
- Recommended change
- Estimated time and cost of the proposed change
- WBS
- List of risks

The final deliverable will be a report that outlines what can be changed, how much it will cost, the expected decrease in the time it will take to place an order, and what work will need to be done to implement the solution.

### High-Level Assumptions *(What is believed to be true or reliable in the situation? What do we believe to be the case but do not have proof or data for? See details in the assumption log.)*

- The existing requirements for the current system (aside from those relating to the speed of order entry) are sufficient and correct for an online ordering system that is four times faster than the current system.
- The current network will be able to support the program changes.
- No new hardware will be required.
- The current subject matter experts and developers have the expertise to evaluate the problem and recommend a solution that will achieve the objectives.
- Internal resources will have the time to work on the project in addition to their current responsibilities.

### High-Level Constraints *(What factors may limit our ability to deliver? What boundaries or parameters will the project have to function within?)*

- WBS must be complete in two weeks.
- Risk register is due in three weeks.
- The scope is limited to identifying a solution that will reduce the time it takes to complete an online order.

### Measurable Project Objectives *(How does the project tie into the organization's strategic goals? What project objectives support those goals? The objectives must be measurable and will depend on the defined priority of the project constraints.)*

The objective of this project is to develop a solution that will improve customer satisfaction rates for online orders to 95 percent by reducing the time customers spend placing orders to 25 percent of the current time. Scope and customer satisfaction are the top priorities on this project, closely followed by schedule and then cost.

- Summary milestone schedule: Due no later than September 1, 20XX
- Preapproved financial resources: $50,000

### Project Approval Requirements *(What items need to be approved for the project, and who will have sign-off authority? What designates success?)*

Approvals for this project include:

- The sponsors will approve the WBS before planning efforts continue.
- The sponsors will approve the list of risks before planning efforts continue.
- The sponsors will give final project approval.

### Overall Project Risks *(Overall potential threats and opportunities for the project)*

- Because this project analyzes customer satisfaction, the project may help generate ideas to improve customer satisfaction, resulting in higher levels of customer retention.
- Because we are using internal resources to analyze and propose a solution, it is possible that they may not be aware of all possible solutions, and the proposed solution may be inadequate to address the problem successfully.
- Because this problem is greatly troubling to our customers, project delay could result in lost customers, further jeopardizing the likelihood of meeting this year's sales goals.
- Because assessment of this system is difficult, implementation of the proposed solution to change the system could impact other business functions.

### Project Exit Criteria *(What needs must be met so that the project manager will be able to close or terminate the project or phase?)*

A final report will include a description of the solution, how much the solution will cost, and the expected decrease in the time it takes to place an order expected to result from implementing the solution. The findings contained in the report must be agreed to by the representatives of Quality Control, Customer Service, and Marketing, in addition to the project team.

## Project Sponsors Authorizing This Project

_____          _____
Alexandra Guyot, Executive Vice President          Christopher Davis, Vice President

## Exercise    Test yourself! Answer the question below.

### What Does the Project Charter Do for the Project Manager?

_____

_____

_____

_____

_____

_____

_____

_____

**Answer**    Do not underestimate the value of the project charter! The project charter is such an important document that a project cannot be started without one. The project charter is your target for the project and serves as a definition of how success will be measured. Without a project charter, the project and project manager cannot be successful. Know the following for the exam.

The project manager may create the project charter, but it is issued (signed off on) by the sponsor as part of project initiating. The project charter should be broad enough that it does not need to change as the project progresses. (Any change to the project charter should call into question whether the project should continue.) It provides, at a minimum, the following benefits:

- The project charter should clarify and encourage understanding between the sponsor and project manager of the major deliverables and milestones. It should also define the key roles and responsibilities on the project. This information should be shared with all stakeholders.

- The project charter formally recognizes (authorizes) the existence of the project, or establishes the project. This means that a project does not exist without a project charter.

- The project charter gives the project manager authority to spend money.

- The project charter gives the project manager authority to commit corporate resources to the project. On the exam, this is a commonly described benefit or use of the project charter. In most project situations, the project team does not report to the project manager in the corporate structure, which can lead to cooperation and performance issues. The project charter helps to prevent these issues.

- The project charter provides the objectives, high-level requirements, and success criteria for the project.

- The process of creating the charter uncovers assumptions about the project, which the project manager can later address in the detailed requirements-gathering, scope-definition, and risk management efforts.

- The project charter links the project to the ongoing work of the organization.

Can you see that the creation of a project charter influences all the project management knowledge areas (scope, schedule, cost, quality, resources, communications, risk, procurement, and stakeholder management)?

## Large Projects

As we've discussed, you need to maintain a large-project perspective when answering questions on the exam. To help you understand this critical concept, review the following project charter for a large project, and then complete the exercise.

NOTE: The following charter example refers to attached documents. These documents are not shown as part of this example.

---

### Project Charter

**Project Title and Description** *(What is the project?)*   **Upgrade the Payroll Systems**
We're a large, multinational organization with more than 20,000 employees, so human resource management is critical to our success. To more efficiently compensate our employees, we want to replace or upgrade the employee payroll systems to better reflect the changing nature of our workforce. Employees now work in various locations (offices and homes) around the world, work simultaneously for multiple business units, and have more varied work schedules than ever before. Current geographically focused payroll systems are not integrated, are inflexible, and require significant clerical time to maintain them manually. With the existing systems, consolidated corporate reporting and analysis is expensive and inefficient.

**Project Manager Assigned and Authority Level** *(Who is given authority to lead the project, and can they determine, manage, and approve changes to budget, schedule, staffing, etc.?)*
Isaiah Higgins will be the project manager for this project. He may request any team members he sees fit and will work with resource managers to secure the needed resources. He has signature authority up to $10,000. Ashley Chan is assigned as assistant project manager.

**Business Case** *(Why is the project being done? On what financial or other basis can we justify doing this project?)*
Administering payroll currently costs $2.4 million annually along with the unmeasured costs of procedural inefficiencies. The industry average payroll processing costs for a global company our size is $100 per employee per year, or $2 million overall per year. Anticipated savings of $400,000 per year (assuming a three-year payback period) justifies the approval of this project. See the detailed business case attached to this charter.

**Resources Preassigned** *(How many or which resources will be provided?)*
The corporate payroll processing group will be closely involved in this project, along with the payroll specialists who work in our local offices. A senior team of business analysts, enterprise architects, and software designers has been identified for the initial research and analysis phase. Procurement and legal representatives will be involved in vendor contract processes, including development of RFPs and contracts when deemed necessary. English will be the primary project language; local language experts will be involved to ensure country-specific regulations and laws are understood. Other required resources must be identified and negotiated for by the project manager.

**Key Stakeholder List** *(Who will affect or be affected by the project [influence the project], as known to date?)*
Attached is a list of stakeholder groups that will be impacted by this project. It includes all employees, divided into payees, corporate management, legal, procurement, and payroll administrators. It also includes outside representatives of government taxing authorities, benefit providers, and suppliers of payroll-processing solutions.

---

139

## Stakeholder Requirements as Known  (*Requirements related to both project and product scope.*)

| Req. Number | High-Level Requirements |
|---|---|
| R1 | Pay employees based on the agreed-upon rate/salary on the agreed-upon schedule. |
| R2 | Adhere to country-specific government requirements related to tax withholding and payment schedules. |
| R3 | Adhere to state, province, county, or other local government requirements related to tax withholding and payment schedules. |
| R4 | Allow the company to provide benefits for employees as approved by the Board of Directors. |
| R5 | Allow the company to collect benefit premium payments from employee pay as agreed to by each employee. |
| R6 | Keep all employee data confidential, secure, and archived as required by law in each jurisdiction. |

## High Level Product Description/Key Deliverables  (*What are the key product deliverables that are wanted and what will be the end result of the project?*)

The result of this project should be one or more systems that support payroll processing for all employees, at or below the industry average cost. Specific desired features include:

- The systems should allow direct deposit of employee pay into any financial institution in the world, along with notification of deposit via email or text message to any device.
- Workers should be able to change their address, number of dependents, tax withholding parameters, and benefit characteristics via a website at any time from any location.
- The systems must support consolidated management and reporting of corporate payroll processing, plus government mandated reporting and payments.

## High-Level Assumptions  (*What is believed to be true or reliable in the situation? What do we believe to be the case but do not have proof or data for? See details in the assumption log.*)

- There are payroll applications available that support the countries in which our employees are located.
- The average cost of $100 per employee per year is accurate for our industry.
- Each employee reports their primary residence in just one country for tax reporting purposes.
- We have internal resources available to evaluate and do the work assigned.

## High-Level Constraints  (*What factors may limit our ability to deliver? What boundaries or parameters will the project have to function within?*)

- The system must be able to comply with all international payroll rules and perform direct deposits globally.
- The solution and the supporting systems must be able to maintain organizational information security standards that meet or exceed individual country standards.
- Year-end tax reporting must be completed by the new system in the year of the implementation (payroll data must be converted).
- Summary milestone schedule: Due no later than October 6, 20XX
- Preapproved financial resources: $1,200,000

## Measurable Project Objectives  (*How does the project tie into the organization's strategic goals? What project objectives support those goals? The objectives need to be measurable and will depend on the defined priority of the project constraints.*)

The main objective of this project is to decrease costs by at least $400,000 annually. A second objective, which supports the first, is to increase productivity for new employees and payroll processing employees.

- Decrease payroll processing costs by 15 percent in two years by decreasing manual clerical processes.
- Decrease the duration of the new worker onboarding process from an average of 5 business days to 2 business days within 18 months.

140

Project Approval Requirements *(What items need to be approved for the project, and who will have sign-off authority? What designates success?)*
Approvals for this project include:
- Decision to purchase application software to support the payroll systems (VP of Operations)
- Choice of vendor application package (Director of HR)
- High-level design of the new systems (Director of HR)
- Global transition plan for new systems rollout (VP of Operations)

Overall Project Risks *(Overall potential threats and opportunities for the project)*
- Because of the complexity of employee pay calculations and the large number of employees, we may have errors in employee payroll during implementation of the new systems. (High impact)
- Because of the number of localities supported and differing regulations, we may have errors in government tax payments and regulatory compliance during implementation of the new systems. (High impact)
- Because of the volatility in the software application marketplace, we may select an unreliable vendor for delivery of the payroll-processing applications. (High impact)

Project Exit Criteria *(What needs must be met so that the project manager will be able to close or terminate the project or phase?)*
- A new payroll processing system that meets the project objectives and requirements and incorporates all key deliverables described herein will be delivered within defined cost and budget constraints.
- *Or,* if it is determined that the project objectives of cost saving cannot be met, the project manager will recommend termination of the project.
- *Or,* if it is determined that another solution will better meet the organizational needs, the sponsor should be notified for closing approval, and a business case will be developed for the new solution.

**Project Sponsors Authorizing This Project**

_____          _____
Muhammad Chauhan, Executive Vice President          Jessica Bouchard, Director of Human Resources

**Exercise**  Make a list of what is different about managing the large project described in this charter versus managing the small project described in the earlier charter example.

| What Would Be Different about Managing the Large Project versus the Small Project? |
| --- |
| |
| |
| |
| |
| |
| |

## What Would Be Different about Managing the Large Project versus the Small Project?

_____

_____

_____

_____

_____

_____

**Answer** The following are some possible answers to this question, although there are certainly other correct answers. The large project:

- Has a larger stakeholder group, and therefore requires more effort to manage relationships and stakeholder expectations and involvement
- Has a more diverse team composition
- Requires a broader and more complex communications management plan to deal with the number of stakeholders and language issues
- Contends with multiple nations, cultures, time zones, languages, and laws
- Will be affected by currency exchange rates
- Requires a more formal change management process to handle the requested changes
- Has thousands of activities to track
- Has larger activities, making it more difficult to develop good duration and cost estimates
- Has a more complex network diagram with many discretionary and external dependencies
- Requires a more robust tracking system for all the project metrics
- Involves multiple contracts, requiring more management of the sellers
- Has much more risk, requiring a more detailed risk management process

Regardless of whether you have a large or small project, developing the project charter requires the following actions:

- Identifying stakeholders
- Meeting with key stakeholders to confirm high-level requirements, project scope, risks, assumptions, and issues
- Defining product scope
- Defining project objectives, constraints, and success criteria
- Documenting risks

Some of the tools and techniques that can be used during this process include data gathering (interviews, brainstorming, focus groups, etc.), conflict management, and meeting management. During meetings with the sponsor and key stakeholders, the project manager can obtain needed information and work with experts to understand and address organizational strategy and develop measurable project objectives.

## Assumption Log

As you might expect, the project charter is the primary output of this process. The other output of this process is the assumption log, which contains a list of all assumptions and constraints that relate to the project. Note that some project managers also include initial assumptions and constraints in the project charter. The assumption log is typically added to during planning and updated throughout the project as assumptions and constraints change and new assumptions are uncovered.

## Develop Project Management Plan   PAGE 82

| | |
|---|---|
| **Process** Develop Project Management Plan | |
| **Process Group** Planning | |
| **Knowledge Area** Integration Management | |

Project managers must plan before they act. Let's first look at what management plans are, and then move on to discuss the project management plan.

## Management Plans

For the exam, it is very important to understand the concept of management plans. Management plans document the strategy and approach for managing the project and the processes related to the knowledge areas of scope, schedule, cost, quality, resources, communications, risk, procurement, and stakeholder management. This means there is a management plan for each knowledge area. These plans are, in essence, a set of documents with processes, procedures, practices, and standards the team will follow to ensure consistent results. When creating a management plan, you ask yourself, "How will I define, plan, manage (execute), and control scope (or schedule, cost, quality, etc.) for the project?" You think ahead, and document how you will plan for each knowledge area (and ultimately the project) based on its particular needs, how you will manage each knowledge area during executing, and how you will monitor and control each knowledge area. This effort should cover all aspects of the project management process. You also need to think about the people involved in the project and how you will manage those people, evaluate their work, and keep them engaged. Management plans are, of necessity, unique to each project in order to address the project's particular needs. The format and level of detail of management plans should be customized to fit the needs of the project, the style of the project manager, and the organizational influences.

If you don't create management plans for your projects or don't create them to the extent described here, this area of the exam may be difficult for you. So, let's consider an example of how you would address planning, executing, and monitoring and controlling cost management. The planning portion of a management plan is where we define the processes and procedures that will be followed when completing planning for the knowledge area. In our cost example, we need to address questions such as: "How will we make sure all costs are identified and estimated?" "Who will be involved in estimating costs?" "What methods of estimating costs will we use?" "What historical records, processes, and organizational requirements will need to be used or met?" "What estimating tools and techniques will we employ?" "What level of accuracy is appropriate?" "How will funding and cost constraints be considered when establishing the budget?" "What data, metrics, and measurements do we need for planning cost?"

The executing portion of a management plan focuses on the processes and procedures for doing the work (note that some knowledge areas, such as cost management, don't have separate executing processes; in such a case, the work performance data related to the knowledge area is gathered as part of Direct and Manage Project Work and must still be planned for). The executing component of a cost management plan

143

answers questions such as: "What cost data is needed?" "Who is responsible for gathering it?" "Where will we capture the raw data that will later be used in monitoring and controlling?"

The monitoring and controlling component of a management plan defines the processes and procedures to measure project progress, compare actual project results to what was planned, and determine how to handle variances that require a change.

The creation of management plans is an integral part of a project manager's job. If you are not familiar with management plans and have no experience creating them, do not just study this concept. Before you read further, spend some time imagining what management plans for scope, schedule, quality, resources, communications, risk, procurement, and stakeholder management might contain for a large project. Many project managers don't realize how big their knowledge gap is regarding management plans until it finds them on the exam. Don't let this happen to you!

 Here is a trick to understanding the topic of management plans for the exam. Know that management plans look forward in time and that there are management plans for all the knowledge areas. There are also the following management plans:

- Change management plan
- Configuration management plan
- Requirements management plan

When taking the exam, assume the project manager has created each of these management plans. For example, if a question refers to a problem on a project, the answer might be for the project manager to look at the management plan for that aspect of the project to see how the plan says such a problem will be handled. Or when the work is being done, the project manager might refer to the cost management plan to see how costs are supposed to be measured and evaluated on the project.

## Project Management Plan

Now let's talk about the project management plan. What do you currently think of as a project management plan or project plan? If you think of such a plan as just a schedule, then it's time to significantly expand your understanding of this concept.

The project management plan integrates all the individual management plans into a cohesive whole, creating a centralized document to describe what is involved in the project. The overall project management plan also includes the baselines for the project. Do you remember the discussion in the Project Management Processes chapter about how the iterations in project planning lead to a realistic project management plan? This means a project management plan is a set of plans and baselines (not just a schedule). The key components of the project management plan are discussed in the following sections.

### Project Life Cycle

The project life cycle describes the phases of work on a project required to produce the deliverables (for example, requirements, design, code, test, implement). Project life cycles range from plan driven to change driven.

### Development Approach

Development approaches to produce the project deliverables range from plan driven to change driven.

### Management Reviews

Milestones will be built into the project management plan, indicating times when management and stakeholders will compare project progress to what was planned and identify needed changes to any of the management plans.

**Project Management Processes That Will Be Used on the Project**   Think about the science of project management for a moment. Would you want to use everything in the *PMBOK® Guide* to the same extent on every project? No! A project manager should determine the extent to which processes need to be used, based on the needs of the project. Tailoring the process to be followed is part of developing the project management plan.

**Knowledge Area Management Plans**   These are the management plans for scope, schedule, cost, quality, resources, communications, risk, procurement, and stakeholder management. (The individual management plans are discussed in more detail in chapters 5 through 13 of this book.)

**Baselines[11] (Performance Measurement Baseline)**   The project management plan includes scope, schedule, and cost baselines, against which the project manager will report project performance. These baselines are created during planning. They are a record of what the project had planned, scheduled, and budgeted for in terms of scope, schedule, and cost performance, and are used to compare the project's actual performance against planned performance. The following are the elements included in each baseline:

- **Scope baseline**   The project scope statement, work breakdown structure (WBS), and WBS dictionary
- **Schedule baseline**   The agreed-upon schedule, including the start and stop dates for each activity, and scheduled milestones
- **Cost baseline**   The time-phased cost budget (the spending plan indicating how much money is approved for the project and when the funds are required and will be available)

Together these baselines are called the performance measurement baseline.

What do baselines mean for the project manager and team? The project manager must be able to clearly, completely, and realistically define scope, schedule, and cost to develop the baselines. That's not all, however. The project performance, and the performance of the project manager, will be measured against the baselines. The project manager and team will watch for deviations from the baselines while the work is being done. If a deviation is discovered, they will assess whether adjustments can be made to the project to deal with the problem. These adjustments might involve submitting a change request for corrective or preventive action or defect repair. Depending on the extent and type of action required, the baselines themselves do not always change. If minor adjustments will not correct the deviation, however, a request to change the baselines might be necessary. A substantial part of project monitoring and controlling is making sure the baselines are achieved, which in turn helps ensure the sponsor and the organization get the complete benefits of the project they chartered. Therefore, as a project manager, your ability to not only plan a project but also to control the project and get it completed as planned is very important.

Requested changes to the baselines are evaluated and approved in the Perform Integrated Change Control process. Baseline changes are so serious that the evolution of the baselines should be documented to show when and why changes were made.

**TRICKS OF THE TRADE®**   The exam tests you at an expert level. You need to understand that deviations from baselines are often due to incomplete risk identification and risk management. Therefore, if the exam asks what to do when a project deviates significantly from established baselines, the correct answer is likely the one about reviewing the project's risk management process. Many project managers do not understand that such an effort should be done. Does it make sense to you now that we've pointed it out?

Baselines are mentioned frequently on the exam. Make sure you understand the concepts described here, including what the project manager's attitude should be regarding the project's baselines and any changes to those baselines.

**Requirements Management Plan**    Part of the scope management process (which is described in the next chapter) involves defining and planning for stakeholders' needs, wants, expectations, and assumptions to determine the requirements for the project. The requirements management plan defines how requirements will be gathered, analyzed, prioritized, evaluated, and documented, as well as how the requirements will be managed and controlled throughout the project.

**Change Management Plan**    Controlling a project to the baselines and the rest of the project management plan is so important that the project manager needs to think in advance about where there might be changes and what to do to limit the negative effects of changes. Are you this focused on change management on your projects? Regardless of whether you work on small or large projects, your role is not to just facilitate changes. Instead, you need to plan the project in a way that minimizes the need for changes and prevents unnecessary changes. You also need to proactively look for needed changes, thereby solving problems before they have a major negative impact on the project. Because making changes is much more costly than including the work from the beginning, changes should not be undertaken lightly.

The change management plan describes how changes will be managed and controlled, and may include:
- Change control procedures (how and who)
- The approval levels for authorizing changes
- The creation of a change control board to approve changes, as well as the roles and responsibilities of those on the board (the change control board is described later in this chapter)
- A plan outlining how changes will be managed and controlled
- Who should attend meetings regarding changes
- The organizational tools to use to track and control changes
- Information on reporting the outcome of change requests
- The emergency change process

Note that a change management plan will often have a separate process for addressing each of the knowledge areas, taking into account the specific needs within each knowledge area.

**Change Control System**    Many organizations have a change control system as part of their project management information system (PMIS). This system includes standardized forms, reports, processes, procedures, and software to track and control changes. It is part of an organization's enterprise environmental factors.

**Configuration Management Plan**    With all the product and project documentation that is part of managing a project and all the changes to this documentation that will occur throughout the life of the project, it is essential to have a plan for making sure everyone knows what version of the scope, schedule, and other components of the project management plan is the latest version. This is the purpose of the configuration management plan. It defines the naming conventions, the version control system, and the document storage and retrieval system, and details how you will manage the changes to the documentation, including which organizational tools you will use in this effort.

**Configuration Management System**[12]    Like the change control system, the configuration management system is part of the project management information system (PMIS). It contains the organization's standardized configuration management tools, processes, and procedures that are used to track and control the evolution of the project documentation.

## Putting the Project Management Plan Together

The project management plan, including the individual management plans and the scope, schedule, and cost baselines, is created by completing the activities described in the Planning column of Rita's Process Chart™. Once the project management plan is complete, the sponsor or key stakeholders review and approve it. The Develop Project Management Plan process must result in a project management plan that is bought into, approved, realistic, and formal. In other words, the project management plan needs to be agreed to by those involved in the project, it needs to be formally approved, everyone needs to believe the project can be done according to the plan, and it needs to remain a formal document that is controlled and used throughout the project. If this is a new concept to you, make sure you spend time thinking about how to accomplish this in the real world.

Let's see how everything connects so far by looking at figure 4.2.

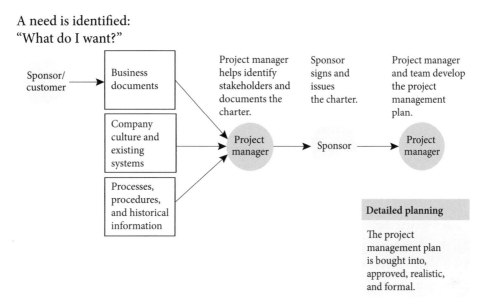

FIGURE 4.2    *Project initiating and planning*

Once the project management plan has been completed, the project manager uses it as a tool to help manage the project on a daily basis. It is not just a document created for the sponsor and other key stakeholders. Although it may evolve over the life of the project through progressive elaboration or approved changes, the project management plan is designed to be as complete as possible when project executing begins.

**Exercise**    Test yourself! Make a list of the specific actions required to create a project management plan that is bought into, approved, realistic, and formal.

_____

_____

_____

_____

_____

147

_____
_____
_____
_____
_____
_____
_____

**Answer**   Some of the possible answers to this exercise include:

- Select the best life cycle and approach for the project.
- Determine a methodology for creating the project management plan.
- Agree on reporting formats and communications plans.
- Agree on processes to report, control, and incorporate changes.
- Make sure the approach and processes are consistent with the PMO and/or program management plan, if the project is part of a program.
- Analyze the stakeholders' needs, wants, expectations, and assumptions.
- Capture the project requirements as completely as possible.
- Analyze the skills and knowledge of all the stakeholders, and determine how you will use them on the project.
- Meet with stakeholders to define their roles on the project.
- Meet with resource managers to get the best resources possible.
- Work with team members to estimate the project.
- Give team members a chance to approve the final schedule that converts the team's activity estimates into a calendar schedule.
- Get resource managers to approve the schedule and confirm when their resources will be used.
- Work through iterations of the plan (for example, update the work breakdown structure after you complete risk analysis).
- Create the necessary project documents.
- Apply risk reserves to the project schedule and budget.
- Look for impacts on your project from other projects.
- Hold meetings or presentations to let the sponsor know if any of the project requirements that were outlined in the project charter cannot be met.
- Perform schedule compression (crash, fast track, change scope or quality, etc.), and present options to the sponsor.

If you included most of the answers in the previous list, you are in good shape. But why is it so important to have a project management plan that is realistic and that everyone believes can be done? Because later in the project management process, you will need to constantly measure progress against the project management plan to see how the project is going. The end date, end cost, and other constraints in the project must be met. There are no excuses. You will use the project management plan (including the scope, schedule, and cost baselines contained in the plan) as a measurement tool to make sure the project delivers within these constraints.

148

So when you think of the project management plan, think of all the facilitations, meetings, sign-offs, interactions with other projects, conflict resolution, negotiations, schedule compressions, etc. that will be required to bring the plan to the point of being bought into, approved, realistic, and formal. Expect questions on the exam about how to use your skills to develop the project management plan, as well as how it makes a difference as you manage work on the project and solve challenges that occur.

## Project Documents

A lot of information needs to be captured on a project, and not all of that information is recorded in the project management plan. The *PMBOK® Guide* uses the term "project documents" to refer to any project-related documents that are not part of the project management plan. They include the assumption and issue logs, cost and duration estimates, lessons learned register, project schedule and resource calendars, quality reports, resource requirements along with requirements documentation, and other such documentation (see page 89 in the *PMBOK® Guide* for a longer list of examples). While the sponsor and/or key stakeholders will see and approve the project management plan, most project documents (excluding some documents such as the charter, agreements, contracts, and statements of work) are created by the project manager for use on the project and typically are not shown to or approved by the sponsor.

Due to the iterative nature of planning and the nature of the work throughout the rest of the project, project documents must be updated frequently. For the exam, know that project documents updates are an output of many of the project management processes, though this book will not cover these updates as an output of every process.

## Project Management Plan Approval

Since the project management plan is a formal document that defines how the project will be managed, executed, and controlled and includes items such as the project completion date, milestones, costs, etc., it typically requires formal approval by management, the sponsor, the project team, and other key stakeholders. Formal approval means sign-off (signatures). If the project manager has identified all stakeholders and their requirements and objectives, included the appropriate project and product scope in the plan, and dealt with conflicting priorities in advance, getting the project management plan approved should be relatively straightforward.

## Kickoff Meeting

Before the Develop Project Management Plan process can be completed and project executing can begin, a kickoff meeting should be held. This is a meeting of the key parties involved in the project (customers, sellers, the project team, senior management, functional management, and the sponsor). The purpose of this meeting is to announce the start of the project, to ensure everyone is familiar with its details—including the project objectives and stakeholders' roles and responsibilities—and to ensure a commitment to the project from everyone. In other words, the meeting is held to make sure everyone is on the same page. In addition to introducing those involved in the project, the meeting may review such items as project milestones, project risks, the communications management plan, and the meeting schedule.

## Direct and Manage Project Work    PAGE 90

> **Process** Direct & Manage Project Work
> **Process Group** Executing
> **Knowledge Area** Integration Management

This process represents the integration aspect of project executing.
In Direct and Manage Project Work, the project manager integrates all the executing work into one coordinated effort to accomplish the project management plan and produce the deliverables. In addition to completing the activities and deliverables in the project management plan, Direct and Manage Project

149

Work involves gathering work performance data, creating and using the issue log, requesting changes, and completing the work resulting from approved change requests.

The Direct and Manage Project Work process involves managing people and keeping them engaged in the project, doing the work, finding ways to work more efficiently, requesting changes, and implementing approved changes. It is about being of service to the team to help them get the work completed, ensuring a common understanding of the project among stakeholders, and keeping everyone focused and informed by documenting and facilitating resolution of issues. In other words, the project manager needs to do things such as facilitate meetings and technical discussions, make sure the stakeholders whose scope was not included in the project understand they will not receive that scope, use the work authorization system[13] to keep the team and functional managers informed of upcoming work assignments and milestones, help remove roadblocks that would prevent the team from completing work, look at improving processes, and inform other departments within the organization how the project may affect their work.

There is another piece of the Direct and Manage Project Work process that you need to be aware of for the exam. When executing the project, the project manager takes time to focus on managing the schedule, budget, risks, quality, and all other knowledge areas. This way of thinking about project executing is not an approach that many project managers take. We just manage the project as a whole, rather than giving individual attention to each knowledge area. This can also mean we do not take the time to properly look at how issues relating to one knowledge area affect other knowledge areas (for example how scope management issues can affect quality and resource management). We may forget to even think about some of the knowledge areas. Integration management requires project managers to keep all the knowledge areas in mind at all times.

The project management information system (PMIS) is used to help the project manager keep track of the many aspects of the project. The PMIS includes automated tools, such as scheduling software, a configuration management system, shared workspaces for file storage or distribution, work authorization software, time-tracking software, procurement management software, and repositories for historical information.

The work authorization system is the project manager's system for authorizing the start of work packages or activities, and it is part of the PMIS. If you have never used such a system, imagine a large construction project with hundreds of people working on the project. Can you have a plumber and an electrician show up to work in one small area at the same time? No. Remember that a project is planned to the level of detail needed for that particular project. There might be instances when the project manager needs to manage to a detailed level, as in the case of the plumber and the electrician. To handle these types of situations, a work authorization system is put in place to make sure work is only started when a formal authorization is given. In many cases, this tool for authorizing work is a company-wide system used on the project, not created just for the project. There will likely only be one question about this on the exam, but the term may be included more frequently as an answer choice.

It is likely that the project manager will also make use of meetings as a tool for keeping the team and stakeholders informed and engaged in the project work during this process. Depending on the needs of the project and the project approach, the format of these meetings can range from informal stand-up sessions to structured meetings with an agenda and a focus on a specific aspect of the project. Within the Direct and Manage Work process, meeting topics may include project updates, lessons learned, upcoming project activities, and, of course, risk management.

The Direct and Manage Project Work process can be illustrated as shown in figure 4.3.

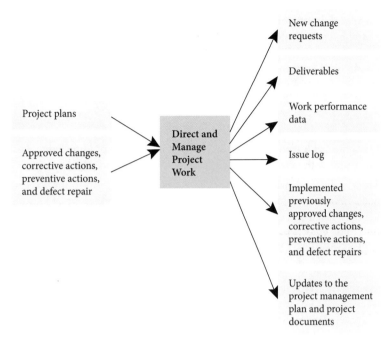

FIGURE 4.3   *Direct and Manage Project Work process*

The outputs of this process include the issue log, any newly discovered work performance data, possible change requests, and deliverables. A deliverable can be any product or result that is produced as part of a project. Other outputs include updates to project management plan components, organizational process assets, and project documents, such as the activity list, assumption log, lessons learned register, stakeholder register, requirements documentation, and risk register.

## Manage Project Knowledge   PAGE 98

| | |
|---|---|
| **Process** | Manage Project Knowledge |
| **Process Group** | Executing |
| **Knowledge Area** | Integration Management |

A project doesn't—or at least shouldn't—exist in a vacuum. Think of the tremendous amount of knowledge required to properly plan and execute a project. Project managers can benefit from the knowledge base of the organization, particularly from the experiences and discoveries of others on past, similar projects. The Manage Project Knowledge process provides a means to take advantage of the knowledge the organization has accumulated over time. In addition, it requires each project to actively contribute to that knowledge base. This includes sharing new processes, successes, etc. internally within the project, as well as making that knowledge accessible throughout the entire organization.

Successful knowledge management requires an organizational culture of trust in which the project manager and stakeholders exchange knowledge without fear of judgment. Some of the knowledge to be shared will involve experiences that did not work out as planned. But we can often learn more from mistakes than successes. Each mistake, each unidentified stakeholder, each missed risk trigger, and each unrealistic schedule teaches us something. What a valuable thing it is to share such information and possibly save another project or individual from the same outcome.

This process includes two distinct types of knowledge—explicit and tacit:

- **Explicit knowledge**   Explicit knowledge is fact-based, and can be easily communicated through words and symbols. However, it may need explanation or context to provide value to recipients of this information. Traditional lessons learned fall under this category of knowledge. Lessons learned are generated and shared as the project is ongoing, and consolidated as part of project closing.
- **Tacit knowledge**   Tacit knowledge, on the other hand, includes emotions, experience, and ability, which are more difficult to communicate clearly. The sharing of this type of knowledge requires the atmosphere of trust discussed earlier.

In this process, the project manager is responsible for managing both knowledge and information.

## Knowledge Management   Collaboration and the sharing of knowledge are key to successful projects. The project manager needs to plan and develop an environment within a project that will support the sharing of tacit knowledge (including the ways people do their work, their experiences and best practices, and how they solved problems they encountered in their work). The availability of online knowledge-sharing tools helps facilitate knowledge sharing among distributed teams, enabling team members and others to benefit from a broad range of experience. Discussion forums and interactive events and meetings, whether in person or virtual, support the sharing of knowledge and experience.

## Information Management   People on projects need to create and share information, or explicit knowledge, as efficiently as possible. Information management tools and techniques can help with this. The processes for capturing explicit knowledge include documentation in the lessons learned register and other repositories of explicit knowledge. Explicit knowledge is shared by making it available in the PMIS, through discussion, and via direct communication.

On the exam, you may encounter situational questions that test your understanding of the need to cultivate and share knowledge and information. You may be asked how to establish an environment that encourages the project team to share tacit and explicit knowledge. Or you may be asked how you would make adjustments to the environment when that doesn't happen as intended. Answers might include such actions as holding retrospective sessions and engaging in interactive communication with individual stakeholders.

Legal and regulatory requirements and constraints such as nondisclosure agreements may limit or impact the gathering or sharing of particular information due to confidentiality or privacy concerns, or may dictate the format and type of information that can be disseminated. It is important for the project manager to be aware of these constraints and to communicate to the team any restrictions regarding the sharing of information they may be exposed to during the project. For example, on a project involving development of banking software, the team may have access to personal and financial information of customers of the bank for which the software is being developed. This is an obvious example of information that team members would not be permitted to share, other than in the context of the project work.

The entire project management plan is an input to the Manage Project Knowledge process. In particular, the communications, stakeholder engagement, and configuration management plans all provide direction for managing knowledge and information by the project manager, team members, and other stakeholders. Do you see why this is an integration process?

One input to this process that might seem confusing at first is deliverables. In fact, deliverables represent great amounts of knowledge regarding all aspects of what it will take to complete them. This might include new knowledge around standards or metrics, or the processes used to create the deliverables.

Knowledge can be shared formally through team training, seminars, and workshops. Other techniques for sharing knowledge include work shadowing and activity observation. Instead of receiving hard-to-understand process documentation, a team member can watch someone doing a particular job or activity to more easily learn the process. A similar technique is storytelling. Simply asking, "Walk me through how you would do this task," can encourage understanding. Informal sharing occurs through the application of interpersonal and team skills, including active listening and networking. Successful and consistent sharing of knowledge and information contributes to a more productive work environment and increases the ability of project teams to achieve project and organizational objectives.

Specific knowledge shared through this process is referred to as lessons learned. You will see the topic of lessons learned mentioned often throughout this book, both as an input to and an output of many processes. As an input, they help improve the current project. As an output, they help make the organization better. Lessons learned are defined as "what was done right, what was done wrong, and what would be done differently if the project could be redone." Accurately and thoroughly documenting lessons learned is a professional responsibility.

You need to collect and review lessons learned from similar projects before starting work on a new project. Why make the same mistakes or face the same problems others have faced? Why not benefit from others' experience? Imagine you could reach into a filing cabinet or access a database to see data for all the projects your company has undertaken. How valuable would that be?

Lessons learned are collected and saved in a lessons learned register, which is the main output of this process. Do not underestimate the value of this shared information! Remember that the lessons learned register is a living document, which is shared throughout the project, as well as when the project is completed. New lessons learned may not only be added to the lessons learned register but may also be incorporated into the organization's recommended practices.

Your organization may have a template for lessons learned documentation, but even if it does not, lessons learned should include an overview of the situation, what was done, the impact of actions taken, and any updates to the project management plan or project documents necessitated by the action.

In the first chapter of this book, we described lessons learned as a PMI-ism. Lessons learned are an essential asset to managing a project, as they are taken into account as well as created throughout a project. Complete the following exercise to test your understanding of lessons learned.

## Exercise   Test yourself! Lessons learned include what type of information?

_____
_____
_____
_____
_____
_____
_____
_____
_____
_____

## Answer

The lessons learned register includes what was done right, what was done wrong, and what could have been done differently. Another way of saying this is that lessons learned include reasons why issues occur, change requests, workarounds, reestimating, preventive and corrective actions, and defect repair the project has faced, as well as the reasoning behind any implemented changes. They also include successes, such as new sources of information, newly developed processes, ways of tracking work, and even new information on resources who demonstrated outstanding skills or were able to contribute to the project in unexpected ways.

To make lessons learned as valuable as possible, use categories to ensure that all are captured. Some categories that should be captured are:

- **Technical aspects of the project** What was right and wrong about how we completed the work to produce the product? What did we learn that will be useful in the future? (Examples include acceptable metrics and variance levels, new processes, improved or revised processes for particular results, and the effectiveness of particular acceptance criteria.)

- **Project management** How did we do with WBS creation, risk planning, etc.? What did we learn that will be useful in the future? (Examples include recommendations for transitioning project results to the business and operations teams, recommended changes to the organization's procurements process, and experiences working with particular sellers.)

- **Management** How did I do with communications and leadership as a project manager? What did we learn that will be useful in the future? (Examples include the results of stakeholder analysis and stakeholder engagement efforts.)

Many project managers do not understand the role of lessons learned on projects. The graphic in figure 4.4 helps explain their function.

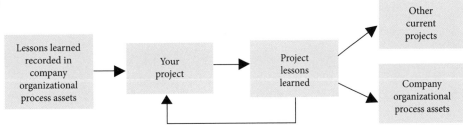

FIGURE 4.4   *Lessons learned on a project*

Remember it is not only knowledge and information that are gained from this process. Equally important is developing the organizational culture to promote growth through the sharing of knowledge and experiences.

## Monitor and Control Project Work   PAGE 105

> **Process** Monitor & Control Project Work
> **Process Group** Monitoring & Controlling
> **Knowledge Area** Integration Management

The Monitor and Control Project Work process involves looking at what is happening on the project and comparing the actual and forecasted performance to what was planned. It is a monitoring and controlling function that is done from project initiating through project closing.

When you think of a large project, it makes sense that the project manager would make a formal effort to monitor and control how the project management and knowledge area processes are going. This process involves aggregating the work performance information from monitoring and controlling knowledge area processes to evaluate and assess how their individual process results are impacting the other knowledge areas and their plans and baselines. For example, scope may be completed on a project but the quality may not be acceptable, or the schedule might be met but at excessive cost. This process also involves monitoring any other performance requirements that were included in the project management plan. Monitoring and controlling project work encourages a holistic view of the project performance and enables the project manager to take appropriate action to keep the project on track.

The integration function of Monitor and Control Project Work also includes activities such as analyzing and tracking risks, performing quality control activities, assessing possible outcomes across the project using data analysis techniques (including alternatives, cost-benefit, earned value, root cause, trend, and variance analysis), and reviewing changes and corrective actions made on the project to see if they were effective.

If the exam talks about monitoring and controlling project work, it may not be referring to the entire monitoring and controlling process group. Instead, it may be referring to the specific integration management process: Monitor and Control Project Work. Remember that monitoring and controlling means measuring against all aspects of the project management plan.

155

Many project managers do not control their projects to the project management plan. If the exam asks what you should do if a work activity on the project takes longer than estimated, the answer is to request corrective action (discussed later in this section) to make up for the delay. Such action keeps the project on or close to schedule and allows the project manager to feel comfortable that the scope will be completed according to the budget and schedule agreed to. This knowledge is the value of controlling the project.

This effort may result in change requests (including recommended corrective and preventive actions and defect repair), work performance reports, and updates to the project management plan and project documents. The change requests from this and other processes are evaluated and approved, rejected, or deferred in the Perform Integrated Change Control process, described later in this chapter.

The following sections highlight some important concepts related to the Monitor and Control Project Work process.

## Change Requests     PAGE 112 AND THROUGHOUT     No matter how well you plan a project, there will always be changes. Change requests can have differing focuses, depending on which process they are generated in. Three main categories of change requests are corrective action, preventive action, and defect repair. Changes may involve additions to the project requested by the customer, changes to the plan that the team believes would make their work more efficient, or even changes to the policies and procedures used on the project.

The need for changes are identified as you manage the execution of the project and as part of monitoring and controlling when you measure project performance against the performance measurement baseline. See the "Perform Integrated Change Control" section for more about changes.

Note that change requests are also outputs of Plan Risk Responses and Plan Procurement Management, both of which are planning processes. Change requests are generated from these processes when the risk response plans or procurement documents are elaborated after the project management plan has been approved. For example, on a three-year project, it is unlikely that all procurement documents can be completed prior to plan approval. If the seller is not needed until year three, notes regarding the procurement and estimates for schedule and budget are accepted in the plan and elaborated later.

## Corrective Action     PAGE 112 AND THROUGHOUT     A corrective action is any action taken to bring expected future project performance in line with the project management plan. Without a realistic performance measurement baseline and/or project management plan, including acceptable variances, you cannot determine when a variance has occurred and when corrective action is needed. Those who have serious problems with this in the real world have problems on the exam. What do you do on your projects? Do you have predetermined areas to measure, and have you identified an acceptable range in which the measurements can fall (control limits) to determine if a project is on schedule and on budget?

You cannot simply jump in and start implementing corrective actions. Instead, you need to:

- Consciously focus on identifying areas that need corrective action.
- Look for problems, using observation, active listening, and measurement, rather than just waiting for them to be brought to your attention.
- Create metrics during project planning that cover all aspects of the project.
- Have a realistic project management plan to measure against.
- Continue to measure throughout the project.
- Know when the project is off track, and requires corrective action.
- Find the root cause of the variance.

- Measure project performance after a corrective action is implemented to evaluate the effectiveness of the corrective action.
- Determine whether there is a need to recommend further corrective action.

Typically, corrective actions are undertaken to adjust performance within the existing project baselines; the actions do not change the baselines. All corrective actions should be reviewed and approved, rejected, or deferred as part of the Perform Integrated Change Control process. All changes that would affect the project management plan, baselines, policies or procedures, charter, contracts, or statements of work need the approval of the change control board or sponsor, as outlined in the change management plan.

As you can see, a significant portion of the project manager's time while the project work is being done is spent measuring performance (to determine the need for corrective action) and implementing corrective actions. Therefore, you can expect many questions about this topic on the exam. Do not expect all these questions to use the words "corrective action," however. Some questions may just describe a situation and ask you, "What is the best thing to do?" To answer those types of questions, you need to know when to look for corrective actions. Try the next exercise to see if you understand when you might identify the need for such actions.

**Exercise** In the following scenarios, which process would generate requests for corrective action?

| When | Process Name |
| --- | --- |
| When meeting with the customer to obtain acceptance of interim deliverables | |
| When measuring project performance against the performance measurement baseline | |
| When making sure people are using the correct processes | |
| When evaluating whether performance reports are meeting stakeholders' needs | |
| When working with the project team | |
| When assessing stakeholder relationships | |
| When you notice that there are many unidentified risks occurring | |
| When evaluating a seller's performance | |
| When evaluating team members' performance | |
| When making sure deliverables meet quality standards | |
| When communicating with stakeholders to resolve issues and manage their perceptions about the project | |

© 2018 RMC Publications, Inc.™ • 952.846.4484 • info@rmcls.com • www.rmcls.com

## Answer

| When | Process Name |
| --- | --- |
| When meeting with the customer to obtain acceptance of interim deliverables | Validate Scope |
| When measuring project performance against the performance measurement baseline | Control Scope, Control Schedule, Control Costs |
| When making sure people are using the correct processes | Manage Quality |
| When evaluating whether performance reports are meeting stakeholders' needs | Monitor Communications |
| When working with the project team | Manage Team |
| When assessing stakeholder relationships | Monitor Stakeholder Engagement |
| When you notice that there are many unidentified risks occurring | Monitor Risks |
| When evaluating a seller's performance | Control Procurements |
| When evaluating team members' performance | Manage Team |
| When making sure deliverables meet quality standards | Control Quality |
| When communicating with stakeholders to resolve issues and manage their perceptions about the project | Manage Stakeholder Engagement |

## Preventive Action   PAGE 112 AND THROUGHOUT   While taking corrective action involves dealing with actual deviations from the performance measurement baseline or other metrics, taking preventive action means dealing with anticipated or possible deviations from the performance measurement baseline and other metrics. The process for taking preventive action is not as clear as it is for taking corrective actions. Knowing when preventive action is needed requires more experience than calculation because you are evaluating trends in the measurement analysis and anticipating that, if they continue, they could lead to deviation from the performance measurement baseline or other metrics. Examples of preventive actions include:

- Adjusting the project to prevent the same problem from occurring again later in the project
- Changing a resource because the resource's last activity nearly failed to meet its acceptance criteria
- Arranging for team members to gain training in a certain area because there is no one with the necessary skills to back up a team member who may unexpectedly get sick

Typically, preventive actions are undertaken to adjust performance within the existing project baselines; the actions do not change the baselines. All preventive actions should be reviewed and approved or rejected as part of the Perform Integrated Change Control process. Proposed changes that would affect the project management plan, baselines, policies or procedures, charter, contracts, or statements of work would likely have to go to the change control board or sponsor for approval, as outlined in the change management plan.

You will see preventive action mentioned throughout the *PMBOK® Guide*. Preventive action can be implemented at any time on any project management process.

**Defect Repair**[14]    PAGE 112 AND THROUGHOUT    Defect repair is another way of saying "rework." Defect repair may be requested when a component of the project does not meet specifications. As with corrective and preventive actions, any defect repairs should be reviewed and approved or rejected as part of the Perform Integrated Change Control process.[15]

## Perform Integrated Change Control    PAGE 113

> **Process** Perform Integrated Change Control
> **Process Group** Monitoring & Controlling
> **Knowledge Area** Integration Management

At any time during the project, changes to any part of the project may be requested. Keep in mind, however, that just because a change is requested does not mean it has to be—or even should be—implemented. All change requests are evaluated and accepted, rejected, or deferred in the Perform Integrated Change Control process. A key focus of integrated change control is to look at the impact of each change on all the project constraints. For example, any scope change needs to be assessed for its impact on quality, risk, schedule, cost, resources, and customer satisfaction. The value of analyzing the impact of changes is to reduce the potential risk of not fulfilling project objectives.

For the changes that are accepted, updates and replanning efforts are required to make sure the project team is working with a completely current and integrated project management plan, performance measurement baseline, and project documents. These updating and replanning efforts take place during Perform Integrated Change Control. The approved changes are then implemented in Direct and Manage Project Work, Control Quality, and Control Procurements.

So do you need to go through Perform Integrated Change Control to make changes to processes or plans that haven't been finalized? No! When developing the project charter, project management plan, and baseline, changes can be made without a formal change request. But after the charter or the project management plan have been approved, requested changes need to be evaluated for resolution in integrated change control. Read exam questions carefully to understand whether a requested change pertains to something that is still in the process of being finalized or has already been finalized. This will help you determine whether integrated change control is required.

Integrated change control can be a difficult topic on the exam for people who do not work on projects that have formal change procedures. It can also be difficult for project managers who simply estimate the cost and/or schedule impact of a change and stop there, rather than looking for the impacts of a change on the other parts of the project. You can check your understanding of this topic with the following example:

> *A stakeholder wants to add scope to the project. You estimate that the change will add two weeks to the project duration. What do you do next?*

Do not simply read on! Try to answer the question. Understanding the Perform Integrated Change Control process is very important. There may be as many as 20 questions on this topic on the exam.

So what is your answer? Is it to look for ways to save time so the change can be accommodated? Or should you get the change approved? How about asking for an extension of time to accommodate the change?

None of the previous choices are the correct answer. Instead, the next thing to do would be to see how the proposed change impacts the project cost, quality, risk, resources, and possibly customer satisfaction. Whenever the exam mentions changes, keep in mind that a change to one of the project constraints should be evaluated for impacts on all the other constraints.

To fully evaluate the impacts of a change, it is necessary to have:

- A realistic project management plan to measure against
- A complete product scope and project scope (see the definitions in the Scope Management chapter)

Are changes bad? In many industries, this can be a controversial question. Changes can have negative effects. In fact, changes can be expensive and can disrupt the project. Some studies have shown that changes made late in the project can be up to 100 times more expensive than if they were made early in the project. The function of each process within the monitoring and controlling process group is to control changes. If there are a lot of changes on a project, it can become impossible for a project manager to coordinate the work, because it is constantly shifting. Team members are frequently pulled off assigned work to help implement or evaluate changes.

Change is inevitable on projects, but a project manager should work to prevent the root cause of changes whenever possible. And in many cases, the root cause may be that the project manager did not properly plan the project. The need for changes may indicate that the project manager did not fully identify stakeholders and uncover their requirements or that they did not properly complete other project management actions. All possible changes must be planned, managed, and controlled.

To control changes on the project, the project manager should:

- Work to obtain complete and thorough requirements as soon as possible.
- Spend enough time on risk management to comprehensively identify the project's risks.
- Establish schedule and cost reserves (see the discussion of reserve analysis in the Schedule Management, Cost Management, and Risk Management chapters).
- Have a process in place to control changes.
- Follow the process to control changes.
- Have a process and templates in place for creating change requests.
- Have clear roles and responsibilities for approving changes.
- Reevaluate the business case in the project charter if the number of changes becomes excessive.
- Consider terminating a project that has excessive changes and starting a new project with a more complete set of requirements.
- Allow only approved changes to be added to the project baselines.

Changes can be grouped into two broad categories—those that affect the project management plan, baselines, policies and procedures, charter, or contracts, or statements of work, and those that do not. If a change does not affect the project management plan, baselines, company policies and procedures, the charter, contracts, or statements of work, a company's change management policies may allow the project manager to approve the change. If, on the other hand, the change does affect those key elements, the change typically needs to go to a change control board and/or sponsor for a decision.

## Change Control Board (CCB)[16]    Why should the project manager always have to be the one to deny a change request? They might not even have the knowledge or expertise to analyze a change request. Depending on the project manager's level of authority, their role might be to facilitate decisions about certain changes, rather than actually make the decisions. For these reasons, many projects have formally established change control boards responsible for reviewing and analyzing change requests in accordance with the change management plan for the project. The CCB then approves, defers, or rejects the changes. The results of the board's decisions are documented in the project's change log. The board may include the project manager, the customer, experts, the sponsor, functional managers, and others. For the exam, assume that most projects have change control boards—with the exception of change-driven projects.

## Process for Making Changes

The exam has many situational questions that deal with how to make changes. Here are two examples.

*Question*    A functional manager wants to make a change to the project. What is the first thing a project manager should do?

*Question*    Someone wants to make a change to the project scope. What is the best thing to do first?

 The answers are the same in either case. A trick for answering questions that ask about the process for making changes is to know that, on a high-level basis, the project manager should follow these steps:

1.  **Evaluate the impact**  Evaluate (assess) the impact of the change on all aspects of the project (for example, this change will add three weeks to the project length, require $20,000 additional funding, and have no effect on resources).

2.  **Identify options**  This can include cutting other activities, compressing the schedule by crashing or fast tracking, or looking at other options. For example, you may be able to decrease the potential effect of the change on the project by spending more time decreasing project risk, or by adding another resource to the project team.

3.  **Get the change request approved internally**

4.  **Get customer buy-in**  (if required)

The process of handling changes is often tested on the exam. Note in the previous steps that changes are always evaluated before any other action is taken. In most cases, evaluation involves using data analysis techniques to determine the impact of the change on all the project constraints.

Next, options to handle the change, such as crashing, fast tracking, reestimating, and using "what if" analysis, are considered and evaluated. (See the Schedule Management chapter for a discussion of crashing, fast tracking, and reestimating.)

Do you remember the following question from earlier in the chapter? It is an example of the type of question you may see on the exam:

*A stakeholder wants to add scope to the project. You estimate that the change will add two weeks to the project duration. What do you do next?*

Notice how the following question is different:

*A change in scope has been determined to have no effect on the project constraints. What is the best thing to do?*

Be careful when reading these questions. Expect the right answer to depend on how the question is written. Sometimes evaluation has been done, so the best thing to do is to look for options. Sometimes evaluation and looking for options have been done, and the best thing to do is to meet with the sponsor or change control board.

In the second question, evaluation (step 1 in the Trick of the Trade above) has been done. The answer would be to look for options (step 2 above), and then meet with the sponsor or change control board (step 3 above) to discuss the change and its lack of impact on the project constraints. After informing the sponsor or change control board, the project manager may inform the customer using the process defined in the communications management plan (step 4 above).

161

**Detailed Process for Making Changes**   Now that you know the high-level process, let's look at a more detailed process for making changes:

1. **Prevent the root cause of changes**  The project manager should not just focus on managing changes; they should proactively eliminate the need for changes.

2. **Identify the need for a change**  Changes can come from the project manager, as a result of measuring against the performance measurement baseline, or from the sponsor, the team, management, the customer, or other stakeholders. The project manager should be actively looking for changes from all these sources because discovering a change early will decrease the impact of the change.

3. **Evaluate the impact of the change within the knowledge area**  If it is a scope change, how will it affect the rest of the scope of the project? If it is a schedule change, how will it affect the rest of the schedule for the project?

4. **Create a change request**  Changes can be made to the product scope, any part of the project management plan, contracts, charter, statements of work, policies and procedures, or even the performance measurement baseline. The process of making a change should follow the change management plan.

5. **Perform integrated change control**  How will the change affect all the other project constraints?

   a. **Assess the change**  Does the change fall within the project charter? If not, it should not be a change to your project; it may be an entirely different project. If the change is not beneficial to the project, it should not be approved. Also note that any change for which a reserve has been created (a previously identified risk event) would be accounted for in the project management plan as part of risk management efforts and should be handled as part of the Implement Risk Responses process rather than Perform Integrated Change Control. The techniques of alternative and cost-benefit analysis are helpful in understanding the full impact of a change request.

   b. **Identify options**  Actions to decrease threats or increase opportunities include compressing the schedule through crashing or fast tracking, changing how the work is performed, adjusting quality, or cutting scope so that the effect of the change will be minimized.

   Sometimes it may be necessary to accept the negative consequences of a change, if the positive impact that would result from the change is more valuable to the project. It is a matter of balancing project constraints. For example, the benefits of adding new scope to the project may outweigh the negative impact of adjusting the schedule to accommodate the additional time the change would require. (See the Schedule Management chapter for a discussion of the critical path.)

   c. **The change is approved, rejected, or deferred**  Again, the project manager may be able to approve many changes. But those that affect the project management plan, baselines, charter, etc. would likely need to go to a change control board and/or the sponsor. Decision-making techniques help in this effort. The approved changes are then implemented in the Direct and Manage Project Work, Control Quality, and Control Procurements processes.

   d. **Update the status of the change in the change log**  This helps everyone know the status of the change. If a change is not approved, the reasons it was rejected should be documented.

   e. **Adjust the project management plan, project documents, and baselines as necessary**  Some approved changes need to be incorporated into the project baselines. The changes could affect other parts of the project management plan or project documents or could affect the way the project manager will manage the project. Project documentation must be updated to reflect the changes. This means replanning must be done to incorporate the impacts of the change into the new version of the documents and plan before the team starts executing the change. For example, if there is a change in scope, the scope baseline (the

© 2018 RMC Publications, Inc.™ • 952.846.4484 • info@rmcls.com • www.rmcls.com

WBS, WBS dictionary, and project scope statement), the project management plan, and the requirements traceability matrix should be updated. If that change in scope affects other areas of the project, the associated documentation (such as the activity list, resource management plan and other resource documentation, schedule, budget, or risk register) also needs to be updated.

6. **Manage stakeholders' expectations by communicating the change to stakeholders affected by the change** How often do you remember to do this? You could think of this, in part, as configuration management (version control to make sure everyone is working off the same project documentation).

7. **Manage the project to the revised project management plan and project documents**

**Exercise** Test yourself! Describe common changes on projects, and determine what you would do to handle each. An example is provided. Because of the wide variety of possible changes, this exercise does not include answers, but it will help you prepare for questions related to change on the exam.

| Common Change | How to Handle It |
|---|---|
| Customer wants to add scope | Make sure you know what the specific scope is and why it is necessary. Make sure all the data required in the change request is filled out. Assess the change, including whether reserves were allocated on the project to accommodate the addition of the scope. Evaluate the impact of the change. Look for options. Have the change reviewed by the change control board if necessary. |
| | |
| | |
| | |
| | |

## Close Project or Phase  PAGE 121

> **Process** Close Project or Phase
> **Process Group** Closing
> **Knowledge Area** Integration Management

Many of the actions of the Close Project or Phase process have already been presented in the Project Management Processes chapter. You need to understand that this effort finalizes all activities across all process groups to formally close out the project or project phase. This process is typically addressed in about 12 questions on the exam.

© 2018 RMC Publications, Inc.™ • 952.846.4484 • info@rmcls.com • www.rmcls.com

Is your project really done when the technical work is done? Not if you don't close it out! The Close Project or Phase process encompasses the actions of closing as outlined in the project management plan. For example, individual contracts are closed as part of the Control Procurements process in monitoring and controlling, and all contracts must be closed out before the project is closed. Close Project or Phase ensures that final contract documentation and customer acceptance have been received.

There are many inputs to this process, including all the accumulated work performance data, information and reports, communications, and updates that have been created during the project, including the following:

- The charter—to confirm that exit criteria was met
- The business case—to validate that it was fulfilled
- The benefits management plan—to evaluate and report on benefits delivery
- The project management plan—to confirm that all planned work was completed within baselines with approved changes
- Deliverables—to complete the final review for acceptance and transition to ongoing business
- The lessons learned register—to archive lessons learned in the lessons learned repository
- The risk register and the risk report, with final data on which risks occurred and how the strategies worked—to confirm that all risks were managed successfully
- The change log—to evaluate the number of changes and the impact of those changes on the project
- Agreements and procurement documentation—to confirm that all contracts are closed

The project manager will work with subject matter experts to analyze the data, including all the documents from the project, and complete the final work to close the project. Regression analysis will be done to examine the project variables—such as the schedule, budget, and risks that occurred—and how they impacted the project and its outcomes. The project manager will look at planned versus actual project results, identify variances to the plan, along with their impacts, and identify additional lessons learned that can be shared or used in the organization.

A project manager must get formal acceptance of the project and its deliverables, issue a final report that shows the project has been successful, issue the final lessons learned, and index and archive all the project records. Do you understand the importance of the items included in Rita's Process Chart™? Make sure you become familiar with all the concepts and actions listed here, and, if you do not currently do these things on your projects, imagine completing these activities in the real world on large projects. For the exam, be sure to remember that you always close out a project, no matter the circumstances under which it stops, is terminated, or is completed!

There are financial, legal, and administrative efforts involved in closing. Let's look again at the activities presented in Rita's Process Chart™.

- Confirm work is done to requirements.
- Complete final procurement closure.
- Gain final acceptance of the product.
- Complete financial closure.
- Hand off completed product.
- Solicit customer's feedback about the project.
- Complete final performance reporting.
- Index and archive records.
- Gather final lessons learned, and update knowledge base.

Note that the Close Project or Phase process involves getting the final, formal acceptance of the project or phase as a whole from the customer, whereas the Validate Scope process in scope management (a monitoring and controlling process) involves getting formal acceptance from the customer for interim deliverables. The project needs both processes.

Does it make sense to you that the Close Project or Phase process is an integration management function? If not, think of the example of final performance reporting. Can you see how you would have to report on all knowledge areas? How about the example of indexing and archiving project records? You need to do so for records from all the knowledge areas.

Take some time to think about project closing and how it applies to proper project management for large projects before you take the exam.

## Practice Exam

1. You are planning communications on a new service development project. Your stakeholder list is large, but not terribly complicated. Not all stakeholders will understand the need for developing an actual communications plan, and you already have good relationships with most stakeholders on this project. What is one of the major driving forces for communication on a project?

   A. Optimization
   B. Integrity
   C. Integration
   D. Differentiation

2. The customer has accepted the completed project scope. However, the lessons learned required by the project management office have not been completed. What is the status of the project?

   A. The project is incomplete because it needs to be replanned.
   B. The project is incomplete until all project and product deliverables are complete and accepted.
   C. The project is complete because the customer has accepted the deliverables.
   D. The project is complete because it has reached its due date.

3. Your well-planned project is likely to encounter a number of change requests and approved changes during its life cycle. In the change management plan, you have outlined the processes that you and others will use to understand the impacts of changes. Getting stakeholder acceptance of the decisions related to change on this project is critical, as a failed project could impact shareholder value and the earning projections for the organization. Your attention is best focused on which of the following regarding changes on your project?

   A. Making changes
   B. Tracking and recording changes
   C. Informing the sponsor of changes
   D. Preventing unnecessary changes

4. The customer on a project tells the project manager they have run out of money to pay for the project. What should the project manager do first?

   A. Shift more of the work to later in the schedule to allow time for the customer to get the funds.
   B. Close Project or Phase.
   C. Stop work.
   D. Release part of the project team.

5. All the following are parts of an effective change management plan except:

   A. Procedures
   B. Standards for reports
   C. Meeting
   D. Lessons learned

6. A work authorization system can be used to:

   A. Manage who does each activity.
   B. Manage when and in what sequence work is done.
   C. Manage when each activity is done.
   D. Manage who does each activity and when it is done.

7. A project is plagued by requested changes to the project charter. Who has the primary responsibility to decide if these changes are necessary?

    A. The project manager
    B. The project team
    C. The sponsor
    D. The stakeholders

8. Effective project integration usually requires an emphasis on:

    A. The careers of the team members
    B. Timely updates to the project management plan
    C. Effective communication at key interface points
    D. Product control

9. Integration is done by the:

    A. Project manager
    B. Team
    C. Sponsor
    D. Stakeholders

10. The project manager's many responsibilities include being of service to the team, integrating new team members as the project progresses, and ensuring that the project meets its objectives within scope, time, budget, and other constraints. Which of the following best describes the project manager's role as an integrator?

    A. Help team members become familiar with the project.
    B. Put all the pieces of a project into a cohesive whole.
    C. Put all the pieces of a project into a program.
    D. Get all team members together into a cohesive whole.

11. Approved corrective actions are an input to which of the following processes?

    A. Validate Scope
    B. Direct and Manage Project Work
    C. Develop Project Charter
    D. Develop Schedule

12. Double declining balance is a form of:

    A. Decelerated depreciation
    B. Straight-line depreciation
    C. Accelerated depreciation
    D. Life cycle costing

13. At various points during project execution, the project manager reviews the project charter. Which of the following best describes what a project charter may be used for when the work is being completed?

    A. To make sure all the team members are rewarded
    B. To help determine if a scope change should be approved
    C. To assess the effectiveness of the change control system
    D. To make sure that all the documentation on the project is completed

14. Which of the following best describes a project management plan?
    A. A printout from project management software
    B. A bar chart
    C. Scope, risk, resource, and other management plans
    D. The project scope

15. You have recently joined an organization that is just beginning to follow formal project management practices. In a meeting, your manager describes your next assignment, a project to select and implement a new telephone system for the customer service department. When you request a signed charter authorizing you to begin work, the manager suggests you "just draft something." Which of the following is true about the development of a project charter?
    A. The sponsor creates the project charter, and the project manager approves it.
    B. The project team creates the project charter, and the PMO approves it.
    C. The executive manager creates the project charter, and the functional manager approves it.
    D. The project manager creates the project charter, and the sponsor approves it.

16. A project management plan should be realistic in order to be used to manage the project. Which of the following is the best method to achieve a realistic project management plan?
    A. The sponsor creates the project management plan based on input from the project manager.
    B. The functional manager creates the project management plan based on input from the project manager.
    C. The project manager creates the project management plan based on input from senior management.
    D. The project manager creates the project management plan based on input from the team.

17. You have taken over a project during project planning and have discovered that six individuals have signed the project charter. Which of the following should most concern you?
    A. Who will be a member of the change control board
    B. Spending more time on configuration management
    C. Getting a single project sponsor
    D. Determining the reporting structure

18. The project manager is working to clearly describe the level of involvement expected from everyone on the project in order to prevent rework, conflict, and coordination problems. Which of the following best describes the project manager's efforts?
    A. Develop Project Management Plan and Plan Quality Management
    B. Manage Stakeholder Engagement and Direct and Manage Project Work
    C. Validate Scope and Control Quality
    D. Identify Risks and Develop Project Team

19. All the following are parts of the Direct and Manage Project Work process except:
    A. Identifying changes
    B. Using a work breakdown structure
    C. Implementing corrective actions
    D. Setting up a project control system

20. A project manager is appointed to head a highly technical project in an area with which this person has limited familiarity. The project manager delegates the processes of Develop Schedule, Estimate Costs, Define Activities, and Estimate Activity Resources to various project team members, and basically serves as an occasional referee and coordinator of activities. The results of this approach are likely to be:

    A. A team functioning throughout the project at a very high level, demonstrating creativity and commitment
    B. A team that initially experiences some amounts of confusion, but that after a period of time becomes a cohesive and effective unit
    C. A team that is not highly productive, but that stays together because of the work environment created by the project manager
    D. A team that is characterized by poor performance, low morale, high levels of conflict, and high turnover

21. You are in the middle of leading a major modification project for an existing manufactured product when you learn that the resources promised at the beginning of the project are not available. According to your plans, these resources will be needed soon, and their unavailability will affect your timeline and possibly other aspects of the project. What is the best thing to do?

    A. Show how the resources were originally promised to your project.
    B. Replan the project without the resources.
    C. Explain the impact if the promised resources are not made available.
    D. Crash the project.

22. The primary customer of a project has requested an application change during user testing. As project manager, how should you address this issue?

    A. Develop a risk mitigation plan.
    B. Create a formal change request.
    C. Inform the project sponsor of changes to scope, cost, and schedule.
    D. Ensure the scope change complies with all relevant contractual provisions.

23. The project manager has just received a change request from the customer that does not affect the project schedule and is easy to complete. What should the project manager do first?

    A. Make the change happen as soon as possible.
    B. Contact the project sponsor for permission.
    C. Go to the change control board.
    D. Evaluate the impacts on other project constraints.

24. You are the project manager for an existing year-long project that must be completed. Your company just won a major new project. It will begin in three months and is valued at $2,000,000. The new project has a greater starting value and is therefore likely to have a higher priority than your project. It may affect your resources. You are concerned about how you will manage your project so that both projects can be implemented successfully. What is the first thing you should do when you hear of the new project?

    A. Ask management how the new project will use resources.
    B. Resource level your project.
    C. Crash your project.
    D. Ask management how the new project will affect your project.

25. You were just assigned to take over a project from another project manager who is leaving the company. The previous project manager tells you that the project is on schedule, but only because he has constantly pushed the team to perform. What is the first thing you should do as the new project manager?

    A. Check risk status.
    B. Check cost performance.
    C. Determine a management strategy.
    D. Tell the team your objectives.

26. You are assigned as the project manager in the middle of the project. The project is within the baselines, but the customer is not happy with the performance of the project. What is the first thing you should do?

    A. Discuss it with the project team.
    B. Recalculate baselines.
    C. Renegotiate the contract.
    D. Meet with the customer.

27. In the middle of the project, the project manager is informed by her scheduler that the project control limits are secure. That same morning, she receives a note from a team member about a problem he is having. The note says, "This activity is driving me crazy, and the manager of the accounting department won't help me until the activity's float is in jeopardy." In addition, the project manager has emails from a minor stakeholder and 14 emails from team members. While she is reading the emails, a team member walks into the project manager's office to tell her a corrective action was implemented by a team member from the project management office, but was not documented. What should the project manager do next?

    A. Report the documentation violation to the project management office, evaluate the security of the control limits, and review the emailing rules in the communications management plan.
    B. Clarify the reasoning behind documentation being a problem, get the accounting department to assist the team member, and respond to the minor stakeholder.
    C. Add the implemented corrective action to the change log, discuss the value of documentation at the next team meeting, and smooth the team member's issue with the accounting department.
    D. Find out who caused the problem with the accounting department, respond to the minor stakeholder before responding to the other emails, and review the process in the communications management plan for reporting concerns with the team member having the documentation problem.

28. The client demands changes to the product specification that will add only two weeks to the critical path. Which of the following is the best thing for the project manager to do?

    A. Compress the schedule to recover the two weeks.
    B. Cut scope to recover the two weeks.
    C. Consult with the sponsor about options.
    D. Advise the client of the impact of the change.

29. During executing, the project manager determines that a change is needed to material purchased for the project. The project manager calls a meeting of the team to plan how to make the change. This is an example of:

    A. Management by objectives
    B. Lack of a change management plan
    C. Good team relations
    D. Lack of a clear work breakdown structure

© 2018 RMC Publications, Inc.™ • 952.846.4484 • info@rmcls.com • www.rmcls.com

30. The project was going well when all of a sudden there were changes to the project coming from multiple stakeholders. After all the changes were determined, the project manager spent time with the stakeholders to find out why there were changes and to discover any more.

    The project work had quieted down when a team member casually mentioned to the project manager that he added functionality to a product of the project. "Do not worry," he said, "I did not impact schedule, cost, or quality!" What should the project manager do first?

    A. Ask the team member how the need for the functionality was determined.
    B. Hold a meeting to review the team member's completed work.
    C. Look for other added functionality.
    D. Ask the team member how he knows there is no schedule, cost, or quality impact.

31. You are asked to prepare a budget for completing a project that was started last year and then shelved for six months. All the following would be included in the project budget except:

    A. Fixed costs
    B. Sunk costs
    C. Direct costs
    D. Variable costs

32. Which of the following sequences represents straight-line depreciation?

    A. $100, $100, $100
    B. $100, $120, $140
    C. $100, $120, $160
    D. $160, $140, $120

33. A project is chartered to determine new ways to extend the product life of one of the company's medium-producing products. The project manager comes from the engineering department, and the team comes from the product management and marketing departments.

    The project scope statement and project planning are completed when a stakeholder notifies the team that there is a better way to complete one of the work packages. The stakeholder supplies a technical review letter from his department proving that the new way to complete the work package will actually be faster than the old way.

    The project manager has had similar experiences with this department on other projects, and was expecting this to happen on this project. What is the first thing the project manager should do?

    A. Contact the department and complain again about their missing the deadline for submission of scope.
    B. Determine how this change will impact the cost to complete the work package and the quality of the product of the work package.
    C. See if there is a way to change from a matrix organization to a functional organization so as to eliminate all the interference from other departments.
    D. Ask the department if they have any other changes.

34. Project A has an internal rate of return (IRR) of 21 percent. Project B has an IRR of 7 percent. Project C has an IRR of 31 percent. Project D has an IRR of 19 percent. Which of these would be the best project?

    A. Project A
    B. Project B
    C. Project C
    D. Project D

35. An output of the Close Project or Phase process is the creation of:
    A. Project archives
    B. A project charter
    C. A project management plan
    D. A risk management plan

36. All the following occur during the Close Project or Phase process except:
    A. Creating lessons learned
    B. Formal acceptance
    C. Performance reporting
    D. Performing cost-benefit analysis

37. Which of the following is included in a project charter?
    A. A risk management strategy
    B. Work package estimates
    C. Detailed resource estimates
    D. The business case for the project

38. A project manager is trying to convince management to use more formal project management procedures and has decided to start improving the company's project management by obtaining a project charter for each of his projects. Which of the following best describes how a project charter would help the project manager?
    A. It describes the details of what needs to be done.
    B. It lists the names of all team members.
    C. It gives the project manager authority.
    D. It describes the history of similar or related projects.

39. Linear programming is an example of what type of project selection criteria?
    A. Constrained optimization
    B. Comparative approach
    C. Benefit measurement
    D. Impact analysis

40. You have been involved in creating the project charter, but could not get it approved. Your manager and his supervisor have asked that the project begin immediately. Which of the following is the best thing to do?
    A. Set up an integrated change control process.
    B. Show your manager the impact of proceeding without approval.
    C. Focus on completing projects that have signed project charters.
    D. Start work on only the critical path activities.

172

41. The engineering department has uncovered a problem with the cost accounting system and has asked the systems department to analyze what is wrong and fix the problem. You are a project manager working with the cost accounting program on another project. Management has issued a change request to the change control board to add the new work to your project.

    Your existing project has a cost performance index (CPI) of 1.2 and a schedule performance index (SPI) of 1.3, so you have some room to add work without delaying your existing project or going over budget. However, you cannot see how the new work fits within the project charter for your existing project. After some analysis, you determine that the new work and existing work do not overlap and can be done concurrently. They also require different skill sets. Which of the following is the best thing to do?

    A. Develop a project charter.
    B. Reestimate the project schedule with input from the engineering department.
    C. Validate the scope of the new work with the help of the stakeholders.
    D. Identify specific changes to the existing work.

42. All technical work is completed on the project. Which of the following remains to be done?

    A. Validate Scope
    B. Plan Risk Responses
    C. Create a staffing management plan
    D. Complete lessons learned

43. The project manager can help to influence the processes that affect change on projects by creating and using the most appropriate planning strategies and tools. Assuming the project manager has created and is executing the best possible project management plan, the project sponsor should help the project manager to protect the project against unnecessary changes. Which of the following best reflects the phrase, "influencing the factors that affect change?"

    A. Telling people that changes are not allowed after planning is complete
    B. Determining the sources of changes and fixing the root causes
    C. Adding more activities to the work breakdown structure to accommodate risks
    D. Calculating the impact of changes to date on the project

44. The organization is about to begin a series of similar projects. The projects will be managed consecutively. Each project involves developing an online cooking video focused on foods appropriate to the month in which they will be released. For example, the summer videos will include picnic food and cool treats, and the December video will feature holiday foods for Hanukkah, Christmas, and Kwanzaa. The project sponsor is adamant that the management plan for each project includes an emphasis on making the best possible use of the lessons learned register. He believes that other projects have not been successful because they failed to take advantage of lessons learned from previously completed projects. The lessons learned register should be updated:

    A. At the end of each project phase
    B. Throughout the project
    C. Weekly
    D. At the end of the project

173

45. Knowledge management is a key responsibility of the project manager. This responsibility includes managing two kinds of knowledge on a project: tacit and explicit. Which of the following definitions are correct?

    A. Tacit knowledge is fact-based and can be easily communicated through words and symbols.
    B. Tacit knowledge may need explanation or context to provide value to recipients of this information.
    C. Tacit knowledge includes emotions, experience, and abilities.
    D. Lessons learned are an example of tacit knowledge.

© 2018 RMC Publications, Inc.™ • 952.846.4484 • info@rmcls.com • www.rmcls.com

## Answers

1. **Answer** C
   **Explanation** The project manager is an integrator. This is a question about your role as an integrator and communicator.

2. **Answer** B
   **Explanation** Replanning is uncalled for by the situation described. Reaching the planned completion date does not mean the project is necessarily finished. A project is complete when all work, including all project management work, is complete, and the product of the project and all project deliverables are accepted. The lessons learned are project management deliverables, and therefore must be completed for the project to be complete.

3. **Answer** D
   **Explanation** Project managers should be proactive. The only proactive answer here is preventing unnecessary changes.

4. **Answer** B
   **Explanation** Every project must be closed, as closure provides benefit to the performing organization. This means simply stopping work is not the best choice. Shifting work and releasing team members will only postpone dealing with the problem, not solve it. The best thing for the project manager to do is begin the Close Project or Phase process.

5. **Answer** D
   **Explanation** A change management plan includes the processes and procedures that allow smooth evaluation and tracking of changes. Lessons learned are reviews of the processes and procedures after the fact—to improve them on future projects.

6. **Answer** B
   **Explanation** Who does each activity is managed with the responsibility assignment matrix. When each activity is done is managed with the project schedule. A work authorization system is used to coordinate when and in what order the work is performed so that work and people may properly interface with other work and other people.

7. **Answer** C
   **Explanation** The sponsor issues the project charter, so they should help the project manager control changes to the charter. The primary responsibility lies with the sponsor. Remember that any change to the project charter should call into question whether the project should continue.

8. **Answer** C
   **Explanation** This question is asking for the most important of the choices. Think about what is involved in integration: project management plan development, project management plan execution, and integrated change control. Updates and product control are parts of project monitoring and controlling, while integration includes more than control. Advancing the careers of team members falls under project executing (the Develop Project Team process). To integrate the project components into a cohesive whole, communication is key whenever one activity will interface with another or one team member will interface with another, and when any other form of interfacing will occur.

9. **Answer** A
   **Explanation** Integration is a key responsibility of the project manager.

10. **Answer** B
    **Explanation** Integration refers to combining activities, not team members.

175

11. **Answer** B

    **Explanation** Direct and Manage Project Work is the only correct response.

12. **Answer** C

    **Explanation** Double declining balance is a form of depreciation. That eliminates the choice of life cycle costing. The choices of decelerated depreciation and straight-line depreciation are also incorrect because double declining balance is a form of accelerated depreciation.

13. **Answer** B

    **Explanation** One way to decide if a change should be approved is to determine whether the work falls within the project charter. If not, it should be rejected, assigned to a more appropriate project, or addressed as a project of its own.

14. **Answer** C

    **Explanation** The project management plan includes more than just a bar chart and the project manager's plan for completing the work. It includes all the management plans for the project.

15. **Answer** D

    **Explanation** The project manager may create the project charter, but it is approved and authorized by the project sponsor, giving the project manager authority to proceed with the project.

16. **Answer** D

    **Explanation** To narrow down the answer options, this question could be rephrased to ask, "Who creates the project management plan?" The best answer is that the project management plan is created by the project manager but requires input from the team.

17. **Answer** B

    **Explanation** Determining who will be on the change control board and determining the reporting structure may have already been done. In any case, these choices are not directly impacted by the number of sponsors who have signed the charter. Having a single project sponsor is not necessary. This situation implies that there are six areas concerned with this project. In addition to focusing on the added communications requirements, you should be concerned with competing needs and requirements impacting your efforts on configuration management.

18. **Answer** A

    **Explanation** Notice that this question uses the words "working to clearly describe" and "prevent." Taken together, they should tell you the project is in project planning. This eliminates all choices except Develop Project Management Plan and Plan Quality Management. Coordination and conflict prevention relate to Develop Project Management Plan, and preventing rework is part of Plan Quality Management.

19. **Answer** D

    **Explanation** A WBS is created in project planning, but can be used to help manage the project during project executing. The wording in the question was not "creating a WBS," but "using a WBS." A project control system is set up during project planning, not during project executing, and therefore is the exception.

20. **Answer** D

    **Explanation** A project manager must manage and integrate all aspects of a project. If all activities are delegated, chaos ensues, and team members will spend more time jockeying for position than completing activities.

21. **Answer** C

    **Explanation** Crashing and replanning are essentially delaying the problem. Instead, the project manager should try to prevent it by showing the consequences if the resources are not available. This is a more effective strategy than saying, "But you gave those resources to me."

22. **Answer** B

    **Explanation** Your first action is to formally document the requested change to the requirements, and then follow the integrated change control process.

23. **Answer** D

    **Explanation** The other impacts to the project should be evaluated first. The change could impact scope, cost, quality, risk, resources, and/or customer satisfaction. Once these are evaluated, the change control board, if one exists, can approve or deny the change.

24. **Answer** D

    **Explanation** You do not have enough information to consider resource leveling or crashing this project. As you work on any project, you need to constantly reevaluate the project objectives and how the project relates to other concurrent projects. Is your project still in line with corporate objectives? If the other project will impact yours, you need to be proactive and work on options now.

25. **Answer** C

    **Explanation** Before you can do anything else, you have to know what you are going to do. Developing the management strategy will provide the framework for all the rest of the choices presented and the other activities that need to be done.

26. **Answer** D

    **Explanation** First, you need to find out why the customer is not happy. Then meet with the team and determine options.

27. **Answer** C

    **Explanation** Notice how much information is thrown at you in this question. It is important to practice reading through questions to discover what is important and what is simply background information. In this question, the only thing relevant was the corrective action taken. Once you discover what the primary issue is, look at the choices to find out which is best for addressing that issue. What is the primary issue here? Did you realize the team member's note is about a non-critical path activity? ("Until the project float is in jeopardy" means there is float; thus, the activity is not on the critical path.) So, is the issue the non-critical path activity or the documentation? You might disagree with the logic, but in this case the answer is the documentation. In the real world, problems often repeat. Without a record of what was done, there is no opportunity to consider the same solution for future problems. Documentation is critical to projects. Because the change log becomes part of the historical records database, it is best to first record the corrective action taken, then discuss the value of documentation at the next team meeting, and, finally, smooth the team member's issue with the accounting department.

28. **Answer** C

    **Explanation** Do you remember what to do when there is a change? Evaluate first. You wouldn't take action before getting approval, so compressing the schedule or cutting scope would happen after consulting the sponsor and/or advising the client of the impact of the change. You would not go to the customer before going to your internal management, so advising the client is not the correct thing to do next. The next step is to discuss options with the sponsor.

29. **Answer**  B

    **Explanation**  The project manager is asking how to make a change. Such a question cannot be resolved using management by objectives, team relations, or a work breakdown structure. The procedures, forms, sign-offs, and other similar requirements for handling changes should have already been determined in the change management plan. Because they were not, the project manager will waste valuable work time trying to figure it out after the fact.

30. **Answer**  D

    **Explanation**  Notice that the first paragraph is extraneous. Also notice that the question states that the change has already been made. The project manager's actions would be different if the change had not been made. The project manager, with the help of others, must determine how the change impacts the project as a whole. Asking the team member how he knows there is no impact on schedule, cost, or quality is the best answer. This begins the project manager's analysis of the impacts to the project as a whole by finding out what analysis has already been done. This change minimally involves a change to the scope baseline, and likely other baselines as well. A change request must ultimately be submitted to integrated change control, but that is not listed as an option.

31. **Answer**  B

    **Explanation**  Sunk costs are expended costs. The rule is that they should not be considered when deciding whether to continue with a troubled project.

32. **Answer**  A

    **Explanation**  Straight-line depreciation uses the same amount each time period.

33. **Answer**  B

    **Explanation**  Complaining about the missed deadline could be done, but it is not proactive. It would be helpful to get to the root cause of why this department always comes up with such ideas or changes after the project begins. However, this is not the immediate problem; the change is the immediate problem, and therefore complaining is not best. The type of project organization described is a matrix organization. There is not anything inherently wrong with such an organization, nor is there anything in this particular situation that would require it to be changed. So, changing the way the company is organized cannot be best. The department's history indicates that asking if the department has other changes is something that should definitely be done, but the proposed change needs more immediate attention. Looking at impacts of the change begins integrated change control.

34. **Answer**  C

    **Explanation**  Remember, the internal rate of return is similar to the interest rate you get from the bank. The higher the rate, the better the return.

35. **Answer**  A

    **Explanation**  The project charter is created in initiating. The project management plan and risk management plan are outputs of project planning. Project records, including the charter and all management plans, are archived in the Close Project or Phase process.

36. **Answer**  D

    **Explanation**  Cost-benefit analysis is done earlier in the project to help select between alternatives. All the other choices are done during the Close Project or Phase process. Therefore, performing cost-benefit analysis must be the best answer.

37. **Answer** D

    **Explanation** A risk management strategy and work package estimates are not created until project planning, but the project charter is created in initiating. A project charter may include the names of some resources (the project manager, for example), but not detailed resource estimates. Of the choices given, only the business case for the project is included in the project charter.

38. **Answer** C

    **Explanation** The exam will ask questions like this to make sure you know the benefits you should be getting out of the processes and tools of project management. The details of what needs to be done are found in the WBS dictionary. The names of team members are included in the responsibility assignment matrix and other documents. Project history is found in the lessons learned and other historical records. A major benefit of a project charter is that it documents the authority given to the project manager.

39. **Answer** A

    **Explanation** Constrained optimization uses mathematical models. Linear programming is a mathematical model.

40. **Answer** B

    **Explanation** The best thing to do would be to show the impact. This is the only choice that prevents future problems—always the best choice. The other choices just pretend the problem does not exist.

41. **Answer** A

    **Explanation** How long did it take you to read this question? Expect long-winded questions like this on the exam. Take another look at the choices before you continue reading.

    This question is essentially asking if the new work should be added to the existing project. There may be many business reasons to try to do this, but from a project management perspective, major additions to the project are generally discouraged. In this case, the new work is a self-contained unit of work, has no overlap with the existing work, does not fit within the project charter, and needs a different skill set. Therefore, it is best to make it a new project.

    The first step to answering this question is to realize that the work should be a separate project. The second step is to look at the choices and see which relates to initiating a new project. Reestimating the project sounds like the best choice only if you did not realize that the new work should be a separate project. Validating scope is done during project monitoring and controlling, and does not relate to the decision of whether to add work to the project. Identifying scope changes also implies that the new work has been accepted as an addition to the existing project. Developing a project charter is among the first steps of initiating a new project, and the best choice in this situation.

42. **Answer** D

    **Explanation** Did you pick Validate Scope? Then you may have forgotten that the Validate Scope process is done during project monitoring and controlling, not project closing. Planning the risk responses and creating the staffing management plan are done earlier in the project. The lessons learned can only be completed after the work is completed.

43. **Answer** B

    **Explanation** A project manager should be looking at where changes are coming from and doing whatever is necessary to limit the negative effects of change on the project. They need to find the root cause, so future changes may be avoided.

44. **Answer** B

    **Explanation** The lessons learned register is a living document. It should be updated throughout the project, for the benefit of the current project, future, similar projects, and the organization as whole. The communications management plan documents how new lessons learned should be shared.

45. **Answer** C

**Explanation** Tacit knowledge includes emotions, experience, and ability. Sharing this type of knowledge requires an atmosphere of trust within the team or organization. The other choices relate to explicit knowledge.

# Scope Management

Scope management is the process of defining what work is required and then making sure all of that work—and only that work—is completed. This is generally an easy topic, but we all have gaps in our knowledge, even regarding things like scope management that we deal with daily. The following are gaps that many people do not know they have. Read through this list, and see if it helps you uncover any gaps in your knowledge.

 **Things to Know about Scope Management for the Exam**

- You must plan how you will determine the scope, as well as how you will manage and control scope. This is part of your scope management plan.

- Scope must be clearly defined and formally approved before work starts.

- Requirements are elicited from all stakeholders, not just the person who assigned the project.

- Requirements elicitation[1] can take a substantial amount of time, especially on large projects, which may involve obtaining requirements from hundreds of people.

- Requirements must be evaluated against the business case, ranked, and prioritized to determine what is in and out of scope.

- A work breakdown structure (WBS)[2] is used on all projects. Using this tool enables you to clarify identified scope as well as find additional scope.

## QUICKTEST

- Product scope
- Project scope
- Scope management process
- Scope management plan
- Requirements management plan
- Data-gathering techniques
  - Brainstorming
  - Interviews
  - Focus groups
  - Questionnaires and surveys
  - Benchmarking
- Requirements documentation
- Project scope statement
- Work breakdown structure (WBS)
  - Decomposition
  - Control account
  - Work package
  - Activity
  - How to create a WBS
  - Benefits of using a WBS
  - Uses for a WBS
- WBS dictionary
- Scope baseline
- Group decision-making
  - Voting
    » Unanimous
    » Autocratic
    » Majority
    » Plurality
  - Multicriteria decision analysis
- Data representation
  - Affinity diagrams
  - Mind maps
- Requirements categories
  - Business
  - Stakeholder
  - Solution
    » Functional
    » Nonfunctional
  - Transition
  - Project
  - Quality
  - Technical
- Interpersonal and team skills
  - Nominal group technique
  - Observation
  - Facilitation
    » Consensus
    » User stories
- Context diagrams
- Prototypes
- Acceptance criteria
- Requirements traceability matrix
- Product analysis
- Deliverables
  - Verified
  - Accepted

181

# Scope Management FIVE

| INITIATING | PLANNING (This is the only process group with a set order.) | EXECUTING | MONITORING & CONTROLLING | CLOSING |
|---|---|---|---|---|
| Select project manager | **Determine development approach, life cycle, and how you will plan for each knowledge area** | Execute work according to the project management plan | **Take action to monitor and control the project** | Confirm work is done to requirements |
| Determine company culture and existing systems | **Define and prioritize requirements** | Produce product deliverables (product scope) | **Measure performance against performance measurement baseline** | Complete final procurement closure |
| Collect processes, procedures, and historical information | **Create project scope statement** | Gather work performance data | **Measure performance against other metrics in the project management plan** | Gain final acceptance of product |
| Divide large projects into phases or smaller projects | Assess what to purchase and create procurement documents | Request changes | **Analyze and evaluate data and performance** | Complete financial closure |
| Understand business case and benefits management plan | Determine planning team | Implement only approved changes | **Determine if variances warrant a corrective action or other change request(s)** | Hand off completed product |
| Uncover initial requirements, assumptions, risks, constraints, and existing agreements | **Create WBS and WBS dictionary** | Continuously improve; perform progressive elaboration | **Influence factors that cause change** | Solicit customer's feedback about the project |
| Assess project and product feasibility within the given constraints | Create activity list | Follow processes | **Request changes** | Complete final performance reporting |
| Create measurable objectives and success criteria | Create network diagram | Determine whether quality plan and processes are correct and effective | Perform integrated change control | Index and archive records |
| Develop project charter | Estimate resource requirements | Perform quality audits and issue quality reports | Approve or reject changes | Gather final lessons learned and update knowledge bases |
| Identify stakeholders and determine their expectations, interest, influence, and impact | Estimate activity durations and costs | Acquire final team and physical resources | **Update project management plan and project documents** | |
| Request changes | Determine critical path | Manage people | Inform stakeholders of all change request results | |
| Develop assumption log | Develop schedule | Evaluate team and individual performance; provide training | Monitor stakeholder engagement | |
| Develop stakeholder register | Develop budget | Hold team-building activities | Confirm configuration compliance | |
| | Determine quality standards, processes, and metrics | Give recognition and rewards | Create forecasts | |
| | **Determine team charter and all roles and responsibilities** | Use issue logs | **Gain customer's acceptance of interim deliverables** | |
| | Plan communications and stakeholder engagement | Facilitate conflict resolution | Perform quality control | |
| | Perform risk identification, qualitative and quantitative risk analysis, and risk response planning | Release resources as work is completed | Perform risk reviews, reassessments, and audits | |
| | **Go back—iterations** | Send and receive information, and solicit feedback | Manage reserves | |
| | Finalize procurement strategy and documents | Report on project performance | Manage, evaluate, and close procurements | |
| | Create change and configuration management plans | Facilitate stakeholder engagement and manage expectations | Evaluate use of physical resources | |
| | **Finalize all management plans** | Hold meetings | | |
| | **Develop realistic and sufficient project management plan and baselines** | Evaluate sellers; negotiate and contract with sellers | | |
| | Gain formal approval of the plan | Use and share project knowledge | | |
| | Hold kickoff meeting | Execute contingency plans | | |
| | Request changes | Update project management plan and project documents | | |

## Rita's Process Chart™
## Scope Management
Where are we in the project management process?

- While the project is being completed, you must check to make sure you are doing all the work included in the project management plan—and only that work.
- Gold plating a project (adding extras) is not allowed.
- Any change to scope must be evaluated for its effect on time, cost, risk, quality, resources, and customer satisfaction.
- Changes to scope require an approved change request.
- Scope changes should not be approved if they relate to work that does not fit within the project charter.
- You need to continuously determine what is and is not included in the project.
- You are responsible for getting acceptance of deliverables throughout the project.

Note that creating a WBS is a required part of project management. A WBS is not a list! If you have never created one or do not currently use a WBS on your projects, this chapter will help you understand how beneficial this tool is and what it can do for you. Remember, the exam asks questions at an expert level and assumes you have experience using the various tools of project management. Therefore, you need to know how the WBS can help you clearly define requirements, plan how you will manage scope, and control scope.

The following should help you understand how each part of scope management fits into the overall project management process:

| The Scope Management Process | Done During |
| --- | --- |
| Plan Scope Management | Planning process group |
| Collect Requirements | Planning process group |
| Define Scope | Planning process group |
| Create WBS | Planning process group |
| Validate Scope | Monitoring and controlling process group |
| Control Scope | Monitoring and controlling process group |

You should understand the following concepts for the exam:

# Product Scope     PAGE 131    Product scope is another way to say "requirements that relate to the product, service, or result of the project." It can also be defined as the product deliverables with their associated features and functions. It answers the question, "What end result is needed?" There may be a separate, preliminary project to determine product scope, or you may define the requirements as part of your project.

Let's look at an example of product scope. On a project to build a new train terminal, the product scope is "a new train terminal that meets these technical specifications." To determine if the project successfully achieved the product scope, the resulting product (the new train terminal) is compared to the product requirements, which were recorded in the requirements documentation and the project scope statement for the project.

# Project Scope     PAGE 131    The project scope is the work the project team will do to deliver the product of the project; it encompasses the product scope. In the train terminal example, the project scope will be "a new train terminal that meets these technical specifications," plus all the work needed to deliver the train terminal. In other words, project scope includes the planning, coordination, and management activities (such as meetings and reports) that ensure the product scope is achieved. These efforts become

part of the scope baseline and scope management plan, which are parts of the project management plan. To determine whether the project scope has been successfully completed, the work accomplished is measured against the scope baseline.

## The Scope Management Process

To avoid the risk that you will read the rest of this chapter and miss an important concept, let's make this point clear right away: there are a lot of acceptable ways to manage scope. If you do it differently than described here, you are not necessarily wrong; you may just be managing scope differently based on the needs of your projects. For the exam, think of the scope management process as including the following steps:

1. Develop a plan for how you will plan, validate, and control scope and requirements on the project.
2. Determine requirements, making sure all requirements support the project's business case as described in the project charter.
3. Sort and balance the needs of stakeholders to determine scope.
4. Create a WBS to break the scope down to smaller, more manageable pieces, and define each piece in the WBS dictionary.
5. Obtain validation (signed acceptance) that the completed scope of work is acceptable to the customer or sponsor.
6. Measure scope performance, and adjust as needed.

Again, this may not be the way scope management is performed in your organization. For example, many organizations establish a separate project to elicit and evaluate requirements and determine what the project will be. This is especially true for work that demands a large requirements-gathering effort and for projects on which the people involved in determining requirements are different from those who will perform the work to produce them. The decision of whether to determine requirements as a separate project should be made based on the needs of the project and the organization.

On change-driven projects, requirements are identified and documented at a sufficient level of detail so they can be prioritized and estimated at a high level. The work is broken into releases and iterations, and the work of each release or iteration is defined in more detail just before the work is done.

 When taking the exam, assume that you will need to determine requirements as part of the project.

If you work as a seller, your process might begin with the receipt of a lengthy technical description (possibly 300 pages) of what the customer wants. In such a case, the requirements step is more about clarifying the product requirements supplied by the customer rather than determining them. However, the project requirements would still need to be determined.

 Assume that you are the project manager for the buyer for all questions on the exam that involve procurement, unless the question specifically states otherwise.

Here is something else to notice about the scope management process. It includes making sure all requirements support the project's business case, as described in the project charter. This means that no one can request or add work that is not related to the reason documented in the charter for initiating the project. Yet, in your real world, do you see people who want work done and try to attach it to any project they can in order to get that work accomplished? Do you see scope on projects that does not support the company's business objectives? It happens all the time. To prevent it, a project manager must be assertive. This is also the attitude you should have when you take the exam. You must be able to say no when someone tries to add unnecessary scope to your project. Unnecessary scope adds time, cost, and risk to the project that you just do not need. You have to be able to say, "That sounds like it is a separate project. It should go through the project approval process, instead of being added to my project." Understanding that a project manager needs to properly plan and protect the project is essential for passing the exam.

## Plan Scope Management   PAGE 134

> **Process**  Plan Scope Management
> **Process Group**  Planning
> **Knowledge Area**  Scope Management

Each of the project management knowledge areas has a management plan. For scope, there are actually two—a scope management plan and a requirements management plan. Together these plans provide direction on how the project and product scope will be defined, managed, and controlled. Before we discuss these plans in more detail, let's look at the inputs to creating them.

The project charter, project life cycle description, and organizational process assets are all inputs to the Plan Scope Management process. The project charter includes a high-level description of the product, service, or result the project is intended to produce. It also documents high-level project requirements.

The project life cycle description breaks the project into the phases that it will go through to produce the product, service, or result. It's also important to note that scope management planning must be performed in accordance with organizational policies and procedures. Historical records and lessons learned from previous, similar projects may be useful for the team in their planning efforts.

In addition to the above inputs, every project has a development approach. This could be plan-driven (predictive or waterfall), change-driven (iterative, adaptive, or agile), or a combination, or hybrid, approach. The development approach influences how requirements will be elicited as well as how the scope statement and WBS will be developed (for the entire project at once, or at a high level for the overall project, and then in more detail for each release).

## Scope Management Plan   PAGE 137   The scope management plan, which is the primary output of the Plan Scope Management process, is part of the project management plan, and the project manager uses it to guide the project until closing. The scope management plan essentially contains three parts which detail how scope will be planned, executed, and controlled. It defines the following:

- How to achieve the scope
- What tools to use to plan how the project will accomplish the scope
- How to create the WBS
- How scope will be managed and controlled to the project management plan
- How to obtain acceptance of deliverables

Each project's scope management plan is unique, but it may cover topics that can be standardized for the company or for the type of project. Therefore, companies can often utilize templates, forms, and standards for scope management. These are valuable assets to have on a project.

The scope management plan can be developed in stages, or iterated, during project planning. The first step is to plan how scope will be defined. As represented in the planning order of Rita's Process Chart™, the project manager and the team will have enough information to decide how the scope will be validated and controlled. Those decisions will then become part of the scope management plan. Another aspect of iterations is that later parts of project planning, such as the Plan Risk Responses process, can result in scope being added to the project, thereby changing the scope management plan, project scope statement, and WBS.

The idea behind the creation of the scope management plan and all management plans is: if you cannot plan it, you cannot do it. Even for a change-driven project, you need to plan some level of scope before work begins. Yet many people make the mistake of starting to work on a project before the product and project scope are defined and before they have properly planned how they will manage scope. Do you? Remember that creating a scope management plan is a required part of project management. The efforts of preparing a scope management plan and a requirements management plan (see the following paragraph) may be repeated, or iterated, throughout the project.

## Requirements Management Plan   PAGE 137   The requirements management plan, the
second and final output of the Plan Scope Management process, also falls under the PMI-ism of "plan before you do." This plan is also referred to as the business analysis plan. In addition to describing the methods you intend to use to identify requirements, the plan should answer the following questions: "Once I have all the requirements, what will I do to analyze, prioritize, manage, and track changes to them? What should I include in the requirements traceability matrix?" (The requirements traceability matrix is described later in this chapter.)

The scope management plan and the requirements management plan are parts of the project management plan. The next process, Collect Requirements, begins to put these plans into action.

## Collect Requirements   PAGE 138

> **Process** Collect Requirements
> **Process Group** Planning
> **Knowledge Area** Scope Management

Requirements are what stakeholders need from a project or product. Remember, work should not be included in a project just because someone wants it. Instead, requirements should relate to solving problems or achieving the objectives outlined in a project charter. Requirements may include requests about how the work is planned and managed. For example, a stakeholder could request that systems not be shut down to accommodate a project during peak business hours. Requirements may include the capabilities stakeholders would like to see in the product, such as a software application that allows multiple users to access it at the same time. Requirements can also relate to the following:

- **Quality**  "The component D must be able to withstand 200 pounds of pressure."
- **Business processes**  "You must track and report the project's expenses in this way."
- **Compliance**  "By law, we have to meet this safety standard."
- **Project management**  "We require risk management procedure X to be used on the project."

The Collect Requirements process looks for all requirements, not just those related to the product of a project. This process is critical to project success, as a missed requirement could mean significant changes and conflict throughout the remainder of a project—and even project failure.

This process involves using the project charter, the assumption log, the stakeholder register, agreements, and organizational process assets to create the requirements document and the requirements traceability matrix. Review these inputs in the following paragraphs, and think through how each of these inputs might help you in collecting requirements.

## Project Charter

The high-level project and product descriptions are defined in the project charter, which was developed during initiating. The Collect Requirements process begins with these descriptions, and elicits more detailed input about what is required.

## Assumption Log

The assumption log documents known stakeholder assumptions related to product and project requirements. Collect Requirements includes refining and adding to this list of assumptions.

## Stakeholder Register

Remember that the stakeholder register was created in initiating. It includes a list of stakeholders identified thus far in the project, as well as their requirements and expectations.

## Agreements

If the project includes procurements, the requirements of the buyers are documented in the contracts. Any agreed-upon requirements included in letters of agreement within an organization are also a source of requirements.

## Organizational Process Assets

Organizational process assets, such as historical records and lessons learned, include requirements from past, similar projects and help identify relevant processes and expectations. For example, historical records may provide data about reporting requirements, project management requirements, system compatibility requirements, and compliance requirements. Lessons learned from other projects, which may identify commonly overlooked areas of scope, can be used to help ensure such requirements are not missed on the current project.

On large projects, there could be hundreds of stakeholders, and no single method of collecting requirements will work for all stakeholders. Since missing a needed requirement can be very expensive and time-consuming and can cause other problems later, a concerted effort must be made to find as many requirements as possible before work starts on a project or development phase.

The Collect Requirements effort also includes eliciting stakeholders' expectations—their beliefs or mental pictures about how the project will turn out—and translating those expectations into requirements as necessary. Collecting requirements may involve using various techniques (described next). The project manager needs to choose the techniques that are the most appropriate for the project and its stakeholders. Note that many of these techniques can also be used in other data-gathering efforts, such as identifying risks during the risk management process.

The following tools and techniques can be used to collect requirements.

## Brainstorming

Be careful here—many people think brainstorming is just a meeting where people discuss ideas, but it is more than that. The purpose of brainstorming is not so much to get individuals to share their thoughts on a topic as it is to encourage participants to build on each other's ideas. One person mentions an idea to solve a problem or, in this case, determine scope. That idea generates an idea from another participant, which leads to yet another idea, and so on. The results of brainstorming sessions vary depending on the participants. It can be highly beneficial to include people with different perspectives or backgrounds. The participants may be internal or external to the project and/or the organization. After all the ideas have been captured, the group can evaluate and rank them using the nominal group technique or multicriteria decision analysis, as described in the following sections.

187

## Interviews

On the exam, this technique may also be referred to as expert interviews. The team or project manager interviews project stakeholders to elicit their requirements for a specific element of the product or project work, or for the overall project. These interviews can take place between two individuals or in group settings. Interviews can also be conducted via email or phone, or using virtual collaboration tools.

## Focus Groups

The focus group technique helps elicit opinions and requirements for the product or an aspect of the project from stakeholders and subject matter experts. Members of a focus group are usually selected from a specific demographic group of customers. They discuss their ideas with each other, and the conversation is directed by a moderator.

## Questionnaires and Surveys

Questionnaires or surveys are typically used for large groups. The questions are asked in such a way as to elicit requirements from the respondents.

## Benchmarking

Another way to help identify and define requirements is to look at what the competition is doing. Benchmarking focuses on measuring an organization's performance against that of other organizations in the same industry. There are limitations to this technique, however. Benchmarking can be very time-consuming and costly. It may also inhibit the team's creativity because the focus is on studying solutions that have been used elsewhere, rather than on developing new, innovative ideas.

## Voting

Soliciting input about requirements from stakeholders often results in conflicting requirements. It is essential to resolve these conflicts, as well as to review, analyze, accept or reject, and prioritize requirements before recording them in project documents. Voting is commonly used to make decisions in a group setting. If the group agrees on a requirement *unanimously* (everyone agrees), the decision is easy. The decision-making process is also simplified if a single person is assigned to make the decision for the entire group. However, this *autocratic* method of decision-making can have negative impacts on the project if the stakeholders do not buy into the decision.

When there are conflicting opinions, groups may also take a *majority* approach. With this approach, the group chooses the decision that more than half of its members support. If there is no majority opinion, the group may go with the decision that has the largest number of supporters. This is known as the *plurality* approach.

## Multicriteria Decision Analysis[3]

Another way to rank ideas is through multicriteria decision analysis. With this technique, stakeholders quantify requirements using a decision matrix based on factors such as expected risk levels, time estimates, and cost and benefit estimates.

## Affinity Diagrams[4]

In this technique, the ideas generated from any other requirements-gathering techniques are grouped by similarities. Each group of requirements is then given a title. This sorting makes it easier to see additional areas of scope (or risks) that have not been identified (see fig. 5.1).

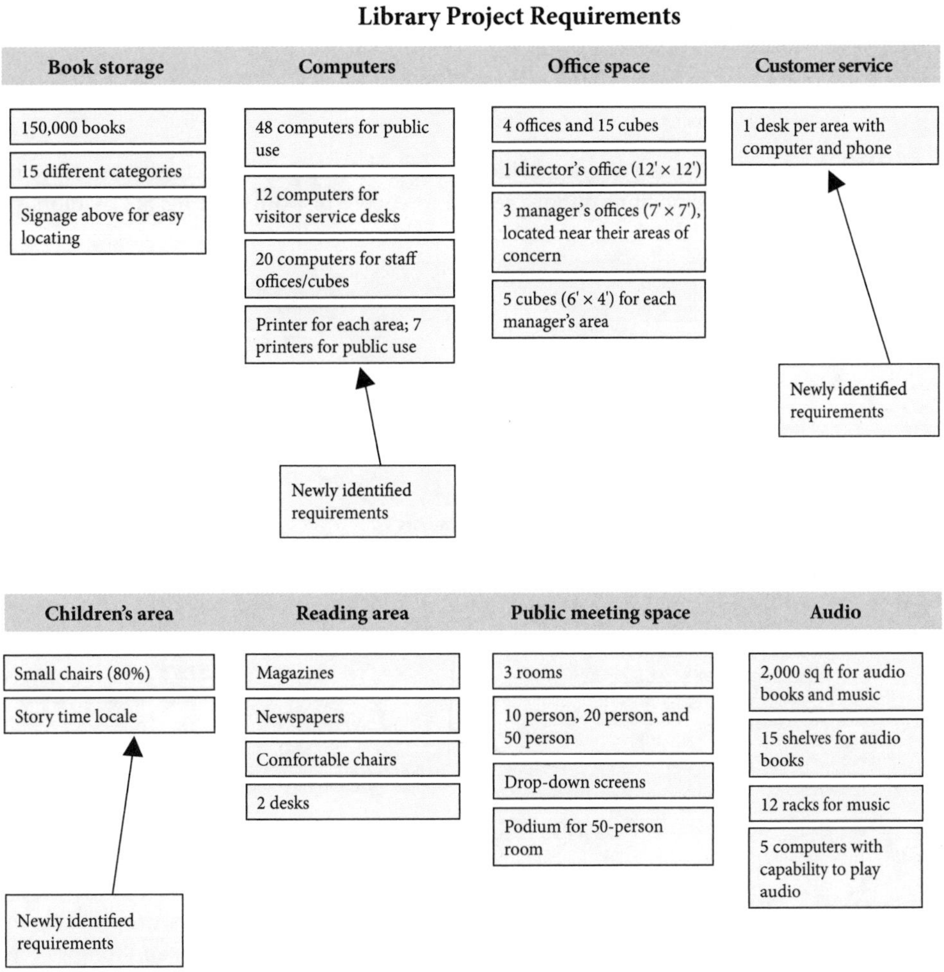

**Library Project Requirements**

| Book storage | Computers | Office space | Customer service |
|---|---|---|---|
| 150,000 books | 48 computers for public use | 4 offices and 15 cubes | 1 desk per area with computer and phone |
| 15 different categories | 12 computers for visitor service desks | 1 director's office (12' × 12') | |
| Signage above for easy locating | 20 computers for staff offices/cubes | 3 manager's offices (7' × 7'), located near their areas of concern | |
| | Printer for each area; 7 printers for public use | 5 cubes (6' × 4') for each manager's area | |

Newly identified requirements (Computers)

Newly identified requirements (Customer service)

| Children's area | Reading area | Public meeting space | Audio |
|---|---|---|---|
| Small chairs (80%) | Magazines | 3 rooms | 2,000 sq ft for audio books and music |
| Story time locale | Newspapers | 10 person, 20 person, and 50 person | 15 shelves for audio books |
| | Comfortable chairs | Drop-down screens | 12 racks for music |
| | 2 desks | Podium for 50-person room | 5 computers with capability to play audio |

Newly identified requirements (Children's area)

FIGURE 5.1  *Affinity diagram*

Affinity diagrams can also be organized by requirements categories. The following are some common categories used when collecting requirements:

- **Business requirements** Why was the project undertaken? What business need is the project intended to address?

- **Stakeholder requirements** What do stakeholders want to gain from the project?

- **Solution requirements** What does the product need to look like? What are its *functional* requirements (how the product should work) and *nonfunctional* requirements (what will make the product effective)?

- **Transition requirements** What types of handoff procedures or training are needed to transfer the product to the customer or organization?

- **Project requirements** How should the project be initiated, planned, executed, controlled, and closed?

189

- **Quality requirements**  What quality measures does the product need to meet? What constitutes a successfully completed deliverable?
- **Technical requirements**  How will the product be built? What are the product specifications?

## Mind Maps[5]

A mind map is a diagram of ideas or notes to help generate, classify, or record information. It looks like several trees branching out of a central core word or words (see fig. 5.2). Colors, pictures, and notations can be used to make the diagram more readable.

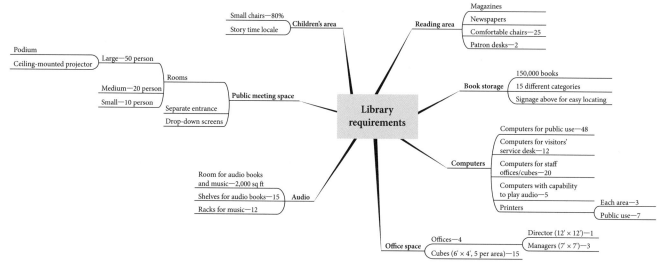

FIGURE 5.2   *Mind map*

## Nominal Group Technique[6]

This technique is usually, but not always, done during the same meeting as brainstorming. It tends to be more structured than other techniques, and follows these four steps: a question or issue is posed, all meeting participants write down and then share their ideas, the group discusses what's been shared, and then ideas are ranked based on which ideas are the most useful.

## Observation

Observation is a great way to learn about business processes and to get a feel for the work environment of stakeholders. This technique generally involves job shadowing—watching a potential user of the product at work and, in some cases, participating in the work to help identify requirements.

## Facilitation

Facilitation brings together stakeholders with different perspectives, such as product designers and end users, to talk about the product and, ultimately, define requirements. This technique uses a *consensus* approach, which achieves general agreement about a decision. Those who would prefer another option are willing to accept the decision supported by most members of the group.

Stakeholders may develop user stories during these facilitated sessions. User stories describe functionality or features that stakeholders hope to see and are often written in the following format:

*As a <role>, I want <functionality/goal> so that <business benefit/motivation>.*

For example: "As a community organizer, I want the new library to offer public meeting spaces so that we have a central place to gather and can expose community members to the benefits of the library through neighborhood events."

Examples of facilitation sessions include the following:

- **Joint application design (JAD) sessions** Used primarily in software development efforts, JAD sessions involve eliciting requirements and input to enhance the processes of developing the software.
- **Quality functional deployment (QFD)** QFD (also referred to as the Voice of the Customer, or VOC) is a technique used to elicit and prioritize customer requirements. It is generally used in the manufacturing industry.

## Context Diagrams[7]
A context diagram, also known as a context level data flow diagram, is frequently used to define and model scope. It shows the boundaries of the product scope by highlighting the product and its interfaces with people, processes, or systems. Figure 5.3 shows an example of a context diagram for the payroll system upgrade described in the second project charter in the Integration Management chapter.

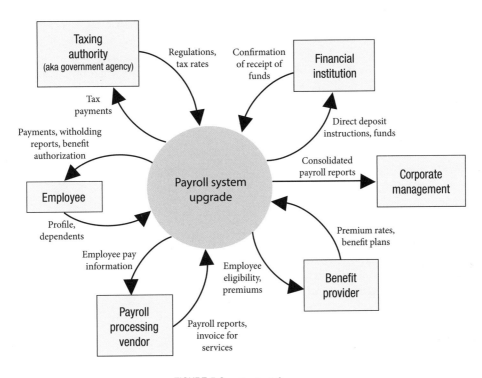

FIGURE 5.3  *Context diagram*

## Prototypes
A prototype is a model of the proposed product that is presented to stakeholders for feedback. The prototype may be updated multiple times to incorporate stakeholders' feedback until the requirements have been solidified for the product.

## Balancing Stakeholder Requirements
This effort is an important aspect of the Collect Requirements process. Part of balancing requirements from stakeholders involves making sure the requirements can be met within the project objectives. If they cannot, then you need to look for options to adjust the competing demands of scope, time, cost, quality, resources, risk, and customer satisfaction. Balancing requirements also involves prioritizing requirements and resolving any conflicts.

The need to balance stakeholder requirements continues beyond the Collect Requirements process. It may only become apparent later in the project that some requirements do not match those of the project or those of other stakeholders. Whenever this occurs, you need to balance the requirements against the interests of the project and resolve any conflicts.

This type of balancing is never easy or fast. It can become impossible if you do not have clear project objectives and if you do not identify and prioritize all requirements from all stakeholders during the Collect Requirements process. Do you try to get as close to final requirements as possible when managing projects? Are your requirements ranked by order of importance? On adaptive projects, do you rank requirements in a backlog? If not, think about how such actions could improve your projects. When you take the exam, assume that every effort has been made by the project manager to uncover all requirements and that those requirements are ranked by order of importance.

**Exercise** This exercise outlines some of the key actions involved in balancing requirements from stakeholders. It goes beyond the Collect Requirements process and looks at this effort throughout the project life cycle. Spend some time thinking about balancing requirements while getting ready for the exam. This exercise will help you determine whether you really understand the process. Go through each topic, and put a check mark next to the actions you understand. Put an X next to the actions you are able to apply in the real world. Then spend time thinking about the unmarked topics.

| Action | Understand ✓ | Can Do X |
|---|---|---|
| Identify all stakeholders; understand their needs, wants, assumptions, and expectations related to the project. | | |
| Work to get requirements as clear and complete as appropriate for the selected development approach before starting project work. | | |
| Use information about stakeholders and their requirements to resolve competing requirements while work is being done on the project. | | |
| Look for competing interests during project planning; don't just wait for competing interests to show up during project executing. | | |
| Look for possible options to resolve competing interests and alternative ways of completing project activities. This may involve using techniques such as brainstorming, schedule compression, reestimating, and other project management and management-related practices. | | |
| Resolve competing requirements from stakeholders based on how the requirements affect the project. (See the guidelines listed in the following discussion.) | | |
| Give priority to the customer. (For the exam, know that if any needs conflict with those of the customer, the customer's needs normally take precedence.) | | |
| Use quality management to support the project's satisfaction of the needs for which it was undertaken. | | |

| Action | Understand ✓ | Can Do X |
|---|---|---|
| Deal with problems and conflicts as soon as they arise through the use of team building, problem-solving, and conflict management techniques. | | |
| Say no to some of the competing interests. (For the exam, assume the project manager has the authority to say no when necessary to protect the project.) | | |
| Fix the project when the project metrics start to deviate from the requirements, rather than changing the requirements to meet the results of the project. | | |
| Work toward fair resolutions of disputes—ones that consider the interests of all stakeholders as well as the needs of the project. | | |
| Hold meetings, interviews, and discussions to facilitate the resolution of competing requirements. | | |
| Call on management to help resolve competing interests when the project manager and the team cannot come up with a fair and equitable solution. | | |
| Use negotiation techniques to resolve disputes between stakeholders. | | |
| Plan and implement effective communication. | | |
| Gather, assess, and integrate information into the project. | | |

**Resolving Competing Requirements**   Many project managers have no idea how to prioritize competing requirements. What if, for example, the engineering department wants your project to focus on decreasing defects while the accounting department wants your project to focus on lowering costs? Can both needs be met? What if the engineering department is the primary stakeholder or even the sponsor of the project? Should that department's needs outweigh the needs of the accounting department? What if the needs of the engineering department actually hurt the accounting department?

Some issues are so complex they cannot be resolved by the project manager alone, and require management intervention. However, there are some standard guidelines for balancing competing requirements. Walk through the following list for each requirement.

You should resolve competing requirements by accepting those that best comply with following:

- The business case stating the reason the project was initiated (market demand, legal requirement, etc.)
- The project charter
- The project scope statement (if this is available at the time of the conflict)
- The project constraints

A stakeholder's request to do or add something to the project that is not related to the reason the project was initiated should be rejected. If a requirement is related to the reason the project was initiated but does not fall within the project charter, this request should also be rejected. Any suggested changes to the project

193

charter must be brought to the sponsor for approval. When considering constraints, if the most important constraint is schedule, then any requirements that would delay the schedule will not likely be accepted. Those that enhance the schedule (without serious impact to other project constraints) will more likely be accepted. Requests that do not fall within these guidelines could become part of a future project instead.

## Requirements Documentation   PAGE 147   After requirements have been collected and finalized, they are documented. Imagine you have elicited requirements from hundreds of people. Can you see how documenting those requirements would be useful? This documentation is an output of the Collect Requirements process and helps to ensure all requirements are clear and unambiguous.

Requirements documentation can contain various types of information, but the one thing that must be included is acceptance criteria. To avoid having requirements that could easily be misunderstood, a great question to ask stakeholders is, "How will we know if the work we do will meet this requirement?" Not only is this a good way to make sure you understand the stakeholder's requirement, but it also helps to ensure the work being done will be acceptable.

It's also important to note that the level of detail of documentation is iterated until each requirement satisfies the criteria of being clear, complete, and measurable. Requirements must be described in such a way that associated deliverables can be tested or measured against the requirements in the Validate Scope process to confirm that the deliverables are acceptable.

## Requirements Traceability Matrix[8]   PAGE 148   Have you ever worked on a project in which some requirements got lost in the details? In the process of determining requirements, one requirement often leads to additional, more refined requirements and clarifications—especially on large projects. It can be difficult to remember where a requirement came from and what its significance is to the project. Losing focus on the reason for a requirement can result in a major strategic or project objective not being met. The requirements traceability matrix, another output of the Collect Requirements process, helps link requirements to the objectives and/or other requirements to ensure the strategic goals are accomplished (see fig. 5.4). The matrix is used throughout the project in analyzing proposed changes to project or product scope.

Information such as requirement identification numbers, the source of each requirement, who is assigned to manage the requirement, and the status of the requirement should be documented in the requirements traceability matrix. For large projects, however, including all this information in the matrix would make it cumbersome and difficult to use. Another option is to store this data in a separate repository, preserving the matrix as an easy-to-reference tool. For the exam, simply understand that the requirements traceability matrix links requirements to objectives and/or other requirements, and that the requirements attributes, such as identification numbers, source, and status, also need to be documented.

Assigning responsibility for management of each requirement is similar to the concept of risk owners, described in the Risk Management chapter. An owner helps ensure the customer receives what they asked for and that the objectives are met. Assigning team members to manage requirements also helps free up the project manager's time. The role of requirement owner is another example of the type of work team members may do on a project in addition to their efforts to produce the product.

| Objectives | Reading area | | | | Book storage | | | Public meeting space | | | Children's area | | Audio | | | Office space | | Computers | | | | |
|---|---|---|---|---|---|---|---|---|---|---|---|---|---|---|---|---|---|---|---|---|---|---|
| | Magazines | Newspapers | Comfortable chairs—25 | Patron desks—2 | 150,000 books | 15 different categories | Signage above for easy locating | Rooms | Separate entrance | Drop-down screens | Small chairs—80% | Story time locale | Room for audio books and music | Shelves for audio books—15 | Racks for music—12 | Offices—4 | Cubes—15 | For public use—48 | For visitor service desk—12 | For staff—20 | With audio capability—5 | Printers |
| Improve access to job resources by 20%. | | X | | X | | | | X | | X | | | | | | | | X | X | | | X |
| Improve local children's reading levels by two grade levels in one year. | | | X | | X | | X | | | | | X | | | | | | X | | | | |
| Provide a pleasant place for community members to meet. | X | X | X | | | | | X | X | | X | | X | X | X | | | | | | | |
| Replace the existing library by end of next quarter. | X | X | X | | X | X | X | | | | | X | | X | | X | X | X | | X | X | X |

FIGURE 5.4  *Requirements traceability matrix*

# Define Scope   PAGE 150

**Process** Define Scope
**Process Group** Planning
**Knowledge Area** Scope Management

The Define Scope process is primarily concerned with what is and is not included in the project and its deliverables. This process uses information from the project charter, scope management plan, the requirements documentation created in the Collect Requirements process, the assumption log, and the risk register to define the project and product scope.

Remember that planning is iterative. When the requirements have been determined and the scope is defined, the project manager follows the project management planning process outlined in Rita's Process Chart™ to determine the schedule and budget. If the resulting schedule and budget do not meet the sponsor's or management's expectations for the project, the project manager needs to balance the requirements (scope) against budget and schedule constraints. Through iterations, options for meeting the scope, schedule, and cost objectives of the project are developed. These options are then presented to management for a decision. This work may include compressing the schedule, identifying alternative ways to perform the work on the project, or adjusting the budget or scope. The result is a realistic schedule and budget that can achieve the project's agreed-upon scope.

The process of scope definition is ongoing throughout the project. The following are two key reasons this process is important on the exam:

- Many project managers complain about unrealistic schedules. For the exam, you need to understand that unrealistic schedules are the project managers' fault because they have not done planning in an iterative way, as described in the previous paragraph. Project managers must reconcile the scope to the schedule and the budget, as well as to other project constraints, to resolve any issues before work begins.

- Project managers spend a large portion of their time during executing and monitoring and controlling looking for options to adjust the project and still meet the project schedule or budget. Therefore, all the analysis tools used in planning to come up with a realistic schedule and budget are also utilized while the work is being done.

Whether a project uses a plan-driven or change-driven approach, the process of Define Scope is iterated as the project progresses. Its purpose is always to determine what scope is and is not in the project.

## Product Analysis   PAGE 153   As noted at the beginning of this section, part of defining scope is determining what the deliverables of the project are. Product analysis is performed to analyze the objectives and description of the product as stated by the customer or sponsor. That information is then used to define tangible deliverables. The work of product analysis may entail analyzing the product description and stated requirements, or using techniques such as systems engineering, value analysis, or value engineering. Product analysis is a critical tool that allows the project manager to make sure the product and project scope are understood and accurate. For the exam, realize you may need to determine and define deliverables as part of the project, rather than receiving a complete list from the customer.

## Project Scope Statement[9]   PAGE 154   The primary result, or output, of the Define Scope process is the project scope statement. This document in effect says, "Here is what we will do on this project." Or it could say, "Here is the approved project and product or service scope for this project." On a plan-driven project, the development of the project scope statement can take a lot of time and involve the expert judgment of many stakeholders and even experts from outside the organization. The project scope statement for a change-driven project will be less detailed, but will still have sufficient detail to define what is in and out of scope. The product scope will be progressively elaborated as needed. While defining requirements and, in turn, defining scope, you should identify areas where people requested scope but it was not approved to be included in the project. You should also clarify areas where the scope could easily be misunderstood. It is a waste of project time and money to create scope that is not needed or approved, yet it is easy for this to occur. One way to avoid this problem is to identify in the project scope statement what is not in the project, to make it clear that such additions are not allowed.

The project scope statement, along with the WBS and WBS dictionary (described in the next section), comprise the scope baseline, which is part of the project management plan. The project scope statement may include the following:

- Product scope
- Project scope, including a description
- Deliverables of the project
- Acceptance criteria
- What is not part of the project
- Assumptions and constraints

## Create WBS   PAGE 156

**Process** Create WBS
**Process Group** Planning
**Knowledge Area** Scope Management

What is a WBS? Correctly understanding this project management tool is essential for successful projects, and for passing the exam.

**Exercise**   Test yourself! What is a WBS?

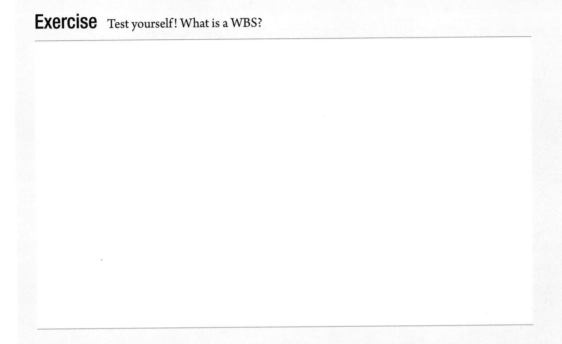

**Answer**   The WBS is a required element of project management. This organizational tool shows all of the scope on a project, broken down into manageable deliverables. Without a WBS, a project can and will take longer, deliverables and the work to produce them are likely to be missed, and your project will be negatively impacted. So, there is no choice. All projects, even small ones, need a WBS. Read the rest of this section to learn more about what a WBS is and how it adds value to projects.

If you have not created a WBS, or do not practice using this tool, you will likely answer questions incorrectly when taking the exam. What if a question described details of a project to you and then asked, "You are in the middle of planning this project, and you are creating a WBS. Which of the following do you most likely need to worry about?" It is difficult to answer such questions with only academic knowledge. You need experience using this tool.

Let's work through the topic of the WBS together. Try the following exercise.

**Exercise**   Many people simply make a list of things to do as their method of defining all the deliverables on a project. This is a mistake; there are enormous advantages to using a WBS instead. Test yourself. Can you explain why the image on the right side (a list) is not as good as the diagram on the left (a WBS)?

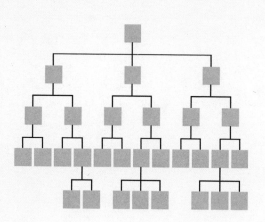

## Vendors

### Custom Vendor Selection

- Agenda for visits
- Evaluation criteria
- Team preparation
- Visit schedule
- Report on visits
- Vendor scores
- Finalist list

### Vendor Reference Checks

- Reference format
- Vendor reference requests
- Reference evaluation forms

FIVE

**Answer** Here are just a few answers that explain why a WBS is better than a list:

- Both the way a list is created and the way it displays information make it easy to overlook some deliverables. In contrast, the construction of a WBS graphically provides a structured vision for a project and helps to ensure that nothing slips through the cracks and no deliverables are forgotten.

- A list can be cumbersome and does not allow you to clearly break down a large project into small enough pieces. With a WBS, you can easily break down deliverables into work packages (smaller deliverables, not activities). A WBS also shows how work packages are derived.

- A list is usually created by one person, whereas a WBS is created with input from the team and stakeholders. Involving the team and stakeholders helps gain buy-in, and increased buy-in leads to improved performance. In contrast, a list can make people wary of a project because they are not able to understand the project by looking at a list, nor do they know how the list was created.

- The process of creating a WBS allows the team to walk through a project in their minds and thus improves project plans. The execution of a project is typically easier and less risky as a result.

- Being involved in the creation of a WBS helps people better understand a project. It also makes a project seem more achievable.

- A WBS shows a complete hierarchy of a project, making it easier to see how one deliverable relates to another. A list is just a list.

Will this be on the exam? Not directly, but you will need to fully understand a WBS, and this discussion describes aspects of using a WBS that many people do not understand.

Review the WBS example in figure 5.5.

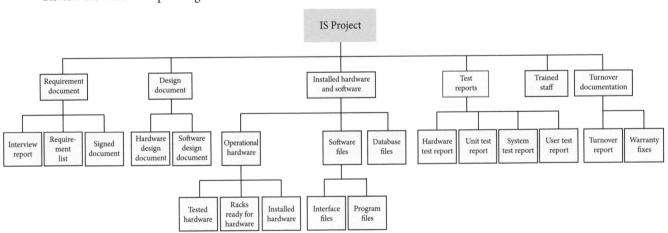

FIGURE 5.5  *A WBS (on a summary level) for a hardware/software creation and installation project*

Most commonly, the project name goes at the top of a WBS. The next level is typically the same as the development life cycle. The subsequent levels break the project into deliverables, which are then broken down again into smaller component deliverables, ultimately to create work packages (described next). Such decomposition continues until reaching the level appropriate to manage the project.

Although a WBS may look like a corporate organizational chart, it is not! It serves a different function. A WBS allows you to break down a seemingly overwhelming project into pieces you can plan, organize, manage, and control. The creation of a WBS is an effort to decompose deliverables into smaller component deliverables called work packages. Decomposition can be done using a top-down approach (starting with the high-level pieces of a project), a bottom-up approach (starting at the work package level), or by following organizational and industry guidelines or templates.

Note that on a WBS, work refers not to an activity, but to the work products or deliverables that result from an activity or group of activities. So, for the exam, note that each work package should consist of nouns—things (deliverables), rather than actions (activities). A WBS is deliverable-oriented. This does not mean that only customer deliverables are included. The complete scope of a project, including product scope, project scope, and project management efforts are included as well.

 Watch out for the word "task." What many people refer to as a "task" in the real world (and in some project management software) is generally called an "activity" on the exam. An activity is a particular piece of work scheduled for a project. For the exam, you should typically expect to manage to the activity level. Tasks are smaller components of work that make up an activity—they can be used to further break down an activity into smaller components of work.

Every WBS is unique, and every project manager will approach creating a WBS in their own way. But there are a few guidelines that every project manager should follow when creating a WBS:

- A WBS should be created by the project manager using input from the team and other stakeholders.
- Each level of a WBS is a breakdown of the previous level.
- An entire project should be included in the highest levels of a WBS. Eventually, some levels will be further broken down.
- A WBS includes only project deliverables that are required; deliverables not included in the WBS are not part of the project.

During planning, the project management team and subject matter experts break down the scope description until the work package level is reached. This occurs when the deliverables:

- Can be realistically and confidently estimated (including the activities, duration, and cost associated with them)
- Can be completed quickly
- Can be completed without interruption and without the need for more information
- May be outsourced

At this point, you might enter the work packages—the items at the lowest level of the WBS—into some sort of project scheduling software. You would not try to finalize the list of work packages by using software, however. That list comes from the creation of the WBS.

The levels in the WBS are often numbered for ease of location later. When the WBS is complete, identification numbers are assigned to help distinguish where a work package is in the WBS. There are many different numbering systems you can use. Figure 5.6 provides an example.

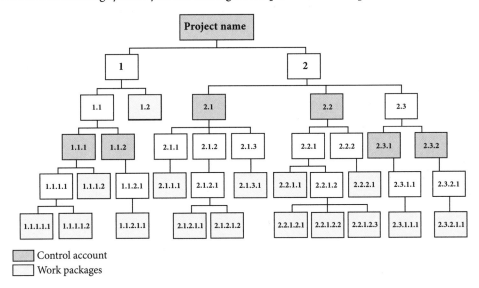

FIGURE 5.6  *Sample WBS numbering system*

You may see the terms "control account"[10] or "planning package" on the exam. Sometimes found at higher levels within the WBS (as shown in figure 5.6), a control account is a tool that allows you to collect and analyze work performance data regarding costs, schedule, and scope. Control accounts, which may include one or more planning packages, provide a way to manage and control costs, schedule, and scope at a higher level than the work package. Each work package in the WBS is assigned to only one control account.

As planning progresses, the team breaks down the work packages from the WBS into the schedule activities (or "activities," for short) that are required to produce the work packages. Note that this further breakdown of the WBS into an activity list is done as part of the schedule management process of Define Activities. The team uses the project scope statement, WBS, and WBS dictionary (described later in this chapter) to help define which activities are required to produce the deliverables.

For example, on small projects, the WBS is often broken down into work packages that take between 4 and 40 hours to complete. Medium-sized projects may have work packages with 8 to 80 hours of work. On large projects, however, the work packages may be much larger and could involve 300 hours of work. Therefore, the Define Activities process is especially important on large projects. Think about how this effort is different on a large project than on a small project.

If your company works on many similar projects, it is important to realize that the WBS from one project may be used as the basis for another. Therefore, the project management office should collect and share WBS examples and encourage the creation of templates. Project WBSs become part of the company's organizational process assets, and may be used by similar projects in the future.

Great project managers not only see the value of the information provided in the WBS, they also recognize the value of the effort involved in creating the WBS. Do you really understand what a WBS is? Try the next exercise. If you miss many of the answers, review this section, and rethink your knowledge before taking the exam.

## Exercise  Test yourself! What are the benefits of using a WBS?

_____

_____

_____

_____

_____

_____

_____

_____

_____

_____

## Answer  This exercise may seem similar to the previous exercise, but it is important to clearly understand the value of a WBS. The following are benefits of using a WBS:

- Helps prevent work from slipping through the cracks
- Provides project team members with an understanding of how deliverables fit into the overall project management plan and gives the project team an indication of the impact of their work on the project as a whole
- Facilitates communication and cooperation between and among the project team and other stakeholders
- Helps manage stakeholder expectations regarding deliverables
- Helps identify risks
- Helps prevent changes
- Focuses the project team's experience on what needs to be done, resulting in increased quality and a project that is easier to manage
- Provides a basis for estimating resources, costs, and schedules
- Provides proof of the need for resources, funds, and schedules
- Helps with planning control efforts and establishing acceptance criteria for deliverables
- Gets team buy-in and builds the project team
- Helps people get their minds around the project

A WBS is the foundation of a project. This means almost everything that occurs in planning after the creation of a WBS is related to the WBS. For example, project costs and schedules are estimated at the work package or activity level, and not for the project as a whole. Also note that a WBS can help a project manager identify more risks by examining a project at the work package level. Work packages are assigned to individuals or parts of the performing organization, depending on the size of the project. Does the WBS shown in figure 5.7 make sense to you?

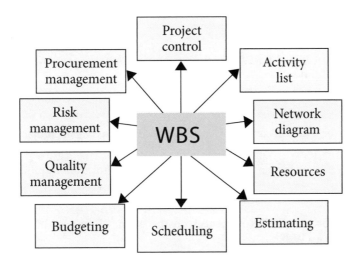

FIGURE 5.7    *The WBS is the foundation of the project.*

Let's think about the project control element in figure 5.7. Many people forget to use the project management tools from project planning while the work is being done. They may create a WBS just because it is a required part of a complete scope baseline, but then forget about it. As a result, they do not get the full benefit of the tool. If an exam question asks what you do with a WBS once it has been created, what will you answer?

**Exercise**   What do you do with a WBS once it has been created?

If you were going to test someone's WBS knowledge, would you ask questions about the basics of creating a WBS, or would you test their knowledge by asking how a WBS can help a project manager to better manage a project? The exam strongly weighs toward the latter. So, take some time to really think about this question.

203

**Answer**  When completed, the WBS can be used any time the scope of a project needs to be reevaluated. For example:

- When there is a scope-related change request, a project manager can use the WBS, along with the project scope statement, to determine if the request is within the planned scope of the project.
- A project manager can use the WBS as part of the integrated change control process to evaluate impacts of changes that relate to scope.
- Project managers can control scope creep[11] by using the WBS to reinforce what work is to be done. (The term "scope creep" refers to scope increasing or varying from what was planned.)
- The WBS can be used as a communications tool when discussing the project with the team or the customer.
- The WBS can be used to help new team members see their roles on the project.

 There may be many WBS references on the exam. To answer these questions correctly, remember that a WBS:

- Is a graphical picture of the hierarchy of a project
- Identifies all deliverables to be completed (if it is not in the WBS, it is not part of the project)
- Is the foundation upon which a project is built
- Is very important and should exist for every project
- Ensures that the project manager thinks through all aspects of a project
- Can be reused for other projects
- Does not show dependencies

 The previous list should help you get a few more tricky questions right on the exam. Now, would you like to get one more right? Many people confuse the terms "WBS" and "decomposition." The best way to think of decomposition[12] is that decomposition is what you are doing, and a WBS is the means to do it. In other words, you decompose a project using a WBS.

 The exam may use the term "deconstruction" instead of "decomposition." Both terms mean the same thing.

## WBS Dictionary

PAGE 162  Think about how a work package is identified in a WBS. It is usually described using only one or two words. But assigning a deliverable with such a brief description to a team member allows for too much possible variation. In other words, it allows for scope creep. A WBS dictionary is the solution to this problem. This document provides a description of the work to be done for each WBS work package, and it lists the acceptance criteria for each deliverable, which ensures the resulting work matches what is needed. Therefore, a project manager can use a WBS dictionary to prevent scope creep before work even starts, rather than dealing with scope creep while the work is being done.

The WBS dictionary is an output of the Create WBS process. This document may be used as part of a work authorization system, which informs team members when their work package is going to start. A WBS dictionary can include descriptions of schedule milestones, acceptance criteria, durations, interdependencies, and other information about work packages. You can also use it to control what work is done when, to prevent scope creep, and to solidify a stakeholder's understanding of the effort required for each work package. The WBS dictionary essentially puts boundaries around what is included in a work package, similar to the way the project scope statement puts boundaries around what is included in a project. Note that some of the entries in a WBS dictionary, such as durations and interdependencies, may be filled in during iterations, rather than when it is first drafted.

A WBS dictionary may look similar to the example shown in figure 5.8.

| **WBS Dictionary** | | | |
|---|---|---|---|
| Control Account ID # | Work Package Name/Number | Date of Update | Responsible Organization/ Individual |
| Work Package Deliverable Description | | | |
| Work Involved to Produce Deliverable | | | |
| Acceptance Criteria (How to know if the deliverable/work is acceptable) | | | |
| Assumptions and Constraints | | | |
| Quality Metrics | | | |
| Technical Source Document | | | |
| Risks | | | |
| Resources Assigned | | | |
| Duration | | | |
| Schedule Milestones | | | |
| Cost | | | |
| Due Date | | | |
| Interdependencies Before this work package _____ After this work package _____ | | | |
| Approved By: Project Manager _____ Date: _____ | | | |

FIGURE 5.8 *WBS dictionary*

## Scope Baseline    PAGE 161

As discussed in the Integration Management chapter, baselines help the project manager control their projects. Baselines are simply the final and approved versions of certain pieces of the project management plan. For scope, the baseline is made up of the final versions of the WBS, the WBS dictionary, and the project scope statement that are approved at the end of planning, before the project work begins. As the work on the project is being done, the project manager reviews how the project is progressing and compares that data to the baseline by answering the following questions:

- How is my project going, and how does that compare to the baseline?
- What scope has been completed on the project?
- Does it match what is defined in the WBS, WBS dictionary, and project scope statement?

If scope is needed that is not in the baseline, a change has to be formally approved through the integrated change control process, and a new item (or items) needs to be added to the WBS, WBS dictionary, and project scope statement to show the scope addition. This updated documentation becomes the new scope baseline for the project. Any other components of the project management plan and project documents that are affected by the change in scope also need to be updated, including requirements documentation and the assumption log.

A project's (and project manager's) measurements of success include whether the project has met all the requirements, including the scope baseline. Because a project manager's performance is evaluated along with the success of the project, it is essential to use the tools, techniques, and practices of project management in the real world. These assets make it so much easier to achieve success on a project and to get a great evaluation of your own performance as the project manager.

## Validate Scope    PAGE 163

| | |
|---|---|
| **Process** | Validate Scope |
| **Process Group** | Monitoring & Controlling |
| **Knowledge Area** | Scope Management |

Many people are confused about what it means to validate scope. If you correctly understand scope validation, you can get five more questions right on the exam. These next few pages will clarify this process and help you find gaps in your knowledge.

 First, think about the name of the process. Many people think Validate Scope means confirming the validity and appropriateness of the scope definition during project planning. This is incorrect, however. The Validate Scope process actually involves frequent, planned meetings with the customer or sponsor to gain formal acceptance of deliverables during project monitoring and controlling. That's a big difference, isn't it?

Let's look at the inputs to this process. Try this exercise.

**Exercise** Can you list the inputs of Validate Scope? (Remember that the word "input" means, "What do I need before I can...?")

_____

_____

_____

_____

_____

_____

_____

## Answer

- Work must be completed and checked before each meeting with the customer; therefore, you must have what are called *verified deliverables* from the Control Quality process.

- It's helpful to have the approved scope with you when you meet with the customer, so you need the *scope baseline* from the project management plan.

- You'll also need to share information about the requirements of the project and show the customer how those requirements have been validated. This information can be found in the *requirements management plan* and the *requirements traceability matrix*.

- In addition, you should have the *requirements documentation* with you, in order to compare the requirements to actual results. You can then determine whether any action or change needs to take place.

- Other project documents, such as *quality reports* and *lessons learned*, should also be reviewed at the start of this process. Quality reports can include information about open or closed issues as well as issue management, while lessons learned can be used to improve the process of validating project deliverables.

- Another component you should have from the project management plan is the *scope management plan*, which shows the previously agreed-upon deliverables and plans for gaining formal acceptance for them.

- Lastly, you will need to refer to *work performance data* from the Direct and Manage Project Work process to assess how well product deliverables are meeting the requirements.

Did you notice that we didn't just list the inputs, but actually described how they will be used? Whenever you think about the inputs of a project management process, make sure you can describe them and explain where they come from and what they can offer. Similarly, make sure you understand how outputs flow logically from each process. For the exam, this deeper understanding will often give you more insight into situational questions, help you distinguish between relevant and extraneous data, and help you select the correct answers.

Now let's try outputs.

**Exercise**   Name the outputs of Validate Scope. (Remember that "output" means, "What will I have when I am done with…?")

**Answer**   Another way of looking at an output is to think about why you are doing this and what the expected result is. Validate Scope is done to help ensure the project is on track from the customer's point of view during the project, rather than just hoping to get final acceptance in project closure. It is better to find changes and issues during the project than at the end. The customer will either accept deliverables or make change requests. In either case, the project documents will need to be updated to reflect completion or changes. Therefore, the outputs are:

- Work performance information (analyzed work performance data)
- Accepted deliverables
- Change requests
- Updates to the lessons learned register, requirements traceability matrix, and requirements documentation

 Beyond the potentially misleading name, there are a few more tricky aspects of the Validate Scope process. First, it can be done at the end of each project phase in the project life cycle (to get formal acceptance of the phase deliverables along the way) and at other points throughout the project as part of monitoring and controlling (to get formal acceptance of any deliverables that require approval in the middle of the phase or project). Therefore, you validate scope with the customer multiple times throughout the life of a project. In a change-driven project, this will happen at the end of each iteration as part of the iteration review with the customer. Second, the difference between the Validate Scope and the Close Project or Phase processes can also be a little tricky. Whereas the Validate Scope process results in formal acceptance by the customer of interim deliverables, part of the reason for the Close Project or Phase process is to get final acceptance or sign-off from the customer for the project or phase as a whole.

The third tricky aspect is understanding how Validate Scope relates to the Control Quality process. See the high-level diagram in figure 5.9.

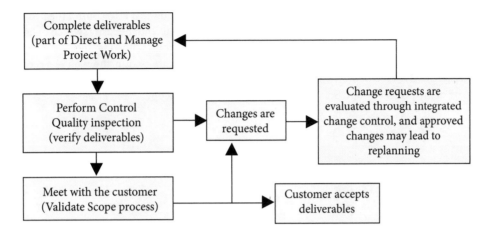

FIGURE 5.9  *Relationship between Validate Scope and Control Quality*

Although Control Quality is generally done first (to make sure the deliverable meets the requirements before it is shown to the customer), the two processes are very similar as both involve checking for the correctness of work. The difference is the focus of the effort and who is doing the checking. In Control Quality, the quality control department checks to see if the requirements specified for the deliverables are met and makes sure the work is correct. In Validate Scope, the customer checks and hopefully accepts the deliverables.

## Control Scope  PAGE 167

| | |
|---|---|
| **Process** | Control Scope |
| **Process Group** | Monitoring & Controlling |
| **Knowledge Area** | Scope Management |

Many project managers do not really control their projects. If this is true for you, you might have some gaps in your knowledge of this process. Control Scope involves measuring and assessing work performance data against the scope baseline and managing scope baseline changes. At any point in a project, the project manager must be sure that the scope is being completed according to the project management plan. As you take the exam, assume that the project manager is controlling scope in this way. Assume proper project management is being done on the project unless the question states otherwise.

To control scope, you first need to have a clear definition of the scope (the scope baseline from the project management plan), and you need to have work completed on the project. You also need to be aware of the original requirements recorded in the requirements documentation and the requirements traceability matrix (inputs to this process). You then have to measure the completed work against the scope baseline, perform data analysis, including analyzing any variances, and determine whether the variances are significant enough to warrant changes. If necessary, you would submit a change request through the Perform Integrated Change Control process to assess the impact the change would have on all aspects of the project. New work performance information may result, along with updates to the project management plan and project documents.

Remember that the Control Scope process is extremely proactive. It includes thinking about where changes to scope are coming from on the project and what can be done to prevent or remove the need for any more changes from that source. Properly using project management tools, techniques, and practices will save you from unnecessary problems throughout the life of a project.

As a project manager, your job is not to just process other people's changes; it is to control the project to the project management plan and to meet all baselines. Therefore, you should not be easily swayed or influenced, and you should not let others add scope or change scope without following the approved change management process and without ensuring the suggested changes are within the planned scope of the project. As discussed earlier, people who want work to be done will try to add it to the project whether it is logically part of the project or not. So, you must control the project scope.

## Practice Exam

1. A project has a number of deliverables that are complex and have to be assembled. As the project manager, you know the work breakdown structure will help stakeholders to see interim deliverables that will be integrated into the final project deliverables. To help manage the individual elements, you have used a work breakdown numbering system. This numbering system allows the project team to:

    A. Systematically estimate costs of work breakdown structure elements.
    B. Provide project justification.
    C. Identify the level at which individual elements are found.
    D. Use it in project management software.

2. The work breakdown structure can best be thought of as an effective aid for _____ communications.

    A. Team
    B. Project manager
    C. Customer
    D. Stakeholder

3. The product of the project has been completed and delivered to the customer by the team. They are informed by the customer that several of the deliverables are not acceptable, as they do not meet the requirements specified early in the project. The project manager and team review the requirements documentation, and are in agreement that the product deliverables meet the customer's requirements as they understand them. The project manager, who is new to the organization, seeks the advice of the project management office in determining what went wrong. After some discussion, the PMO realizes that the Validate Scope process was not performed appropriately by the project manager. Which of the following is a key output of the Validate Scope process?

    A. A more complete scope management plan
    B. Customer acceptance of project deliverables
    C. Requirements analysis
    D. Confirmation of the project scope statement

4. During project executing, a team member comes to the project manager because he is not sure what work he needs to accomplish on the project. Which of the following documents contains detailed descriptions of work packages?

    A. WBS dictionary
    B. Activity list
    C. Project scope statement
    D. Scope management plan

5. During which part of the project management process is the project scope statement created?

    A. Initiating
    B. Planning
    C. Executing
    D. Monitoring and controlling

6. The program was planned years ago, before there was a massive introduction of new technology. While planning the next project in this program, the project manager has expanded the scope management plan because as a project becomes more complex, the level of uncertainty in the scope:

A. Remains the same
B. Decreases
C. Decreases then increases
D. Increases

7. During a meeting with some of the project stakeholders, the project manager is asked to add work to the project scope. The project manager had access to correspondence about the project before the project charter was signed and remembers that the project sponsor specifically denied funding for the scope mentioned by these stakeholders. The best thing for the project manager to do is to:

A. Let the sponsor know of the stakeholders' request.
B. Evaluate the impact of adding the scope.
C. Tell the stakeholders the scope cannot be added.
D. Add the work if there is time available in the project schedule.

8. A new project manager is being mentored by a more experienced PMP-certified project manager. The new project manager is having difficulty finding enough time to manage the project because the project scope is being progressively elaborated. The PMP-certified project manager advises that the basic tools for project management, such as a work breakdown structure, can be used during project executing to assist the project manager. For which of the following can a work breakdown structure be used?

A. Communicating with the customer
B. Showing calendar dates for each work package
C. Identifying the functional managers for each team member
D. Describing the business need for the project

9. During a project team meeting, a team member suggests an enhancement to the scope that is beyond the scope of the project charter. The project manager points out that the team needs to concentrate on completing all the work and only the work required. This is an example of:

A. Change management
B. Scope management
C. Quality analysis
D. Scope decomposition

10. A project has just started the second phase, in which work packages are being created. A new team member has completed his work packages for this phase and has asked the project manager to validate the scope of his work packages. The team member is anxious to have the customer see his work packages. The project manager, although confident in this new team member, wants the team member to gain confidence after the customer sees his work packages. When should the Validate Scope process be done?

A. At the end of the project
B. At the beginning of the project
C. At the end of each phase of the project
D. During the planning processes

11. The project is mostly complete. The project has a schedule variance of 300 and a cost variance of -900. All but one of the quality control inspections have been completed, and all have met the quality requirements. All items in the issue log have been resolved. Many of the resources have been released. The sponsor is about to call a meeting to obtain product validation when the customer notifies the project manager that they want to make a major change to the scope. The project manager should:

    A. Meet with the project team to determine if this change can be made.
    B. Ask the customer for a description of the change.
    C. Explain that the change cannot be made at this point in the process.
    D. Inform management.

12. You have just joined the project management office after five years of working on projects. One of the things you want to introduce to your company is the value of creating and utilizing work breakdown structures. Some of the project managers are angry that you are asking them to do "extra work." Which of the following is the best thing you could tell the project managers to convince them to use work breakdown structures?

    A. Work breakdown structures will prevent work from slipping through the cracks.
    B. Work breakdown structures are of greater value on large projects.
    C. Work breakdown structures are best when the project involves contracts.
    D. Work breakdown structures are the only way to identify risks.

13. A new project manager has asked you for advice on creating a work breakdown structure. After you explain the process to her, she asks you what software she should use to create the WBS and what she should do with it when it is completed. You might respond that the picture is not the most valuable result of creating a WBS. The most valuable result of a WBS is:

    A. A bar chart
    B. Team buy-in
    C. Activities
    D. A list of risks

14. To manage a project effectively, work should be broken down into small pieces. Which of the following does not describe how far to decompose the work?

    A. Until it has a meaningful conclusion
    B. Until it cannot be logically subdivided further
    C. Until it can be done by one person
    D. Until it can be realistically estimated

15. A project manager may use _____ to make sure the team members clearly know what is included in each of their work packages.

    A. The project scope statement
    B. The product scope
    C. The WBS dictionary
    D. The schedule

16. On an agile software development project, the project manager asks business stakeholders to create user stories, which will be used in the development and testing of the new application. The main purpose of a user story is:

    A. To document features or functions required by stakeholders
    B. To create a record of issues encountered on the project
    C. To perform what-if analysis
    D. To communicate progress

17. The development phase of a new software product is near completion. A number of quality issues have increased the cost of building the product, but the project manager and team feel these costs will be inconsequential once the project gets to market. The next phases are testing and implementation. The project is two weeks ahead of schedule. Which of the following processes should the project manager be most concerned with before moving into the next phase?

    A. Validate Scope
    B. Control Quality
    C. Manage Communications
    D. Control Costs

18. You are managing a six-month project and have held biweekly meetings with your project stakeholders. After five-and-a-half months of work, the project is on schedule and budget, but the stakeholders are not satisfied with the deliverables. This situation will delay the project completion by one month. The most important process that could have prevented this situation is:

    A. Monitor Risks
    B. Control Schedule
    C. Define Scope
    D. Control Scope

19. All of the following are parts of the scope baseline except the:

    A. Scope management plan
    B. Project scope statement
    C. Work breakdown structure
    D. WBS dictionary

20. One of the stakeholders on the project contacts the project manager to discuss some additional scope they would like to add to the project. The project manager asks for details in writing and then works through the Control Scope process. What should the project manager do next when the evaluation of the requested scope is complete?

    A. Ask the stakeholder if any more changes are expected.
    B. Complete integrated change control.
    C. Make sure the impact of the change is understood by the stakeholder.
    D. Find out the root cause of why the scope was not identified during project planning.

21. During the completion of project work, the sponsor asks the project manager to report on how the project is going. In order to prepare the report, the project manager asks each of the team members what percent complete their work is. There is one team member who has been hard to manage from the beginning. In response to being asked what percent complete he is, the team member asks, "Percent complete of what?" Tired of such comments, the project manager reports to the team member's manager that the team member is not cooperating. Which of the following is most likely the real problem?

    A. The project manager did not get buy-in from the manager for the resources on the project.
    B. The project manager did not create an adequate reward system for team members to improve their cooperation.
    C. The project manager should have had a meeting with the team member's manager the first time the team member caused trouble.
    D. The project manager did not assign work packages.

22. Being prepared to do a complete job of developing and finalizing the scope baseline requires that you have done a thorough and timely job of identifying and analyzing stakeholders, and of collecting requirements. The development of the scope baseline can best be described as involving:

    A. The functional managers
    B. The project team
    C. All the stakeholders
    D. The business analyst

23. Which of the following is an output of the Collect Requirements process?

    A. Requirements traceability matrix
    B. Project scope statement
    C. Work breakdown structure
    D. Change requests

24. The cost performance index (CPI) on the project is 1.13, and the benefit-cost ratio is 1.2. The project scope was created by the team and stakeholders. Requirements have been changing throughout the project. No matter what the project manager has tried to accomplish in managing the project, which of the following is he most likely to face in the future?

    A. Having to cut costs on the project and increase benefits
    B. Making sure the customer has approved the project scope
    C. Not being able to measure completion of the product of the project
    D. Having to add resources to the project

25. Validate Scope is closely related to:

    A. Control Quality
    B. Sequence Activities
    C. Manage Quality
    D. Schedule Management

26. A highway renewal project you are managing appears to have some missing scope. Your understanding of the scope was that the highway was to be resurfaced. Now, one of the construction foremen has come to ask why he finds no mention of repainting the lines on the repaved road. He also wants to know if there are any guard rail replacement work packages in the project. You have seen some of the resurfaced road that is completed, with the new lines painted on them. Which of the following is most likely to have caused the misinterpretation of the project scope statement?

    A. Imprecise language
    B. Poor pattern, structure, and chronological order
    C. Variations in size of work packages or detail of work
    D. Too much detail

27. Which of the following is correct in regard to the Control Scope process?

    A. Effective scope definition can lead to a more complete project scope statement.
    B. The Control Scope process must be done before scope planning.
    C. The Control Scope process must be integrated with other control processes.
    D. Controlling the schedule is the most effective way of controlling scope.

28. Which of the following best describes the Validate Scope process?

    A. It provides assurances that the deliverable meets the specifications, is an input to the project management plan, and is an output of Control Quality.
    B. It ensures the deliverable is completed on time, ensures customer acceptance, and shows the deliverable meets specifications.
    C. It ensures customer acceptance, shows the deliverable meets specifications, and provides a chance for differences of opinion to come to light.
    D. It is an output of Control Quality, occurs before Define Scope, and ensures customer acceptance.

29. Which of the following best describes product analysis?

    A. Working with the customer to determine the product description
    B. Mathematically analyzing the quality desired for the project
    C. Gaining a better understanding of the product of the project in order to create the project scope statement
    D. Determining whether the quality standards on the project can be met

30. Which of the following best describes the difference between the Control Scope process and the Perform Integrated Change Control process?

    A. Control Scope focuses on making changes to the product scope, and Perform Integrated Change Control focuses on making changes to integration.
    B. Control Scope focuses on controlling the scope of the project, and Perform Integrated Change Control focuses on determining the impact of a change of scope on time, cost, quality, risk, resources, and customer satisfaction.
    C. Control Scope focuses on controlling the scope of the project, and Perform Integrated Change Control focuses on making changes to integration.
    D. Control Scope focuses on making changes to the product scope, and Perform Integrated Change Control focuses on determining the impact of a change to scope, time, cost, quality, risk, resources, and customer satisfaction.

31. The project was tasked to develop a new software to be used by three sales channels of an auto parts company. The project was consistently on time and within budget, and the stakeholders approved prototypes of the software. However, when the completed software was installed and beta tested, a problem was discovered. Although the software performed as expected on in-store and call center–assisted purchases, it was found to be incompatible with other software necessary to complete online transactions. Therefore, the customer refused to accept the final deliverable, and the team was left to find a new software package that would accommodate all the customer's needs.

    Which of the following did the team not do?

    A. Collect requirements from the right stakeholders.
    B. Test interim deliverables.
    C. Control stakeholder engagement.
    D. Accurately define product scope.

# Answers

1. **Answer** C

   **Explanation** The numbering system allows team members to quickly identify the level in the work breakdown structure where the specific element is found. It also helps to locate the element in the WBS dictionary.

2. **Answer** D

   **Explanation** The term "stakeholder" encompasses all the other choices. In this case, it is the best answer since the WBS can be used as a communications tool for all stakeholders to see what is included in the project.

3. **Answer** B

   **Explanation** The output of the Validate Scope process is customer acceptance of project deliverables. The other choices all happen during project planning, well before the time the Validate Scope process takes place.

4. **Answer** A

   **Explanation** The WBS dictionary defines each element in the WBS. Therefore, descriptions of the work packages are in the WBS dictionary. Activity lists may identify the work package they relate to, but they do not contain detailed descriptions of the work packages. The project scope statement defines the project scope, but it does not describe the work a team member is assigned. The scope management plan describes how scope will be planned, managed, and controlled. It does not include a description of each work package.

5. **Answer** B

   **Explanation** The project scope statement is an output of the Define Scope process, which occurs during project planning.

6. **Answer** D

   **Explanation** Not all questions will be difficult. The level of uncertainty in scope increases based on the scale of effort required to identify all the scope. On larger projects, it is more difficult to catch everything.

7. **Answer** C

   **Explanation** Although one could let the sponsor know about the stakeholders' request, the best choice listed would be to say no, as this was already considered. An even better choice would be to find the root cause of the problem, but that choice is not offered here.

8. **Answer** A

   **Explanation** A WBS does not show dates or responsibility assignments. The business need is described in the project charter. In this situation, the project scope is being fine-tuned. It would save the project manager time in effectively managing progressive elaboration if the WBS was used as a communications tool. Using the WBS helps ensure everyone (including the customer) understands the scope of the work.

9. **Answer** B

   **Explanation** The team member is suggesting an enhancement that is outside the scope of the project charter. Scope management involves focusing on doing all the work and only the work in the project management plan that meets the objectives of the project charter. The project manager is performing scope management.

10. **Answer** C

    **Explanation** The Validate Scope process occurs during project monitoring and controlling. It is done at the end of each project phase to get approval for phase deliverables, as well as at other points to get approval for interim deliverables.

11. **Answer** B

    **Explanation** Do not jump into the problem without thinking. The customer only notified the project manager that they want to make a change. They did not describe the change. The project manager should not say no until they know more about the potential change, nor should the project manager go to management without more information. The project manager must understand the nature of the change and have time to evaluate the impact of that change before doing anything else. Of these choices, the first thing to do is to determine what the change is. The project manager might then analyze the potential change with the team, but only if their input is required.

12. **Answer** A

    **Explanation** Work breakdown structures are required on projects of every size, regardless of whether contracts are involved. Work breakdown structures can be used to help identify risks, but risks can be identified using other methods as well. Preventing work from being forgotten (slipping through the cracks) is one of the main reasons the tool is used, and is the best choice offered here.

13. **Answer** B

    **Explanation** The WBS is an input to all of these choices. However, team buy-in is a direct result of the WBS creation process, while the other choices use the WBS to assist in their completion. Involving the team in creating the WBS provides project team members with an understanding of where their pieces fit into the overall project management plan and gives them an indication of the impact of their work on the project as a whole.

14. **Answer** C

    **Explanation** The lowest level of the WBS is a work package, which can be completed by more than one person. The other choices are aspects of a work package.

15. **Answer** C

    **Explanation** The project scope statement describes work on a high-level basis. Work packages need to be specific to enable team members to complete their work without gold plating. The product scope does not tell team members what work is assigned to them. The team should have a copy of the schedule, but a schedule does not show them what work is included in each of their work packages. Work packages are described in the WBS dictionary. NOTE: Do not think of the WBS dictionary as a dictionary of terms.

16. **Answer** A

    **Explanation** A user story is a way of stating a requirement, often using the following format: As a <role>, I want <functionality/goal>, so that <business benefit/motivation>. User stories may be developed in facilitation sessions or as part of other requirements-gathering activities.

17. **Answer** A

    **Explanation** The Validate Scope process deals with acceptance by the customer. Without this acceptance, the project manager will not be able to move into the next project phase.

18. **Answer** C

    **Explanation** Monitor Risks, Control Schedule, and Control Scope are monitoring and controlling processes. This situation asks how to prevent the problem, which would have been done during planning. The project deliverables are defined in the Define Scope process, which is a part of project planning. Good planning reduces the likelihood of a situation like the one described in the question, by including the right people and spending adequate time clarifying the project scope.

19. **Answer** A

    **Explanation** The scope baseline includes the WBS, WBS dictionary, and the project scope statement. The scope management plan is not part of the scope baseline.

20. **Answer** B

    **Explanation** Notice that there are many things the project manager could do listed in the choices; however, the question asks what the project manager should do next. Management of the change is not complete when the Control Scope process is completed. It is important to look at the impact of the change on other parts of the project, such as schedule and budget. Therefore, performing integrated change control is the best thing to do next. This would probably be followed by making sure the impact of the change is understood by the stakeholder, then determining why this scope was not identified in planning, and asking the stakeholder if more changes are expected.

21. **Answer** D

    **Explanation** The project manager is not losing resources (which is implied by not getting the manager's buy-in). Although a reward system would help with cooperation, the real problem here is not cooperation. Meeting with the team member and his manager cannot be the answer because it also does not solve the problem at hand (the team member not knowing what he is to do). If you selected this choice, be very careful! You can get 10 to 20 questions wrong on the exam simply because you do not see the real problem! The whole discussion of the team member and his actions is a distractor. The real problem in this scenario is not that the team member is being uncooperative. He is asking a question that many team members want to ask in the real world. "How can I tell you how things are going if I do not know what work I am being asked to do?" The real problem is the lack of a WBS and work packages. If there were a WBS and work packages for the project, the team member would not have to ask such a question.

22. **Answer** B

    **Explanation** After obtaining input from the customer and other stakeholders, the project team is responsible for developing the scope baseline. Remember that the scope baseline includes the WBS, WBS dictionary, and project scope statement.

23. **Answer** A

    **Explanation** The project scope statement is an output of the Define Scope process. The work breakdown structure is an output of the Create WBS process. Scope change requests are outputs of the Validate Scope and Control Scope processes. The requirements traceability matrix is an output of the Collect Requirements process, and is used to track the requirements throughout the life of the project.

24. **Answer** C

    **Explanation** There are many pieces of data in this question that are distractors from the real issue. Though it is common to have to cut costs and add resources to a project, nothing in the question should lead you to think these will be required in this situation. Customers do not generally approve the project scope (what you are going to do to complete their requirements); instead, they approve the product scope (their requirements). Since requirements are used to measure the completion of the product of the project, not having complete requirements will make such measurement impossible.

25. **Answer**  A

    **Explanation**  Control Quality checks for correctness, and Validate Scope checks for acceptance.

26. **Answer**  A

    **Explanation**  Much of the work on the project is dictated by the project scope statement. Any imprecision in such a key document will lead to differing interpretations.

27. **Answer**  C

    **Explanation**  Though it is correct that effective scope definition can lead to a more complete project scope statement, this cannot be the answer, because it does not deal with control. Scope planning occurs before the Control Scope process, not after it. Controlling the schedule is not the best way to control scope, so that is not the best answer. The control processes do not act in isolation. A change to one will most likely affect the others. Therefore, the need to integrate the Control Scope process with other control processes is the best answer.

28. **Answer**  C

    **Explanation**  The project management plan is completed before the Validate Scope process. The Validate Scope process does not deal with time, but rather with acceptance. The Validate Scope process does not occur before the Define Scope process. The choice stating that the Validate Scope process ensures customer acceptance, shows the deliverable meets specifications, and provides a chance for differences of opinion to come to light is entirely correct, making that the best answer.

29. **Answer**  C

    **Explanation**  You need to have a product description before you can do product analysis. Analyzing the level of quality desired is related to the Plan Quality Management process. Determining whether the quality standards on the project can be met is done in the Manage Quality process. Product analysis includes gaining a better understanding of the product of the project in order to create the project scope statement.

30. **Answer**  B

    **Explanation**  Notice how the choices are similar to each other? Simply look at the first part of each choice "Control Scope focuses on . . ." and see which version of the first part of the statement is correct. Then read the second part of each choice. The only statement that is entirely correct is: Control Scope focuses on controlling the scope of the project, and Perform Integrated Change Control focuses on determining the impact of a change of scope on time, cost, quality, risk, resources, and customer satisfaction.

31. **Answer**  B

    **Explanation**  Based on the scenario presented, the team was aware of the high-level requirement that the software perform in all three sales channels. It seems that they had collected requirements from the right stakeholders, and accurately defined the scope. Somehow in the development of the software, an important requirement was overlooked, or was not properly developed. If the software had been tested in all three channels before it was delivered to the customer, the issue would have been identified, and the change control process to fix the problem would have been followed. Testing is an important aspect of the Control Scope process.

# Schedule Management

## SIX

This chapter can be difficult for those who do not realize that an unrealistic schedule is the project manager's fault. Yes, it's true! One of the key responsibilities of a project manager is ensuring that the needed end date for a project can be met and to create options to make it happen—all before project executing starts. If you know the many options for compressing a project schedule, and understand that a project schedule must be realistic before project executing begins, this chapter should not be difficult for you.

To answer schedule management questions correctly, you should thoroughly understand the process of scheduling a project. Although most project managers use some type of software to assist with scheduling, the exam has often required test takers to manually draw network diagrams to answer questions about network diagrams and scheduling. Therefore, you need to know some things that normally go on behind the scenes when using project management software.

Watch out! The term "project management software" can be misleading. Software can be extremely helpful and save you time scheduling, analyzing what-if scenarios, and performing status reporting functions, particularly on large projects, but you cannot rely on it to manage a project. When taking the exam—and when working on projects—you must recognize the limitations of software. Software does not take into account the unique nature of each project management process. Relying on software may limit your understanding of project management, which could cause you problems in identifying the best answer choices on the exam.

Make sure you recognize where each schedule management process falls within the project management process, and check your knowledge as you proceed through this chapter. Particularly if you rely on software on your projects, you may not have the knowledge and experience in schedule management, such as performing schedule analysis and creating network diagrams, that you will need to pass the exam.

## QUICKTEST

- Schedule management process
- Schedule baseline
- Schedule compression
  - Crashing
  - Fast tracking
- Activity list
- Network diagram
- Dependencies
  - Mandatory
  - Discretionary
  - External
  - Internal
- Precedence diagramming method (PDM)
- Critical path
- Float (Schedule flexibility)
  - Total float
  - Free float
  - Project float
- Three-point estimating
  - Beta distribution
  - Triangular distribution
- Monte Carlo analysis
- Bar charts
- Schedule model
- Project management information systems (PMIS)
- Schedule management plan
- Critical path method
- Near-critical path
- Leads and lags
- Milestones, milestone list, and charts
- Resource breakdown structure (RBS)
- Reserve analysis
- Padding
- Analogous estimating
- Parametric estimating
- Heuristics
- Activity attributes
- Reestimating
- Rolling wave planning
- Progressive elaboration
- Alternatives analysis

# Schedule Management S I X

| INITIATING | PLANNING (This is the only process group with a set order.) | EXECUTING | MONITORING & CONTROLLING | CLOSING |
|---|---|---|---|---|
| Select project manager | **Determine development approach, life cycle, and how you will plan for each knowledge area** | Execute work according to the project management plan | **Take action to monitor and control the project** | Confirm work is done to requirements |
| Determine company culture and existing systems | Define and prioritize requirements | Produce product deliverables (product scope) | **Measure performance against performance measurement baseline** | Complete final procurement closure |
| Collect processes, procedures, and historical information | Create project scope statement | Gather work performance data | **Measure performance against other metrics in the project management plan** | Gain final acceptance of product |
| Divide large projects into phases or smaller projects | Assess what to purchase and create procurement documents | Request changes | **Analyze and evaluate data and performance** | Complete financial closure |
| Understand business case and benefits management plan | Determine planning team | Implement only approved changes | **Determine if variances warrant a corrective action or other change request(s)** | Hand off completed product |
| Uncover initial requirements, assumptions, risks, constraints, and existing agreements | Create WBS and WBS dictionary | Continuously improve; perform progressive elaboration | **Influence factors that cause change** | Solicit customer's feedback about the project |
| Assess project and product feasibility within the given constraints | **Create activity list** | Follow processes | **Request changes** | Complete final performance reporting |
| Create measurable objectives and success criteria | **Create network diagram** | Determine whether quality plan and processes are correct and effective | Perform integrated change control | Index and archive records |
| Develop project charter | Estimate resource requirements | Perform quality audits and issue quality reports | Approve or reject changes | Gather final lessons learned and update knowledge bases |
| Identify stakeholders and determine their expectations, interest, influence, and impact | **Estimate activity durations and costs** | Acquire final team and physical resources | **Update project management plan and project documents** | |
| Request changes | **Determine critical path** | Manage people | Inform stakeholders of all change request results | |
| Develop assumption log | **Develop schedule** | Evaluate team and individual performance; provide training | Monitor stakeholder engagement | |
| Develop stakeholder register | Develop budget | Hold team-building activities | Confirm configuration compliance | |
| | Determine quality standards, processes, and metrics | Give recognition and rewards | **Create forecasts** | |
| | **Determine team charter and all roles and responsibilities** | Use issue logs | Gain customer's acceptance of interim deliverables | |
| | Plan communications and stakeholder engagement | Facilitate conflict resolution | Perform quality control | |
| | Perform risk identification, qualitative and quantitative risk analysis, and risk response planning | Release resources as work is completed | Perform risk reviews, reassessments, and audits | |
| | **Go back—iterations** | Send and receive information, and solicit feedback | Manage reserves | |
| | Finalize procurement strategy and documents | Report on project performance | Manage, evaluate, and close procurements | |
| | Create change and configuration management plans | Facilitate stakeholder engagement and manage expectations | Evaluate use of physical resources | |
| | **Finalize all management plans** | Hold meetings | | |
| | **Develop realistic and sufficient project management plan and baselines** | Evaluate sellers; negotiate and contract with sellers | | |
| | Gain formal approval of the plan | Use and share project knowledge | | |
| | Hold kickoff meeting | Execute contingency plans | | |
| | **Request changes** | Update project management plan and project documents | | |

**Rita's Process Chart™
Schedule Management**
Where are we in the project management process?

© 2018 RMC Publications, Inc.™ • 952.846.4484 • info@rmcls.com • www.rmcls.com

The following should help you understand how each part of schedule management fits into the overall project management process:

| The Schedule Management Process | Done During |
| --- | --- |
| Plan Schedule Management | Planning process group |
| Define Activities | Planning process group |
| Sequence Activities | Planning process group |
| Estimate Activity Durations | Planning process group |
| Develop Schedule | Planning process group |
| Control Schedule | Monitoring and controlling process group |

## Plan Schedule Management    PAGE 179

**Process** Plan Schedule Management
**Process Group** Planning
**Knowledge Area** Schedule Management

The Plan Schedule Management process involves documenting how you will plan, manage, and control the project to the schedule baseline, and how you will manage schedule variances. Many project managers just work on the project and hope the project meets the deadline, but proper schedule management requires you to develop and follow a plan, measuring progress along the way. So as part of planning, you need to determine in advance what the measures of performance will be, how and when you will capture the data you need to evaluate schedule performance, how you will use the data to keep the project on track, and what you will do when variances occur. Plan Schedule Management answers questions such as: "Who will be involved, and what approach will we take to plan the schedule for the project?" and "What processes and procedures will we use to create the schedule?"

The project life cycle and development approach agreed on in the Develop Project Management plan process (in integration management) will influence the level and type of schedule management planning you will do on a project. You will also consider existing enterprise environmental factors. Is there a work authorization system in place for the project to use? Does the organization have a preferred project management software to use for scheduling? If not, will the work of the project include creating a work authorization system or selecting a scheduling software product? How does the company culture and the overall structure of the organization impact the work of scheduling the project?

Also keep in mind that expert judgment and data analysis techniques, such as alternatives analysis, may be used in planning the methodology you will use to arrive at a final schedule. To plan the schedule, you might also need to review the project charter or hold meetings that include the project sponsor, team members, and other stakeholders.

## Schedule Management Plan    PAGE 181    The key output of this process is a schedule management plan, which can be formal or informal. It is part of the project management plan, and it helps make the estimating and schedule development process faster by specifying the following:

- The scheduling methodology and scheduling software to be used on the project
- Rules for how estimates should be stated; for example, should estimates be in hours, days, or weeks? Should estimators identify both the effort (the amount of labor involved in completing an activity; for example, 12 hours) and duration (the amount of work periods the effort will span; for example, 1.5 days) needed to complete an activity?
- A schedule baseline for measuring against as part of project monitoring and controlling
- A threshold for acceptable variance

- Performance measures that will be used on the project, to identify variances early
- A plan for how schedule variances will be managed
- A process for determining whether a variance must be acted upon
- Identification of schedule change control procedures
- Types of reports required on the project relating to schedule
- Formats and frequency of project reporting
- The length of releases and iterations (in an adaptive life cycle)

## Define Activities    PAGE 183

> **Process** Define Activities
> **Process Group** Planning
> **Knowledge Area** Schedule Management

This process involves taking the work packages created in the WBS and decomposing them into the activities that are required to produce the work package deliverables and thus achieve the project objectives. The activities should be at a level small enough to estimate, schedule, monitor, and control. These activities are then sequenced in the next process: Sequence Activities. (Note that breaking down the project work into the work packages in the WBS is part of scope management, and the identification of activities is part of schedule management.)

Defining activities is not always done as a separate process. Many project managers combine this effort with creating a WBS and WBS dictionary; they decompose work packages into the activities required to produce them, rather than stopping at the work package level.

So what do you need in order to define activities? The schedule management plan, created in the previous process, gives you important information about the approved methodology for scheduling. The scope baseline (project scope statement, WBS, and WBS dictionary) from scope management provides information about what is included in your project scope. This is the work you will now break down into project activities. You may also refer to organizational process assets including existing templates, historical information, such as activity lists from other similar projects, and any standards, such as a prescribed scheduling methodology. Involving the team in this process helps define the activities completely and accurately and therefore makes the estimates, created later in the planning process, more accurate.

**TRICKS OF THE TRADE®** Decomposition is used in the Define Activities process in schedule management, as well as in the Create WBS process in scope management. When you see the term used on the exam, it is important to look at the context of what is being decomposed. When deliverables are being decomposed into smaller deliverables, or work packages, you know the question is referring to the Create WBS process. When work packages are being decomposed into the activities to produce them, the question is referring to the Define Activities process. Be sure to choose an answer choice that aligns with the appropriate process.

## Rolling Wave Planning[1]

Have you ever worked on a project that seemed to have too many unknown components to adequately break down the work and schedule it? Be careful—when that is the case, you might really have more than one project (see the definition of a project in the Project Management Framework chapter). Or, it might simply be a project for which it is better to not plan the entire project to the smallest detail in advance, but instead to plan to a higher level and then develop more detailed plans when the work is to be done. This practice is called "rolling wave planning" and is a form of progressive elaboration. Remember that progressive elaboration refers to the process of clarifying and refining plans as the project progresses. With this method, you plan activities to the detail needed to manage the work just before you are ready to start that part of the project. This technique is used to varying degrees on both change-driven and plan-driven projects.

Iterations of rolling wave planning during the project may result in additional activities being added, and in the further elaboration of other activities. Therefore, rolling wave planning may create the need for updates to the project management plan, specifically the schedule, scope, and/or cost baselines. These changes require integrated change control, beginning with a change request.

But remember—the option of rolling wave planning does not eliminate the need to ensure all the scope that can be known is known before starting work!

**Milestones** The Define Activities process also involves determining milestones to use on the project. Milestones are significant events within the project schedule. They are not work activities, and have no duration. For example, a completed design, customer-imposed due dates for interim deliverables, or a company-required checkpoint, phase gate, or stage gate could be milestones. Initial milestones are documented in the project charter. The project manager can also insert milestones as checkpoints to help control the project. If a milestone in the schedule is reached and any of the planned work has not been completed, it indicates the project is not progressing as planned. The milestone list is part of the project documents.

When completed, the Define Activities process results in an activity list, which includes all activities required to complete the project, and activity attributes, or details regarding project activities. At this time, known attributes may be limited to the activity name and ID number. As the project progresses, additional attributes—such as planned completion date, leads and lags, and predecessor and successor activities—may be added.

Define Activities is one of only a few planning processes with an output of change requests specifically listed in the *PMBOK® Guide*. Refer back to the discussion of rolling wave planning, and you will see that, as the project progresses, early planning efforts may need to be iterated, potentially resulting in changes to the project baselines.

## Sequence Activities PAGE 187

| | |
|---|---|
| **Process** | Sequence Activities |
| **Process Group** | Planning |
| **Knowledge Area** | Schedule Management |

The next process involves taking the activities and sequencing them in the order in which the work will be performed. The result is a network diagram (also referred to as a project schedule network diagram), which is illustrated in figure 6.1. There are several exercises designed to help you learn how to draw and interpret network diagrams later in this chapter.

If you need extra help understanding how to create and interpret network diagrams, please visit the website that accompanies this book: rmcls.com/extras.

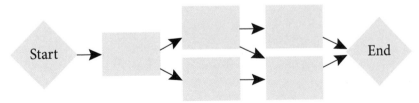

FIGURE 6.1 *Network diagram*

225

For the exam, know that in its pure form, the network diagram shows just dependencies (logical relationships). If activity duration estimates (estimates) and leads and lags are added to the diagram later in the schedule management process, it can also show the critical path. If plotted out against time (or placed against a calendar-based scale), the network diagram is a time-scaled schedule network diagram.

Factors that may influence dependencies in the sequencing of activities include the assumption log, activity attributes, and milestone list.

## Methods to Draw Network Diagrams[2]
In the past, the arrow diagramming method[3] (ADM) and the graphical evaluation and review technique (GERT)[4] method were commonly used to draw network diagrams. Today most network diagrams are created using the precedence diagramming method (PDM).

### Precedence Diagramming Method (PDM)[5]
In this method, nodes (or boxes) are used to represent activities, and arrows show activity dependencies, as shown in figure 6.2.

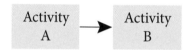

FIGURE 6.2    *Precedence diagramming method*

This type of drawing can have four types of logical relationships between activities (see fig. 6.3):

- **Finish-to-start (FS)** An activity must finish before the successor can start. This is the most commonly used relationship. Example: You must finish digging a hole before you can start the next activity of planting a tree.

- **Start-to-start (SS)** An activity must start before the successor can start. Example: You must start designing and wait for two weeks' lag in order to have enough of the design completed to start coding.

- **Finish-to-finish (FF)** An activity must finish before the successor can finish. Example: You must finish testing before you can finish documentation.

- **Start-to-finish (SF)** An activity must start before the successor can finish. This dependency is rarely used.

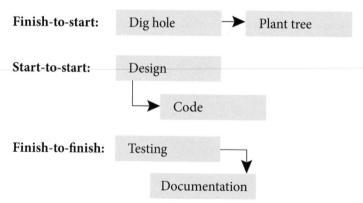

FIGURE 6.3    *Finish-to-start, start-to-start, and finish-to-finish dependencies*

226

## Types of Dependencies[6]

The sequence of activities is determined based on the following dependencies:

- **Mandatory dependency (hard logic)** A mandatory dependency is inherent in the nature of the work (for example, you must design before you can construct) or is required by a contract.
- **Discretionary dependency (preferred, preferential, or soft logic)** This is the way an organization has chosen to have work performed. There are other ways it could be done, but this is the preferred approach. Whereas you cannot easily change the other types of dependencies, you can change a discretionary dependency if necessary. Discretionary dependencies are important when analyzing how to compress the schedule to decrease the project duration (fast track the project).
- **External dependency** This dependency is based on the needs or desires of a party outside the project (for example, government or suppliers).
- **Internal dependency** This dependency is based on the needs of the project and may be something the project team can control.

More than one dependency can be identified for the same work. Combinations include mandatory external, mandatory internal, discretionary external, and discretionary internal.

The project team identifies mandatory and discretionary dependencies; the project manager identifies external and internal dependencies. (Remember, when we use the term "project manager" in this book, we're referring to anyone doing project management activities on the project, which could include not just the lead project manager but also supporting members of the project management team.)

## Leads and Lags    PAGE 192

A lead may be used to indicate that an activity can start before its predecessor activity is completed. For example, web page design might be able to start five days before the database design is finished. A lag is waiting time inserted between activities, such as needing to wait three days after pouring concrete before constructing the frame for a house. When project activities are first being sequenced, the duration of the activities, and required leads and lags, may be uncertain.

Also keep in mind, when creating complex project schedule network diagrams that include leads and lags as well as other dependencies, an automated scheduling system that is part of the PMIS can be used. This is especially helpful on large projects.

## Project Schedule Network Diagram    PAGE 194

A project schedule network diagram is an image depicting the flow of project activities in the logical order in which they will be performed. All activities after Start should be connected to at least one predecessor activity. All activities on the network diagram before Finish should be connected to at least one successor activity. In addition to sequencing activities, the network diagram helps you to plan which activities can be completed in parallel and to see where leads or lags are required. Of course, the more complex the project, the more likely it is that activities will overlap. When an activity has two or more activities directly preceding it, this is referred to as path convergence. When an activity has two or more successor activities directly following it, this is referred to as path divergence. Both path convergence and path divergence are indicators of greater risk within the impacted activities.

Now it's time to test your knowledge. Rather than just knowing what a network diagram is, you will be expected to answer harder, more sophisticated questions when taking the exam. You need to have worked with network diagrams to accurately answer such questions. See how you do with the next exercise.

**Exercise**　Describe how the network diagram can help you on the project.

_____

_____

_____

_____

_____

_____

_____

_____

**Answer**　You should know that network diagrams can be used in many ways. For example, they can be used to:

- Help justify your time estimate for the project.
- Aid in effectively planning, organizing, and controlling the project.
- Show interdependencies of all activities, and thereby identify riskier activities.
- Show workflow so the team will know what activities need to happen in a specific sequence.
- Identify opportunities to compress the schedule in planning and throughout the life of the project (explained later in this chapter).
- Show project progress (when used for controlling the schedule and reporting).

Project schedule network diagrams may also be referred to as network diagrams or activity network diagrams.

In addition to a network diagram, the Sequence Activities process may result in updates to project documents such as the activity list, activity attributes, assumption log, and the milestone list. Sequencing the activities can also reveal new risks, resulting in changes to the risk register.

**TRICKS OF THE TRADE®** **Things to Know about Estimating for the Exam**　The Estimate Activity Durations and the Estimate Costs process (see the Cost Management chapter) as well as the Estimate Activity Resources process (see the Resource Management chapter) all involve estimating. The following are important points to understand about estimating for the exam:

- Management plans provide the approach for estimating.
- The project manager and team may use one or many techniques to estimate project work.
- Estimating should be based on a WBS to improve accuracy.
- Duration, cost, and resource estimates are interrelated; for example, duration and resource estimates could impact cost estimates.
- Identified risks must be considered when estimating the duration, cost, and resource requirements of project work.

228

- Estimating duration, cost, and resource requirements may uncover additional, previously unidentified risks.
- Whenever possible, estimating should be done by the person doing the work (or the person most familiar with the work) to improve accuracy.
- Historical information from past projects (part of organizational process assets) is key to improving estimates.
- Estimates are more accurate if smaller-size work components are estimated.
- A project manager should never just accept constraints from management, but should instead analyze the needs of the project, develop estimates with input from the team members doing the work when possible, and reconcile any differences to produce a realistic plan.
- The project manager may periodically recalculate the estimate to complete (ETC) for the project to make sure adequate time, funds, and resources, are available for the project.
- Plans based on estimates should be revised, with approved changes, during completion of the work, as necessary.
- There is a process for creating the most accurate estimate possible.
- Padding estimates is not an acceptable project management practice.
- The project manager must meet any agreed-upon estimates.
- Estimates must be reviewed when they are received from team members or sellers to see if they are reasonable and to check for padding and risks.
- Estimates must be kept realistic through the life of the project by reestimating and reviewing them periodically.
- Estimates can be impacted by reducing or eliminating risks.
- The project manager has a professional responsibility to provide estimates that are as accurate as feasible and to maintain the integrity of those estimates throughout the life of the project.

In the past, the exam has focused on the practices required to produce good estimates, more than it has focused on calculations. Therefore, make sure you take some time to think about these points. Remember, incorrect project management practices will be listed as choices on the exam. Project managers who do not adequately understand and manage their projects in this way have difficulty on the exam.

## Estimate Activity Durations   PAGE 195

> **Process** Estimate Activity Durations
> **Process Group** Planning
> **Knowledge Area** Schedule Management

When the activities have been defined and sequenced, the next step
is to estimate how long each activity will take. This is the Estimate Activity Durations process. When possible, the estimators should be those who will be doing the work. On large projects, however, the estimators are more often the members of the project management team, as it is known during planning, who are most familiar with the work that needs to be done. To come up with realistic time estimates, these individuals need to have access to the following inputs:

- **Activity list and activity attributes** The relevant inputs may include the time for required leads or lags between activities, which must be factored into duration estimates.
- **Assumption log** Assumptions or constraints that contribute to risk within the activities to be estimated can be found in the assumption log.
- **Lessons learned register**[7] Information relevant to estimating the duration of schedule activities include lessons learned from earlier in the current project or from past, similar projects performed by the organization.

229

- **Resource breakdown structure**[8]  Created in the Estimate Activity Resources process of Resource Management, the resource breakdown structure represents categories of resources required for the project.

- **Resource requirements**  These requirements indicate the skill levels of resources required to perform specific project work.

- **Project team assignments**  Project team assignments should include the number and experience level of individuals who have been committed to the project.

- **Resource calendars**  These calendars provide information on when key resources with specialized skills needed for project activities will be available. If the resources are not available within the timeframe of your project, you may need to add extra time to some activity estimates, allowing for less experienced resources to do the work.

- **Risk register**  The risk register may include identified threats and/or opportunities that should be reflected in the estimates.

Now let's think about how estimating works on your projects for a moment. Do your team members feel like this?

This response is an example of padding. Do you consider this practice normal or appropriate? It is not. Many project managers rely on this practice, but padding undermines the professional responsibility of a project manager to develop a realistic schedule and budget. This is another point that is essential to understand for the exam.

So what is wrong with padding? A pad is extra time or cost added to an estimate because the estimator does not have enough information.

In cases where the estimator has many unknowns and the information required to clarify the unknowns is unavailable, the potential need for additional time or funds should be addressed with reserves through the risk management process. Through risk management, the uncertainties are turned into identifiable opportunities and threats (risks). They should not remain hidden; instead, estimators need to identify and openly address uncertainties with the project manager.

What happens if all or many of your estimates are padded? Quite simply, you have a schedule or budget that no one believes. And if that is the case, why even bother creating a schedule or a budget? In the real world, we need the schedule and the budget to manage the project against. So we need them to be as believable and realistic as possible, and we need to adhere to them. To be a successful project manager, you need to be able to meet the agreed-upon project completion date and budget. It is important to understand that padding is a sign of poor project management and that it can damage your reputation and the credibility of the project management profession as a whole.

You may see questions on the exam that include padding as a solution to an estimating scenario. Just remember, padding is never a viable way to plan a project or to solve a problem—on the exam or in the real world!

In a properly managed project, the estimators have a WBS and may even have helped create it. They also have a description of each work package (the WBS dictionary) and may have helped create that as well. They may even have helped create the activity list from the work packages. They know there will be time and cost reserves on the project that will be determined through actual calculations—not arbitrary guesses—to address identified risks or unknowns. With all that information, they should not need to pad their estimates!

If you allow padding on your projects now, and consider it to be an appropriate practice, please make sure you reread this section and carefully review the Risk Management chapter. You need to recognize the difference between padding and creating reserves, and understand how padding can be detrimental to your project. The exam questions in this area are designed to identify those who make common project management errors, such as padding.

## How Is Estimating Done?
As stated earlier in this chapter, those who will be doing the work, or those most familiar with the activities to be done, should create the activity estimates. They may use one or many techniques, which were identified in the schedule management plan.

Before we discuss estimating techniques, let's look at the project manager's role in this process. If other people are creating the estimates, then what is the project manager doing?

The role of the project manager in estimating is to:
- Provide the team with enough information to properly estimate each activity.
- Let those doing the estimating know how refined their estimates must be.
- Complete a sanity check of the estimates.
- Prevent padding.
- Formulate a reserve (more on this later—in the reserve analysis discussion in this section and in the Risk Management chapter).
- Make sure assumptions made during estimating are recorded for later review.

Now let's look at estimating techniques that may be used on a project.

## One-Point Estimating
When estimating time using a one-point estimate, the estimator submits one estimate per activity. For example, the person doing the estimating says that the activity will take five weeks. The time estimate may be based on expert judgment or historical information, or it could be just a guess. As a result, this technique can be problematic.

Although one-point estimating is often not the best method to use, it is an easy way to illustrate how to draw network diagrams and find the critical path. Using one-point estimates also allows for quick calculation on the exam and demonstrates that you understand concepts such as the critical path. You may see references to one-point estimating on the exam, as shown in the exercises later in this chapter.

One-point estimating can have the following negative effects on the project:
- Being limited to making a one-point estimate may encourage people to pad their estimates.
- A one-point estimate doesn't provide the project manager with important information about risks and uncertainties they need in order to better plan and control the project.
- One-point estimating can result in a schedule that no one believes in, thus decreasing buy-in to the project management process.
- When a person uses one-point estimating to develop an estimate that an activity will take 20 days and it is completed in 15 days, it can make the person who provided the estimate look unreliable.

### Analogous Estimating[9] (Top-Down)   PAGE 200   Applicable to duration, cost, and resource estimating, analogous estimating uses expert judgment and historical information to predict the future. Management or the sponsor might use analogous estimating to create the overall project constraint/estimate given to the project manager as the project is chartered. The project manager may use analogous estimating at the project level, using historical data from past, similar projects. (For example, the last five projects similar to this one each took eight months, so this one should as well.) Analogous estimating can also be used at the activity level, if the activity has been done on previous projects and if there is substantial historical data to support the accuracy of such an estimate. (For example, the last two times this activity was completed each took three days; since we have no other information to go on, we will use three days as the estimate for this activity and review the estimate when more details become available.) Be aware for the exam that analogous estimating can be done at various times, and the level of accuracy depends on how closely the project or activity matches the historical data used.

### Parametric Estimating   PAGE 200   Parametric estimating involves creating a mathematical equation using data from historical records or other sources, such as industry requirements or standard metrics, to create estimates. The technique analyzes relationships between historical data and other variables to estimate duration or cost. It can be applied to some or all the activities within a project. For example, when estimating activity duration, the estimator may use measures such as time per line of code, time per linear meter, or time per installation. When used in cost estimating, the measures include cost as one of the variables. So the measures would be cost per line of code, cost per linear meter, etc.

An estimator might create parametric estimates using the following:

- **Regression analysis[10] (scatter diagram)**  This diagram tracks two variables to see if they are related; the diagram is then used to create a mathematical formula to use in future parametric estimating (see fig. 6.4).

- **Learning curve**  Example: The 100th room painted will take less time than the first room because of improved efficiency.

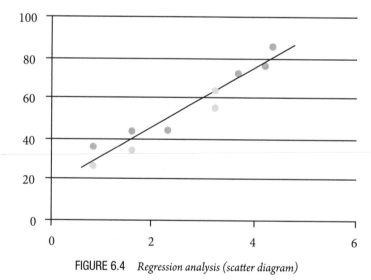

FIGURE 6.4   *Regression analysis (scatter diagram)*

### Heuristics[11]   A heuristic means a generally accepted rule, or best practice. An example of a heuristic is the 80/20 rule. A schedule heuristic might be, "Design work is always 15 percent of the total project length." The results of parametric estimating can become heuristics.

232

## Three-Point Estimating[12]  PAGE 201

Statistically, there is a very small probability of completing a project on exactly any one date. As we know, things do not always go according to plan. Therefore, it is often best to state estimates in a range using three-point estimates. Analyzing what could go right (opportunities) and what could go wrong (threats) can help estimators determine an expected range for each activity. By analyzing this range of time or cost estimates, the project manager can better understand the potential variation of the activity estimates. With the three-point technique, estimators give an optimistic (O), pessimistic (P), and most likely (M) estimate for each activity. Three-point estimating allows more consideration of both the uncertainty of estimating and the risks associated with the activities being estimated. A wide range between the optimistic and pessimistic estimates can indicate uncertainty—and therefore risk—associated with the activity.

Ultimately, three-point estimates can be used to calculate a risk-based expected duration estimate for an activity by taking either a simple average or a weighted average of three estimates. See the following information and formulas.

### Triangular Distribution (Simple Average)

A simple average of the three-point estimates can be calculated using the formula $(P + O + M)/3$. The use of simple averaging gives equal weight to each of the three-point estimates when calculating the expected activity duration or cost. Using this formula, the risks (P and O estimates) are considered equally along with the most likely (M) estimate.

### Beta Distribution (Weighted Average)[13]

The use of beta distribution (a weighted average) gives stronger consideration to the most likely estimate. Derived from the program evaluation and review technique (PERT),[14] this technique uses a formula to create a weighted average for the work to be done: $(P + 4M + O)/6$. Since the most likely estimate is multiplied by 4, it weights the average toward that estimate. This method of estimating leverages the benefits of risk management in reducing the uncertainty of estimates. When a good risk management process is followed, the most likely estimates are more accurate because risk response plans have been developed to deal with identified opportunities and threats that have been factored into the pessimistic and optimistic estimates.

 **TRICKS OF THE TRADE®**  For the exam, it's important to know the formulas for both triangular and beta distribution and to understand that if you are asked to calculate the activity duration or cost, you will need to read the situation carefully to determine which formula to use. Terms like "simple" or "straight" refer to triangular distribution, "weighted" refers to beta distribution. Knowing this will help you choose the correct formula.

You may be asked to perform calculations using the formulas, or to analyze information to determine which calculation is best for the situation presented. If the scenario indicates that you don't have a lot of experience or historical info, you would use triangular distribution, which provides a straight average. Beta distribution is used when there are historical data or samples to work with. The exercises that follow can help you prepare for three-point estimating questions on the exam. But first, review the formulas, shown again in figure 6.5.

 You must memorize these formulas and remember that they can be used for both time and cost estimates.

| Expected activity duration (triangular distribution) | Expected activity duration (beta distribution) |
|:---:|:---:|
| $$\frac{P + M + O}{3}$$ | $$\frac{P + 4M + O}{6}$$ |

Legend: P = Pessimistic, M = Most likely, O = Optimistic

FIGURE 6.5  *Triangular distribution and beta distribution formulas for three-point estimating*

**Exercise** Calculate the expected activity duration using triangular distribution. It is best to calculate to three decimal places. All estimates are in hours.

| Activity | P | M | O | Expected Activity Duration (Triangular Distribution) |
|----------|-----|-----|-----|-----|
| A | 47 | 27 | 14 | |
| B | 89 | 60 | 41 | |
| C | 48 | 44 | 39 | |
| D | 42 | 37 | 29 | |

## Answer

| Activity | P | M | O | Expected Activity Duration (Triangular Distribution) |
|----------|-----|-----|-----|-----|
| A | 47 | 27 | 14 | 29.333 |
| B | 89 | 60 | 41 | 63.333 |
| C | 48 | 44 | 39 | 43.666 |
| D | 42 | 37 | 29 | 36 |

**Exercise** Calculate the expected activity duration using beta distribution. Calculate to three decimal places. All estimates are in hours.

| Activity | P | M | O | Expected Activity Duration (Beta Distribution) |
|----------|-----|-----|-----|-----|
| A | 47 | 27 | 14 | |
| B | 89 | 60 | 41 | |
| C | 48 | 44 | 39 | |
| D | 42 | 37 | 29 | |

## Answer

| Activity | P | M | O | Expected Activity Duration (Beta Distribution) |
|----------|-----|-----|-----|-----|
| A | 47 | 27 | 14 | 28.167 |
| B | 89 | 60 | 41 | 61.667 |
| C | 48 | 44 | 39 | 43.833 |
| D | 42 | 37 | 29 | 36.500 |

Compare the answers in the "Expected Activity Duration (Beta Distribution)" column to the answers in the "Expected Activity Duration (Triangular Distribution)" column in the previous exercise. Notice that the results are not significantly different. However, if you do not select the right formula for a question that requires the calculation of expected activity duration, you could end up choosing the wrong answer.

These exercises are provided for understanding and do not necessarily represent the complexity of questions on the exam. Most of the questions on the exam relating to three-point estimating are relatively simple and may require assessment, but not calculations.

Activity standard deviation[15] is the possible range for the estimate. For example, an activity estimate of 30 hours that has a standard deviation of $+/-2$ is expected to take between 28 hours and 32 hours. The formula for beta activity standard deviation is $(P - O)/6$. Calculation using these formula is not a focus of the exam, but understanding and interpreting standard deviation in a situational question is important.

Although there is a standard deviation formula for triangular distribution, it's complicated and is unlikely to be on the exam so we are not showing it here. What you need to remember for the exam is that the greater the standard deviation, the greater the risk.

To establish a range for an individual activity estimate using weighted (beta) averaging, you need to know the beta expected activity duration (EAD) and the beta activity standard deviation (SD). You calculate the range using beta EAD $+/-$ SD. The start of the range is beta EAD $-$ SD, and the end of the range is beta EAD $+$ SD. Review the following table to see how the information is presented. Keep in mind that the exam scenario may include information for you to do the same evaluation with triangular distribution.

| Activity | P | M | O | Expected Activity Duration (Beta Distribution) | Beta Activity Standard Deviation | Range of the Estimate |
|----------|----|----|----|------------------|------------------|------------------------------------|
| A | 47 | 27 | 14 | 28.167 | 5.500 | 22.667 to 33.667, or 28.167 +/− 5.500 |
| B | 89 | 60 | 41 | 61.667 | 8.000 | 53.667 to 69.667, or 61.667 +/− 8.000 |
| C | 48 | 44 | 39 | 43.833 | 1.500 | 42.333 to 45.333, or 43.833 +/− 1.500 |
| D | 42 | 37 | 29 | 36.500 | 2.167 | 34.333 to 38.667, or 36.500 +/− 2.167 |

Note that the formulas we've been discussing relate to activities, rather than the overall project, and that the exam concentrates on using three-point estimating to find ranges for activity duration and cost estimates. You can also use this information to calculate the overall project estimate and the project standard deviation to help manage a project successfully. Consider how these ranges might affect the estimate of the overall project duration and cost, and use this knowledge to effectively address variations on your project.

For the exam, you should be able to do simple calculations using the formulas, understand that estimates of time (or cost) should be in a range, and interpret the information to answer situational questions. You may also see beta total project duration (for example, the project duration is 35 months plus or minus 3 months) used in questions that require you to evaluate the situation, rather than complete a calculation, to answer the questions correctly. Remember that, just like with an activity, the greater the range for the project as a whole, the greater the risk.

Why do project managers need to understand expected durations, range estimates, and standard deviations? The main purpose is to use these concepts to better monitor and control projects. These calculations help you know the potential variances on your project and determine appropriate courses of action.

You can use estimate ranges and standard deviation to assess risk. Looking back at the table presenting beta standard deviation in this section, which activity has the most risk? The answer is Activity B. It has the widest range and the highest standard deviation, and is therefore likely to have the greatest risk. These calculations are based on the pessimistic, optimistic, and most likely estimates for an activity. The further away from the mean these estimates are, the more that could go right or wrong and affect the activity. Therefore, you can assess and compare the risk of various activities by looking at activity ranges and standard deviations.

Don't forget that these concepts also apply to cost. Let's say you have estimated that a portion of your project will cost $1 million with a standard deviation of $200,000. You need to decide whether to use a fixed-price contract to outsource that piece of the project work. The standard deviation indicates there is a 40 percent range in the cost estimate for the work. Therefore, you would not likely choose a fixed-price contract, since this large standard deviation suggests there is not a firm definition of the scope of the work to be done. (See the Procurement Management chapter for information about types of contracts.)

### Bottom-Up Estimating    PAGE 202    This technique involves creating detailed estimates for each part of an activity (if available) or work package (if activities are not defined). Doing this type of estimating well requires an accurate WBS. The estimates are then rolled up into control accounts and finally into an overall project estimate.

Make sure you have a general understanding of these estimating concepts. If you are still struggling with this topic, review this section again.

### Data Analysis    PAGE 202    Estimate Activity Durations uses two forms of data analysis; alternatives analysis and reserve analysis.

### Alternatives Analysis    When activity estimates are not acceptable within the constraints of the project, alternatives analysis is used to look more closely at the variables that impact the estimates. For example, comparing options such as outsourcing work versus completing it internally to meet a schedule constraint, or purchasing testing software to decrease the time of manually testing components. Alternatives analysis involves evaluating the impact of each option on project constraints, including financial investment versus time saved and level of risk. This process will result in the determination of the best approach to completing project work within the constraints.

### Reserve Analysis    Now let's connect the topics of estimating and risk management. Estimating helps to identify more risks. Risk management reduces the uncertainty in time and cost estimates. This is accomplished by evaluating and planning for significant opportunities and threats, including how they will be dealt with if they occur. Risk management saves the project time and money!

Project managers have a professional responsibility to establish a reserve to accommodate the risks that remain after the risk management planning processes are completed. Often in the risk management process, an initial reserve is estimated, the Plan Risk Responses process is performed to reduce the risk, and then a revised reserve is created. This is another example of the iterative nature of project planning.

As described in the Risk Management chapter, two types of reserves can be added to the project schedule: contingency reserves and management reserves.[16]

Contingency reserves for schedule are allocated for the identified risks remaining after the Plan Risk Responses process (known unknowns). These reserves are included in the project schedule baseline.

Significant risks to critical path activities may be managed by allocating a specific amount of schedule reserve. The amount of this schedule reserve is based on the impact of identified risks on the activity as well as the contingency plans to deal with it.

The expected values of each contingency plan are added together to create a schedule contingency reserve. The project manager employs the contingency plan and uses the contingency reserve when identified risks occur. This keeps the project within the schedule baseline. (See the Risk Management chapter for a more detailed discussion of reserves.)

Management reserves are additional funds and time to cover unforeseen risks that could impact the project's ability to meet the schedule. (These risks are referred to as unknown unknowns.) Management reserves are not part of the schedule baseline. These reserves may not be applied at the project manager's discretion, but rather require approval of a formal change request. The Risk Management chapter explains how these reserves are calculated.

For the exam, you should understand the major difference between the practice of creating reserves and the practice of padding. In creating reserves, the project manager has the information necessary to reliably calculate what additional time or funds the project may need, whereas with padding, team members arbitrarily determine how much of a pad they want to attach to their estimates.

## Decision-Making    PAGE 203    Involving team members in estimating can be beneficial on many levels. Those doing the work are most likely to have a good understanding of the time required to complete the effort. Additionally, including team members in the estimating process increases their buy-in to the resulting schedule.

Voting is a method that can be used during decision-making—giving every participant the opportunity to weigh in on a decision regarding an activity estimate or amount of reserve needed. On plan-driven projects, voting may result in a decision based on plurality, majority, or unanimity. A voting technique commonly used on change-driven projects is "fist of five," also called "fist to five". In this variation, team members are asked to physically show their level of support for a decision. A closed fist indicates a zero (no support) and an open fist indicates five (full support). Team members who are not supportive, and showed two or fewer fingers in the vote, are allowed to share why they are not in support of the option. Voting is repeated until everyone in the group indicates their support by showing at least three fingers.

When the Estimate Activity Durations process is completed, you will of course have estimates, including reserves. But remember that you may also update or make changes to the project documents, including activity attributes, assumption log, and lessons learned register as a result of this process.

Another output of this process is the basis of estimates. The basis of estimates is an explanation of how the estimates were derived, what assumptions and constraints were included, and what risks were taken into consideration in the estimation process. Basis of estimates also includes the confidence level of the estimators, expressed as a range, such as plus or minus 20 percent within which the actual project results are expected to fall.

## Process for Achieving a Realistic Schedule or Budget    Project managers often complain about unrealistic schedules and budgets and put the blame on senior management. They do not realize that a major reason for having a project manager on a project is to make the schedule and budget realistic. How do you go about achieving a realistic schedule or budget? Let's think about the process logically.

# Schedule Management

If you need more help with scheduling or handling unrealistic schedules, visit rmcls.com for free tips and information about courses on these topics.

First, you analyze the work needed to complete the project. You then estimate the duration and cost of the work, and calculate an end date and budget for the project. You try to optimize that date and budget, and then compare your results to any schedule or budget constraints. If there is a difference, you analyze the project and provide options on how to change it to meet schedule and budget constraints or negotiate a change to the end date or budget; in other words, you balance the constraints. This is your professional responsibility as a project manager!

Do you follow the process we just described? If not, take some time now to truly understand it, and think about how you can implement these practices on your projects.

## Develop Schedule    PAGE 205

**Process** Develop Schedule
**Process Group** Planning
**Knowledge Area** Schedule Management

After network diagram and activity duration estimates are completed, it is time to put this information into the scheduling software within the project management information system (PMIS) to create a schedule model.[17] The schedule model includes all the project data that will be used to calculate the schedule, such as the activities, duration estimates, dependencies, and leads and lags. The project schedule is the output of the schedule model, and it consolidates all the schedule data. Representations of the schedule include bar charts and milestone charts. The approved project schedule is the baseline (a version of the schedule model that can only be changed with change control procedures), and is part of the project management plan.

The schedule is calendar-based, approved, and realistic as it includes all the activities needed to complete the work of the project, as well as contingency reserves to manage risk events. Consider what is involved in creating a schedule, and complete the following exercises. Hint: Think about the outputs of the previous schedule management processes!

**Exercise**   Let's start at the beginning. What do you need before you can develop a schedule for your project?

_____

_____

_____

_____

_____

_____

_____

_____

_____

_____

_____

238

**Answer**   To develop a schedule, you need to have:

- Historical records of previous, similar projects including lessons learned
- Components of the project management plan needed to develop a realistic schedule (schedule management plan and scope baseline)
- Defined activities (activity list and attributes)
- Milestone list
- Assumption log
- The order in which the work will be done (network diagram)
- Basis of estimates
- An estimate of the duration of each activity (activity duration estimates)
- An estimate of the resources needed (resource requirements)
- An understanding of the availability of resources (resource calendars)
- The required resources by category (resource breakdown structure)
- A company calendar identifying working and nonworking days
- A list of resources already assigned to specific project activities by management or agreement/contract (project team assignments)
- A list of risks that could impact the schedule (risk register)

**Exercise**   As a project manager, you need to use the estimating data and other inputs to create a schedule that you will be able to stake your reputation on meeting. What do you need to do to create such a schedule?

239

**Answer**  Let's go beyond the *PMBOK® Guide*. The Develop Schedule process really includes everything you need to do to develop a finalized schedule that is bought into, approved, realistic, and formal. This is what developing the schedule is all about. What do you need to do to get it to that level?

- Work with stakeholders' priorities.
- Look for alternative ways to complete the work.
- Look for impacts on other projects.
- Take into consideration the skill levels and availability of resources assigned to the team by management, or agreed-upon through negotiations in the Acquire Resources process in resource management.
- Apply leads and lags to the schedule.
- Compress the schedule by crashing, fast tracking, and reestimating.
- Adjust components of the project management plan as necessary (for example, change the WBS to reflect planned risk responses).
- Input the data into a scheduling tool and perform calculations to determine the optimum schedule.
- Simulate the project using Monte Carlo and other analysis techniques to determine the likelihood of completing the project as scheduled.
- Optimize resources if necessary.
- Give the team a chance to approve the final schedule; they should review the calendar allocation of their estimates to see if they are still feasible.
- Conduct meetings and conversations to gain stakeholder buy-in and formal management approval.

The Develop Schedule process is iterative and can occur many times over the life of the project (at least once per project life cycle phase on a large project). The Develop Schedule process is a source of problems on the exam for many project managers. The exam will test you as an expert in handling schedule development during project planning and whenever there are changes to the project.

## Schedule Network Analysis    PAGE 209    Schedule network analysis is used to create the schedule model, and, ultimately, to finalize the project schedule. This analysis may use one or more of the following techniques:

- Critical path method
- Schedule compression
- What-if/Monte Carlo analysis
- Resource optimization
- Agile release planning

## Critical Path Method[18]    PAGE 210    The critical path method involves determining the longest duration path through the network diagram, the earliest and latest an activity can start, and the earliest and latest it can be completed. To use this method, you need to understand the following basic concepts.

**Critical Path**   The critical path is the longest duration path through a network diagram, and it determines the shortest time it could take to complete the project.

The easiest way to find the critical path is to identify all paths through the network and add the activity durations along each path. The path with the longest duration is the critical path. Be careful that you do the exercises that follow and practice doing this manual work for the exam.

**Near-Critical Path**[19]   In addition to the critical path, you should be familiar with the concept of a near-critical path. This path is closest in duration to the critical path. Something could happen that shortens the critical path or lengthens the near-critical path to the point where the near-critical path becomes critical. The closer in length the near-critical and critical paths are, the more risk the project has. You need to focus time and effort monitoring and controlling activities on both the critical and near-critical paths (yes, there can be more than one) so there is no delay to project completion.

**Float**[20] **(Schedule Flexibility)**   You should understand float and be able to calculate it manually for the exam. Note that the terms "float" and "slack" mean the same thing. Slack is an older term for this concept, and is rarely used in project management. It is unlikely that you will see the term "slack" used on the exam.

The three types of float to know for the exam are:

- **Total float**  Total float is the amount of time an activity can be delayed without delaying the project end date or an intermediary milestone, while still adhering to any imposed schedule constraints. This is the primary type of float, but there are others.
- **Free float**  Free float is the amount of time an activity can be delayed without delaying the early start date of its successor(s) while still adhering to any imposed schedule constraints.
- **Project float**  Project float (also referred to as positive total float) is the amount of time a project can be delayed without delaying the externally imposed project completion date required by the customer or management, or the date previously committed to by the project manager.

Activities on the critical path have zero float. Critical path activities that are delayed or have an imposed completion date can result in negative float. This must be addressed before the project begins, as the project manager is responsible to ensure that the project schedule is realistic and achievable. Negative float analysis results in options to bring the schedule back within the baseline.

Float is an asset on a project, as it provides schedule flexibility. If you know where you have float, you can use it to help organize and manage the project. Do you do this on your projects? If not, study this section carefully.

When you know the critical path and any near-critical paths, you can use float as a way to focus your management of a project and to achieve better allocation of resources. For example, if you have a resource who is not very experienced but whom you must use for the project, you can assign them (assuming they have the skill set) to work on the activity with the most float. This gives you some level of security; even if their activity takes longer, the project is less likely to be delayed.

Knowing the float also helps team members juggle their work on multiple projects. They of course need to get approval from the project manager for any delays from the plan, but the amount of float tells them how much time flexibility they may have for each activity they are working on.

Sometimes the exam questions are presented in such a way that you can simply see the amount of float, but other times you will need to calculate it. Float is calculated using either of the following equations:

- Float = Late start (LS) – Early start (ES)
- Float = Late finish (LF) – Early finish (EF)

Either formula gets you the same answer. Do you want to remember them without any further study? Just know the following:

"There is a start formula and a finish formula, and we always begin late." Notice that the formula uses either two start or two finish data elements and each begins with late.

| Start Formula (Used in Forward Pass) | Finish Formula (Used in Backward Pass) |
|---|---|
| Float = LS – ES | Float = LF – EF |

You determine whether to use the start or finish formula based on the information available. For example, if an exam question states that you have a late start of 30, an early start of 18, and a late finish of 34, how do you find the float? Using the previous trick, you know to subtract the two starts or the two finishes. Since you do not have two finishes, you use the equation 30 – 18, which equals 12.

## Exercise    Test yourself! How does the critical path help you as a project manager?

_____

_____

_____

_____

_____

_____

_____

_____

_____

_____

242

## Answer The critical path:

- Helps prove how long the project will take
- Shows which activities have float and can therefore be delayed without delaying the project
- Provides information needed to compress the schedule during project planning and whenever there are changes
- Helps determine where to focus your project management efforts
- Helps determine which activities have more risk associated with them
- Helps determine if a delayed activity needs immediate attention

**Using the Critical Path Method**    Now that we have discussed the basic concepts, let's look at how the critical path method works. We'll use the network diagram in figure 6.6 as an example. Note that the critical path is identified by the bold arrows.

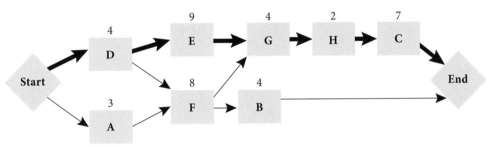

FIGURE 6.6    *Critical path method*

To determine the earliest and latest each activity can start and the earliest and latest each activity can be completed, you need to perform a forward and backward pass through the network diagram. The "early" figures are found by calculating from the beginning of the project to the end of the project, following the dependencies in the network diagram—a forward pass through the network diagram. The "late" figures are found by moving from the end of the project, following the dependencies to the beginning of the project—a backward pass.

The first activity in the diagram normally has an early start of zero. Some people, however, use 1 as the early start of the first activity. There is no right way to start calculating through network diagrams for the early and late starts; either method will get you the right answer. Just pick one method, and use it consistently. We use zero as the early start because it saves a bit of calculation and people consistently find it easier when learning this concept.

Let's start with the forward pass. You need to move through the activities from the start until you reach the end, determining the early starts and early finishes, as illustrated in figure 6.7. This example uses zero as the early start for the first activities.

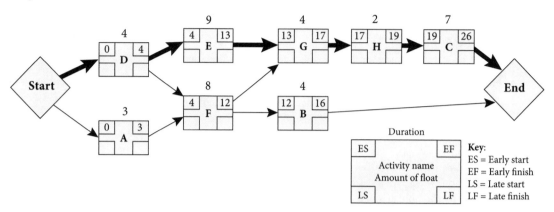

FIGURE 6.7   *Forward pass through network diagram*

It is important to look at where paths converge (path convergence). To compute the early start and the early finish in a forward pass, you have to take into account all the paths that lead into that activity (see activity F and activity G in figure 6.7). The same concept applies to the backward pass; to compute the late finish and late start you need to consider all the paths that flow backward into an activity (see activity D and activity F in figure 6.7). In this diagram, paths converge during the forward pass at activity F and at activity G. So you need to do the forward pass on both paths leading up to activity F, calculating the early finishes for activities D (EF = 4) and A (EF = 3). You then select the later early finish of activities D and A to use as the early start for activity F, since activity F cannot start until both activities D and A are complete. Therefore, the early start of activity F is 4. You use the same process for calculating the early finish of activities E (EF = 13) and F (EF = 12) before determining the early start of activity G (ES = 13).

Once you have completed the forward pass, you can begin the backward pass, computing the late finish and late start for each activity. The backward pass uses the duration of the critical path (in this case, 26) as the late finish of the last activity or activities in the network. See figure 6.8 for the late start and late finish data.

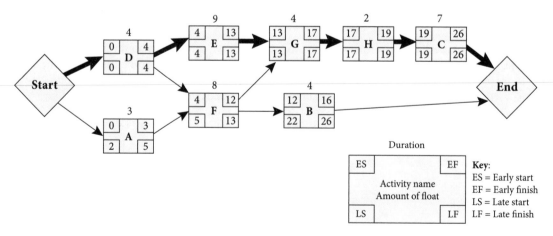

FIGURE 6.8   *Backward pass through network diagram*

Again, you need to be careful at points of convergence as you move through the network diagram. There is convergence at activity F and at activity D. You work from the end back to these by first computing the late start of activities B (LS = 22) and G (LS = 13). Select the earlier late start to use for the late finish of activity F, since activity F must be finished before either activity B or G can start.

Therefore, the late finish of activity F is 13. This same process should be used on activities E (LS = 4) and F (LS =5) before calculating the late finish for activity D (LF = 4).

Once you finish calculating the starts and finishes, you have the data required to calculate float. It's time to use those formulas. What was that trick again? "There is a start formula and a finish formula, and we always begin late." Therefore, the formulas are:

| Start Formula (Used in Forward Pass) | Finish Formula (Used in Backward Pass) |
| --- | --- |
| Float = LS – ES | Float = LF – EF |

> If you want additional practice, there are more questions on float and critical path in RMC's PM FASTrack® exam simulator.

The activities with zero float are on the critical path (identified by the bold arrows). See figure 6.9 for the float of each activity.

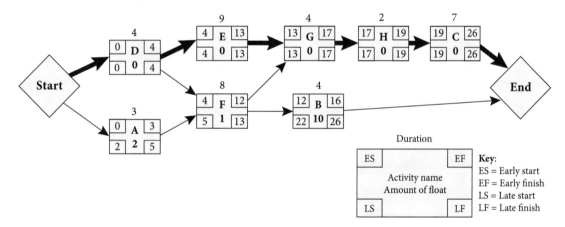

FIGURE 6.9    *Float of activities on network diagram*

The next few exercises should help you better understand these concepts. As you do the exercises, think about how knowing float helps you in managing your projects.

Be prepared for different types of exam questions. Some questions may be substantially similar to the following exercises, and others may be more situational and wordy. Not all questions will require you to draw a network diagram.

**Exercise**   Test yourself. Draw a network diagram, and then answer the following questions.

- You are the project manager for a new project and have figured out the following dependencies: Activity 1 can start immediately and has an estimated duration of 3 weeks.

- Activity 2 can start after activity 1 is completed and has an estimated duration of 3 weeks.

- Activity 3 can start after activity 1 is completed and has an estimated duration of 6 weeks.

- Activity 4 can start after activity 2 is completed and has an estimated duration of 8 weeks.

- Activity 5 can start after activity 4 is completed and after activity 3 is completed. This activity takes 4 weeks.

1. What is the duration of the critical path?

2. What is the float of activity 3?

3. What is the float of activity 2?

4. What is the float of the path with the longest float?

5. The resource working on activity 3 is replaced with another resource who is less experienced. The activity will now take 10 weeks. How will this affect the project?

6. After some arguing between stakeholders, a new activity 6 is added to the project. It will take 11 weeks to complete and must be completed before activity 5 and after activity 3. Management is concerned that adding the activity will add 11 weeks to the project. Another stakeholder argues the time will be less than 11 weeks. Who is correct? Use the original information (without the change to activity 3 listed in the previous question) to answer this question.

7. Based on the information in question 6, how much longer will the project take?

**Answer**   There are many ways to answer these questions. If you learned another way in your project management training and are comfortable with that method, use it. Here is a simple way to compute the answers.

1. The length of the critical path is 18. There are two paths here:

| Paths | Duration |
|-------|----------|
| Start, 1, 2, 4, 5, End | 18 |
| Start, 1, 3, 5, End | 13 |

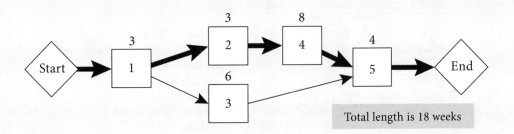

Total length is 18 weeks

Start, 1, 2, 4, 5, End (shown with the bold arrows in the diagram) is the longest duration path and is therefore the critical path. The durations of the activities add up to 18, so the critical path is 18 weeks long.

2.  The float of activity 3 is 5 weeks, per the following diagram, which shows how to calculate float using the forward and backward pass.

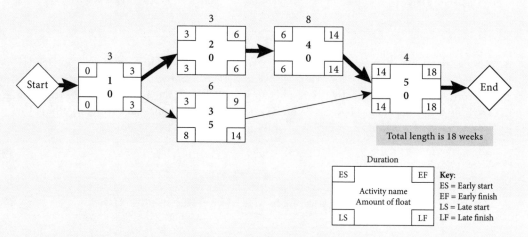

Total length is 18 weeks

|  | Duration | |
| --- | --- | --- |
| ES | | EF |
| | Activity name<br>Amount of float | |
| LS | | LF |

**Key:**
ES = Early start
EF = Early finish
LS = Late start
LF = Late finish

You can use either float formula to compute float. Late finish – Early finish = 14 – 9 = 5, or Late start – Early start = 8 – 3 = 5.

3.  The float of activity 2 is zero; it is on the critical path. An activity on the critical path generally has no float.

4.  The float of the path with the longest float is 5 weeks. There are only two paths in this example: Start, 1, 2, 4, 5, End and Start, 1, 3, 5, End. Only the non-critical path (Start, 1, 3, 5, End) will have float. You can calculate the float for this path by adding the float for each activity: 0 + 5 + 0 = 5. Therefore, the total float of the path with the longest float is 5.

5.  The resource change on activity 3 will have no effect. The length of path activities 1, 3, and 5 is 13. Adding 4 more weeks to the length of activity 3 will make that path 17. Since that path is still shorter than the critical path, the critical path does not change. The length of the critical path is still 18 weeks because activity 3 is not on the critical path.

6.  The stakeholder who says that the time that will be added to the project will be less than 11 weeks is correct. The new activity will be added to a non-critical path that has a float of 5 weeks. Therefore, adding 11 weeks will make this path the new critical path. The overall effect of adding an activity that takes 11 weeks will be a delay to the project of 6 weeks.

7.  The project will take 6 weeks longer. (Note: If you answered 24, you did not read the question correctly!) Follow the bold arrows in the following diagram.

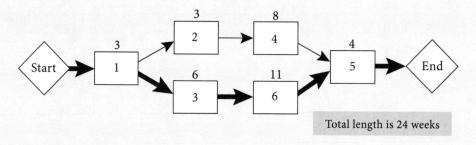

Total length is 24 weeks

**Exercise**   Use the data in this table to answer the questions that follow.

| Activity | Preceding Activity | Estimate in Months |
|----------|--------------------|--------------------|
| Start    |                    | 0                  |
| D        | Start              | 4                  |
| A        | Start              | 6                  |
| F        | D, A               | 7                  |
| E        | D                  | 8                  |
| G        | F, E               | 5                  |
| B        | F                  | 5                  |
| H        | G                  | 7                  |
| C        | H                  | 8                  |
| End      | C, B               | 0                  |

1.  What is the duration of the critical path?

2.  What is the float of activity B?

3.  What is the float of activity E?

4.  What is the float of activity D?

5.  To shorten the length of the project, the sponsor has offered to remove the work of activity E from the project, making activity D the predecessor to activities G and F. What will be the effect?

## Answer

1. The critical path (project duration) is 33 months.

| Paths | Duration |
|---|---|
| Start, D, E, G, H, C, End | 32 |
| Start, D, F, G, H, C, End | 31 |
| Start, D, F, B, End | 16 |
| Start, A, F, G, H, C, End | 33 |
| Start, A, F, B, End | 18 |

2. The float of activity B is 15 months, per the following diagram.

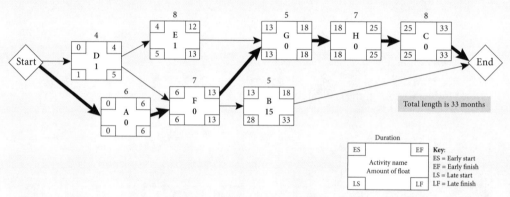

3. The float of activity E is one month. Once you have finished calculating using the long way, all the other answers are usually quick. Just look at the diagram to see the float of any activity.

    Watch out here for the float of activity E. The project must be completed by the end of month 33. Activity E must be completed before activities G, H, and C can start. So the late finish for E is 33 – 8 – 7 – 5, or 13.

    Activity E must be completed after activity D. So the early finish is 4 + 8, or 12. Float = Late finish – Early finish, so 13 – 12 = 1.

    Float = Late finish – Early finish, so 13 – 12 = 1.

4. The float of activity D is one month.

    Now let's look at using a calculation to determine the float for activity D. The project must be completed by the end of month 33. Activity D must be completed before activities E, F, G, H, C, and B can start. Looking backward through the dependencies, the late finish is 33 – 8 – 7 – 5, but then we run into a problem. Normally we would go along the critical path, but look at activities E and F. Activity E is longer than activity F, so we must go along the longest duration path, from activity G to activity E, making the late finish 33 – 8 – 7 – 5 – 8, or 5.

    Early finish is easier. There are no predecessors, so the early finish is the end of month 4.

    Float = 5 – 4, or 1 month.

5. Removing the work of activity E will have no effect on the critical path. The paths are now:

| Paths | Duration |
|---|---|
| Start, D, G, H, C, End | 24 |
| Start, D, F, G, H, C, End | 31 |
| Start, D, F, B, End | 16 |
| Start, A, F, G, H, C, End | 33 |
| Start, A, F, B, End | 18 |

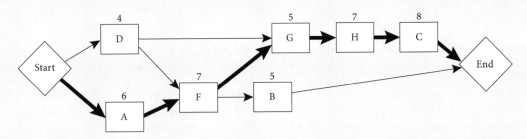

You survived! Hopefully it was not too hard.

 **TRICKS OF THE TRADE®** The following are good questions to test your knowledge about critical paths, float, and network diagrams:

- **Can there be more than one critical path?** Yes, you can have two, three, or many critical paths.

- **Do you want there to be?** No; having more than one critical path increases risk.

- **Can a critical path change?** Yes.

- **Can there be negative float?** Yes; it means you are behind.

- **How much float does the critical path have?** In planning, the critical path generally has zero total float. During project executing, if an activity on the critical path is completed earlier or later than planned, the critical path may then have positive or negative float. Negative float on the critical path requires corrective action or changes to the project to bring it back in line with the plan.

- **Does the network diagram change when the end date changes?** No, not automatically, but the project manager should investigate schedule compression options such as fast tracking and crashing the schedule to meet the new date. Then, with approved changes, the project manager should change the network diagram accordingly.

- **Would you leave the project with negative float?** No; you would compress the schedule. If schedule compression efforts do not result in zero or positive float, you need to request a change to adjust the baseline.

 **TRICKS OF THE TRADE®** When you manually create a network diagram while taking the exam, label it with the question number, in case you want to go back to it later. You may be able to reuse the same network diagram to answer additional questions later in the exam.

It is easy to miss paths through a network diagram. When attempting to identify the critical path, carefully calculate the duration of each path, to ensure you look at all paths before determining which is critical.

**Schedule Compression**[21]  PAGE 215  One of the most common problems on projects is an unrealistic timeframe. This problem can arise during project planning when management or the customer requires a completion date that cannot be met, or during project executing when the project manager needs to bring the project back in line with the schedule baseline or adjust the project for changes. As we discussed earlier, many project managers blame their sponsors or executives for unrealistic schedules, but project managers have a professional responsibility to push back, present options, and make sure the project is achievable by properly planning the project and using schedule network analysis techniques such as schedule compression.

Also keep in mind that schedule compression is a way to utilize float by fast tracking activities that are on the critical path. This means adjusting the network diagram so critical path activities that were originally planned to be completed in a series are replanned to be done in parallel. As we discuss below, fast tracking can save time, but it also adds risk to the project.

During project planning, schedule compression can help a project manager determine if the desired completion date can be met and, if not, what can be changed to meet the requested date.

Later in the project, schedule compression may be used during Perform Integrated Change Control and Control Schedule to evaluate options to manage the impacts of changes. The objective of this technique is to manage the schedule without changing the schedule baseline. This isn't always possible, but we try.

**Fast Tracking**  This technique involves taking critical path activities that were originally planned in a series and doing them instead in parallel for some or all of their duration (see fig. 6.10). Fast tracking often results in rework, usually increases risk, and requires more attention to communication.

FIGURE 6.10  *Fast tracking*

For example, which activity in figure 6.11 would you fast track to shorten the project length?

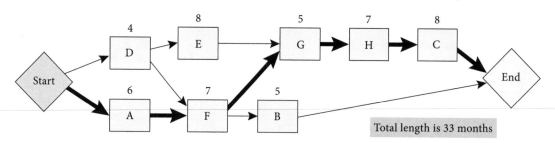

FIGURE 6.11  *Which activity would you fast track?*

Assuming the dependencies are discretionary, activity H could be fast tracked by making it occur at the same time as, or in parallel with, activity G. Any other pair of activities on the critical path could be fast tracked. Activities C and H could also be fast tracked by having part of activity C done concurrently with activity H.

252

**Crashing**[22]    This technique involves adding or adjusting resources in order to compress the schedule while maintaining the original project scope. Crashing, by definition, always results in increased costs, and may increase risk. It trades time for money.

For example, in the network diagram in figure 6.11, a contract resource could supplement the internal resource's efforts on a critical path activity (assuming this is logical, based on the nature of the work). Another option to crash the project might be to buy a software application; the purchase adds cost to the project but helps the team work more efficiently, thus saving time.

If you have negative project float (meaning the estimated completion date is after the desired date), would your first choice be to tell the customer the date cannot be met and to ask for more time? No; the first choice would be to analyze what could be done about the negative float by compressing the schedule. In crashing or fast tracking, it is best to see all potential choices and then select the option or options that have the least negative impact on the project. For the exam, remember that you need to identify all the possible options and, if given a choice between crashing or fast tracking options, select the choice or combination of choices with the least negative impact on the project. This tip can help you on exam questions that seem to have two right answers.

In the real world, many project managers use the network diagram to manage the day-to-day operations of the project and to make adjustments when changes occur. You should expect this to be reflected on the exam in terms of the number of questions involving network diagrams, calculations, and "What do you do in this situation?" scenarios.

Let's make sure you are prepared to deal with unrealistic schedules on the exam. This issue is so important that you can expect to see more than 10 questions about it. Most project managers have some gaps in their knowledge in this area, and it shows on their score sheets. To remedy this, let's try an exercise.

**Exercise**    During project planning, the project duration is estimated to be 33 months. However, now you have been given a constraint of 30 months. Using the following network diagram, identify options for shortening the schedule to 30 months.

This is a general exercise with little detail. Make any assumptions you need to make in order to come up with as many options as possible.

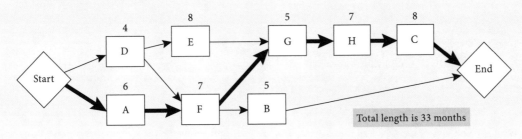

| Option | How to Achieve It | Explanation (Including Assumptions Made) |
| --- | --- | --- |
| | | |
| | | |
| | | |
| | | |
| | | |
| | | |
| | | |

| Option | How to Achieve It | Explanation (Including Assumptions Made) |
|--------|-------------------|------------------------------------------|
|        |                   |                                          |

**Answer**   Did this situation make sense? If it did, you are in good shape. If not, you should study a little more. Notice how this analysis allows the project manager to proactively deal with the reality of the project and take action to be sure the project constraint can be met. The following are possible options for shortening the schedule.

| Option | How to Achieve It | Explanation (Including Assumptions Made) |
|--------|-------------------|------------------------------------------|
| Reestimate. | Review risks. | Now it is time to look at the estimates and see which contain hidden risks. By reducing the risks, the estimate can be lowered, and the project finished faster. It is never an option to just cut 10 percent off of the estimate. |
| Execute activities H and C in parallel. | Fast track (schedule compression). | We assume that the dependency between activities H and C is a discretionary one. |
| Add resources from within the organization (at additional cost to the project) to activity G. | Crash (schedule compression). | We assume that adding resources to activity G would, in fact, be practical and that there are resources available. |
| Cut activity H. | Reduce scope. | Although not the first choice, as it will likely affect the customer, reducing scope should be considered an option. |
| Hire consultants to assist on activity G, H, or C (at additional cost to the project). | Crash (schedule compression). | We assume that adding external resources to these activities would be practical and that there are resources available. |
| Move more experienced people to activities on the critical path (activities G, H, or C). | Compress the schedule. | We assume that some of the critical path activities are being done by less experienced people. |
| Cut time. | Lower quality standards. | Do not get excited. Quality is a project constraint, and lowering quality standards is an option. In this case, it would probably be easier—and thus faster—to complete the project with the lowered quality standards. |

| Option | How to Achieve It | Explanation (Including Assumptions Made) |
|---|---|---|
| Say no; the project must have 33 months. | Stand your ground. | This is not a viable option until other alternatives are exhausted. |
| Get more work done with the same amount of resources. | Work overtime. | This is not an option during project planning. There are too many other ways to compress the schedule that do not have the negative effects of overtime. Save it for a last resort. |

Which of the options listed is the best? To answer the question, think of the impacts on the project of each one. Is the best option to cut time by lowering quality standards? What are the impacts of cutting quality? Is there another option? Why not do what many project managers do—ask for more resources? But adding resources may also add cost. Why not work overtime? Most organizations are working at close to 100 percent capacity. Having your project team work overtime limits the possibility of resources responding to emergencies for any other project they are working on, thereby putting other projects at risk. Besides, how much overtime can a person take? Overtime is not free.

The best choice is to look at risks and then reestimate. Once it is known that the schedule (or budget) must be reduced, a project manager can investigate the activity estimates that contain the most unknowns, eliminate or reduce these risks, and thus decrease the estimate. Eliminate risks in the risk management process and everyone wins! If this is not enough, the project manager would continue the effort to shorten the schedule by using other schedule compression techniques.

Let's look at these concepts again with a few more exercises.

**Exercise**   What are the impacts of the schedule-shortening options listed in the following table?

| Option | General Impacts on the Project |
|---|---|
| Fast track | |
| Crash | |
| Reduce scope | |
| Cut quality | |

## Answer

| Option | General Impacts on the Project |
|---|---|
| **Fast track** | • Always adds risk<br>• May add management time for the project manager |
| **Crash** | • Always adds cost<br>• May add management time for the project manager<br>• May add risk |
| **Reduce scope** | • May save cost, resources, and time<br>• May negatively impact customer satisfaction |
| **Cut quality** | • May save cost, resources, and time<br>• May increase risk<br>• Requires good metrics on current and desired levels of quality to be effective<br>• May negatively impact customer satisfaction |

## Exercise    Here is another chance to test yourself on schedule compression.

| Activity | Original Duration (Months) | Crash Duration (Months) | Time Savings | Original Cost (Dollars) | Crash Cost (Dollars) | Extra Cost (Dollars) | Cost per Month |
|---|---|---|---|---|---|---|---|
| J | 14 | 12 | 2 | $10,000 | $14,000 | $4,000 | $2,000 |
| K | 9 | 8 | 1 | $17,000 | $27,000 | $10,000 | $10,000 |
| N | 3 | 2 | 1 | $25,000 | $26,000 | $1,000 | $1,000 |
| L | 7 | 5 | 2 | $14,000 | $20,000 | $6,000 | $3,000 |
| M | 11 | 8 | 3 | $27,000 | $36,000 | $9,000 | $3,000 |

1.  Imagine that this project has a project float of −3 months. Which activity or activities presented above would you crash to save three months on the project, assuming that the activities listed above represent critical path activities?




2.  How much would it cost to crash this project?

## Answer

1. The following activities could be crashed to save three months on the project:

| Activities | Cost |
|------------|----------|
| J and K | $14,000 |
| J and N | $5,000 |
| K and L | $16,000 |
| L and N | $7,000 |
| M | $9,000 |

Crashing activities J and N is the least expensive option, and because there is nothing in the question to eliminate it, the option to crash activities J and N is the best answer. Any time you have negative project float, it means that the project is not going to meet its deliverable date. The answer, depending on how the question is worded, involves crashing or fast tracking the project and coming up with options, or telling the customer the date cannot be met.

2. Crashing activities J and N would result in the least added cost—only $5,000. The "Cost per Month" column in this exercise is a distractor; you can answer this question with just the "Activity," "Time Savings," and "Extra Cost" columns. Don't assume you will need all the data provided to you in questions on the exam.

## Exercise  Consider the following question:

*Question*  Management has told you to get the project completed two weeks early. What is the best thing for you to do?

    A. Consult the project sponsor
    B. Crash
    C. Fast track
    D. Advise management of the impact of the change

## Answer  Did you get fooled by this question? Did you think you had to choose between crashing and fast tracking? There is no information provided to help you determine which one is better. Therefore, the best choice presented is D, advise management of the impact of the change.

The exam will include many such questions requiring you to know that a project manager needs to analyze first, create options to deal with the change, and then let management, the sponsor, the customer, or other parties know the impacts of their request (see the four-step process for handling changes in the Integration Management chapter). A project manager does not just say yes! Instead, after analyzing the change for its impact on all areas of the project (cost, risk, resources, etc.), they could say something like, "Yes, I would be happy to make the change, but the project will be delayed two weeks. And I will need two more resources, or the project will cost $25,000 more."

WARNING: For questions about changes to the network diagram, make sure you look for shifts to new critical paths caused by the changes to the network diagram or to activity durations.

**Data Analysis/Simulation**   PAGE 213   In creating a finalized, realistic schedule, it is helpful to ask, "What if a particular factor changed on the project? Would that produce a shorter schedule?" The assumptions for each activity can change and, therefore, the activity durations can also change. One of the ways to calculate the effect of these changes is through what-if scenario analysis.

**Monte Carlo Analysis**[23]   This technique uses computer software to simulate the outcome of a project, based on the three-point estimates (optimistic, pessimistic, and most likely) for each activity and the network diagram. The simulation can tell you:

- The probability of completing the project on any specific day
- The probability of completing the project for any specific cost
- The probability of any activity actually being on the critical path
- An indication of the overall project risk

Monte Carlo analysis is another way of putting together the details of three-point estimates into a project estimate. It is more accurate than other methods because it simulates the actual details of the project and calculates probability.

Monte Carlo analysis can help deal with "path convergence," places in the network diagram where multiple paths converge into one or more activities, thus adding risk to the project (see fig. 6.12). Monte Carlo analysis is also used as a risk management tool to quantitatively analyze risks (see the Risk Management chapter).

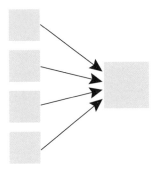

FIGURE 6.12   *Path convergence*

**Resource Optimization**[24]   PAGE 211   Resource optimization refers to finding ways to adjust the use of resources. There are two techniques that can achieve this outcome.

- **Resource Leveling**[25]   Resource leveling is used to produce a resource-limited schedule. Leveling lengthens the schedule and increases cost to deal with a limited number of resources, resource availability, and other resource constraints. A little-used function in project management software, this technique allows you to level the peaks and valleys of the schedule from one month to another, resulting in a more stable number of resources used on your project.

  You might level the resources if your project used 5 resources one month, 15 the next, and 3 the next, or some other up-and-down pattern that was not acceptable. Leveling could also be used if you did not have 15 resources available and preferred to lengthen the project (which is a result of leveling) instead of hiring more resources.

- **Resource Smoothing**[26]  Resource smoothing is a modified form of resource leveling, where resources are leveled only within the limits of the float of their activities, so the completion dates of activities are not delayed.

### Agile Release Planning   PAGE 216

In agile—or change-driven—projects, work to develop the product of the project is broken down into iterations and releases. Agile release planning provides a high-level schedule that includes the frequency of releases and the number of iterations that will be completed as a part of each release. The planning efforts result in a timeline, which indicates the features to be included in each release.

## Outputs of Develop Schedule   PAGE 217

The Develop Schedule process results in the project schedule, the schedule baseline, schedule data, change requests, and updates to any related project documents. The following sections describe these outputs.

### Project Schedule

The project schedule is the result of the previous planning processes and the schedule network analysis that is performed as part of the Develop Schedule process. As planning progresses, the schedule will be iterated in response to risk management and other parts of project planning until an acceptable and realistic schedule can be agreed upon. The iterated and realistic schedule that results from this effort is called the schedule baseline, which becomes part of the project management plan.

The project schedule includes project activities with assigned dates for each activity, and includes milestones inserted by the project manager or management. The project schedule may be represented in formats such as bar charts or network diagrams.

The project schedule can be shown with or without dependencies (logical relationships) and can be shown in any of the following presentations created from the schedule model, depending on the needs of the project:

- Network diagram (described earlier in this chapter)
- Milestone chart
- Bar chart

### Milestone Charts[27]

These are similar to bar charts (described next), but they only show major events. Remember that milestones have no duration; they simply represent the completion of activities. Milestones, which may include "requirements are complete" or "design is finished," are part of the inputs to the Sequence Activities process. Milestone charts are good tools for reporting to management and to the customer. See the example in figure 6.13.

| ID | Milestone | December | January | February | March | April |
|----|-----------|----------|---------|----------|-------|-------|
| 1 | Start | ◆12/14 | | | | |
| 2 | Requirements gathered | | ◆12/31 | | | |
| 3 | Design complete | | ◆1/17 | | | |
| 4 | Coding complete | | | ◆2/15 | | |
| 5 | Testing complete | | | | ◆3/15 | |
| 6 | Implementation complete | | | | | ◆4/4 |
| 7 | End | | | | | ◆4/15 |

FIGURE 6.13    *Milestone chart*

**Bar Charts**[28]    Bar charts are weak planning tools, but they are effective for progress reporting and control. They are not project management plans. Figure 6.14 shows a sample bar chart.

| ID | Activity Name | Duration | Start | Finish | August | September | October |
|----|---------------|----------|-------|--------|--------|-----------|---------|
| 1 | Start | 0 days | Mon 8/26 | Mon 8/26 | ◆ | | |
| 2 | D | 4 days | Mon 8/26 | Thu 8/29 | | | |
| 3 | A | 6 days | Mon 8/26 | Mon 9/2 | | | |
| 4 | F | 7 days | Mon 9/2 | Tue 9/10 | | | |
| 5 | E | 8 days | Fri 8/30 | Tue 9/10 | | | |
| 6 | G | 5 days | Wed 9/11 | Wed 9/18 | | | |
| 7 | B | 5 days | Wed 9/11 | Wed 9/18 | | | |
| 8 | H | 7 days | Wed 9/18 | Thu 9/26 | | | |
| 9 | C | 8 days | Fri 9/27 | Tue 10/8 | | | |
| 10 | Finish | 0 days | Tue 10/8 | Tue 10/8 | | | ◆ |

FIGURE 6.14    *Bar chart*

Notice that there are no lines between activities to show interdependencies, nor are assigned resources shown. Bar charts do not help organize the project as effectively as a WBS and network diagrams do. They are completed after the WBS and the network diagram in the project management process.

# Schedule Management

**Understanding the Benefits of Different Presentation Formats**    No matter how much you know about project management, there are always questions on the exam that will be tricky if you have never thought about them before. The different types of schedule presentations can be one of those areas. Think through the next exercise. Make sure you look for anything you did not know, and organize your knowledge according to the exercise answers. You can get quite a few questions right on the exam if you know what each of the schedule presentations is used for.

### Exercise    Test yourself! Answer the following questions in the spaces provided.

| Question | Answer |
|---|---|
| Under what circumstances would you use a network diagram? | |
| Under what circumstances would you use a milestone chart? | |
| Under what circumstances would you use a bar chart? | |

### Answer    See the answers in the following table.

| Question | Answer |
|---|---|
| Under what circumstances would you use a network diagram? | • To show interdependencies between activities |
| Under what circumstances would you use a milestone chart? | • To report to senior management |
| Under what circumstances would you use a bar chart? | • To track progress<br>• To report to the team |

**Schedule Baseline**    PAGE 217    The schedule baseline is the version of the schedule model used to manage the project; it is what the project team's performance is measured against. Remember that the baseline can only be changed as a result of formally approved changes. Meeting the schedule baseline is one of the measures of project success. If the project can be done faster than the customer requested, there may be a difference between the schedule baseline and the end date required by the customer. This difference is project float.

**Schedule Data**    Schedule data encompasses all the data used to create the schedule model, including milestones, project activities, activity attributes, duration estimates, dependencies, and the assumptions and constraints used in creating the schedule.

**Change Requests**    This is another planning process with change requests as an output. As the project progresses, any changes to the schedule may necessitate changes to other parts of the project management plan. Change requests are addressed through the integrated change control process.

**Project Documents Updates**   The process of creating a final and realistic schedule could result in updates to project documents including duration estimates, resource requirements, activity attributes, risk register, assumption log, and the lessons learned register.

## Control Schedule   PAGE 222

| | |
|---|---|
| **Process** | Control Schedule |
| **Process Group** | Monitoring & Controlling |
| **Knowledge Area** | Schedule Management |

Controlling the project was discussed in the Project Management Processes chapter, and is an important part of every knowledge area (scope, schedule, cost, quality, etc.). We will spend a little more time talking about it here. Control means measure; you measure against the plan. You need to stay in control of your project and know how it is performing compared to the plan. Do you do this on your projects? If not, pay particular attention to the concept of monitoring and controlling in this chapter and throughout this book. Make sure you understand that such actions are done as part of basic project management. When answering exam questions, you need to assume proper project management was done unless the question states otherwise. On properly managed projects, a project manager does not have to spend all their time dealing with problems, because most of those problems were prevented through appropriate planning and risk management. Project managers are measuring against the plan and taking action as needed to control the project.

The project (and the project manager) will be unsuccessful if the schedule baseline—the end date agreed to in planning and adjusted for approved changes—is not met. So monitoring and controlling efforts go beyond measuring; they also involve taking corrective and preventive action over and over again during the life of the project to keep the project in line with the plan. Do you do this? If not, why not? Without such work, all the efforts in planning to create a realistic schedule could be wasted.

Schedule control also means looking for the things that are causing changes and influencing the sources, or root causes, of the changes. For example, if there is one person or one piece of work causing a lot of changes, the project manager must do something about it, rather than let the issues and the high number of changes continue. A project manager must be proactive.

If the project can no longer meet the agreed-upon completion date, and achieving the completion date is a critical factor for success of the project, the project manager might recommend the termination of the project before any more company time is wasted. In other words, the project manager might have to influence directors and senior executives in the organization to control the project. Schedule control is more than just issuing updated schedules!

Make sure you really understand what is involved in schedule control. Think of protecting the hard work of all those involved in planning to make sure what was planned occurs as close to the plan as possible. Think of being constantly on the lookout for anything that might be affecting the schedule. This is what it means to control the schedule, and the project.

The following are some additional activities that can be used to control the schedule:

- Access the PMIS to review current work performance data and compare actual progress to what was planned.
- Reestimate the remaining components of the project partway through the project (see the following discussion).
- Conduct performance reviews by formally analyzing how the project is doing (see the "Earned Value Measurement" discussion in the Cost Management chapter).
- Perform data analysis (this can include earned value analysis, trend analysis, variance analysis, and what-if scenario analysis) of project performance.

263

- Confirm that critical path activities are being completed within the schedule baseline. If they are not, adjust the critical path by taking advantage of available float.
- Adjust future parts of the project to deal with delays, rather than asking for a schedule extension (using schedule compression techniques such as using leads and lags, crashing, and fast tracking).
- Consider making adjustments to optimize resources assigned to activities to improve the performance.
- Continue efforts to optimize the schedule.
- Adjust metrics that are not giving the project manager the information needed to properly understand performance and manage the project. Add new metrics if needed.
- Adjust the format or required content of reports as needed to capture the information necessary to control and manage the project (see the "Progress Reporting" discussion in the Cost Management chapter).
- Identify the need for changes, including corrective and preventive actions.
- Follow the change control process.

Efforts to control the schedule when the project is using a change-driven approach include:

- Comparing work actually completed to what was predicted to be complete within a given work cycle using an Iteration burndown chart
- Holding retrospectives to address possible process improvements
- Reprioritizing the backlog of work
- Identifying and managing changes as they arise

## Reestimating
One of the roles of a project manager is to make sure the project meets the project objectives. Although you did your best to understand the project well enough to estimate it sufficiently in planning, there are always changes that occur during a project that impact those plans. Therefore, it is standard practice to reestimate the remaining work at least once during the life of the project to make sure you can still satisfy the project objectives within the schedule, budget, and other project constraints, and to adjust the project if you cannot. Again, assume proper project management was done when answering questions on the exam unless the question provides specific information to indicate it was not.

The Control Schedule process results in work performance information, schedule forecasts, and sometimes change requests. For example, a change to the schedule might require additional resources or a change in scope. Such changes must be handled as part of the Perform Integrated Change Control process. Make sure you review this important process in the Integration Management chapter.

This process may also result in updates to the schedule management plan and performance measurement baseline in addition to project documents such as the assumption log, risk register, and lessons learned register, and changes to any other part of the project.

## Practice Exam

1. A project manager is informed midway through project planning that she was given inaccurate data regarding new regulations affecting the required end date of her project. She may need to make a few adjustments, but she thinks she can still manage the project to complete it before the regulations take effect. She confirms this by analyzing the sequence of activities with the least amount of scheduling flexibility. What technique is she using?

    A. Critical path method
    B. Flowchart
    C. Precedence diagramming
    D. Work breakdown structure

2. A design engineer is helping to ensure that the dependencies within her area of expertise are properly defined on the project. The design of several deliverables must be complete before manufacturing can begin. This is an example of what type of dependency?

    A. Discretionary dependency
    B. External dependency
    C. Mandatory dependency
    D. Scope dependency

3. Your sponsor and stakeholders have made it clear they wish to be kept informed on the project status. There are many aspects of the project on which you will report, and you want to choose the most appropriate tool to use in each case. Which of the following are generally illustrated better by bar charts than network diagrams?

    A. Logical relationships
    B. Critical paths
    C. Resource trade-offs
    D. Progress or status

4. A heuristic is best described as a:

    A. Control tool
    B. Scheduling method
    C. Planning tool
    D. Generally accepted rule

5. Lag means:

    A. The amount of time an activity can be delayed without delaying the project finish date
    B. The amount of time an activity can be delayed without delaying the early start date of its successor
    C. Waiting time
    D. The product of a forward and backward pass

265

6. A project manager is new to the company but has 10 years of project management experience. She is given a medium-sized project and is asked to plan so it is finished as quickly as possible because the company has a large list of projects to complete in the coming year. She will be given another project to manage as soon as she has this one baselined. She needs to report on the longest time the project will take. Which of the following is the best project management tool to use to determine this?

    A. Work breakdown structure
    B. Network diagram
    C. Bar chart
    D. Project charter

7. Which of the following is correct?

    A. The critical path helps prove how long the project will take.
    B. There can be only one critical path.
    C. The network diagram will change every time the end date changes.
    D. A project can never have negative float.

8. A new project manager is walking you through the schedule she has created for her project. She asks you about the duration of a particular milestone, so she knows how to properly schedule it. What will you tell her about a milestone's duration?

    A. It is shorter than the duration of the longest activity.
    B. It is shorter than the activity it represents.
    C. It has no duration.
    D. It is the same length as the activity it represents.

9. Which of the following best describes the relationship between standard deviation and risk?

    A. There is no relationship.
    B. Standard deviation tells you if the estimate is accurate.
    C. Standard deviation tells you how uncertain the estimate is.
    D. Standard deviation tells you if the estimate includes a pad.

10. The float of an activity is determined by:

    A. Performing a Monte Carlo analysis
    B. Determining the waiting time between activities
    C. Determining lag
    D. Determining the length of time the activity can be delayed without delaying the critical path

11. To help them determine the schedule baseline, the team has drafted a network diagram. The project manager adds the time estimates for each activity to establish the critical path for the project. They discover the project has three critical paths. Which of the following best describes how this discovery will affect the project?

    A. It makes it easier to manage.
    B. It increases the project risk.
    C. It requires more people.
    D. It makes it more expensive.

12. The team is working on a project to develop or procure a customized software package that will be used by delivery drivers for a new chain of pizza restaurants. There are multiple stakeholders on this project. Because of other ongoing projects to design, build, and equip brick-and-mortar restaurant locations, you are informed that there is no rush to complete this software development work. If project time and cost are not as important as the number of resources used each month, which of the following is the best thing to do?

    A. Perform a Monte Carlo analysis.
    B. Fast track the project.
    C. Perform resource optimization.
    D. Analyze the life cycle costs.

13. You have identified a diverse group of stakeholders, and you will need to report information in a variety of ways to meet their different communications needs. When will you use a milestone chart instead of a bar chart?

    A. Project planning
    B. Reporting to team members
    C. Reporting to management
    D. Risk analysis

14. The organization is committed to rolling out a new cell phone accessory at an industry trade show in six months. The sponsor has made it clear that this product, to be created by your project team, must meet a long list of requirements, adhere to high quality standards, and, most importantly, be ready in time for the trade show. The sponsor has promised to commit as many resources as necessary for you to complete the project within these constraints. Your project management plan results in a project schedule that is too long. If the project network diagram cannot change but you have extra personnel resources, what is the best thing to do?

    A. Fast track the project.
    B. Level the resources.
    C. Crash the project.
    D. Perform Monte Carlo analysis.

15. Your team worked hard throughout project planning, thoroughly defining and estimating each activity required to complete the work. The resulting network diagram supported the end date that was approved by the team, management, and the stakeholders. As work has progressed, most milestones have been met. On two occasions, workarounds were needed to deal with the occurrence of unidentified risk events. With continued attention to detail, you have been successful in keeping the project on schedule and within budget. Now, an opportunity is identified that can only be realized if the project is completed two days ahead of schedule. Which of the following is the best thing to do when asked to complete a project two days earlier than planned?

    A. Tell senior management that the project's critical path does not allow the project to be finished earlier.
    B. Tell your manager.
    C. Meet with the team to look at options for crashing or fast tracking the critical path.
    D. Work hard and see what the project status is next month.

© 2018 RMC Publications, Inc.™ • 952.846.4484 • info@rmcls.com • www.rmcls.com

16. Although the customer agreed to the original project schedule, they are now asking for an earlier project finish. They are being pressured by their own customers. The project manager's sponsor thinks finishing early is not only a viable option but also a good idea for your organization because it will enable you to start another project sooner. In attempting to complete the project faster, the project manager looks at the cost associated with crashing each activity. The best approach to crashing would also include looking at the:

A. Risk impact of crashing each activity
B. Customer's opinion of which activities to crash
C. Sponsor's opinion of which activities to crash and in what order
D. Project life cycle phase in which the activity is due to occur

17. You are working collaboratively with the team to plan a project. You have obtained estimates from team members on the activities for which they each will be responsible. You are currently reaching agreement on the calendar dates for each activity. Which of the following processes are you working on?

A. Sequence Activities
B. Develop Schedule
C. Define Scope
D. Develop Project Charter

18. A project manager is in the middle of executing a large construction project when he discovers the time needed to complete the project is longer than the time available. What is the best thing to do?

A. Cut product scope.
B. Meet with management, and tell them the required date cannot be met.
C. Work overtime.
D. Determine options for schedule compression, and present management with the recommended option.

19. During project planning, you estimate the time needed for each activity and then total the estimates to create the project estimate. You commit to completing the project by this date. What is wrong with this scenario?

A. The team did not create the estimate, and estimating takes too long using that method.
B. The team did not create the estimate, and a network diagram was not used.
C. The estimate is too long and should be created by management.
D. The project estimate should be the same as the customer's required completion date.

20. You are a project manager on a $5,000,000 software development project. While working with your project team to develop a network diagram, you notice a series of activities that can be worked in parallel but must finish in a specific sequence. What type of activity sequencing method is required for these activities?

A. Precedence diagramming method
B. Arrow diagramming method
C. Critical path method
D. Operational diagramming method

21. You are a project manager on a US $5,000,000 software development project. While working with your project team to develop a network diagram, your data architects suggest that quality could be improved if the data model is approved by senior management before moving on to other design elements. They support this suggestion with an article from a leading software development journal. Which of the following best describes this type of input?

    A. Mandatory external dependency
    B. Discretionary external dependency
    C. External regulatory dependency
    D. Heuristic

22. Based on the following, if you needed to shorten the duration of the project, which activity would you try to shorten?

| Activity | Preceding Activity | Duration in Weeks |
|---|---|---|
| Start | None | 0 |
| A | Start | 1 |
| B | Start | 2 |
| C | Start | 6 |
| D | A | 10 |
| E | B, C | 1 |
| F | C | 2 |
| G | D | 3 |
| H | E | 9 |
| I | F | 1 |
| End | G, H, I | 0 |

    A. Activity B
    B. Activity D
    C. Activity H
    D. Activity C

23. You have a project with the following activities: Activity A takes 40 hours and can start after the project starts. Activity B takes 25 hours and should happen after the project starts. Activity C must happen after activity A and takes 35 hours. Activity D must happen after activities B and C and takes 30 hours. Activity E must take place after activity C and takes 10 hours. Activity F takes place after Activity E and takes 22 hours. Activities F and D are the last activities of the project. Which of the following is true if activity B actually takes 37 hours?

    A. The critical path is 67 hours.
    B. The critical path changes to Start, B, D, End.
    C. The critical path is Start, A, C, E, F, End.
    D. The critical path increases by 12 hours.

24. A project manager has received activity duration estimates from his team. Which of the following does he need in order to complete the Develop Schedule process?

    A. Earned value analysis
    B. Schedule change control system
    C. Trend analysis
    D. Reserves

25. A project manager is taking over a project from another project manager during project planning. If the new project manager wants to see what the previous project manager planned for managing changes to the schedule, it would be best to look at the:

    A. Communications management plan
    B. Update management plan
    C. Staffing management plan
    D. Schedule management plan

26. A project manager is using weighted average duration estimates to perform schedule network analysis. Which type of mathematical analysis is being used?

    A. Critical path method
    B. Beta distribution
    C. Monte Carlo
    D. Resource leveling

27. The WBS, estimates for each work package, and the network diagram are completed. The next thing for the project manager to do is:

    A. Sequence the activities.
    B. Validate that they have the correct scope.
    C. Create a preliminary schedule and get the team's approval.
    D. Complete risk management.

28. A new product development project has four levels in the work breakdown structure and has been sequenced using the precedence diagramming method. The activity duration estimates have been received. What should be done next?

    A. Create an activity list.
    B. Begin the work breakdown structure.
    C. Finalize the schedule.
    D. Compress the schedule.

29. You are the project manager for a new product development project that has four levels in the work breakdown structure. The network diagram and duration estimates have been created, and a schedule has been developed and compressed. Which schedule management activity should you do next?

    A. Control the schedule.
    B. Determine dependencies.
    C. Analogously estimate the schedule.
    D. Gain approval.

30. A team member from research and development tells you that her work is too creative to provide you with a fixed single estimate for the activity. You both decide to use the average labor hours (from past, similar projects) to develop a prototype. This is an example of which of the following?

    A. Parametric estimating
    B. Three-point estimating
    C. Analogous estimating
    D. Monte Carlo analysis

31. As part of a project manager's due diligence, he reviews the schedule, focusing on each activity as its start time approaches. He also monitors activities as they progress. He is currently looking at an activity that has an early start (ES) of day 3, a late start (LS) of day 13, an early finish (EF) of day 9, and a late finish (LF) of day 19. In all likelihood, this activity:

    A. Is on the critical path
    B. Has a lag
    C. Is progressing well
    D. Is not on the critical path

32. The project is calculated to be completed four days after the desired completion date. You do not have access to additional resources. The project is low risk, the benefit-cost ratio is expected to be 1.6, and the dependencies are preferential. Under these circumstances, what is the best thing to do?

    A. Cut resources from an activity.
    B. Make more activities concurrent.
    C. Move resources from the preferential dependencies to the external dependencies.
    D. Remove an activity from the project.

33. A project manager for a small construction company has a project that was budgeted for $130,000 over a six-week period. According to the schedule, the project should have cost $60,000 to date. However, it has cost $90,000 to date. The project is also behind schedule, because the original estimates were not accurate. Who has the primary responsibility to solve this problem?

    A. Project manager
    B. Senior management
    C. Project sponsor
    D. Manager of the project management office

34. Senior management is complaining that they are not able to easily determine the status of ongoing projects in the organization. Which of the following types of reports would help provide summary information to senior management?

    A. Detailed cost estimates
    B. Project management plans
    C. Bar charts
    D. Milestone reports

35. Rearranging resources so that a constant number of resources is used each month is called:

    A. Crashing
    B. Floating
    C. Leveling
    D. Fast tracking

271

36. The team is helping the project manager estimate activities on their project. They are experienced and skilled, and many members have been with the company for some time. There are several activities they need to estimate that have not been previously done by the company. What is the best method of estimating these activities?

    A. Analogous estimating
    B. Three-point estimating
    C. Monte Carlo analysis
    D. Parametric estimating

37. During project executing, a large number of changes are made to the project. Several of the change requests have come from the customer, significantly changing the functionality of the originally requested product. Six project team members have been reassigned by management to a higher-priority project, and they have been replaced. As project work has progressed, many of the identified risks have occurred and have been successfully mitigated. However, three contingency plans have been adjusted and will be implemented if identified risks recur during the remainder of the project. The project manager should:

    A. Wait until all changes are known, and then print out a new schedule.
    B. Make sure the project charter is still valid.
    C. Change the schedule baseline.
    D. Talk to management before any changes are made.

# Answers

1. **Answer** A

   **Explanation** There are only two choices related to scheduling: critical path method and precedence diagramming. Precedence diagramming is a diagramming technique that deals with the relationship between activities, not schedule flexibility. The project manager is analyzing the critical path.

2. **Answer** C

   **Explanation** No mention is made that the dependency comes from a source outside the project, so this is not an external dependency. Scope dependency is not a defined term. The key words in the question are "must be complete." Since the dependency is required, it could not be discretionary and therefore must be mandatory. The question defines a mandatory dependency.

3. **Answer** D

   **Explanation** The bar chart is designed to show a relationship to time. This is best used when demonstrating progress or status as a factor of time.

4. **Answer** D

   **Explanation** A heuristic is a generally accepted rule. Examples are cost per line of code and cost per square foot of floor space.

5. **Answer** C

   **Explanation** Total float and free float are the time an activity can be delayed without impacting the entire project or the next activity. A forward or backward pass refers to a network analysis technique, not waiting time. Waiting time is the correct definition of lag.

6. **Answer** B

   **Explanation** The bar chart may show an end date, but it is not used to determine dates. The project charter also may include a required end date but not a logical determination of how long the project will take. The network diagram shows dependencies between activities on the project activity list. The dependencies allow us to look at the various paths through the diagram to determine the longest duration (critical) path. The network diagram is the best answer.

7. **Answer** A

   **Explanation** This question tests your knowledge about a number of topics. There can often be more than one critical path, but you might adjust the plan in order to decrease risk and have only one critical path. The network diagram may or may not change when the end date changes, depending on the amount of schedule reserve and the reason for the change to the schedule. You can have negative float if you are behind schedule. The critical path helps prove how long the project will take. This is the only correct statement of the choices given.

8. **Answer** C

   **Explanation** A milestone represents the completion of a series of activities or work packages. Milestones represent significant events within the project schedule. They are not work activities, and they have no duration

9. **Answer** C

   **Explanation** An estimate can have a wide range and still be accurate if the item estimated includes identified risks. There is no such thing as a pad in proper project management. An estimate might be inflated, but it is a calculated reserve to account for risks, not arbitrary padding. The standard deviation tells you the amount of uncertainty or risk involved in the estimate for the activity.

10. **Answer** D

    **Explanation** The float of an activity is the length of time the activity can be delayed without delaying the critical path.

11. **Answer** B

    **Explanation** Although having three critical paths could require more people or cost more, the answer that is always true is that it increases project risk. Because you need to manage three critical paths, there is more risk that something could happen to delay the project.

12. **Answer** C

    **Explanation** Fast tracking affects both time and cost but may not help even out resource usage. Monte Carlo analysis and analysis of life cycle costs do not directly deal with resources. Resource optimization is the only choice that will definitely affect resources.

13. **Answer** C

    **Explanation** Both types of charts are used in project planning. Team members need to see details, so they need a bar chart rather than a milestone chart. Risk analysis could make use of both charts. A milestone chart is used instead of a bar chart for any situation where you want to report in a less detailed way. Since bar charts can intimidate people with their complexity—and often show too much detail to be worthwhile on a management level—milestone charts are more effective for reporting to management.

14. **Answer** C

    **Explanation** Leveling resources generally extends the schedule. Monte Carlo analysis does not directly address the constraints of this situation. To compress the schedule, you could either crash or fast track. However, the situation says that the network diagram cannot change. This eliminates fast tracking, which leaves crashing the project as the best answer.

15. **Answer** C

    **Explanation** This is another question that asks about problem-solving. Neither telling your manager nor waiting to see the status next month will address the real problem. It would be inaccurate to report that the project cannot be finished earlier. Only meeting with the team to look for options for compressing the schedule (by crashing or fast tracking) relates to problem-solving.

16. **Answer** A

    **Explanation** You may or may not need your customer's or your sponsor's input, but you will definitely need to include an analysis of risk.

17. **Answer** B

    **Explanation** By the time this process is taking place, Develop Project Charter, Define Scope, and Sequence Activities would be completed. The process defined in the question is Develop Schedule.

18. **Answer** D

    **Explanation** This question tests whether you know how to solve problems. Cutting product scope negatively affects the customer, and is therefore not best. A project manager's job is to determine options for meeting any end date; therefore, simply telling management the required date cannot be met is not correct. Working overtime is expensive and unnecessary when there are many other choices that could be considered first. Determining options for schedule compression would have the least negative effect on the project.

19. **Answer** B

    **Explanation** Time estimates for the activities should be created by the team and should not be added together to create the project estimate. Some activities may take place concurrently; these would be identified in the network diagram.

20. **Answer** A

    **Explanation** The question implies a finish-to-finish relationship between activities. The arrow diagramming method is not a commonly used diagramming method, and it does not support that type of relationship. Critical path is not a diagramming method, and operational diagramming method is a made-up term. The precedence diagramming method is most appropriate in this case.

21. **Answer** B

    **Explanation** A heuristic is a general rule that can be used consistently. This situation is a unique occurrence in which a preferred method is being suggested. Dependencies are often described with two terms, either mandatory or discretionary, and either internal or external. The input in this scenario is discretionary, as it is a suggestion, rather than a required method of doing the work. Since the input comes from a source outside the organization, it is considered external.

22. **Answer** D

    **Explanation** This is an example of a two-stage question you may find on the exam. First you need to draw the network diagram and find the critical path, and then make a decision. The network diagram would be:

| Paths | Duration in Weeks |
|-------|-------------------|
| Start, A, D, G, End | 14 |
| Start, B, E, H, End | 12 |
| Start, C, E, H, End | 16 |
| Start, C, F, I, End | 9 |

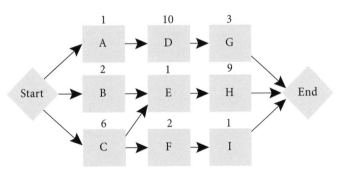

The critical path is 16 (Start, C, E, H, End). Many people immediately look for the longest duration activity on the project to cut. Here activity D is the longest, at 10 weeks. However, that activity is not on the critical path, and cutting it would not shorten the project's duration. You must change the critical path. In this case, both activity C and activity H are on the critical path. If you have a choice, all things being equal, choose the earlier option. Therefore, activity C is the best answer.

23. **Answer** C

**Explanation** Did you notice how difficult this question was to read? Such wording is intentional—to prepare you for interpreting questions on the real exam. Looking at this situation, you see there are three paths through the network, as shown in the following table. If the duration of activity B changes from 25 to 37, the activity will take 12 hours longer. As the activity is only on the third path, it will only change the duration of that path from 55 to 55 + 12, or 67 hours. Since the duration of the critical path is 107 hours, the delay with activity B will have no impact on the project timeline or the current critical path.

| Paths | Duration in Hours |
|---|---|
| Start, A, C, E, F, End | 107 |
| Start, A, C, D, End | 105 |
| Start, B, D, End | 55 |

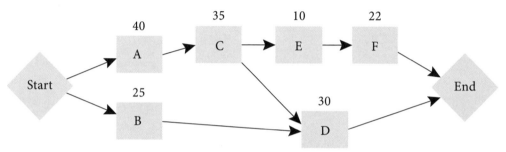

24. **Answer** D

**Explanation** The Develop Schedule process includes all work and uses all inputs needed to come up with a finalized, realistic schedule. As part of the Estimate Activity Durations process, reserves are created to cover identified and unknown schedule risks. All the other items are parts of Control Schedule and occur after the Develop Schedule process.

25. **Answer** D

**Explanation** The schedule management plan is the most correct answer. It includes plans for how schedule changes will be managed.

26. **Answer** B

**Explanation** Beta distribution uses weighted averages to compute activity durations.

27. **Answer** C

**Explanation** Sequencing the activities is the same thing as creating a network diagram, so that has already been done. The Validate Scope process is done during project monitoring and controlling, not during project planning. Since a schedule is an input to risk management, risk management comes after the creation of a preliminary schedule, and so that is not the next thing to do. Creating the preliminary schedule is next.

28. **Answer** D

**Explanation** The question is really asking, "What is done after the Estimate Activity Durations process?" The work breakdown structure and activity list are done before Estimate Activity Durations. The schedule is not finalized until after schedule compression. Therefore, compressing the schedule is done next.

29. **Answer** D

    **Explanation** Notice how this question and the previous one seem similar. This is intended to prepare you for similar questions on the exam. Determining dependencies and analogously estimating the schedule should have already been completed. The situation described is within the Develop Schedule process of schedule management. Control Schedule is the next schedule management process after Develop Schedule, but the Develop Schedule process is not yet finished. Final approval of the schedule by the stakeholders is needed before one has a project schedule.

30. **Answer** A

    **Explanation** Monte Carlo analysis is a modeling, or simulation, technique. Three-point estimating uses three time estimates per activity. One could use data from past projects to come up with the estimate (analogous estimating), but the best answer is parametric estimating because history is being used to calculate an estimate.

31. **Answer** D

    **Explanation** There is no information presented about lag or progress. The activity described has float because there is a difference between the early start and late start. An activity that has float is probably not on the critical path.

32. **Answer** B

    **Explanation** Cutting resources from an activity would not save time, nor would moving resources from the preferential dependencies to the external dependencies. Removing an activity from the project is a possibility, but because the dependencies are preferential and the risk is low, the best choice is to make more activities concurrent, as this would have less impact on the project.

33. **Answer** A

    **Explanation** Did you get lost looking at all the numbers presented in this question? Notice that there are no calculations required, simply an understanding of what the problem is. This question describes schedule management, which is a responsibility of the project manager.

34. **Answer** D

    **Explanation** Detailed cost estimates have nothing to do with the situation described. Project management plans include more detail than is necessary for the situation described, and may distract from the conversation if used in this situation. Bar charts are most effective for reporting to the team. The best answer is milestone reports, which present the right level of detail for upper management.

35. **Answer** C

    **Explanation** The key to this question is the phrase "constant number of resources used each month." Only leveling has such an effect on the schedule.

36. **Answer** B

    **Explanation** Analogous estimating can be used when you have done similar work previously. Monte Carlo analysis is a schedule development technique. Parametric estimating includes the use of history and productivity rates for the work, which would not be available if you had not done the activity before. Three-point estimating is the best method to use in this case because it allows you to estimate in a range—optimistic, pessimistic, and most likely.

37. **Answer** B

   **Explanation**  Waiting until all changes are known and then printing out a new schedule is a common error many project managers make. Instead, the project manager should be controlling the project throughout its completion. The situation in the question does not provide a reason to believe the schedule baseline must be changed. A project manager must be in control of the project, rather than consulting with management before making any changes. Whenever a large number of changes occur on a project, it is wise to confirm that the business case, as stated in the project charter, is still valid.

# Cost Management

## SEVEN

Do you create a budget for your projects? Do you have practical experience managing and controlling project costs? The questions on the exam are written to test whether you have such experience. If these efforts are not part of how you manage your real-world projects, make sure you read this chapter carefully and fully understand the concepts discussed.

Many people are nervous about questions relating to earned value. This chapter should help ease your mind. There have typically been 15 to 20 questions on earned value on the exam. Not all these questions have required earned value calculations. Some questions may only require you to interpret earned value terminology and analysis results. With a little study, earned value questions should be easy.

On the exam, there is a strong connection between cost management and schedule management. Some topics (including planning, estimating, and monitoring and controlling) covered here in the Cost Management chapter also apply to the Schedule Management chapter. The Schedule Management chapter included information on estimating techniques that can be used for both schedule and cost estimating. Earned value analysis is discussed later in this chapter, and is another example of a technique that can be used for both cost and schedule.

## QUICKTEST

- Cost management process
- Earned value analysis
  - PV
  - EV
  - AC
  - CPI
  - SPI
  - BAC
  - EAC
  - ETC
  - VAC
  - CV
  - SV
  - TCPI
- Cost baseline
- Cost budget
- Performance measurement baseline
- Three-point estimating
- Analogous estimating
- Bottom-up estimating
- Parametric estimating
- Inputs to estimating costs
- Cost management plan
- Rough order of magnitude (ROM) estimate
- Definitive estimate
- Budget estimate
- Reserve analysis
- Contingency reserves
- Management reserves
- Cost risk
- Variable/fixed costs
- Direct/indirect costs
- Life cycle costing
- Value analysis
- Control thresholds
- Progress reporting
- Cost of quality
- Return on investment (ROI)
- Discounted cash flow

The Schedule Management chapter describes the decomposition of work packages into smaller components, or activities. For many projects, cost estimates are created at the activity level. On some large projects, however, it might be more practical to estimate and control costs at a higher level, called a control account. (See the Scope Management chapter for more on control accounts.)

279

# Cost Management  SEVEN

| INITIATING | PLANNING (This is the only process group with a set order.) | EXECUTING | MONITORING & CONTROLLING | CLOSING |
|---|---|---|---|---|
| Select project manager | **Determine development approach, life cycle, and how you will plan for each knowledge area** | Execute work according to the project management plan | **Take action to monitor and control the project** | Confirm work is done to requirements |
| Determine company culture and existing systems | Define and prioritize requirements | Produce product deliverables (product scope) | **Measure performance against the performance measurement baseline** | Complete final procurement closure |
| Collect processes, procedures, and historical information | Create project scope statement | Gather work performance data | **Measure performance against other metrics in the project management plan** | Gain final acceptance of product |
| Divide large projects into phases or smaller projects | Assess what to purchase and create procurement documents | Request changes | **Analyze and evaluate data and performance** | Complete financial closure |
| Understand business case and benefits management plan | Determine planning team | Implement only approved changes | **Determine if variances warrant a corrective action or other change request(s)** | Hand off completed product |
| Uncover initial requirements, assumptions, risks, constraints, and existing agreements | Create WBS and WBS dictionary | Continuously improve; perform progressive elaboration | **Influence factors that cause change** | Solicit customer's feedback about the project |
| Assess project and product feasibility within the given constraints | Create activity list | Follow processes | **Request changes** | Complete final performance reporting |
| Create measurable objectives and success criteria | Create network diagram | Determine whether quality plan and processes are correct and effective | Perform integrated change control | Index and archive records |
| Develop project charter | Estimate resource requirements | Perform quality audits and issue quality reports | Approve or reject changes | Gather final lessons learned and update knowledge bases |
| Identify stakeholders and determine their expectations, interest, influence, and impact | **Estimate activity durations and costs** | Acquire final team and physical resources | **Update project management plan and project documents** | |
| Request changes | Determine critical path | Manage people | Inform stakeholders of all change request results | |
| Develop assumption log | Develop schedule | Evaluate team and individual performance; provide training | Monitor stakeholder engagement | |
| Develop stakeholder register | **Develop budget** | Hold team-building activities | Confirm configuration compliance | |
| | Determine quality standards, processes, and metrics | Give recognition and rewards | **Create forecasts** | |
| | **Determine team charter and all roles and responsibilities** | Use issue logs | Gain customer's acceptance of interim deliverables | |
| | Plan communications and stakeholder engagement | Facilitate conflict resolution | Perform quality control | |
| | Perform risk identification, qualitative and quantitative risk analysis, and risk response planning | Release resources as work is completed | Perform risk reviews, reassessments, and audits | |
| | **Go back—iterations** | Send and receive information, and solicit feedback | Manage reserves | |
| | Finalize procurement strategy and documents | Report on project performance | Manage, evaluate, and close procurements | |
| | Create change and configuration management plans | Facilitate stakeholder engagement and manage expectations | Evaluate use of physical resources | |
| | **Finalize all management plans** | Hold meetings | | |
| | **Develop realistic and sufficient project management plan and baselines** | Evaluate sellers; negotiate and contract with sellers | | |
| | Gain formal approval of the plan | Use and share project knowledge | | |
| | Hold kickoff meeting | Execute contingency plans | | |
| | Request changes | Update project management plan and project documents | | |

**Rita's Process Chart™**
**Cost Management**
Where are we in the project management process?

The following should help you understand how each part of cost management fits into the overall project management process:

| The Cost Management Process | Done During |
|---|---|
| Plan Cost Management | Planning process group |
| Estimate Costs | Planning process group |
| Determine Budget | Planning process group |
| Control Costs | Monitoring and controlling process group |

Although they are not currently found in the *PMBOK® Guide,* you should be familiar with the following cost management concepts.

### Life Cycle Costing[1]

This concept involves looking at costs over the entire life of the product, not just the cost of the project to create the product. For example, assume you plan the project to produce the product at a lower level of quality and save $9,000. After the project is completed, the maintenance costs are $100,000 over the life of the product, instead of the $20,000 in maintenance it could have cost had you built the product to a higher quality standard. Your $9,000 project "savings" cost the company $80,000 (or $71,000 in additional cost). This is the concept of life cycle costing—looking at the cost of the whole life of the product, not just the cost of the project. You may encounter questions on the exam requiring you to consider life cycle cost when selecting the cost option with the least negative impact.

### Value Analysis[2]

This concept is sometimes referred to as value engineering. Its focus is on finding a less costly way to do the same work. In other words, this technique is used to answer the question, "How can we decrease cost on the project while maintaining the same scope?" Value analysis refers to finding ways to provide required features at the lowest overall cost without loss of performance.

### Cost Risk[3]

In the Integration Management chapter (and other chapters), we have discussed how some topics cross the boundaries between knowledge areas. The concept of cost risk involves cost, risk, and procurement management. This term means just what its name implies—cost-related risk. Because such topics cross knowledge areas, so do the questions on the exam about the topics. See the following sample question.

*Question*    Who has the cost risk in a fixed-price contract—the buyer or the seller?

*Answer*    The seller

### Plan Cost Management    PAGE 235

> **Process** Plan Cost Management
> **Process Group** Planning
> **Knowledge Area** Cost Management

The Plan Cost Management process involves identifying how you're going to plan (including estimating and budgeting), manage, and monitor and control project costs, including the cost of resources. This process answers the questions, "How will I go about planning cost for the project?" and "How will I effectively manage the project to the cost baseline, control costs, and manage cost variances?"

281

The project charter includes a high-level cost constraint as well as other requirements regarding cost management on the project. Organizational process assets used in this process include cost data and lessons learned from previous projects as well as organizational standards and policies for estimating and budgeting.

In some organizations, the Plan Cost Management process can involve determining whether the project will be paid for with the organization's existing funds or will be funded through equity or debt. It can also include decisions about how to finance project resources—such as choosing whether to purchase or lease equipment.

Net present value, return on investment, payback period, and internal rate of return are calculations that may be used to make such determinations. Do you remember these techniques from the Integration Management chapter? If not, you may want to return to that chapter now and review them. In integration, they were used as project selection measures, and they are also useful in planning cost management. As we get detailed estimates and develop the budget, we will use them to evaluate whether the project is still feasible within the charter and whether the measurable project objectives can be achieved.

Another useful calculation here is discounted cash flow. This technique is used in project selection to estimate the attractiveness of an investment by predicting how much money will be received in the future and then discounting it to its current value. In cost management planning, it is used to evaluate the potential revenue to be earned from specific project work.

Can you see how decisions about funding and financing resources might affect project risks and other project constraints? These decisions will influence how you plan the project across all knowledge areas and how work will be completed. If you haven't had to deal with these concerns on your own projects, it's easy to miss questions on the exam about how cost-related decisions could impact the rest of the project. As you read through this chapter, don't just focus on memorizing the formulas for earned value management. Make sure you truly understand what project management efforts you should be doing when it comes to cost management and what those efforts mean to the project.

## Cost Management Plan    PAGE 238    The output of this process is the cost management plan, which could also be called the "budget management plan" or "budget plan." The cost management plan is similar to other management plans (a PMI-ism). It can be formal or informal, but it is part of the project management plan. Once again, you can see that such a plan requires thinking in advance about how you will plan, manage, and monitor and control project costs. This is a concept many project managers miss.

The cost management plan may include the following:
- Specifications for how estimates should be stated (in what currency)
- The levels of accuracy and precision needed for estimates
- Approved estimating techniques
- Reporting formats to be used
- Rules for measuring cost performance
- Guidance regarding whether costs will include indirect costs (costs not directly attributable to any one project, such as overhead costs) in addition to direct costs (those costs directly attributable to the project)
- Guidelines for the establishment of a cost baseline for measuring against as part of project monitoring and controlling (the cost baseline will ultimately be established in Determine Budget)
- Control thresholds
- Cost change control procedures
- Information on control accounts or other ways to monitor spending on the project

- Funding decisions
- Methods for documenting costs
- Guidelines for dealing with potential fluctuations in resource costs and exchange rates
- Roles and responsibilities for various cost activities

Notice the inclusion of control thresholds. The creation of the cost management plan (like any other management plan in project management) requires thinking ahead about how you will control costs. If an actual cost comes in higher than expected, will you need to take action? What if it's a two-dollar difference? Control thresholds are the amount of variation allowed before you need to take action. You determine these thresholds in planning while creating the cost management plan.

## Estimate Costs   PAGE 240

> **Process** Estimate Costs
> **Process Group** Planning
> **Knowledge Area** Cost Management

This process involves coming up with cost estimates for all project activities and resources required to complete them. These estimates will be combined into one time-phased spending plan in the next process: Determine Budget.

In the Schedule Management chapter, we included some Tricks of the Trade® titled, "Things to Know about Estimating for the Exam." As noted in that chapter, those concepts apply to both cost and schedule estimating. Take some time now to review that list. It is helpful to have those concepts fresh in your mind before continuing to read about the Estimate Costs process.

So what costs should you estimate? To put it simply, you need to estimate the costs of all the efforts to complete the project. This includes costs directly associated with the project, such as labor, equipment, materials, and training for the project, as well as the following:

- Costs of quality efforts
- Costs of risk efforts
- Costs of the project manager's time
- Costs of project management activities
- Expenses for physical office spaces used directly for the project
- Overhead costs, such as management salaries and general office expenses

In addition, when the project involves a procurement, the buyer estimates the amount of profit they are paying the seller when purchasing goods or services. The seller estimates the amount of profit to build into the cost of providing the goods or services.

### Types of Cost   There are several ways to look at costs when creating an estimate. In the past, the exam has only asked a few questions regarding types of cost. The following information should help you answer such questions.

A cost can be either variable or fixed:

- **Variable costs** These costs change with the amount of production or the amount of work. Examples include the cost of material, supplies, and wages.
- **Fixed costs** These costs do not change as production changes. Examples include the cost of setup, rent, utilities, etc.

A cost can be either direct or indirect:

- **Direct costs**  These costs are directly attributable to the work on the project. Examples are team wages, team travel and recognition expenses, and costs of material used on the project.

- **Indirect costs**  Indirect costs are overhead items or costs incurred for the benefit of more than one project. Examples include taxes, fringe benefits, and janitorial services.

## Inputs to Estimating Costs    PAGE 241    These inputs help you create estimates more quickly and accurately. For example, imagine having access to a repository containing all the previous WBSs for projects similar to yours, along with the estimates and actual costs for each activity. Can you see how that might be helpful in creating more accurate estimates on your own project? Having highly accurate estimates will help you better control the project later and, therefore, save you effort. So, read through the following list of inputs, and think through how each might help you estimate costs:

- **Cost management plan**  This plan, developed in the Plan Cost Management process, documents the methods you'll use to estimate costs, as well as the levels of accuracy and precision required for estimates.

- **Quality management plan**  This plan outlines all the activities the team must perform (as well as any required resources) in order to achieve the expected level of quality. These quality activities have cost associated with them.

- **Scope baseline**  To create a cost estimate, you need to know the details of what project and product scope you are estimating; this includes knowing what is out of scope and what cost-related constraints have been placed on the project scope. This information can be found by looking at all the components of the scope baseline (the project scope statement, WBS, and WBS dictionary).

- **Lessons learned register**  Lessons learned from estimates made in earlier phases of the current project (if you are using rolling wave planning) should have been documented in the project's lessons learned register. Also, historical lessons learned regarding estimates from previous similar projects should be available. You can use these lessons to help you create more accurate estimates for the remaining parts of your project.

- **Project schedule**  The project schedule includes a list of activities, the resources needed to complete the work, and information about when the work will occur. There are two reasons you need a schedule before you can come up with a budget. First, the timing of when you buy something may affect its cost. For example, the price of material or a piece of equipment may vary due to factors such as availability, seasonal pricing fluctuations, or new model releases. If you know something will be more expensive at the time it is scheduled to be purchased, you may consider changing the schedule to be able to purchase the material or equipment at a different time, for a lower price. As another example, the cost of human resources may be impacted by their availability. If a lower-priced resource is not available, you may have to pay more for a higher-priced one. Second, you need to develop a time-phased spending plan to monitor and control project expenditures (a budget) so you know how much money will be spent during specific periods of time (weeks, months, etc.) This is the process of iterative planning, as shown in Rita's Process Chart™.

- **Resource requirements**  The resource management plan lists the human resources (including the quantity of resources needed and their skills) required on the project, as well as all the other resources (such as materials and equipment) necessary to complete each activity. Of course, these resources have costs associated with them. The project manager should have access to the rates paid to everyone who works on the project. Recognition and rewards given to team members can increase productivity and save money, but they are still a cost item and need to be estimated. The resource management plan is discussed in more detail in the Resource Management chapter.

- **Risk register**  The risk management process can save time and money, but there are costs associated with the efforts to deal proactively with risks (both opportunities and threats). Risks are an input to this process because they influence how costs are estimated. They can also be an output because our choices related to estimating costs have associated risks. Again, planning is iterative.

- **Policies and historical records related to estimating, templates, processes, procedures, lessons learned, and historical information (organizational process assets)**  As noted earlier, records from past projects can be highly beneficial in creating estimates for a current project. Organizational policies and standardized templates, such as preferred estimation methods and forms to document estimates, can also make this effort faster and easier.

- **Company culture and existing systems that the project will have to deal with or can use (enterprise environmental factors)**  For cost estimating, this includes marketplace conditions, commercial cost databases, exchange rates, and inflation. You also might review the sources from which supplies might be procured and at what costs as part of estimating.

- **Project management costs**  It is important to understand that part of the expense of a project comes from the costs of project management activities. Although project management efforts save money on projects overall, they also result in costs, and should be included in the project cost estimates. These include not only costs associated with the efforts of the project manager but also those associated with status reports, change analysis, etc.

**Exercise**  Test yourself! Try to recreate the list of inputs to estimating in the space below. For the answer, refer back to the previous list. Spend some time thinking about any inputs you forgot, to make sure you really understand these inputs for the exam.

285

# Cost Management   S E V E N

**How Is Estimating Done?**   Costs can be estimated using the same techniques described in the Schedule Management chapter: one-point estimating, analogous estimating, parametric estimating, bottom-up estimating,[4] and three-point estimating.

**Exercise**   Test yourself! See if you understand the differences between top-down (analogous) and bottom-up estimating by identifying the advantages and disadvantages of each technique. (These estimating techniques were described in the Schedule Management chapter.)

| What Are the Advantages of Top-Down (Analogous) Estimating? | What Are the Disadvantages of Top-Down (Analogous) Estimating? |
|---|---|
| | |

| What Are the Advantages of Bottom-Up Estimating? | What Are the Disadvantages of Bottom-Up Estimating? |
|---|---|
| | |

286

| What Are the Advantages of Bottom-Up Estimating? | What Are the Disadvantages of Bottom-Up Estimating? |
|---|---|
| | |
| | |
| | |

**Answer** There are many possible answers to these questions. The purpose of this exercise is to get you thinking about the differences so you can answer any questions on the topic of estimating, no matter how they may be worded. When taking the exam, look at the context of the question to determine whether it is referring to early, high-level estimating or more detailed, bottom-up estimating.

| Advantages of Top-Down (Analogous) Estimating | Disadvantages of Top-Down (Analogous) Estimating |
|---|---|
| Quick | Less accurate |
| Activities do not need to be identified | Estimates are prepared with a limited amount of detailed information and understanding of the project or key deliverables |
| Less costly to create | Requires considerable experience to do well |
| Cost constraints created by management in project initiating give the project manager data to evaluate high-level project feasibility | There may be infighting to gain the biggest piece of the budget without being able to justify the need |
| Overall project costs will be capped for a project analogous estimate | Extremely difficult for projects with uncertainty or where there is no history of similar projects for the subject matter expert to reference |
| | Does not take into account the differences between projects |

| Advantages of Bottom-Up Estimating | Disadvantages of Bottom-Up Estimating |
|---|---|
| More accurate, as it uses analogous, three-point, or parametric estimating at the activity level | Takes time and money to use this estimating technique |
| Gains buy-in from the team because the team creates estimates they can live with | Tendency for the team to pad estimates unless they understand the use of reserves |
| Based on a detailed analysis of the project and the deliverables | Requires that the project be defined and well understood before estimating begins |
| Provides a basis for monitoring and controlling, performance measurement, and management | Requires time to break the project down into smaller pieces |

287

### Accuracy of Estimates
Think about someone walking into your office and asking you to estimate the total cost of a new project. The first question you would probably ask is, "How accurate do you want me to be?" Estimates made in the early part of the project will be less accurate than those made later, when more is known about the project. Estimates should be in a range, as it is very unlikely an activity will be completed for the exact amount estimated. In the early part of the project, you typically provide wide-ranging estimates. They are top-down in nature. Over time, as you determine more information about the project during planning, you can narrow the estimate range. These top-down estimates evolve into bottom-up estimates.

### Project Management Information System
A Project Management Information System (PMIS) is made up of tools to support information documentation, storage, and retrieval on the project. It includes estimating spreadsheets and software, and integrates finance and accounting, scheduling, quality, and risk tools. These tools can significantly speed up calculations and analysis related to estimating.

### Determining Resource Cost Rates
Although many project managers do not have access to this information on their projects, the exam assumes a project manager knows the actual cost of labor when performing detailed cost estimating. Resources are not limited to internal human resources. The work of estimating resource costs might also involve estimating the work of consultants, sellers, and suppliers.

When the project includes plans to outsource pieces of work, the Estimate Costs and Plan Procurement Management processes impact each other and require iterations as planning progresses. This same relationship exists between Plan Procurement Management and the other estimating processes, such as Estimate Activity Resources and Estimate Activity Durations.

### Alternatives Analysis
In this process, alternatives analysis involves assessing the cost of various ways to accomplish the project work. This could include make-or-buy analysis or other types of analysis regarding how to accomplish the project outcomes within cost constraints or practices of the organization.

### Reserve Analysis
Proper project management requires the use of reserves to cover the schedule, cost, and other areas of risk in a project estimate. As discussed in the Schedule Management chapter, reserve analysis involves identifying which activities on the project have significant risk and determining how much time and money to set aside to account for those risks in case they occur. Contingency reserves are used for known risks, which are specifically identified risks. A management reserve is used to accommodate unknown, or unidentified, risks. See the Risk Management chapter to learn how these reserves are calculated.

### Cost of Quality
The cost of work added to the project to accommodate quality efforts should be included in the project estimate.

### Decision-Making
As is the case with schedule estimates, involving team members in estimating costs improves accuracy because they are the ones most likely to understand what's involved in the effort. Examples of group decision-making techniques include voting, brainstorming, and the nominal group technique, all of which were described in the Scope Management chapter of this book.

**Estimate Ranges**    Organizations often have different standards for different ranges—from preliminary to conceptual to feasibility to order of magnitude to definitive estimates. Such ranges tell you how much time and effort need to go into estimating to make sure the actual cost is within the range of the estimate. The standard ranges of the order of magnitude estimate, budget estimate, and definitive estimate are shown below:

- **Rough order of magnitude (ROM) estimate**[5]    This type of estimate is usually made during project initiating. A typical range for ROM estimates is –25 to +75 percent, but this range can vary depending on how much is known about the project when creating the estimates.

- **Budget estimate**    As a best practice, it is a good idea to narrow the range of the estimate before you begin iterating the plan. A budget estimate is in the range of –10 to +25 percent.

- **Definitive estimate**    As project planning progresses, the estimate will become even more refined. Some project managers use the range of +/–10 percent, while others use –5 to +10 percent.

**TRICKS OF THE TRADE®**    The concept of ranges often appears on the exam. Make sure you understand that estimates become more detailed as project planning progresses. Remember that organizations have different rules for the acceptable range of estimate for an activity or the project and that what you see here may be different than your experience. It is wise to estimate in a range, based on the level of uncertainty remaining in the estimate. Even the approved baseline may be expressed as a range, for example: $1,000,000 (–5 to +10 percent).

When completed, the Estimate Costs process results in cost estimates and an explanation of how those estimates were derived (known as the basis of estimates). It can also result in changes or updates to project documents, such as the risk register, assumption log, and lessons learned register.

## Determine Budget    PAGE 248

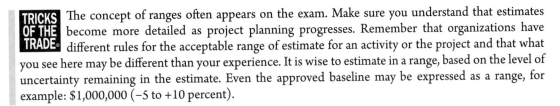

| | |
|---|---|
| **Process** | Determine Budget |
| **Process Group** | Planning |
| **Knowledge Area** | Cost Management |

In this part of cost management, the project manager calculates the total cost of the project to determine the amount of funds the organization needs to have available for the project. The result of this calculation is the budget. The cost baseline is the portion of the budget the project manager will have control over. Meeting the cost baseline will be a measure of project success, so the budget should be in a form the project manager can use while the work is being done to control costs and, therefore, control the overall project.

To begin the Determine Budget process, the project manager should review the business case and the benefits management plan for the project. The business case includes the business need and reason the project is being done. This may be expressed in financial terms, such as expected return on investment. The benefits management plan can be used to finalize the budget and compare it to the economic benefits expected from the project.

Many of the inputs to the Estimate Costs process are used here as well: the cost management plan, the scope baseline, the project schedule, the risk register, and organizational process assets (existing policies on cost control and cost budgeting, for example). Two outputs from Estimate Costs—cost estimates and the basis of estimates—are also essential inputs to this process. You'll also need information about when and for how long resources will be needed (and at what rates—which can be found in the resource management plan), and any agreements regarding the purchase of services or products for the project.

In estimating the total cost of a project (determining the project's budget), a project manager must perform risk management activities and include reserves in their estimates. The cost baseline includes contingency reserves; it represents the funds the project manager has authority to manage and control. The cost budget is the cost baseline plus the management reserves.

To create a budget, activity cost estimates are rolled up to work package cost estimates. Work package costs are then rolled up to control account costs and finally to project costs. This process is called cost aggregation. Contingency reserves are added to determine the cost baseline. These can be added at the project level, as described here and depicted in figure 7.1, but note it is also possible to add contingency reserves at the activity level. In the final step, the management reserves are added.

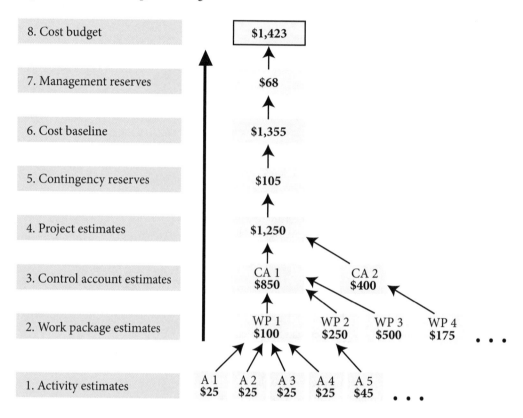

FIGURE 7.1    *Creating a budget*

After the cost baseline and cost budget are estimated, the project manager may compare these numbers to parametric estimates or to expert judgment; alternatively, the project manager may perform a historical information review, comparing their estimates to those of past, similar projects. For example, a general rule for a high-level parametric estimate in some industries is that design should be 15 percent of the cost of construction. Other industries estimate the cost of design to be 60 percent of the project budget. The project manager needs to investigate and justify any significant differences between the project estimates and the reference data to ensure the estimates are reasonable and as accurate as possible.

The next thing to check is cash flow (part of funding limit reconciliation[6]). Funding may not be available when it is needed on the project, causing changes to the other parts of the project and iterations of the project documents or project management plan. For example, if equipment costing $500,000 is scheduled to be purchased on June 1 but the money for the purchase is not available until July 1, the activities dependent on that equipment will have to be moved to later points in the schedule. The cost baseline, therefore, is time-phased and may be shown as an S-curve.[7]

The project manager needs to perform another reconciliation before the proposed cost baseline and cost budget can become final: reconciling with any cost constraints in the charter. If, after all of the project manager's work, the project estimate still exceeds the constraints, the project manager must meet with management, explain why their cost requirement cannot be met, and propose options to decrease costs. Pay particular attention to that last sentence.

Such actions are a required part of project management. If a proposed budget is unrealistic, it is the project manager's job to address it early in planning. As with the schedule, project managers have a professional responsibility to reconcile the budget in this way.

Financing refers to obtaining the needed funds for a project. This means all funds, both internal and external. External funds are obtained from sources outside the performing organization, and are typically needed for major long-term projects. These funds are included in the cost baseline.

When the Determine Budget process is complete, the cost baseline, including all funding requirements, is established. As in the other processes we have discussed, the efforts involved in determining the budget may create the need for updates to project documentation including cost estimates, the risk register, and the project schedule.

## Control Costs   PAGE 257

| | |
|---|---|
| **Process** | Control Costs |
| **Process Group** | Monitoring & Controlling |
| **Knowledge Area** | Cost Management |

The Control Costs process is similar to the ongoing process of control in other knowledge areas, with a focus on cost. Complete the following exercise and imagine how this would apply to real-world projects.

**Exercise**   What actions should a project manager take to control costs? (This is an important topic, so be sure to take your time to think about this question.)

**Answer**  Was one of your answers "follow the cost management plan"? That is an excellent answer! The cost management plan includes your plan for how you will control the costs of the project, which may include items such as meetings on cost, reports, measurements that will be made, and the frequency with which you will measure. The control part of the management plan is customized to the needs of the project.

If you understand the idea behind PMI-isms, you might also have answered something like "look at organizational process assets." That is also a good answer. You need to consider policies, procedures, tools, or reporting formats related to controlling costs that are available or required by your company.

Was another one of your answers "manage changes"? This is generally correct, but make sure you understand the complexity of this effort. What about preventing unnecessary changes and influencing the things causing costs to rise? What about letting people know which changes are approved and which are not so everyone is working with the same project information? You need to make sure the project goes according to the plan; controlling all aspects of the project is essential to achieve overall project success. Think of yourself as a detective looking for anything that can get in the way of project success. This mindset will help you choose the best choice when answering questions that seem to have more than one correct answer.

Also keep in mind that control means measure. When taking the exam, assume the project manager is measuring the project, even if you do not do this on your real-world projects. Measurement helps you see if there are any variances. You can then determine if those variances require changes, including corrective or preventive actions. The cost management plan should include what you will measure, when, and what amount of variation between planned and actual will require action (your control limits). In other words, you plan what you will do to control the project before you get started. Do you do this on your projects? Assume that you do, and assume that all proper project management is being done when you take the exam unless the question tells you (directly or indirectly) that proper project management was not done.

## Progress Reporting    PAGE 264    The project manager can use information about project progress to help control the schedule and costs and to assess whether the project is on track through earned value analysis (a data analysis technique described later in this section). Some project managers use alternative means of determining progress that don't rely on earned value analysis, such as asking team members for an estimate of percent complete for each work package or activity. On projects where work is not objectively measured, the estimates the team members are able to provide are simply guesswork. The method of asking for percent complete is time-consuming and generally a waste of time because it does not result in a realistic estimate of the project's progress.

Another way to track progress without using earned value analysis is to accurately measure deliverable completion (evaluating how much has been done to complete the deliverable based on the work package and the cost and schedule estimates). Typically, with a WBS, 80 hours is a small enough increment of work to be able to track progress against and still have accurate data. For the exam, remember that projects planned using proper project management make use of a WBS, and the activities to produce the work package deliverable are broken down to an appropriate level for monitoring and controlling. Because such work packages are completed relatively quickly and frequently, the project manager can monitor completion of work packages as a way to show progress on deliverables within the time and cost allotted to them in the plan.

## Reserve Analysis   PAGE 265   Remember the contingency reserves that get factored into the cost baseline to address known risks? Part of controlling costs involves analyzing whether those contingency reserves are still necessary or whether new reserves are required. For example, let's say a project team identifies a highly ranked risk and sets aside a contingency reserve to address that risk, should the need arise. If the risk does not occur and it is determined the risk is no longer a threat, the contingency reserve can be removed from the cost baseline (and subsequently the cost budget). Or, a risk review on a project may identify new risks, which could lead to a decision to increase the contingency reserves. Both of these examples require a change request being submitted through integrated change control. It may also be necessary to reassess the amount of management reserve that was set aside to address unknown risks. Maybe too little or too much was set aside for management reserves in the cost management plan.

Reserve analysis allows you to identify and apply lessons learned in the Control Costs process. Analysis of the management reserves may indicate too many unknown risk events are occurring, suggesting that the risk management efforts in planning were inadequate and need to be redone. Management reserves, if you recall, are separate from the cost baseline, so changes to them will change the cost budget. If an unknown risk event occurs, management reserves will pay for the workaround; a change request is required to move those management reserve funds into the cost baseline and to add any additional funds required to complete the reestimated project work within the new parameters of the project.

## Earned Value Measurement[8]   PAGE 261   You already know earned value, as a concept and a technique, is on the exam. Are you worried about it? Don't be. We are going to make it easier.

First, think about this: How valuable would it be to know how your project is really going? Could you sleep better at night? Would you be able to spend your time in more productive ways than worrying? These are the benefits of the methodology of earned value management. If you currently rely on hope, guesses, or a general percent complete estimate to assess how your project is faring, you probably know from experience that these methods do not tell you much, nor are they very accurate. And they may regularly result in the need to work overtime at the end of the project because of the lack of control along the way. Keep the benefits of earned value as an analysis technique in mind as you read this section, and go through it slowly if it seems confusing.

Earned value analysis is used in performance reviews to measure project performance against the scope, schedule, and cost baselines. Note that earned value analysis uses a combination of these three baselines, known as the performance measurement baseline. The measurements resulting from an earned value analysis of the project indicate whether there are any potential deviations from the performance measurement baseline. Many project managers manage their project's performance by comparing planned to actual results. With this method, however, you could easily be on time but overspend according to your plan. Using earned value analysis is better, because it integrates cost, time, and the work done (or scope), and it can be used to forecast future performance and project completion dates and costs.

Using the work performance information gathered through earned value analysis, a project manager can create reports, including cost forecasts, and other communications related to the project's progress. Earned value analysis may also result in change requests to the project.

# Cost Management SEVEN

 **Terms to Know**    Here are the earned value terms you need to know.

| Acronym | Term | Interpretation |
|---|---|---|
| PV | Planned value | As of today, what is the estimated value of the work planned to be done? |
| EV | Earned value | As of today, what is the estimated value of the work actually accomplished? |
| AC | Actual cost (total cost) | As of today, what is the actual cost incurred for the work accomplished? |
| BAC | Budget at completion (the cost baseline) | How much did we budget for the total project effort? |
| EAC | Estimate at completion | What do we currently expect the total project to cost (a forecast)? |
| ETC | Estimate to complete | From this point on, how much more do we expect it to cost to finish the project (a forecast)? |
| VAC | Variance at completion | As of today, how much over or under budget do we expect to be at the end of the project? |

**Formulas and Interpretations to Memorize**    The exam focuses not just on calculations, but also on knowing what the numbers mean. Therefore, you should know all the formulas in the following table. Note that most exam questions relating to these formulas will refer to cumulative analysis data from the beginning of the project to the point in time when it is being measured.

| Name | Formula | Interpretation |
|---|---|---|
| Cost variance (CV) | $EV - AC$ | Negative is over budget; positive is under budget. |
| Schedule variance (SV) | $EV - PV$ | Negative is behind schedule; positive is ahead of schedule. |
| Cost performance index[9] (CPI) | $\dfrac{EV}{AC}$ | We are getting $ _____ worth of work out of every $1 spent. Funds are or are not being used efficiently. Greater than one is good; less than one is bad. |
| Schedule performance index (SPI) | $\dfrac{EV}{PV}$ | We are (only) progressing at _____ percent of the rate originally planned. Greater than one is good; less than one is bad. |

294

| Name | Formula | Interpretation |
|---|---|---|
| Estimate at completion (EAC) | | As of now, how much do we expect the total project to cost? $_____. |
| **NOTE:** *There are many ways to calculate EAC, depending on the assumptions made. Notice how the purpose of the formulas really is to create forecasts based on past performance of the project. Exam questions may require you to determine which EAC formula is appropriate. Pay attention to the information provided in the question. It will help you determine which formula to use.* | AC + Bottom-up ETC | This formula calculates actual costs to date plus a revised estimate for all the remaining work. It is used when the original estimate was fundamentally flawed. |
| | $\dfrac{BAC}{CPI^C}$ | This formula is used if no variances from the BAC have occurred or if you will continue at the same rate of spending (as calculated in your cumulative CPI or based on the trends that have led to the current CPI). |
| | AC + (BAC – EV) | This formula calculates actual costs to date plus remaining budget. It is used when current variances are thought to be atypical of the future. It is essentially AC plus the remaining value of work to perform. |
| | $AC + \dfrac{(BAC - EV)}{(CPI^C \times SPI^C)}$ | This formula calculates actual to date plus the remaining budget modified by performance. It is used when current variances are thought to be typical of the future and when project schedule constraints will influence the completion of the remaining effort. So for example, it might be used when the cumulative CPI is less than one and a firm completion date must be met. |
| To-complete performance index (TCPI) | $\dfrac{(BAC - EV)}{(BAC - AC)}$ | This formula divides the value of the work remaining to be done by the money remaining to do it. It answers the question "To stay within budget, what rate do we need to meet for the remaining work?" |
| | | Greater than one is bad; less than 1 is good. |
| Estimate to complete (ETC) | | How much more will the project cost? |
| **NOTE:** *You can determine ETC by either using the formula listed here or reestimating the cost of the work remaining.* | EAC – AC | This formula calculates the total project cost as of today minus what has been spent to date. |
| | Reestimate | Reestimate the remaining work from the bottom up. |
| Variance at completion (VAC) | BAC – EAC | How much over or under budget will we be at the end of the project? |

295

Make sure you understand and memorize the following about CV, SV, CPI, and SPI:

- EV comes first in each of these formulas. Remembering this one fact alone should help you get about half the earned value questions right.
- If it is a variance (difference), the formula is EV minus AC or PV.
- If it is an index (ratio), the formula is EV divided by AC or PV.
- If the formula relates to cost, use AC.
- If the formula relates to schedule, use PV.
- For variances interpretation: negative is bad and positive is good. Thus a –200 cost variance means you spent more than planned (over budget). A –200 schedule variance means you are behind schedule. This also applies to VAC.
- For indices interpretation: greater than one is good and less than one is bad. Remember, this only applies to CPI and SPI. The opposite is true of TCPI.

People often incorrectly answer questions requiring them to interpret earned value terms or acronyms because they fail to understand the meanings of the terms. Figure 7.2 illustrates some of the differences. Notice that planned value (PV; what the value was expected to be at this point in the project according to the plan) and actual cost (AC; what the cost has actually been on the project to this point) look backward at the project. Budget at completion (BAC), estimate to complete (ETC), and estimate at completion (EAC) look forward. BAC refers to the project's planned budget; it indicates what the end cost of the project would be if everything went according to plan. ETC and EAC forecast future performance based on what has actually occurred on the project, taking into account any variances from the plan the project has already experienced. ETC is an estimate of how much more the remainder of the project will cost to complete. EAC indicates what the total project cost is forecasted to be.

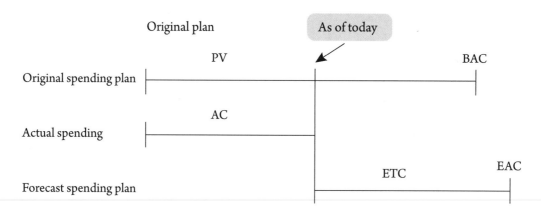

**FIGURE 7.2**　*Understanding earned value concepts by looking backward and forward on a project*

### Earned Value in Action

Earned value is an effective tool for measuring performance and determining the need to request changes. The following is a sample team meeting conversation on this subject.

*The project manager calls a team meeting and says, "We are six months into this million-dollar project, and my latest analysis shows a CPI of 1.2 and an SPI of 0.89. This means we are getting 1.2 dollars for every dollar we put into the project, but only progressing at 89 percent of the rate originally planned. Let's look for options to correct this problem."*

*The network specialist suggests that she could be removed from the project team and replaced with someone less expensive.*

*The project manager replies, "Not only would it sadden me to lose you, but your suggestion would improve costs, not schedule. You are the company's best network specialist. Someone else would not be as proficient as you in completing the work."*

*The IT coordinator suggests either removing the purchase of new computers from the project, or telling the customer the project will be two weeks late.*

*The project manager responds, "Canceling the new computers would save us money, not time. We need to focus on time. We cannot change the project schedule baseline arbitrarily. That would be unethical."*

*Another team member suggests that since the project is doing well on cost, the project manager could bring in another programmer from the IT department to work on the project to get the next two activities completed more quickly.*

*The project manager says, "That sounds like the most effective choice in this situation. Let's see if we can find someone who will improve performance, at the lowest cost. Thanks for your help."*

The best way to learn the earned value analysis technique is to use it. The following exercises are designed to give you a chance to practice both calculations and interpretation. Earned value questions on the exam have generally required fewer calculations per question than these exercises.

**Exercise**   The cost performance index (CPI) and the schedule performance index (SPI) can be charted each month to show the project trends. Based on the diagram, what would you be more concerned about—cost or schedule—if you were taking over this project from another project manager?

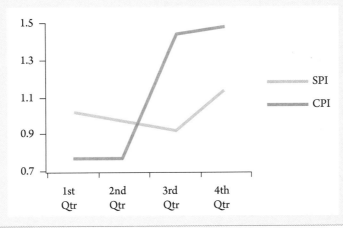

**Answer**   Since these calculations were made in the past, the data in the chart is historical data. The last, most current measurement was in the fourth quarter, which shows both SPI and CPI being above one (good). As of the fourth quarter, the SPI is lower. Therefore, the answer is schedule. An easy way to answer performance index questions that ask whether cost or schedule should concern you most is to pick the option with the lowest index.

**Exercise**   **The Fence #1**   You have a project to build a new fence. The fence will form a square, as shown at right. Each side is to take one day to build, and $1,000 has been budgeted per side. The sides are planned to be completed one after the other. Today is the end of day 3.

Using the following project status chart, calculate PV, EV, etc. in the spaces provided. Then check your answers. Interpretation is also important on the exam. Can you interpret what each answer means?

Do the calculations to three decimal places on the exercises. On the real exam, round the results of your calculations to two decimal places when you are ready to check your answers against the choices provided.

| Activity | Day 1 | Day 2 | Day 3 | Day 4 | Status End of Day 3 |
|----------|-------|-------|-------|-------|---------------------|
| Side 1 | S---------F | | | | Complete, spent $1,000 |
| Side 2 | | S--------PF | ----F | | Complete, spent $1,200 |
| Side 3 | | | PS--S---PF | | 50% done, spent $600 |
| Side 4 | | | | PS--------PF | Not yet started |

**Key**   S = Actual Start, F = Actual Finish, PS = Planned Start, and PF = Planned Finish

| | What Is: | Calculation | Answer | Interpretation of the Answer |
|---|----------|-------------|--------|------------------------------|
| 1 | PV | | | |
| 2 | EV | | | |
| 3 | AC | | | |
| 4 | BAC | | | |
| 5 | CV | | | |
| 6 | CPI | | | |
| 7 | SV | | | |
| 8 | SPI | | | |
| 9 | EAC | | | |
| 10 | ETC | | | |
| 11 | VAC | | | |

298

## Answer   The Fence #1

| | What Is: | Calculation | Answer | Interpretation of the Answer |
|---|---|---|---|---|
| 1 | PV | $1,000 plus $1,000 plus $1,000 | $3,000 | We should have done $3,000 worth of work. |
| 2 | EV | Complete, complete, and half done, or $1,000 plus $1,000 plus $500 | $2,500 | We have actually completed $2,500 worth of work. |
| 3 | AC | $1,000 plus $1,200 plus $600 | $2,800 | We have actually spent $2,800. |
| 4 | BAC | $1,000 plus $1,000 plus $1,000 plus $1,000 | $4,000 | Our project budget is $4,000. |
| 5 | CV | $2,500 minus $2,800 | −$300 | We are over budget by $300. |
| 6 | CPI | $2,500 divided by $2,800 | 0.893 | We are only getting about 89 cents out of every dollar we put into the project. |
| 7 | SV | $2,500 minus $3,000 | −$500 | We are behind schedule. |
| 8 | SPI | $2,500 divided by $3,000 | 0.833 | We are only progressing at about 83 percent of the rate planned. |
| 9 | EAC | $4,000 divided by $0.893 | $4,479 | We currently estimate that the total project will cost $4,479. |
| 10 | ETC | $4,479 minus $2,800 | $1,679 | We need to spend an additional $1,679 to finish the project. |
| 11 | VAC | $4,000 minus $4,479 | −$479 | We currently expect to be $479 over budget when the project is completed. |

Did you select the correct EAC formula? If not, did you miss information in the question that could have guided you to the correct formula? In this example, side 2 cost $1,200. Side 3 is 50 percent complete and has cost $600. This suggests a trend that indicates side 4 is likely to cost $1,200 when complete. When there is a trend and no other information to indicate the trend will not continue, it's most appropriate to use the BAC/CPI formula.

## Exercise   The Fence #2   You have a project to build a new fence. The fence will form a square, as shown at right. Each side is to take one day to build, and $1,000 has been budgeted per side. The sides were planned to be completed one after the other; however, circumstances changed on the project, and work on the sides was able to proceed in parallel. Assume therefore that the sides have a finish-to-finish relationship instead of a finish-to-start relationship, so more than one side can be worked on at the same time. Today is the end of day 3.

Using the following project status chart, calculate PV, EV, etc. in the spaces provided. Then check your answers.

| Activity | Day 1 | Day 2 | Day 3 | Day 4 | Status End of Day 3 |
|----------|-------|-------|-------|-------|---------------------|
| Side 1 | S---------F | | | | Complete, spent $1,000 |
| Side 2 | | S----F----PF | | | Complete, spent $900 |
| Side 3 | | S---- | PS-------PF | | 50% done, spent $600 |
| Side 4 | | | S---- | PS--------PF | 75% done, spent $600 |

**Key**   S = Actual Start, F = Actual Finish, PS = Planned Start, and PF = Planned Finish

| | What Is: | Calculation | Answer | Interpretation of the Answer |
|---|----------|-------------|--------|------------------------------|
| 1 | PV | | | |
| 2 | EV | | | |
| 3 | AC | | | |
| 4 | BAC | | | |
| 5 | CV | | | |
| 6 | CPI | | | |
| 7 | SV | | | |
| 8 | SPI | | | |
| 9 | EAC | | | |
| 10 | ETC | | | |
| 11 | VAC | | | |

## Answer   The Fence #2

| | What Is: | Calculation | Answer | Interpretation of the Answer |
|---|----------|-------------|--------|------------------------------|
| 1 | PV | $1,000 plus $1,000 plus $1,000 | $3,000 | We should have done $3,000 worth of work. |
| 2 | EV | Complete, complete, half done, and 75% done, or $1,000 plus $1,000 plus $500 plus $750 | $3,250 | We have actually completed $3,250 worth of work. |

| | What Is: | Calculation | Answer | Interpretation of the Answer |
|---|---|---|---|---|
| 3 | AC | $1,000 plus $900 plus $600 plus $600 | $3,100 | We have actually spent $3,100. |
| 4 | BAC | $1,000 plus $1,000 plus $1,000 plus $1,000 | $4,000 | Our project budget is $4,000. |
| 5 | CV | $3,250 minus $3,100 | $150 | We are under budget by $150. |
| 6 | CPI | $3,250 divided by $3,100 | 1.048 | We are getting about $1.05 out of every dollar we put into the project. |
| 7 | SV | $3,250 minus $3,000 | $250 | We are ahead of schedule. |
| 8 | SPI | $3,250 divided by $3,000 | 1.083 | We are progressing at about 108 percent of the rate planned. |
| 9 | EAC | $4,000 divided by $1.048 | $3,817 | We currently estimate that the total project will cost $3,817. |
| 10 | ETC | $3,817 minus $3,100 | $717 | We need to spend an additional $717 to finish the project. |
| 11 | VAC | $4,000 minus $3,817 | $183 | We currently expect to be $183 under budget when the project is completed. |

In this example, you are looking for the value of the work that has actually been done. The finish-to-finish relationship allowed the team to work on more than one side at the same time. In this case, work is being done on both sides 3 and 4 at the same time. Since the value of each side is $1,000, we look at how much of each side is complete and apply that percent to the value. Here sides 1 and 2 are completed, so each receives a value of $1,000. It doesn't matter what it actually cost—just the value. Side 3 is 50 percent done and receives a value of $500 (50 percent of $1,000). Side 4 is 75 percent done and receives a value of $750 (75 percent of $1,000). The earned value to date is $3,250.

Understanding the meaning of the results of each calculation is as important as knowing how to calculate them.

Expect questions on the exam such as: "The CPI is 0.9, and the SPI is 0.92. What should you do?" You will need to interpret this and other data in the question and then determine which choice would address the issue(s) described. In the fence example, there are both cost and schedule problems.

You may also see questions on the exam that require you to perform multiple calculations (for example, you need to perform one calculation to come up with a result that can be used as an input for a second calculation). We have a few exercises coming up that will help you understand how to answer these questions, but it's helpful to first consider the following useful tip.

**TRICKS OF THE TRADE®** Here's a quick trick for finding EV when a question provides partial information. Depending on the information you're given in a question, you can reverse the formulas you know for CV, SV, CPI, or SPI so you can isolate EV on its own side of the equation, which will make it much easier to solve. For example, say a question gives you CV and AC and asks you to solve for EV. You already know that CV = EV − AC, so now you can reverse this formula by adding AC to both sides of the equation as follows:

CV = EV − AC

CV + AC = EV − AC + AC

CV + AC = EV

Do you understand why we added AC to both sides of the equation? You're trying to isolate EV on one side of the equation. By adding AC to the right side of the equation, you cancel out the −AC, so you end up with EV on its own. But whatever you do on the right-hand side of the equation, you have to do on the left-hand side as well. (Here's a little algebra refresher: you can perform an operation—such as adding, subtracting, dividing, or multiplying—on one side of the equation so long as you do the exact same thing on the other side as well. This allows you to manipulate an equation to make it easier to solve.)

So now, to solve for EV, all you have to do is add CV and AC.

Similarly, say a question gives you CPI and AC and asks you to determine EV. You already know the formula for CPI (CPI = EV/AC), but how can you isolate EV on one side of the equation? Instead of adding AC to both sides of the equation, in this case, you would multiply both sides by AC:

$$CPI = \frac{EV}{AC}$$

$$CPI \times AC = \frac{EV}{AC} \times AC$$

$$CPI \times AC = EV$$

You can also simply memorize the reverse formulas in the table below.

| Original Formula | Reverse Formula to Determine EV |
|---|---|
| CV = EV − AC | EV = CV + AC |
| SV = EV − PV | EV = SV + PV |
| $CPI = \dfrac{EV}{AC}$ | EV = CPI × AC |
| $SPI = \dfrac{EV}{PV}$ | EV = SPI × PV |

Just keep in mind that this quick trick for reversing the formula only works for EV. Although you can reverse other earned value formulas, to do so would generally require multiple steps.

**Exercise**  What is the EV if your CPI is 1.1, your SPI is .92, and your AC is $10,000? Which reverse formula would you use?

**Answer**  Since the question gives us the CPI and AC, we can reverse the CPI formula to get to the EV. So the reverse formula would be EV = CPI × AC, or EV = 1.1 × $10,000, which works out to $11,000. For this question, there was no need to use the SPI information.

**Exercise**  What is the SPI if the CV is $10,000, the SV is −$3,000, and the PV is $100,000?

**Answer** To find the SPI, you actually need to perform two calculations here. The formula for SPI is SPI = EV/PV; we know what the PV is, but we don't know the EV. Luckily, we can figure it out using the information given in the question. We're given the SV and PV, so we can use the following reverse formula to determine EV.

EV = SV + PV

EV = −$3,000 + $100,000

EV = $97,000

We can then plug the PV and EV into the SPI formula as follows.

$$SPI = \frac{EV}{PV}$$

$$SPI = \frac{\$97,000}{\$100,000}$$

SPI = .97

If your equation requires you to solve for something other than EV (for example, AC or PV), the math will be slightly more complicated, but don't worry: we've got an exercise to help you understand what to do.

**Exercise** Using the information from the previous exercise, determine AC.

**Answer** We need to look at the information from the previous exercise to determine what formula to use to figure out AC. We know the CV is $10,000 and the EV is $97,000 (from the calculation we performed in the previous exercise). With this information, we can determine the AC by using the formula CV = EV − AC. To do this, we first plug the information we know into the formula:

CV = EV − AC

$10,000 = $97,000 − AC

To solve for AC, we need to get AC alone on one side of the equation. First, add AC to both sides of the equation:

$10,000 + AC = $97,000 − AC + AC

$10,000 + AC = $97,000

The −AC and +AC on the right-hand side of the equation canceled each other out. But we still need to isolate AC on the left-hand side of the equation. To do this, we're going to subtract $10,000 from both sides.

$10,000 + AC − $10,000 = $97,000 − $10,000

AC = $87,000

**Exercise**   In the latest earned value report for your project, you see the CPI is 1.2, the SPI is 0.8, the PV is $600,000, and the SV is −$120,000. You can't find the CV in the report, so you need to calculate it based on the information given. What is the CV?

**Answer**   The formula for CV is CV = EV − AC. Therefore, we need to find EV and AC to calculate CV. We can do this by using one of the reverse formulas we learned earlier. Since we know the values for SPI (0.8) and PV ($600,000), we can use EV = SPI × PV (this is the reverse formula for SPI = EV/PV).

EV = SPI × PV

EV = 0.8 × $600,000

EV = $480,000

Now we need AC, which we can get from the EV we just determined and the CPI given in the question (1.2).

The formula is $CPI = \dfrac{EV}{AC}$ or $1.2 = \dfrac{\$480,000}{AC}$.

We need to isolate AC on one side of the equation to figure out what it is. Start by multiplying both sides of the equation by AC.

$$1.2 \times AC = \frac{\$480,000}{AC} \times AC.$$

The resulting equation is:

$$1.2 \times AC = \$480,000$$

To get AC on its own, we need to divide both sides by 1.2.

$$\frac{(1.2 \times AC)}{1.2} = \frac{\$480,000}{1.2}$$

The resulting equation is:

$$AC = \frac{\$480,000}{1.2}$$

So, AC = $400,000.

Now that we know the EV and the AC, we can figure out what the CV is:

$$CV = EV - AC$$

$$CV = \$480,000 - \$400,000$$

$$CV = \$80,000$$

Earned value analysis enables the project manager and team to identify and analyze trends in cost performance, as well as variances that may require action to bring project results in line with what was planned. Earned value analysis also includes monitoring the use of contingency reserves to ensure the amount of reserves remaining is adequate. It may identify the need to request additional reserve funds through integrated change control.

The Control Costs process provides measurements that indicate how the work is progressing and allow the project manager to create reliable forecasts and take action to control the project. This process may result in requested changes to the cost management plan, performance measurement baseline, and other parts of the project management plan, recommended corrective or preventive actions, and updates to project documents.

## Practice Exam

1. One common way to compute estimate at completion (EAC) is to take the budget at completion (BAC) and:
   A. Divide by SPI.
   B. Multiply by SPI.
   C. Multiply by CPI.
   D. Divide by CPI.

2. The finance department requires that you keep them updated on the costs being spent on the capital project you are leading. You were required to submit a funding plan, and monthly forecasts are necessary so that any changes to the funding plan can be requested in advance and evaluated. Exceeding the budget limit is unacceptable, as it will impact the stock value. You have successfully implemented processes and practices to anticipate funding changes, and you evaluate them to minimize problems and increase the efficient use of funds. You have employed a variety of reporting and analysis techniques to meet the finance department requirements. One of them is EAC, which is a periodic evaluation of:
   A. The cost of work completed
   B. The value of work performed
   C. The anticipated total cost at project completion
   D. What it will cost to finish the project

3. If earned value (EV) = 350, actual cost (AC) = 400, and planned value (PV) = 325, what is the cost variance (CV)?
   A. 350
   B. –75
   C. 400
   D. –50

4. The customer responsible for overseeing your project asks you to provide a written cost estimate that is 30 percent higher than your estimate of the project's cost. He explains that the budgeting process requires managers to estimate pessimistically to ensure enough money is allocated for projects. What is the best way to handle this?
   A. Add the 30 percent as a lump sum contingency fund to handle project risks.
   B. Add the 30 percent to your cost estimate by spreading it evenly across all project activities.
   C. Create one cost baseline for budget allocation and a second one for the actual project management plan.
   D. Ask for information on risks that would cause your estimate to be too low.

5. You've recently been assigned to manage a marketing project to brand a sustainable development program. Even though you are just starting your efforts, the sponsors are concerned about the likelihood of reaching planned milestones during the project. They are wondering how you will go about estimating. Analogous estimating:
   A. Uses bottom-up estimating techniques
   B. Is used most frequently during project executing
   C. Uses top-down estimating techniques
   D. Calculates estimates using actual detailed historical costs

307

6. You have been working with the subject matter experts to estimate the activity durations and costs on the project. All the following are outputs of the Estimate Costs process except:
   A. An understanding of the cost risk in the work that has been estimated
   B. The prevention of inappropriate changes from being included in the cost baseline
   C. An indication of the range of possible costs for the project
   D. Documentation of any assumptions made during the Estimate Costs process

7. The product your project team is working on is a replacement of a device the company launched a couple of years ago. That device did not meet market projections for sales, even though it was revolutionary in its capabilities. The reason it did not meet projections was that the life cycle costing was not fully considered and analyzed during the device development. When the original device was offered to the market, it had initial success until a trade publication analyzed the life cycle costs and determined they were unreasonably high. Sales lagged due to the negative reports. Internal tests showed that the trade publication was correct. This time the team is taking life cycle costs into consideration as they develop the product. The main focus of life cycle costing is to:
   A. Estimate installation costs.
   B. Estimate the cost of operations and maintenance.
   C. Consider installation costs when planning the project costs.
   D. Consider operations and maintenance costs in making project decisions.

8. You're managing a project to develop a new mobile application for the inventory-tracking-and-control system of a restaurant franchise organization. Schedule is the highest-priority constraint for the leadership team, but the franchise owners are most concerned about cost and the quality of the application. If there are bugs and errors in the system, they will pay higher costs on waste or lost sales. But investing a lot of effort into delivering great functionality could be expensive. It was decided that an adaptive approach to the project life cycle would likely be the best way to balance the competing priorities and deliver a working, cost-effective application. The franchise decision team has been meeting with the development team. The groups feel good about the project's progress, but they are hearing concerns from other stakeholders about what the impact will be to the bottom line and whether the system will be ready for launch. These concerns were anticipated in planning, and will be managed with cost performance measurement. Cost performance measurement is best done through which of the following?
   A. Asking for a percent complete from each team member and reporting that in the monthly progress report
   B. Calculating earned value, and using indexes and other calculations to report past performance and forecast future performance
   C. Using the 50/50 rule, and making sure the life cycle cost is less than the project cost
   D. Focusing on the amount expended last month and what will be expended the following month

9. A cost performance index (CPI) of 0.89 means:
   A. At this time, we expect the total project to cost 89 percent more than planned.
   B. When the project is completed, we will have spent 89 percent more than planned.
   C. The project is progressing at 89 percent of the rate planned.
   D. The project is getting 89 cents out of every dollar invested.

10. The team's attitude toward the project is very positive. They are excited about the research and development work they are doing. The value of the work completed today is $60 million. The potential consumers from the product testing and focus groups have stated "the product will be amazing" and "they would absolutely buy it." The phase gate review board has received the reports and is asking for market projections and launch plans. They are wondering when this product can start returning value to the organization. The project is budgeted to cost $77 million. The value of the work planned to be done to this point is $78.9 million. What does the schedule performance index (SPI) for this project tell you?

    A. You are over budget.
    B. You are ahead of schedule.
    C. You are progressing at 76 percent of the rate originally planned.
    D. You are progressing at 24 percent of the rate originally planned.

11. The project management team is busy breaking down deliverables, and the procurement department has started looking for possible sellers to help produce the deliverables. There are departmental concerns that the project could go over budget because the scope will be iterated and the planning and development will be done in increments. At a recent company gathering, the sponsor asked questions of the project manager and the project management staff team about how changes in scope will affect the estimates. The sponsor wanted to know how the project estimates could be relied upon, given that they were planning to iterate the scope. The project manager reassured them that the team has the right tools with which to provide accurate estimates, and will utilize the tools throughout the project. Which of the following is not needed in order to come up with a project estimate?

    A. A WBS
    B. A network diagram
    C. Risks
    D. Change requests

12. Which of the following is an example of a parametric estimate?

    A. Dollars per module
    B. Learning bend
    C. Bottom-up
    D. CPM

13. A rough order of magnitude (ROM) estimate is made during which project management process group?

    A. Planning
    B. Closing
    C. Executing
    D. Initiating

© 2018 RMC Publications, Inc.™ • 952.846.4484 • info@rmcls.com • www.rmcls.com

14. For each activity on your project, you have worked with designers, engineers, technical experts, and consultants to come up with details on the resources needed to complete the activity. For some of the activities the lists are quite long, as you need raw and finished materials, equipment, and people. You have a limited amount of warehousing available, so you have to coordinate the deliveries and work so that the materials and equipment are delivered as close to the start of an activity as possible. You and the project management team have identified the amount of time and money needed for each of the activities, which you have then aggregated and analyzed with their help. These efforts will eventually result in the creation of a cost baseline for the project. A senior manager is trying to better understand the work of project management and has asked which process produces the cost baseline. What is the correct response?

    A. Estimate Activity Resources
    B. Estimate Costs
    C. Determine Budget
    D. Control Costs

15. During which project management process group are budget forecasts created?

    A. Monitoring and controlling
    B. Planning
    C. Initiating
    D. Executing

16. Which type of cost is team training?

    A. Direct
    B. NPV
    C. Indirect
    D. Fixed

17. Project setup costs are an example of:

    A. Variable costs
    B. Fixed costs
    C. Overhead costs
    D. Opportunity costs

18. The quality efforts on the project have gone through some changes during the first four months of project work. Two processes in particular have undergone extensive change. The customer is happy with the work to date, but has heard that the competition is working on a similar product. The team has been asked to analyze and create options for the customer. Value analysis is performed to get:

    A. More value from the cost analysis
    B. Management to buy into the project
    C. The team to buy into the project
    D. A less costly way of doing the same work

19. Which estimating method tends to be most costly for creating a project cost estimate?

    A. Bottom-up
    B. Analogous
    C. Parametric
    D. 50/50

20. To gain a clear indication of how the project is progressing, the buyer expects periodic reporting that includes analysis of the work that has been accomplished according to plan, the dollars that have been spent and how they reflect the planned expenses, the accepted deliverables, and evaluation of the risk events that have occurred. Which of the following represents the estimated value of the work actually accomplished?

    A. Earned value (EV)
    B. Planned value (PV)
    C. Actual cost (AC)
    D. Cost variance (CV)

21. Which of the following are all items included in the cost management plan?

    A. The level of accuracy needed for estimates, rules for measuring cost performance, and specifications for how duration estimates should be stated
    B. Specifications for how estimates should be stated, rules for measuring cost performance, and the level of accuracy needed for estimates
    C. Rules for measuring team performance, the level of accuracy needed for estimates, and specifications for how estimates should be stated
    D. Specifications for how estimates should be stated, the level of risk needed for estimates, and rules for measuring cost performance

22. Your project has a medium amount of risk and is not very well defined. The sponsor hands you a project charter and asks you to confirm that the project can be completed within the project cost budget. What is the best method to handle this?

    A. Develop an estimate in the form of a range of possible results.
    B. Ask the team members to help estimate the cost based on the project charter.
    C. Based on the information you have, calculate a parametric estimate.
    D. Provide an analogous estimate based on past history.

23. You are leading a project to introduce a new healthcare appointment scheduling application. As you are creating plans detailing how the team will respond to possible events that may impact the project, you and the team determine the amount of cost contingency reserve needed. The cost contingency reserve should be:

    A. Hidden to prevent management from disallowing the reserve
    B. Added to each activity to provide the customer with a shorter critical path
    C. Maintained by management to cover cost overruns
    D. Added to the cost of the project to account for risks

24. You are having difficulty estimating the cost of a project. Which of the following best describes the most probable cause of your difficulty?

    A. Inadequate scope definition
    B. Unavailability of desired resources
    C. Lack of historical records from previous projects
    D. Lack of company processes

25. Your cost forecast shows you will have a cost overrun at the end of the project. Which of the following should you do?

    A. Eliminate risks in estimates and reestimate.
    B. Meet with the sponsor to find out what work can be done sooner.
    C. Cut quality.
    D. Decrease scope.

311

26. Early in the life of your project, you are having a discussion with the sponsor about what estimating techniques should be used. You want a form of expert judgment, but the sponsor argues for analogous estimating. It would be best to:

   A. Agree to analogous estimating, as it is a form of expert judgment.
   B. Suggest life cycle costing as a compromise.
   C. Determine why the sponsor wants such an accurate estimate.
   D. Try to convince the sponsor to allow expert judgment because it is typically more accurate.

27. You have just completed the initiating processes of a small project and are moving into project planning when a project stakeholder asks you for the project's budget and cost baseline. What should you tell her?

   A. The project budget can be found in the project charter, which has just been completed.
   B. The project budget and baseline will not be finalized and accepted until the planning processes are completed.
   C. The project management plan will not contain the project's budget and baseline; this is a small project.
   D. It is impossible to complete an estimate before the project management plan is created.

28. The project manager is working with cost estimates in order to establish a baseline for measuring project performance. What process is this?

   A. Cost Management
   B. Estimate Costs
   C. Determine Budget
   D. Control Costs

29. Monitoring cost expended to date in order to detect variances from the plan occurs during:

   A. The creation of the cost change control system
   B. Recommending corrective actions
   C. Updating the cost baseline
   D. Project performance reviews

30. You're thinking through what approach will make it easiest for the team to take responsibility for providing work performance data for all aspects of the project. As part of this approach, you believe it will be helpful to make sure the team understands how and why the data will be analyzed. You explain to the team that the cost management plan contains a description of:

   A. The project costs
   B. How resources are allocated
   C. The budgets and how they were calculated
   D. The WBS level at which earned value will be calculated

31. A manufacturing project has a schedule performance index (SPI) of 0.89 and a cost performance index (CPI) of 0.91. Generally, what is the most likely explanation for why this occurred?

   A. The scope was changed.
   B. A supplier went out of business, and a new one needed to be found.
   C. Additional equipment needed to be purchased.
   D. A critical path activity took longer and needed more labor hours to complete.

32. Although the stakeholders thought there was enough money in the budget, halfway through the project the cost performance index (CPI) is 0.7. To determine the root cause, several stakeholders audit the project and discover the project cost budget was estimated analogously. Although the activity estimates add up to the project estimate, the stakeholders think something was missing in how the estimate was completed. Which of the following describes what was missing?
    A. Estimated costs should be used to measure CPI.
    B. SPI should be used, not CPI.
    C. Bottom-up estimating should have been used.
    D. Past history was not taken into account.

33. In analyzing problems that have occurred during testing, the team discovered that cause-and-effect diagramming is helpful in identifying the best place to focus their efforts. Their coordination of the interrelationships of the deliverables has improved, and the team has discovered efficiencies that have been shared with other projects and the organization for process improvement. This has made a difference in how well the project is aligning to the performance measurement baseline. Stakeholders are anticipating that control efforts and reporting on future projects will be easier. Earned value analysis is the basis for:
    A. Performance reporting
    B. Planning control
    C. Ishikawa diagrams
    D. Integrating the project components into a whole

34. The replacement of the inventory management and portion control system for an international restaurant chain has been prioritized as a key strategic objective for the organization. Stakeholders are very concerned about many aspects of the project. They have shared these concerns and ideas in workshops, focus groups, emails, and surveys. Identified risks are:
    A. An input to the Estimate Costs process
    B. An output of the Estimate Costs process
    C. Not related to the Estimate Costs process
    D. Both an input to and an output of the Estimate Costs process

35. There is confusion among some of the stakeholders about how the cost forecasts will be calculated on the project. They also have concerns about whether enough money has been set aside to cover the cost of risk responses. You are planning to share information in the upcoming team meeting and in reports to stakeholders to clear up the confusion. You are referencing the stakeholder and communications management plans to determine how best to communicate with the stakeholders. You will explain that the difference between the cost baseline and the cost budget can be best described as:
    A. The management reserves
    B. The contingency reserves
    C. The project cost estimate
    D. The cost account

36. You provide a project cost estimate for the project to the project sponsor. He is unhappy with the estimate, because he thinks the price should be lower. He asks you to cut 15 percent off the project estimate. What should you do?
    A. Start the project and constantly look for cost savings.
    B. Tell all the team members to cut 15 percent from their estimates.
    C. Inform the sponsor of the activities to be cut.
    D. Add additional resources with low hourly rates.

313

37. Cost risk means:

    A. There are risks that will cost the project money.
    B. The project is too risky from a cost perspective.
    C. There is a risk that project costs could go higher than planned.
    D. There is a risk that the cost of the project will be lower than planned.

38. A project manager is analyzing the project to find ways to decrease costs. It would be best if the project manager looks at:

    A. Variable costs and fixed costs
    B. Fixed costs and indirect costs
    C. Direct costs and variable costs
    D. Indirect costs and direct costs

## Answers

1. **Answer** D

   **Explanation** The formula BAC/CPI is used to calculate EAC if no variances from the BAC have occurred or if you will continue at the same rate of spending (as calculated in your cumulative CPI).

2. **Answer** C

   **Explanation** When you look at earned value, many of the terms have similar definitions. This could get you into trouble. EAC means the estimate at completion. What it will cost to finish the project is the definition of ETC, or estimate to complete.

3. **Answer** D

   **Explanation** The formula is CV = EV − AC. Therefore, CV = 350 − 400, or CV = −50. PV is not a factor in this calculation.

4. **Answer** D

   **Explanation** Presenting anything other than your original estimate (allocating more to the budget) is inaccurate and calls into question your competence and integrity as a project manager. The customer should list potential changes and risks related to your estimate. If the costs and risks are justified, you can ethically increase the budget.

5. **Answer** C

   **Explanation** Analogous estimating is used most frequently during project initiating and planning, not project executing. Parametric estimating involves calculations based on historical records. Analogous estimating early in the project uses top-down estimating techniques.

6. **Answer** B

   **Explanation** This question is asking, "When you finish estimating costs, what do you have?" Many people who do not realize that estimates should be in a range choose that option. Documentation of assumptions is included in the basis of estimates, which is an output of Estimate Costs. The prevention of inappropriate changes is more correctly part of the cost management plan and the change control system.

7. **Answer** D

   **Explanation** Life cycle costing looks at operations and maintenance costs and balances them with the project costs to try to reduce the cost across the entire life of the product.

8. **Answer** B

   **Explanation** Asking percent complete is not a best practice since it is usually a guess. If the easiest work is done first on a project, it can throw off any percentage calculations of work remaining. The life cycle cost cannot be lower than the project cost, as the life cycle cost includes the project cost. Focusing on the amount spent last month and what will be spent in the next month is often done by inexperienced project managers. Not only does this provide little information, but the data cannot be used to predict the future. Earned value analysis and other calculations is the best answer since this choice looks at the past and uses that information to estimate future costs.

9. **Answer** D

   **Explanation** The CPI is less than one, so the situation is bad. The project is only getting 89 cents out of every dollar invested.

315

10. **Answer** C

    **Explanation** This earned value question is asking you to calculate the schedule performance index (SPI) and interpret the results. The formula for SPI is EV/PV. The EV in this question is the estimated value of the work already completed, or $60 million. The planned value, the estimated value of the work planned to be done is $78.9 million. Therefore SPI = $60/$78.9 = 0.76. This tells you the project is progressing at 76 percent of the rate planned.

11. **Answer** D

    **Explanation** You need the WBS to define the activities, the network diagram to see the dependencies, and the risks to determine contingencies. NOTE: These are high-level risks, not the detailed risks that are identified later in project planning. Change requests are not required to obtain estimates, although they could cause existing estimates to be adjusted. Without the other three choices, you cannot develop good estimates.

12. **Answer** A

    **Explanation** Parametric estimates use a mathematical model to predict project cost or time.

13. **Answer** D

    **Explanation** This estimate has a wide range. It is done during project initiating, when very little is known about the project.

14. **Answer** C

    **Explanation** A cost baseline is an output of the Determine Budget process.

15. **Answer** A

    **Explanation** Budget forecasts are an output of Control Costs, which is part of monitoring and controlling.

16. **Answer** A

    **Explanation** You are training the team on skills required for the project. The cost is directly related to the project and is therefore a direct cost.

17. **Answer** B

    **Explanation** Setup costs do not change as production on the project changes. Therefore, they are fixed costs.

18. **Answer** D

    **Explanation** Value analysis seeks to decrease cost while maintaining the same scope.

19. **Answer** A

    **Explanation** Because you need project details to estimate this way, the effort expended will be greater with bottom-up estimating.

20. **Answer** A

    **Explanation** It can be confusing to differentiate earned value terms from each other. The estimated value of the work actually completed is the definition of EV, or earned value.

21. **Answer** B

    **Explanation** Notice how one item in each of the incorrect options makes the entire choice incorrect. Duration estimates are created during schedule management, and measuring team performance is a part of resource management. There is no level of risk required for estimates. Specifications for how estimates should be stated, rules for measuring cost performance, and the level of accuracy needed for estimates are all parts of the cost management plan.

22. **Answer** A

    **Explanation** With such limited information, it is best to estimate in a range. The range can be narrowed as planning progresses and risks are addressed.

23. **Answer** D

    **Explanation** Hiding the reserve is an inappropriate action. Adding cost to each activity will not shorten the critical path, and is an incorrect statement. Management reserves, not contingency reserves, are maintained by management to cover cost overruns. During the risk management process, you determine appropriate contingency reserves to cover the cost of identified risks. These costs are included in the project cost baseline.

24. **Answer** A

    **Explanation** Although all choices could cause difficulty, only inadequate scope definition makes estimating impossible.

25. **Answer** A

    **Explanation** Look for the choice that would have the least negative impact on this situation. You would not need to meet with the sponsor to determine which work can be done sooner, and changing the order of activities is unlikely to eliminate the cost overrun. Cutting quality and decreasing scope always have negative effects. The choice with the least negative impact is to eliminate risks in estimates and reestimate.

26. **Answer** A

    **Explanation** This is a tricky question. Determining why the sponsor wants such an accurate estimate sounds like a good idea at first. However, analogous estimates are less accurate than other forms of estimating, as they are prepared with a limited amount of detailed information. Reading every word of this choice helps eliminate it. To pick the best answer, you need to realize that analogous estimating is a form of expert judgment.

27. **Answer** B

    **Explanation** The overall project budget may be included in the project charter but not the detailed costs. Even small projects should have a budget and schedule. It is not impossible to create a project budget before the project management plan is created. However, it is not wise to do so, as the budget will not be accurate. The project budget and baseline are not finalized and accepted until the planning processes are completed.

28. **Answer** C

    **Explanation** Cost Management is too general. The estimates are already created in this situation, so the answer is not Estimate Costs. The answer is not Control Costs, because the baseline has not yet been created. The work described is the Determine Budget process.

29. **Answer** D

    **Explanation** Recommending corrective actions and possible updates to the cost baseline result from project performance reviews; they are not concurrent with them. Monitoring costs is part of change control, but not part of creating the change control system. The correct choice is project performance reviews.

30. **Answer** D

    **Explanation** The exam may ask you what the management plans include in order to test whether you really understand them. The cost management plan identifies the WBS level at which earned value will be calculated.

317

31. **Answer** D

    **Explanation** To answer this question, you must look for a choice that would take longer and cost more. Notice one of the choices says scope was changed, but that does not necessarily mean it was added to. If the change was to reduce the scope, it might also have reduced cost. Although it would take time to handle the issue of the need to find a new supplier, the impacted activity might not be on the critical path and might not affect time. Purchasing additional equipment definitely adds cost, but not necessarily time. A critical path activity taking longer and requiring more labor hours to complete would negatively affect both time and cost.

32. **Answer** C

    **Explanation** Actual costs are used to measure CPI, and there is no reason to use SPI in this situation. Using past history is another way of saying "analogous." The most detailed way to estimate is bottom-up. Such estimating would have improved the overall quality of the activity estimates.

33. **Answer** A

    **Explanation** Earned value is a great way to communicate the value of work already accomplished. With it, you can show where you stand on budget and schedule, as well as provide forecasts for the rest of the project.

34. **Answer** D

    **Explanation** Identified risks are listed in the risk register, an input to the Estimate Costs process. In completing the Estimate Costs process, additional risks may be uncovered. These are added to the risk register as project documents updates.

35. **Answer** A

    **Explanation** The costs of activities are included in the project cost estimate, and the contingency reserves (to cover identified risks) are added to that to come up with the cost baseline. Thereafter, the management reserves (to cover unknown, or unidentified, risks) are added to come up with the cost budget. The management reserves make up the difference between the cost baseline and the cost budget.

36. **Answer** C

    **Explanation** To answer the question, you must first realize that it is never appropriate for a project manager to just cut estimates across the board. You should have created a project estimate based on realistic work package estimates that do not include padding. Then, if costs must be decreased, you can look to cut quality, decrease risk, cut scope, or use cheaper resources (and at the same time closely monitor the impact of changes on the project schedule).

    One of the worst things a project manager can do is to start a project knowing that the schedule or cost for the project is unrealistic. Did you notice the choice of adding additional resources? Even though they have lower hourly rates, that would add cost. Evaluating, looking for alternatives, and then reporting the impact of cost cutting to the sponsor is the best action to take.

37. **Answer** C

    **Explanation** While it is true that risk will cost the project money, that is not the definition of cost risk. Stating that the project is too risky from a cost perspective assumes the risk is too great to do the project. Cost risk is the risk that project costs could go higher than planned.

38. **Answer** C

    **Explanation** Direct costs are directly attributable to the project, and variable costs are costs that vary with the amount of work accomplished. It is best to look at decreasing these costs on the project.

# Quality Management

EIGHT

Before you read this chapter, think about the quality management plan on your project. If you do not have a quality management plan, or if you do not manage quality now, this could be a difficult topic for you on the exam. This chapter will help you understand quality and its role in the project management process.

Some people argue that project managers do not have time to spend managing quality, and many organizations do not require their project managers to have quality management plans. But think about the impact of managing quality on your projects. A lack of attention to quality results in rework or defects. The more rework you have to do, the more time and money you are wasting, and the less likely you are to meet the project schedule and cost baselines. With a focus on quality, you can spend time preventing—rather than dealing with—problems. You can actually save time on the project that you would have otherwise spent on rework and problem-solving.

Projects and organizations determine their approach to quality management. For some, that may mean simply responding to customer complaints about the quality of deliverables. Others inspect their deliverables for quality before they reach the customer. More informed organizations not only inspect their deliverables, but also evaluate and adjust their quality management processes in an effort to identify the causes of defects. An even better approach includes these quality management and process improvements, as well as planning quality into projects. Ideally, an organization embraces all these efforts as part of a total commitment to providing the required level of quality. This chapter will improve your understanding of the efforts required to address quality at the most effective level.

## QUICKTEST

- Quality management process
- Definition of quality
- Gold plating
- Prevention over inspection
- Continuous improvement
- Just in time (JIT)
- Responsibility for quality
- Interviews
- Brainstorming
- Benchmarking
- Cost-benefit analysis
- Impact of poor quality
- Cost of quality
- Costs of conformance and nonconformance
- Marginal analysis
- Logical data models
- Flowcharts
- Test and inspection planning
- Checklists
- Quality metrics
- Quality management plan
- Cause-and-effect diagrams
- Histograms
- Pareto diagrams
- Scatter diagrams
- Document analysis
- Alternatives analysis
- Design of experiments
- Process analysis
- Root cause analysis
- Failure analysis
- Multicriteria decision analysis
- Affinity diagrams
- Audits
- Design for X
- Problem-solving
- Test and evaluation documents
- Quality reports
- Mutual exclusivity
- Probability
- Normal distribution
- Statistical independence
- Standard deviation
- 3 or 6 sigma
- Checksheets
- Statistical sampling
- Questionnaires and surveys
- Performance reviews
- Inspection
- Control charts
  - Assignable cause/special cause variation
  - Control limits
  - Mean
  - Specification limits
  - Out of control
  - Rule of seven

# Quality Management E I G H T

| INITIATING | PLANNING<br>(This is the only process group<br>with a set order.) | EXECUTING | MONITORING &<br>CONTROLLING | CLOSING |
|---|---|---|---|---|
| Select project manager | **Determine development approach, life cycle, and how you will plan for each knowledge area** | Execute work according to the project management plan | **Take action to monitor and control the project** | Confirm work is done to requirements |
| Determine company culture and existing systems | Define and prioritize requirements | Produce product deliverables (product scope) | Measure performance against performance measurement baseline | Complete final procurement closure |
| Collect processes, procedures, and historical information | Create project scope statement | Gather work performance data | **Measure performance against other metrics in the project management plan** | Gain final acceptance of product |
| Divide large projects into phases or smaller projects | Assess what to purchase and create procurement documents | **Request changes** | **Analyze and evaluate data and performance** | Complete financial closure |
| Understand business case and benefits management plan | Determine planning team | Implement only approved changes | **Determine if variances warrant a corrective action or other change request(s)** | Hand off completed product |
| Uncover initial requirements, assumptions, risks, constraints, and existing agreements | Create WBS and WBS dictionary | **Continuously improve; perform progressive elaboration** | **Influence factors that cause change** | Solicit customer's feedback about the project |
| Assess project and product feasibility within the given constraints | Create activity list | **Follow processes** | **Request changes** | Complete final performance reporting |
| Create measurable objectives and success criteria | Create network diagram | **Determine whether quality plan and processes are correct and effective** | Perform integrated change control | Index and archive records |
| Develop project charter | Estimate resource requirements | **Perform quality audits and issue quality reports** | Approve or reject changes | Gather final lessons learned and update knowledge bases |
| Identify stakeholders and determine their expectations, interest, influence, and impact | Estimate activity durations and costs | Acquire final team and physical resources | **Update project management plan and project documents** | |
| Request changes | Determine critical path | Manage people | Inform stakeholders of all change request results | |
| Develop assumption log | Develop schedule | Evaluate team and individual performance; provide training | Monitor stakeholder engagement | |
| Develop stakeholder register | Develop budget | Hold team-building activities | Confirm configuration compliance | |
| | **Determine quality standards, processes, and metrics** | Give recognition and rewards | Create forecasts | |
| | **Determine team charter and all roles and responsibilities** | **Use issue logs** | Gain customer's acceptance of interim deliverables | |
| | Plan communications and stakeholder engagement | Facilitate conflict resolution | **Perform quality control** | |
| | Perform risk identification, qualitative and quantitative risk analysis, and risk response planning | Release resources as work is completed | Perform risk reviews, reassessments, and audits | |
| | **Go back—iterations** | Send and receive information, and solicit feedback | Manage reserves | |
| | Finalize procurement strategy and documents | Report on project performance | Manage, evaluate, and close procurements | |
| | Create change and configuration management plans | Facilitate stakeholder engagement and manage expectations | Evaluate use of physical resources | |
| | **Finalize all management plans** | Hold meetings | | |
| | **Develop realistic and sufficient project management plan and baselines** | Evaluate sellers; negotiate and contract with sellers | | |
| | Gain formal approval of the plan | **Use and share project knowledge** | | |
| | Hold kickoff meeting | Execute contingency plans | | |
| | Request changes | **Update project management plan and project documents** | | |

**Rita's Process Chart™**
**Quality Management**
Where are we in the project
management process?

© 2018 RMC Publications, Inc.™ • 952.846.4484 • info@rmcls.com • www.rmcls.com

If asked, "Is it better to plan in quality or to inspect to find quality problems?" almost everyone will answer correctly that it is better to plan in quality. However, that is not how most of the quality-related questions are presented on the exam. Instead, exam questions focus on situations to see if you know what to do. For example:

> *The project manager finds that one of his team members has created their own process for installing hardware. What should the project manager do?*

Beginning project managers might choose a response that relates to thanking the team member for the effort. More experienced project managers might select a choice that relates to finding out if the process was a good one. The best project managers select the choice that relates to investigating the quality management plan to determine if a standard process should have been followed.

People without quality management experience generally have a hard time with such questions. Fortunately, not all the quality questions on the exam are that difficult. Expect to see exam questions that refer to different project environments (for example, the project manager works for a manufacturer of tables). This does not mean you have to learn about all industries. The exam may highlight manufacturing because quality is an important factor in that industry, and manufacturing examples tend to be understandable to all. Focus on the situation that is being described. Also expect questions about the process of quality management and how quality relates to the project constraints, as defined in this book.

Imagine a project to build a stadium. The concrete part of the work is two-thirds done when the buyer arrives one day and tests the strength of the concrete. The buyer finds that the concrete does not meet the clearly stated quality requirements for strength in the contract. You can imagine the problems when the buyer says, "Rip out the concrete; it is not acceptable." Whose fault is this? Why did this occur?

Could we say it is the buyer's fault for not testing the concrete sooner? You might argue that case, but isn't the real fault with the seller for not testing the quality throughout the project? Where was their quality plan? They should have noted the requirement and determined when and how they would confirm they had met it. Lack of attention to quality in this scenario needlessly added considerable risk to the project, which resulted in a tremendous amount of rework and additional expense.

Here is something else to consider. Have any of your customers ever said one of your deliverables was not acceptable, even though they had not provided you with a definition of what was acceptable? It is important to know—in advance—what acceptable quality is and how it will be measured on the project. You can then determine what you will do to make sure the project meets those requirements. It is the project manager's responsibility to make sure that quality is defined in the plan. If you do not take these steps, you will have unclear acceptance criteria, such as "the customer likes it." Performing the quality management process well helps you avoid many issues later in the project.

The following should help you understand how each part of quality management fits into the overall project management process:

| The Quality Management Process | Done During |
| --- | --- |
| Plan Quality Management | Planning process group |
| Manage Quality | Executing process group |
| Control Quality | Monitoring and controlling process group |

Before we start discussing these three processes in detail, let's look at some basic quality management concepts that you should understand for the exam.

321

### Definition of Quality
What is quality? Know the short definition for the exam. Quality is defined as the degree to which the project fulfills requirements. Memorize this phrase; it may help you with up to four questions on the exam.

Now here is a story about quality. A student in one of RMC's classes looked out the window during class and noticed someone painting the limestone of an old building white. The student said, "That is not quality!" Let's think about the student's statement for a moment. Why would such painting not be "quality"? If the painting contract required the painter to use a certain kind of paint and follow painting standards, and he was doing so, the work met the quality requirements. The issue the student really had was that the wonderful old stone was being painted instead of cleaned. In other words, this was a disagreement with the requirements, not the quality of the work.

Let's review the definition of quality again: the degree to which the project fulfills requirements. In a plan-driven, or predictive, environment, can you achieve quality if you do not have all the stated and unstated requirements defined in the project scope statement and requirements documentation? Of course not. This makes the requirements-gathering effort (from scope management), the requirements documentation, and the project scope statement very important to the quality management effort. In a change-driven, or adaptive, environment, we capture quality requirements and acceptance criteria in user stories. As user stories are prioritized, quality efforts will be planned in detail for releases and iterations.

You may see situational questions on the exam that use the term "grade" in discussing quality. Whereas quality is the degree to which a project (or deliverable) fulfills requirements, grade refers to a general category or classification of a deliverable or resource that indicates common function, but varying technical specifications. For example, a low grade of concrete that supports limited weight might be sufficient for a project's needs and could be of acceptable quality if it meets the established quality requirements, such as having zero defects. Likewise, a high grade of concrete intended to sustain more weight could be of unacceptable quality if it is mixed or poured to low standards, or otherwise fails to meet the established quality metrics.

## Definition of Quality Management
Quality management includes creating and following organizational policies and procedures and tailoring them to ensure the project also meets the needs of the customer. We could also say it means ensuring a project is completed in compliance with the project requirements. Quality management includes the processes of Plan Quality Management, Manage Quality, and Control Quality.

### Quality-Related PMI-isms
Quality-related questions can be confusing because many of the topics on the exam are not covered in the *PMBOK® Guide*. The exam may test your understanding of the need to satisfy project requirements, as opposed to giving the customer extras. It is important to apply this approach to quality management in order to answer exam questions correctly. Know the following PMI-isms related to quality:

- Quality means meeting requirements, not adding extras.
- The project manager must determine the metrics to be used to measure quality before the project work begins.
- The project manager must define quality management processes for the project and put into place a plan for continually improving them.
- The project manager should recommend improvements to the performing organization's standards, policies, and processes. Such recommendations are expected and welcomed by management.

322

- Quality should be checked before an activity or work package is completed.
- The project manager must ensure that authorized approaches and processes are followed.
- Quality should be considered whenever there is a change to any of the project constraints.
- The project manager must ensure that the quality standards and processes on the project are adequate to meet quality requirements.
- Some quality activities may be performed by a quality department.

## Quality Management in the Real World

Many people getting ready for this exam have limited quality management experience, so they struggle with envisioning how quality management efforts fit into managing a project in the real world. The following scenario, along with the diagram in figure 8.1, will help clarify these concepts:

1. The customer determines their requirements.
2. The project team clarifies those requirements.
3. The project team defines what work will be done to meet those requirements (project scope).
4. The project manager determines the existing standards, policies, and procedures that might be available for the project. The quality department might assist in identifying the relevant standards.
5. The project manager creates other standards and processes that may be needed.
6. The project manager develops the quality management plan, encompassing relevant standards and processes.
7. The project manager integrates quality with other knowledge area plans to get an approved project management plan.
8. The team begins executing the project management plan.
   - 8a. The team or the quality department evaluates the quality of project deliverables against planned metrics and standards. (Control Quality)
   - 8b. The team or the quality department audits the project work periodically as part of the executing process, looking for indications that the standards, policies, plans, and procedures are not being followed or need to be changed. (Manage Quality)
   - 8c. Results are analyzed.
9. Deliverables are verified.
10. Lessons learned are documented and shared.
11. Change requests, including corrective and preventive action and defect repair, are sent to integrated change control.
12. Change requests, including corrective and preventive action and defect repair, are approved or rejected in integrated change control.
13. The team adjusts plans as needed to accommodate approved or rejected changes and returns to step 7 until project deliverables are complete and verified.
14. New organizational process assets, including lessons learned, are shared with the organization.
15. Verified deliverables are accepted by the customer, the project is completed, quality targets are reached, and the customer is happy.

The quality management process is represented by the shaded area of figure 8.1.

323

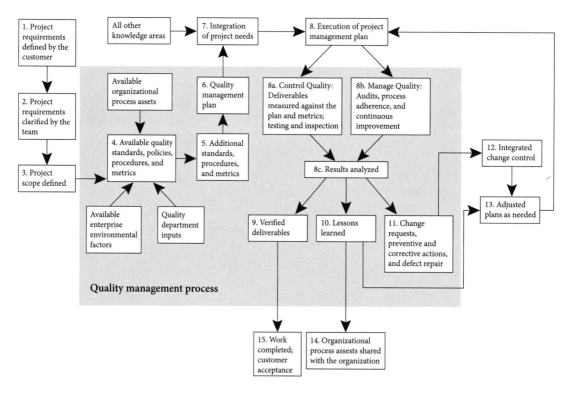

FIGURE 8.1   *Quality management*

## Gold Plating[1]
Do you remember a time on a project when one of your team members delivered more than what was needed? Can you think of a time when you've had trouble keeping a project from producing the Taj Mahal when all you needed was a garage, for example?

Gold plating refers to giving the customer extras (extra functionality, higher-quality components, extra scope, or better performance). Although your company might have a policy that promotes gold plating (for example, "Meet and exceed customers' expectations."), advanced quality thinking does not recommend "exceeding" as a best practice. Gold plating is often the team's impression of what is valued by the customer, and the customer might not agree. It is also a problem because so few projects provide what the customer wanted. Since most projects have difficulty meeting the project objectives, all available effort should go into achieving those objectives, instead of into gold plating.

Sometimes gold plating is not planned, but rather arises out of a team member's efforts to do the best they can. The project might not call for the best, however, just what was asked for. Therefore, the project manager must be on the lookout for team members providing extra functionality, extra work, or higher quality than is required for the project.

## Prevention over Inspection
Is it better to inspect work to find problems or to prevent them in the first place? Which takes less effort and is less costly? Remember that quality must be planned in, not inspected in! The concept of prevention over inspection was advocated by quality theorist Philip Crosby. You may see exam questions that test your understanding that failure to plan quality into a project will lead to problems later in the project.

324

## Continuous Improvement

Continuous improvement involves continuously looking for ways to improve the quality of work, processes, and results. The terms "continuous improvement" and *"Kaizen"* are taken to mean the same thing on the exam; however, in Japan, *Kaizen*[2] means to alter *(kai)* and make better or improve *(zen)*. *Kaizen* is a general term, while continuous improvement is a quality movement. In the United States and most of Western Europe, continuous improvement focuses on major improvements. In Japan, the emphasis is on smaller improvements. Continuous improvement of project management within an organization can include analysis of how quality management is planned and utilized on projects.

Similarly, the philosophy of total quality management[3] developed by quality expert W. Edwards Deming encourages companies and their employees to focus on finding ways to continuously improve the quality of their products and their business practices at every level of the organization.

Another approach to continuous improvement is Six Sigma[4]—a methodology for achieving organizational process improvement and high levels of correctness with extremely reduced variances. Sigma is another name for standard deviation. It indicates how much variance from the mean has been established as permissible in a process. The higher the sigma, the fewer deviations (less variance) in the process. The level of quality required by an organization is usually represented by 3 or 6 sigma.

## Just in Time (JIT)[5]

Many companies find that holding raw materials or other resources in inventory is not only too expensive but also unnecessary. Instead, they have their suppliers deliver resources just before they are needed, thus decreasing inventory to nearly zero. A company using JIT must achieve a high level of quality in their practices; otherwise, there will not be enough materials or equipment to meet production requirements because of waste and rework. A JIT system forces attention on quality as well as schedule.

## Responsibility for Quality

The project manager has the ultimate responsibility for the quality of the product of the project, but each team member must check their work by inspecting it themselves. It is not acceptable for team members to simply complete the work and then turn it over to the project manager or their manager to be checked. Work should meet the project requirements, and testing should be done whenever appropriate before submitting the work.

According to W. Edwards Deming, 85 percent of the quality problems on a project are attributable to the management environment and the system in which the team works. Therefore, senior management is responsible for promoting an organizational approach that supports quality efforts. This often includes a quality department that determines quality management methodologies the project manager is required to follow.

## Understanding the Difference between Plan Quality Management, Manage Quality, and Control Quality

One of the major challenges people have while studying this topic is understanding the difference between Plan Quality Management, Manage Quality, and Control Quality. Some of this confusion may be a result of differences between what companies call these processes and what the exam calls them. It may also be a result of the confusing nature of some of the questions in this knowledge area.

For purposes of the exam, here is a brief description of the three processes:

- **Plan Quality Management**  This process focuses on defining quality for the project, the product, and project management, and planning how it will be achieved.

- **Manage Quality**  Because it is an executing process, the Manage Quality process is focused on the work being done on the project. Its purpose is to ensure the team is following organizational policies, standards, and processes as planned to produce the project's deliverables. The project manager also evaluates whether the quality management plan or processes need to be improved or modified.

325

- **Control Quality** Control Quality, a monitoring and controlling process, includes examining the actual deliverables produced on the project to ensure they are correct and meet the planned level of quality, evaluating variances, finding the source of problems, and recommending ways to address them.

**TRICKS OF THE TRADE®** The following chart presents a trick for understanding the three quality management processes. Study it now to gain a clearer understanding of the focuses of each process before reading the rest of this chapter. In the detailed descriptions, you will see combinations of actions and outputs. Can you spot them? You may want to review this chart after you read the in-depth discussions of each of the processes.

| Plan Quality Management | Manage Quality | Control Quality |
|---|---|---|
| **Process Group** | | |
| Project planning | Project executing | Project monitoring and controlling |
| **High-Level Description of What Each Process Focuses On** | | |
| • What is quality? <br> • How will we ensure it? | • Are we following the policies, metrics, procedures, and processes as planned? <br> • Are the procedures and processes giving us the intended results? <br> • Will we meet the quality objectives? | • Are the results of our work meeting the standards and required metrics? <br> • Is the variance within acceptable limits, or do we have to take action? |
| **More Detailed Description of What Each Process Focuses On** | | |
| • Review management plans and project documents to understand quality requirements on the project. <br> • Identify quality practices as well as internal and external standards relevant to the product, project, and project management efforts (OPAs and EEFs). <br> • Create additional project-specific processes, standards, and metrics. <br> • Determine the processes that will be used on the project. <br> • Determine what work you will do to meet the standards. <br> • Determine how you will measure to make sure you meet the standards. <br> • Plan for process improvement. | • Use measurements from Control Quality to confirm that: <br> – Policies and processes are being followed <br> – Policies, metrics, and processes are still appropriate for the project <br> – Policies and processes are effective in achieving planned quality results <br> • Use data-representation techniques to analyze results of quality testing. <br> • Determine the root cause of quality problems/ variances from plan. <br> • Perform continuous improvement to increase efficiency and effectiveness. <br> • Create test and evaluation documents for use in Control Quality. | • Inspect and measure the quality of deliverables to determine whether they meet requirements. <br> • Use the PMIS to track deviations from planned quality. <br> • Identify the need for quality improvements (corrective or preventive action, and defect repair). <br> • Complete checklists and checksheets, perform tests, and evaluate results. <br> • Graphically document results of testing and evaluation using data-representation techniques. <br> • Verify deliverables. <br> • Validate approved changes. <br> • Recommend improvements to testing processes. |

| Plan Quality Management | Manage Quality | Control Quality |
|---|---|---|
| **More Detailed Description of What Each Process Focuses On** | | |

**Plan Quality Management**

- Perform cost of quality, cost-benefit, and other analysis work to make certain the appropriate level of quality will be planned in.
- Determine roles and responsibilities for achieving quality requirements and objectives.
- Plan for testing and inspection to check that requirements, performance, reliability, and quality goals and objectives are achieved.
- Interface the quality management plan with other management plans to balance the needs of quality with scope, cost, time, risk, resources, and customer satisfaction requirements.
- Finalize a quality management plan as part of the project management plan.

**Manage Quality**

- Determine if project activities comply with organizational and project policies, processes, and procedures—perform a quality audit.
- Solve problems.
- Produce reports.
- Share good practices with others in the organization.
- Submit change requests.
- Update the project management plan and project documents.

**Control Quality**

- Use and update lessons learned.
- Submit change requests.
- Update the project management plan and project documents.

## Plan Quality Management   PAGE 277

> **Process** Plan Quality Management
> **Process Group** Planning
> **Knowledge Area** Quality Management

The objectives of the Plan Quality Management process are to identify all relevant organizational or industry practices, standards, and requirements for the quality of the project, the product of the project, and the project management efforts, and then to plan how to meet those quality standards and requirements. The main result of this process is a quality management plan.

It is important to keep in mind that the level of quality efforts should be appropriate to the needs of the project. There is no reason to negatively impact project scope, time, or cost if higher quality is not required on the project. Quality must be balanced with the other project constraints. That sounds easy, right? Often, however, it is not. The project scope statement, WBS, and WBS dictionary (the scope baseline) help the project manager maintain the proper perspective and plan quality to the appropriate level.

327

On many projects and in many organizations, practices are not standardized. If this is true on your projects, take some time now to imagine what such standardized practices would be for your projects and how they might be helpful to you. For example, a construction company could choose to establish a standardized practice for installing wallpaper on home construction projects. Imagine all the wallpaper installers within that organization putting together their best ideas to make the work of installing wallpaper easier on future projects. That would be a valuable effort. As another example, the *PMBOK® Guide* is a practice standard for project management. Standardization can come from within the organization or from government or professional associations. The performing organization or the project may adopt these practices as they apply to the work of the project. As part of the Plan Quality Management process, the project manager needs to look for any such standards that will help the project avoid "reinventing the wheel," so to speak, and achieve the level of quality that is required. Some available standards include:

- **The United Nations Convention on Contracts for International Sale of Goods (CISG)**[6] The CISG is the standard that governs international sales transactions.

- **ISO 9000**[7] This family of standards was created by the International Organization for Standardization (ISO) to help ensure that organizations have quality procedures and that they follow them. Many people incorrectly believe that ISO 9000 tells you what quality should be, or describes a recommended quality system.

- **Occupational Safety and Health Administration (OSHA)** OSHA sets standards for the safety of American workers.

Organizational process assets and enterprise environmental factors inform the project manager of relevant standards, policies, and procedures. They include lessons learned from previous projects and the performing organization's idea of the best way to accomplish work.

The project manager must plan the project so it also meets the customer's quality standards, which might be outlined in an agreement (contract) or need to be discovered as part of the Collect Requirements process. Quality requirements are documented, analyzed, and prioritized according to the requirements management plan. Examples of such standards are the acceptable number of software bugs per module, the strength of concrete, or the average time per installation. These measures of quality will help the project manager know when the project is out of control and when to request changes, including corrective actions and preventive actions designed to prevent the problem from reoccurring.

Once existing practices and standards are identified, the project manager must create any additional project-specific standards and procedures that are needed.

A project manager may create standards and procedures based on how quality is defined for each piece of work. For the exam, you should understand that this effort could also include defining processes for how project management activities should be done, and suggesting improvements to existing processes. The new practices cannot violate other relevant standards.

After the standards and procedures have been identified or created, the project manager needs to determine what work is required to meet those standards. Additional testing may need to be planned into the project, resources may need to be moved around, or the descriptions of products to be purchased may need to be changed. The project manager should also determine the specific measurements that will be made each week or each month, or for each deliverable, to ensure compliance with all standards.

Management plans and documentation that influence quality planning include the stakeholder engagement plan and stakeholder register, a list of the major project deliverables (requirements management plan), risk thresholds (risk management plan), and approval requirements (project charter). The assumption log provides insight into the level of quality that is assumed to be acceptable on the project. The requirements traceability matrix shows the origin of requirements related to quality and will be used to confirm that quality requirements, particularly external compliance requirements, have been achieved.

## Plan Quality Management Tools and Techniques
PAGE 281   The following are some tools and techniques used in the Plan Quality Management process. Remember that the objective of using these tools and techniques is to determine what quality requirements, procedures, and standards for the project and product should be.

### Interviews, Brainstorming, and Benchmarking[8]
There are numerous tools and techniques you can use to identify existing standards, processes, and metrics or to create new ones. Interviews and brainstorming can help identify appropriate ways to measure quality on the project along with the metrics or processes to be used. You may recall learning about these techniques in the Scope Management chapter.

Benchmarking was also discussed as a technique used in scope management. Here, benchmarking is used to review methodologies used by comparable projects or organizations to establish quality metrics and acceptable variance ranges, and to measure quality.

### Decision-Making
An important aspect of planning is determining priorities and choosing between options. In the Plan Quality Management process, key decisions might include selecting the most critical metrics or prioritizing quality requirements. Decision-making tools and techniques for planning quality include multicriteria decision analysis and prioritization matrices.

### Cost-Benefit Analysis[9]
Using this data analysis technique, the project manager analyzes the benefits versus the costs of quality efforts to determine the appropriate quality level and requirements for the project. As noted in the Integration Management chapter, this technique can also be used in project selection and in other planning efforts, including assessing the costs and benefits of potential risk responses.

The exam will test your knowledge about the effects of quality efforts, or the lack thereof. Note that if you have poor quality, you might also have:

- Increased costs
- Decreased profits
- Low morale
- Low customer satisfaction
- Increased risk
- Rework

### Cost of Quality (COQ)[10]
Evaluating the cost of quality means making sure the project is not spending too much to achieve a particular level of quality. It involves looking at what the costs of conformance and nonconformance[11] to quality will be on the project and creating an appropriate balance. This concept was popularized by the quality expert Philip Crosby. The following table provides some examples of the costs of conformance and nonconformance to quality.

| Cost of Conformance | Cost of Nonconformance |
| --- | --- |
| Quality training | Rework of deliverables not meeting quality standards |
| Studies | Scrap |
| Measuring quality of interim deliverables | Inventory costs |
| Customer satisfaction surveys (and work to respond to issues raised) | Warranty costs |
| Efforts to ensure everyone knows the processes to use to complete their work | Lost business |

329

The costs of conformance should be lower than the costs of nonconformance. Otherwise, why spend time improving quality? Cost of quality is planned in the Plan Quality Management process and then monitored and measured throughout the life of the project.

A term related to this concept is marginal analysis,[12] which is analysis focused on finding the point at which the benefits or revenue to be received from improving quality equals the incremental cost to achieve that quality. Sometimes added attention to something such as quality does not produce added value. When that point is reached, you should stop trying to improve quality.

## Logical Data Models
The logical data model can be presented using an entity relationship diagram—a method of representing and analyzing data. A logical data model contains a description of the quality needs of the project. It is used to understand the requirements, clarify business rules, and define processes. It can be used to create and refine quality plans that best meet the needs of the project.

## Matrix Diagrams[13]
A matrix diagram is a visual representation of the relationship between two or more sets of items. In the Plan Quality Management process, matrix diagrams can be used to sort quality requirements and identify the requirements that are most critical to the project. With this information, appropriate metrics may be planned to track and measure project progress.

A type of matrix diagram, a prioritization matrix is useful for decision analysis about quality management plan components (organizational policies, processes, and requirements) that may need to change.

An example of a matrix diagram is the probability and impact matrix shown in the Risk Management chapter of this book as a tool of qualitative risk analysis.

## Mind Mapping
As discussed in the Scope Management chapter, a mind map is a diagram of ideas or notes to help generate, classify, or record information. It is used here to facilitate the gathering of quality requirements and illustrate their impacts on other parts of project planning.

## Flowcharts
Flowcharts may also be referred to as process flows or process maps. They show how a process or system flows from beginning to end, how the elements interrelate, alternative paths the process can take, and how the process translates inputs into outputs. A common flowchart model is a SIPOC, which shows the connections between the supplier, input, process, output, and customer in a process. Flowcharts can be used in many parts of project management. In the Plan Quality Management process, flowcharts can help determine the cost of quality by mapping the expected monetary value of pursuing paths of conformance and nonconformance to quality.

Flowcharts are also useful for defining and communicating processes that will be used on the project. Also, they can be analyzed to determine how processes will be measured for conformance and effectiveness.

You can also use this tool in Plan Quality Management to visualize a process and find potential quality problems or quality control issues. Imagine that work results are passed to four departments for approval. Might this lead to quality problems? What about an unfinished fragile product in a manufacturing environment? Would the quality of the product be reduced if it needed to be passed by hand from person to person?

A generic example of a flowchart is shown in figure 8.2.

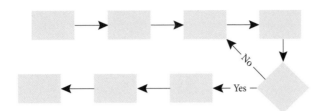

FIGURE 8.2   *Flowchart*

**Test and Inspection Planning**   Plan Quality Management includes determining how the team will confirm that the required level of quality has been achieved in the completed project deliverables, as well as how the deliverables will be evaluated for performance and reliability. Testing methods, which vary depending upon the type of product, service, or result being created by the project, are used in the Control Quality process.

**Meetings**   Developing management plans requires the collaboration of the project manager and team. The project manager may hold meetings specifically focused on project planning. Note that any of the tools and techniques discussed in this section may be used within those meetings as part of quality management planning.

## Outputs of Plan Quality Management   PAGE 286   The Plan Quality Management Process results in the following outputs.

**Quality Management Plan**   Remember that the purpose of the Plan Quality Management process is to determine what quality is and to put a plan in place to deliver that level of quality. This plan is called the quality management plan. It also includes analyzing processes to find ways to increase efficiency and prevent problems, which saves money and increases the probability that the customer will be satisfied.

Most quality management plans include the following:
- The quality practices and standards that apply to the project
- Who will be involved in managing quality, when, and what their specific duties will be
- What processes will be followed to help ensure quality
- A review of earlier decisions to make sure those decisions are correct
- The meetings that will be held regarding quality
- The reports that will address quality
- What metrics will be used to measure quality
- What parts of the project or deliverables will be measured and when

**Quality Metrics**   Throughout this book, there is an underlying theme that the project manager must know how the project is performing compared to what was planned and be able to determine when to request changes. The only way to effectively do this is to determine metrics in advance. This means the project manager needs to think through the areas on the project that are important to measure and (in most cases) decide what range of variation is acceptable. The following are some examples of quality metrics:
- The number of changes (to help measure the quality of the project management planning process)
- The variance related to resources utilization

331

- The number of items that fail inspection
- The variance of the weight of a product produced by the project compared to the planned weight
- The number of bugs found in software that is being developed as part of the project

As a project manager, you must know what processes are being used on the project, analyze their effectiveness, and create additional processes as necessary, while also improving those processes as they are being used. This plan for analysis and improvement of these processes is included in the quality management plan. Improving existing processes saves time by increasing efficiency and preventing problems. It also saves money and increases the probability that the customer will be satisfied.

### Project Management Plan and Project Documents Updates
The Plan Quality Management process will result in additions or changes (iterations) to the project management plan and project documents. For example, quality management work may be added to the project. This work is documented in the scope baseline (WBS and WBS dictionary) as well as in the requirements traceability matrix, and may necessitate adjustments to the project activity list, schedule, budget, and resource assignments. Additional risks related to quality may be added to the risk register, and risk management efforts may be added to the project management plan.

### Manage Quality   PAGE 288

> **Process** Manage Quality
> **Process Group** Executing
> **Knowledge Area** Quality Management

Manage Quality is performed while the project work is being done.
A group outside the project team, such as a quality department, often handles this work on a project. The efforts of this process focus on making certain that the project work, the processes followed, and the deliverables that are produced conform to the quality management plan.

Do you remember the discussion of conformance and nonconformance to quality in the "Plan Quality Management" section of this chapter? The items included in the list of costs of conformance (for example, quality training, measuring interim deliverables, and ensuring the project team understands and follows the accepted processes) refer to the work of both the Manage Quality and Control Quality processes.

Processes to ensure quality standards will be met are reviewed to make sure they are effective, and are being followed correctly. Quality audits, failure analysis, and design of experiments (described later in this chapter) may be done to see if the quality management plan with the standards, metrics, processes, and procedures may need to change. Test and evaluation documents, for use in Control Quality, are prepared as a part of Manage Quality.

This process uses the quality management plan, including quality requirements, and analyzes measurements gathered in Control Quality to answer the following questions:

- Are the quality requirements, organizational policies, and processes identified in the quality management plan giving us the results we intended?
- Based on what we know now, is the work we planned the right quality work for this project and the right work to meet customer requirements?
- Are we following the procedures and processes as planned?
- Can the processes and procedures be improved?
- How can we increase efficiency and prevent problems?

The process of managing quality also includes evaluating all aspects of the product design to confirm that the end result will meet quality requirements and identifying possible improvements to the design or the process of producing it.

The work performed in Manage Quality will uncover any processes that may be resulting in a level of quality that is not acceptable according to the quality management plan.

## Manage Quality Tools and Techniques  PAGE 292  The quality management plan is created to prevent quality issues. The following tools and techniques are used to evaluate the success of our planning efforts. You will see that many of these accomplish the same thing, but in different ways. Not all of these tools and techniques will be used on every project. The choice depends on the preferences of the project manager, and organizational requirements regarding quality management, as well as the needs of a particular project.

### Checklists  In Manage Quality, a checklist can be used to confirm that the steps of a process have all been completed. It may also be used to analyze defects discovered in quality inspections, looking for issues within the process, and to assess whether a deliverable meets the acceptance criteria.

### Cause-and-Effect (Fishbone, Ishikawa, or Why-Why) Diagrams[14]  A project manager can use cause-and-effect diagrams to confirm that policies and procedures are being followed and that metrics are being used correctly, and that they were adequate to produce the required level of quality in project deliverables. Figure 8.4 in the "Control Quality" section of this chapter is an example of a cause-and-effect diagram.

### Histograms[15]  In this process, histograms are used to analyze the type and frequency of defects in order to identify where the quality plan and processes may need improvement as the project moves forward. Figure 8.5 and figure 8.6 in the Control Quality section of this chapter are both examples of histograms.

### Scatter Diagrams[16]  This diagram tracks two variables to determine their relationship to the quality of the results. Figure 8.7 in the "Control Quality" section of this chapter shows three examples of scatter diagrams.

### Document Analysis  Document analysis involves reviewing the results of testing and other quality reports to identify ways in which the quality management plan and processes may not be supporting the production of deliverables that meet the project quality requirements.

### Alternatives Analysis  It is important to consider all the ways to solve an issue or problem. In Manage Quality, alternatives analysis may be used to evaluate which action would best impact the results of quality management efforts or processes. For example, would a new automated testing tool be of more benefit than redefining the testing process?

Design of experiments (DOE)[17] is a technique that can be used to analyze alternatives. Experimentation is performed to determine statistically what variables will improve quality; for example, DOE can be used to look for ways to deliver the same level of quality for less cost. DOE is a fast and accurate technique that allows you to systematically change the important factors in a process and see which combinations have an optimal impact on the project deliverables. For example, designers might use DOE to determine which combination of materials, structure, and construction will produce the highest-quality product. Performing DOE can help decrease the time and effort required to discover the optimal conditions in which to produce a quality deliverable. An alternative to DOE is to perform individual experiments for each variable in a process to assess their impacts on quality, but this can be time-consuming and can overlook interactions among variables.

### Process Analysis[18]
Quality management can also include process analysis. Have you ever worked on a project where some of the activities or work packages were repeated? This often happens when projects have multiple installations, such as a project to install software onto hundreds of computers. The lessons learned on the first few installations are used to improve the process for the remaining installations. Though this often happens naturally, formal process analysis should be planned in at certain points in the project (for example, after every 10 installations). Process analysis is a part of the continuous improvement effort on a project and focuses on identifying improvements that might be needed in project processes.

### Root Cause Analysis
Root cause analysis in Manage Quality seeks to identify the processes, procedures, and policies within the plan that may not be working or that may need adjustment. Identifying the root cause of a quality problem or defect helps the team determine how to prevent it from recurring.

Failure analysis is a specific type of root cause analysis. It analyzes failed components of deliverables or failed processes to determine what led to that failure. Corrective action or change requests are likely outcomes of this type of analysis.

### Multicriteria Decision Analysis
The project manager must facilitate a number of decisions regarding quality. There are several decision-making techniques that may be used. Multicriteria decision analysis is a complex method of numerically assessing options based on criteria such as time, cost, and quality. It can be used throughout a project to help the team reach agreement regarding the best way to solve a problem or improve quality. For example, in Manage Quality, the team may use this technique when considering whether to adjust the quality management plan or specific processes or procedures.

A simpler decision-making technique is a prioritization matrix. A prioritization matrix can be used to numerically assess available options, ranking them based on predetermined criteria.

### Flowcharts[19]
In the Plan Quality Management process, we discussed flowcharts as a tool to determine the cost of quality and identify potential quality problems. In Manage Quality, flowcharts may be used to study the steps of a process leading up to a quality defect. It is possible that this analysis would uncover confusion among the team or point out ways the process needs to be adjusted to make it more effective.

### Affinity Diagrams
We first saw this technique in the Collect Requirements process. In Manage Quality, affinity diagrams can help you organize and group the results of root cause analysis. For example, in Control Quality you may have determined the cause of a variance, product defect, or a deliverable not meeting requirements. You can use this information in the Manage Quality process to determine whether a change to the policies, procedure, and standards in the quality management plan would best address the root cause of the problems.

### Audits
Imagine a team of auditors walking into your office one day to check up on you and the project. Their job is to see if you are complying with company policies, processes, practices, and procedures as defined in the quality management plan, and to determine whether those being used are efficient and effective. This scenario represents a quality audit, and it serves as an example of how seriously companies take quality. Do not think of a quality audit as a negative event. Instead, a good quality audit will look for new lessons learned and effective practices that your project can contribute to the performing organization. The work of a project is not only to produce the product of the project; it could also be said that a project should contribute to the best practices within the organization and, therefore, make the organization better. A quality audit may identify gaps or areas in need of improvement. Making these changes will enhance your ability to meet quality objectives.

If you do not have a team of auditors from the quality department coming to see you on your projects, do you take on the responsibility of looking for opportunities to identify lessons learned and best practices on your projects? Although quality audits are usually done by the quality department, the project manager can lead this effort if the performing organization does not have such a department.

### Design for X

Design for X is another way of analyzing variables to evaluate both the effectiveness of the quality management plan and the team's ability to meet objectives. The X in the name Design for X can represent an attribute of quality, such as reliability, security, or serviceability. If the plan is not delivering the intended results in relation to the variable being analyzed, Design for X can help determine what changes or adjustments are needed.

### Problem-Solving

Think of how important this technique might be when you encounter quality problems. Gaining a good understanding of the real problem is the first step towards finding an effective and long-lasting solution. Problem-solving can be used when considering quality improvements or to determine how best to respond to deficiencies identified in quality audits.

The following are the steps used to analyze quality (and other) problems:

1. Define the real or root problem—not what is presented to you or what appears to be the problem.
2. Analyze the problem.
3. Identify solutions.
4. Pick a solution.
5. Implement a solution.
6. Review the solution, and confirm that the solution solved the problem.

## Outputs of Manage Quality

PAGE 296 To understand the value of the Manage Quality process, you need to know that it leads to the following outputs.

### Test and Evaluation Documents

Test and evaluation documents are identified or created in Manage Quality and used in Control Quality. They provide a format with which to evaluate whether quality objectives have been met. Control charts, checklists, test plans, or project documents such as a requirements traceability matrix from scope management, may also be used here. Larger organizations, or organizations that work on many similar projects, may develop templates for such testing and evaluation work.

### Quality Reports

These types of reports interpret and document the results of Manage Quality and Control Quality activities. They can present information in a number of formats. Information in quality reports is used to identify necessary changes to plans, policies, and processes to ensure that quality requirements will be met throughout the life of a project.

### Change Requests and Project Management Plan Updates

Changes and updates to components of the project management plan—including the quality management plan and the scope, schedule, or cost baselines—may result from the work of this process.

### Project Documents Updates

Newly discovered issues will be added to the issue log. The lessons learned register and risk register will be updated as needed.

## Control Quality   PAGE 298

**Process**  Control Quality
**Process Group**  Monitoring & Controlling
**Knowledge Area**  Quality Management

Control Quality is the process of ensuring a certain level of quality in a deliverable, whether it be a product, service, or result. Control means measure, and that is the major function of the Control Quality process. Aspects of products, services, or results are measured to determine whether they meet the quality standards. This process helps ensure customer acceptance, as it involves confirming and documenting the achievement of agreed-upon requirements.

It is important to note that Control Quality is closely related to the previous process, Manage Quality. Many of the tools and techniques used in Control Quality—as well as the resulting measurements—are also used in Manage Quality, but with a different focus. Control addresses the quality of product. Defects are detected and corrected. Manage Quality addresses the effectiveness of quality management plans, processes, and procedures, and whether the project is on track to meet quality objectives. Quality defects are assumed to indicate issues with those plans, processes, and procedures.

Inputs to this process include the quality management plan, quality metrics (the agreed-upon measures of quality), test and evaluation documents (developed in Manage Quality to be used in this process), work performance data and deliverables (from Direct and Manage Project Work in integration management), approved change requests from integrated change control, and project documents.

Although a project manager must be involved and concerned about quality control, a quality department may complete much of this work in large companies. The department then informs the project manager about quality issues through change requests, which are accompanied by any necessary documentation and reports to detail the quality issues. The project manager must be able to read and understand quality measurement reports.

It is during Control Quality that the height of doors in a manufacturing process or the number of bugs per module will be measured. Quality control helps answer the following questions:

- Are the results of our work meeting the agreed-upon standards and thereby meeting project requirements?
- What is the actual variance from the standards?
- Is the variance from standards or processes outside of acceptable limits?
- Are people using the checklists to support meeting the metrics established for the process?
- What changes in the project should be considered?

To better understand questions relating to Control Quality, you should be familiar with the following terms.

## Mutual Exclusivity
The exam may reference statistical terms such as "mutual exclusivity." Two events are said to be mutually exclusive if they cannot both occur in a single trial. For example, flipping a coin once cannot result in both a head and a tail.

## Probability
This term refers to the likelihood that something will occur. Probability is usually expressed as a decimal or a fraction.

## Normal Distribution
A normal distribution is the most common probability density distribution chart. It is in the shape of a bell curve and is used to measure variations (see the example in the control chart exercise later in this chapter).

## Statistical Independence
Another confusing statistical term you may see on the exam is "statistical independence." This means the probability of one event occurring does not affect the probability of another event occurring. For example, the probability of rolling a six on a die is statistically independent from the probability of getting a five on the next roll.

## Standard Deviation (or Sigma)
As we've already discussed, one measure of a range is its standard deviation. It denotes what would be considered a statistically stable process or output. This concept is also sometimes stated as a measure of how far you are from the mean (not the median). (Remember $(P - O)/6$ is the beta distribution formula for standard deviation, using pessimistic and optimistic estimates, as described in the Schedule Management chapter.)

## Control Quality Tools and Techniques
There are many tools and techniques that may be used in this process. However, it is helpful to realize that regardless of the method used, the ultimate goal is the same: to test (verify) that each deliverable meets the metrics and requirements as stated in the plan, including the customer's acceptance criteria, and that it is ready to move to the Validate Scope process.

### Checklists
Information about the quality of interim deliverables can be gathered using quality checklists. A quality checklist can be a list of items to inspect, a list of steps to be performed, or a picture of the item to be inspected, with space to note any defects found.

In Control Quality, checklists are used to determine that all required features and functions are included, and that they meet acceptance criteria. Checklists may be a part of the test and evaluation documents created in Manage Quality. Checklist templates for commonly performed work, deliverables, or processes may be organizational process assets of the organization.

### Checksheets
A checksheet is a type of checklist that can be used to keep track of data, such as quality problems uncovered during inspections, as well as to document how often a particular defect occurs, as illustrated in figure 8.3.

| Defect | Frequency |
|---|---|
| Too long | IIII II |
| Too narrow | III |
| Too wide | IIII III |
| Too short | II |

FIGURE 8.3   *Checksheet*

### Statistical Sampling
Let's think about the process of manufacturing doors. There would likely be some allowable variation in the height and weight of the doors being manufactured. Even so, the doors must be checked to see if they meet quality standards on the project. What if inspecting each door would cause damage or take too much time? Then you may need to take a statistically valid sample. It is best to take a sample of a population if you believe there are not many defects, or if studying the entire population would:

- Take too long
- Cost too much
- Be too destructive

The sample size and frequency of measurements are determined as part of the Plan Quality Management process, and the actual sampling is done in Control Quality. Keep in mind that statistical sampling can also be done for project management activities. For example, you may initially check the on-time status for 5 out of 50 of a group's activities. If you find issues in those 5, you can assume there will be more issues in the remaining 45 activities.

### Questionnaires and Surveys
Questionnaires and surveys may be used in Control Quality to gather data on details of problems or defects, or to confirm that customers or end users are satisfied with deliverables that have been deployed on the project. The results can be used to determine whether conformance to quality has been achieved.

### Performance Reviews
The project manager or quality department may conduct periodic performance reviews to formally assess how the project is doing in terms of following the quality management plan and meeting quality requirements. Such a review involves comparing the results of control measurements to metrics identified in the quality management plan. It may bring to light changes necessary to achieve quality requirements.

### Root Cause Analysis
Root cause analysis is used to identify the cause of quality problems, including defects, to determine how they can be remedied.

### Inspection
Inspections are used to verify that deliverables meet the requirements. Inspections may be referred to as audits or walkthroughs, and generally include measurement of project deliverables. Quality tools, such as checklists and control charts, may be used to capture the data. Inspections are also used to check that previously approved changes have been made correctly, and that the changes have provided the intended results (validated changes).

### Control Charts[20]
Much of what the exam focuses on regarding control charts is not in the *PMBOK® Guide*. But don't worry; the information in the following sections, along with the exercise that follows, will help you understand this tool, even if control charts are new to you. Once you understand control charts, it is generally easy to get questions about them right on the exam. Note that there's an example of a control chart in the exercise.

Control charts are established in Manage Quality, and the parameters such as the mean, specification limits, and control limits (all defined later in this section) are determined. Control charts are used in Control Quality to help determine if the results of a process are within acceptable limits.

To better understand the need for control charts, imagine a door manufacturer is undertaking a project to create a new production line. To make sure the production facility will create doors that meet quality standards, it's essential to monitor the processes and output so the new production line can become an ongoing business operation. Would each door be the same exact height? Weight? Not likely. Instead there is a range, however small, that is acceptable. Each door should be within the range of normal and acceptable limits.

During the Control Quality process, samples are taken and plotted on the chart (see the small squares shown on the control chart in the following exercise). The control chart shows whether the samples are within acceptable limits. If the data does not fall within the acceptable range, the results are considered to be "out of control," which indicates a problem that needs to be handled.

A control chart can also be used to represent and monitor data on project performance, such as cost and schedule variances.

Now that we have discussed the basic concepts of a control chart, let's look at some of the related terms you should know for the exam. You will see questions on this topic, but they should be fairly straightforward. The following can be indicated on a control chart.

**Upper and Lower Control Limits**[21]  Control limits are often shown as two dashed lines on a control chart. These limits are the acceptable range of variation of a process or measurement's results. Control limits indicate what is stable versus unstable (out of control) in the process. Every process is expected to have some variation in its results; for example, each door manufactured will not be exactly the same size. The project manager and stakeholders determine the appropriate upper and lower control limits for quality metrics on a project. Data points within this range are generally thought of as "in control," excluding the rule of seven (described later in this section), and are an acceptable range of variation. Data points outside this range indicate the process is out of control.

The concept of control limits is also important outside of a control chart. A project manager can have control limits for many things. How about for a work package? Is one hour late in its delivery a problem? How about one day? Such control limits help the project manager know when to take action.

**Mean (Average)**  The mean is indicated by a line in the middle of the control chart. It shows the middle of the range of acceptable variation. A normal distribution curve represents the acceptable range of variance around a mean, and it falls within the boundaries of the control limits.

**Specification Limits**[22]  While control limits represent the performing organization's standards for quality, specification limits represent the customer's expectations—or the contractual requirements—for performance and quality on the project. Specification limits are characteristics of the measured process and are not inherent. In other words, specification limits are not calculated based on the control chart; instead, they are inputs from the customer. Therefore, they can appear either inside or outside of the control limits. To meet the customer's specification limits, the performing organization's standards for quality (control limits) must be stricter than those of the customer. Agreeing to do a project when your work does not meet the customer's quality standards adds waste and extra management to the project to sort out acceptable items. Therefore, on the exam, assume that specification limits are outside the upper and lower control limits.

**Out of Control**  The process is out of a state of statistical control under either of two circumstances:

- A data point falls outside of the upper or lower control limit.
- There are nonrandom data points; these may be within the upper and lower control limits, such as the rule of seven (described next).

Think of "out of control" as a lack of consistency and predictability in the process or its results.

**Rule of Seven**[23]   The rule of seven is a general rule, or heuristic. It refers to a group or series of nonrandom data points that total seven on one side of the mean. The rule of seven tells you that, although none of these points are outside of the control limits, they are not random and the process is out of control. The project manager should investigate this type of situation and find a cause.

**Assignable Cause/Special Cause Variation**[24]   An assignable cause or special cause variation signifies that a process is out of control. If there is an assignable cause or special cause variation, it means a data point, or a series of data points, requires investigation to determine the cause of the variation. The project manager could use additional tools, such as a cause-and-effect diagram, to try to uncover the root cause of the variation.

**Exercise**   Now try this exercise. On the following charts, label the examples of each of the ten listed items by placing the item number next to its location on the chart(s). If you are unsure, take a guess, and then review the control chart discussion. The pictures represent two different control charts.

When you are able to pick out all the items on the control charts, you should be ready to answer questions about control charts on the exam.

NOTE: The questions on the exam relating to control charts may be easier to answer if you can picture a control chart in your mind. It is unlikely one will be shown to you on the exam. Instead, the exam will use the terms in situational questions, and you will need to know what they mean. (For example: "A team member tells you that one sample is outside the lower control limit. What should you do?"). This exercise is designed to help you visualize control charts and make sure you understand these tools so you can answer questions about them.

Identify the following on the charts:

1. Upper control limit
2. Lower control limit
3. Assignable cause/special cause
4. The process is out of control
5. Normal and expected variation in the process

6. Rule of seven
7. Specification limits
8. Three sigma
9. Six sigma
10. Normal distribution curve

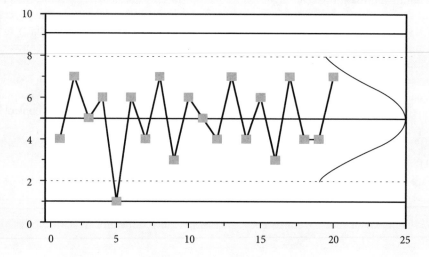

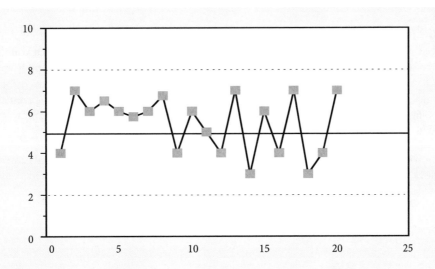

## Answer

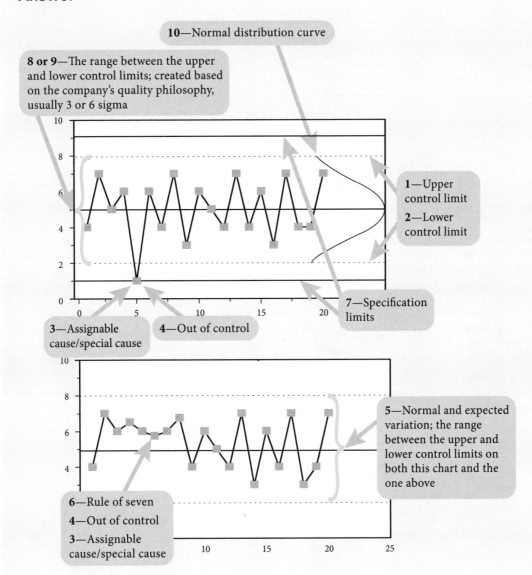

**10**—Normal distribution curve

**8 or 9**—The range between the upper and lower control limits; created based on the company's quality philosophy, usually 3 or 6 sigma

**1**—Upper control limit

**2**—Lower control limit

**7**—Specification limits

**3**—Assignable cause/special cause

**4**—Out of control

**5**—Normal and expected variation; the range between the upper and lower control limits on both this chart and the one above

**6**—Rule of seven

**4**—Out of control

**3**—Assignable cause/special cause

341

### Cause-and-Effect (Fishbone, Ishikawa, or Why-Why) Diagrams

Is it better to fix a defect or get to the root cause of the defect? Think about this question for a moment. The answer is that you should do both, and a cause-and-effect diagram can help you. In Manage Quality, we discussed the application of the cause-and-effect diagram in determining the root cause of quality issues relating to plans, processes, or procedures. In Control Quality, this tool can be used to look backward at what may have contributed to quality problems on the project, as well as to analyze the impact of defects on the quality and acceptability of a deliverable.

Figure 8.4 shows the defect "system will not install" on the right and then lists the potential causes, such as hardware issues, software issues, etc. Various subcauses of each potential cause are also listed in an effort to find the root cause of the defect.

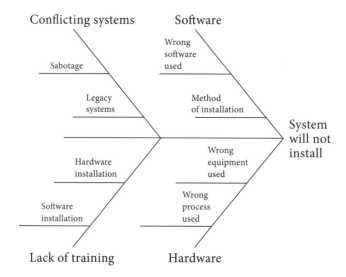

**FIGURE 8.4** *Cause-and-effect diagram*

Examples of phrasing the exam may use to describe cause-and-effect diagrams include the following:

- A creative way to look at the causes of a problem
- Helps stimulate thinking, organize thoughts, and generate discussion

### Histograms

As shown in figure 8.5, a histogram shows data in the form of bars or columns. A typical histogram presents data in no particular order and without reference to time. The results of measurements taken in Control Quality are displayed on a histogram to determine the problems that need the most immediate attention or that are most likely to prevent the project from achieving its quality requirements. The Manage Quality process will analyze these problems and defects to determine if the cause is related to processes or the quality management plan.

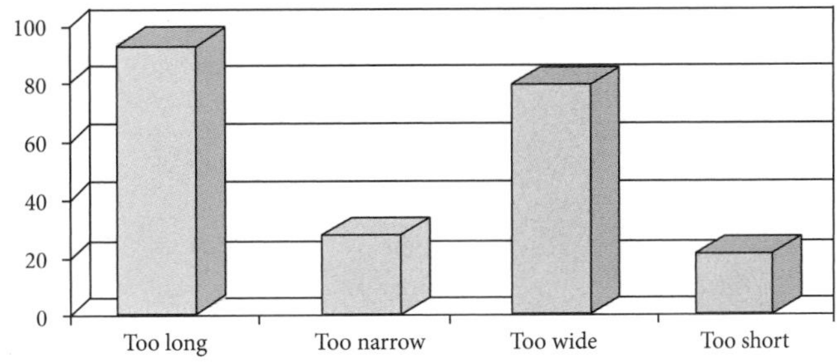

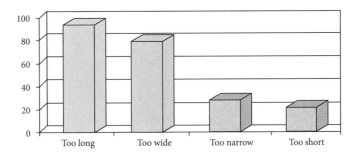

FIGURE 8.5   *Histogram*

**Pareto Charts**[25]   A Pareto diagram or Pareto chart is a commonly used type of histogram that arranges the results from most frequent to least frequent to help identify which root causes are resulting in the most problems. Joseph Juran adapted Vilfredo Pareto's 80/20 rule to create the 80/20 principle (also known as the Pareto Principle), which states that 80 percent of problems are due to 20 percent of the root causes. Addressing the root cause of the most frequent problems makes the greatest impact on quality.

In Plan Quality Management, you can identify potential problems (using, for example, historical information from past projects) and document them on a Pareto diagram, as shown in figure 8.6. In Control Quality, you measure the data and represent it on the diagram to help analyze the situation and determine where to focus corrective action.

FIGURE 8.6   *Pareto diagram*

**Scatter Diagrams**   As discussed in Manage Quality, a scatter diagram is used to determine the relationship between variables and the quality of the results. In Control Quality, a scatter diagram can be used to compare actual results to what was anticipated, and to estimate and forecast future outcomes of the process.

A scatter diagram tracks two variables to determine their relationship. Imagine that our door manufacturer has a project to develop a new painted door product line. Scatter diagrams may be used to determine the relationship of independent variables, such as paint quantity, dryer fan speed, and door weight, to the dependent variable of drying time, or to correlate defects to other variables in the process.

A regression line (or trend line) is calculated to show the correlation of variables, and can then be used for estimating and forecasting. Figure 8.7 depicts the possible resulting patterns: a proportional or positive correlation of paint quantity to drying time, an inverse or negative correlation of dryer fan speed to drying time, and no correlation between door weight and drying time.

343

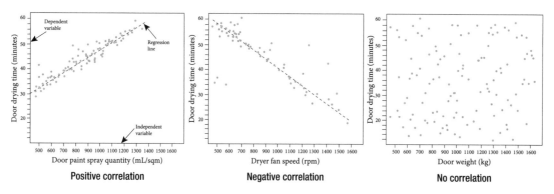

FIGURE 8.7   *Scatter diagrams*

**Meetings**    Lessons learned or retrospectives are meetings conducted as part of Control Quality to assess what was done right and what could have been done differently to make the project more successful.

Approved change request reviews are meetings in which the team evaluates whether approved change requests have been completed, and whether they have returned the results intended.

## Outputs of Control Quality    PAGE 305   When you have completed the Control Quality process, you will have the following outputs:

- Measurements
- Validated changes
- Work performance information
- Updates to the project management plan (including the quality management plan) and project documents (including the issue log, test and evaluation documents, risk register, and lessons learned register)
- Change requests, including recommended corrective and preventive actions and defect repair
- Verified deliverables

## Putting It All Together    Do you think you understand quality management now? If not, don't worry; we are not finished with this chapter yet. The following exercises will help you review the information you have learned. Take this opportunity to solidify your understanding of what quality management is and how it fits into the overall project management process.

**Exercise**   List the specific actions required to ensure quality on the project.

344

_____

**Answer**   There are a lot of possible answers. Did you come up with these?

- Review the project management plan, particularly the project baselines, and relevant project documents as they relate to quality on the project.

- Make sure you know and understand the customer's definition of quality.

- Identify the desired levels of performance in the product and components of the product.

- Identify at what level you should control the project (for example, the work package, activity, or a more detailed level).

- Identify any quality standards and processes that are applicable to the project.

- Identify the required level of quality for project management activities.

- Determine the quality standards and processes to use, when, and on what parts of the project.

- Set standards to reach the level of desired performance for activities and the project.

- Set metrics to measure quality from the customer's and the organization's perspective.

- Decide what you will do to make sure the processes are followed and the standards are met.

- Determine how you will improve the processes on the project.

- Test the validity of assumptions before they result in problems.

- Make sure team members understand what "quality" means for their work.

- Review problems, errors, and complaints to determine what can be done to prevent them from reoccurring on the project.

- Have the team follow planned efforts to evaluate the project to look for quality improvements.
- Inspect work as it is being done, not after.
- Perform quality reviews.
- Measure performance against standards.
- Hold meetings, issue reports, measure, and perform calculations to evaluate variances.
- Reassess the quality standards.
- Evaluate the effectiveness of the quality control system.
- Manage quality with the same effort as time, cost, or scope.
- Request changes, including corrective and preventive actions and defect repairs.
- Update organizational process assets with information and data learned from process improvement and control efforts.
- Include quality issues in lessons learned.
- Feed lessons learned back into the project.

## Understanding the Tools and Techniques Used in Quality Management As you have read through this chapter, have you found yourself asking questions like, "Now, when are all these tools and techniques used?" or "What are the differences between the three parts of the quality management process again?" People tend to struggle with these concepts. The following exercises will help.

**Exercise** Take a moment to research in this book the different tools and techniques that are created or used in each of the quality management processes. Then complete the following table, indicating the process in which each tool is used. Remember that some tools and techniques are used in more than one quality management process. Think about the ways they are used for different purposes in each process.

| Tool | Used in Plan Quality Management | Used in Manage Quality | Used in Control Quality |
|---|---|---|---|
| Affinity diagrams | | | |
| Alternatives analysis | | | |
| Benchmarking | | | |
| Brainstorming | | | |
| Cause-and-effect diagrams | | | |
| Checklists | | | |
| Checksheets | | | |
| Control charts | | | |
| Cost of quality | | | |
| Cost-benefit analysis | | | |
| Design for X | | | |
| Document analysis | | | |
| Flowcharts | | | |

| Tool | Used in Plan Quality Management | Used in Manage Quality | Used in Control Quality |
|---|---|---|---|
| Histograms | | | |
| Inspection | | | |
| Interviews | | | |
| Logical data model | | | |
| Matrix diagrams | | | |
| Meetings | | | |
| Mind mapping | | | |
| Multicriteria decision analysis | | | |
| Performance reviews | | | |
| Problem-solving | | | |
| Process analysis | | | |
| Questionnaires and surveys | | | |
| Root cause analysis | | | |
| Scatter diagrams | | | |
| Statistical sampling | | | |
| Test and inspection planning | | | |
| Testing/product evaluations | | | |

## Answer

| Tool | Used in Plan Quality Management | Used in Manage Quality | Used in Control Quality |
|---|---|---|---|
| Affinity diagrams | | X | |
| Alternatives analysis | | X | |
| Benchmarking | X | | |
| Brainstorming | X | | |
| Cause-and-effect diagrams | | X | X |
| Checklists | | X | X |
| Checksheets | | | X |
| Control charts | | | X |
| Cost of quality | X | | |
| Cost-benefit analysis | X | | |
| Design for X | | X | |
| Document analysis | | X | |
| Flowcharts | X | X | |
| Histograms | | X | X |

| Tool | Used in Plan Quality Management | Used in Manage Quality | Used in Control Quality |
|---|---|---|---|
| Inspection | | | X |
| Interviews | X | | |
| Logical data model | X | | |
| Matrix diagrams | X | X | |
| Meetings | X | | X |
| Mind mapping | X | | |
| Multicriteria decision analysis | X | X | |
| Performance reviews | | | X |
| Problem-solving | | X | |
| Process analysis | | X | |
| Questionnaires and surveys | | | X |
| Root cause analysis | | X | X |
| Scatter diagrams | | X | X |
| Statistical sampling | | | X |
| Test and inspection planning | X | | |
| Testing/product evaluations | | | X |

**TRICKS OF THE TRADE®** Here is a trick: If the situation is looking forward in time, it is most likely a planning function. If it is looking back in time at project results, it is most likely part of quality control. If it is looking back in time at processes and procedures, it is most likely part of managing quality.

## Exercise
Now take what you have learned and see if you can apply it in a different way. This exercise should help prepare you for questions on the exam, regardless of how they are written.

| | Situation | What Tool/ Technique Is Being Referred To? | What Part of the Quality Management Process Are You In? |
|---|---|---|---|
| 1 | Looking at the project practices of comparable projects | | |
| 2 | Measuring 4 of the doors produced, rather than all 400 | | |
| 3 | Evaluating the factors that influence particular variables in a product or process | | |
| 4 | Analyzing a chart of problems to find the most frequent one(s) to determine whether processes need to be improved | | |

© 2018 RMC Publications, Inc.™ • 952.846.4484 • info@rmcls.com • www.rmcls.com

| Situation | What Tool/ Technique Is Being Referred To? | What Part of the Quality Management Process Are You In? |
|---|---|---|
| 5  Comparing the expense of quality efforts to the return on that investment | | |
| 6  Determining what will be an acceptable range of performance | | |
| 7  Comparing what was done to what was documented in the plans | | |
| 8  Graphically representing a process to determine where a process that is achieving low-quality results might need adjustment | | |
| 9  Taking measurements and comparing them to the upper and lower thresholds of acceptable variance | | |
| 10  Collecting data about defects discovered during inspection | | |
| 11  Analyzing a graphic displaying issues that might have caused a defect, to determine whether the proper process was followed | | |
| 12  Showing data in the form of bars to measure and plot how frequently a problem occurred | | |
| 13  Collecting many data points to look at the pattern of relationships or correlation between two variables | | |
| 14  Using a bar chart to show how many problems occurred for each cause and arranging them according to the frequency at which the problems occurred | | |
| 15  Creating a list of items to be checked during inspections | | |
| 16  Reviewing a graphic displaying issues or potential issues that might have led to a defect or problem | | |
| 17  Examining a work product to make sure it meets standards | | |

**Answer**  Remember that the tools and techniques can be described in many ways on the exam. Get used to the idea that the exam will ask questions indirectly, and be able to differentiate between the tools or techniques and their uses.

349

| | Situation | What Tool/ Technique Is Being Referred To? | What Part of the Quality Management Process Are You In? |
|---|---|---|---|
| 1 | Looking at the project practices of comparable projects | Benchmarking | Plan Quality Management |
| 2 | Measuring 4 of the doors produced, rather than all 400 | Statistical sampling | Control Quality |
| 3 | Evaluating the factors that influence particular variables in a product or process | Design of experiments (part of process analysis) | Manage Quality |
| 4 | Analyzing a chart of problems to find the most frequent one(s) to determine whether processes need to be improved | Histograms | Manage Quality |
| 5 | Comparing the expense of quality efforts to the return on that investment | Cost-benefit analysis | Plan Quality Management |
| 6 | Determining what will be an acceptable range of performance | Control charts | Plan Quality Management |
| 7 | Comparing what was done to what was documented in the plans | Checklists | Control Quality |
| 8 | Graphically representing a process to determine where a process that is achieving low-quality results might need adjustment | Flowcharts | Manage Quality |
| 9 | Taking measurements and comparing them to the upper and lower thresholds of acceptable variance | Control charts | Control Quality |
| 10 | Collecting data about defects discovered during inspection | Checksheets | Control Quality |
| 11 | Analyzing a graphic with an organized series of lines displaying issues that might have caused a defect to determine whether the proper process was followed | Cause-and-effect diagrams | Manage Quality |
| 12 | Showing data in the form of bars to measure and plot how frequently a problem occurred | Histograms | Control Quality |
| 13 | Collecting many data points to look at the pattern of relationships or correlation between two variables | Scatter diagrams | Control Quality |
| 14 | Using a bar chart to show how many problems occurred for each cause and arranging them according to the frequency at which the problems occurred | Histograms (Pareto diagram) | Control Quality |
| 15 | Creating a list of items to be checked during inspections | Checklists | Plan Quality Management |

| | Situation | What Tool/ Technique Is Being Referred To? | What Part of the Quality Management Process Are You In? |
|---|---|---|---|
| 16 | Reviewing a graphic with an organized series of lines displaying issues or potential issues that might have led to a defect or problem | Cause-and-effect diagrams | Control Quality |
| 17 | Examining a work product to make sure it meets standards | Inspection | Control Quality |

**TRICKS OF THE TRADE®** **Understanding the Differences between the Three Parts of the Quality Management Process** Are you still unsure about the difference between Plan Quality Management, Manage Quality, and Control Quality? Think through what you have learned in this chapter, and see if you can recreate the chart shown earlier by filling in the following table.

| Plan Quality Management | Manage Quality | Control Quality |
|---|---|---|
| | Process Group | |
| | | |
| | High-Level Description of What Each Process Focuses On | |
| | | |
| | More Detailed Description of What Each Process Focuses On | |
| | | |

351

| Plan Quality Management | Manage Quality | Control Quality |
| --- | --- | --- |
| | | |

When you are finished, check your answers against the chart on pages 326-327. Having a clear understanding of what happens in each process will make it easier for you to answer quality-related questions on the exam. You will still have to read the questions carefully to determine which quality management process is being described.

© 2018 RMC Publications, Inc.™ • 952.846.4484 • info@rmcls.com • www.rmcls.com

## Practice Exam

1. When a product or service completely meets a customer's requirements:
    A. Quality is achieved.
    B. The cost of quality is high.
    C. The cost of quality is low.
    D. The customer pays the minimum price.

2. To what does the following definition refer? "A type of analysis focused on finding the point at which the benefits or revenue to be received from improving quality equals the incremental cost to achieve that quality."
    A. Quality control analysis
    B. Marginal analysis
    C. Standard quality analysis
    D. Conformance analysis

3. Who is ultimately responsible for quality management on the project?
    A. The project engineer
    B. The project manager
    C. The quality manager
    D. The team member

4. A project has faced major difficulties in the quality of its deliverables. Management now states that quality is the most important project constraint. If another problem with quality were to occur, what would be the best thing for the project manager to do?
    A. Fix the problem as soon as possible.
    B. Allow the schedule to slip by cutting cost.
    C. Allow cost to increase by fixing the root cause of the problem.
    D. Allow risk to increase by cutting cost.

5. A manager notices that a project manager is holding a meeting with some of the team and some stakeholders to discuss the quality of the project. The project schedule has been compressed, and the CPI is 1.1. The team has worked hard on the project and has been rewarded according to the reward system the project manager put in place. Overall, there is a strong sense of team. The manager suggests that the project manager does not have enough time to hold meetings about quality when the schedule is so compressed. Which of the following best describes why the manager is wrong?
    A. Improved quality leads to increased productivity, increased cost effectiveness, and decreased cost risk.
    B. Improved quality leads to increased productivity, decreased cost effectiveness, and increased cost risk.
    C. Improved quality leads to increased productivity, increased cost effectiveness, and increased cost risk.
    D. Improved quality leads to increased productivity, decreased cost effectiveness, and decreased cost risk.

353

6. Quality is:

    A. Meeting and exceeding the customer's expectations

    B. Adding extras to make the customer happy

    C. The degree to which the project meets requirements

    D. Conformance to management's objectives

7. All the following are tools and techniques of Control Quality except:

    A. Inspection

    B. Cost of quality

    C. Histogram

    D. Cause-and-effect diagram

8. A project manager is experiencing a great deal of frustration because a lot of rework has been required. It seems as though the team has significant differences of opinion related to interpretation of the requirements. The project manager is trying to determine what changes need to be made to meet the quality requirements and reduce future rework. He seeks the advice of his manager, who asks if he has created a histogram. Histograms help the project manager:

    A. Focus on the most critical issues to improve quality.

    B. Focus on stimulating thinking.

    C. Analyze the cause of a quality problem.

    D. Determine if a process is out of control.

9. A control chart helps the project manager:

    A. Focus on the most critical issues to improve quality.

    B. Focus on stimulating thinking.

    C. Analyze the cause of a quality problem.

    D. Determine if a process is functioning within established metrics.

10. Testing the entire population would:

    A. Take too long

    B. Provide more information than wanted

    C. Be mutually exclusive

    D. Show many defects

11. Cost has been determined to be the highest priority constraint on a project to design and produce a new tool that will be used in restaurant kitchens. The project team has included random sampling of these tools in their quality plan. Although cost is a key factor, the product must also meet high quality standards. All the following are examples of the cost of nonconformance except:

    A. Rework

    B. Quality training

    C. Scrap

    D. Warranty costs

12. Standard deviation is a measure of:

    A. How far the estimate is from the highest estimate

    B. How far the measurement is from the mean

    C. How correct the sample is

    D. How much time remains in the project

13. All the following result from quality audits except:

    A. Determination of whether project activities comply with organizational policies
    B. Improved processes to increase productivity
    C. Creation of quality metrics
    D. Confirmation of the implementation of approved change requests

14. A control chart shows seven data points in a row on one side of the mean. What should the project manager do?

    A. Perform a design of experiments.
    B. Adjust the chart to reflect the new mean.
    C. Find an assignable cause.
    D. Nothing. This is the rule of seven and can be ignored.

15. You are managing a project in a just in time environment. This will require more attention because the amount of inventory in such an environment is generally:

    A. 45 percent
    B. 10 percent
    C. 12 percent
    D. 0 percent

16. There are several executing activities underway on your project. You are beginning to get concerned about the accuracy of the progress reporting your team members are doing. How could you verify whether there is a problem?

    A. Perform a quality audit.
    B. Create risk quantification reports.
    C. Perform regression analysis.
    D. Perform Monte Carlo analysis.

17. A project manager and team from a firm that designs railroad equipment are tasked to design a machine to load stone onto railroad cars. The design allows for 2 percent spillage, amounting to over two tons of spilled rock per day. In which of the following does the project manager document this for the project?

    A. Quality management plan
    B. Quality policy
    C. Control charts
    D. Quality audit documentation

18. During a team meeting, the team adds a specific area of extra work to the project because they have determined it would benefit the customer. What is wrong in this situation?

    A. The team is not following the project management plan.
    B. These efforts shouldn't be done in meetings.
    C. Nothing. This is how to meet and exceed customer expectations.
    D. Nothing. The project manager is in control of the situation.

19. The project team has created a plan for how they will implement the quality policy, addressing responsibilities, procedures, and other details. If this plan changes during the project, which of the following plans will also change?

    A. Quality assurance plan
    B. Quality management plan
    C. Project management plan
    D. Quality control plan

20. You are a project manager for a major information systems project. Someone from the quality department comes to see you about beginning a quality audit of your project. The team, already under pressure to complete the project as soon as possible, objects to the audit. You should explain to the team that the purpose of a quality audit is:

    A. To check whether measurements of project deliverables are within specification limits
    B. To check if the customer is following the quality process
    C. To identify inefficient and ineffective policies
    D. To check the accuracy of costs submitted by the team

21. You are in the middle of a major facility construction project. The structural steel is already in place, and the heating conduits are being put into place when a senior manager informs you that he is worried the project will not meet the quality standards. What should you do in this situation?

    A. Assure senior management that during the Plan Quality Management process, it was determined that the project would meet the quality standards.
    B. Analogously estimate future results.
    C. Involve the quality team.
    D. Check the results from the last quality management plan.

22. You are asked to select tools and techniques to supplement existing quality control activities. Which of the following would not be appropriate for this purpose?

    A. Performance reviews
    B. Statistical sampling
    C. Pareto diagrams
    D. Focus groups

23. The new software installation project is in progress. The project manager is working with the quality department to improve stakeholders' confidence that the project will satisfy the quality standards. Which of the following must they have before they start this process?

    A. Quality problems
    B. Quality improvement
    C. Quality control measurements
    D. Rework

24. A project manager has just taken over the project from another project manager during project executing. The previous project manager created a project budget, determined communications requirements, and went on to the complete work packages task. What should the new project manager do next?

    A. Coordinate completion of work packages.
    B. Identify quality standards.
    C. Begin the Identify Risks process.
    D. Validate scope.

25. An experienced project manager is working with a team chartered to build a bridge near the Arctic Circle. In addition to the usual concerns of safety and longevity, the team must also take into account the extreme weather conditions and their potential impact on the bridge. The sponsor meets with the project manager regarding her progress on this work. The sponsor is pleased to learn that the project manager is planning to conduct a design of experiments as part of quality planning. Design of experiments:

    A. Identifies which variables will have the most influence on a quality outcome
    B. Helps to identify the root cause of quality problems
    C. Determines what a quality outcome is
    D. Determines methods to be used for research and development

26. At the end of the project, the project manager reports that the project has added four unexpected areas of functionality and three areas of performance. The customer has expressed satisfaction with the project. What does this mean in terms of the success of the project?

    A. The project was an unqualified success.
    B. The project was unsuccessful because it was gold plated.
    C. The project was unsuccessful because the customer being happy means they would have paid more for the work.
    D. The project was successful because the team had a chance to learn new areas of functionality and the customer was satisfied.

27. During project executing, a project team member informs the project manager that a work package has not met the quality metric, and that she believes it is not possible to meet it. The project manager meets with all concerned parties to analyze the situation. Which part of the quality management process is the project manager involved in?

    A. Manage Quality
    B. Perform Integrated Change Control
    C. Control Quality
    D. Plan Quality Management

28. The project manager notices that the project activities being completed by one department are all taking slightly longer than planned. To date, none of the activities in the work packages have been on the critical path. The project manager is bothered by the problem, since four of the next five critical path activities are being completed by this department.

    After making three calls, the project manager is finally able to talk with the department manager to determine what is going on. The conversation is slow because both speak different native languages, and they are trying to converse in French, a shared language. To make communication easier, the project manager frequently asks the department manager to repeat back what has been said.

    The department manager communicates that his staff is following a company policy that requires two levels of testing. During the conversation, the department manager also makes a comment that leads the project manager to believe the policy may include excessive work. This is the fourth time the project manager has heard such a comment. What is the best thing to do?

    A. Create a better communications management plan that requires one universal language on the project and have translators readily available on a moment's notice.
    B. Contact someone else in the department who speaks the project manager's native language better to confirm the department manager's opinion.
    C. Find out if the upcoming activities should be reestimated.
    D. Work on increasing the effectiveness of the performing organization by recommending continuous improvement of the policy in question.

357

29. As the project manager, you are preparing your quality management plan. You are looking for a tool that can demonstrate the relationship between events and their resulting effects. You want to use this tool to depict the events that cause a negative effect on quality. Which of the following is the best choice for accomplishing your objective?

    A. Scatter diagram
    B. Pareto diagram
    C. Why-why diagram
    D. Control chart

30. Which of the following explains why quality should be planned in and not inspected in?

    A. It reduces quality and is less expensive.
    B. It improves quality and is more expensive.
    C. It reduces quality and is more expensive.
    D. It improves quality and is less expensive.

31. Work on a project is ongoing when the project manager overhears two workers arguing over what a set of instructions means. The project manager investigates and discovers that the instructions for the construction of the concrete footings currently being poured were poorly translated between the different languages in use on the project. Which of the following is the best thing for the project manager to do first?

    A. Get the instructions translated by a more experienced party.
    B. Look for quality impacts of the poor translation of the instructions for the footings.
    C. Bring the issue to the attention of the team, and ask them to look for other translation problems.
    D. Inform the sponsor of the problem in the next project report.

32. While performing quality planning for the design and manufacture of a new medical device, the team has identified the need to keep variances to a minimum because the end product must be of the highest quality possible. They are researching the practices of comparable projects for ideas on how to achieve this requirement. The team is using which of the following techniques?

    A. Benchmarking
    B. Pareto analysis
    C. Design for X
    D. Cost-benefit analysis

33. Which of the following would generally lead to the least amount of quality improvement?

    A. Total quality management
    B. Quality planning
    C. Implementing an ISO 9000 standard
    D. Inspection

34. In a meeting to gain approval of the quality management plan, a stakeholder points out what he believes to be an error in the plan. He notes that the plan includes using some of the same techniques in more than one of the quality processes. Which of the following quality management techniques can be used in two of the three quality management processes?

    A. Cause-and-effect diagrams
    B. Interviews
    C. Checksheets
    D. Logical data model

358

# Answers

1. **Answer** A

   **Explanation** As a general rule, one cannot say that quality (as defined in the question) is either of high or low cost. Quality provides what the customer wanted, which may not be the highest or lowest cost. When a product or service completely meets a customer's needs, quality is achieved.

2. **Answer** B

   **Explanation** This is the definition of marginal analysis. Know the term so you will be able to answer questions that deal with this concept. The other choices may sound good, but they are made-up terms.

3. **Answer** B

   **Explanation** Although each person working on the project should check their own work, the project manager ultimately has the responsibility for quality on the project as a whole.

4. **Answer** C

   **Explanation** If a problem with quality were to occur again, many people would opt to fix the problem as soon as possible. It is proactive, but some other project constraint(s) must change to accommodate fixing the root cause of the problem. It may not be necessary to allow the schedule to slip, because the project manager might be able to compress the schedule in other areas. Cutting cost does not necessarily cause the schedule to slip, nor would that necessarily fix the problem at hand. Allowing risk to increase by cutting cost is not the best choice, because a quality problem is most likely to create additional cost, rather than cut cost. Allowing the cost to increase by fixing the root cause of the problem addresses both the need to find the cause and the probable impact of dealing with the problem.

5. **Answer** A

   **Explanation** Did you notice there is a lot of data not relevant to answering the question? Expect distractors to appear in many questions on the exam. Quality efforts should produce a decrease rather than an increase in cost risk as a result of less rework. Quality efforts should also provide increased cost effectiveness due to less rework. This leaves the best answer: "Improved quality leads to increased productivity, increased cost effectiveness, and decreased cost risk."

6. **Answer** C

   **Explanation** There can be a cost impact (as well as an impact on other project constraints) of exceeding expectations or adding extras. Quality is the degree to which the project meets requirements.

7. **Answer** B

   **Explanation** Inspection, histograms, and cause-and-effect diagrams are all tools that can be used in Control Quality. Cost of quality is part of Plan Quality Management, making sure the project is not spending too much to achieve a particular level of quality.

8. **Answer** A

   **Explanation** Cause-and-effect (or why-why) diagrams are often used to stimulate thinking and to analyze the cause of quality problems. Determining whether a process is out of control is a function of control charts. Only focusing on critical issues to improve quality relates to histograms.

9. **Answer** D

   **Explanation** Focusing on the most critical issues to improve quality relates to histograms. Stimulating thinking and analyzing the cause of quality problems relate to cause-and-effect diagrams. Only determining if a process is functioning within established metrics relates to control charts.

10. **Answer** A

    **Explanation** The length of time it takes to test a whole population is one of the reasons to test a sample of the deliverables, rather than all of them. The sample size and frequency of measurements are determined as part of the Plan Quality Management process, and the actual sampling is done in Control Quality.

11. **Answer** B

    **Explanation** Quality training is a cost of conformance to quality. All the other choices are costs of nonconformance to quality.

12. **Answer** B

    **Explanation** Standard deviation is the measurement of a range around the mean.

13. **Answer** C

    **Explanation** Quality metrics are an output of the Plan Quality Management process. They are an input to the Manage Quality process, the process in which quality audits take place.

14. **Answer** C

    **Explanation** The rule of seven applies here. If you have seven data points in a row on the same side of the mean, statistically the mean has shifted, calling for action to correct the problem.

15. **Answer** D

    **Explanation** In a just in time environment, supplies are delivered when you need them and not before. Therefore, you have little or no inventory.

16. **Answer** A

    **Explanation** Quality audits are a necessary part of the Manage Quality process. They help you assess whether the processes are being followed correctly on the project.

17. **Answer** A

    **Explanation** The defined level of acceptable spillage would be documented in the quality management plan. The quality policy and control charts are components of a quality management plan. Quality audit documentation is created in Manage Quality, while the work of the project is being done. The amount of acceptable spillage would have been determined in the Plan Quality Management process.

18. **Answer** A

    **Explanation** This is an example of gold plating. The team should provide only what was included in the approved project management plan. The team does not know if their change will provide benefit to the customer. Any such changes must be evaluated in integrated change control. Instead of adding extras, the team should focus their efforts on fulfilling the requirements.

19. **Answer** C

    **Explanation** The plan described is the quality management plan. Since the quality management plan is included in the project management plan, changing the quality management plan will also change the project management plan. The other choices are not actual plans.

20. **Answer** C

    **Explanation** Control charts show whether measurements of project deliverables are within specification limits, and are used in the Control Quality process. The seller cannot generally control or review the customer's quality process. Checking the accuracy of costs submitted by the team is more representative of a cost audit than a quality audit, so that option cannot be the best choice. Manage Quality, of which an audit is part, focuses on processes, procedures, and standards. One purpose of a quality audit is to identify inefficient and ineffective policies.

21. **Answer** C

    **Explanation** Assuring management that it was determined in planning that the project would meet quality standards is not productive, since it does not solve the problem. An analogous estimate looks at the past history of other projects. This would not be appropriate to determine how the current project is going. The quality management plan does not provide results. The quality team could help to determine whether the team is following the correct process to satisfy the relevant quality standards.

22. **Answer** D

    **Explanation** Focus groups are a tool of the Collect Requirements process, and would not be useful in Control Quality. The other choices are all tools and techniques of the Control Quality process.

23. **Answer** C

    **Explanation** Although quality problems may lead to quality improvement efforts, they are not a prerequisite for quality improvement. Quality improvement is a result of Manage Quality and Control Quality, not an input. Rework (or requested defect repair) can be an output of Control Quality. That leaves only quality control measurements, which are inputs to the Manage Quality process.

24. **Answer** B

    **Explanation** Completion of work packages is done after project planning. Since Validate Scope is a monitoring and controlling process, that is not next. Identify Risks sounds like a good choice; however, identifying quality standards occurs before the Identify Risks process. You may have misread the question and assumed communication planning was complete, but notice it only says that communications requirements have been determined. Communications planning still needs to be completed, as do other aspects of planning. Identify quality standards is the best answer choice offered.

25. **Answer** A

    **Explanation** Design of experiments is performed in quality planning, and uses experimentation to determine statistically what variables will improve quality. It allows the project manager to focus attention on the factors that are most important. Design of experiments is also used in Manage Quality to help decrease the time and effort required to discover the optimal conditions in which to produce a quality deliverable.

26. **Answer** B

    **Explanation** The unexpected functionality reported by the project manager is outside the scope of the project. Adding extra functionality is the definition of gold plating. Gold plating a project wastes time and probably cost. It makes the project unsuccessful.

27. **Answer** C

    **Explanation** Measuring is part of the Control Quality process. Perform Integrated Change Control is an integration management process. It is likely that the scenario described will result in a change request submitted to Integrated Change Control.

28. **Answer** D

    **Explanation** Changing the communications management plan may not be needed, and it does not deal with the problem at hand—the policy that is slowing things down. Confirming the department manager's opinion with someone else in the department is not the best choice, as the project manager already has heard the opinion on many other occasions. It is already confirmed. Determining whether upcoming activities should be reestimated is just being reactive. A good project manager will find the root cause and deal with that, even if it means attempting to improve the company's policies and processes. Yes, recommending improvement of the policy is the best answer. This is continuous improvement. Because there are several activities affected by the policy, it would best serve the project to get to the root cause of the problem and solve it.

361

29. **Answer** C

**Explanation** All reports and diagrams are communications tools. This question asks you to pick the most appropriate quality tool to help communications. A why-why diagram, also called a cause-and-effect or Ishikawa diagram, is more appropriate than a Pareto diagram since you are trying to determine the causes. Once causes are known and you have data on occurrences, the data can be displayed in a Pareto diagram.

30. **Answer** D

**Explanation** Look for the proactive approach. When we plan for quality, we define the appropriate level of quality needed, which will improve quality overall and will likely be less expensive in the long run. NOTE: You may spend more initially on determining the right level of quality and doing the work to produce the required level of quality, but you will save through reduced rework, waste, and scrap.

31. **Answer** B

**Explanation** Although all these choices are correct things to do, the question asks what to do first. What is the most immediate problem? Getting the instructions translated by a more experienced party could be done, but it does not address the critical concern of the footings that have already been poured according to the poorly translated instructions. Asking the team to look for other translation issues is an excellent idea. However, it does not address the immediate problem. Informing the sponsor is also not taking action to solve the problem. Isn't it most urgent to find out whether the concrete footings meet your project requirements? Are they adequate? Only the option of looking for quality impacts of the poor translation will help you determine that.

32. **Answer** A

**Explanation** The team is using the benchmarking technique to review methodologies used by comparable projects or organizations to establish quality metrics and acceptable variance ranges, and to measure quality.

33. **Answer** D

**Explanation** Quality cannot be inspected in; you must plan for and execute a quality strategy. Increasing inspection is the only answer that is not proactive.

34. **Answer** A

**Explanation** Interviews are used in Plan Quality Management to identify existing standards, processes, and metrics—or to create new ones. A logical data model is also used in Plan Quality Management. Its purpose is to help the team understand the requirements, and define the appropriate quality management processes. Checksheets are used in Control Quality to track data such as the type and frequency of quality problems uncovered during inspections. Cause-and-effect diagrams are used in Manage Quality to confirm that the policies, procedures, and metrics are adequate to produce the required level of quality in project deliverables. In Control Quality, cause-and-effect diagrams can be used to uncover the root cause of a variation in the quality of deliverables.

# Resource Management

NINE

As you might expect, resource management includes the project manager's responsibilities for planning, acquiring, and managing the project team. But there is more. In this chapter—and on the PMP exam—the term "resources" refers to more than the team and other people from within or outside the organization who may be working on the project. It also encompasses the facilities, equipment, and materials (physical resources) that are required to perform the work of the project. You will see in this chapter that most of the processes of resource management include the project manager's responsibilities with regard to both human and physical resources.

Many topics covered in this chapter may seem easy, but you need to identify any misperceptions, and expand your project management knowledge. Review the following list of the most common knowledge gaps people have about resource management, and look for others that apply to you as you read the rest of this chapter:

- "Resources" refers to more than just human resources; it also includes materials, equipment, supplies, and anything else needed to complete the project.

- Creating a recognition and reward system is an important resource management function, and such systems are a required part of project management.

- The project manager is responsible for improving the competencies of team members so they are able to perform the work on the project most effectively.

- The project manager's resource management activities are formal and require documentation.

- There should be clear roles and responsibilities on the project. For example, who should be assigned to assist the project manager, who should take on specific responsibilities at meetings, and who should be completing other work not directly related to project activities?

# Resource Management NINE

| INITIATING | PLANNING (This is the only process group with a set order.) | EXECUTING | MONITORING & CONTROLLING | CLOSING |
|---|---|---|---|---|
| Select project manager | **Determine development approach, life cycle, and how you will plan for each knowledge area** | Execute work according to the project management plan | **Take action to monitor and control the project** | Confirm work is done to requirements |
| Determine company culture and existing systems | Define and prioritize requirements | Produce product deliverables (product scope) | Measure performance against performance measurement baseline | Complete final procurement closure |
| Collect processes, procedures, and historical information | Create project scope statement | Gather work performance data | **Measure performance against other metrics in the project management plan** | Gain final acceptance of product |
| Divide large projects into phases or smaller projects | Assess what to purchase and create procurement documents | **Request changes** | **Analyze and evaluate data and performance** | Complete financial closure |
| Understand business case and benefits management plan | **Determine planning team** | Implement only approved changes | **Determine if variances warrant a corrective action or other change request(s)** | Hand off completed product |
| Uncover initial requirements, assumptions, risks, constraints, and existing agreements | Create WBS and WBS dictionary | Continuously improve; perform progressive elaboration | **Influence factors that cause change** | Solicit customer's feedback about the project |
| Assess project and product feasibility within the given constraints | Create activity list | Follow processes | **Request changes** | Complete final performance reporting |
| Create measurable objectives and success criteria | Create network diagram | Determine whether quality plan and processes are correct and effective | Perform integrated change control | Index and archive records |
| Develop project charter | **Estimate resource requirements** | Perform quality audits and issue quality reports | Approve or reject changes | Gather final lessons learned and update knowledge bases |
| Identify stakeholders and determine their expectations, interest, influence, and impact | Estimate activity durations and costs | **Acquire final team and physical resources** | Update project management plan and project documents | |
| Request changes | Determine critical path | **Manage people** | Inform stakeholders of all change request results | |
| Develop assumption log | Develop schedule | **Evaluate team and individual performance; provide training** | Monitor stakeholder engagement | |
| Develop stakeholder register | Develop budget | **Hold team-building activities** | Confirm configuration compliance | |
| | Determine quality standards, processes, and metrics | **Give recognition and rewards** | Create forecasts | |
| | **Determine team charter and all roles and responsibilities** | **Use issue logs** | Gain customer's acceptance of interim deliverables | |
| | Plan communications and stakeholder engagement | **Facilitate conflict resolution** | Perform quality control | |
| | Perform risk identification, qualitative and quantitative risk analysis, and risk response planning | **Release resources as work is completed** | Perform risk reviews, reassessments, and audits | |
| | **Go back—iterations** | Send and receive information, and solicit feedback | Manage reserves | |
| | Finalize procurement strategy and documents | Report on project performance | Manage, evaluate, and close procurements | |
| | Create change and configuration management plans | Facilitate stakeholder engagement and manage expectations | **Evaluate use of physical resources** | |
| | **Finalize all management plans** | Hold meetings | | |
| | **Develop realistic and sufficient project management plan and baselines** | Evaluate sellers; negotiate and contract with sellers | | |
| | Gain formal approval of the plan | **Use and share project knowledge** | | |
| | Hold kickoff meeting | Execute contingency plans | | |
| | Request changes | **Update project management plan and project documents** | | |

**Rita's Process Chart™**
**Resource Management**
Where are we in the project management process?

- The exam assumes, unless stated otherwise, that the project is operating in a matrix environment. Therefore, topics such as motivation, conflict management, and powers of the project manager are more challenging than you might expect. These items need to be planned for and managed throughout the project.

- Projects are planned by the team and coordinated by the project manager.

- The project manager must continually confirm resource availability.

- On large projects, the project manager might have some team members help with project management activities. These people are called the project management team. So, the project team consists of the project manager, the project management team, and the other members of the team who will be doing the work of the project.

- The project manager formally plans team-building activities in advance; these activities are a required part of project management.

- The processes of resource management are repeated and updated throughout the project.

- Geographically and culturally diverse teams require additional attention and planning by the project manager.

- The project manager is responsible for controlling physical resources on the project; this is not only the responsibility of procurement or other departments that may provide physical resources.

If you manage small projects (those lasting only a few months or those that involve less than 20 people), keep in mind that resource management responsibilities increase as the size of the project increases. The resource management process takes time and effort to plan. You must do things such as identify all resources needed to complete the project (including the required skills of team resources and the required quality and grade of material or equipment), define everyone's roles, create reward systems, provide training and motivation for team members, manage the use of physical resources, and track performance.

 Many of the topics described in this chapter are not directly tested on the exam. It is best to read this chapter two or three times and make a list of the gaps in your knowledge as you read. After a couple of passes through this chapter, you will likely know the concepts well enough to be able to understand the ways in which they are applied in questions on the exam.

The following should help you understand how each part of resource management fits into the overall project management process:

| The Resource Management Process | Done During |
| --- | --- |
| Plan Resource Management | Planning process group |
| Estimate Activity Resources | Planning process group |
| Acquire Resources | Executing process group |
| Develop Team | Executing process group |
| Manage Team | Executing process group |
| Control Resources | Monitoring and controlling process group |

## Roles and Responsibilities

Roles and responsibilities go far beyond just a title. You know you are the project manager, but what does that mean as the project work is being done? Do you know what decisions you can make and enforce, and when you need the approval of someone higher in the organization? Do you know what to expect from functional managers and your project sponsor? What about the team? Do they know their responsibilities, and when they need to escalate a situation?

Project roles and responsibilities, and the authority that goes with them, are agreed upon in planning, and documented in the resource management plan.

The following exercise tests your knowledge of some typical roles on a project.

**Exercise** Did you complete the exercise on project roles in the Project Management Framework chapter? Your understanding of that content will impact how well you do on this exercise. You may want to review those pages before starting this exercise, or use the information in that exercise to fill your gaps.

This exercise is designed to help you answer situational questions on the exam dealing with project roles and responsibilities. If you disagree with some of the answers, make sure you are not reading something into the question, and assess whether it indicates a gap in your project management knowledge.

In the following table, write the initials of the key role responsible for solving each of the problems listed. Because much of the confusion of roles is between the team members (T), the project manager (PM), the sponsor (SP), and the functional manager (FM), this exercise is limited to those roles. Consider what you have learned about project roles, and remember to keep matrix organizations in mind when reading through these situations.

| | Situation | Key Role |
|---|---|---|
| 1 | Two project team members are having a disagreement. | |
| 2 | There is a change to the overall project deliverable. | |
| 3 | A functional manager is trying to pull a team member off the project to do other work. | |
| 4 | The project manager does not have the authority to get things done. | |
| 5 | There are not enough resources to complete the project. | |
| 6 | The team is unsure of what needs to happen when. | |
| 7 | An activity needs more time and will cause the project to be delayed. | |
| 8 | An activity needs more time without causing the project to be delayed. | |
| 9 | A team member is not performing. | |
| 10 | The team is not sure who is in charge of the project. | |
| 11 | There is talk that the project may no longer be needed. | |
| 12 | The sponsor provides an unrealistic schedule objective. | |
| 13 | The team is in conflict over priorities between activities. | |
| 14 | The project is behind schedule. | |
| 15 | A team member determines that another method should be used to complete an activity. | |
| 16 | The project is running out of funds. | |
| 17 | Additional work that will increase cost and that was not identified during the risk management process is added to the project. | |

366

## Answer

| | Situation | Key Role |
|---|---|---|
| 1 | Two project team members are having a disagreement. | T |
| | *The people involved in the conflict should attempt to solve it themselves.* | |
| 2 | There is a change to the overall project deliverable. | SP |
| | *A change to the project deliverable is a change to the project charter. Only the sponsor can approve changes to the project charter.* | |
| 3 | A functional manager is trying to pull a team member off the project to do other work. | T |
| | *The project manager must give team members enough information (such as the schedule, network diagram, project management plan, and identified risks) so they can manage their own workloads. Because the word "trying" is used, we know this situation is occurring at the present time. If the question used the words "has pulled," the answer would be the project manager. Read situational questions carefully.* | |
| 4 | The project manager does not have the authority to get things done. | SP |
| | *It is the sponsor's role to give the project manager authority via the project charter.* | |
| 5 | There are not enough resources to complete the project. | SP/FM |
| | *The sponsor and functional manager control resources.* | |
| 6 | The team is unsure of what needs to happen when. | PM |
| | *It is the project manager's role to take the individual estimates, combine them into the project schedule, and communicate that schedule to team members.* | |
| 7 | An activity needs more time and will cause the project to be delayed. | SP |
| | *Notice the word "will." This means the evaluation by the team is completed and there is no available reserve, since the project completion date is most likely included in the project charter. Any such changes are changes to the project charter and require sponsor involvement.* | |
| 8 | An activity needs more time without causing the project to be delayed. | PM |
| | *Think about integrated change control here. It is the project manager's role to look for impacts to the other project constraints.* | |
| 9 | A team member is not performing. | PM/FM |
| | *In a matrix environment, the project manager and the functional manager share responsibility for directing resources.* | |
| 10 | The team is not sure who is in charge of the project. | SP |
| | *The sponsor designates the project manager in the project charter.* | |
| 11 | There is talk that the project may no longer be needed. | SP |
| | *It is the sponsor's role to protect the project from changes, including such a large change as termination (unless it becomes clear that the project is no longer meeting the objectives of the organization).* | |

| | Situation | Key Role |
|---|---|---|
| 12 | The sponsor provides an unrealistic schedule objective. <br> *Only the sponsor can make a change to the project charter (including schedule objectives or constraints). The project manager must provide evidence that the schedule is unrealistic and work with the sponsor to resolve it.* | SP |
| 13 | The team is in conflict over priorities between activities. <br> *It is the project manager's role to settle any such conflicts and to provide a network diagram and critical path. It is the sponsor's or program/portfolio manager's role to set priorities between projects.* | PM |
| 14 | The project is behind schedule. <br> *Only the project manager can control the overall project schedule.* | PM |
| 15 | A team member determines that another method should be used to complete an activity. <br> *The team member has control over their activities as long as the team member meets the time, quality, cost, and scope objectives in the project management plan. The team member must keep the project manager informed of these changes, however, so the project manager can integrate them into the rest of the project and look for any impacts.* | T |
| 16 | The project is running out of funds. <br> *It is the sponsor's role to provide funding for the project.* | SP |
| 17 | Additional work that will increase cost and that was not identified during the risk management process is added to the project. <br> *The fact that the change was not identified in the risk management process and is additional work means it was not included in the original project budget (or the contingency reserve). Therefore, the sponsor must be involved in providing additional funds.* | SP |

If you got many of the answers wrong, reread the discussions of roles and responsibilities in the Project Management Framework chapter, and review the exact wording of the situations presented here. With such a brief description, it can be easy to misinterpret a question. Although this exercise asked you to identify the key role responsible for solving the problems, you may have preferred the word "decide" or the words "make the final decision" to describe what should happen in some of the situations. This exercise should help prepare you to interpret questions on the exam. It is meant to make you think!

**Resource Responsibilities for Project Managers**    This chapter and the Stakeholder Management, Communications Management, and the Professional and Social Responsibility chapters discuss how a project manager needs to manage and interact with team members, other stakeholders, and managers. Make sure you connect the ideas in these chapters in your mind.

 A trick to correctly answering exam questions on this topic is to realize that as a project manager, you have responsibilities regarding resources. Some of these are ethical responsibilities, as described in the Professional and Social Responsibility chapter, while others are administrative. The best way to approach administrative responsibilities is to think of your team as if they are employees who report directly to you. Project managers have some responsibilities similar to those of a manager.

The following is a list of project manager responsibilities to keep in mind when taking the exam:

- Determine what human and physical resources you will need.
- Negotiate with resource managers for the optimal available resources.
- Work with the procurement department if necessary.
- Confirm availability of assigned resources.
- Create a project team directory.
- Create project job descriptions for team members and other stakeholders.
- Make sure all roles and responsibilities on the project are clearly assigned.
- Understand the team members' training needs related to their work on the project, and make sure team members get any necessary training.
- Create a formal plan—the resource management plan—covering topics such as how the team will be involved in the project and what roles they will perform.
- Send out letters of commendation to team members and their managers to recognize exceptional performance of project work.
- Make sure the needs of all team members are acknowledged and considered.
- Create recognition and reward systems.
- Use emotional intelligence (EI).
- In a change-driven environment, encourage self-organizing teams and provide support as needed.
- Plan for and manage communications challenges specific to virtual teams.
- Tailor the resource management plan as appropriate to the needs of the project.
- Encourage collaboration among team members.
- Determine what physical resources will be needed on the project, and when they will be needed.
- Determine the quality, grade, and amount of physical resources needed on the project.
- Plan ahead to ensure physical resources are available and accessible when needed.
- Use resources efficiently.
- Look for ways to improve resource utilization.
- Evaluate and select appropriate methods of managing physical resources.

## Plan Resource Management   PAGE 312

> **Process** Plan Resource Management
> **Process Group** Planning
> **Knowledge Area** Resource Management

This plan encompasses the management of human resources as well as physical resources. For both types of resources, the plan must answer questions such as the following:

- What resources are required?
- What quantity of each type of resource is needed to complete the work of the project?
- When and for how long will each resource be needed?
- How will the resources be acquired?
- Are these resources available internally, or will the procurement department need to be involved?
- What will be the cost of these resources?
- Is there a limited time during which the resources will be available for the project?
- How will resources be managed throughout the project?

Early in the project, the project manager will have to determine the approach they will take to managing the project, unless this has been determined in advance by management. As discussed earlier in the Project Management Processes chapter, two common approaches to projects are plan-driven and change-driven. On a project following a plan-driven approach, as much resource management planning as possible will be done early in the project. On a project following a change-driven approach, planning and securing resources will likely occur as a part of each iteration or release. The concepts discussed in the next three sections are often associated with change-driven projects.

## Lean

The term "lean" comes from the concept of lean manufacturing, a practice that is over 100 years old. The principle behind lean is to remove waste from a process. Agile is a derivative of this approach, which has evolved to encompass the efficient use of human as well as physical resources. The goal of lean management is to eliminate waste of time, effort, and resources, as shown in figure 9.1.

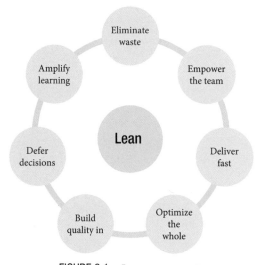

**FIGURE 9.1**   *Lean core concepts*

## Kaizen

The Japanese term *kaizen* is synonymous with continuous improvement. It literally means to alter *(kai)* and improve or make better *(zen)*. This term is used in quality management, but it also applies to other aspects of a project, including resource management.

## Just in Time (JIT)

If the project is using a just in time (JIT) system for physical resources, the strategy to manage those resources will be different than if all the inventory, materials, and supplies are purchased and delivered at the beginning of the project.

A common complaint of team members is that roles and responsibilities are not clearly defined on a project. Therefore, the definition of roles and responsibilities is a critical part of the Plan Resource Management process. Project work often includes more than just completing work packages. It may also include responsibilities such as assisting with risk, quality, and project management activities. Team members need to know what work packages and activities they are assigned to, when they are expected to report, what meetings they will be required to attend, and any other "work" they will be asked to do on the project. In a functional or matrix environment, the managers of team resources also need to understand when and for how long these resources will be needed on the project.

In terms of physical resources, the project manager needs to determine what is needed and where the resources will come from. If the resources are available from departments within the organization, the project manager must work with the managers of those departments to reach an agreement on delivery dates as well as on quantity and quality of resources. If the resources will be obtained from external sources, the project manager must work with the procurement department, creating a purchase order or bid documents to facilitate the purchase. The project manager will likely be involved in the procurement process.

In the Plan Resource Management process, a project manager uses a variety of items, which are discussed in the following sections.

## Project Charter    PAGE 314    The project charter documents high-level requirements for the project. It may include a list of key stakeholders and preassigned resources, as well as budgetary constraints that must be considered when planning resource management.

## Project Management Plan    PAGE 314    The existing components of the project management plan are going to help you plan human resource management. Before you can define roles, responsibilities, reporting structure, and so forth, you'll need to consider information about the life cycle and processes already determined for the project, how work will be done, the communication needs of stakeholders, and other factors from the project management plan.

The scope baseline includes descriptions of the project deliverables, which helps the project manager determine the resources needed to create those deliverables.

The quality management plan includes the agreed-upon level of quality and grade of physical resources needed to satisfy the requirements of the project. These decisions will impact the team's options in terms of how and where they will obtain those resources.

The stakeholder engagement plan includes the approach to involving stakeholders—including the team. It provides direction for engaging stakeholders in the planning, decision-making, and work on the project. The stakeholder register lists the individuals and groups who are project stakeholders, and it includes analysis of factors such as each stakeholder's power and interest related to the project.

The procurement management plan describes how the project manager should interact with that department to facilitate the procurement of needed human or physical resources for the project.

## Project Documents    PAGE 314    Documents that can be used in planning resource management include requirements documentation, the project schedule, and the risk and stakeholder registers. These documents provide key information, such as the timeline for needed resources, what type of resources will be needed to complete project work, and how many resources will be required to get the work done.

## Enterprise Environmental Factors    PAGE 315    Before you develop a resource management plan, you need to understand what enterprise environmental factors may come into play. Remember that the term "enterprise environmental factors" refers to the company culture and existing systems the project will have to deal with or can make use of. For this process, you should take into account factors such as the following:

- What organizations will be involved in the project?
- Are there hidden agendas?
- Is there anyone who does not want the project?
- Are assigned and potential team members colocated or based in different offices and/or countries?
- What is the availability of contract help?
- What is the availability of training for project team members?

371

For most experienced project managers, this is common sense. They already consider such things on their projects, even if they have not called them enterprise environmental factors.

## Organizational Process Assets   PAGE 315   When developing the resource management plan, you may use organizational process assets such as a resource management plan template that describes the standard responsibilities on projects, and existing policies and procedures for resource management. These assets, along with historical information, such as lessons learned from similar projects, can help increase the efficiency of the Plan Resource Management process, as well as the effectiveness of the resulting plan.

## Plan Resource Management Tools and Techniques   A comprehensive resource management plan includes documentation of all project responsibilities and assignments on the project. There are a lot of methods that can be used to document and communicate roles and responsibilities of management, team members, and other stakeholders. Examples include a responsibility assignment matrix (RAM), a RACI chart, an organizational breakdown structure, a resource breakdown structure (RBS), the WBS, and written position descriptions. Additional tools and techniques used in the plan resource management process include physical resource documentation and organizational theory.

Any roles and responsibilities that are expected of team members, such as project management team assignments, reporting requirements, or meeting attendance, need to be clearly assigned, in addition to the project activities the team members are expected to complete. In other words, all efforts the project team might expend should be determined in advance. If you work on small projects, you might never have taken the time to do this. Spend a moment now thinking about how much time this effort might take on a large project.

For the exam, know the tools presented in the following sections, including the information each tool displays so that you can answer questions such as the following:

Question   A responsibility assignment matrix does not show _____.

Answer   When people will do their jobs (time)

### Responsibility Assignment Matrix (RAM)[1]   This chart cross-references team members with the activities or work packages they are to accomplish. Figure 9.2 is an example of a RAM.

| Activity | Team Member | | | |
| --- | --- | --- | --- | --- |
| | Karla | Patrick | Muhammad | Trisha |
| A | P | | S | |
| B | | S | | P |

Key: P = Primary responsibility, S = Secondary responsibility

FIGURE 9.2   *Responsibility assignment matrix*

### RACI Chart[2] (Responsible, Accountable, Consult, and Inform)   This chart is a type of responsibility assignment matrix that defines role assignments more clearly than the example shown in figure 9.2. Instead of the P and S shown in the figure, the letters R for Responsible, A for Accountable, C for Consult, and I for Inform are used. Note that multiple resources may be responsible, informed, or consulted, but only one person is held accountable.

### Organizational Breakdown Structure[3]

An organizational breakdown structure can be used to assign project responsibilities to divisions or departments within the organization, such as marketing, product development, or IT. In a matrix organization, the project manager will have to interface with the managers of each department involved in the project to coordinate availability and scheduling of human and physical resources that will be used on the project. Figure 9.3 is an example of an organizational breakdown structure.

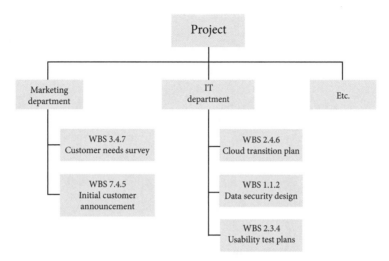

FIGURE 9.3 *Organizational breakdown structure*

### Resource Breakdown Structure[4]

The resource breakdown structure breaks the work down by type of resource (see fig. 9.4).

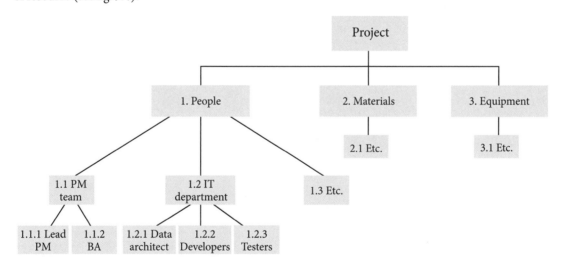

FIGURE 9.4 *Resource breakdown structure*

### Work Breakdown Structure

Are you surprised to see the WBS here? Can you think of how the WBS could be a valuable tool in creating the resource management plan? In the Scope Management chapter, we said that all project work must be represented in the WBS. It follows, then, that the WBS is a great tool to ensure that each work package has an "owner"—a team member responsible to complete that work.

**Position Descriptions**    Position descriptions are usually documented in text format rather than charts. If you haven't used these on your projects, imagine a typical job description, but created only for project work.

**Physical Resource Documentation**    In addition to mapping out the roles and responsibilities of human resources on the project, the project manager must plan ahead for usage of physical resources. This aspect of planning is as important as planning for the management of human resources!

The project manager must document the physical resource needs, which may involve adapting tools and techniques often used for other purposes. For example, since the WBS shows the project deliverables broken down into work packages, it could be used to plan resource requirements for each of those work packages. The WBS could also be used as a reference to ensure that all necessary physical resources for each work package have been secured.

**Organizational Theory**    PAGE 318    Organizational theory studies organizations to identify how they solve problems and how they maximize efficiency and productivity and meet the expectations of stakeholders. Such analysis helps the organization develop effective resource management policies and procedures for the acquisition, management, and evaluation of human and physical resources. Adopting practices such as JIT, Lean, Kaizen, or Six Sigma influences how projects will handle the management of physical resources.

The outputs of the plan resource management process are discussed in the following sections.

**Resource Management Plan**    PAGE 318    The primary result (output) of the Plan Resource Management process is, of course, a resource management plan. If you manage small projects, think for a moment about what the resource management effort would involve on a large project that has hundreds of assigned resources. Would it take more work than you are doing now to manage all the resources on your project? Large projects require a plan for when and how resources will be added, managed, and released from the project. This is what the resource management plan provides.

Components of the resource management plan include the following:
- Human Resources
  - Identification of human resource requirements (who, when, how many, what skills, what level of expertise, duration)
  - Roles and responsibilities (described earlier in this chapter)
  - Project organizational charts (described earlier in this chapter)
  - Process for acquiring human resources (internal or procurement)
  - Training, team development, and recognition (goals, what, when)
  - Project team management (team charter, ground rules, engagement, communications)
  - Compliance (How will the project comply with any rules related to human resources?)
  - Safety (policies to protect the resources)
  - Release of human resources
- Physical Resources
  - Identification of physical resource requirements (what, when, how many, what type, quality, grade, duration)
  - Process for acquiring physical resources (internal or procurement)
  - Inventory management
  - Release of resources

A project manager must motivate their team, especially when working on a project in a matrix organization. Have you ever wondered, "How do I get improved performance from people who do not report directly to me in the organization?" If your team members are not motivated, it is nearly impossible to be effective as a project manager. This is not to say that great project managers do not have issues with motivating people, but they have the tools and knowledge to prevent and to deal with such problems. Recognizing individual and team accomplishments is one of the most effective ways to motivate and gain cooperation from your team, regardless of the reporting relationship. Excellent project managers include a plan to do so as part of their resource management plan. Developing such a plan can be a significant effort, as it should include when and how resources will be recognized, and what actions or achievements will be rewarded.

Everyone likes to feel appreciated. A good start to planning how to use recognition and rewards[5] is to make a conscious effort to personally acknowledge the efforts of team members. A smile and a "thank you" are often more meaningful than a so-called reward. But you need to go beyond that in your planning. To make the rewards more personal, consider asking what your team members and stakeholders want to get out of the project, on a professional and personal level. They might respond with such things as, "I want to learn more about XYZ," "I want to decrease the time I am allocated to this project," "I want to make sure I leave work on time on Tuesday nights because I have a family obligation," or "I want to be assigned a certain piece of the project work."

After gathering such information, a project manager creates a plan that includes what recognition and rewards will be given, to whom, and when. As the project progresses, the plan may be iterated as new team members are added, and as the project manager becomes more familiar with the team and what motivates them.

Recognizing and rewarding the team might include performing the following actions on an ongoing basis, while project work is being done:

- Saying "thank you" more often
- Awarding prizes for performance
- Recommending team members for raises or choice of work assignments, even though such actions by the project manager may not officially be part of the team members' performance reviews
- Sending notes about great performance to team members' managers
- Planning milestone parties or other celebrations
- Adjusting the project to assign people to activities they want to work on
- Assigning a team member to a non-critical-path activity so that they can gain more knowledge in that area

The list could go on and on, but ask yourself, "Do I do any of these things? Do I do them systematically?" Creating a recognition plan requires planning in advance of any project work, and then iterating that plan as the project progresses.

## Team Charter   PAGE 319   This document is a working agreement developed by the members of the project team. It describes the approach the team will take regarding communications, decision-making, and conflict resolution, as well as ground rules for team meetings. The team charter is a project document and can be referenced at any time during the project.

Setting ground rules can help eliminate conflicts or problems with the team during the project because everyone knows what is expected of them. And if team members have input on the creation of the ground rules, they're more likely to follow them. Ground rules can be especially important when the team is managed virtually.

The ground rules may include items such as the following:

- How a team member should resolve a conflict with another team member
- When a team member should notify the project manager that they are having difficulty with an activity
- Rules for meetings
- Who is authorized to give direction to contractors
- How the team will decide work assignments
- When and how to provide status updates to the project manager
- Methods for coordinating and approving changes to team members' calendars, both in normal and emergency situations

## Project Document Updates    PAGE 320    The assumption log is updated to reflect assumptions made in planning regarding resources. These may include assumptions made about the availability, quantity, quality, or type of human and/or physical resources. Other assumptions made might relate to what type of rewards and recognition will be effective, and how the releasing of resources should be managed. Assumptions can change as the project progresses, and should be regularly assessed for validity. Incorrect assumptions may create risks on the project.

Another document that may need to be updated is the risk register. Risks related to resources should be added to the risk register, and then analyzed and prioritized along with other documented risks in the risk management process.

## Estimate Activity Resources    PAGE 320

| Process | Estimate Activity Resources |
| --- | --- |
| Process Group | Planning |
| Knowledge Area | Resource Management |

In the Estimate Activity Resources process, the project manager and team determine the type and quantity of all resources needed to complete project work. This includes human resources to perform the work packages that were created in the WBS and broken down in the activity list. It also includes any equipment or materials needed, space in which to meet and perform project work, and anything else needed to fulfill the requirements of the project.

The resource management plan is an input to all the processes (with the exception of Plan Resource Management) within Resource Management. Here, it provides documentation on the estimating methods to be used. Other inputs include the scope baseline (the project scope description, WBS, and WBS dictionary), and the activity list from Schedule Management. These enable estimating needed resources at the work package level and activity level, respectively, and are important elements to creating accurate estimates. Another input from Schedule Management is activity attributes. Attributes provide specific information about each activity, such as the type and amount of human and physical resources expected to be required to complete them.

Cost estimates provide constraints in terms of resource estimating, as the resource costs must fall within the cost baseline. Resource calendars identify organizational work hours and company holidays, and show the availability of potential resources—both human and physical. Organizational process assets include policies the project must follow when arranging for staff and needed equipment.

In the Schedule and Cost Management chapters, we discussed estimating techniques used to develop the schedule and budget. Several of those techniques may also be used to estimate activity resources. Let's briefly review them:

- **Bottom-up estimating** This technique involves creating detailed estimates for each part of an activity or work package and then rolling the estimates into work packages and control accounts and, finally, into an overall project estimate.

- **Analogous estimating** Analogous estimating uses expert judgment and historical information to predict the future.

- **Parametric estimating** Parametric estimating creates an equation that uses historical information from other estimates, actual results, and variables—such as the number of hours to complete the work or the number of resources with the associated skill level, quality, or grade—to create estimates.

- **Alternatives analysis** Bottom-up, analogous, and parametric estimating can be used to generate estimates for various options—such as the costs to make versus buy software for a project, the costs of internal versus external team members, or the impact of using various materials to produce components of the product of the project. Alternatives analysis can then be used to assess the impact of each option on project constraints such as schedule, cost, quality, and risk.

Another tool you can use to estimate resources is a resource histogram. A resource histogram is a way to visualize resource requirements, and compare needed resources and their availability, to better enable estimating. As depicted in figure 9.5, a resource histogram is a bar chart that shows the number of resources needed per time period; it also illustrates where there is a spike in the need for resources. If the materials, equipment, or human resources are not available when they are needed, the project manager must evaluate available options, which may include negotiating with another department to provide the resources, procuring the resources from an external source, or adjusting the project schedule to do the work when the resources are available.

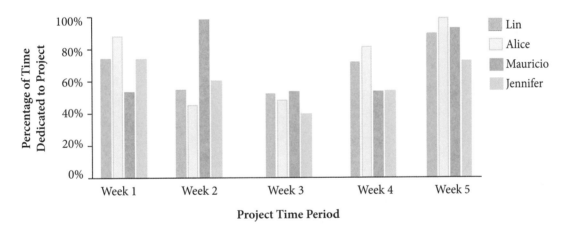

FIGURE 9.5    *Resource histogram*

Do you remember the discussion of resource leveling in the Schedule Management chapter? It is a technique to change the project to minimize the peaks and valleys of resource usage (level the resources). The project manager could use a histogram to help in performing that activity if resources are limited.

At the end of this process, the team will have determined resource requirements for project activities, including the cost, quantity, and availability of human and physical resources. They may choose to document the requirements in a resource breakdown structure. You may remember that the RBS was also discussed as a Plan Resource Management tool that is used to break down the work by the type of resource required. As planning continues, and more detail is gathered, the RBS is expanded and augmented in Estimate Activity Resources. The RBS in this process is an iteration of the document that was originally created in Plan Resource Management.

**Exercise** In the following table, identify which activities are involved in the Estimate Activity Resources process. Simply write yes or no in the right-hand column. Then check your answers against the answer table. (As you complete this exercise, assume the full project management process is being used on a large project.)

| | Action | Is It Part of Estimate Activity Resources? |
|---|---|---|
| 1 | Review project management plan. | |
| 2 | Review scope baseline. | |
| 3 | Review resource availability. | |
| 4 | Review cost estimates. | |
| 5 | Get one time estimate per activity. | |
| 6 | Complete an analysis of the reserves needed on the project. | |
| 7 | Create a company calendar identifying working and nonworking days. | |
| 8 | Create milestones. | |
| 9 | Review the WBS, activity list, and activity attributes. | |
| 10 | Review the risk register and assumption log. | |
| 11 | Identify potentially available resources and their skill levels. | |
| 12 | Review historical information about the use of resources on similar projects. | |
| 13 | Review organizational policies on resource use. | |
| 14 | See how leads and lags affect the time estimate. | |
| 15 | Solicit expert judgment on what resources are needed and available. | |
| 16 | Create bottom-up, analogous, or parametric estimates. | |
| 17 | Analyze alternative equipment or methods to use in completing the work and approaches to better utilize resources. | |
| 18 | Show network dependencies per activity. | |
| 19 | Identify areas of the project that cannot be completed internally or would otherwise be more efficiently achieved through outsourcing. This information will be shared with the procurement department. | |
| 20 | Crash the project. | |
| 21 | Break the activity down further if the activity is too complex to estimate resources (bottom-up estimating). | |
| 22 | Quantify resource requirements by activity. | |
| 23 | Create a hierarchical image that organizes the planned resources by their category and type (a resource breakdown structure). | |
| 24 | Fast track the project. | |
| 25 | Develop the schedule. | |
| 26 | Develop a plan as to what types of resources will be used. | |
| 27 | Update project documents. | |

## Answer

| | Action | Is It Part of Estimate Activity Resources? |
|---|---|---|
| 1 | Review project management plan. | Yes |
| 2 | Review scope baseline. | Yes |
| 3 | Review resource availability. | Yes |
| 4 | Review cost estimates. | Yes |
| 5 | Get one time estimate per activity. | No |
| 6 | Complete an analysis of the reserves needed on the project. | No |
| 7 | Create a company calendar identifying working and nonworking days. | No |
| 8 | Create milestones. | No |
| 9 | Review the WBS, activity list, and activity attributes. | Yes |
| 10 | Review the risk register and assumption log. | Yes |
| 11 | Identify potentially available resources and their skill levels. | Yes |
| 12 | Review historical information about the use of resources on similar projects. | Yes |
| 13 | Review organizational policies on resource use. | Yes |
| 14 | See how leads and lags affect the time estimate. | No |
| 15 | Solicit expert judgment on what resources are needed and available. | Yes |
| 16 | Create bottom-up, analogous, or parametric estimates. | Yes |
| 17 | Analyze alternative equipment or methods to use in completing the work and approaches to better utilize resources. | Yes |
| 18 | Show network dependencies per activity. | No |
| 19 | Identify areas of the project that cannot be completed internally or would otherwise be more efficiently achieved through outsourcing. This information will be shared with the procurement department. | Yes |
| 20 | Crash the project. | No |
| 21 | Break the activity down further if the activity is too complex to estimate resources (bottom-up estimating). | Yes |
| 22 | Quantify resource requirements by activity. | Yes |
| 23 | Create a hierarchical image that organizes the planned resources by their category and type (a resource breakdown structure). | Yes |
| 24 | Fast track the project. | No |
| 25 | Develop the schedule. | No |
| 26 | Develop a plan as to what types of resources will be used. | Yes |
| 27 | Update project documents. | Yes |

## Acquire Resources   PAGE 328

| | |
|---|---|
| **Process** | Acquire Resources |
| **Process Group** | Executing |
| **Knowledge Area** | Resource Management |

This process involves following the resource management plan to secure the human and physical resources needed for the project. The resource management plan describes how resources will be acquired and released, and the resource requirements documentation tells the project manager what types of resources are needed. The project schedule and cost baseline provide essential information regarding when resources will be required and the amount of funds budgeted to pay for them.

To understand why this is an executing process, think of a large project that may last several years and require hundreds of people and lots of physical resources. A planning team is acquired early in planning to help the project manager. However, many of the people and other resources needed to do the work may not be needed until long after planning starts. The final list of resources might include contractors, sellers, and people who will work on the project years into the future and may not even be employed by the company until needed. Likewise, the physical resources may be purchased closer to the time they are needed, to avoid the need to warehouse inventory. Acquiring the planned resources as they are needed is an example of rolling wave planning.

 You should read the process name "Acquire Resources" as "Acquire Final Resources."

Acquiring resources begins by using the planning and estimating work, which identified the type and quantity of resources needed. Let's look first at the process of acquiring the team, and then at acquiring physical resources.

When it is time to finalize the human resources who will perform the work of the project, the project manager may be required to negotiate with functional (resource) managers, other project managers, and the resources themselves in order to arrange their participation on the project. If the resources must be hired or contracted, work with the human resource or procurement departments may be necessary.

The project manager will also use the resource requirements documentation as a reference in acquiring physical resources. Often this involves working with the procurement or inventory management department.

A project manager has to work with the resources they are given, or acquire those that are needed. Resource availability (as indicated by resource calendars) and the project schedule must be coordinated to ensure that the right resources will be available when they are required.

To review, acquiring project resources includes all the following:

- Knowing which resources are preassigned to the project and confirming their availability
- Negotiating for the best possible resources
- Hiring new employees
- Hiring resources through the contracting process from outside the performing organization—outsourcing
- Using JIT, Lean, or other methods as required by the organization
- Managing the risk of resources becoming unavailable

## Types of Teams

The makeup of the final project team can take one or a combination of forms, such as the following:

- **Dedicated**  Most of the team members work full-time and exclusively on the project. From the perspective of the project manager, this is the easiest form of team to work with, as team members can dedicate most of their energy to the project and often report directly to the project manager. Dedicated teams are most common in projectized organizations, but can also be found in matrix organizations; they're least likely to exist in functional organizations.

- **Part-time**  Team members and the project manager spend a portion of their time working on the project while also working on other projects and/or their usual (non-project-related) work responsibilities. Part-time teams are most often seen in functional and matrix organizations.

- **Partnership**  In cases where several organizations undertake a project, the teams are likely to consist of people from each of the participating organizations, plus the project manager from the organization taking the lead on the project. Such teams may offer advantages, such as cost savings, but they can be difficult to manage.

- **Virtual**  When multiple organizations, offices, groups, or individuals are involved on a project, the geographic distance of these organizations can necessitate the creation of virtual teams (see the "Virtual Teams" section of this chapter).

For the exam, be aware of how the type of team described in a situational question could impact the project manager's work. For example, with a dedicated team, the project manager will have more control over the team members. With a part-time team, the project manager will likely have to negotiate with functional managers and leadership to acquire and retain team members. With a partnership or virtual team, coordination among the various organizations or locations might require increased risk management work, more effort to coordinate communication, and so on.

Let's review several of the ways a project manager may obtain resources.

## Preassignment

As noted earlier, sometimes resources are assigned before the project begins. Preassigned resources are documented in the project charter. This relates to both physical and team resources.

## Negotiation

When resources are not preassigned, they may be acquired through negotiation. You will see negotiation referenced frequently on the exam as it relates to gaining resources from within your organization and in procurement situations. To negotiate for human or physical resources from within the organization, the project manager should do the following:

- Know the needs of the project and its priority within the organization.

- Be able to express how the resource's manager will benefit from assisting the project manager.

- Understand that the resource's manager has their own work to do and that the individual may not gain benefits from supporting the project.

- Do not ask for the best resources if the project does not need them.

- Be able to prove, using project management tools such as the network diagram and project schedule, why the project requires the stated quantity and quality of resources.

- Use negotiation as an opportunity to discover what the resource's manager will need from the project manager in order to manage their own resources.

- Build a relationship so the project manager can call on the expertise of the resource's manager later in the project if necessary.

- Work with the resource's manager to deal with situations as they arise.

Notice the previous list goes beyond traditional negotiation strategy and includes elements of professional responsibility. Although chapter 14 focuses on professional and social responsibility, the topic is discussed throughout this book and is relevant in every part of a project manager's job.

When resources must be acquired from outside the organization from external vendors, suppliers, or contractors, the project manager is required to follow procurement and negotiating policies and procedures for the acquisition of resources. (See the Procurement Management chapter for information related to procuring resources from outside sources.)

## Virtual Teams
Not all teams meet face-to-face. Virtual teams have to rely on other forms of communication to work together. Although virtual teams can be more challenging to manage because of communication issues and differences in schedules, languages, and/or culture, they offer the opportunity to benefit from the expertise of team members who are in distant locations or who are otherwise unavailable to participate with the team onsite. There may be questions on the exam that ask why virtual teams might be necessary as well as some that describe situations that involve acquiring and managing virtual teams. You may also encounter situational questions for which choosing the correct answer depends on your understanding that a virtual team might require a different approach than a colocated team.

## Multicriteria Decision Analysis
When acquiring resources, the project manager may establish a set of criteria to help choose potential team members or physical resources. Factors that address the needs of the project, such as availability, cost, experience, location, and/or a required skill set, are weighted by importance, and potential resources are evaluated based on the selected criteria.

A potential issue to be aware of when dealing with team members is something called the "halo effect," which refers to a tendency to rate team members high or low on all factors due to the impression of a high or low rating on one specific factor. Because of the halo effect, a project manager might say to a team member, "You are a great programmer. Therefore, we will make you a leader of a team within the project and expect you to be great at that as well." Since a person who is a great programmer may not, in fact, be qualified to be a team leader, such assumptions can have a negative impact on the project schedule, cost, and quality, and should be avoided.

## Outputs of Acquire Resources
The outputs of the Acquire Resources process include physical resource assignments, project or work assignments, and resource calendars that show the planned utilization and availability of project resources. Here are some things to remember about the outputs of this process:

- If decisions made in this process require changes to approved management plans or project documents, change requests are submitted to integrated change control. Affected documents and plans may include any of the plans or baselines within the project management plan.

- The resource management plan may be changed based on the project experience to date. For example, the plan for acquiring future resources may need to be adjusted if it doesn't work as expected.

- The project schedule may need to be adjusted to accommodate the availability of resources with specific expertise needed by the project. The cost baseline may be impacted if hourly rates or material prices will need adjustment from what was estimated.

- Project documents will need to be updated or changed, with new team members added or information changed in the stakeholder register. The resource breakdown structure is iterated to include specific information about human or physical resources that have been committed to the project.

- Newly identified risks related to human and physical resources are added to the risk register, reviewed, and analyzed. For example, a resource with unique qualifications could be called away during the project, or the equipment purchased or rented may have a higher failure rate than anticipated. Resource requirements, including the type, quantity, skill level, or quality and grade may change.

- There are usually lessons learned to be captured, integrated into the project for future acquisitions, and shared with the organization.

## Develop Team    PAGE 336

| | |
|---|---|
| **Process** Develop Team | |
| **Process Group** Executing | |
| **Knowledge Area** Resource Management | |

The Develop Team process is ongoing throughout project work.
This process should result in decreased turnover, enhanced individual knowledge and skills, and improved teamwork. The project manager works to lead, empower, and motivate the team to achieve high performance and to meet project objectives. This is accomplished through efforts to create an environment conducive to building trust and cooperation, and by providing training and support to the team. Team members are recognized for their efforts.

A plan for making all of this happen is included in the resource management plan. The project manager can also make use of lessons learned earlier in the project and on other, similar projects to enhance their ability to effectively develop the team.

**Exercise**    What do you think a project manager needs to do to develop a team?

383

**Answer**   An exercise like this can be tempting to skip. But remember that the only effective way to find gaps in your knowledge is to test your knowledge and understanding of the goals, actions, and benefits of the process before you look at the answers.

You may do some of the activities listed below on your projects, but you might not plan them in or do them consistently or consciously. These activities are part of proper project management. Keep them in mind for the exam to help you understand the situations described and select the best answer choices. Remember to assume that proper project management was done—unless the exam situation indicates otherwise.

A major part of being a project manager is ensuring the project team is working together as effectively and efficiently as possible. Your answer could include any of the following:

- Using soft skills, such as mentoring, leadership, negotiation, empathy, and communication
- Encouraging teamwork
- Communicating honestly, effectively, and in a timely manner with the people assigned to your team
- Assessing team members' strengths and weaknesses, preferences, and learning styles to help the team work together
- Establishing and maintaining trust between the project manager and each team member, and among all stakeholders
- Collaborating with the team to make good, bought-into decisions and to find mutually beneficial solutions to problems
- Capitalizing on cultural differences
- Holding team-building activities
- Providing training for team members as needed
- Encouraging team members to uphold the agreements documented in the team charter
- Assisting the team with conflict resolution when needed
- Giving recognition and rewards
- Placing team members in the same location, if possible (colocation)
- Facilitating communication between team members
- Evaluating and working to improve team performance
- Motivating team members
- Improving team members' knowledge
- Encouraging a positive team culture

Remember that on a properly managed project, team members need to have input into the project, including what work needs to be done, when, at what cost, what the risks may be, etc.—no matter when they get involved in the project. Great project managers will invite new team members to review their part of the project for changes before they start work. People perform better when they have input, rather than simply being told what to do.

384

## Interpersonal and Team Skills  PAGE 341

**Motivation Theory[7]**  Since most projects operate in a matrix environment, the team members often do not report directly to the project manager. To gain the cooperation of team members, the project manager must understand how to motivate them.

As you have read in this chapter, one of the best ways to gain cooperation is to give rewards. How can we reward people if we do not understand what motivates them? Questions on the exam related to this topic do not directly quote motivation theorists. The questions may simply describe situations and ask you what to do. The answer might depend on understanding that the person in the situation is a Theory X manager, or that the project manager was using an ineffective motivation technique.

Following are explanations of four motivation theories that you can help you understand situations for the exam.

**McGregor's Theory of X and Y[8]**  McGregor believed that all workers fit into one of two groups: X and Y. The exam may describe this concept in many different ways. It can be confusing to determine which answer is correct or even what the choices are saying. For those of you with strong visual memories, here is a trick to answering questions on these theories.

**Theory X**  Based on the picture, take a guess as to what Theory X is.

**Answer**  Managers who accept this theory believe that people need to be watched every minute. They believe employees are incapable, avoid responsibility, and avoid work whenever possible.

**Theory Y**  Based on the picture, take a guess as to what Theory Y is.

**Answer**  Managers who accept this theory believe that people are willing to work without supervision, and want to achieve. They believe employees can direct their own efforts. It's a PMI-ism that this is indeed how team members behave, so unless directed otherwise, assume this perspective when responding to exam questions.

**Maslow's Hierarchy of Needs[9]**  Maslow's message is that people are not most motivated to work by security or money. Instead, the highest motivation for most people is to contribute and to use their skills. Maslow called this "self-actualization." He created a hierarchy of needs to explain how people are motivated and stated that a person cannot ascend to the next level until the levels below are fulfilled. See figure 9.6.

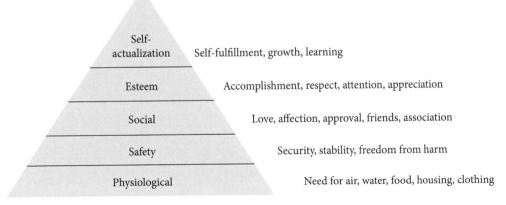

FIGURE 9.6  *A representation of Maslow's hierarchy of needs*

### McClelland's Theory of Needs[10] (or Acquired Needs Theory)    This theory states that people are most motivated by one of three needs. A person falling into one need category would be managed differently than a person falling into another category. The following table explains the three need categories.

| Primary Need | Behavioral Style |
|---|---|
| Achievement | These people should be given projects that are challenging but are reachable. They like recognition. |
| Affiliation | These people work best when cooperating with others. They seek approval rather than recognition. |
| Power | People whose need for power is socially oriented, rather than personally oriented, are effective leaders and should be allowed to manage others. These people like to organize and influence others. |

### Herzberg's Two-Factor Theory of Motivation[11]    Herzberg's theory deals with hygiene factors and motivating agents.

### Hygiene Factors    Poor hygiene factors may destroy motivation, but improving them, under most circumstances, will not improve motivation. Hygiene factors are not sufficient to motivate people.

Examples of hygiene factors include the following:

- Working conditions
- Salary
- Personal life
- Relationships at work
- Security
- Status

### Motivating Agents    People are motivated, energized, and engaged by the work itself, including factors such as the following:

- Responsibility
- Self-actualization
- Professional growth
- Recognition

So, the lesson here is that motivating people is best done by rewarding them and letting them grow. Giving raises is not the most effective motivator. This is generally good news for project managers, as they often do not have any influence over the pay raises of their team members. Solving an individual or team issue may mean that you have to make certain that basic needs are met within the project. Then you can use rewards, recognition, and the roles and responsibilities assigned to individuals and teams.

**Team Building**    Team building can play a major role in team development—helping to form the project team into a cohesive group working for the best interests of the project and enhancing project performance. Make sure you know the following key points about team building:

- It is the project manager's job to guide, manage, and improve the interactions of team members.
- The project manager should work to improve trust and cohesiveness among the team members.
- The project manager should incorporate team-building activities into project activities.
- Team building requires a concerted effort and continued attention throughout the life of the project.
- WBS creation is a team-building activity because it allows team members to actively engage in the planning and ownership of the project; similar benefits occur when the team is involved in other planning efforts, as well.
- Team building should start early in the life of the project.

Let's spend a little more time on the concept of trust. First think of project problems you have recently experienced. Now ask yourself the following questions: "Could these problems be caused by a lack of trust? Do team members trust each other? Do they trust me?" Your team needs to feel that you are working in the best interests of the project, the company, and them—rather than in your own best interests. Trust is gained or lost from the minute you meet each team member for the first time. If the team does not trust you, you cannot easily be successful. The team will not take your direction or follow your instructions, and the project will suffer. Once you have trust, it can be lost if you are not honest and consistent. Assuming you work in a matrix organization, how do you get people to cooperate if you do not have the ability to give them a raise or a promotion? Trust, as well as a recognition and reward system, are the answers.

Trust also affects, and is affected by, your reputation. Do you know what your reputation is? Many of the people you meet know. Why not ask them about it, so you can deal with any changes you need to make?

Team building helps build trust, and it is a concept that appears throughout the exam. It is an attitude, as well as an action. Do you have the attitude of helping to build the team, or do you think the team members should just follow instructions and accept what they are told? Some project managers think team building is a minor activity; they bring in lunch for the team a couple times during their three-year project and believe they have done team building.

Team building, like many parts of project management, is, in part, a science. The Tuckman ladder model formally identifies the following stages of team formation and development:[12]

- **Forming** People are brought together as a team.
- **Storming** There are disagreements as people learn to work together.
- **Norming** Team members begin to build good working relationships and learn to trust the project manager and each other.
- **Performing** The team becomes efficient and works effectively together. This is the point when the project manager can give the most attention to developing individual team members.
- **Adjourning** The project ends, and the team is disbanded.

New teams may go through each step, while teams that have worked together before may experience a shortened version, possibly even skipping some of the early steps.

387

Project managers who feel they do not have time for team building typically are not using project management best practices on their projects. Practices such as properly planning a project and managing risks and quality save significant amounts of time on a project, freeing up the project manager to do other important things, like team-building activities. When you take the exam, assume the project manager featured in the questions has a team-building plan appropriate to the size and characteristics of the team.

Team-building activities can include the following:

- Involving team members in planning the project, including creating the WBS as a group
- Taking classes together
- Retrospectives by the team to evaluate and improve their processes and interactions
- Collaborative problem-solving
- Milestone parties
- Holiday and birthday celebrations
- Skills assessments and development

### Negotiation

Negotiation can provide value in developing the team, while working to build consensus on project decisions. Including the team members in the decision-making process shows that the project manager values and considers their input.

### Conflict Management

On any project, there may be conflicts among team members or between team members and the project manager. This is especially true as a team is moving through the forming and storming stages of development on the Tuckman ladder, discussed previously. It is a responsibility of the project manager to address such conflicts, and facilitate resolution in a way that satisfies everyone involved. We will further discuss conflict management in the "Manage Team" section.

### Influencing

"Influencing" is a rather ambiguous term, but it is an important aspect of a project manager's role that begins with the project manager actively listening to differing viewpoints expressed by team members. Acknowledging those different perspectives and using communication and persuasive skills helps the project manager develop mutual trust and, eventually, agreement within the team.

## Individual and Team Assessments   PAGE 342

### Individual Assessments

The more you know about each person on the project team, the easier it is to build trust, improve team communication, and encourage cooperation among team members. Personnel assessment tools can help you learn more about team members by revealing how they make decisions, interact with others, and process information. This information can give you insight into how to lead and guide the team. Formal and informal assessment of team members by the project manager should continue throughout the project.

### Team Assessments

The project manager completes formal and informal team performance assessments as part of developing the project team. These assessments are meant to evaluate and enhance the effectiveness of the team as a whole. They may include an analysis of how much team members' skills have improved over the course of the project; how well the team is performing, interacting, and dealing with conflict; and how they are progressing through the stages of team development. The assessments also help identify needed support or intervention by the project manager. Such assessments should be ongoing while project work is being done. The results of team assessments can be used to recognize the team's progress or to motivate them to improve. Think of team performance assessment as looking at team effectiveness. The results of these assessments are also inputs to the Manage Team process, in which the project manager uses them to address issues identified.

## Training    PAGE 342    Team members may require training to perform on the project or to enhance their performance. Such training can help team members, while also decreasing the overall project cost and schedule through increased efficiency. If the training will benefit the organization in the long run and/or can be used on future projects, it may be covered as an organizational cost. Otherwise, it is paid for by the project and documented in the resource management plan and included in the project budget.

## Project Performance Appraisals    On the exam, you may also see a mention of project performance appraisals, which are evaluations of individual team member performance. In this effort, the project manager collects information from team members' supervisors (often members of the project management team) and adjusts the project accordingly. For example, the project manager might decide, as a result of an appraisal, to provide some kind of reward to recognize a team member's diligence. On the other hand, an appraisal might bring to the project manager's attention the need to provide additional training or encouragement to a team member. Note that the focus of this appraisal is on the individual's performance of their assigned responsibilities, rather than on team performance.

Because the Develop Team and Manage Team processes are performed at the same time, it is sometimes difficult to determine what happens in which process. It is our interpretation that project performance appraisals are actually performed as part of Manage Team, and the rewards and additional training indicated by the results of those appraisals are given as part of Develop Team.

## Colocation[13]    PAGE 340    A project manager might try to arrange for the entire team in each city to have offices together in one place or one room. This is called colocation, and it helps improve communication, decreases the impact of conflict (since all parties are right there), and improves project identity for the project team and for management in a matrix organization. The project charter, WBS, network diagram, and schedule may be posted on the walls to keep everyone focused on the work of the project.

## Virtual Teams    PAGE 340    The efforts of the project manager to develop the team have an added level of complexity when the team is not colocated. Extra efforts will be required to keep everyone on a virtual team informed, engaged, and committed to the project work. Such efforts include an emphasis on communication.

## Communications Technology    PAGE 340    Technology provides many ways to keep in touch during a project, including the following:

- A shared portal, such as a website, enables access to current project documents at any time and from any location.
- Video or audio conferencing can be used to conduct virtual meetings when team members are working from remote locations.
- Email, text, and online chat are familiar ways for the project manager and team to communicate.

Communications technology is a valuable asset on any project, but particularly on virtual projects. The project manager can use technology to build and support team efforts, even among team members who may not ever have the opportunity to work in the same physical location. Of course, communications technology also helps colocated team members stay in contact with each other and provide timely updates to other team members as needed. The resource management plan includes specifics of how the project manager will use available communications technology to meet the development needs of the team.

389

### Recognition and Rewards
PAGE 341   In the Develop Team process, the project manager appraises performance and provides recognition and rewards in response to the work of the team or individual team members. To be effective, such rewards should be determined based on the project manager's understanding of what is valuable to the team member or group being recognized. In addition to recognizing past accomplishments, rewards provide incentive for ongoing achievement and efforts.

### Outputs of Develop Team
The results of team performance assessments are an output of this process. As you will read in the next section, these results are an input to the Manage Team process, and they provide insight to the project manager regarding continuous improvement of the team's performance. If the project manager determines that changes to any of the project plans are necessary, change requests are processed through integrated change control. Project documents including the project schedule, team assignments, and resource calendars may require such formal changes.

Organizational process assets updates may include changes to training requirements, newly adopted team-building exercises, and revisions to existing templates for individual and team assessments. This process may also result in updates to documents such as the team charter and lessons learned register.

### Manage Team   PAGE 345

> **Process**  Manage Team
> **Process Group**  Executing
> **Knowledge Area**  Resource Management

Like the Develop Team process, the Manage Team process is done during project executing. The Develop Team and Manage Team processes are performed simultaneously throughout the project.

Manage Team involves all the day-to-day management activities that you are likely already doing on your projects. But there may be more to managing a team than you realize. Not knowing the responsibilities of a project manager as described in this chapter could cause you to get questions wrong on the exam.

### Inputs to Manage Team
PAGE 347   Details related to team-management activities are included in the resource management plan. Other inputs to this process include the issue log (specifically issues related to the team), project team assignments (documented in a RACI chart), and the team charter. Work performance reports provide an indication of project progress as compared to the project management plan. The project manager uses this information to identify necessary corrective actions. Results of team performance assessments from the Develop Team process are analyzed to identify successes that need to be recognized, areas in which the team may need additional support or assistance, and issues or conflicts that need to be resolved in this process. Ultimately, team members are released as their work is completed.

In the Manage Team process, the project manager should perform the following activities to help challenge team members to be part of a high performing team:
- Tracking and evaluating team performance
- Providing leadership
- Dealing with team issues
- Facilitating conflict resolution
- Negotiating and influencing
- Adjusting plans based on performance data
- Managing risks to team success
- Observing what is happening

390

- Using an issue log to track resolution
- Actively looking for and helping to resolve conflicts that team members cannot resolve on their own

Part of supporting a high-performing team is assessing how each team member is fulfilling their responsibilities. Project performance appraisals provide this information on individual team members.

Every project is different and presents unique challenges to the project manager. Factors such as the size and makeup of the team, the experience level of the team, and the complexity of the actual project work must be considered by the project manager in their efforts to get the best from the team.

Consider the following question:

| | |
|---|---|
| *Question* | You were just assigned to take over a project from another project manager who is leaving the company. The previous project manager tells you that the project is on schedule, but only because he has constantly pushed the team to perform. What is the first thing you should do as the new project manager? |

A. Check risk status.
B. Check cost performance.
C. Determine a management strategy.
D. Tell the team your objectives.

| | |
|---|---|
| *Answer* | C |
| *Explanation* | Before you can do anything else, you need to find a more effective management strategy. A management strategy that encourages performance and buy-in to achieving project objectives, rather than relying on micromanagement of the team, will provide a sustainable framework for a motivated team to accomplish the required work. This may require requesting a change to the resource management plan that includes adding team-building activities as well as a recognition and reward system as part of the Develop Team and Manage Team processes. |

Because a goal of managing the team is to engage team members and encourage them to do their best work on the project, involving them in decisions about the work is an excellent strategy. On a properly managed project, the team has helped to create the project management plan. Because they were involved in developing the plan, the team members will be more likely to take on the attitude of, "I helped create this plan, so I do not mind being held to what is included in it." This collaboration between the project manager and team should continue in the Manage Team process.

If, on your projects, you have had difficulty gaining cooperation, could it have been due to a lack of trust, a poor (or nonexistent) recognition and reward system, a micromanaging style of leadership, or the lack of team member and stakeholder involvement in project decisions?

Managing the team takes planning and a focused effort throughout the project that includes keeping in touch with the team, addressing issues before they become problems, listening, communicating, and maintaining relationships.

If you were an observer of your project management work, what would you see? Do you have a tendency to busy yourself issuing reports, rather than really seeing what the team is doing, how team members are interacting, what they feel is missing or doesn't work, and what is generating problems? Whether your team is colocated or virtual, paying attention to the tone of interactions, including emails and phone conversations will tell you more about what is going on than simply analyzing data. A project manager should observe what is happening and talk to people to understand how things are going.

**Issue Log**　Many project managers use issue logs, also known as issue registers or action item logs, to record problems and their resolutions. You have seen the issue log used in integration and quality processes, and you will also see it in other knowledge areas within this book. Because it is updated to reflect new issues as well as the resolution of issues, it is frequently an input and an output of the same processes.

As part of managing team members and stakeholders, the issue log can be used to communicate about issues on the project. It facilitates the assessment of the causes of issues, the impact of issues on scope, schedule, cost, risk, and other aspects of the project, and the recommendation of corrective actions that could be taken. Such a log indicates to people that their needs will be considered, even if they are not addressed at the time the issue arises. Effective project managers control issues so they do not impact the project. The issue log is updated as part of project documents updates throughout the project.

An issue log might look like the one shown in figure 9.7.

| Issue # | Issue | Date Added | Raised By | Person Assigned | Resolution Due Date | Status | Date Resolved | Resolution |
|---------|-------|------------|-----------|-----------------|---------------------|--------|---------------|------------|
|         |       |            |           |                 |                     |        |               |            |
|         |       |            |           |                 |                     |        |               |            |
|         |       |            |           |                 |                     |        |               |            |

FIGURE 9.7　*Issue log*

An issue log should be customized to meet the needs of the people that will be using it. For example, an issue log could include more detail—such as a description or the category of the issue (such as team, schedule, or technical)—as preferred by the team.

Many concepts related to managing people can appear on the exam. The next several pages include information and exercises related to some important topics.

# Management and Leadership Styles　The exam refers to management and leadership styles using the terms and concepts discussed in this section. However, there is no one right way to lead or manage that fits all situations or all project managers. Project managers should know the science of project management and make educated decisions about what they are doing, even when it comes to interacting with and managing people. To choose the most effective approach when answering exam questions, you must consider the information in the scenario, including whether the management and leadership of the project manager have been effective up to this point, what the skill levels, experience, and needs of your team members are, and how complex the project work is.

**TRICKS OF THE TRADE®**　You will likely need to use many leadership approaches throughout the life of a project. The term "situational leadership" refers to a manager using different leadership styles based on the people and project work they are dealing with. For example, there is a general consensus that a project manager needs to provide more direction (directing leadership style) at the beginning of the project because the project manager knows the project management work that must be done to plan the project. During project executing, the project manager needs to do more coaching, facilitating, supporting, influencing, and delegating.

You should be aware of some key terms related to management and leadership styles in the context of managing a project. On the exam, expect questions that describe a situation and then ask what you should do. The options might include solutions that involve using various forms of leadership styles; you will need to select the best answer based on the situation presented. The three bulleted lists that follow include important terms and definitions. Read the definitions two or three times so you are familiar with the terms before you see them used on the exam.

Some of the primary styles that you may see described in situational questions include the following:

- **Directing** The project manager uses their expertise to guide team members in what to do.
- **Facilitating** The project manager enables communication and helps remove roadblocks.
- **Coaching** The project manager advises and makes recommendations, helping the team and other stakeholders achieve their goals.
- **Supporting** The project manager encourages and provides assistance to team members and stakeholders in working through the situations they encounter.
- **Influencing** The project manager emphasizes teamwork, team building, and team decision-making, and works with their team to influence collaborative, successful project implementation.
- **Delegating** The project manager establishes goals and then gives the project team sufficient authority to complete the work. For basic project management, the manager involves the team in the planning process and assigns or delegates planning and executing work to team members. Delegating can be hard for some people because they feel they can do the work better themselves. Using proper project management practices should help a project manager feel comfortable that others know what needs to be done and that the project can be successful.

The following management and leadership styles may be particularly effective when the team is dealing with issues such as resolving conflicts, negotiating, prioritizing, or other decision-making activities:

- **Consultative** This bottom-up approach uses influence to achieve results. The project manager considers others' opinions and acts as the servant-leader for the team.
- **Consensus** The project manager encourages problem-solving in a group and makes decisions based on group agreement.
- **Democratic or participative** This style involves encouraging team participation in the decision-making process. Team members "own" the decisions made by the group, resulting in improved teamwork and cooperation.
- **Bureaucratic** This style focuses on following procedures exactly. The bureaucratic style may be appropriate for work in which details are critical or when specific safety or other regulations must be strictly adhered to.
- **Analytical** This style depends on the manager's own technical knowledge and ability. Analytical managers often make the technical decisions for the project and then communicate those decisions to their teams. Interview-style communication, in which the project manager asks questions to get the facts, is common with this management style.

Some management and leadership styles that may be described in situational questions or answer choices are not inherently bad, but they may create challenges for the project manager, team, and other stakeholders. For example, if the success of a project team is based on the charisma of its project manager, rather than on a strong management plan, and that project manager leaves the organization mid-project, the team may falter. Or, if a project manager takes a laissez-faire approach, and the team is not sufficiently skilled or motivated, it may be difficult to get the work done as planned. The following management and leadership styles are ones that have the potential to create such challenges:

- **Charismatic** Charismatic managers energize and encourage their teams in performing project work. With this style, project success may become dependent on the presence of the charismatic leader, with the team relying on the leader for motivation.
- **Autocratic** This is a top-down approach. The manager may coach or delegate, but everyone does what the manager tells them to do.

- **Consultative-autocratic**  In this style, the project manager solicits input from team members, but retains decision-making authority.
- **Laissez-faire**  The French term "laissez-faire" has been translated as meaning "allow to act," "allow to do," or "leave alone." A laissez-faire manager is not directly involved in the work of the team, but manages and consults as necessary. This style can be appropriate with a highly skilled team.
- **Driver**  A manager with a driver style is constantly giving directions. Their competitive attitude drives the team to win.

## Powers of the Project Manager    This section could be titled, "How to Get Cooperation from the Team and Stakeholders." Project managers can have difficulty getting people to cooperate and perform, especially if they are working in a matrix organization. Understanding the following types of power can help:

- **Formal (legitimate)**  This power is based on your position. Example: "I understand you disagree. However, after careful evaluation, I believe my decision is in the best interest of the team, and this is what we are going to do."
- **Reward**  This power stems from the ability to give rewards. Example: "I understand that you want to participate in the acceptance testing of this project. Because of your performance, I will assign you as part of that team."
- **Penalty (coercive)**  This power comes from the ability to penalize team members. Example: "If this does not get done on time, I will remove you from the group traveling to the customer meeting."
- **Expert**  This power comes from being the technical or project management expert. Example: "This project manager has been successful on other projects. Let's give her a chance!"
- **Referent**  This power comes from another person liking you, respecting you, or wanting to be like you. It is the power of charisma and fame. Example: The most-liked and respected project manager in the organization says, "I think we should change the content of our standard project charter."

NOTE: The best forms of power are expert and reward. Penalty power is generally the least effective. Formal, reward, and penalty are powers derived from your position in the company. Expert power is earned on your own.

On the exam, expect questions that describe a situation and then ask what you should do. The options might include solutions using various forms of power. You'll then need to select the best answer based on the situation presented. To answer these questions, know that penalty is generally an incorrect choice, but make sure it isn't the most appropriate choice for the particular situation described.

## Conflict Management    PAGE 348    Many situational questions on the exam describe conflicts. Therefore, to be able to pick the best choice from many "right" answers, you should understand different conflict resolution techniques and be able to determine which one is best for the situation described.

First, let's think about conflict. Is it bad? Should we spend time preventing the root causes of conflict? Who should resolve the conflict?

Try to answer the questions just posed. Get them right, and you are likely to do well on this part of the exam. The answers are:

- No, conflict is not inherently bad.
- Yes, it is important to identify and deal with the root causes of conflict.
- Conflict should be resolved by those who are involved, possibly assisted by the project manager.

Although we often think conflict is bad, it actually presents opportunities for improvement. This is another topic many people have a different understanding about than what is supported by currently accepted research. Make sure your basic thinking about conflict is on the new side and not the old.

| Changing Views of Conflict | |
| --- | --- |
| Old | New |
| Conflict is dysfunctional and caused by personality differences or a failure of leadership. | Conflict is an inevitable consequence of organizational interactions. |
| Conflict is to be avoided. | Conflict can be beneficial. |
| Conflict is resolved by physical separation or the intervention of upper management. | Conflict is resolved through openness, identifying the causes, and problem-solving by the people involved and their immediate managers. |

Conflict is inevitable, in part, because of the following factors:

- The nature of projects, which attempt to address the needs and requirements of many stakeholders
- Organizational limitations on the power of the project manager
- The necessity of obtaining resources from functional (resource) managers

The project manager has a professional responsibility as part of basic project management to attempt to avoid conflicts through the following actions:

- Keeping the team informed about the following:
  - Exactly where the project is headed
  - Project constraints and objectives
  - The contents of the project charter
  - All key decisions
  - Changes
- Clearly assigning work without ambiguity or overlapping responsibilities
- Making work assignments interesting and challenging
- Following good project management and project planning practices

Note what we just stated: many conflicts can be avoided. Do you do the things on the previous list? Did you realize the project manager has a professional responsibility to do such things? They are not optional; they are good project management.

Many people think the main source of conflict on a project is personality differences. They may be surprised to learn that this is rarely the case. It only becomes personal if the root cause of the problem is not resolved. The following describes the seven sources of conflict in order of frequency (note that personality is last):

1. Schedules (unrealistic, resources not available)
2. Project priorities
3. Resources
4. Technical opinions
5. Administrative procedures
6. Cost
7. Personality

Conflict is best resolved by those involved in the conflict. The project manager should generally try to facilitate the resolution of problems and conflict as long as they have authority over those in conflict or over the issues in conflict. If not, the sponsor or functional managers may be called in to assist. There is one exception. In instances related to professional and social responsibility (someone breaking laws, not following policies, or acting unethically), the project manager must take the issue to someone higher in the organization.

 When you have questions on the exam relating to conflict management, make sure you first think, "Who generally has authority over the situation described in this question?" Another good question to remember is, "What resolution of this problem would best serve the customer's interests?" Also, ask yourself, "What is the urgency with which I need to solve the conflict?" Would it be best to let everyone cool down before intervening? Or is this something that must be resolved immediately? What would happen if you didn't get involved? What will be the long-term repercussions if you involve yourself in the conflict?

The following are the main conflict resolution techniques to know for the exam. Notice that some have more than one title; you should know both.

- **Collaborating (problem-solving)** With this technique, the parties openly discuss differences and try to incorporate multiple viewpoints to arrive at a consensus. Collaboration leads to a win-win situation.

- **Compromising (reconciling)** This technique involves finding solutions that bring some degree of satisfaction to both parties. This is a lose-lose situation, since no party gets everything. Did you know that compromise is not the best choice, but rather second to collaborating?

- **Withdrawal (avoidance)** With this technique, the parties retreat or postpone a decision on a problem. Dealing with problems is a PMI-ism; therefore, withdrawal is not usually the best choice for resolving conflict, though there may be situations where it is necessary.

- **Smoothing (accommodating)** This technique includes making some concessions, and it emphasizes agreement rather than differences of opinion. It does not result in a permanent or complete resolution of the conflict.

- **Forcing (directing)** This technique involves pushing one viewpoint at the expense of another. It is a win-lose situation.

 Remember to look for collaborating or problem-solving choices as generally the best answers. Forcing is usually the worst, but remember that the answer depends on the situation described. There could be situations in which withdrawal is the best option.

**Exercise** Read the description of a conflict resolution, and try to determine which of the techniques is being used.

| Description | Form of Conflict Resolution This Represents |
|---|---|
| 1 "Do it my way!" | |
| 2 "Let's calm down and get the job done!" | |
| 3 "Let us do a little of what both of you suggest." | |
| 4 "Let's deal with this issue next week." | |
| 5 "Miguel and Kathleen, both of you want this project to cause as little distraction to your departments as possible. With that in mind, I am sure we can come to an agreement on the purchase of equipment and what is best for the project." | |
| 6 "We have talked about new computers enough. I do not want to get the computers, and that is it!" | |
| 7 "Miguel, you say the project should include the purchase of new computers, and Kathleen, you say the project can use existing equipment. I suggest we perform the following test on the existing equipment to determine if it needs to be replaced." | |
| 8 "Let's see what everyone thinks, and try to reach a consensus." | |
| 9 "Since we cannot decide on the purchase of new computers, we will have to wait until our meeting next month." | |
| 10 "Miguel, what if we get new computers for the design activity on the project and use the existing computers for the monitoring functions?" | |

## Answer

| Description | Form of Conflict Resolution This Represents |
|---|---|
| 1 "Do it my way!" | Forcing |
| 2 "Let's calm down and get the job done!" | Smoothing |
| 3 "Let us do a little of what both of you suggest." | Compromising |
| 4 "Let's deal with this issue next week." | Withdrawal |
| 5 "Miguel and Kathleen, both of you want this project to cause as little distraction to your departments as possible. With that in mind, I am sure we can come to an agreement on the purchase of equipment and what is best for the project." | Smoothing |
| 6 "We have talked about new computers enough. I do not want to get the computers, and that is it!" | Forcing |

| | Description | Form of Conflict Resolution This Represents |
|---|---|---|
| 7 | "Miguel, you say the project should include the purchase of new computers, and Kathleen, you say the project can use existing equipment. I suggest we perform the following test on the existing equipment to determine if it needs to be replaced." | Collaborating |
| 8 | "Let's see what everyone thinks, and try to reach a consensus." | Collaborating |
| 9 | "Since we cannot decide on the purchase of new computers, we will have to wait until our meeting next month." | Withdrawal |
| 10 | "Miguel, what if we get new computers for the design activity on the project and use the existing computers for the monitoring functions?" | Compromising |

## Emotional Intelligence

PAGE 349   Emotional intelligence is the ability to recognize and express one's emotions appropriately, and to perceive and manage the emotions being expressed by others using observation, communication, and interpersonal skills. An emotionally intelligent project manager is able to establish and maintain positive relationships by adjusting communications and anticipating the needs of others. They understand how emotion can drive the behavior of others and are able to use this understanding when dealing with issues and concerns of the team. Emotionally intelligent project managers are able to effectively use conflict resolution techniques—such as collaborating or smoothing, rather than forcing—because they are perceived as being trustworthy and fair.

Emotional intelligence enables a project manager to bring out the best in coworkers and team members by making them feel valued and important. Clearly, this trait is an asset for a project manager. Emotional intelligence can be developed and increased with study and practice.

## Other Important Terms

One of the things that drives people crazy about the exam is that they see terms they do not know. The following discussion of topics related to human resource management should help you get more familiar with some terms that have been on the exam but which you may not have run across previously. Note that the exam can have made-up terms and processes as answer choices. But remember, if you are well trained in project management and you see a term on the exam that you do not recognize, chances are it is not the right answer!

- **Expectancy theory**[14]   Employees who believe their efforts will lead to effective performance and who expect to be rewarded for their accomplishments will remain productive as rewards meet their expectations.

- **Arbitration**   In arbitration, a neutral party hears and resolves a dispute.

- **Perquisites (perks)**   Some employees receive special rewards, such as assigned parking spaces, corner offices, organizational logo apparel, and executive dining.

- **Fringe benefits**[15]   These are the standard benefits formally given to all employees, such as education benefits, insurance, and profit sharing.

398

## Outputs of Manage Team
Plans for releasing team members are included in the resource management plan. Because the length and focus of assigned work varies, team members may be released at different times throughout the project, as their work is completed. Whenever it occurs, release of team members is considered a part of this process.

As an output of this process, change requests may be needed to reflect changes in resource assignments, costs, schedule, or any other part of the project management plan or project documents. Examples include changes to plans for recognition and rewards, or newly identified needs for team training.

The issue log and lessons learned may be updated based on results of team management efforts. In addition, the existing systems for human resource management appraisals and evaluations may be updated.

## Control Resources   PAGE 352

| | |
|---|---|
| **Process** | Control Resources |
| **Process Group** | Monitoring & Controlling |
| **Knowledge Area** | Resource Management |

While the previous two resource management processes involved human resources, the Control Resources process relates to physical resources being used on the project. To control physical resources, the project manager must ensure that the physical resources assigned to the project are available when they are needed—in the right place and in the right quantity.

In this process, the project manager also monitors the amount, costs, and quality of resources being used, and compares that to what was planned. If there are any discrepancies between the planned versus actual utilization, corrective action may be necessary.

Remember the concept of integration and how the project processes are related. Imagine a team of construction workers arriving on site only to find that the building materials and construction equipment have not yet arrived. An issue with the management of physical resources could impact not only the resource management plan, but also schedule and cost, and potentially scope and quality.

The resource management plan indicates how physical resources should be utilized, controlled, and eventually released. Other inputs to assist the project manager in controlling resources include project documents, agreements and contracts, and work performance data—all of which are discussed in the following sections.

## Project Documents   PAGE 354
Use the following project documents to determine how you will control resources.

- **Issue log** This document provides information about current issues regarding resource usage on the project. Issues might include availability (over- or under-supply), usage (more or less resources being used than what was planned), quality discrepancies, and cost overruns related to resource usage.
- **Lessons learned register** The project manager may be able to benefit from previous project experience with resource control efforts and from historical lessons learned from other similar projects.
- **Resource assignments** Resource assignments show anticipated resource usage and where the resources are coming from.
- **Project schedule** The project schedule indicates what resources are planned to be used, on which activities, and when they are needed.

- **Resource breakdown structure**  Resource requirements are likely documented in a resource breakdown structure, which may be referenced by the project manager when a physical resource needs to be reordered or replaced.
- **Resource requirements**  Resource requirements include what materials, supplies, and equipment are needed.
- **Risk register**  The risk register includes information on potential risks related to the acquisition and use of physical resources. The project manager and team must be aware of these risks, so they are able to recognize risk triggers and initiate risk responses. Newly identified risks to physical resources may be added to the risk register throughout this process.

## Agreements/Contracts   PAGE 355

If any of the physical resources being used on the project were obtained from a source external to the project, a contract includes details on the procurement as well as the seller's contact information, which can be important in case issues arise related to the delivery or quality of the resources, or if additional resources are needed from the same source.

## Work Performance Data   PAGE 355

This documentation provides a measurement of resources used, dates they arrived, and whether they worked as intended. Analysis of work performance data, the issue log, and other inputs gives the project manager an idea of how actual resource usage compares to the plan. The tools and techniques discussed in the following sections are used to evaluate ways to address any variances from the plan.

The following tools and techniques may be used as part of the Control Resources process.

## Performance Reviews

The project manager may undertake a performance review to analyze actual versus planned resource usage and performance. Cost and schedule data may be included in this analysis to determine possible causes of variance from the resource management plan.

## Trend Analysis

The project manager may compare measurements taken throughout the project to assess resource usage and then use that information to extrapolate potential future usage. This process also compares data to determine whether resource performance is improving or worsening.

## Alternatives Analysis

Options for dealing with variances—such as purchasing more or different resources or adding staff to expedite the use of those resources—may be evaluated to determine the most effective way to bring physical resource utilization back to what was planned, or to accommodate improvements in usage. For each option, the project manager might consider factors such as availability, quality, cost, and speed. The options are weighed to determine the most beneficial and cost-effective solution.

Also note that the project manager may use cost-benefit analysis to determine the most cost-effective way to correct a problem or improve a situation. This may be performed as part of alternatives analysis.

## Project Management Information System (PMIS)

You have seen throughout this book that the PMIS is used in many areas of project management. In this process, it can be used to track, access, and analyze data on the use of resources and to problem-solve issues regarding resource management. The results of these efforts will be stored in the PMIS so they are accessible throughout the organization.

## Problem-Solving Method
As with many other topics in this chapter, you likely have some experience with problem-solving methods. However, you may not use the terms or processes tested on the exam, and you might not have learned the methods as a science. Many people solve problems using an incorrect method. Try the next exercise to test your problem-solving knowledge.

**Exercise** What steps would you use to solve a problem?

_____

_____

_____

_____

_____

_____

_____

**Answer** The important thing to realize about problems is that they typically continue until the root cause is discovered and addressed. Many people prefer to avoid conflict (withdraw) instead of solving the problem. Imagine a senior manager who is arbitrarily reassigning physical resources that were committed to your project. Would you deal with it, or delay action? Would you deal directly with the person or try to avoid doing so?

Questions in this area are not always easy. Before you read on, keep in mind that people have failed the exam because they did not "see" the problems explained in questions or they solved the problems the wrong way. So, let's look at a preferred problem-solving method that will help you when answering exam questions. Note that the *PMBOK® Guide* includes more than one version of the problem-solving method, although the progression through the steps of the technique are similar in each version.

1. Define the real or root problem, not what is presented to you or what appears to be the problem.
2. Analyze the problem.
3. Identify solutions.
4. Pick a solution.
5. Implement a solution.
6. Review the solution, and confirm that the solution solved the problem.

As you have been studying, you might have been saying to yourself, "I do not have time to do that!" The issue may not be that you do not have time, but that you are spending your time focused on the wrong areas. How can you afford not to identify and solve the real problem? Think about step 6 from the previous list. If you do not make sure the problem is resolved, it could just return and take up more of your valuable time.

**TRICKS OF THE TRADE®**   When questions on the exam require you to solve problems, ask yourself, "What is the real problem behind the situation presented?" Here is an example:

*During project executing, the construction manager notifies the project manager that the grade of materials in the shipment received from the supplier today is different than that of the previous shipments in the order. This is the third of five shipments from the supplier. What should the project manager do?*

What would you do? Would you call the seller, and investigate why the quality was different? If so, you would get the answer wrong on the exam. This situation combines procurement with resource management. The situation requires the project manager to know the terms of the contract and determine if the delivery of a different grade of material is allowable based on the terms of the contract.

As part of the Control Resources and Control Procurements processes, the project manager would check the resource requirements and the resource assignments, and possibly work with the procurement manager to determine if a breach by the seller has occurred. If a breach has not occurred, the project manager would communicate to the construction manager that the shipment is in alignment with the contract terms. If the shipment does not meet agreed-upon specifications, the seller has breached the contract by not doing something required in the contract. The required legal action for a breach is to send written notification of the breach first, not call the seller to ask why. You need to understand both your responsibility as a project manager and the real problem.

While root cause analysis and problem-solving are extremely important, they are not the best answer in every situation. Some questions indicate that there is a "fire," and ask you what to do about it. You might choose the answer that amounts to "find out why there is a fire" even though you should choose the choice that relates to "get out of the danger zone" as your first response. This could be followed by root cause analysis to identify and solve the cause of that particular fire.

Making sure you are solving the right problem is extremely important. It is a significant issue for many people who take the exam, especially those who have never managed projects that are more than a few months long or who have not had formal training in project management.

The outputs of the Control Resources process include work performance information, change requests, and updates to project documents and the project management plan.

## Work Performance Information
Did you notice that work performance data is an input to this process, and work performance information is an output? The difference is that the work performance data is raw data. It is analyzed in this process, and used to compare actual to planned results to create work performance information.

## Project Documents
The documents that were inputs to this process may be updated based on the work of monitoring and controlling resources. These documents may include the issue log, the lessons learned register, resource assignments, the project schedule and risk register, and the resource breakdown structure.

## Project Management Plan
Components of the project management plan, specifically the resource management plan, may be updated to reflect minor changes in the usage, availability, and quality of resources. In addition to the resource management plan, the project schedule, cost baselines, and quality management plan may be changed as a result of this process.

## Practice Exam

1. All the following are forms of power derived from the project manager's position except:
   A. Formal
   B. Reward
   C. Penalty
   D. Expert

2. The highest point of Maslow's hierarchy of needs is:
   A. Physiological satisfaction
   B. Attainment of survival
   C. Need for association
   D. Esteem

3. Senior management has been extremely impressed by a new team member on the software development project. The team member has enthusiastically and efficiently completed his assigned activities. He has also demonstrated courtesy, respect, and consideration to everyone around him. For these reasons, management is planning to promote the team member to a business analyst position that is currently open on the project. The halo effect refers to the tendency to:
   A. Promote from within.
   B. Hire the best.
   C. Move people into new roles or new technical fields because they are good in their current technical field.
   D. Move people into project management because they have had project management training.

4. The replacement of an important legacy system in the organization will be challenging because there are offices in seven countries, and the business operations cannot be interrupted. Your objective is to have the system updated before new regulations go into effect in one of the participating countries. There are many opinions on how the system should be changed. Some stakeholders are expecting that the new system will encompass more capabilities than the current system. Both internal team members and consultants will be involved in making the hardware and software changes. The sponsor is hoping to keep costs down by using organizational team members to perform the testing and installation activities. You are defining the roles and responsibilities of the stakeholders on the project. The sponsor's role on a project is best described as:
   A. Helping to plan activities
   B. Helping to prevent unnecessary changes to project objectives
   C. Identifying unnecessary project constraints
   D. Helping to develop the project management plan

5. The project is expected to take four years. The project team members will not all be coming on at the start of the project, but rather will join and leave the team as needed. Historically, projects similar to this one have been volatile, and the work intense. Therefore, conflict between team members is almost inevitable. Which of the following conflict resolution techniques will generate the most lasting solution?
   A. Forcing
   B. Smoothing
   C. Compromise
   D. Problem-solving

6. The most common causes of conflict on a project are schedules, project priorities, and:

    A. Personalities
    B. Resources
    C. Cost
    D. Management

7. Two stakeholders are disagreeing via a series of emails as to whether a deliverable meets the acceptance criteria. One of the stakeholders wanted different criteria, but the cost-benefit analysis done in planning did not support delivering that level of performance. The stakeholders agreed that the higher level of performance was not required and was not cost effective. A team member has just informed you that a problem with her work has occurred. The deliverable she is working on must be shipped today, or there will be a project breach. One of the stakeholders having the email disagreement comes to you to complain about the other. You say, "I cannot deal with this issue right now." Which of the following techniques are you using?

    A. Problem-solving
    B. Forcing
    C. Withdrawal
    D. Compromising

8. What does a resource histogram show that a responsibility assignment matrix does not?

    A. Time
    B. Activities
    C. Interrelationships
    D. The person in charge of each activity

9. You have just been assigned as project manager for a large telecommunications project. This one-year project is about halfway done. The project team consists of 5 sellers and 20 of your company's employees. You want to understand who is responsible for doing what on the project. Where would you find this information?

    A. Responsibility assignment matrix
    B. Resource histogram
    C. Bar chart
    D. Project organizational chart

10. During project planning in a matrix organization, the project manager determines that additional human resources are needed. From whom would she request these resources?

    A. The PMO manager
    B. The functional manager
    C. The team
    D. The project sponsor

11. A project manager must publish a project schedule. Activities, start/end times, and resources are identified. What should the project manager do next?

    A. Distribute the project schedule according to the communications management plan.
    B. Confirm the availability of the resources.
    C. Refine the project management plan to reflect more accurate costing information.
    D. Publish a bar chart illustrating the timeline.

12. During every project team meeting, the project manager asks each team member to describe the work they are doing, and then assigns new activities to team members. The length of these meetings has increased because there are many different activities to assign. This could be happening for all the following reasons except:
    A. Lack of a WBS
    B. Lack of a responsibility assignment matrix
    C. Lack of resource leveling
    D. Lack of team involvement in project planning

13. You are a project manager leading a cross-functional project team in a weak matrix environment. None of your project team members report to you functionally, and you do not have the ability to directly reward their performance. The project is difficult, involving tight schedule constraints and challenging quality standards. Which of the following types of project management power will likely be the most effective in this situation?
    A. Referent
    B. Expert
    C. Penalty
    D. Formal

14. A team member is not performing well on the project because they are inexperienced in system development work. There is no one else available who is better qualified to do the work. What is the best solution for the project manager?
    A. Consult with the functional manager to determine project completion incentives for the team member.
    B. Obtain a new resource more skilled in development work.
    C. Arrange for the team member to get training.
    D. Allocate some of the project schedule reserve.

15. A project has several teams. Team C has repeatedly missed deadlines in the past. This has caused team D to have to crash the critical path several times. As the team leader for team D, you should meet with:
    A. The leader of team C
    B. The project manager
    C. The project manager and management
    D. The project manager and the leader of team C

405

16. The project manager and the team are excited about the new project. This is the project manager's first assignment as project manager, and the team feels they will be able to complete work that has never been tried before. There are 29 people contributing to the product description, and the team consists of nine experienced experts in their fields.

    Part way through planning, three highly skilled technical team members are disagreeing about the scope of two of the deliverables. One is pointing to the draft WBS and saying that two additional work packages should be added. Another is saying that a particular work package should not even be done. The third team member agrees with both of them. How should the project manager best deal with the conflict?

    A. She should listen to the differences of opinion, determine the best choice, and implement that choice.

    B. She should postpone further discussions, meet with each individual, and determine the best approach.

    C. She should listen to the differences of opinion, encourage logical discussions, and facilitate an agreement.

    D. She should help the team focus on points on which they agree and build unity by using relaxation techniques and common-focus team building.

17. The project is just starting out and consists of people from 14 different departments. The project charter was signed by one person and contains over 30 major project requirements. The sponsor has informed the project manager that the SPI must be kept between 0.95 and 1.1. A few minutes of investigation resulted in the identification of 34 stakeholders, and the schedule objectives on the project are constrained. The project manager has just been hired. Which of the following types of power will best help the project manager gain the cooperation of others?

    A. Formal
    B. Referent
    C. Penalty
    D. Expert

18. A project manager is trying to settle a dispute between two team members. One says the systems should be integrated before testing, and the other maintains each system should be tested before integration. The project involves over 30 people, and 12 systems need to be integrated. The sponsor is demanding that integration happen on time. What is the best statement the project manager can make to resolve the conflict?

    A. Do it my way.
    B. Let's calm down and get the job done.
    C. Let's deal with this again next week after we all calm down.
    D. Let's do limited testing before integration and finish testing after integration.

19. A project is in the middle of the executing effort when a stakeholder suggests a change that would result in the third major overhaul of the project. At the same time, the project manager discovers that a large work package was not completed because a team member's manager moved her to another project that had a higher priority. Of the following, who is the best person for the project manager to address these issues with?

    A. The team
    B. Senior management
    C. The customer
    D. The sponsor

20. The installation project has a CPI of 1.03 and an SPI of 1.0. There are 14 team members, and each team member had input into the final project management plan. The customer has accepted the three deliverables completed so far without complaint, and the responsibility assignment matrix has not changed since the project began. The project is being completed in a matrix environment, and there are no contracts needed for the project.

    Although the sponsor is happy with the status of the project, one of the team members is always complaining about how much time his project work is taking. Which of the following is the best thing for the project manager to do?

    A. Review the reward system for the project.
    B. Try to improve schedule performance of the project.
    C. Meet with the customer to try to extend the schedule.
    D. Gain formal acceptance in writing from the customer.

21. The project has been challenging to manage. Everyone has been on edge due to pressure to complete the project on time. Unfortunately, the tension has grown to the point where team meetings have become shouting matches, with little work accomplished during the meetings. One team member asks to be excused from future team meetings, as all the shouting upsets him. Meanwhile, the sponsor has expressed interest in attending future team meetings to hear how the project is going and to better understand the issues involved in completing the project. In addition, the customer has started discussions about adding scope to the project. In this situation, it would be best for the project manager to:

    A. Ask the sponsor if the information needed could be sent in a report rather than have her attend the meetings.
    B. Inform the team member who asked to be excused from the meetings of the value of communication in such meetings.
    C. Involve the team in creating ground rules for the meetings.
    D. Hold a team-building exercise that involves all the team members.

22. Project performance appraisals are different from team performance assessments in that project performance appraisals focus on:

    A. How an individual team member is performing on the project
    B. An evaluation of the project team's effectiveness
    C. A team-building effort
    D. Reducing the staff turnover rate

23. A project manager had a complex problem to solve and facilitated a team decision about what needed to be done. A few months later, the problem resurfaced. What did the project manager most likely not do?

    A. Perform proper risk analysis.
    B. Confirm the decision solved the problem.
    C. Have the project sponsor validate the decision.
    D. Use an Ishikawa diagram.

24. The project cost performance index (CPI) is 1.02, the benefit-cost ratio is 1.7, and the latest round of performance reviews identified few required adjustments. The project team was colocated in a new building when the project started. Everyone commented on how excited they were to have all new facilities. The sponsor is providing adequate support for the project, and few unidentified risks have occurred. In an attempt to improve performance, the project manager spends part of the project budget on new chairs for the team members and adds the term "senior" to each team member's job title.

    Which of the following is the most correct thing that can be said of this project or the project manager?

    A. The project manager has misunderstood Herzberg's theory.
    B. The project is slowly spending more money than it should. The project manager should begin to watch cost more carefully.
    C. The performance review should be handled better to find more adjustments.
    D. The project manager should use good judgment to determine which variances are important.

25. You just found out that a major subcontractor for your project consistently provides deliverables late. The subcontractor approaches you and asks you to continue accepting late deliverables in exchange for a decrease in project costs. This offer is an example of:

    A. Confronting
    B. Compromise
    C. Smoothing
    D. Forcing

26. During the first half of the project, five team members left for other projects without being replaced, two team members went on vacation without informing you, and other team members expressed uncertainty about the work they were to complete. In this situation, it is best if you update which of the following for the second half of the project?

    A. Communications management plan
    B. Resource histogram
    C. Resource management plan
    D. Responsibility assignment matrix

27. The project manager is looking at the project's resource needs and lessons learned from past projects. This information causes the project manager to be concerned about her ability to acquire enough resources for the project in six months. Which of the following would be the least effective preventive action?

    A. Make sure functional managers have a copy of the resource histogram.
    B. Show the sponsor the data, and explain the project manager's concern.
    C. Determine metrics to use as an early warning sign that resources will not be available.
    D. Ask functional managers for their opinions.

28. A large project is underway when one of the team members reviews the project status report. He sees the project is currently running late. As he looks at the report further, he notices the delay will cause one of his activities to be scheduled during a time he will be out of the country and will be unable to work on the activity. This is of great concern to the team member because he is committed to the success of the project and does not want to be the cause of the project being further delayed. What is the best thing for him to do?

    A. Contact the project manager immediately to provide the project manager with his schedule.
    B. Include the information in his next report.
    C. Request that the issue be added to the project issue log.
    D. Recommend preventive action.

408

29. Many work packages have been successfully completed on the project, and the sponsor has made some recommendations for improvements. The project is on schedule to meet an aggressive deadline when the successor activity to a critical path activity suffers a major setback. The activity has 14 days of float and is being completed by four people. There are two other team members with the skill set to assist the troubled activity, if needed.

    The project manager finds out that three other team members are attempting to be removed from the project because they do not feel the project can be successful. When the project manager investigates, she discovers that those team members have issues that have not been addressed.

    Which of the following is the best thing to do to improve the project?
    A. Have the team members immediately assist the troubled activity.
    B. Investigate why the project schedule is aggressive.
    C. See who can replace the three team members.
    D. Create an issue log.

30. In determining the physical resource requirements of the project, the team has identified the need for a highly specialized piece of testing equipment that will be used for approximately six months. The organization only owns one of these units, and it has been committed to other projects during the time this team will need it. Purchasing another similar unit is assumed to be cost-prohibitive. Which of the following is the least effective action for the project manager to take?
    A. Negotiate with the project manager that has reserved the equipment during the time it is needed by this team.
    B. Consult with the procurement department about the possibility of leasing a similar unit.
    C. Request that the sponsor intervene on behalf of the project.
    D. Adjust the schedule so that the work requiring the equipment can be done when the equipment is available.

31. A project is being completed by a virtual team with team members from six countries. From their various locations, the team members are arguing about which office will take the lead on the project, disagreeing over meeting schedules, and questioning the abilities of individuals whom they have not worked with before. In which stage of the Tuckman ladder is this team functioning?
    A. Forming
    B. Reforming
    C. Storming
    D. Resourcing

32. A team member has missed the last two team meetings. Several of his assigned deliverables were completed late, and not all were of acceptable quality. He requests a meeting with the project manager, where he explains that he has been dealing with a number of personal issues, which he realizes have affected his work. Although this has been concerning for the project manager, as he has had to smooth the irritation of other team members and even taken on some of the team member's responsibilities, the project manager shows concern to the team member. He works with the team member to reschedule his work to allow him long weekends to deal with his personal situation. This is an example of:
    A. Expectancy theory
    B. Theory Y management
    C. Emotional intelligence
    D. Problem-solving

## Answers

1. **Answer**  D
   **Explanation**  When someone is given the job of project manager, they will have formal, reward, and penalty power. But just having the position does not make the project manager either a technical or project management expert. Expert power has to be earned.

2. **Answer**  D
   **Explanation**  This question is asking which of the *following* is the highest. Self-actualization is not listed, so the next best choice is esteem.

3. **Answer**  C
   **Explanation**  The halo effect refers to the tendency to rate team members high or low on all factors due to the impression of a high or low rating on one specific factor. It can result in a decision to move people into a different technical field because they are good in their current technical field. However, just because a person is good in one technical field does not mean they will also be good in another technical field.

4. **Answer**  B
   **Explanation**  Although the sponsor may help plan some of the activities, it is not their exclusive duty. Some project constraints come from the sponsor, but they should be considered necessary. The project management plan is created with the team and approved by the sponsor and other management. Since the project objectives are stated in the project charter, and it is the sponsor who issues the project charter, helping to prevent unnecessary changes to project objectives is the correct answer.

5. **Answer**  D
   **Explanation**  Problem-solving (also referred to as collaborating) normally takes more time, but it gets buy-in from everyone, generating a more lasting solution.

6. **Answer**  B
   **Explanation**  Know the top four sources of conflict on projects (schedules, project priorities, resources, and technical opinions) so you can be prepared to answer questions that relate to sources of conflict and how to deal with them. Don't be fooled because "personality" is on the list. It is not a major cause of conflict.

7. **Answer**  C
   **Explanation**  Delaying the issue is called withdrawal.

8. **Answer**  A
   **Explanation**  The responsibility assignment matrix maps specific resources to the work packages from the WBS. On a resource histogram, the use of resources is shown individually or by groups over time.

9. **Answer**  A
   **Explanation**  The resource histogram shows the number of resources used in each time period. In its pure form, a bar chart shows only activity and calendar date. The organizational chart shows who reports to whom. The responsibility assignment matrix shows who will do the work.

10. **Answer**  B
    **Explanation**  In a matrix organization, power is shared between the functional manager and the project manager, so the project manager needs to negotiate with the functional manager for the resources.

11. **Answer**  B
    **Explanation**  The project schedule remains preliminary until resource assignments are confirmed.

12. **Answer**  C

    **Explanation**  The lack of a WBS, responsibility assignment matrix, or team involvement in planning could contribute to excessively long meetings during which resources are assigned to activities. Resource leveling refers to maintaining the same number of resources on the project for each time period and would not impact the length of meetings.

13. **Answer**  B

    **Explanation**  Reward and expert are the best types of power to use in such a situation. Reward is not listed as a choice, and the question says the project manager has limited ability to reward the team members. Therefore, expert power is the correct answer.

14. **Answer**  C

    **Explanation**  The job of the project manager includes providing or obtaining project-specific training for team members. This kind of training may be a direct cost of the project.

15. **Answer**  D

    **Explanation**  Those involved in the problem should resolve the problem. The fact that team D has had to crash the critical path several times implies that team D has already tried to deal with this problem. In this case, the two team leaders need to meet. The extent of this situation requires the project manager's involvement as well.

16. **Answer**  C

    **Explanation**  Do not get confused by the wordiness of the question. Ask yourself what the best way is to resolve any conflict, and you can get the answer. Most of the details provided are distractors. Problem-solving (collaborating) and compromising are the two most important conflict resolution techniques. Conflict management is a key interpersonal and team skill.

17. **Answer**  A

    **Explanation**  Generally, the best forms of power are reward or expert. The project manager has not had time to become a recognized expert in the company, and reward power is not included as a choice here. This leaves formal power as the only logical answer.

18. **Answer**  D

    **Explanation**  Doing limited testing before integration and finishing testing after integration is an example of compromising. This is the best way for the project manager to resolve the conflict in this situation.

19. **Answer**  D

    **Explanation**  It is the sponsor's role to prevent unnecessary changes and to set priorities among projects. The situation described in this question implies that such work is not being done. The project manager must therefore go to the root of the problem: the sponsor.

20. **Answer**  A

    **Explanation**  Improving schedule performance relates to getting the project completed sooner. Although it would seem to be a good idea to improve schedule performance, this project's performance is fine. The schedule has been approved as it is. It would be better for the project manager to spend more time controlling the project to make sure it finishes according to plan than to improve schedule performance.

    If you chose attempting to extend the schedule, look at the SPI. There is nothing wrong with the schedule performance of the project that would require an extension. Gaining formal acceptance from the customer will need to be done, as it provides an opportunity for the team to check if everything is going well. This action will not affect the team member's dissatisfaction, however.

411

The only real problem presented in this situation is that the team member is complaining. If you read the question completely, you will notice that the team member was involved in creating and approving the project management plan, which included details about his own involvement in the project. Because the responsibility assignment matrix has not changed, the team member has not even been assigned different duties since the project began. There must be something else causing the team member to complain. The project manager should investigate and find out if the reward system is ineffective.

21. **Answer** C

    **Explanation** Here is a situation in which all four choices could be done, but there is one best answer. Asking the sponsor if the information could be sent in a report does not solve the root cause of the problem described. Informing the team member of the value of communication in meetings merely dismisses the concerns of the team member. A team-building exercise would take planning, so it could not be done right away. Remember, the sponsor might be attending the next meeting, and at least one team member might not attend because of past problems. The best thing to do would be to set up new ground rules governing team behavior and then plan a team-building exercise.

22. **Answer** A

    **Explanation** The best thing to do is to look at the two terms used here (project performance appraisals and team performance assessments), and review in your mind what each means before looking at the choices. Team performance assessments evaluate the project team's effectiveness as a whole. Project performance appraisals deal with how each team member is performing on the project.

23. **Answer** B

    **Explanation** Notice the phrasing of this question, "most likely not do." Expect to see questions worded on the exam in ways that can cause you to misinterpret them. You will also see questions about things we forget to do in the real world. "Who has time," you might say, "to determine if each problem is really solved?" One could respond with, "Who has time not to do this? Who has time to deal with the same problem twice?" The final steps of problem-solving include implementing a decision, reviewing it, and confirming that the decision solved the problem.

24. **Answer** A

    **Explanation** The option of the project manager watching cost more closely could trick you into selecting it if you are unsure of the real answer. There is no indication that the costs are trending in any particular direction. There is no reason to think that performance reviews would turn up more adjustments. The project manager should always use good judgment but because nothing in this question talks about judgment regarding variances, this cannot be the best choice. In this situation, the project manager is making great working conditions better by buying new chairs and enhancing the team members' titles. According to Herzberg's theory, fixing bad working conditions will help motivate the team, but making good ones better will not improve motivation. The project manager needs to focus on the motivating agents and not the hygiene factors.

25. **Answer** B

    **Explanation** Both parties are giving up something. This is a compromise.

26. **Answer** C

    **Explanation** The resource histogram shows the resources used per time period, but it would provide limited benefit in this situation. The responsibility assignment matrix cross-references resources with the activities or work packages they are to accomplish to help give clarity to the team members on their assignments, but it does not show when they will be required to do their work. The resource management plan, which describes when resources will be brought onto and taken off the project as well as how team members should communicate with the project manager, would provide the most benefit for this project.

27. **Answer** A

**Explanation** Sending data without pointing out the issue does not mean the communication will be adequately decoded by the recipient. The other choices describe more effective communication in this instance.

28. **Answer** D

**Explanation** Notice that this question asks what the team member should do. It is important for the project manager to understand the team member's role and possibly even instruct team members on how to work on projects and what is expected of them. Providing the project manager with his schedule, including the information in a report, and requesting that the issue be added to the issue log have one thing in common. They involve the team member asking the project manager to do something. In reality, it may well be the team member who will come up with a solution (for example, decreasing the scope of the activity, fast tracking, or specific suggestions about changes to predecessor activities). Therefore, recommending preventive action is the best choice for the team member. Note that recommended corrective or preventive actions can come from the team or stakeholders in addition to the project manager.

29. **Answer** D

**Explanation** Sometimes complex problems are caused by not doing simple things. After you read the answer options, you should realize that the data in the first paragraph is completely extraneous. The troubled activity has float and so does not need immediate attention. It may not be necessary for additional team members to assist the troubled activity, but none of the choices suggest investigating whether the amount of float is enough to cover any delay caused by the trouble. Rather, the choices take you in different directions.

Investigating why the schedule is so aggressive should have been done before the project began. Replacing team members does not solve the root cause of the problem. Could there be something the project manager is doing wrong, or could be doing that she is not, that would solve the problem without losing resources? Wouldn't it be more effective to discover the root cause of those team members' concerns so the problem does not surface again later? The creation of an issue log will let the troubled team members know their concerns have been heard, are noted, and will be resolved. This might be enough to stop them from leaving and avoid the resultant project delays and confusion if new team members must be added.

30. **Answer** C

**Explanation** It is a professional responsibility of the project manager to consider the needs of the entire organization, not only those of his project. It is also the project manager's responsibility to attempt to deal with the situation before involving the sponsor. For these reasons, involving the sponsor is not the best thing to do. All the other choices are options the project manager should consider first.

31. **Answer** C

**Explanation** The team's disagreements are indicative of the storming stage of development. As they continue working together, they will move into the norming stage.

32. **Answer** C

**Explanation** Emotional intelligence enables a project manager to bring out the best in coworkers and team members by making them feel valued and important. In this case, he was able to show empathy while still working out a plan for the team member to fulfill his project responsibilities.

# Communications Management

## TEN

How often do you delete a voicemail without listening to the very end of the message? Is your inbox typically flooded with emails? How many times has a team member on one of your projects not received an important piece of information that could have impacted their work? These types of occurrences happen all too often on projects and indicate a need to better plan and manage communications. Think about your real-world projects. How much time do you spend planning and managing communications?

When surveyed, project managers typically identify communication-related issues as the problem they experience most frequently on projects. Communication is an incredibly important part of managing a project, so shouldn't we make sure we plan, manage, and monitor our messages?

Many beginning project managers only communicate using status reports. As project managers gain experience, they often recognize the need for a more structured approach to communications. Effective project managers create a communications management plan that goes beyond merely sending status reports and includes asking stakeholders what they need communicated to them and identifying what communications need to be received from the stakeholders. Effective project managers also frequently revisit communications at team meetings to limit the potential for communication problems. To pass the exam, you should have this type of mindset about communicating on projects.

Although this chapter is not particularly difficult, it is one you should take seriously. Be sure to find your gaps regarding communications, and be aware that communications questions are frequently combined with other topics. For example, a WBS can be used as a communications tool (see the Scope Management chapter), and risk response strategies should be communicated to the stakeholders (see the Risk Management chapter).

## QUICKTEST

- Communications management process
- Communications management plan
- Flow of communication
- Communication types
  - Formal/informal written
  - Formal/informal verbal
- Communication models
  - Interactive
  - Noise
  - Effective communication
  - Nonverbal
  - Verbal
  - Active listening
  - Effective listening
  - Feedback
- Communications technology
- Communication methods
  - Interactive communication
  - Push communication
  - Pull communication
- Meetings
- Communication channels
- Project reporting
  - What should be reported
  - Types of reports
    » Status report
    » Progress report
    » Trend report
    » Forecasting report
    » Variance report
    » Earned value report
    » Lessons learned documentation
- Communication blockers
- Monitoring communications

415

# Communications Management   T E N

## Rita's Process Chart™
## Communications Management
Where are we in the project management process?

416

You may also see questions linking communications management to stakeholder management. As you might expect, these two are closely related: managing stakeholder engagement and keeping stakeholders informed and involved requires well-thought-out communications. See the Stakeholder Management chapter for more information.

The following should help you understand how each part of communications management fits into the overall project management process:

| The Communications Management Process | Done During |
| --- | --- |
| Plan Communications Management | Planning process group |
| Manage Communications | Executing process group |
| Monitor Communications | Monitoring and controlling process group |

## Plan Communications Management   PAGE 366

**Process** Plan Communications Management
**Process Group** Planning
**Knowledge Area** Communications Management

The Plan Communications Management process considers how to develop a plan for project communications activities. This plan should be based on the information needs of stakeholders and on the needs of the project. The plan identifies what systems and processes are already in place to support communication needs, as well as what processes and documents must be created to maximize the effectiveness and efficiency of communications on the project. This effort includes planning what information will be communicated, to whom, when, using what method, and how frequently. The major output of this process is the communications management plan, which will guide the project manager and the team in managing and monitoring communications to ensure information is getting to the people who need it, is clear and understandable, and allows stakeholders to take action as necessary.

To create an effective communications management plan, you must understand communications technology, methods, and models. You must also take into account the performing organization's established processes and procedures for communicating about projects, its historical records and lessons learned from previous projects, and other stored information (organizational process assets). In addition, you must consider the performing organization's environment and approved communication systems, including its culture and expectations (enterprise environmental factors). You'll need to refer to the project charter and relevant project documents, such as requirements documentation and the stakeholder register. You will also need to consider the project management plan—specifically, plans for resource management and stakeholder engagement. The resource management plan may indicate communications requirements of project team members and resource managers. The stakeholder engagement plan may provide information on planned strategies to engage stakeholders, which likely emphasize communication efforts. Your communications management plan must detail how your project communications will support those plans.

In planning communication on a project, it's essential that you determine and analyze stakeholders' communications requirements. Different stakeholders need to receive different information in various formats, and you must figure out in advance what each stakeholder needs when it comes to communication. On your projects, do you take the time to ask stakeholders about their communications requirements? Remember, you need to gather requirements from your stakeholders that relate not only to how they want the product of the project to function, but also to how they want to communicate and be communicated with on the project. These communications requirements need to be analyzed to determine how they can be met and to make sure that meeting them will add value to the project and will be worth the effort and cost involved.

417

# Communications Management

If you have only managed small projects, you might believe you need to spend just a few minutes thinking about what information people may need. Having this attitude when taking the exam is a mistake, however. Rather, imagine a team of 300 people spread throughout the world, speaking many different languages and with diverse approaches to communication that are influenced by their culture. This example should help you to recognize how much work goes into planning communications and how critical it is to thoroughly plan communications for a large project. Many project managers fail to recognize not only the impact of communications on a project but also the complexity of sharing information. When we teach communication in our Project Management Tricks of the Trade® class, this topic is one that most people are not initially interested in, yet they find the communication activities we offer in class to be some of the most valuable.

This topic is important on the exam, but luckily it is not difficult—as long as you think in terms of large projects. A basic concept of communications is that they should be efficient (providing only the information needed) and effective (providing information in the right format at the right time), and should add value to the project. Think about your real-world communications. Do you do the following?

- Ask people what information they need and when (this overlaps with stakeholder management).
- Plan communications for all stakeholders.
- Customize standardized communication practices within your organization to meet the needs of the project.
- Use multiple methods of communicating.
- Plan how you will confirm communication is actually received and understood.
- Realize that communication goes in multiple directions, to and from people at all levels within and external to the organization.
- Analyze how factors such as location, culture, security, privacy, and language will impact communication on the project.
- Plan communication with each stakeholder based on the individual's needs and interests.
- Have a system for storing, maintaining, and retrieving project information.

## Exercise
Test yourself! What information and documents need to be communicated on a project?

_____

_____

_____

_____

_____

_____

_____

_____

_____

_____

_____

_____

418

## Answer

Some possible answers are:

- Project charter
- Project management plan and project documents
- Impacts to and from other projects
- WBS, network diagram, and dependencies
- When resources will be needed
- Meeting schedule
- Work assignments
- Status
- New risks uncovered
- Uncertainties
- Problems
- Successes
- Changes to project scope and product scope
- Schedule of planned reviews of the project management plan, including when updates are likely to be issued
- Updates to the project management plan and project documents
- Results of change requests
- Upcoming work
- Delays
- The date of the next milestone completion
- Performance reports
- Lessons learned
- Issue logs
- Configuration management issues
- What types of emails will be sent to each stakeholder
- Contact information for all stakeholders
- Method of updating the communications management plan

 Project communications occur internally and externally to the core project team—vertically (up and down the levels of the organization) and horizontally (between peers). Make sure your planning includes communicating in all directions, as shown in figure 10.1.

419

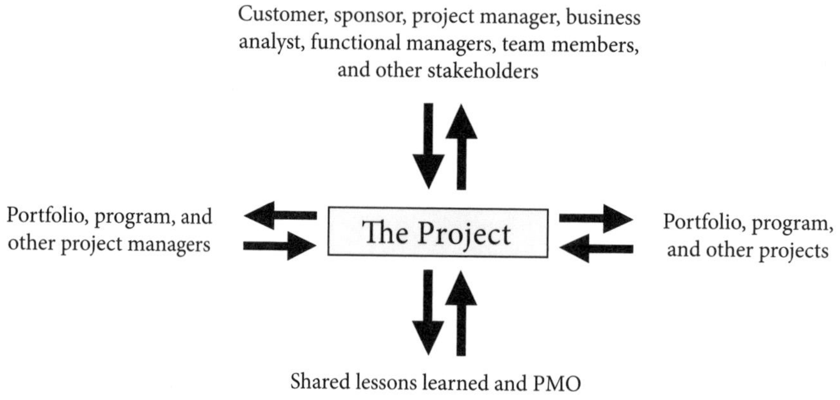

**FIGURE 10.1**  *Flow of communication on a project*

To communicate effectively, you need to handle communications in a structured way and choose the best type of communication for each situation. Information can be expressed in different ways—formally or informally, written or verbal. You need to decide what approach to use for each instance of communication. Make sure you understand the following chart.

| Communication Type | When Used |
|---|---|
| Formal written | Project management plan, other formal documentation (such as the project charter), and reports; can be both physical and electronic |
| Formal verbal | Planned meetings and stakeholder briefings; can be face-to-face or remote |
| Informal written | Email, handwritten notes, text messages, instant messaging, social media, and websites |
| Informal verbal | Unscheduled meetings, conversations, and other casual discussions |

## Exercise  Test yourself! What is the best type of communication in the following situations?

| Situation | Communication Type |
|---|---|
| Updating the project management plan | |
| Giving presentations to management | |
| Trying to solve a complex problem | |
| Making notes regarding a telephone conversation | |
| Making changes to a contract | |
| Informing a team member about poor performance (first notice) | |
| Informing a team member about poor performance (second notice) | |
| Scheduling a meeting | |
| Clarifying a work package | |
| Requesting additional resources | |
| Trying to discover the root cause of a problem | |

420

| Situation | Communication Type |
|---|---|
| Sending an email to ask for clarification of an issue | |
| Holding a milestone party | |
| Conducting an online bidder conference | |

**Answer**   Imagine these as situational questions. Exam questions may have more words, but they will boil down to straightforward situations like the ones described in the following table.

| Situation | Communication Type |
|---|---|
| Updating the project management plan | Formal written |
| Giving presentations to management | Formal verbal |
| Trying to solve a complex problem | Formal written |
| Making notes regarding a telephone conversation | Informal written |
| Making changes to a contract | Formal written |
| Informing a team member about poor performance (first notice) | Informal verbal |
| Informing a team member about poor performance (second notice) | Formal written |
| Scheduling a meeting | Informal written |
| Clarifying a work package | Formal written |
| Requesting additional resources | Formal written |
| Trying to discover the root cause of a problem | Informal verbal |
| Sending an email to ask for clarification of an issue | Informal written |
| Holding a milestone party | Informal verbal |
| Conducting an online bidder conference | Formal written |

## The Five Cs of Communication   Certain qualities of written communication enhance the likelihood that communications will be correctly interpreted and understood by the recipients. The following qualities should be incorporated by the project manager to ensure that messages are effective:

- Correct grammar and spelling
- Concise and well-crafted
- Clear and purposeful
- Coherent and logical
- Controlled flow of words and ideas

## Communication Models

PAGE 371  Many of us do not think scientifically about our communications. We just send an email and expect that it will be read and interpreted properly. The most basic communication model only ensures that a message has been delivered, but excellent project communication requires a more structured approach to communications.

A more comprehensive communication model, interactive communication, includes three main components: the sender, the receiver, and the confirmation that the message is correctly understood. Each message is encoded by the sender and decoded by the receiver. The receiver acknowledges receipt of the message, and both the sender and receiver are responsible for confirming that it has been properly interpreted by the receiver.

Factors such as the receiver's perception of the message, everyday distractions, or even a lack of interest can affect the way the receiver decodes a message. Communication models often refer to these types of factors as "noise" because they interfere with the receiver's ability to understand the message.

More complicated communication models exist, and different models may be appropriate for different projects or components of a single project. The model or models that will be used on the project are described in the communications management plan. Keep the interactive model of communication in mind when answering communications questions on the exam.

### Effective Communication

The sender should determine which communication method to use to send a message, and then encode the message carefully and confirm that it is understood. When encoding the message, the sender needs to be aware of the following communication factors:

- **Nonverbal** A significant portion of in-person communication is nonverbal; this can include gestures, facial expressions, and body language.
- **Verbal** There are two important aspects of verbal communication:
  - The words and phrases a sender chooses are essential components of the message, but their meaning can be obscured by the accompanying nonverbal factors.
  - Pitch and tone of voice also help to convey a spoken message.

To confirm the message is understood, it's helpful for the sender to ask for feedback using questions such as, "Could you rephrase what I've said in your own words?" But it's also up to the receiver to make sure they have received and understood the entire message.

This is especially true in situations involving cross-cultural communication. Senders and receivers of communications must be cognizant of cultural differences, including age, gender, and nationality, and take those factors into account when planning, transmitting, and interpreting communications.

The previous paragraphs apply to individual interactions as well as to project communication. It's possible to plan not just the types of communications to be used, but also ways for the sender to confirm the receiver has interpreted the message as intended. The communications management plan provides guidance to stakeholders regarding what to communicate and when to communicate it. It also includes direction on how to confirm understanding of communications.

### Effective Listening

So what should a receiver do during in-person communication to accurately decode a message and confirm it has been understood? The receiver should pay attention to the sender's gestures and facial expressions, and try to focus on the content of the message without distraction. It's also important that a receiver practices active listening. Active listening means the receiver confirms they are listening, expresses agreement or disagreement, and asks for clarification when necessary.

If a message is not understood, the receiver should acknowledge the message by saying something like, "I am not sure I understand. Can you explain that again?" Like the sender, the receiver needs to encode their response carefully, keeping in mind the potential effects of verbal and nonverbal communication, when giving feedback to the sender, as illustrated in figure 10.2.

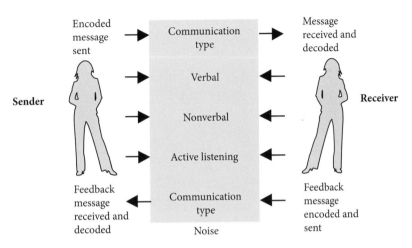

FIGURE 10.2   *The interactive communication model*

 **Communications Technology**   PAGE 370   Communication can take place in many ways: face-to-face, over the phone, in writing, through instant messaging, and via email. These means of communicating are collectively referred to as communications technology. Another aspect of planning communications is determining the optimal technology with which to communicate information. To determine the appropriate technology to use, ask questions such as:

- Would it be better to communicate this information in person or virtually?
- Would it be better to communicate the information through an email or a phone call?
- What technology is the team familiar and comfortable with?
- How quickly does the information need to be communicated?
- Are there security or confidentiality issues that should be considered when choosing a means of communicating information?
- Would a letter sent through the mail get more attention?

**TRICKS OF THE TRADE®**   As you read this chapter, you may come across many new terms. You can learn most of these terms without memorization as long as you understand the concept that project communications must be planned to include all stakeholders—who may be in several different countries. For example, can you guess what push communication might be without reading the next section? You will see many of the terms we use in this chapter on the exam, but do not waste time memorizing them. Just read this chapter over once or twice, and you should understand the concepts for the exam.

## Communication Methods   PAGE 374   When planning communications, it is also important to determine the communication method. These methods can be grouped into the following categories:[1]

- **Interactive communication**   This method is reciprocal and involves two or more people. One person provides information; others receive it and then respond to the information. Examples of interactive communication include conversations, phone calls, meetings, instant messaging, and video calls.

- **Push communication** This method involves a one-way stream of information. The sender provides information to the people who need it but does not expect feedback from the recipients. Examples of push communication are status reports, emailed updates, blogs, and company memos.
- **Pull communication** In this method, the sender places the information in a central location. The recipients are then responsible for retrieving the information from that location. This method is often used to distribute large documents or to provide information to many people.

In choosing a communication method, you should consider whether feedback is needed or if it is enough to simply provide the information. Where possible, it's worth involving stakeholders in the final decision about which methods will meet their communication needs. Such decisions will support the stakeholder engagement efforts on the project.

## Meetings

Early in the project, the project manager is likely to conduct meetings with the team to plan how information will be communicated on the project. Planning for communication should also involve thinking ahead about when, how, and how often meetings will be used throughout the project.

Meetings are a problem in the real world because many project managers manage by doing everything in meetings, and most meetings are not efficient. Thinking ahead about how and when meetings will be conducted, when they're appropriate and when a less disruptive form of communication could be substituted, and who needs to attend meetings can go a long way toward addressing this problem.

When planning meetings, consider the following rules:

- Schedule recurring meetings in advance.
- Meet with the team regularly, but not too often.
- Have a purpose for each meeting.

## Communications Requirements Analysis

PAGE 369   Requirements analysis will help you correctly understand stakeholders' information requirements. Understanding and fulfilling these requirements will help you maintain stakeholder engagement by ensuring that communication needs are met. If you skip this step, you risk not meeting the communication needs of stakeholders, and potentially misunderstanding requirements altogether.

Use the following information to determine and analyze communication requirements:

- Stakeholder register
- Stakeholder engagement plan
- Locations of stakeholders
- Number of communication channels

**Communication Channels**[2]   A quick note on communication channels. When you add one more person to the team, does the number of communication channels simply increase by one? No. In fact, there is a substantial increase in communication channels. As a result, communication needs can grow rapidly with each added stakeholder.

Communication channels can be calculated using the following formula:

$$\frac{n(n-1)}{2} \qquad n = \text{the number of stakeholders}$$

Note that $n$ equals the total number of stakeholders, and keep in mind during the exam that you may have to add yourself as a stakeholder if a question does not acknowledge the project manager.

Let's practice using this formula with an example. If you have four people on your project (including you, the project manager) and you add one more, how many more communication channels do you have? To get the answer you calculate the number of communication channels with a team of four and with a team of five, and then subtract to identify the difference.

For a team of four: calculate 4 times 3 (which is $n-1$) to get 12, and then divide by 2 to reach the answer, which is 6. For a team of five: calculate 5 times 4 (which is $n-1$) to get 20, and then divide by 2 to reach the answer, which is 10. The difference between 10 and 6 is 4. Simple!

You may or may not see this formula when taking the exam. But just in case, be sure to understand the concept, and know how to calculate the number of communication channels.

## Communications Management Plan   PAGE 377   The primary output of the Plan Communications Management process is a communications management plan that documents both the communications needs of stakeholders and a strategy to meet those needs. Components of the plan may include what communications should be prepared, disseminated, and received among all project stakeholders, how communications should be named and stored, who has access to the communications, who has the ability to edit communications, and who has responsibility for sending and receiving project communications. The plan also includes information on how the effectiveness of project communications will be evaluated.

Figure 10.3 shows a portion of what you might find in a communications management plan.

| What Needs to Be Communicated | Why | Between Whom | Best Method for Communicating | Responsibility for Sending | When and How Often |
|---|---|---|---|---|---|
| | | | | | |
| | | | | | |

FIGURE 10.3   *Sample portion of a communications management plan*

Because communications are so complex, a communications management plan should be in writing for most projects. It must address the needs of all the stakeholders, and should account for any language and cultural differences on the project. The communications management plan is part of the project management plan.

## Manage Communications   PAGE 379

**Process**  Manage Communications
**Process Group**  Executing
**Knowledge Area**  Communications Management

Throughout the life of a project, many stakeholders will require information about the project. The communications needs of stakeholders are determined in planning and documented in the communications management plan. These needs are met in Manage Communications, through the distribution of communications artifacts, such as reports, graphics, and emails, as well as through meetings and other in-person communication.

The resource, communications, and stakeholder management plans all document communication needs that must be managed. In addition, the quality and risk management processes generate reports that are disseminated to stakeholders through this process.

The Manage Communications process also includes making sure information is flowing back and forth on the project in accordance with the communications management plan. This process is about facilitating effective communication and practicing flexible approaches when managing communications. Managing communications also includes providing opportunities for stakeholders to request additional information and clarification. Also note that project reports and other formal written communications are archived as part of the project's historical records.

## Communication Blockers[3]

Project managers may unknowingly introduce communication blockers during their projects. Communication blockers can range from a lack of cultural sensitivity to a failure to provide concise messages. Blockers cause miscommunication and can lead to disagreement and confusion. The exam has often included one or two questions that ask, "What can get in the way of communication?" or "The following has occurred; what is wrong?" The correct answer may include:

- Noisy surroundings
- Distance between those trying to communicate
- Improper encoding of messages
- Language
- Culture

Using the technology, models, and methods established in the communications management plan to meet the communication needs of the project is vital to successful communications management. It is important to make sure communications are received, effective, efficient, and understandable. Along with the communications management plan, project documents and work performance reports will give you information about what needs to be communicated. Whether it's information from recent risk reviews, forecasts on project performance, or details about changes that have gone through the integrated change control process, a project manager will need to follow the communications management plan to effectively share information.

The following tools and techniques can be used to manage communications.

## Communication and Interpersonal Skills   PAGES 384 AND 386

What communication skills do you use? Do you practice active listening? How do you handle conflict? Do you pay attention to cultural differences between stakeholders? Utilizing a range of communication skills, as well as relying on interpersonal skills can help you better manage communications.

Although the communications management plan may suggest good practices for project communications, it is a responsibility of the project manager and team to tailor their communications approach in response to feedback from stakeholders. Also keep in mind that the culture of the organization and the political environment within which the project and its stakeholders exist will need to be regularly assessed, and the project manager and team must be flexible in their adaptation to any significant changes. A project manager and all stakeholders on a project must use their skills to reduce or resolve conflicts and to promote effective communicating.

# Meetings    PAGE 386

As discussed in the "Plan Communications Management" section of this chapter, meetings are often key elements of the effort to manage communications. When handled properly, they provide a means to communicate efficiently with stakeholders. Review the following rules for conducting meetings:

- Set a time limit, and keep to it.
- Create an agenda with team input.
- Distribute the agenda beforehand.
- Stick to the agenda.
- Let attendees know their responsibilities in advance.
- Bring the right people together.
- Chair and lead the meeting with a set of rules.
- Assign deliverables and time limits for all work assignments that result from meetings.
- Document and publish meeting minutes.

# Project Reporting    PAGE 385

A big part of managing communications focuses on project reporting, which involves communicating to stakeholders about how the project is going. Much of that information comes from work performance reports, an output of the Monitor and Control Project Work process. It also involves asking for feedback from stakeholders to ensure they have received the information they need and have understood it, and to determine whether they need more. This communication may take the form of presentations, blog updates, or reports, as outlined in the communications management plan. There probably is not much here that you do not already know, but make sure you remember the following:

- Reports should provide the kinds of information and the level of detail required by stakeholders.
- Reports should be designed for the needs of the project.
- Use the most appropriate communication method when sending information.
- Reports should include measurements against the performance measurement baseline set in the project management plan. For the exam, it is expected that a project manager will have this information and will communicate it to their stakeholders.
- Reports must be truthful and not hide what is really going on. This seems logical, but because of scandals related to untruthful reporting from companies around the world, there may be a few questions on the exam describing such situations.
- Cost, schedule, scope, and quality performance (not just schedule) should be reported.
- Reports help team members know where they need to recommend and implement corrective actions.
- Reporting performance includes looking into the future. Using forecasts, the team and sponsor can determine what preventive actions are needed.
- Feedback from stakeholders who receive reports as part of this process should be analyzed to allow for tailoring of future communications to better meet the needs of stakeholders.

There are different types of reports used in project management. For the exam, think in terms of a large project, and recognize that a project manager might issue the following types of reports:

- **Status report**  This report describes where the project currently stands in relation to the performance measurement baseline.
- **Progress report**  A progress report describes what has been accomplished.
- **Trend report**[4]  This report examines project results over time to see if performance is improving or deteriorating.
- **Forecasting report**[5]  This report predicts future project status and performance.
- **Variance report**[6]  A variance report compares actual results to baselines.
- **Earned value report**[7]  An earned value report integrates scope, cost, and schedule measurements to assess project performance.
- **Lessons learned documentation**  Reports on performance are used as lessons learned for future projects.

The Manage Communications process results in the distribution of project communications, such as performance reports, status reports, and presentations, as well as other forms of communications. The communications management plan may be updated to reflect changes in the approach to managing communications on the project. The stakeholder engagement plan and stakeholder register may be updated to reflect changes in stakeholder communications requirements or changes in the project's strategy to fulfill their requirements. Issues regarding communications are documented in the issue log and, possibly, in the lessons learned register. The project schedule may need to be changed to accommodate implementation of changes to the communications management process.

## Monitor Communications  PAGE 388

| | |
|---|---|
| **Process** | Monitor Communications |
| **Process Group** | Monitoring & Controlling |
| **Knowledge Area** | Communications Management |

In the Monitor Communications process, the project manager and team assess how communications are going throughout the project to ensure information is flowing as planned—in the right way, to the right people, and at the right time—to effectively keep stakeholders informed and maintain the desired levels of stakeholder engagement. The communications management plan provides details on how to measure the effectiveness and efficiency of communications. If you're not familiar with formal data collection and evaluation techniques, you'll need to think about how you would use them on a large project.

This process involves measuring to determine whether the communications management plan is being followed and whether communications are meeting the needs of the stakeholders. If not, you need to identify where communication is breaking down, and then respond and adjust as necessary to meet the stakeholders' communication needs. How can you tell if communication is breaking down? In addition to the metrics you've established in your communications management plan, you'll need to rely on some soft skills. Some problems will be obvious. People will let you know, for example, if they're not getting the reports or information they're meant to receive. Or you'll know people aren't reading meeting minutes if they're not following up on action items. But you'll also benefit from encouraging stakeholders to tell you whether the project communications are meeting their needs.

As mentioned earlier, you should ask stakeholders for feedback on the reports and other communications they receive. Also, project team members should report any communication problems they experience, and help to identify ways communications can be improved on the project.

**Exercise**   Test yourself! Based on what you've learned, do you have a sense of what you need in order to monitor communications and why? For this exercise, we'll give you the inputs (what you need to monitor communications); you'll need to determine how they are used in the Monitor Communications process.

| Input | How Is It Used in Monitor Communications? |
|---|---|
| Project management plan | |
| Project communications | |
| Issue log | |
| Lessons learned register | |
| Work performance data | |
| Enterprise environmental factors | |
| Organizational process assets | |

## Answer

| Input | How Is It Used in Monitor Communications? |
|---|---|
| Project management plan | The communications management plan and other pieces of the project management plan are important to this process because they allow you to compare actual communication on the project against planned communication. They provide details on what needs to be distributed, why, how, when, and to whom, along with information on roles and responsibilities. |
| Project communications | You'll need to compare the actual project communications to the communications management plan. How do the various reports and other communications hold up against what you planned? Are they giving you the intended results? |
| Issue log | An issue log can be used to document and track issues on the project—areas of confusion, disagreement, conflict, and concern that require attention. It is also updated to reflect resolution of those issues. The issue log helps you assess the causes of the issues and their impacts on the project; it can also help when planning corrective actions. This is a useful tool that lets you capture and communicate about issues, so you're handling them proactively rather than reactively, with the goal of preventing problems and change requests. |
| Lessons learned register | Actively documenting lessons learned during a project can help you learn from previous problems, and avoid repeating the same mistakes. Lessons learned should be shared with other ongoing projects as appropriate. They become part of the historical records of the project and the organization's lessons learned repository, and thereby provide the benefit of past experience with communications issues to future projects. |

| Input | How Is It Used in Monitor Communications? |
|---|---|
| Work performance data | Work performance data is raw communications data about what has occurred during a project. The data can help you measure the efficiency and effectiveness of communications against planned metrics. You can also use the data in root cause analysis to evaluate the cause of poor communications or to analyze variances from the plan to determine if changes are necessary. |
| Enterprise environmental factors | Organizational culture, existing communications tools and systems, and common practices for communicating are influencing factors that need to be considered when evaluating the effectiveness of communications and the communications management plan. |
| Organizational process assets | You need to refer to your organization's available or required procedures, reporting formats, standards, tools, and security policies related to communication to make sure communications are meeting organizational expectations. |

Monitoring communications will result in work performance information (an analysis of raw work performance data), possible change requests, and possible updates to the project management plan and project documents.

This concludes the Communications Management chapter. For the exam, keep in mind that communication is essential to success and affects all areas of a project. Poor communication can cause major problems and rework. Therefore, a project manager should take a structured approach to communication by creating a communications management plan. As the project work is being done, the project manager and the project stakeholders need to follow the communications management plan to distribute information about the project, make sure communication is flowing as planned, and adjust the communications approach as necessary.

## Practice Exam

1. A team member has been late to several recent team meetings, and the last two deliverables he submitted were not acceptable. The project manager decides he can no longer wait for things to improve and must address the issue with the team member. What is the best form of communication for addressing this problem?
    A. Formal written communication
    B. Formal verbal communication
    C. Informal written communication
    D. Informal verbal communication

2. Extensive use of _____ communication is most likely to aid in solving complex problems.
    A. Formal verbal
    B. Informal written
    C. Formal written
    D. Nonverbal

3. The new project manager has a team including several individuals for whom English is not their first language. He frequently uses technical jargon from his former company, which is unfamiliar to these team members, when discussing work activities with his team members. The most likely result of communication blockers is that:
    A. The project is delayed.
    B. The trust level is enhanced.
    C. Conflict occurs.
    D. Senior management is displeased.

4. Communications are often enhanced when the sender _____ the receiver.
    A. Speaks up to
    B. Uses gestures when speaking to
    C. Speaks slowly to
    D. Shows concern for the perspective of

5. Formal written correspondence with the customer is required when:
    A. Defects are detected.
    B. The customer requests additional work not covered under contract.
    C. The project has a schedule slippage that includes changes to the critical path.
    D. The project has cost overruns.

6. You are managing a project on which considerable negotiations will be involved. You are confident that these negotiations will go well and that all agreements will be finalized into formal, written contracts. When you are engaged in negotiations, nonverbal communication skills are of:
    A. Little importance
    B. Major importance
    C. Importance only when cost and schedule objectives are involved
    D. Importance to ensure you win the negotiation

© 2018 RMC Publications, Inc.™ • 952.846.4484 • info@rmcls.com • www.rmcls.com

7. A large, one-year telecommunications project is about halfway done when you take the place of the previous project manager. The project involves three different sellers and a project team of 30 people. You would like to see the project's communications requirements and what technology is being used to aid in project communications. Where will you find this information?

    A. The stakeholder management plan
    B. The information distribution plan
    C. The bar chart
    D. The communications management plan

8. Changes to some project deliverables have been documented in the project management plan. These changes, along with other project information, have been distributed according to the communications management plan. One stakeholder expressed surprise to the project manager upon hearing of a documented change to a project deliverable. All stakeholders received the communication providing notification of the change. What should the project manager do?

    A. Determine why the stakeholder did not receive the information, and let him know when it was published.
    B. Ask the functional manager why the stakeholder did not understand his responsibility.
    C. Review the communications management plan, and make revisions if necessary.
    D. Address the situation in the next steering committee meeting, so others do not miss published changes.

9. Communication is key to the success of a project. As the project manager, you had three stakeholders with whom you needed to communicate. Therefore, you had six channels of communication. A new stakeholder has been added with whom you also need to communicate. How many communication channels do you have now?

    A. 7
    B. 10
    C. 12
    D. 16

10. Two people are arguing about what needs to be done to complete a work package. In addition to the words being spoken, if the project manager wants to know what is going on, she should pay most attention to:

    A. What is being said and when
    B. What is being said, who is saying it, and the time of day
    C. Physical mannerisms and when during the schedule this discussion is taking place
    D. The pitch and tone of their voices, along with their gestures

11. A project manager has a project team consisting of people in four countries. The project is very important to the company, and the project manager is concerned about its success. The length of the project schedule is acceptable. What type of communication should he use?

    A. Informal verbal communication
    B. Formal written communication
    C. Formal verbal communication
    D. Informal written communication

12. The project team meeting is not going well. Many attendees are talking at the same time, there are people who are not participating, and many topics are being discussed at random. Which of the following rules for effective meetings is not being adhered to?

    A. Demonstrate courtesy and consideration of each other, and control who is allowed to speak.
    B. Schedule meetings in advance.
    C. Have a purpose for the meeting, with the right people in attendance.
    D. Create and publish an agenda and a set of rules for controlling the meeting.

13. You have just been assigned as project manager for a large manufacturing project. This one-year project is about halfway done. It involves five different sellers and 20 members of your company on the project team. You want to quickly review where the project now stands. Which of the following reports would be the most helpful in finding such information?

    A. Work status
    B. Progress
    C. Forecast
    D. Communications

14. A team member is visiting the manufacturing plant of one of the suppliers. Which of the following is the most important thing to be done in any telephone calls the project manager might make to the team member?

    A. Ask the team member to repeat back what the project manager says.
    B. Review the list of contact information for all stakeholders.
    C. Ask the team member to look for change requests.
    D. Review the upcoming meeting schedule.

15. A project manager overhears a conversation between two stakeholders who are discussing how unhappy they are with the impacts of the project on their own departments. Stakeholder A asks if the project is on time, and stakeholder B replies that the SPI is 1.05. Stakeholder A asks if the project manager for the project knows of stakeholder B's concern. Stakeholder B responds that he is not sure. What is the best thing for the project manager to do?

    A. Make sure the stakeholders are aware that the project manager overheard. Then ask them to direct any questions to the project manager in writing.
    B. Make a presentation to all the stakeholders regarding the status of the project.
    C. Send both stakeholders a copy of the issue log, and ask for additional comments.
    D. Arrange a meeting with both stakeholders to allow them to voice any concerns they may have.

16. Things have been going well on the project. The work authorization system has allowed people to know when to start work, and the issue log has helped keep track of stakeholders' concerns. The sponsor has expressed his appreciation for the team members' efforts by hosting a milestone party. The project manager gets a call from a team member saying the results from the completion of her activity's predecessor are two days late. Which of the following reasons would best describe why this occurred?

    A. The project manager was focusing on the sponsor's needs.
    B. Functional management was not included in the communications management plan.
    C. The successor activities should have been monitored, not the predecessors.
    D. The right people were not invited to the milestone party.

17. A project manager has just been assigned a team comprised of team members from many countries including Brazil, Japan, the United States, and Britain. What is her best tool for success?
    A. The responsibility assignment matrix (RAM)
    B. The teleconference
    C. Team communication with the WBS
    D. Well-developed interpersonal skills

18. The project has 13 team members and affects more than 15 departments in the organization. Because the project is 20 percent complete to date and the team has had successful performance reports from five of the affected departments, the project manager holds a party to celebrate. The project manager invites key stakeholders from all of the departments to the party in order to give those providing good reviews an informal opportunity to communicate good things to those departments that have not yet been affected by the project. At the party, the project manager walks around to try to discover any relevant information that would help her make the project even more successful. She happens to hear a manager of one of the departments talking about setting up more regular meetings on the project.

    The best thing for the project manager to do would be to first:
    A. Record the effectiveness of the party in the project lessons learned.
    B. Review the effectiveness of the project's communications management plan.
    C. Hold a meeting of all the stakeholders to discuss their concerns.
    D. Make sure the manager has a copy of the communications management plan so that he is reminded that such concerns should be sent to the project manager.

19. The requirements of many stakeholders were not approved for inclusion in your project. Therefore, you had a difficult time gaining formal approval of the project management plan. The stakeholders argued and held up the project while they held meeting after meeting about their requirements. The project was finally approved and work began six months ago. All of the following would be good preventive actions to implement except:
    A. Keep a file of what requirements were not included in the project.
    B. Make sure the change control process is not used as a vehicle to add the requirements back into the project.
    C. Maintain an issue log.
    D. Hold meetings with the stakeholders to go over the work that will not be added to the project.

20. The project manager is expecting a deliverable to be submitted by email from a team member today. At the end of the day, the project manager contacts the team member to notify him that it has not been received. The team member apologizes and explains that he was not able to email the deliverable, and it was sent through the mail instead. The team member goes on to remind the project manager that he had informed the project manager during a phone conversation that this would occur. "Was that the conversation we had when I told you I could not hear you well due to poor cell phone coverage?" asks the project manager. "Yes," replies the team member. What could have been done to avoid this problem?
    A. Verbal communication
    B. Adding to the issue log after the phone call
    C. Better attention to determining communications requirements
    D. Feedback during the communication

21. A project manager at a large consulting firm is asked to report on the actual project results versus planned results. The project is going well, and the marketing department wants to see if the current results can be used in a future marketing campaign. This project manager should prepare a:

    A. Trend report
    B. Forecasting report
    C. Status report
    D. Variance report

22. A successful project manager is required to use knowledge, skills, and abilities in a number of different areas of expertise. Planning ability is very important, as is the ability to execute, manage and control the project according to the project management plan. Which area of expertise is most important for a project manager?

    A. Communication
    B. Team building
    C. Technical expertise
    D. Project control

23. The project manager is trying to recall a stakeholder's preferred communication method. Where can she find that information?

    A. RACI chart
    B. Stakeholder engagement assessment matrix
    C. Stakeholder engagement plan
    D. Resource management plan

© 2018 RMC Publications, Inc.™ • 952.846.4484 • info@rmcls.com • www.rmcls.com

## Answers

1. **Answer** D

   **Explanation** It is best to start this discussion informally. The project manager should also document the problem and include a summary of the conversation with the team member. If informal communication does not solve the problem, formal written communication is the next course of action.

2. **Answer** C

   **Explanation** Formal written communication allows your words to be documented and ensures they will go to everyone in the same form. When there are complex problems, you want everyone to receive the same information.

3. **Answer** C

   **Explanation** Communication blockers can range from a lack of cultural sensitivity to a failure to provide concise messages. Blockers cause miscommunication and can lead to disagreement and confusion. The major result of communication blockers and miscommunication as a whole is conflict.

4. **Answer** D

   **Explanation** An understanding of the receiver's perspective allows the sender to direct the communication to meet the receiver's needs.

5. **Answer** B

   **Explanation** Everything we do is more formal in a procurement environment than in other project activities. Therefore, formal written communication is required when the customer requests work not covered under the contract.

6. **Answer** B

   **Explanation** Nonverbal communication carries a significant portion of the message you send. With so much at stake, nonverbal communication is of major importance.

7. **Answer** D

   **Explanation** This information is found in the communications management plan.

8. **Answer** C

   **Explanation** The question states that all stakeholders received the information, so the issue is not that this stakeholder did not receive it. The problem presented here illustrates that there is something missing in the communications management plan. The best answer is to review the communications management plan in order to prevent future problems and to find any instances of similar problems.

9. **Answer** B

   **Explanation** Did you remember that the project manager needs to be included when calculating the number of communication channels? Therefore, there are actually four stakeholders to begin with and six channels of communication. The question is asking how many total channels of communication you have with a team of five people. The formula is $[n \times (n - 1)]/2$ or $(5 \times 4)/2 = 10$.

10. **Answer** D

    **Explanation** Nonverbal communication represents a major part of all communication. The choice including verbal communication (pitch and tone) as well as gestures is the best choice.

11. **Answer** B

    **Explanation** Because of the differences in culture and the distance between team members, formal written communication is needed.

436

12. **Answer** D

    **Explanation** Courtesy and consideration is not a "rule" for effective meetings. Since there is no indication that the meeting was not scheduled in advance or that there isn't a purpose, these cannot be the best answers. "Discussed at random" implies no agenda. If an agenda is issued beforehand, people will follow the outline and should not need random discussions.

13. **Answer** B

    **Explanation** The key word is quickly. The status report is too detailed for a quick look. The forecast report only looks into the future. The progress report summarizes project status, and would be the most helpful for a quick review.

14. **Answer** A

    **Explanation** There are many choices that are reasonably correct. Look for the most immediate need. Here, the team member is in a manufacturing environment. That means communications will most likely be blocked by noise. It is best for the project manager to ask the team member to repeat back what he says, to ensure the team member correctly heard what the project manager communicated.

15. **Answer** D

    **Explanation** This is another question with more than one right answer. Would asking for something in writing be the best way to communicate? In this particular situation, asking for the concern to be put into writing might alienate the stakeholders. The issue log is where the issue should be listed, but the situation does not say if the project manager knows what the stakeholders' concern is. Therefore, using the issue log cannot be the best choice. Why not make a presentation to all the stakeholders regarding the status of the project? The concern was being voiced only by stakeholders A and B, so it is unnecessary to involve all the stakeholders. This problem would likely require informal verbal communication to discover the real problem. Arranging a meeting with the concerned stakeholders is therefore the best choice.

16. **Answer** B

    **Explanation** Since there is no information about the sponsor or his needs in this situation, focusing on his needs cannot be best. The statement that successor activities should have been watched, rather than the predecessors, is not a correct statement. A project manager should watch both predecessor and successor activities. Attendance at the party and the issue at hand (the late results) are not related. Often forgotten in communications management plans are the managers of team members (functional management, in a matrix organization). Including the managers of team members in communications planning, requirements gathering, risk management, and other areas of project management helps make the project better. In addition, it helps the functional managers manage their resources effectively. If the functional manager of the team member assigned to the predecessor activity had been included in the project planning processes, he would have known when the team member was needed to do work for the project and the impact, if any, of delay. The communications management plan should also have included a method to communicate potential delays.

17. **Answer** D

    **Explanation** Working with people from different cultures who may have different values and beliefs necessitates an understanding of both basic definitions and areas of cultural impact. Project managers need good interpersonal skills and a willingness to adapt to other cultures.

18. **Answer** B

    **Explanation** Many of these choices could be done, but ask yourself, "What is the most effective thing to do?" The party may well generate lessons learned, and recording them would certainly be a good idea, but the question asked what to do first. There is a more immediate issue—the manager. Meeting with all the stakeholders could be useful, but there is only one stakeholder, the manager, who definitely has an issue. Besides, a good project manager would be holding regular meetings with the stakeholders already. Making sure the manager has a copy of the communications management plan might be a good idea, as the manager apparently is not communicating with the project manager. However, this would not be enough to ensure the manager does communicate.

    The manager is, in effect, saying he is not getting the information he needs, which is causing him to suggest more meetings. However, too many meetings can be a problem on projects. A great project manager does not just add meetings, but rather solves the real problem in the best way.

    A goal of communications management is to get information to those who need it. The project manager may decide to adjust her communications management process by changing the format of a report or sending existing reports to the manager with the issue, rather than adding meetings. Therefore, the correct choice is to review the methods of providing project information to the stakeholders.

19. **Answer** D

    **Explanation** This issue should be over, but since there were so many meetings and arguments about the requirements being removed, it is unlikely the issue will be dropped by the stakeholders. However, as it has not come up again and the project was started six months ago, spending time in a meeting is excessive. The other choices are easier, have less impact on the project, and are, therefore, things that could be done.

20. **Answer** D

    **Explanation** The pitch and tone of voice (verbal communication) is not relevant here, as the project manager could not even hear all that was being said. There were no issues recognized after the conversation, so none could be added to the issue log. This issue is not related to communications requirements, so that choice cannot be best. Saying, "I am not sure I properly heard what you said," during the conversation or repeating the message back to the team member would have prevented this problem. Giving and requesting feedback during the communication is the best option.

21. **Answer** D

    **Explanation** This situation describes the need to compare. A trend report shows performance over time. A forecasting report looks only to the future. A status report is generally static (relating to a moment in time). The only choice that compares project results is a variance analysis.

22. **Answer** A

    **Explanation** Project managers can spend 90 percent of their time communicating, so the correct choice must be communication.

23. **Answer** C

    **Explanation** Stakeholders' individual communication requirements are documented in the stakeholder engagement plan.

# Risk Management

## ELEVEN

Let's start this chapter with a story. A project manager was working on a hardware/software installation in an area where hurricanes are a relatively frequent occurrence when a hurricane struck.

Not long after the hurricane was over, the project manager was telling people what a great job his team had done and how quickly they had recovered from the disaster. Would you have been proud of yourself if you were the project manager? Before you answer, consider the following information:

- The activity the team was working on required three days to complete.

- The project manager had warning that the hurricane was coming.

- They had to recover from the disaster.

Instead of being excited about how quickly his team was able to recover from the hurricane, the project manager—and the sponsor—should have questioned the wisdom of scheduling the implementation at a time when there was a strong probability of a hurricane coming.

A project manager's work should not focus on dealing with problems; it should focus on preventing them. Had the project manager performed risk management[1] on his project, he would have considered the threat of a hurricane and worked with his team as part of the project planning effort to identify possible actions to take if a hurricane was forecast for implementation weekend. Then, when one actually was forecast, the team could have reacted according to the plan, probably moving the implementation to another weekend and avoiding the damage and rework that resulted from the disaster. This is the value of risk management.

## QUICKTEST

- Definition of risk management
- Risk management process
- Threats
- Opportunities
- Risk factors
- Risk appetite
- Risk threshold
- Risk averse
- Inputs to risk management
- Risk register
- Risk management plan
- Risk report
- Risk categories
- Risk breakdown structure (RBS)
- Overall project risk
- Individual project risk
- Types of risk
- Probability and impact matrix
  - Watch list
  - Variance and trend analysis
- Risk urgency assessment
- Risk response strategies
  - Avoid
  - Mitigate
  - Transfer
  - Exploit
  - Share
- Enhance
- Accept
- Escalate
- Residual risks
- Contingency plans
- Fallback plans
- Risk owner
- Secondary risks
- Risk trigger
- Workarounds
- Reserve analysis
- Risk reviews
- Risk audits
- Simulation
- Checklist analysis
- Assumption and constraint analysis
- Documentation reviews
- Risk data quality assessment
- Prompt list
- Monte Carlo analysis
- SWOT analysis
- Sensitivity analysis
- Decision tree
- Expected value
- Expected monetary value
- Common risk management mistakes
- Representations of risk uncertainty

439

| INITIATING | PLANNING (This is the only process group with a set order.) | EXECUTING | MONITORING & CONTROLLING | CLOSING |
|---|---|---|---|---|
| Select project manager | **Determine development approach, life cycle, and how you will plan for each knowledge area** | Execute work according to the project management plan | **Take action to monitor and control the project** | Confirm work is done to requirements |
| Determine company culture and existing systems | Define and prioritize requirements | Produce product deliverables (product scope) | Measure performance against performance measurement baseline | Complete final procurement closure |
| Collect processes, procedures, and historical information | Create project scope statement | Gather work performance data | **Measure performance against other metrics in the project management plan** | Gain final acceptance of product |
| Divide large projects into phases or smaller projects | Assess what to purchase and create procurement documents | **Request changes** | **Analyze and evaluate data and performance** | Complete financial closure |
| Understand business case and benefits management plan | Determine planning team | Implement only approved changes | **Determine if variances warrant a corrective action or other change request(s)** | Hand off completed product |
| Uncover initial requirements, assumptions, risks, constraints, and existing agreements | Create WBS and WBS dictionary | Continuously improve; perform progressive elaboration | **Influence factors that cause change** | Solicit customer's feedback about the project |
| Assess project and product feasibility within the given constraints | Create activity list | Follow processes | **Request changes** | Complete final performance reporting |
| Create measurable objectives and success criteria | Create network diagram | Determine whether quality plan and processes are correct and effective | Perform integrated change control | Index and archive records |
| Develop project charter | Estimate resource requirements | Perform quality audits and issue quality reports | Approve or reject changes | Gather final lessons learned and update knowledge bases |
| Identify stakeholders and determine their expectations, interest, influence, and impact | Estimate activity durations and costs | Acquire final team and physical resources | **Update project management plan and project documents** | |
| Request changes | Determine critical path | Manage people | Inform stakeholders of all change request results | |
| Develop assumption log | Develop schedule | Evaluate team and individual performance; provide training | Monitor stakeholder engagement | |
| Develop stakeholder register | Develop budget | Hold team-building activities | Confirm configuration compliance | |
| | Determine quality standards, processes, and metrics | Give recognition and rewards | Create forecasts | |
| | **Determine team charter and all roles and responsibilities** | **Use issue logs** | Gain customer's acceptance of interim deliverables | |
| | Plan communications and stakeholder engagement | **Facilitate conflict resolution** | Perform quality control | |
| | **Perform risk identification, qualitative and quantitative risk analysis, and risk response planning** | Release resources as work is completed | **Perform risk reviews, reassessments, and audits** | |
| | **Go back—iterations** | Send and receive information, and solicit feedback | **Manage reserves** | |
| | Finalize procurement strategy and documents | Report on project performance | Manage, evaluate, and close procurements | |
| | Create change and configuration management plans | Facilitate stakeholder engagement and manage expectations | Evaluate use of physical resources | |
| | **Finalize all management plans** | Hold meetings | | |
| | **Develop realistic and sufficient project management plan and baselines** | Evaluate sellers; negotiate and contract with sellers | | |
| | Gain formal approval of the plan | **Use and share project knowledge** | | |
| | Hold kickoff meeting | **Execute contingency plans** | | |
| | **Request changes** | **Update project management plan and project documents** | | |

## Rita's Process Chart™
## Risk Management
Where are we in the project management process?

Think about your own projects. How would it feel if you could say, "No problem; we anticipated this, and we have a plan in place that will resolve it," whenever a problem occurs? How good would you look to your manager and sponsor? How much time and money would you save that would have otherwise been spent addressing the problem? How much less stress would you have in your life? Performing risk management helps prevent many problems on projects and helps make other problems less likely or less impactful. Conversely, effective risk management helps to increase the probability and/or impact of positive risks, or opportunities. And when you eliminate threats and increase opportunities, project schedule and cost estimates can be decreased, reflecting the results of risk management efforts. These are the benefits of risk management and the reasons risk management is a required part of proper project management.

If you do not practice risk management on your projects, this may be a difficult chapter for you. The exam asks questions on this topic at a sophisticated level, and you need to recognize that risk management activities are an integral part of a project manager's daily work. The everyday impact of risk management on projects and the project manager is an incredibly important concept that you need understand before you take the exam. Through risk management, the project manager can stay in control of the project, rather than being controlled by it.

The exam tests your knowledge of the process of risk management. This process is very logical. You may be given a situation on the exam and then asked to determine which risk management process is being performed, based on the information provided. So, you must understand the actions you and your team should take in each part of the risk management process. Also expect questions on the exam that require you to analyze a situation and determine what should be done next.

If you want additional training in risk management, please consider our online or instructor-led risk management courses. Find more information at our website, rmcls.com.

We cannot stress the value of risk management enough. This chapter will provide the overview of this topic that you need for the exam. You should realize, however, there are more tools and techniques for real-world risk management than are covered here. If you are like many project managers and do not currently practice risk management on your projects, we encourage you to seek more knowledge or training on risk management. Proper risk management can greatly improve the efficiency and effectiveness of your projects and reduce stress for you and your team.

The following should help you understand how each part of risk management fits into the overall project management process:

| The Risk Management Process | Done During |
| --- | --- |
| Plan Risk Management | Planning process group |
| Identify Risks | Planning process group |
| Perform Qualitative Risk Analysis | Planning process group |
| Perform Quantitative Risk Analysis | Planning process group |
| Plan Risk Responses | Planning process group |
| Implement Risk Responses | Executing process group |
| Monitor Risks | Monitoring and controlling process group |

**Defining the Concepts**   As you read this chapter, remember the basic, yet very important, concepts discussed next. Make sure you are prepared to deal with exam questions that test your knowledge of such concepts at an expert level.

### Risk Management  PAGE 395  Risk management is the process of identifying, evaluating, and planning responses to events, both positive and negative, that might occur throughout the course of a project. Through risk management, you increase the probability and impact of opportunities on the project (positive events), while decreasing the probability and impact of threats to the project (negative events).

Risks are identified and managed starting in initiating and are kept up to date while the project is underway. The project manager and the team look at what has happened on the project, the current status of the project, and what is yet to come—and then reassess the potential threats and opportunities.

Also, given the iterative nature of project management, a response strategy for a newly discovered risk may create other project risks, which must be identified and managed. You must be prepared for exam questions that test your knowledge and understanding of these concepts.

### Threats and Opportunities  A risk event is something identified in advance that may or may not happen. If it does happen, it can have positive or negative impacts on the project. Project managers often just focus on threats—what can go wrong and negatively impact the project. Do not forget that there can also be positive impacts—good risks, called opportunities! Opportunities can include such things as:

- If we can combine orders for the ZYX equipment to buy more than 20 items at once, the cost will be 20 percent less per item than planned.

- If we provide a training class to improve efficiency, work package number 3.4 could be completed two days faster than expected.

- If we can obtain a resource with more experience and a higher level of productivity in May, work on the critical path activity 4.7.2 could be done 10 percent faster.

Up to 90 percent of the threats identified and investigated in the risk management process can be eliminated by changing how the project work is planned and performed. Strategies such as using an adaptive life cycle, outsourcing some or all of the work, or selecting more skilled people within the organization to do the work may reduce risk on a project.

### Uncertainty  Uncertainty is a lack of knowledge about an event that reduces confidence in conclusions drawn from the data. The work that needs to be done, the cost, the time, the quality needs, the communications needs, etc. can be uncertain. The investigation of uncertainties may help identify risks.

### Risk Factors  When assessing risk, it's necessary to determine the following:

- The probability that a risk event will occur (how likely)
- The range of possible outcomes (impact or amount at stake)
- Expected timing for it to occur in the project life cycle (when)
- The anticipated frequency of risk events from that source (how often)

### Risk Appetites and Thresholds  These terms refer to the level of risk an individual or group is willing to accept. Risk *appetite* (which is also referred to as risk tolerance) is a general, high-level description of the level of risk acceptable to an individual or an organization. For example, a sponsor is willing to accept little risk to the schedule on this project. Risk *threshold* refers to the specific point at which risk becomes unacceptable. For example, the sponsor will not accept a risk of the schedule being delayed 15 days or longer. Risk appetites and thresholds vary depending on the individual or organization and the risk area. For example, an organization may have more tolerance for cost-related risks than for risks that affect customer satisfaction or their reputation in the marketplace. Risk areas can include any project constraints (scope, schedule, cost, quality, etc.), as well as risks to reputation, customer satisfaction, and other intangibles.

442

Look for information about individual and organizational risk appetites and thresholds to answer situational exam questions related to risk response[2] strategies.

### Risk Averse
Someone who does not want to be negatively impacted by threats is *risk averse*.

### Inputs to Risk Management
Risk management is very process-oriented. Expect to see risk management input and output questions on the exam; however, you should not need to memorize the inputs and outputs. As you go through this chapter, keep in mind that many of the inputs to each risk management process are the outputs of the processes that came before it.

Remember, inputs are merely, "What do I need to do this well?" or "What do I need before I can begin…?"

The next exercise will help you understand the inputs to the risk management effort. If you know Rita's Process Chart™, you should not need to spend much time studying these inputs.

### Exercise
Test yourself! Explain why each of the following inputs to risk management is needed before you can adequately perform the risk management process. This is an important test. The answer table includes what you should know for the exam. Note that definitions of these inputs will not be repeated later in this chapter.

| | Inputs to Risk Management | This Is an Input of What Process? | Why Is This Input Needed, and What is Included Within This Input? |
|---|---|---|---|
| 1 | Project charter | | |
| 2 | Project management plan | | |

| | Inputs to Risk Management | This Is an Input of What Process? | Why Is This Input Needed, and What is Included Within This Input? |
|---|---|---|---|
| 3 | Project documents | | |
| 4 | Enterprise environmental factors | | |
| 5 | Organizational process assets | | |
| 6 | Agreements | | |
| 7 | Procurement documentation | | |
| 8 | Work performance data and reports | | |

444

**Answer**   There can be many answers. Here are some possible ones.

| | Inputs to Risk Management | This Is an Input of What Process? | Why Is This Input Needed, and What Is Included Within This Input? |
|---|---|---|---|
| 1 | Project charter | Plan Risk Management | The project charter indicates the initial, high-level risks identified on the project and helps you see if the overall project objectives and constraints are generally risky or not. The charter also helps identify risks based on what is and what is not included in the project. |
| 2 | Project management plan | Plan Risk Management | The project management plan includes: individual knowledge area management plans; additional plans for configuration, change, and requirements; baselines for time, cost, and scope; information on the development approach and project life cycle; and the performance measurement baseline. These components are used in all the risk processes because the information included is beneficial in planning for, dealing with, and monitoring risk on projects.<br><br>The following specific management plans and components of the project management plan listed below are frequently used during risk management. |
| | | Identify Risks | **Requirements management plan**  The requirements management plan may include a list of the project objectives along with identified prioritization and an indication of the most critical opportunities and threats. The approach to how all the requirements are gathered, documented, and prioritized will provide vital information for the risk team. |
| | | Identify Risks | **Schedule management plan**  The aggressiveness of schedule objectives provides an indication of the risk of meeting those objectives. Schedule-related assumptions may indicate areas of uncertainty. |
| | | Identify Risks | **Cost management plan**  This plan details cost processes and assumptions that may indicate areas of uncertainty. |
| | | Identify Risks, Plan Risk Responses | **Resource management plan**  The resource management plan describes what resources are needed, identifies the resources available to the project, outlines assumptions, and explains how the resources will be managed. Knowing this information will help you to identify risks related to resources and assign allocation of resources to responses. |

445

| Inputs to Risk Management | This Is an Input of What Process? | Why Is This Input Needed, and What Is Included Within This Input? |
|---|---|---|
| | Identify Risks, Perform Qualitative Risk Analysis, Perform Quantitative Risk Analysis, Plan Risk Responses, Implement Risk Responses, Monitor Risks | **Risk management plan** The risk management plan will define the project's approach to risk management and detail how risk management efforts will be conducted throughout the project, with specifics about the methods and tools to be used. |
| | Identify Risks | **Quality management plan** The requirements and assumptions included in this plan—along with information on the degree of confidence that the requirements will be achieved and the metrics that will be measured—will help you identify quality risks. The documented processes in this plan can also help minimize threats or enhance opportunities, and can help you manage risks. |
| | Identify Risks, Perform Quantitative Risk Analysis | **Scope baseline** The scope baseline can help you assess how complex the project will be and what level of risk management effort is appropriate. The baseline includes information about boundaries, acceptance criteria, constraints, and assumptions, which can indicate risks to the project. |
| | Identify Risks, Perform Quantitative Risk Analysis | **Schedule baseline** Use the schedule baseline to find any dates (deliverable deadlines or milestones, for example) that may not be completely determined. Imposed schedule constraints, dependencies between activities, and a lack of clarity regarding milestone dates or estimates are indicators of risk. |
| | Identify Risks, Perform Quantitative Risk Analysis, Plan Risk Responses | **Cost baseline** Use the cost baseline to find any costs (for example, funding requirements) that may not be completely determined. Imposed budget constraints and a lack of clarity regarding funding requirements or cost estimates are indicators of risk. The amount of contingency reserve allocated to respond to risks is another important piece of information. |
| 3 Project documents | | Project documents that can be inputs include things such as registers, logs, estimates, requirements, and forecasts. The following are project documents associated with risk management. |

| Inputs to Risk Management | This Is an Input of What Process? | Why Is This Input Needed, and What Is Included Within This Input? |
|---|---|---|
| | Plan Risk Management, Identify Risks, Perform Qualitative Risk Analysis, Plan Risk Responses | **Stakeholder register** Stakeholders will view the project from different perspectives and thus will be able to see risks that the team cannot. Stakeholders are involved in many aspects of risk management. |
| | Identify Risks, Plan Risk Responses, Implement Risk Responses, Monitor Risks | **Lessons learned register** The lessons learned register provides information about what worked and what didn't work on the current project and on past, similar projects. Lessons learned can be used to reduce the risk of repeating the same mistakes and take full advantage of potential opportunities. |
| | Identify Risks, Perform Qualitative Risk Analysis, Perform Quantitative Risk Analysis | **Assumption log** Reviewing this log to analyze assumptions and constraints will help to identify risks on the project. |
| | Identify Risks, Monitor Risks | **Issue log** Reviewing this log to understand when confusion and disagreement has occurred, or where it is currently occurring on the project, can help to further identify risks on the project. |
| | Identify Risks, Perform Quantitative Risk Analysis | **Cost, duration, and basis of estimates** Knowing the estimates as well as the basis of those estimates helps you determine the risk of the project not meeting the time and cost objectives. |
| | Identify Risks | **Requirements documentation** This list of project requirements can be used to identify requirements that are poorly defined or that present other sources of risk for the project. |
| | Identify Risks, Perform Quantitative Risk Analysis | **Resource requirements** The resource requirements of a project should include some quantitative assessments, which can indicate the level of risk. For example, after reviewing the resource requirements, a project manager has determined there is risk because the project does not have enough resources. |
| | Plan Risk Responses | **Resource calendars** Resource calendars will show a project manager when a resource is available. Review this calendar to verify that all resources are available as scheduled to avoid threats and find opportunities. |

447

| Inputs to Risk Management | This Is an Input of What Process? | Why Is This Input Needed, and What Is Included Within This Input? |
|---|---|---|
| | Perform Qualitative Risk Analysis, Perform Quantitative Risk Analysis, Plan Risk Responses, Implement Risk Responses, Monitor Risks | **Risk register** The risk register is the repository of information on identified risks for the project; as such, it is an important input for prioritizing and analyzing risks, planning and implementing risk responses, and monitoring risks. |
| | Perform Quantitative Risk Analysis, Plan Risk Responses, Implement Risk Responses, Monitor Risks | **Risk report** The risk report is iterated throughout the project, and may include information about overall project risk, risk response strategies, and planned responses to individual risks. This report can also include the number of risks, types of risks, risk trends, metrics, and risk sources. Analysis of this information helps to determine which risks could have the most impact on project risk exposure. |
| | Perform Quantitative Risk Analysis | **Cost and schedule forecasts** Cost forecasts can be compared or reviewed against the cost risk analysis, and the schedule forecasts can be reviewed along with the schedule risk analysis. These comparisons can give you insight into whether the cost and schedule estimates are realistic and likely to be achieved, and they can help you determine any associated risk. |
| | Perform Quantitative Risk Analysis | **Milestone list** The milestone list provides a register of key events that will occur during the project. Use this list, along with the schedule risk analysis, to determine whether or not the schedule is realistic. |
| | Plan Risk Responses | **Project schedule** Use the project schedule to figure out how risk responses will be performed without disrupting project activities. |
| | Plan Risk Responses | **Project team assignments** These assignments list the resources that may be utilized for risk work, such as the agreed-upon risk responses. |
| 4 Enterprise environmental factors | Plan Risk Management, Identify Risks, Perform Qualitative Risk Analysis, Perform Quantitative Risk Analysis, Plan Risk Responses | Knowing the degree of risk the organization is willing to accept—as well as the specific areas for which there is willingness to accept risk (organizational risk appetites, tolerances, and thresholds)—helps you to identify the impact of risks, rank risks, and determine which risk response strategies to use. A company's culture can add or diminish risk and should be considered when identifying risks. |

| | Inputs to Risk Management | This Is an Input of What Process? | Why Is This Input Needed, and What Is Included Within This Input? |
|---|---|---|---|
| 5 | Organizational process assets | Plan Risk Management, Identify Risks, Perform Qualitative Risk Analysis, Perform Quantitative Risk Analysis, Plan Risk Responses, Implement Risk Responses | These records may have information about risks from past, similar projects—including risk categories, formats for stating risks, risk management templates, and lessons learned—that are relevant to managing risk on the current project. Company processes and procedures for project management and risk management, or the lack of such standardized procedures, may help identify additional risks. |
| 6 | Agreements | Identify Risks | Agreements, such as a contract with an external resource, will list information that may relate to or present threats or opportunities. |
| 7 | Procurement documentation | Identify Risks | Procurement documentation provides the answer to questions including the following: How many contracts are there likely to be on the project? What is the level of expertise of those handling the contracts? Was the project manager involved before any contracts were signed? (If not, the project will have more risk and is likely to cost more.) Contracts are a way to mitigate or transfer risks in risk response planning, but they can also create risk if not managed well. |
| 8 | Work performance data and reports | Monitor Risks | Project work generates raw data and measurements (work performance data), which are analyzed to evaluate the impact of the risks that have occurred and the plans that have been implemented, determine if risks should be closed, identify updates to triggers, and look for variance and its relationship to other identified risks. Work performance reports provide the analyzed data from various control processes in a format that can be used to do risk reassessment, reserve analysis, analysis of trends and variance, etc. |

There are a few additional project management plan components that are not specifically listed as inputs to this process within the *PMBOK® Guide* that may have a significant impact when planning risk management:

- **Project background information** Correspondence from before the project was approved, articles written about similar projects, and other such information will help identify risks. (Project background information is part of organizational process assets.)

- **Network diagram** The network diagram is the only place where paths that converge into one activity can be easily seen. Such path convergence makes an activity riskier than if there was no path convergence. The network diagram also helps determine the critical path and any near-critical paths. The tighter the schedule, the more risk the project has. (The network diagram is part of project documents.)

449

- **Communications management plan** The communications management plan can be used to structure communications around risk. It can also help identify risks. The communications management plan helps answer questions such as, "Are there a lot of stakeholders to communicate with?" and "Where in the project are communications so important that communication errors can actually add risk to the project?" There is a strong connection between planning communications and decreasing risk.

## The Risk Management Process
It is very important to understand the risk management process for the exam. You must know what happens when and understand how risk management can change the way projects are managed. On large, properly managed projects where risk management has been an integral part of planning, the following occurs:

- There are no longer huge "fires" to put out every day—they are eliminated with risk response plans.
- Risks are reviewed in every meeting, triggers are monitored, and risks are addressed before they happen.
- Normally, if a risk event does occur, there is a plan in place to deal with it. Hectic meetings to develop responses are a rarity, and are only needed when an unknown risk event occurs and requires the development of a workaround.
- As a result, the project manager has time for efforts such as:
  - Monitoring and controlling the various aspects of the project, looking for deviations and trends to find them early
  - Implementing a reward system
  - Developing the team
  - Keeping stakeholders informed of project progress
  - Staying ahead of the project

 The seven risk management processes are:
- Plan Risk Management
- Identify Risks
- Perform Qualitative Risk Analysis
- Perform Quantitative Risk Analysis
- Plan Risk Responses
- Implement Risk Responses
- Monitor Risks

Although the initiating and planning processes are more likely done in sequence, remember that they are often repeated during the course of the project. Risks can be identified at any time, as can responses to new risks. If a risk is uncovered after the initial risk identification process, it still must be analyzed, and responses must be planned. The risk management process is iterative.

## Plan Risk Management PAGE 401

| | |
|---|---|
| **Process** | Plan Risk Management |
| **Process Group** | Planning |
| **Knowledge Area** | Risk Management |

The project manager, sponsor, team, customer, other stakeholders, and experts may be involved in the Plan Risk Management process. They define how risk management will be structured and performed for the project. Since risk management is critical to the success of a project, wouldn't it be wise to think about how you will approach risk management before you do it? Plan before you act. Part of that planning involves determining at a high level the amount and areas of potential risk on the project. Risk management efforts should be appropriate not only to the size and complexity of the project but also to the experience and skill of the project team. Successful risk management cannot be done with just a standardized checklist of risks from past projects. Although such a checklist can be helpful in creating a plan and identifying risks, the necessary risk management effort needs to be performed on each project.

The Plan Risk Management process answers the question of how much time should be spent on risk management based on the needs of the project. This includes the risk appetite of management and other key stakeholders. This process also identifies who will be involved and how the team will go about performing risk management. Organizational procedures and templates related to risk, such as standard probability and impact matrices, are identified as part of this process and then adapted to the needs of the project.

## Outputs of Plan Risk Management   PAGE 405   When you have completed risk management planning, you should, of course, have a risk management plan.

### Risk Management Plan    The risk management plan may include:

- **Risk strategy**  This is an overall approach to managing risk throughout the life of the project.

- **Methodology**  This section of the plan defines how risk management will be performed to meet the needs of the specific project. Low-priority projects will likely warrant less of a risk management effort than high-priority projects.

- **Roles and responsibilities**  This section explains who will do what risk management work. Did you realize that stakeholders outside the project team may have roles and responsibilities regarding risk management?

- **Funding**  This section includes the cost of the risk management process. Yes, there is a cost of doing risk management, but overall, risk management saves the project time and money by avoiding or reducing threats and by taking advantage of opportunities. This section also includes a plan for utilizing reserves in response to risks on the project.

- **Timing**  This section of the plan talks about when to do risk management for the project. Risk management should start as soon as you have the appropriate inputs and should be repeated throughout the life of the project, since new risks can be identified as the project progresses and the degree of risk can change over the course of a project. Also note that time needs to be allocated in the schedule for risk management activities.

- **Risk categories**  See the discussion of risk categories on the next page.

- **Stakeholder risk appetite/thresholds**  Remember that risk appetite is a high-level description of an individual or group's openness to risk. Thresholds are measurable amounts of risk that an individual or group are willing to accept within a specific category—such as risk to the project schedule, budget, or the achievement of a particular project objective. The risk appetites and thresholds of key stakeholders are documented and considered in the risk management plan. This information is also considered when ranking risks based on probability and impacts, and when prioritizing which risks will be addressed in risk response planning.

- **Definitions of probability and impact**  Would everyone who rates the probability of a particular risk a 7 in qualitative risk analysis mean the same thing? A person who is risk averse might think of 7 as very high, while someone who is risk prone might think of 7 as a low figure. The definitions and the probability and impact matrix (discussed later in this chapter) help standardize these interpretations and also help compare risks between projects.

451

- **Reporting** This section of the plan describes reports related to the risk management effort on the project that will be created, what they will include, and to whom they will be sent. In addition, the composition of the risk register for the project is defined here.

- **Tracking** The tracking section of the plan describes how the risk management process will be audited and how the results of risk management efforts will be documented.

## Risk Categories
A standard list of risk categories can help ensure areas of risk are not forgotten on your projects. These categories are broad, common areas or sources of risk that the company or similar projects have experienced. They can include things such as technology changes, lack of resources, regulatory hurdles, or cultural issues. Organizations and project management offices should maintain standard lists of risk categories that all projects can use to help identify and group individual project risks. When leading risk identification efforts, you should make sure each category is considered. A risk breakdown structure (RBS) is an organizational chart that can help you identify and document risk categories.

Risk can be classified or categorized in many ways, including:

- **External** Regulatory, environmental, or governmental issues; market shifts; problems with project sites, etc.

- **Internal** Changes to schedule or budget; scope changes; inexperienced team members; issues with people, staffing, materials, and equipment, etc.

- **Technical** Changes in technology, technical processes, or interfaces, etc.

- **Commercial** Customer stability, terms and conditions within contracts, vendors, etc.

- **Unforeseeable** Only a small portion of risks (about 10 percent) are actually unforeseeable.

Research has shown over 300 potential categories of risk, including risks caused by:

- The customer
- Lack of project management effort (yes, a lack of project management effort can add risk)
- Lack of knowledge of project management by the project manager and stakeholders
- The customer's customers
- Suppliers
- Resistance to change
- Cultural differences

The following are additional examples of sources of risk:

- **Schedule** "The hardware may arrive earlier than planned, allowing work package XYZ to start three days earlier."

- **Cost** "Because the hardware may arrive later than planned, we may need to extend our lease on the staging area—at a cost of $20,000."

- **Quality** "The concrete may dry to our quality standards before winter weather sets in, allowing us to start successor work packages earlier than planned."

- **Scope** "We might not have correctly defined the scope for the computer installation. If that proves true, we will have to add work packages at a cost of $20,000."

- **Resources** "Our designer may be called away to work on the new project everyone is so excited about. If that occurs, we will have to use someone else, and our schedule will slip between 100 and 275 hours."

- **Customer satisfaction (stakeholder satisfaction)** "There is a chance the customer will tell us they are unhappy with the XYZ deliverable, causing at least a 20 percent increase in time to rework the deliverable and test plans."

Expect the phrases "sources of risk" and "risk categories" to be used interchangeably on the exam.

In addition to risk categories, risks can be classified under two main types:

- **Business risk**  Risk of a gain or loss
- **Pure (insurable) risk**  Only a risk of loss (such as fire, theft, or personal injury, etc.)

You may also see references to risks described as non-event risks, which fall under the following categories:

- **Variability**  Risks caused by the inability to predict future changes
- **Ambiguity**  Risks caused by a lack of understanding

## Identify Risks  PAGE 409

> **Process**  Identify Risks
> **Process Group**  Planning
> **Knowledge Area**  Risk Management

In this process, risks to the project are identified. This effort should involve all stakeholders and might even include literature reviews, research, and communicating with nonstakeholders. Sometimes, the core team will begin the process and then other team members will become involved, or there could be a special, dedicated risk team—a part of the project team focused on risk management efforts.

 When you get a question about who should be involved in risk identification, the best answer is "everyone"! Each stakeholder has a different perspective of the project and can provide thoughts on opportunities and threats.

Project managers should begin looking for risks as soon as a project is first discussed. In fact, an assessment of overall project risk is included in the project charter. However, the major risk identification effort occurs during planning. The project manager will need to have skills to facilitate the identification of all risks (or as many risks as reasonably possible).

Because risk identification primarily occurs during project initiating and planning, the exam has often said that the major part of risk identification happens at the onset of the project. But keep in mind that smaller numbers of risks may also be identified later in the project. Risks should be continually reassessed. For the exam, understand that risk identification is done during integrated change control, when working with contracts, when working with resources, and when dealing with project issues.

### Tools and Techniques of Identify Risks  PAGE 414  The following sections discuss some risk identification tools and techniques.

#### Brainstorming  Brainstorming is usually done in a meeting where one idea helps generate another. Tools such as the risk breakdown structure, risk categories, and prompt lists can help to identify risks.

#### Checklist Analysis  Over time, organizations may compile lists of risks encountered on projects, which they review to help them identify relevant sources of risk for current projects. This technique also includes reviewing a checklist of generic risk categories, which is used to help identify specific risks to the project from each category.

453

**Interviewing**   Also called "expert interviewing" on the exam, this technique consists of the risk team or project manager interviewing project participants, stakeholders, or experts to identify risks to the overall project or to a specific element of work.

**Root Cause Analysis[3]**   In root cause analysis, the identified risks are reorganized by their root causes to help identify more risks.

**Assumption Analysis**   Identifying and analyzing assumptions that have been made on the project, and whether those assumptions are valid, may lead to the identification of more risks.

**Constraint Analysis**   Constraints such as schedule or budget limitations are examined to determine the level of risk they pose.

**Strengths, Weaknesses, Opportunities, and Threats (SWOT) Analysis[4]**   This analysis examines the project to identify its strengths and weaknesses as well as the opportunities and threats that could originate from those strengths and weaknesses.

**Documentation Reviews**   What is and is not included in project documentation, such as the project charter, contracts, and planning documentation, can help identify risks. Those involved in risk identification might look at project documentation, as well as lessons learned, articles, and other sources, to help uncover risks. This technique used to be an RMC Trick of the Trade® for risk management and has proven to be so beneficial that it has now become standard practice.

**Prompt Lists**   This is a list of categories that have been identified as possible sources of risk to the project. The project team can use a prompt list when identifying risks to individual elements of the project as well as risks to the overall project.

**Facilitation**   Facilitation skills are used by the project manager in conducting meetings to identify individual and overall project risks. As a part of such a meeting, the project manager may use any of the other risk identification techniques discussed earlier in this section.

## Outputs of Identify Risks   PAGE 417   The Identify Risks process results in the creation of the risk register and the risk report.

**Risk Register[5]**   Think of the risk register as one document for the entire risk management process that will be constantly updated with information as the risk management processes are completed. The risk register becomes part of the project documents and is included in historical records that will be used for future projects.

**TRICKS OF THE TRADE®**   Notice that the risk register, including updates, is an output of several of the risk management processes. (The *PMBOK® Guide* lists the updated risk register under project documents updates.) Read exam questions carefully, and remember that the risk register contains different information at different points in the risk management process. For example, if the project has just started and you are in the Identify Risks process, the risk register will contain the identified risks and potential responses, not the response plans actually selected for the project, which come later.

At this point in the risk management process, the risk register includes:

- **List of risks** Risks should be stated as clearly and specifically as possible using a cause-risk-effect format.

- **Potential risk owners** This information is noted in the risk register as potential risk owners are identified.

- **Potential risk responses** Although risk response planning occurs later, one of the things experienced risk managers know is that it is not always logical to separate the work of each part of risk management. There will be times when a response is identified at the same time as a risk. These potential responses should be added to the risk register as they are identified, and analyzed later as part of risk response planning.

- **Root causes of risks** The root causes of risks provide valuable information for use in later efforts to plan risk responses and reassess risk on the project, and as historical records to be used on future projects. Until the root cause of a risk is determined and addressed, it is likely to reoccur.

- **Updated risk categories** You will notice a lot of places where historical records and company records are updated throughout the project management process. Make sure you are aware that documenting lessons learned and communicating information to other projects do not just happen at the end of the project. As part of the risk identification effort, the project provides feedback to the rest of the company regarding new categories of risk to add to the checklist.

Other information that can be documented in the risk register includes risk triggers, potential impact of identified threats and opportunities, when each risk could occur, and when each risk will no longer present a threat or opportunity.

 A tricky question on the exam might ask, "When in the risk management process are risk responses documented?" The answer is both during Identify Risks (as potential responses) and during Plan Risk Responses (as selected response plans).

**Risk Report**    A risk report is generated and disseminated to stakeholders to keep them apprised of risk management efforts and outcomes. After the Identify Risks process, contents of the risk register would include an overview of information about the threats and opportunities that have been identified. Updated risk reports will be updates to the remaining risk management processes.

## Perform Qualitative Risk Analysis[6]    PAGE 419

| | |
|---|---|
| **Process** | Perform Qualitative Risk Analysis |
| **Process Group** | Planning |
| **Knowledge Area** | Risk Management |

As you begin this process, you should have a long list of risks documented in the risk register. But it would be too expensive, and it would take too much time, to plan responses to all these risks. You need to analyze the risks, including their probability and potential impact on the project, to determine which ones warrant a response. The Perform Qualitative Risk Analysis process involves doing this analysis and creating a shortened list of the previously identified individual project risks. The risks on this list may then be further analyzed in the Perform Quantitative Risk Analysis process, or they may move into the Plan Risk Responses process.

Remember that qualitative risk analysis is a subjective analysis of the risks identified in the risk register. Keep in mind that this process is repeated as new risks are uncovered throughout the project.

To perform this analysis, the following must be determined:

- The probability of each risk occurring, using a standard scale (common subjective analysis scales include Low, Medium, High and 1 to 10)

- The impact (the amount at stake or the positive or negative consequences) of each risk occurring, using a standard scale, such as Low, Medium, High or 1 to 10

455

### Risk Data Quality Assessment   PAGE 423   Before you can use the risk information collected on the project, you must analyze the precision of the data. You assess the accuracy and reliability of the data, and determine if the risk is valid and whether more research is needed to understand the risk. Imagine, for example, a risk given to you anonymously. You might allow for anonymous contributions during risk identification, but all the identified risks must be defined well enough to perform a qualitative assessment.

A risk data quality assessment may include determining the following for each risk:

- Extent of the understanding of the risk
- Data available about the risk
- Quality of the data
- Reliability and integrity of the data

### Risk Categorization   PAGE 425   Risk categorization examines the questions of "What will we find if we regroup the risks by categories? By source? By work packages?" Think about how useful it would be to have not only a subjective assessment of the total amount of risk on the project, but also a breakdown of the risks that shows which work packages, processes, people, or other potential causes have the most risk associated with them. Such data will be helpful in risk response planning, potentially allowing you to eliminate many risks at once by eliminating one cause. Risk categories and sources of risks can be organized in a risk breakdown structure.

### Probability and Impact Matrix[7]   PAGE 425   A probability and impact matrix is a data representation technique that can be used during this process. Because qualitative risk analysis is based on subjective evaluation, the rating of any one risk can vary depending on the bias of the person doing the rating and how risk averse they are. For example, one person's score of 3 might be another person's 7. Therefore, organizations frequently have a standard rating system to promote a common understanding of what each risk rating means. This standard is shown in a probability and impact matrix (see fig.11.1).

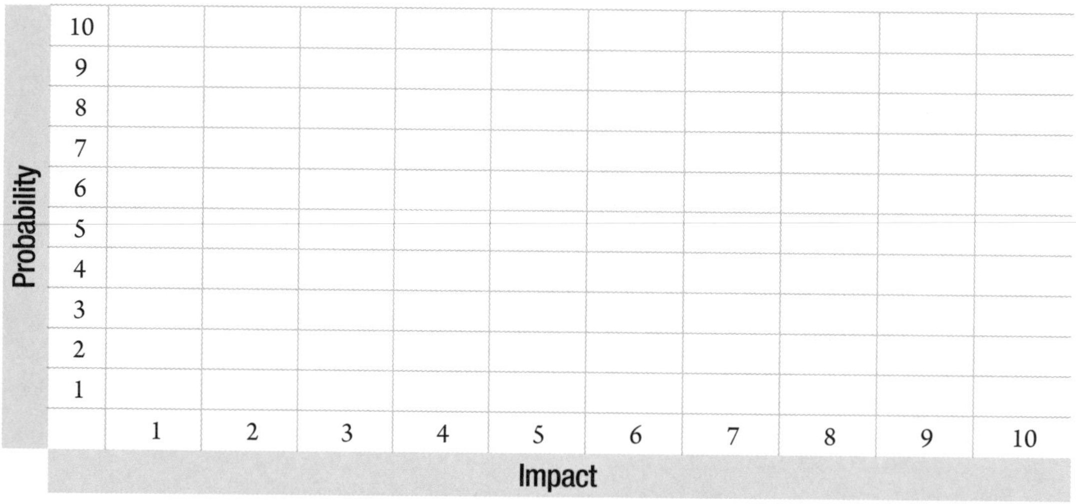

FIGURE 11.1   *Probability and impact matrix*

A key for understanding the ratings on this matrix might be documented as shown in figure 11.2.

| Scale for Probability | |
| --- | --- |
| **Rating** | **Interpretation** |
| 1–2 | Low |
| 3–4 | Medium |
| 5–6 | Medium-High |
| 7–8 | High |
| 9–10 | Fact |

| Scale for Impact | |
| --- | --- |
| **Rating** | **Interpretation** |
| 1 | No real impact |
| 2 | Small reduction of time or cost reserves |
| 3 | Medium reduction of time or cost reserves |
| 4 | Large reduction of time or cost reserves |
| 5 | Slightly over budget |
| 6 | Over budget by 10% to 20% or project delayed by 10% to 20% |
| 7 | Over budget by 20% to 30% or project delayed by 20% to 30% |
| 8 | Over budget by 30% to 40% or project delayed by 30% to 40% |
| 9 | Over budget by 40% or project delayed by 40% |
| 10 | Project failure |

FIGURE 11.2    *Ratings interpretation for probability and impact matrix*

The probability and impact matrix may be used to sort or rate risks to determine which ones warrant an immediate response (and will therefore be moved on through the risk process) and which ones should be put on the watch list (described later). The matrix may be standardized within the company or department, or it may be customized to the needs of the project. Such a matrix results in a consistent evaluation of low, medium, or high (or some other scale) for the project or for all projects. Use of a standardized matrix makes the risk rating process more consistent across projects.

Different charts, such as a hierarchical-type chart, can be used for cost, time, and scope if the thresholds for each type of risk are different or when risks have been categorized with more than two parameters.

## Risk Parameters Assessments    PAGE 423    In addition to creating a short list of risks, qualitative risk analysis includes identifying risks that should move more quickly through the process than others due to factors that are referred to as risk parameters. Some examples of risk parameters include the following:

- **Urgency** The urgency parameter indicates if the risk is likely to occur soon (requiring the response to be implemented quickly) or if the risk requires a particularly long time to plan a response. Urgent risks may be moved directly into risk response planning while the remaining risks continue through quantitative risk analysis, or the urgent risks may simply be the first ones for which you plan a response in risk response planning.

- **Dormancy** Dormancy refers to the anticipated time between when a risk occurs and when its impact is felt on the project.

- **Manageability and controllability** The manageability and controllability parameter indicates the level of difficulty involved in dealing with an identified risk, should it occur.

- **Strategic impact** Strategic impact refers to the degree to which the occurrence of a risk would affect the strategic goals of the performing organization.

457

## Outputs of Perform Qualitative Risk Analysis PAGE 427 This process results in project documents updates. Some examples are discussed in the following sections.

### Assumption Log
Assumption log updates, or updates to the assumptions in the project scope statement, include new information or clarifications about documented assumptions and constraints made about the project.

### Issue log
The issue log should be updated to include any new issues or changes to current issues that have already been included in the log.

### Risk Register
The risk register should be updated to add the results of qualitative risk analysis, including:

- **Risk ranking for the project compared to other projects** Qualitative risk analysis can lead to a number to be used to rank the project in comparison to other projects (for example, this project has a risk score of 8.3). This ranking allows you to redo qualitative risk analysis after you have completed risk response planning and prove the value of your efforts. You can report, "The project now has a risk score of 4.8." Think how this will help you prove the value of project management!
- **List of prioritized risks and their probability and impact ratings**
- **Results of other risk parameter assessments**
- **Risks grouped by categories**
- **List of risks for additional analysis and response** These are the risks that will move forward into quantitative risk analysis and/or risk response planning.
- **List of risks requiring additional analysis in the near term**
- **Watch list (noncritical risks)** These risks are documented in the risk register for observation or later review.

### Risk Report Updates
At the end of this process, the risk report includes the results of risk prioritization and a list of the highest-ranking risks.

Qualitative risk analysis can be used to do the following:
- Compare the risk of the project to the overall risk of other projects.
- Determine whether the project should be continued or terminated.
- Determine whether to proceed to the Perform Quantitative Risk Analysis or Plan Risk Responses processes (depending on the needs of the project and the performing organization).

## Perform Quantitative Risk Analysis[8] PAGE 428

> **Process** Perform Quantitative Risk Analysis
> **Process Group** Planning
> **Knowledge Area** Risk Management

The Perform Quantitative Risk Analysis process involves numerically analyzing the probability and impact (the amount at stake or the consequences) of risks that ranked highest in qualitative risk analysis. Quantitative risk analysis also looks at how risks could affect the objectives of the project. The purpose of quantitative risk analysis is to:

- Determine which risk events warrant a response.
- Determine overall project risk (risk exposure).

458

- Determine the quantified probability of meeting project objectives (for example, "We only have an 80 percent chance of completing the project within the six months required by the customer," or "We only have a 75 percent chance of completing the project within the $80,000 budget.").
- Determine cost and schedule reserves.
- Identify risks requiring the most attention.
- Create realistic and achievable cost, schedule, or scope targets.

 Many people confuse qualitative and quantitative risk analysis. Remember that qualitative risk analysis is a subjective evaluation, even though numbers are used for the rating. In contrast, quantitative risk analysis is a more objective or numerical evaluation; the rating of each risk is based on an attempt to measure the actual probability and amount at stake (impact). Therefore, while the rating for a risk in qualitative risk analysis might be a 5, that same risk might be quantified as a $40,000 cost impact in quantitative risk analysis.

As a project manager, you should always do qualitative risk analysis. Quantitative risk analysis is not required for all projects or for all risks. It may be skipped in favor of moving on to risk response planning. You should proceed with quantitative risk analysis only if it is worth the time and money. For some projects, you may have a subset of risks identified that require further quantitative analysis. But why spend time quantitatively assessing risks for a low-priority or short-term project or when the effort will provide minimal return?

The Perform Quantitative Risk Analysis process can include a lot of calculation and analysis. Luckily, the details of these efforts are not a focus of the exam. You need to know that the following actions are part of quantitative risk analysis but not how to do them beyond what is explained in this chapter:

- Further investigate the highest rated risks on the project.
- Perform data analysis to determine which risks have the most impact on the project.
- Determine how much quantified risk the project has through data analysis (that will be described later in this section).

## Inputs to Perform Quantitative Risk Analysis    PAGE 430    These inputs include the project management plan and scope, schedule, and cost baselines. The project management plan indicates whether, and under what circumstances, quantitative risk analysis will be performed. This includes what is detailed in the risk management plan. The baselines have data that is necessary for the numerical analysis and are used in the simulations and other tools.

The assumption log, which includes both assumptions and constraints, is reviewed to determine any assumptions or constraints that have the potential to add a degree of risk that warrants quantitative analysis.

Also note that project estimates and forecasts include milestones that must be achieved. If there is a risk that any of these are unrealistic, or if there is uncertainty that they will be able to be met, that risk may be analyzed in this process. Lastly, the risk register and risk reports include identified risks and the results of qualitative analysis of those risks. The risks with the highest probabilities and impacts are likely to require quantitative assessment.

## Tools and Techniques of Quantitative Risk Analysis    PAGE 431    Quantitative probability and impact can be determined in a variety of ways that make use of some or all of the following:

- Expert judgment from trained risk specialists and team members
- Data-gathering techniques, such as interviewing

- Data analysis techniques, such as simulations (like Monte Carlo), sensitivity analysis, decision tree analysis, and influence diagrams
- Interpersonal and team skills
- Representations of uncertainty
- Cost and schedule estimating
- Use of historical records from previous projects

**Simulations**    Imagine if you could prove to the sponsor that even if the project were to be done 5,000 times, there is only a low probability that the end date they desire would be met? Would this be valuable? This is what the results of simulation techniques such as Monte Carlo analysis are all about. A Monte Carlo analysis uses the network diagram and schedule or cost estimates to "perform" the project many times and to simulate the cost or schedule results of the project. (Also see the discussion of this topic in the Schedule Management chapter.)

This technique can be extremely valuable, but there have traditionally been only one or two questions about Monte Carlo analysis on the exam. It is, however, mentioned as an answer choice a little more frequently.

 You do not need to know how to perform this calculation for the exam. Rather, you should just understand that Monte Carlo analysis:

- Is usually done with a computer program because of the intricacies of the calculations
- Evaluates the overall risk in the project
- Determines the probability of completing the project on any specific day or for any specific cost
- Determines the probability of any activity actually being on the critical path
- Takes into account path convergence (places in the network diagram where many paths converge into one activity)
- Translates uncertainties into impacts to the total project
- Can be used to assess cost and schedule impacts
- Results in a probability distribution

**Sensitivity Analysis**[9]    Sensitivity analysis is a technique to analyze and compare the potential impacts of identified risks. A tornado diagram[10] may be used to graphically depict the results of this analysis. Risks are represented by horizontal bars: the longest and uppermost bar represents the greatest risk, and progressively shorter horizontal bars beneath represent lower-ranked risks. The resulting graphic resembles a funnel cloud, or tornado. Figure 11.3 depicts a tornado diagram representing the impact of the threats and opportunities surrounding various milestones on the installation of a new computer system.

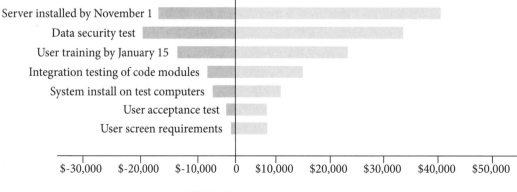

FIGURE 11.3   *Tornado diagram*

460

**Decision Tree[11] Analysis**   If you have to choose between many alternatives, you should analyze how each choice benefits or hurts the project before making the decision. Decision trees can help you in this type of analysis. They are models of real situations and are used to make informed decisions about things like, "Which option should I choose?" or "How will I solve this problem?" by taking into account the associated risks, probabilities, and impacts.

There have traditionally been only one or two questions about decision trees on the exam. You should know what a decision tree is and be able to calculate a simple one from data within an exam question. The exam could also ask you to calculate the expected monetary value for cost, the expected value (or just "value") for the schedule of a path, or the value of your decision.

Make sure you understand that a decision tree is analyzed by calculating the value of each branch. The outcome of this calculation will show the best option to select. Let's quickly go through this value calculation, and then complete a simple exercise to calculate expected monetary value.

To evaluate a risk, you can look at the probability or the impact, but the expected value is a better measure to determine an overall ranking of risks. The formula for expected value is simply probability (P) multiplied by impact (I). The calculation for schedule results in the expected value (EV, not to be confused with Earned Value). Expected monetary value (EMV) is used for cost.

$$EMV = P \times I$$

Questions on the exam can ask, "What is the expected monetary value of the following?" Expected monetary value can also appear in questions in conjunction with decision trees and in calculating contingency reserves (both described later in this chapter).

**Exercise**   Do not think of this as another formula you need to memorize—it is too easy. Test yourself! Complete the following chart, and you will understand this calculation for the exam without memorization.

| Work Package | Probability | Impact | Expected Monetary Value |
|---|---|---|---|
| A | 10% | $20,000 | |
| B | 30% | $45,000 | |
| C | 68% | $18,000 | |

**Answer**   See the answers in the following table.

| Work Package | Probability | Impact | Expected Monetary Value |
|---|---|---|---|
| A | 10% | $20,000 | $2,000 |
| B | 30% | $45,000 | $13,500 |
| C | 68% | $18,000 | $12,240 |

Note that for opportunities, expected monetary value is often presented as a positive amount (e.g., $3,000), whereas threats are usually presented as a negative number (e.g., –$3,000).

The calculation of expected value is performed during quantitative risk analysis and revised during risk response planning when calculating contingency reserves for schedule and costs.

You should also know the following about decision trees for the exam:

- A decision tree takes into account future events in making a decision today.
- It calculates the expected value (probability multiplied by impact) in more complex situations than the expected monetary value example previously presented. With a decision tree, you could evaluate the costs (or schedule implications) and benefits of several risk responses at once to determine which is the best option.
- It involves mutual exclusivity (previously explained in the Quality Management chapter).

 Some examples of decision trees have the costs occurring only at the end of the project, while others have costs occurring early or in the middle of the project. Because a decision tree models all the possible choices to resolve an issue, costs can appear anywhere in the diagram, not just at the end. When you are taking the exam, don't get confused when you look at examples of decision trees. Pay attention to the data provided in the question so you can correctly interpret the answer.

The following two exercises include decision trees. The box represents a decision to be made, and the circles represent what can happen as a result of the decision.

**Exercise** A company is trying to determine if prototyping is worthwhile on a project. They have come up with the following impacts (see the diagram) of whether the equipment works or fails. Based on the information provided in the diagram, what is the expected monetary value of each option? Which is the cheaper option—to prototype or not to prototype?

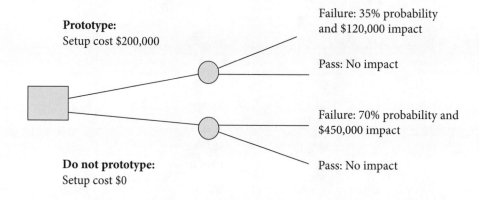

**Prototype:**
Setup cost $200,000

Failure: 35% probability and $120,000 impact

Pass: No impact

Failure: 70% probability and $450,000 impact

Pass: No impact

**Do not prototype:**
Setup cost $0

**Answer**   If you just look at the setup cost of prototyping, it would seem like an unwise decision to spend money on prototyping. However, the analysis proves differently. Taking into account only the one future event of whether the equipment works or fails, the decision tree reveals that it would be cheaper to do the prototyping. The expected monetary value of prototyping is $242,000; the expected monetary value of not prototyping is $315,000.

| | |
|---|---|
| **Prototype** | $35\% \times \$120,000 = \$42,000$ <br> $\$42,000 + \$200,000 = \$242,000$ |
| **Do Not Prototype** | $70\% \times \$450,000 = \$315,000$ |

**Exercise**   You need to fly from one city to another. You can take airline A or B. Considering the data provided, which airline should you take, and what is the expected monetary value of your decision?

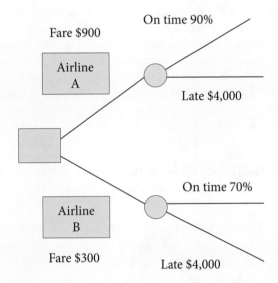

**Answer** If you just look at the cost of the airfare, you would choose airline B because it is cheaper. However, the airlines have different on-time-arrival rates. If the on-time-arrival rate for airline A is 90 percent, it must be late 10 percent of the time. Airline B is on time 70 percent of the time, and is therefore late 30 percent of the time. We have a $4,000 impact for being late. The result is that you should choose airline A, with an expected monetary value of $1,300 as shown below.

| Airline A | $(10\% \times \$4,000) + \$900$ <br> $\$400 + \$900 = \$1,300$ |
| --- | --- |
| Airline B | $(30\% \times \$4,000) + \$300$ <br> $\$1,200 + \$300 = \$1,500$ |

 **Proving the Value of Project Management** Project management saves time and money on projects. Getting your organization's executives to understand that fact can be difficult at times. How beneficial would it be if you could prove the value of project management?

Imagine that you have just done the first calculation of the expected value of all the risks that were assigned high ranking and priority in qualitative risk analysis, or that you have completed a Monte Carlo analysis for the project. In either case, you calculate that you need a $98,000 contingency reserve on the project to accommodate risks. Let's try this example. The team moves on to the Plan Risk Responses process and eliminates some risks and reduces the probability or impact of others. The expected monetary value calculation or Monte Carlo analysis is then redone, showing a revised need for only a $12,000 reserve. You have just saved $86,000, and you have not even started the project yet! Can you imagine how information like that will help you gain support for project management in the real world?

## Outputs of Perform Quantitative Risk Analysis PAGE 436 The Perform Quantitative Risk Analysis process results in updates to the risk register and other project documents.

**Risk Register Updates** The risk register and the risk report are updated to add the results of quantitative risk analysis, including:

- **Prioritized list of quantified individual project risks** What risks are most likely to cause trouble in terms of their effect on the critical path? What risks need the most contingency reserve?

- **The quantified probability of meeting project objectives** For example, "We only have an 80 percent chance of completing the project within the six months required by the customer." Or, "We only have a 75 percent chance of completing the project within the $800,000 budget."

- **Trends in quantitative risk analysis** As you repeat quantitative risk analysis during project planning and when changes are proposed, you can track changes to the overall risk of the project and see any trends.

- **Initial contingency time and cost reserves needed** For example, "The project requires an additional $50,000 and two months of time to accommodate the risks on the project." Reserves will be finalized during Plan Risk Responses.

- **Assessment of overall project risk exposure** Use overall project success (how likely it is that the project will achieve all key objectives) and any variables that may still affect the project to fully understand, at a high level, the overall risk exposure of the project.

- **Possible realistic and achievable completion dates and project costs, with confidence levels, versus the time and cost objectives for the project** For example, "We are 95 percent confident that we can complete this project on May 25th for $989,000."

- **Recommended risk responses** After quantitative risk analysis is performed, the risk register may include suggested responses to overall project risks and individual project risks.

## Plan Risk Responses  PAGE 437

| | |
|---|---|
| **Process** | Plan Risk Responses |
| **Process Group** | Planning |
| **Knowledge Area** | Risk Management |

The Plan Risk Responses process involves figuring out, "What are we going to do about each top risk?" In risk response planning, you find ways to reduce or eliminate threats, and you find ways to make opportunities more likely or increase their impact. The project's risk responses may include doing one or a combination of the following for each top risk:

- Do something to eliminate the threats before they happen.

- Do something to make sure the opportunities happen.

- Decrease the probability and/or impact of threats.

- Increase the probability and/or impact of opportunities.

For the remaining (residual) threats that cannot be eliminated:

- Do something if the risk happens (contingency plans). Contingency plans should be measurable so you can evaluate their effectiveness.

- Do something if contingency plans are not effective or are only partially effective (fallback plans).

Stop here for a moment to think about what we just described. To pass the exam, you will need to be able to envision a world that is not a reality for every project manager; you need to envision a world in which proper risk management is done. Think about the power of risk response planning. You eliminate problems (threats) while still in the planning process on your project. Had they not been eliminated, these problems could have caused stress, delays, and/or added cost to the project. Can you see the value of such efforts in your real world?

This is what risk management is all about. If a change to a team member's availability is a top risk, you can investigate the possibility of replacing that team member with another team member who has similar skills. If a work package is causing a large amount of risk, you might look at changing the deliverable, modifying the work to produce it, or removing scope from the project. There are always options to respond to risks.

Risk management goes further than the examples just described, however. In addition to avoiding or exploiting risks, you and the team determine what to do about each of the residual risks (those that cannot be eliminated or exploited through risk response strategies). This might mean accepting these residual risks, or planning additional risk responses. You then assign the work involved in the responses to risk owners—individuals who watch out for the occurrence of a risk and implement preplanned responses.

If, while reading this book, you have found yourself thinking, "I do not have time to do that," remember what project management can do for you. As with many other areas of project management, risk management does not really take additional time; rather, it saves huge amounts of time on projects. When you have done risk management, your project will go smoother and faster, with significantly fewer complications because avoidable problems were solved before they happened. You now have time to spend implementing reward systems, updating organizational process assets, creating lessons learned, preventing problems, assisting, coaching, and completing all the other work you might have thought you did not have time for.

465

When you are taking the exam, assume that all major potential problems that could have been identified in advance as risks were determined before they occurred and that there was a plan for each of these risks. With this in mind, the best answer to a question describing a major problem on the project will be the choice that talks about implementing a contingency plan, rather than one that involves discussing possible solutions to a problem after it has occurred. Many people have said that these types of questions were the reason they failed the exam. They simply made the wrong choices in situational questions. Be sure to make the transition to this way of thinking if it is unfamiliar to you.

Here are a couple of other points that can be tricky on the exam:

- Can you eliminate all threats on a project? Remember that threats can be eliminated and opportunities exploited, but the time and trouble involved in eliminating all the threats and exploiting all the opportunities on a project would probably not be worthwhile.

- Qualitative risk analysis, quantitative risk analysis, and risk response planning do not end once you begin work on a project. As noted in other parts of this book, planning is iterative. You need to review risks throughout the project, including while the project work is being done or when checking results. When you identify new risks, you then need to spend time analyzing them and planning responses, if appropriate. Risk ratings and response strategies for existing risks can change as more information about the risks and the selected response strategies becomes known. Therefore, you must review risk ratings and response strategies for appropriateness over the life of the project. This is the iterative nature of risk management. Approved change requests create the need to look for new risks that may be caused by the implemented change.

Now that you understand the philosophy of what a project manager is trying to do in the Plan Risk Responses process, let's look at the details you will need to know.

The primary input to this process is the project risk register. It has been updated throughout the risk management process, and now includes a list of risks that have been qualitatively (and possibly quantitatively) analyzed. The risks have been prioritized based on their probability and impact, among other factors. These are the risks for which responses will be planned. Another important input to this process is the cost baseline, which describes the contingency reserve that will be used in addressing identified risks. (See the discussion on reserves later in this chapter.)

## Risk Response Strategies  PAGE 442  When completing risk response planning, a thorough analysis must be done of the potential responses for each risk. The team, guided by the risk owner, may uncover many strategies for dealing with risks. Some of these risk response strategies, also known as risk mitigation strategies or strategies for threats and opportunities, involve changing the planned approach to completing the project, such as changes to the WBS, quality management plan, resources, communications, schedule, or budget. Other strategies, called contingency plans, involve coming up with a plan to be implemented when and if a risk occurs. It is important to make sure all options are investigated.

The choices of response strategies for threats include:

- **Avoid** Eliminate the threat by eliminating the cause, such as removing the work package or changing the person assigned to do work. Avoiding the threat might even involve expanding the scope of the project. Imagine, for example, your project team estimates there's a 75 percent likelihood of a threat occurring, but an additional level of testing or an additional activity would likely prevent this threat; expanding the scope of the project in this way would help avoid the threat.

  On an overall project level, if the threat is beyond the organization's risk threshold, the project manager will need to take action to make the project acceptable. This could include removing pieces of the project that are too risky in order to avoid cancelling the entire project.

© 2018 RMC Publications, Inc.™ • 952.846.4484 • info@rmcls.com • www.rmcls.com

- **Mitigate**  Reduce the probability and/or the impact of an individual or overall project threat, thereby making it a smaller risk and possibly removing it from the list of top risks on the project. Options for reducing the probability are considered separately from options for reducing the impact. Any reduction will make a difference, but the option with the most probability and/or impact reduction is often the option selected.
- **Transfer (deflect, allocate)**  Make a party outside of the project responsible for the threat by purchasing insurance, performance bonds, warranties, or guarantees, or by outsourcing the work. Here is where the strong connection between risk and procurement (contracts) begins. In the world of properly practiced project management, risk analysis is completed before a contract is signed, and transference of risk is included in the terms and conditions of the contract.

Avoidance and mitigation are generally used for high-priority, high-impact risks. Transference, escalation (discussed below), and acceptance (also discussed below) may be appropriate for low-priority, low-impact risks as well as those with higher impact.

A response to pure risks[12]—such as fire, property damage, or personal injury—is to purchase insurance. Insurance exchanges an unknown cost impact of a known risk for a known cost impact. In the example of a risk of fire, the cost impact of the risk is unknown depending on the extent of the fire. But when insurance is purchased, the cost impact of a risk of fire becomes known; it is the cost of the insurance and the deductible. Transferring the risk by purchasing insurance does not eliminate all impacts. There may still be residual risks. For example, a project could experience schedule delays due to a fire even if fire insurance was purchased, or the cost of damage caused by the fire could exceed the amount of insurance purchased.

Transferring a risk will also leave some risk behind. For example, there is a risk that if the third party has trouble, they could cause a schedule delay. So you still need to decide what to do about any such secondary risks.

The choices of response strategies for opportunities include:

- **Exploit (the reverse of avoid)**  Add work or change to the project to make sure the opportunity occurs. This could be on the individual project risk level or on the overall project risk level.
- **Enhance (the reverse of mitigate)**  Increase the likelihood (probability) and/or positive impacts of the opportunity occurring. This could be related to the overall approach to scope and schedule, resources used, and project replanning as well as to individual project risks.
- **Share**  Allocate ownership or partial ownership of the individual or overall project opportunity to a third party (forming a partnership, team, or joint venture) that is best able to achieve the opportunity.

Response strategies for both threats and opportunities include:

- **Escalate**  A threat or an opportunity should be escalated if it is outside the scope of the project or beyond the project manager's authority. Any risks that are escalated will typically be managed at the program or portfolio level—not at the project level. Remember that escalated risk needs to be accepted by the program or portfolio manager, at which point, data on the escalation is documented, and the risk is no longer monitored at the project level.
- **Accept**  Passive acceptance means to do nothing and to essentially say, "If it happens, it happens." This leaves actions to be determined as needed (workarounds) if the risk occurs. Active acceptance involves creating contingency plans to be implemented if the risk occurs and allocating time and cost reserves to the project.

Whether responding to threats or opportunities:

- Strategies must be timely.
- The effort selected must be appropriate to the severity of the risk—avoid spending more money preventing the risk than the impact of the risk would cost if it occurred.
- One response can be used to address more than one risk.
- More than one response can be used to address the same risk.
- A response can address the root cause of risk and thereby address more than one risk.
- The team, other stakeholders, and experts should be involved in selecting a strategy.

Watch out for questions about communicating risk-related information on the exam! Your risk response strategies must be communicated to the sponsor, management, and stakeholders. These parties will need to know that you are in control of the project even if there is a problem, and they may need to approve the resources to make the risk response strategies happen. Communicating about risk is essential for gaining buy-in to the strategy.

**Exercise** Now let's see if you can apply what you have learned. Identify the type of risk response strategy (avoid, mitigate the probability, mitigate the impact, transfer, exploit, enhance the probability, enhance the impact, share, escalate or accept) being described.

| | Description | Risk Response Strategy |
|---|---|---|
| 1 | Remove a work package or activity from the project. | |
| 2 | Assign a team member to frequently visit the seller's manufacturing facilities to learn about problems with deliveries as early as possible. | |
| 3 | Move a work package to a date when a more experienced resource is available to be assigned to the project. | |
| 4 | Begin negotiation for the equipment earlier than planned so as to secure a lower price. | |
| 5 | Outsource a work package so as to gain an opportunity. | |
| 6 | Notify management that there could be a cost increase if a risk occurs because no action is being taken to prevent the risk. | |
| 7 | Remove a troublesome resource from the project. | |
| 8 | Provide a team member who has limited experience with additional training. | |
| 9 | Train the team on conflict resolution strategies. | |
| 10 | Outsource difficult work to a more experienced company. | |
| 11 | Ask the client to handle some of the work. | |
| 12 | Prototype a risky piece of equipment. | |
| 13 | Notify the PMO that the testing software needed for the project could be used by three other IT groups if the enterprise solution is purchased. | |

## Answer

| | Description | Risk Response Strategy |
|---|---|---|
| 1 | Remove a work package or activity from the project. | Avoid |
| 2 | Assign a team member to frequently visit the seller's manufacturing facilities to learn about problems with deliveries as early as possible. | Mitigate the impact |
| 3 | Move a work package to a date when a more experienced resource is available to be assigned to the project. | Exploit |
| 4 | Begin negotiation for the equipment earlier than planned so as to secure a lower price. | Enhance the impact |
| 5 | Outsource a work package so as to gain an opportunity. | Share |
| 6 | Notify management that there could be a cost increase if a risk occurs because no action is being taken to prevent the risk. | Accept |
| 7 | Remove a troublesome resource from the project. | Avoid |
| 8 | Provide a team member who has limited experience with additional training. | Mitigate the probability |
| 9 | Train the team on conflict resolution strategies. | Mitigate the impact |
| 10 | Outsource difficult work to a more experienced company. | Transfer |
| 11 | Ask the client to handle some of the work. | Transfer |
| 12 | Prototype a risky piece of equipment. | Mitigate the probability |
| 13 | Notify the PMO that the testing software for the project could be used by three other IT groups if the enterprise solution is purchased. | Escalate |

 **TRICKS OF THE TRADE®** Potential risk response strategies and contingency plans must be analyzed to determine which strategy or strategies are most cost-effective and most likely to address the risk. Cost-benefit analysis and multicriteria analysis are techniques to evaluate and rank potential risk responses. You may see a question on the exam asking you to compare the cost effectiveness of various risk response options.

## Outputs of Plan Risk Responses    PAGE 447    The outputs of the Plan Risk Responses process are change requests, updates to the project management plan, and project documents updates.

**Project Management Plan Updates**    The efforts spent in risk management can result in updates to the project management plan. After careful consideration and evaluation, planned risk responses may require changes to management plans that have been drafted in planning—at the overall project risk level as well as at the individual project risk level. Spend a moment now thinking about how risk response planning might lead to adjustments to the schedule, cost, quality, procurement, communications, and resource management plans, as well as to the scope, schedule, and cost baselines for the project. This concept is critical for understanding the impact risk management has on projects, especially if you don't currently do risk management on your projects.

Remember also that planning is iterative. To help you answer questions correctly on the exam and understand the flow of the planning processes, Rita's Process Chart™ represents this analysis, evaluation, and integration of the management plan changes during project planning as part of "Go back—iterations." It is expected that in the planning process, the project manager will lead the subject matter experts, assisting with project planning through many iterations of the management plans before coming up with a realistic, formal project management plan that is bought into and approved. Risk response strategies for opportunities and threats could have a wide variety of impacts on the project management plan, often necessitating refinement of management plans.

Other documents a project manager has created to help manage the project may also change as a result of risk response planning. These documents may include the assumption log, cost forecasts, the lessons learned register, the project schedule, project team assignments, the risk register, and the risk report. The risk report is updated to communicate the risks of greatest threat or opportunity, the overall project risk exposure, and the outcomes of planning related to risk responses and any anticipated changes. Can you imagine how risk response planning might affect the roles and responsibilities on a project, your stakeholder management strategy, or your quality metrics?

### Risk Register Updates
The risk register is updated to add the results of risk response planning, including:

- **Residual risks[13]** These are the risks that remain after risk response planning. After you have avoided, exploited, mitigated, enhanced, transferred, shared, escalated, and accepted risks (and created related contingency plans and fallback plans), there will still be risks that remain. Those residual risks that are passively accepted should be properly documented and reviewed throughout the project to see if their ranking has changed.

- **Contingency plans** Contingency plans are plans describing the specific actions that will be taken if the opportunity or threat occurs.

- **Fallback plans** These plans are specific actions that will be taken if the contingency plans are not effective. Think how prepared you will feel if you have plans for what to do if a risk occurs and what to do if the original plan does not work.

- **Risk owners** A key concept in risk response planning is that the project manager does not have to do it all, and neither does the team. Each risk must be assigned to someone who will help lead the development of the risk response and who will be assigned to carry out the risk response or "own" the risk. The risk owner can be a stakeholder other than a team member. Think about how the application of risk management could change real-world projects. The risk occurs; the risk owner takes the preapproved action determined in project planning and informs the project manager. No meeting is needed—just action! This can be very powerful.

- **Secondary risks** Any new risks created by the implementation of selected risk responses should also be analyzed as part of risk response planning. Frequently, a response to one risk will create the possibility of new risks that would otherwise not have occurred. For example, if a portion of the project work is outsourced to a seller because the project team does not have the expertise to complete the work efficiently, there may be a secondary risk of the seller going out of business. This was not a risk to the project prior to outsourcing. The discovery of secondary risks may require additional risk response planning.

- **Risk triggers[14]** These are events that trigger the contingency response. The early warning signs for each risk on a project should be identified so risk owners know when to take action.

- **Contracts** Before a contract is finalized, the project manager should have completed a risk analysis and included contract terms and conditions required to mitigate threats and enhance opportunities. Any contracts issued to deal with risks should be noted in the risk register.

- **Reserves (contingency)**[15] Having reserves for time and cost is a required part of project management. You cannot come up with a schedule or budget for the project without them. Reserves are covered in the Cost Management chapter, but let's look at them again here.

Time and cost each have two types of reserves: contingency reserves and management reserves. Contingency reserves account for "known unknowns" (or simply "knowns"); these are items you identified in risk management. Management reserves account for "unknown unknowns" (or simply "unknowns"); these are items you did not or could not identify in risk management. Projects can have both kinds of reserves. As shown in the diagram in figure 11.4 (also shown in the Cost Management chapter), contingency reserves are calculated and become part of the cost baseline. Management reserves are estimated (for example, 5 percent of the project cost), and then these reserves are added to the cost baseline to get the project budget. The project manager has control of the cost baseline and can approve use of the contingency reserves, but management approval is needed to use management reserves. The same applies to reserves in the schedule.

Make sure you understand that reserves are not an additional cost to a project. The risk management process should result in a decrease to the project's estimated time and cost. As threats are eliminated or their probability or impact reduced, there should be a reduction to the project's schedule and budget. Contingency reserves are allocated for the contingency plans and fallback plans to deal with the associated, accepted opportunities and threats that remain after the risk management planning processes have been completed. No matter what you do, risks will remain in the project, and there should be a time or cost allotment for them, just as time or cost is allotted to work activities on the project.

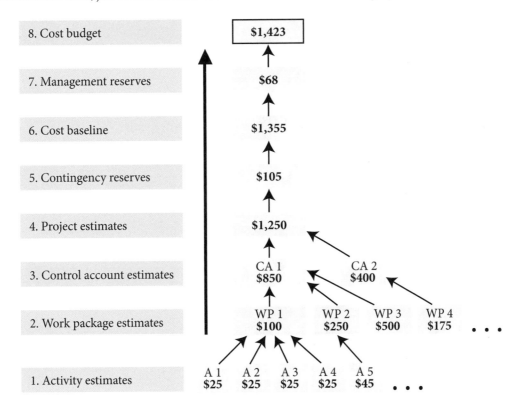

FIGURE 11.4   *Creating a budget*

There may be questions on the exam that ask you to calculate the contingency reserve for several risk events, which may be a combination of opportunities and threats. To do this, you must calculate the value of each risk using the equation for expected value ($P \times I$). On the exam, you may have to calculate contingency reserves for either schedule (expected value) or cost (expected monetary value). But think about this a minute. Let's use the example for cost impacts to projects. Can you just add all the expected monetary value amounts of the opportunities and threats together and come up with one grand total for the budget? No! You'll need to subtract the total expected monetary value of the opportunities from the total expected monetary value of the threats. Why?

Opportunities will save money and time on the project if they occur. This can reduce the cost or schedule baselines. Conversely, the threats will add cost and time to the project.

We're telling you to subtract opportunities here, but didn't we tell you earlier that expected value is often presented as a positive amount for opportunities and a negative amount for threats? That's often true when the values are depicted on something like a decision tree, so you can easily identify positive and negative outcomes and their overall effect on project costs or schedule. But here we're specifically looking to determine how much money or time to set aside for the contingency reserves. Threats will require increasing the amount of contingency reserves, whereas opportunities will decrease the required reserves.

Let's try an example of calculating a contingency reserve in the next exercise.

**Exercise**  Imagine you are planning the manufacture of modifications to an existing product. Your analysis has come up with the following information. What cost contingency reserve would you use?

| Project Data | Cost Contingency Reserve Calculations |
| --- | --- |
| There is a 30 percent probability of a delay in the receipt of parts, with a cost to the project of $9,000. | |
| There is a 20 percent probability that the parts will cost $10,000 less than expected. | |
| There is a 25 percent probability that two parts will not fit together when installed, costing an extra $3,500. | |
| There is a 30 percent probability that the manufacture may be simpler than expected, saving $2,500. | |
| There is a 5 percent probability of a design defect, causing $5,000 of rework. | |
| Total Cost Contingency Reserve | |

**Answer**  You use the expected monetary value calculation (EMV = P × I) to determine the contingency reserve. The answer is $1,075 for the total cost contingency reserve. See the following table for the detailed calculations.

| Project Data | Cost Contingency Reserve Calculations |
| --- | --- |
| There is a 30 percent probability of a delay in the receipt of parts, with a cost to the project of $9,000. | 30% × $9,000 = $2,700 <br> Add $2,700 |
| There is a 20 percent probability that the parts will cost $10,000 less than expected. | 20% × $10,000 = $2,000 <br> Subtract $2,000 |

| Project Data | Cost Contingency Reserve Calculations |
|---|---|
| There is a 25 percent probability that two parts will not fit together when installed, costing an extra $3,500. | 25% × $3,500 = $875 Add $875 |
| There is a 30 percent probability that the manufacture may be simpler than expected, saving $2,500. | 30% × $2,500 = $750 Subtract $750 |
| There is a 5 percent probability of a design defect, causing $5,000 of rework. | 5% × $5,000 = $250 Add $250 |
| Total Cost Contingency Reserve | $1,075 |

Think about this exercise for a minute. Let's assume that the exercise had examples of threats and opportunities to the schedule. If you had a 30 percent probability of a 15-day activity delay, the expected value would be 4.5 days, which would be added to the schedule. And if the probability of an activity taking 10 days less than planned was 20 percent, the expected value would be -2 days. The resulting contingency for these two risks would be 2.5 days.

Now let's try another exercise. If the risk management process is new to you, the following exercise should help you put it all together by looking at it in a chart form.

**Exercise** Create a flowchart of the risk process from Identify Risks through Plan Risk Responses.

**Answer** Creating this chart will help you check whether you have understood what you read in this chapter. Your flowchart could be different than the following depiction.

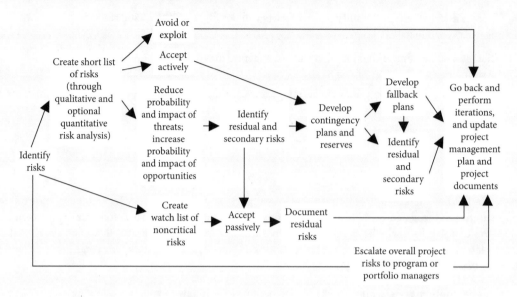

You are nearing the end of the "Plan Risk Responses" section! But first, let's examine some important concepts for the exam in this group of questions and answers. Take a few moments to test yourself.

| | |
|---|---|
| *Question* | What do you do with noncritical risks? |
| *Answer* | Document them in a watch list, and revisit them periodically. |
| *Question* | Would you choose only one risk response strategy? |
| *Answer* | No, you can select a combination of choices. |
| *Question* | What risk management activities are done during the execution of the project? |
| *Answer* | Watching out for watch-listed (noncritical) risks that increase in importance, and looking for new risks; implement contingency plans if triggers indicate the risk is about to occur or is occurring. |
| *Question* | What is the most important item to address in project team meetings? |
| *Answer* | Risk. |
| *Question* | How would risks be addressed in project meetings? |
| *Answer* | By asking, "What is the status of risks? Are there any new risks? Is there any change to the order of importance?" |

## Implement Risk Responses   PAGE 449

> **Process** Implement Risk Responses
> **Process Group** Executing
> **Knowledge Area** Risk Management

Implementing risk responses is a new process within the *PMBOK® Guide*, but it is not new within risk management. Although it has not previously been called out as a separate process, it is really the heart of risk management, and where the value of proper risk management becomes most apparent. When the preliminary work has been done well, the Implement Risk Responses process can be handled smoothly, since the previously documented plans allow for timely and effective responses to risk events.

The key to success is identifying risks in advance and then planning and preparing for their potential occurrence. Lessons learned from the current project or past, similar projects provide insight into the success of previous response plan implementation, and provide valuable input to this process.

Throughout the project, the risk register and risk report are reviewed regularly, ensuring everyone is aware of potential risks and ready to implement the planned responses as needed. Information on triggers enables the project manager, risk owner, and the team to recognize indications that a risk event is imminent. At that point, the risk owner, supported by the project manager, leads previously assigned resources in performing response activities. The consequences of threats are averted, or opportunities are taken advantage of. Risk thresholds[16] are documented in the plan along with an indication of what amount of relief is required from risk responses, so the success of the implementation can be evaluated.

The beginning of this chapter included the story of a project manager who was managing a hardware/software installation during a hurricane. Let's revisit that example.

If the project manager had performed proper risk management, he would have had a plan in place to avoid the risk of a hurricane impacting his project. For example, the scheduled hardware/software implementation could have been moved to before or after the forecasted hurricane. If the project manager and the risk owners had actively monitored known risk triggers (such as weather reports, including wind speeds and the projected path of the hurricane) and then implemented a risk response plan before the hurricane reached the area, they could have successfully avoided the rework and delays, along with the costs, resulting from the hurricane. Such preparation is critical to successfully implementing a risk response.

Even though we do our best, sometimes our carefully developed plans don't have the expected result. For example, let's assume that a risk owner or the project manager in the previous story implemented a risk response plan to reschedule the implementation, causing the schedule to be extended. Although the plan was executed as intended, the hurricane caused more damage than anticipated, and the schedule had to be extended beyond the planned number of days. Such unforeseen results are managed through change requests to the cost and schedule management plans.

Project documents are updated as a result of the Implement Risk Responses process. The risk register and risk report are updated with information on responses taken, describing details on how well the responses addressed the risk and suggesting changes to future risk response plans. The project manager adds information to the lessons learned register about what worked and what didn't work when the risk response was implemented. The risk report is updated with changes to the project's risk exposure and changes to planned risk responses. Ongoing issues, such as confusion or disagreement regarding the response as it was implemented, are added to the issue log.

## Monitor Risks    PAGE 453

**Process** Monitor Risks
**Process Group** Monitoring & Controlling
**Knowledge Area** Risk Management

Risk-related questions on the exam assume that the project manager has done proper project management, including assigning risk owners, putting contingency plans in place, and taking actions as outlined in the plan. The exam also assumes the project is substantially less risky than it would have been if the project manager had not planned the project and properly handled risk management. If you do not have experience using risk management in the real world, these exam questions may be difficult. Try the next exercise. It will help you understand what project management is like when it includes risk management.

**Exercise** Think about the previous paragraph. Because a project manager has completed risk management activities, they are no longer focusing on dealing with problems and figuring out what should be done. So what is the project manager doing?

Spend time really thinking through the actions involved in monitoring risks. Once you have completed your own list of actions, look at our list to make sure you do them all or at least understand what they are and why they are helpful to the project. You could include things on your list that are not on ours, but check each one of those items to determine if they are accurate.

| Actions Involved in Monitoring Risks | Included Below? |
|---|---|
| | |
| | |
| | |
| | |
| | |
| | |
| | |
| | |
| | |
| | |
| | |
| | |
| | |
| | |

**Answer** With risk management and proper project management, you are not doing things like figuring out what work needs to be done on the project or determining who will do a piece of work. Those efforts were already done in project planning. You are not spending much time solving problems, because you already have a plan in place for major problems. Even well-trained and experienced project managers do not always do enough to monitor risk. Read this list over carefully, and make sure you understand each of the actions. This is not a time for memorization; you are simply assessing what you know and do not know so that you can better understand these concepts and correctly answer situational questions on the exam.

The following is our list of actions involved in monitoring risks:

- Look for the occurrence of risk triggers.

- Monitor residual risks.

- Identify new risks and then analyze and plan for them. (Remember, risks can be identified anytime during the project, along with plans for how to handle the newly identified risks.)

- Evaluate the effectiveness of the risk management plan. Is it working? Does it need adjustment?

- Develop new risk responses. If a plan no longer seems like it will work, based on experience or new information, an alternate risk response or responses may be more appropriate. This review and analysis may lead to change requests.

- Collect and communicate risk status: "Four identified risks occurred last month, and all risk response plans were implemented successfully. Next month eight other risks may occur. Risk reserves are still considered adequate for covering the identified risks on this project."

- Communicate with stakeholders about risks: "Remember that one of the major risks on the project could occur next week."

- Determine if assumptions are still valid.

- Ensure proper risk management procedures are being followed.

- Revisit the watch list to see if additional risk responses need to be determined: "This change to the product scope might increase the impact of risk X, currently on our watch list. Let's analyze it."

- Recommend corrective actions to adjust to the severity of actual risk events: "This risk did not have the impact we expected, so let's adjust the contingency plan and change what we will do if the risk reoccurs."

- Look for any unexpected effects or consequences of risk events: "We did not expect this risk to damage the construction site. We need to decide how to fix the damage after we finish implementing the already agreed-upon contingency plan."

- Reevaluate risk identification and qualitative and quantitative risk analysis when the project deviates from the baseline: "The project cost is over the cost baseline (or over the schedule baseline). This implies we missed some major risks. Let's hold another risk identification session."

- Update risk management and response plans.

- Look at the changes, including recommended corrective actions, to see if they lead to identifying more risks: "We keep having to take corrective action related to this problem. Let's look for the root cause and identify any risks to the remainder of the project that relate to the problem."

- Submit change requests to integrated change control.

- Update the project management plan and project documents with approved changes and any relevant information from the analysis of work performance data.

- Create a database of risk data and lessons learned that may be used throughout the organization on other projects.

- Perform variance and trend analysis on project performance data.

- Use contingency reserves and adjust for approved changes.

- Update the risk register and risk report with current risk exposure.

- Reevaluate assumptions and constraints, capture new issues, and update existing ones.

- Close out risks.

Other work that is part of the Monitor Risks process is outlined in the following sections.

## Workarounds

If the project has deviated from the baselines, the team may take corrective action to bring it back in line. Recommendations for such corrective actions may include workarounds. Whereas contingency responses are developed in advance, workarounds are unplanned responses developed to deal with the occurrence of unanticipated events or problems on a project (or to deal with risks that had been accepted because of unlikelihood of occurrence and/or minimal impact). Project managers who do not perform risk management spend a lot of their time creating workarounds.

## Risk Reassessments

Questions always seem to come up on the exam that require you to know that the team needs to periodically review the risk management plan and risk register and adjust the documentation as required. It is important to determine whether any changes or adjustments need to be made to what was planned based on information that becomes apparent once work begins. Reassessing risk is a good topic for a team meeting or even a separate meeting. Many of the actions in the previous exercise relate to this. Remember, the results of such reassessments are part of risk reviews along with newly identified risks, closing risks, additional qualitative or quantitative risk analysis of new and/or previously identified risks, and further risk response planning.

## Reserve Analysis

While the work is being done, reserve analysis is simply a matter of checking to see how much reserve remains and how much might be needed. It is like checking the balance in your bank account. Reserves must be protected throughout the project life cycle.

Now let's talk about a concept that can be tricky on the exam, especially for those who are not experienced in using risk management. People wanting to change the project in response to problems that have occurred may suggest using the reserves instead of adding cost or time to the project. It is important to know that a contingency reserve may only be used to handle the impact of the specific risk it was set aside for. So, if the change is part of the risk response plan that was previously accounted for in the budget, the reserve designated for that response may be used. If it is not, the project manager must take preventive or corrective action, fast track, crash, or otherwise adjust the project to accommodate or make up for the impact of the problem and its resulting changes.

Under certain circumstances, usually determined by the performing organization, management reserves may be used for situations that are within the scope of the project but were not previously identified. For example, assume that a change to the order functionality on a website has exposed a data-sharing incompatibility with the legacy inventory management system's real-time inventory data that was not previously identified. A workaround needs to be created to keep the project on track, and management reserves will be used to hire experts to fix the problem and keep the project close to the current schedule.

If identified risks do not occur, the associated time or cost reserves should be returned to the company, rather than used to address other issues on the project. Reserves are not a free amount of time or cost that can be used at will by the project manager for any needs! If you are inexperienced with risk management, make sure you understand how reserves are used and protected.

## Technical Performance Analysis

Technical performance analysis uses project data to compare planned versus actual completion of technical requirements to determine if there is any variance from what was planned. Any variance could indicate possible risks to the project, either opportunities or threats.

## Meetings

Do you use "go around the room" status meetings on your projects? Are they an effective use of everyone's time? If you have 30 people in a room and each person gets a few minutes to report status on activities that do not directly impact others in the meeting, most people in the room will consider the meeting a waste of time. Status updates can often be collected through other means, such as reports or quick one-on-one conversations between the project manager and the team member. Instead, for the exam, think of status meetings as team meetings in which the project manager can perform risk reviews and risk audits, as discussed next:

- **Risk reviews** Risk reviews are held regularly to discuss the effectiveness of planned risk responses that have been implemented on the project, and may result in the identification of new risks, secondary risks created by risk response plans, and risks that are no longer applicable. Closing of risks allows the team to focus on managing the risks that are still open. The closing of a risk will likely result in the associated risk reserve being returned to the company.

- **Risk audits**[17] These audits can be performed during meetings to assess the overall process of risk management on the project. The auditing process is documented in the risk management plan.

## Outputs of Monitor Risks    PAGE 457    As with the previous risk management processes, updates to the risk report and other project documents are a result of Monitor Risks, along with additional outputs listed here.

## Work Performance Information

This is the analysis of the work performance data gathered as part of project control. Examples include results of risk reviews and audits of how well risk processes are working for the project, performance measurements on schedule progress, comparisons of planned versus actual risk data, determinations of which risks can be closed or are likely to close in the near future, and variance analyses comparing the planned versus actual time and cost of implemented risk responses. This information may be added as updates to the risk register, other project documents, and the project management plan, or it could be the basis of change requests.

## Risk Register Updates

The Monitor Risks process will add the following to the risk register:

- Outcomes of risk reassessments and risk audits
- Results of implemented risk responses
- Updates to previous parts of risk management, including the identification of new risks
- Closing of risks that are no longer applicable
- Details of what happened when risks occurred
- Lessons learned

## Change Requests

The Monitor Risks process will uncover needed project changes, including changes to the cost and schedule baselines due to overall and individual project risks.

479

Read situational questions describing suggested changes resulting from risk processes carefully to determine whether the actual work of the project has begun. You will have to determine what efforts are generating the change requests to help you evaluate answer choices that you may encounter. If the work of monitoring risks is being performed, new risks may be identified or planned risk responses may need to be adjusted based on project knowledge or an evaluation of risk processes. As a result of approved changes, risk planning must again be performed appropriately, and new risks must be evaluated and ranked, which may result in more risk response planning. This will generate change requests to integrated change control. The trick here is to remember that the approved project management plan and baselines are not static while work is performed, and changes to them must go through integrated change control.

## Project Management Plan Updates
This process can result in updates to any component of the project management plan, including the schedule, cost, quality, and procurement management plans, as well as the resource management plan and the scope, schedule, and cost baselines for the project. These changes generally reflect approved preventive or corrective actions or changes to the plans.

## Organizational Process Assets Updates
The Monitor Risks process may include the creation or enhancement of risk templates, such as the risk register, checklists, and risk report, as well as updates to risk management processes and procedures. The project's risk breakdown structure and other data may be added to organizational process assets as historical records for future projects.

 ## Common Risk Management Mistakes
The exam may describe situations where the wrong thing is being done as a way of testing whether you realize it is wrong. The following are some of the common risk management mistakes people make:

- Risk identification is completed without knowing enough about the project.
- Overall project risk is evaluated using only a questionnaire, interview, or Monte Carlo analysis and thus does not identify specific individual project risks.
- Risk identification ends too soon, resulting in a brief list (20 risks) rather than an extensive list (hundreds of risks).
- Padding is used instead of the risk management process.
- The processes of Identify Risks through Perform Quantitative Risk Analysis are blended, resulting in risks that are evaluated or judged as they come to light. This decreases the number of total risks identified and causes people to stop participating in risk identification.
- The risks identified are general rather than specific (for example, "communications" rather than "poor communication of customer's needs regarding installation of system XYZ could cause two weeks of rework").
- Some things considered to be risks are not uncertain; they are facts, and are therefore not risks.
- Whole categories of risks (such as technological, cultural, marketplace, etc.) are missed.
- Only one method is used to identify risks (for example, only using a checklist) rather than a combination of methods. A combination helps ensure that more risks are identified.
- The first risk response strategy identified is selected without looking at other options and finding the best option or combination of options.
- Risk management is not given enough attention.
- Project managers do not explain the risk management process to their team during project planning.
- Contracts are signed long before risks to the project are discussed.

**Exercise** **The Risk Management Process** There may be many questions about the process of risk management on the exam. The following exercise tests if you understand what you have read.

Recreate the risk management process, including the outputs, in the tables on the following pages. Check your answers against our answers when you are done. Even with one reading of this chapter, you should get most of the actions and outputs correct. After reading the chapter a second and a third time, you should be almost 100 percent accurate. Focus on remembering the key parts of risk management, not on memorization. Create these charts three times, and you should know the process well enough for the exam.

| Plan Risk Management | Identify Risks | Perform Qualitative Risk Analysis | Perform Quantitative Risk Analysis | Plan Risk Responses | Implement Risk Responses | Monitor Risks |
|---|---|---|---|---|---|---|
| | | Actions | | | | |
| | | | | | | |

| Plan Risk Management | Identify Risks | Perform Qualitative Risk Analysis | Perform Quantitative Risk Analysis | Plan Risk Responses | Implement Risk Responses | Monitor Risks |
|---|---|---|---|---|---|---|
| | | | Outputs | | | |

## Answer

| Plan Risk Management | Identify Risks | Perform Qualitative Risk Analysis | Perform Quantitative Risk Analysis | Plan Risk Responses | Implement Risk Responses | Monitor Risks |
|---|---|---|---|---|---|---|
| | | | Actions | | | |
| • Answer the following questions:<br>– How will you perform risk management on the project?<br>– What risk management policies or procedures exist, and what new ones are needed?<br>– When will the processes and procedures of risk management be performed?<br>– How will risks be identified, and what tools will be used?<br>– What are stakeholders' roles and responsibilities for risk management?<br>– How will you budget for risk management?<br>– What are the appetites and thresholds for risk? | • Identify all the risks on the project.<br>• Use tools such as brainstorming, root cause analysis, documentation review, checklists, interviews, SWOT analysis, assumptions and constraints analysis, and prompt lists to facilitate risk identification.<br>• Involve and engage stakeholders in the risk management process. | • Qualitatively determine which risk events warrant a response.<br>• Assess the quality of the risk data.<br>• Complete a risk urgency assessment.<br>• Subjectively determine the probability and impact of all risks.<br>• Determine if you will perform quantitative risk analysis or proceed directly to risk response planning.<br>• Find ways to represent the analyzed data from qualitative risk analysis.<br>• Document the watch list (noncritical risks).<br>• Determine the overall risk ranking for the project. | • Numerically evaluate the top risks.<br>• Quantitatively determine which risks warrant a response.<br>• Determine initial reserves.<br>• Create realistic time and cost objectives.<br>• Determine the probability of meeting project objectives. | • Use risk response strategies to decrease project threats and increase opportunities.<br>• Create contingency and fallback plans.<br>• Determine secondary and residual risks.<br>• Calculate final reserves.<br>• Determine risk owners (if not already done).<br>• Identify risk triggers.<br>• Accept or escalate risks, where appropriate. | • Implement contingency and fallback plans (risk owner and resources).<br>• Answer questions and facilitate clarification of plan details.<br>• Communicate with stakeholders according to the plan. | • Respond to risk triggers.<br>• Monitor residual risks.<br>• Create workarounds.<br>• Evaluate effectiveness of plans.<br>• Look for additional risks; then qualify, quantify, and plan responses for them as necessary.<br>• Revisit the watch list.<br>• Analyze work performance data and look for trends.<br>• Update plans.<br>• Communicate risk status.<br>• Close risks.<br>• Recommend changes, including corrective and preventive actions.<br>• Perform risk audits and risk reviews.<br>• Perform reserve analysis. |

483

| Plan Risk Management | Identify Risks | Perform Qualitative Risk Analysis | Perform Quantitative Risk Analysis | Plan Risk Responses | Implement Risk Responses | Monitor Risks |
|---|---|---|---|---|---|---|
| | | | Outputs | | | |
| • Risk management plan | • Risk register updates, including:<br>– List of risks<br>– Potential risk owners<br>– List of potential risk responses<br>• Risk report with summary information on risk details and the sources of overall project risk<br>• Project documents updates, such as lessons learned in the identification of risks for the project, any issues, and new or existing assumption and constraint information<br><br>.. | • Risk register updates, including:<br>– Risk ranking of the project as compared to other projects<br>– List of prioritized risks<br>– Risks by category<br>– Risks needing additional analysis and response<br>– Watch list<br>– Data on probability and impact analysis<br>– Data on risk urgency<br>– Assumptions and constraints analysis updates in assumption log | • Project document updates, including the following updates to the risk report:<br>– Assessment of overall project risk exposure<br>– Probability of meeting objectives<br>– Interpreted quantitative analysis results, such as key sources of overall project risk<br>– Prioritized list of individual project risks<br>– Trends in quantitative risk analysis results<br>– Recommended risk responses<br>– Initial reserves<br>• Updates to the risk register on the specific analysis for individual project risks | • Change requests<br>• Updates to the project management plan and project documents, including:<br>– Assumption log<br>– Cost forecasts<br>– Lessons learned register<br>– Project schedule<br>– Project team assignments<br>– Risk report<br>• Updates to the risk register, including:<br>– Residual and secondary risks<br>– Contingency and fallback plans<br>– Risk owners<br>– Triggers<br>– Final reserves<br>– Contracts<br>– Accepted risks | • Change requests to project management plan, including schedule and cost baselines<br>• Updates to project lessons learned register, including the effectiveness of risk responses and recommendations for managing future risks<br>• Updates to the issue log regarding areas of confusion or disagreement<br>• Updates to the risk report regarding:<br>– Overall project risk exposure after implementing planned responses<br>– Changes to planned risk responses<br>• Updates to the risk register, including data on risk response implementations | • Work performance information<br>• Updates to the risk register and other project documents, including:<br>– Outcomes of risk reviews and audits<br>– New risks<br>– Closed risks<br>– Details of risk occurrences<br>– Lessons learned<br>• Workarounds<br>• Change requests, including recommended corrective and preventive actions<br>• Updates to the project management plan and organizational process assets<br>• Updates to the risk report |

## Practice Exam

1. Your team has worked diligently to identify a large number of risks on a pharmaceutical development project. At this time, the risk register includes risks related to government regulations, risks involved in production and testing, and risks related to introducing a new product to the already flooded market, as well as many other areas of potential risk. Before proceeding with the project, these risks must be assessed, and risk response plans must be developed for the highest-ranking risks. All the following are factors in the assessment of project risk except:

    A. Risk events
    B. Risk probability
    C. Amount at stake
    D. Insurance premiums

2. If a project has a 60 percent chance of a $100,000 profit and a 40 percent chance of a $100,000 loss, the expected monetary value (EMV) for the project is:

    A. $100,000 profit
    B. $60,000 loss
    C. $20,000 profit
    D. $40,000 loss

3. Assuming the ends of a range of estimates are +/− 3 sigma from the mean, which of the following range estimates involves the least risk?

    A. 30 days, plus or minus 5 days
    B. 22 to 30 days
    C. Optimistic = 26 days, most likely = 30 days, pessimistic = 33 days
    D. Mean of 28 days

4. Which of the following risk events is most likely to interfere with attaining a project's schedule objective?

    A. Delays in obtaining required approvals
    B. Substantial increases in the cost of purchased materials
    C. Contract disputes that generate claims for increased payments
    D. Slippage of the planned post-implementation review meeting

5. If a risk has a 20 percent chance of happening in a given month, and the project is expected to last five months, what is the probability that this risk event will occur during the fourth month of the project?

    A. Less than 1 percent
    B. 20 percent
    C. 60 percent
    D. 80 percent

6. If a risk event has a 90 percent chance of occurring, and the consequences will be $10,000, what does $9,000 represent?

    A. Risk value
    B. Present value
    C. Expected monetary value
    D. Contingency budget

485

7. Most of the project risks will be identified during which risk management processes?

    A. Perform Quantitative Risk Analysis and Identify Risks
    B. Identify Risks and Monitor Risks
    C. Perform Qualitative Risk Analysis and Monitor Risks
    D. Identify Risks and Perform Qualitative Risk Analysis

8. You are iterating the project management plan and will be meeting with the sponsors to get approval. There have been some problems on recent projects because the projects were started quickly and it was assumed that there would be few challenges. You know that the sponsors will want assurances that this project will not have similar issues. You have evaluated the approach and have planned the project, including how you will manage risk, in order to deliver a better outcome. You have a few minor risks on the watch list. What, if anything, should be done with those risks?

    A. Document them for historical use on other projects.
    B. Document them and revisit them during project monitoring and controlling.
    C. Document them and set them aside because they are already covered in your contingency plans.
    D. Document them and give them to the customer.

9. You are embarking on a new technology upgrade project that is considered key to future growth of the business. Because of the critical nature of the project, you recognize the importance of performing thorough risk management, and you want to make sure you have considered all relevant project information before beginning. All the following are always inputs to the risk management process except:

    A. Historical information
    B. Lessons learned
    C. Work breakdown structure
    D. Project status reports

10. Risk thresholds are determined to help:

    A. The team rank the project risks
    B. The project manager estimate the project
    C. The team schedule the project
    D. Management know how other managers will act on the project

11. A new project manager is beginning work on her first project. She is planning to use her training to implement many risk identification methods. She realizes that some identified risks will be managed throughout the project, while others will not be considered important enough to deal with. She is aware that risk management is ongoing throughout the project, as new risks may be identified, risk ratings may change, and the project itself may change. She realizes that all the following are common results of risk management except:

    A. Contract terms and conditions are created.
    B. The project management plan is changed.
    C. The communications management plan is changed.
    D. The project charter is changed.

12. You have identified several risks on your project for which purchasing insurance is a possibility. The insurance company your firm uses has quoted reasonable rates, and your analysis shows that purchasing insurance makes sense as a contingency plan in these cases. Your organization has a low threshold for risk but wants to keep costs in line as the profit margin on the product of this project is low. The strategy of purchasing insurance is best considered an example of risk:

    A. Escalation
    B. Transference
    C. Acceptance
    D. Avoidance

13. The project has been chartered to address concerns of low levels of customer satisfaction with the help desk of a large online retailer. You and your team are considering options including upgrading computer systems and software programs, adding additional help desk staff, and improving help desk training. You realize the impact of such changes will be difficult to measure, and you are finding it challenging to evaluate the exact cost impact of risks and responses the team has identified. You should evaluate on a(n):

    A. Quantitative basis
    B. Numerical basis
    C. Qualitative basis
    D. Econometric basis

14. Outputs of the Plan Risk Responses process include:

    A. Residual risks, fallback plans, and contingency reserves
    B. Risk triggers, contracts, and a risk list
    C. Secondary risks, process updates, and risk owners
    D. Contingency plans, project management plan updates, and sensitivity analysis

15. Workarounds are determined during which risk management process?

    A. Identify Risks
    B. Perform Quantitative Risk Analysis
    C. Plan Risk Responses
    D. Monitor Risks

16. During which risk management process is a determination made to transfer a risk?

    A. Identify Risks
    B. Implement Risk Responses
    C. Plan Risk Responses
    D. Monitor Risks

17. A project manager has just finished the risk response plan for a $387,000 engineering project. Which of the following should he probably do next?

    A. Determine the overall risk rating of the project.
    B. Begin to analyze the risks that show up in the project drawings.
    C. Add work packages to the project work breakdown structure.
    D. Hold a project risk review.

18. A project manager analyzed the quality of risk data and asked various stakeholders to determine the probability and impact of a number of risks. He is about to move to the next process of risk management. Based on this information, what has the project manager forgotten to do?

    A. Evaluate trends in risk analysis.
    B. Identify triggers.
    C. Provide a standardized risk rating matrix.
    D. Create a fallback plan.

19. A project manager has assembled the project team. They have identified 56 risks on the project, determined what would trigger the risks, rated them on a risk rating matrix, tested their assumptions, and assessed the quality of the data used. The team is continuing to move through the risk management process. What has the project manager forgotten to do?

    A. Conduct a simulation.
    B. Perform risk mitigation.
    C. Determine the overall risk ranking for the project.
    D. Involve other stakeholders.

20. You are a project manager for the construction of a major new manufacturing plant that is unlike any that has been done before. The project cost is estimated at $30,000,000, and the project will make use of three sellers. Once begun, the project cannot be cancelled, as there will be a large expenditure on plant and equipment. When managing a project, it is most important to carefully:

    A. Review all cost proposals from the sellers.
    B. Examine the budget reserves.
    C. Complete the project charter.
    D. Perform an identification of risks.

21. Your team has come up with 434 risks and 16 major causes of those risks. The project is the last in a series of projects that the team has worked on together. The sponsor is very supportive, and a lot of time was invested in making sure the project work was complete and signed off by all key stakeholders.

    During project planning, the team cannot come up with an effective way to mitigate or insure against a risk. It is not work that can be outsourced, nor can it be deleted. What would be the best solution?

    A. Accept the risk.
    B. Continue to investigate ways to mitigate the risk.
    C. Look for ways to avoid the risk.
    D. Look for ways to transfer the risk.

22. A project manager is quantifying risk for her project. Several of her experts are off-site, but wish to be included. How can this be done?

    A. Perform Monte Carlo analysis using the internet as a tool.
    B. Apply the critical path method.
    C. Determine options for recommended corrective action.
    D. Use facilitation techniques.

23. Having just been hired to manage a project to improve the efficiency of data processing in the accounting department, the project manager is most concerned about managing risk on the project. The timeline is short, and the sponsor's expectations are high. Which of the following would best help the project manager in her initial assessment of risks on the project?

    A. A sensitivity analysis
    B. Her project scope statement from the project planning process
    C. A review of enterprise environmental factors
    D. A conversation with a project manager who worked on a similar project

24. You have been appointed as the manager of a new, large, and complex project. Because this project is business-critical and highly visible, senior management has told you to analyze the project's risks and prepare response strategies for them as soon as possible. The organization has risk management procedures that are seldom used or followed, and has had a history of handling risks badly. The project's first milestone is in two weeks. In preparing the risk response plan, input from which of the following is generally least important?

    A. Project team members
    B. Project sponsor
    C. Individuals responsible for risk management policies and templates
    D. Key stakeholders

25. You were in the middle of a two-year project to deploy new technology to field offices across the country. A hurricane caused power outages just when the upgrade was near completion. When the power was restored, all the project reports and historical data were lost, with no way of retrieving them. What should have been done to prevent this problem?

    A. Purchase insurance.
    B. Plan for a reserve fund.
    C. Monitor the weather and have a contingency plan.
    D. Schedule the installation outside of the hurricane season.

26. A system development project is nearing project closing when a previously unidentified risk is discovered. This could potentially affect the project's overall ability to deliver. What should be done next?

    A. Alert the project sponsor of potential impacts to cost, scope, or schedule.
    B. Qualify the risk.
    C. Mitigate this risk by developing a risk response plan.
    D. Develop a workaround.

27. The cost performance index (CPI) of a project is 0.6, and the schedule performance index (SPI) is 0.71. The project has 625 work packages and is being completed over a four-year period. The team members are inexperienced, and the project received little support for proper planning. Which of the following is the best thing to do?

    A. Update risk identification and analysis.
    B. Spend more time improving the cost estimates.
    C. Remove as many work packages as possible.
    D. Reorganize the responsibility assignment matrix.

28. You believe that the project you have undertaken is relatively straightforward, with less risk than most other projects you have worked on. Therefore, you do not spend a long time on risk identification. While preparing your risk responses, you identify secondary risks that could result in serious consequences later in the project. What should you do?

    A. Add reserves to the project to accommodate the new risks and notify management.
    B. Document the risk items, and calculate the expected monetary value based on the probability and impact of the occurrences.
    C. Determine the risk events and the associated costs, then add the cost to the project budget as a reserve.
    D. Add a 10 percent contingency to the project budget, and notify the customer.

29. During project executing, a team member is coordinating with a supplier, and identifies a risk that is not in the risk register. It appears that the pieces of heavy equipment you have ordered from a supplier are larger than anticipated, and they may not all fit into the warehouse the team has leased to store them until they are needed. What should you do?

    A. Get further information on how the team member identified the risk because you already performed a detailed analysis and did not identify this risk.
    B. Disregard the risk because risks were identified during project planning.
    C. Inform the customer about the risk.
    D. Analyze the risk.

30. During project executing, the team member who is most experienced in the programming work required for the project informs you that he has accepted a new position at another company, and has given his two weeks' notice. This is a major problem that was not included in the risk register. What should you do first?

    A. Create a workaround.
    B. Reevaluate the Identify Risks process.
    C. Look for any unexpected effects of the problem.
    D. Tell management.

31. Which of the following is the primary responsibility of a risk owner?

    A. Identify new risks and create workarounds.
    B. Respond to risk triggers and implement the planned risk responses.
    C. Report to the project manager that a risk has occurred, and note the consequences.
    D. Quantitatively analyze risks as assigned by the project manager.

32. A project has had some problems, but now seems under control. In the last few months, almost all the reserve has been used, and most of the negative impacts of events that had been predicted have occurred. There are only four activities left, and two of them are on the critical path.

    Management now informs the project manager that it would be in the performing organization's best interest to finish the project two weeks earlier than scheduled in order to receive an additional profit. In response, the project manager sends out a request for proposal for some work that the team was going to do, hoping to find another company that might be able to do the work faster. The project manager can best be said to be attempting to work with:

    A. Reserves
    B. Opportunities
    C. Scope validation
    D. Threats

33. Monte Carlo analysis is used to:

    A. Get an indication of the risk involved in the project.
    B. Estimate an activity's length.
    C. Simulate possible quality issues on the project.
    D. Prove to management that extra staff is needed.

34. A project team is creating a project management plan when management asks them to identify project risks and provide some form of qualitative output as soon as possible. What should the project team provide?

    A. Risk triggers
    B. Prioritized list of risks
    C. Contingency reserves
    D. Probability of achieving the time and cost objectives

35. A project manager is creating a risk response plan. However, every time a risk response is suggested, another risk is identified that is caused by the response. Which of the following is the best thing for the project manager to do?

    A. Get more people involved in the Identify Risks process, since risks have been missed.
    B. Make sure the project work is better understood.
    C. Spend more time making sure the risk responses are clearly defined.
    D. Document the new risks and continue the Plan Risk Responses process.

36. A watch list is an output of which risk management process?

    A. Plan Risk Responses
    B. Perform Quantitative Risk Analysis
    C. Perform Qualitative Risk Analysis
    D. Implement Risk Responses

37. During the Identify Risks process, a project manager and stakeholders used various methods to identify risks and created a long list of those risks. The project manager then made sure all the risks were understood and that triggers had been identified. Later, in the Plan Risk Responses process, he took all the risks identified by the stakeholders and determined ways to mitigate them. What has he done wrong?

    A. The project manager should have waited until the Perform Qualitative Risk Analysis process to get the stakeholders involved.
    B. More people should have been involved in the Plan Risk Responses process.
    C. The project manager should have created workarounds.
    D. Triggers should not be identified until the Implement Risk Responses process.

38. Since a template for team meetings does not appear to be available, you are creating one. You think it could also be used for future projects. You want to generalize the agenda template to include topics all project managers would use. Which of the following must be included as an agenda item at all team meetings?

    A. Discussion of project risks
    B. Status of current activities
    C. Identification of new activities
    D. Review of project problems

491

## Answers

1. **Answer** D
   **Explanation** Insurance premiums are not factors in assessing project risk. They come into play when you determine which risk response strategy you will use.

2. **Answer** C
   **Explanation** Expected monetary value is calculated by EMV = probability × impact. We need to calculate both positive and negative values and then add them:
   $$0.6 \times \$100,000 = \$60,000$$
   $$0.4 \times (\$100,000) = (\$40,000)$$
   Expected monetary value = $60,000 – $40,000 = $20,000 profit

3. **Answer** C
   **Explanation** A mean of 28 days is not a range estimate, and so must be eliminated as a possible answer. When you look at the ranges of each of the other choices, you will see that 30 days, plus or minus 5 days = a range of 10 days. The range of 22 to 30 days = a range of 8 days. An optimistic estimate of 26 days, most likely estimate of 30 days, and pessimistic estimate of 33 days represents a range of 7 days. The estimate with the smallest range is the least risky, and is therefore the correct choice. Did you realize the words "+/– 3 sigma" are extraneous? Practice reading questions that are wordy and have extraneous data.

4. **Answer** A
   **Explanation** Cost increases and contract disputes for payments will not necessarily interfere with schedule. If a post-implementation review meeting slips, it may not interfere with the project schedule. Delays in obtaining required approvals always cause time delays, and are therefore the most likely to threaten the project schedule.

5. **Answer** B
   **Explanation** No calculation is needed. If there is a 20 percent chance in any one month, the chance in the fourth month is 20 percent.

6. **Answer** C
   **Explanation** Expected monetary value is calculated by multiplying the probability times the impact. In this case, EMV = 0.9 × $10,000 = $9,000.

7. **Answer** B
   **Explanation** This is a tricky question. Although risks can be identified at any time throughout the project, most risks are identified during the Identify Risks process. Newly emerging risks are identified in the Monitor Risks process.

8. **Answer** B
   **Explanation** Risks change throughout the project. You need to review risks at intervals during the project to ensure noncritical risks on the watch list have not become critical.

9. **Answer** D
   **Explanation** Project status reports can be an input to risk management. However, when completing risk management for the first time, you would not have project status reports. Therefore, project status reports are not always an input to risk management.

10. **Answer** A

    **Explanation** If you know the risk thresholds of the stakeholders, you can determine how they might react to different situations and risk events. You use this information to help assign levels of risk to each work package or activity based on their probability and impact.

11. **Answer** D

    **Explanation** A contract is a tool to transfer risk. The project management plan could change to include a modified WBS and new work packages related to mitigating risk. The communications management plan could change as a way to address a risk. A change to the charter is a fundamental change to the project and may require a major adjustment to all aspects of the project management plan. It is not a common result of risk management efforts.

12. **Answer** B

    **Explanation** A risk is only escalated if it is outside the scope of the project or beyond the project manager's authority, which is not the case in this scenario. Acceptance of risk means doing nothing (if it happens, it happens, or contingency plans are created). Avoidance of risk means we change the way we will execute the project so the risk is no longer a factor. Transference is passing the risk off to another party. Many people think of using insurance as a way of decreasing impact. However, purchasing insurance transfers the risk to another party.

13. **Answer** C

    **Explanation** If you cannot determine an exact cost impact of the event, use qualitative estimates such as Low, Medium, and High.

14. **Answer** A

    **Explanation** A risk list, process updates, and sensitivity analysis are not outputs of the Plan Risk Responses process. Residual risks, fallback plans, and contingency reserves are all outputs of the Plan Risk Responses process, making this the correct answer.

15. **Answer** D

    **Explanation** Creating a workaround involves determining how to handle a risk that has occurred but that was not included in the risk register. The project must be in the Monitor Risks process if risks have occurred.

16. **Answer** C

    **Explanation** Transference is a risk response strategy. Risk response strategies are determined in the Plan Risk Responses process.

17. **Answer** C

    **Explanation** This situation is occurring during project planning. Planning must be completed before moving on. Determining the risk rating of the project is done during Perform Qualitative Risk Analysis, and should have already been done. Project risk reviews occur during Monitor Risks. Adding work packages that are part of the newly planned risk responses comes next in project planning. This is an example of iterating the project management plan.

18. **Answer** C

    **Explanation** The project manager is in the Perform Qualitative Risk Analysis process. This process includes risk data quality assessment along with probability and impact matrix development. It appears the project manager has not yet completed the matrix, which is used to sort risks based on their probability and impact ratings. Trend analysis, the identification of triggers, and the development of fallback plans will occur later in risk management.

19. **Answer** D

**Explanation** The process the project manager has used so far is fine, except the input of other stakeholders is needed in order to identify more risks.

20. **Answer** D

**Explanation** A review of cost proposals could be done, but it is not a pressing issue based on the situation provided. Examining the budget reserves could also be done, but not until risk response planning is completed. It is always important to carefully complete a project charter, but there are other issues needing detailed attention in this situation. Since a project like this has never been done before, and there will be a large cost outlay, it would be best for the project manager to spend more time on risk management. Risk identification is the most proactive response and will have the greatest positive impact on the project.

21. **Answer** A

**Explanation** This question relates real-world situations to risk types. Did you realize the entire first paragraph is extraneous? Based on the question, you cannot remove the work to avoid it, nor can you insure or outsource it to transfer the risk. This leaves acceptance as the only correct choice.

22. **Answer** D

**Explanation** Current technology makes it possible to take advantage of input from experts, even when they are off-site. Virtual interviews or group meetings can be facilitated by the project manager for this purpose.

23. **Answer** D

**Explanation** Sensitivity analysis is a tool of quantitative risk analysis, and is used to compare risks to the project that have already been identified. Reviewing the scope statement is a good idea, but it will only provide an assessment of risk on that aspect of the project. Enterprise environmental factors involve company culture and organization, which also are not adequate to assess overall project risk. A conversation with a project manager who worked on a similar project would provide the most value, as the risks she dealt with on that project are likely to be similar to what the project manager will experience on this project.

24. **Answer** B

**Explanation** Team members will have knowledge of the project as well as the product of the project and will thus have a lot to contribute to risk responses. Those responsible for risk templates will be able to provide the templates from past projects (historical records) and will, therefore, be very important. Key stakeholders will know more about the technical work of the project and can help plan "What are we going to do about it?" Because of that, they are not likely to be the least important. The sponsor may have the least knowledge of what will work to address risks. Sponsors need to be involved in the project and help identify risks. They may even approve the response plans created by others, but they are not generally major contributors to response plans.

25. **Answer** C

**Explanation** The risk is the loss of data due to a power outage. Purchasing insurance is not related to preventing the problem. It transfers the risk. Creating a reserve fund is acceptance of the risk, and would help address the cost factors after the power failure, but it would not reduce the probability or impact of the power failure. Avoiding the hurricane by scheduling the installation at a different time reduces the power outage risk, but could have a large negative impact on the project schedule and so is not the best choice. The best choice of the options provided is to monitor the weather and know when to implement the contingency plan.

26. **Answer** B

    **Explanation** A workaround is an unplanned response to an event that is occurring. The risk discussed in the question has been identified, but it is not occurring at this time, so there is no need to take the action of creating a workaround. You need to analyze the problem before talking to the sponsor. You cannot mitigate the risk until you qualify it. Qualifying the risk will help you determine how to proceed.

27. **Answer** A

    **Explanation** This project has deviated so far from the baseline that updated risk identification and risk analysis should be performed.

28. **Answer** B

    **Explanation** When new risks are identified, they should go through the risk management process. You need to subjectively determine the probability and impact of the risks, and if the risks are determined to pose significant threats to the project, attempt to diminish the threats through the Plan Risk Responses process. Only after these efforts should you consider adding reserves for time and/or cost. Any reserves should be based on a detailed analysis of risk. Calculating the expected monetary value of the risks is an important part of the risk management process, and the best choice presented here.

29. **Answer** D

    **Explanation** First, you need to determine what the risk entails and the impact to the project, then determine what actions you will take regarding the risk.

30. **Answer** A

    **Explanation** Because an unidentified problem or risk occurred, it is important to reevaluate the Identify Risks process as well as to look for unexpected effects of the problem. However, they are not your first choices. You might need to inform management, but this is reactive, not proactive, and also not the first thing you should do. Since this is a problem that has occurred, rather than a problem that has just been identified, the first thing you must do is address the risk by creating a workaround.

31. **Answer** B

    **Explanation** A risk owner may be involved in developing risk responses for their assigned risk. They are also responsible for monitoring the project for triggers that indicate the risk is imminent and for managing implementation of the planned risk response.

32. **Answer** B

    **Explanation** The wording of this question can be confusing. Scope validation involves meeting with the customer to gain formal acceptance, so that cannot be the best choice. Reserve is mentioned in the situation, but the use of reserves is not the primary concern. The project manager is working to make a positive impact on the project more likely to occur. Therefore, he is working with an opportunity. This may include analyzing the appropriateness of using management reserves to cover the cost of exploiting the opportunity.

33. **Answer** A

    **Explanation** A Monte Carlo analysis could indicate that an estimate for an activity needs to change, but it does not indicate what the activity estimate should be. Monte Carlo is a simulation, but it does not specifically address quality. It does not deal directly with staff or resource needs either. Project risk can be assessed using Monte Carlo analysis. By considering the inputs to the weighted estimates along with the network diagram, you can get a better idea of the overall project risk.

495

34. **Answer** B

    **Explanation** This question essentially asks, "What is an output of Perform Qualitative Risk Analysis?" The probability of achieving time and cost objectives is determined during the Perform Quantitative Risk Analysis process. Risk triggers and contingency reserves are parts of the Plan Risk Responses process. A prioritized list of risks is an output of Perform Qualitative Risk Analysis.

35. **Answer** D

    **Explanation** Did you realize this question describes secondary risks? Identifying secondary risks is an important part of completing the Plan Risk Responses process. With that in mind, the best thing to do is to document the newly identified risks and continue the Plan Risk Responses process.

36. **Answer** C

    **Explanation** A watch list is made up of low-priority risks that, in the Perform Qualitative Risk Analysis process, were determined to be of too low priority or low impact to require further attention at this time.

37. **Answer** B

    **Explanation** Stakeholders should be included in the Identify Risks process. Some triggers may be identified in the Identify Risks process, but they are generally identified and added to the risk register in the Plan Risk Responses process. Workarounds are created as unidentified risk events occur. The project manager's error was not including others in the Plan Risk Responses process. Plan Risk Responses must include the involvement of all risk owners and possibly other stakeholders as well.

38. **Answer** A

    **Explanation** Risk is so important that it must be discussed at all team meetings.

© 2018 RMC Publications, Inc.™ • 952.846.4484 • info@rmcls.com • www.rmcls.com

# Procurement Management

A very experienced student in an RMC class was upset about a situation at work. He said he had arranged a meeting with a seller, and the seller did not show up. He then rescheduled the meeting, and the seller still did not show up. When the instructor asked what kind of contract he was working with, the student had to contact his office to find out he had a fixed-price contract. The instructor then asked him where in the contract it said the seller had to attend such meetings. After some investigation, the student determined that meetings were not listed in the contract. Why would a seller attend a meeting if he was not getting paid for it?

Think about what procurement management means on a project. We are not talking about the role of an attorney or a contracting or procurement office. We are talking about the project manager's role.

The basic procurement management skills required of a project manager include being able to help create, read, and manage contracts and any supporting documentation.

For some people, procurement management is one of the hardest knowledge areas on the exam. If you have worked with contracts before, you might have to fine-tune your knowledge and learn new terms for what you already do. You might also have to understand the project manager's role a little better, but you should score well on these questions. If you are like many other people, however, you may have little experience in procurement. Regardless of your real-world experience, the PMP exam will test you as if you were an expert. This chapter walks you through the procurement process and suggests ways you can most effectively study this topic and prepare for the exam.

## QUICKTEST

- Procurement management process
- Procurement management plan
- Procurement strategy
- Types of agreements
- Contract types
  - Fixed-price
  - Time and material
  - Cost-reimbursable
- Advantages/disadvantages of each contract type
- Contract change control system
- Termination
- Bid documents
- Make-or-buy analysis
- Source selection criteria
- Noncompetitive forms of procurement
- Types of procurement SOW
- Procurement performance review
- Claims administration
- Closed procurements
- Bidder conferences
- Proposal evaluation
- Risk and contract type
- Make-or-buy decisions
- Weighting system
- Screening system
- Independent cost estimates
- Incentives
- Special provisions
- Standard contract
- Terms and conditions
- Change requests
- Breach
- Waivers
- Claims
- Product validation
- Procurement conflicts
- Procurement audit
- Formal acceptance
- Records management system
- Privity
- Qualified seller list
- Centralized/decentralized contracting
- Price
- Profit
- Cost
- Target price
- Sharing ratio
- Ceiling price
- Letter of intent
- Presentations
- Nondisclosure agreement
- What makes a legal contract
- Force majeure

497

# Procurement Management TWELVE

| INITIATING | PLANNING<br>(This is the only process group with a set order.) | EXECUTING | MONITORING & CONTROLLING | CLOSING |
|---|---|---|---|---|
| Select project manager | **Determine development approach, life cycle, and how you will plan for each knowledge area** | Execute work according to the project management plan | **Take action to monitor and control the project** | Confirm work is done to requirements |
| Determine company culture and existing systems | Define and prioritize requirements | Produce product deliverables (product scope) | Measure performance against performance measurement baseline | Complete final procurement closure |
| Collect processes, procedures, and historical information | Create project scope statement | Gather work performance data | **Measure performance against other metrics in the project management plan** | Gain final acceptance of product |
| Divide large projects into phases or smaller projects | **Assess what to purchase and create procurement documents** | **Request changes** | **Analyze and evaluate data and performance** | Complete financial closure |
| Understand business case and benefits management plan | Determine planning team | Implement only approved changes | **Determine if variances warrant a corrective action or other change request(s)** | Hand off completed product |
| Uncover initial requirements, assumptions, risks, constraints, and existing agreements | Create WBS and WBS dictionary | Continuously improve; perform progressive elaboration | **Influence factors that cause change** | Solicit customer's feedback about the project |
| Assess project and product feasibility within the given constraints | Create activity list | Follow processes | **Request changes** | Complete final performance reporting |
| Create measurable objectives and success criteria | Create network diagram | Determine whether quality plan and processes are correct and effective | Perform integrated change control | Index and archive records |
| Develop project charter | Estimate resource requirements | Perform quality audits and issue quality reports | Approve or reject changes | Gather final lessons learned and update knowledge bases |
| Identify stakeholders and determine their expectations, interest, influence, and impact | Estimate activity durations and costs | Acquire final team and physical resources | **Update project management plan and project documents** | |
| Request changes | Determine critical path | Manage people | Inform stakeholders of all change request results | |
| Develop assumption log | Develop schedule | Evaluate team and individual performance; provide training | Monitor stakeholder engagement | |
| Develop stakeholder register | Develop budget | Hold team-building activities | Confirm configuration compliance | |
| | Determine quality standards, processes, and metrics | Give recognition and rewards | Create forecasts | |
| | **Determine team charter and all roles and responsibilities** | Use issue logs | Gain customer's acceptance of interim deliverables | |
| | Plan communications and stakeholder engagement | Facilitate conflict resolution | Perform quality control | |
| | Perform risk identification, qualitative and quantitative risk analysis, and risk response planning | Release resources as work is completed | Perform risk reviews, reassessments, and audits | |
| | **Go back—iterations** | Send and receive information, and solicit feedback | Manage reserves | |
| | **Finalize procurement strategy and documents** | Report on project performance | **Manage, evaluate, and close procurements** | |
| | Create change and configuration management plans | Facilitate stakeholder engagement and manage expectations | Evaluate use of physical resources | |
| | **Finalize all management plans** | Hold meetings | | |
| | **Develop realistic and sufficient project management plan and baselines** | **Evaluate sellers; negotiate and contract with sellers** | | |
| | Gain formal approval of the plan | **Use and share project knowledge** | | |
| | Hold kickoff meeting | Execute contingency plans | | |
| | **Request changes** | **Update project management plan and project documents** | | |

**Rita's Process Chart™
Procurement Management**
Where are we in the project management process?

**TRICKS OF THE TRADE®** The *PMBOK® Guide* uses the terms "contract" and "agreement," so you need to be prepared to see both on the exam and understand what each means. Contracts can be written or verbal, are typically created with an external entity, and involve an exchange of goods or services for some type of compensation (usually monetary). The contract forms the legal relationship between the entities; it is mutually binding and provides the framework for how a failure by one side will be addressed and ultimately remedied in court.

The broader term "agreement" encompasses documents or communications that outline internal or external relationships and their intentions. A contract is a type of agreement, but an agreement isn't necessarily a contract. Imagine that the international division and the US division of a company want to leverage their resources to achieve a shared strategic objective; they would create an agreement, but likely not a contract. Agreements can be used to express and outline the intentions of projects. The charter and the project management plans are examples of agreements that are not contracts; they are internal agreements. Some other examples of agreements are service level agreements, memos of intent, letters of intent, letters of agreement, emails, and verbal agreements.

So what does this mean for you? The way you communicate, escalate, and solve problems will vary depending on whether your actions are governed by a contract or an internal agreement. For example, notifying a seller of a default on a contract term or condition should be done through formal written communication to create a record and ensure appropriate legal action can be taken if necessary. In comparison, for an internal agreement, failure to meet a term of the agreement might be handled in a conversation followed up by an email. For the exam, understanding whether a situational question describes an internal agreement or a contract with an outside party might help you select the right answer. In this chapter, we primarily use the term "contract," because the procurement process is used to acquire necessary resources that are outside the project team and involve legal documents between the buyer and seller.

**TRICKS OF THE TRADE®** If you have little or no experience working with contracts, you should obtain from your company some sample contracts, requests for proposals, and the resulting sellers' proposals. Spend some time reviewing them before reading on. It might also be valuable to contact your organization's contracts, procurement, or legal department. The exam assumes that you have a close working relationship with these departments, that as a project manager you have specific involvement in the procurement process even if you do not lead that process, and that the procurement process cannot occur without your involvement. You have an opportunity to build an extremely worthwhile relationship with these other departments when you ask, "What should I know about contracts?" Plus, you can improve your working relationship by explaining the project management process to them. Try it!

The following should help you understand how each part of procurement management fits into the overall project management process:

| The Procurement Management Process | Done During |
| --- | --- |
| Plan Procurement Management | Planning process group |
| Conduct Procurements | Executing process group |
| Control Procurements | Monitoring and controlling process group |

## Overview of the Procurement Management[1] Process

Typically, procurement is a formal process to obtain goods and services. Private companies have a lot of flexibility in their procurement practices. Because government entities are spending public funds, however, they normally have to comply with laws, rules, and regulations that specifically govern each step of the procurement process. Private companies that use public funds from the government may also be required to comply with some or all of these regulations. If the work or result of the project is regulated (as in medical, pharmaceutical, food manufacturing, or construction, for example), the laws and regulations must be adhered to.

To help you better understand procurement, we will start with an overview of the process. Do not just read the description provided! Instead, imagine what it would take to make this happen in the real world. The rest of this chapter discusses the process in more detail. Make sure you understand the overview and can generally describe the procurement process before you continue reading the chapter. Know that there can be multiple procurements on a project and that this process is done for every procurement on the project. Also, remember that contract life cycles begin and end throughout the life of a project.

When a project is planned, the scope is analyzed to determine whether the entire project scope can be completed internally, or if any of the work, deliverables, materials, equipment, etc. will need to be outsourced. This analysis results in make-or-buy decisions. If one or more procurements are needed, the procurement department gets involved in the project to manage the procurement process.

This department may also be referred to as the contracting, purchasing, or legal department, but for simplicity, we'll call it the "procurement department." Managing procurements requires legal knowledge, negotiation skills, and an understanding of the procurement process. Although project managers are not often expected to take the lead in legal matters, negotiations, or managing the procurement process, they must be familiar with all of these aspects of procurement. Project managers must understand what the procurement experts will need from them, provide the experts with that information, and then work with the procurement department throughout the life of the procurements. If there is not a procurement department in the organization, the responsibilities of managing procurements are assumed by the project manager.

When a decision has been made to procure goods or services from an outside source, the project manager will facilitate the creation of a plan for the overall procurement process (a procurement management plan), a plan for how each contract will be managed (a procurement strategy), and a description of the work to be done by each seller (a procurement statement of work).

The procurement department may review the scope of the work for completeness (always a good idea), and the project manager might add scope related to project management activities (such as specific reporting requirements or required attendance at meetings), resulting in the finalized procurement statement of work. This procurement statement of work should be combined with the contract terms to make up the finalized bid documents (RFP, RFI, or RFQ) that are sent to prospective sellers. All of these make up common procurement documents.[2]

The procurement manager will determine what type of contract, bid document, and statement of work should be used. The most common bid documents are request for proposal (RFP), request for information (RFI), and request for quotation (RFQ). The type of bid document used is influenced by the contract type selected and the content within the procurement statement of work. As you will see later in this chapter, different types of contracts require project managers to focus their management activities on different areas.

At this point, the prospective sellers take action, and the buyer waits for their responses. The prospective sellers review the bid documents and determine whether they are interested in submitting a response or proposal to try to win the work. They may have the opportunity to participate in a bidder conference or a pre-proposal meeting. As part of the procurement process, prospective sellers may also have the opportunity to submit questions; buyer responses are then shared with all prospective sellers. As a best practice, all questions should be in writing and should relate to the bid documents. Sellers need to submit these questions to the buyer before the submission deadline for bids or proposals.

The prospective sellers carefully review the buyer's statement of work and all the terms of the proposed contract contained in the bid documents, including the selection criteria. During this review, the sellers develop a full understanding of what the buyer wants, and assess the risks involved in the project. If the scope is incomplete or unclear, if a prospective seller is aware of the buyer having a history of poorly managing projects, or if any other risks are identified, a prospective seller may decide not to respond, or may adjust the price and/or schedule submitted to the buyer to account for these risks. When a fixed-price contract is required, sellers should include these risks in the total detailed cost estimate, as well as other costs, such as overhead, and then add profit to come up with a bid or quote. In any case, the risk of the project is formally or informally assessed before sending the bid or proposal to the buyer. (Do you see the increased risk for the seller caused by unclear requirements if the seller does not get completely defined data before bidding on the work?)

The amount of time that a prospective seller may need to respond to the bid documents can be substantial (sometimes taking several months), and the buyer's project manager must plan this time into the project schedule.

Organizations may use several different methods to select a seller. These methods may be dictated by law or internal policies. If a buyer receives competing submissions from many prospective sellers, the buyer might ask for presentations from all the candidates. Another option is to shorten the list of prospective sellers first and then request presentations. If presentations will not add value for the buyer, the buyer may just move into negotiations with the preferred seller or sellers. All terms and conditions in the proposed contract, the entire procurement statement of work, and any other components of the bid documents can be negotiated. Negotiations can take a lot of time, and they require the involvement of the project manager.

At the end of negotiations, one or more sellers are selected, and a contract is signed. The procurement management plan and procurement strategy created earlier may also be updated.

Once the contract is signed, the procurement must be managed and controlled. This involves making sure all the requirements of the contract are met. It also means keeping control of the contract and making only approved changes. As the procurement work is being completed, questions may arise, such as, "What is and what is not in the contract?" or "What does a particular section of the contract really mean?" The procurement department will help the project manager resolve these issues.

When the procurement work is complete, the procurement will be closed. The required actions to close each procurement need to be done soon after the final deliverables of the procurement are accepted. This can happen within any phase of the project life cycle, as the contracted work is completed. For example, in a project to renovate a house, a seller may be contracted to install new plumbing, another may be contracted to install new landscaping, and still another may be contracted to paint the house. Activities to close out a procurement include an analysis of the procurement process to determine lessons learned (formally called a procurement audit). Final reports are submitted, lessons learned are documented, and final payment is made.

Could you now describe the procurement process to someone else? Be sure this overview makes sense to you before continuing with the chapter.

**Buyers and Sellers**    In the real world, the company or person who provides services and goods can be called a contractor, subcontractor, supplier, designer, or vendor. The *PMBOK® Guide* primarily uses the term "seller," but the exam may use any of the above terms. The company or person who purchases the services is called the buyer. Many companies are a buyer in one procurement and a seller in another.

 Read exam questions carefully to see if the situation described in the question is from the buyer's or seller's point of view. If no point of view is mentioned, assume you are on the buyer's side of the project. Make sure you know the actions that you would take as the project manager for the buyer. This is an especially important concept to understand when taking the exam. If you are on the seller's side of the project, the issues and impacts of many situations are completely different.

501

For large projects, sellers will typically provide the full complement of a solution, rather than just augmenting a project team with additional resources. For example, whereas on a small or medium-size project, you might add contract developers to your internal staff to do the coding, on a large project you would likely outsource all that development work to an external resource who would plan and manage all developers, testers, etc. Unless an exam question indicates otherwise, assume the seller is providing all of the work external to the buyer's team rather than supplying resources to supplement the team.

### Tricks for Answering Procurement Questions

When answering situational questions involving contracts, keep in mind the following general rules, especially if the answer to the question is not immediately apparent:

- Contracts require formality. What this means is that any correspondence, clarification, and notifications related to the contracts should be formal written communication, which can be followed up with verbal communication, if necessary. If issues develop that require arbitration, mediation, or litigation, the formal written communications will be more enforceable and supportable than verbal communications.

- All product and project management requirements for the procurement work should be specifically stated in the contract.

- If it is not in the contract, it can only be required to be done if a formal change order to the contract is issued.

- If it is in the contract, it must be done or a formal change order to remove it must be approved by both parties.

- Changes to contracts must be submitted and approved in writing.

- Contracts are legally binding; the seller must perform as agreed in the contract, or face the consequences for breach of contract.

- Contracts should help diminish project risk.

- Most governments back all contracts that fall within their jurisdiction by providing a court system for dispute resolution.

Remembering these pointers can help you get about four more questions right!

 **Note to Students Outside the United States**   In the past, the PMP exam has had very few references to international contracts. Be aware that government contracting specialists in the United States wrote many of the questions on the exam. PMI's process for procurement management closely follows what is done in the United States, but it is different from the way procurement is handled in other parts of the world. In many places, the contract is an informal document, and the relationship between the parties is more important than the contract. If you are not from the United States, a key trick is to take a more formal approach to the procurement process when answering questions. The contract is most important. It must be followed, and everything provided in it must be done. Study this chapter carefully.

**Centralized/Decentralized Contracting**   In a centralized contracting environment, there is one procurement department, and the procurement manager reports organizationally to the head of the procurement department, not to the project manager. The procurement manager may handle procurements on many projects. When working with a procurement manager, you should know what authority the procurement manager has and how the procurement department is organized. In a centralized contracting environment, the project manager contacts the department when they need help or to ask questions.

502

In a decentralized contracting environment, there is no procurement department or procurement manager assigned. The project manager may be responsible not only for creating the procurement management plan but also for conducting and monitoring work on all procurements. There may be little standardization of procurement processes and contract language without a procurement department to regulate standards, improve knowledge, and increase professionalism in procurement management.

 When answering exam questions, assume a centralized contracting environment unless otherwise stated. Remember that whether contracting is centralized or decentralized, the project manager is responsible for knowing their required level of involvement. Use the scenario described in the question to determine how involved the project manager should be.

Try the following exercise.

**Exercise**  Identify the advantages and disadvantages of a centralized contracting environment. This exercise will help you recognize a centralized contracting environment when taking the exam.

### Centralized Contracting

| Advantages | Disadvantages |
|---|---|
| | |

## Answer

### Centralized Contracting

| Advantages | Disadvantages |
|---|---|
| Because they are part of a department that focuses on procurements, centralized contracting can result in procurement managers with higher levels of expertise. | One procurement manager may work on many projects, so this individual must divide their attention among all of those projects. The procurement manager will likely have less time to spend working on your project and understanding its unique needs, and is more likely to forget important details about the project. |

| Centralized Contracting | |
|---|---|
| **Advantages** | **Disadvantages** |
| A procurement department will provide its employees with continuous improvement, training, and shared lessons learned. | It may be more difficult for the project manager to obtain contracting help when needed. |
| Standardized company practices allow efficiency and help improve understanding. | |
| Individuals in this department have a clearly defined career path in procurement. | |

## The Project Manager's Role in Procurement

You might ask yourself, "If there is a procurement manager, why would a project manager need to be involved in procurements?" This is an important question, and you must fully understand the answer before you take the exam. Here are a few tricks to help you.

 **TRICKS OF THE TRADE®** Remember that it is the project manager's project. There are certain things that cannot be done effectively without the project manager, and the project manager's expertise is needed so the organization can fully realize the project's benefits. This is so important that typically a large percentage of the questions on the exam are focused on testing whether you know what you should do.

Here is a quick summary. Do not memorize it; instead, make sure you understand it.

- Know the procurement process so you understand what will happen when and can make the necessary plans.

- Make sure the contract includes all the scope of work and all the project management requirements, such as attendance at meetings, reports, actions, and communications deemed necessary to minimize problems and miscommunications with the seller(s).

- Identify risks, and incorporate mitigation and allocation of risks into the contract to decrease project risk.

- While it is being written, help tailor the contract to the unique needs of the project.

- Estimate the time and cost of each procurement, including the time required to complete the procurement process, and include these estimates in the project schedule and budget.

- Be involved during contract negotiations to protect the relationship with the seller. A contentious negotiation process—often created when the seller feels that they have had to give up too much profit or agree to terms and conditions they do not like in order to win the contract—can create a win-lose relationship with the procurement manager and the seller, which can negatively affect the project. The project manager will have to manage the seller's delivery to the contract, and bad feelings on the part of the seller can create extra challenges. By staying involved in the negotiations, the project manager can promote the best interests of the project.

- Protect the integrity of the project and the ability to get the work done by making sure the procurement process goes as smoothly as possible.

- Understand what contract terms and conditions mean so you can read and understand contracts. This will help you plan and manage the monitoring and controlling of procurements.

- Help make sure all the work in the contract is done, such as reporting, inspections, and legal deliverables, including the release of liens and ownership of materials, not just the technical scope.

- Do not ask for something that is not in the contract without making a corresponding change to the contract.

- Work with the procurement department to manage necessary changes to the contract.

**TRICKS OF THE TRADE®** Project managers should be assigned on both the buyer's and seller's sides before a contract is signed! Many companies that sell their services make a huge but common mistake by not involving the project manager in the bidding and proposal process. Instead, only marketing and sales are involved until after the contract is signed. The project manager is then handed a project with a contract that may include unrealistic time or cost constraints. The project starts out in trouble.

Involving the project manager early in the procurement process is so important that the exam will test you to see if you know when the project manager should be involved, and why. For example, the project manager is often uniquely capable of answering (or getting answers to) many of the technical and project management questions that arise during bidder conferences. If the sellers' questions are answered incorrectly or incompletely, there may be an inadvertent change to a specification or the scope of the contract that was never intended by the buyer.

## The Procurement Management Process

Project managers often tell procurement managers that they need a seller as soon as possible. And procurement managers want project managers to know that there is a procurement process designed to obtain the best seller at the most reasonable price. That process includes the time it takes for sellers to look at your needs and respond, which can take several months. Understanding the procurement process includes understanding why this time must be accounted for within the project schedule. It is a critical part of both the procurement process and the procurement concepts that are tested on the exam. Not only does the project manager need to be involved along the way, assisting the procurement department with project input, they must also plan for the amount of time procurements take. The remainder of this chapter follows the procurement process from start to finish. You must know what happens when, how procurement management works on a properly managed project, and how it relates to the project life cycle and the project management process.

The three procurement management processes are:

1. Plan Procurement Management
2. Conduct Procurements
3. Control Procurements

## Plan Procurement Management   PAGE 466

| **Process** Plan Procurement Management |
| **Process Group** Planning |
| **Knowledge Area** Procurement Management |

The Plan Procurement Management process answers these questions: "How will make-or-buy analysis be performed?" "What goods and services do we need to buy for this project?" "How will we purchase them?" "Who are potential sellers to consider?"

This process involves putting together the bid documents that will be sent to prospective sellers describing the buyer's need, how to respond, and the criteria the buyer will use to select a seller. Note that the term "bid documents" is used in reference to requests for proposal (RFPs) and requests for quotation (RFQs). You may also see the term used in reference to requests for information (RFIs) as well as invitations for bid (IFBs).[3]

Allowing adequate time for the procurement process is critical to project success.

The Plan Procurement Management process includes the following activities:

- Performing make-or-buy analysis[4]
- Creating a procurement management plan
- Creating a procurement strategy for each procurement
- Creating a procurement statement of work for each procurement

- Selecting the appropriate contract type for each procurement
- Creating the bid documents
- Determining the source selection criteria

## Inputs to Plan Procurement Management   PAGE 468   When planning procurement management, it is important to consider business documents like the benefits management plan and the business case. Also keep in mind the project charter, components of the project management plan, project documents, and any relevant enterprise environmental factors and organizational process assets. Review these inputs in the following sections to determine what is needed before you begin planning procurement management.

### Project Charter   You'll need to review important information found in the project charter, such as any preapproved financial resources, the overall project description, and the project objectives, in order to create the procurement management plan.

### Business Documents   Important business documents that are inputs to the Plan Procurement Management process include the following:

- The benefits management plan lists the benefits of the project and details when they are to be delivered. This information is used to determine what procurements are needed, when procurements must be entered into, and what dates should be included in the bid documents and, ultimately, project contracts.
- The business case reflects the reason the project was undertaken, and must be in alignment with the procurement strategy.

### Project Management Plan   The components of the project management plan, including the scope, quality, and resource management plans as well as the scope baseline, help those involved in the procurement process identify where procurements are necessary and understand any constraints on potential procurement efforts.

### Project Documents   Documents such as the milestone list and the requirements traceability matrix can help you plan procurement management. You'll also want to review the project schedule and any relevant procurements already in place. Other documents used to plan procurements include the following:

- **Project team assignments**  Team assignments will include information on who can help the project manager with procurement planning. If the project team does not have the necessary skills—such as developing bid documents—to complete procurement management activities, team members may require training or need assistance from the procurement department or outside sources.
- **Requirements documentation**  This is where you'll find the scope-related requirements that will help to define the end product, service, or result provided by a seller. In addition, this documentation includes requirements for compliance, safety, communications, project management practices, reporting, quality, and risk management that are likely to be important to the procurement process.
- **Resource requirements**  Resource requirements describe the skills, number, and type of resources that will be needed on the project. If the required team resources, products, materials, equipment, or services are not available within the performing organization, they will need to be procured.
- **Risk register**  The risk register provides an understanding of the individual and overall project risks uncovered to date, as well as the risk responses that involve procurements. Remember, risk analysis of the project should be done before contracts are signed.

506

- **Stakeholder register** The stakeholder register will help identify those who will be impacted by the procurement process as well as those who will have input into or will guide this process, such as the procurement manager, regulatory bodies, and attorneys.

## Enterprise Environmental Factors
These factors include company culture and existing systems your project will have to deal with or can use. For procurement, they include marketplace conditions, the services that are available to be purchased, and the existing culture and structures surrounding the organization's approach to procurements.

## Organizational Process Assets
The organizational process assets that are used in procurement can include procurement procedures and documents, standard contract types used by the organization, statement of work templates, lessons learned from past procurements and projects, and lists of prequalified sellers. Note that selecting the right contract type for each procurement is critical to the success of the project. We will define the most common contract types and discuss their advantages and disadvantages later in this chapter.

## Preapproved Seller List
The process of finding prospective sellers can take months. Another option, especially if a buyer purchases the same type of service often, is to identify and check the credentials of prospective sellers in advance, and maintain a list of preapproved sellers. This will speed up the purchase and help ensure the sellers' qualifications are well researched before they are awarded procurements. If such a list is in place (as part of organizational process assets), the procurement documents for specific projects are then sent only to the preapproved sellers. The preapproved seller list is also sometimes referred to as a prequalified seller list.

Some organizations use master service agreements, which are contracts between two parties including standard terms that will govern future transactions. This is a time-saving approach when a buyer frequently works with the same seller. The overall terms of working together are already agreed to and signed by both buyer and seller. Terms may include the types of services or goods that are included in the agreement, costs, and payment and delivery terms.

**Exercise** Now try to recreate what you just read. If you miss any of the inputs, spend some time thinking about these items to make sure you do not forget them when taking the exam.

| List the Plan Procurement Management Process Inputs | |
|---|---|
| | |
| | |
| | |
| | |
| | |
| | |
| | |

There are two primary types of analysis that can be useful during the Plan Procurement Management process: make-or-buy analysis and source selection analysis. Let's review both.

## Make-or-Buy Analysis  PAGE 473

During planning, you must decide whether the project team will do all of the project work, or if some or all of the work will be outsourced. You will also need to determine if all required materials or equipment are available within the performing organization. Ask questions like, "How are resources currently distributed?" and "What are the capabilities of our resources?" The answers to these types of questions can help you find out information about what can be done internally, and what will need to be done by or procured from outside resources. Make-or-buy analysis is completed early in the planning process to avoid wasted time planning work that will ultimately be outsourced. Also note that this type of analysis enables make-or-buy decisions, which are documented in the procurement management plan.

### Logistics and Supply Chain Management

An important consideration in make-or-buy analysis is the required lead time for materials and equipment to be purchased. Specialty items, custom products, and items ordered internationally will take more time, which must be built into the project schedule.

### Economic Models

Economic models may be used to analyze and support make-or-buy decisions. Examples include the following:

- Payback period
- Return on investment
- Internal rate of return
- Discounted cash flow
- Net present value
- Cost-benefit analysis

Note that these models, which were defined in the Integration Management chapter, are also used in project selection.

Expect to see questions on the exam that refer to make-or-buy analysis, or even questions that require you to calculate buy-or-lease situations, such as:

*Question*   You are trying to decide whether to lease or buy an item for your project. The daily lease cost is $120. To purchase the item, the investment cost is $1,000, and the daily maintenance cost is $20. How long will it take for the lease cost to be the same as the purchase cost?

*Answer*   Let D equal the number of days when the purchase and lease costs are equal.

$120D = $1,000 + $20D

$120D − $20D = $1,000

$100D = $1,000

D = 10

This calculation helps a project manager decide whether it is better to buy or lease. The calculation says that the costs are the same after 10 days. Therefore, if you are planning to use the item for fewer than 10 days, you should lease. If you are planning to use it for more than 10 days, it would be cheaper to buy the item. These costs are then included in the project cost estimate.

## Source Selection Analysis

PAGE 473 Determining the criteria that will be used to select a seller is an important part of procurement planning. To make this determination, project constraints must be analyzed. For example, is schedule the most important criteria or is cost the critical factor? You may want to review the project constraints represented in the graphic in the Project Management Framework chapter to get an idea of possible selection criteria.

If the buyer is purchasing a commodity, such as linear meters of wood, the source selection criteria may just be the lowest price. If the buyer is procuring construction services, the source selection criteria may be price plus experience. If the buyer is purchasing services only, the source selection analysis will be more extensive. In the latter case, source selection criteria may include:

- Number of years in business
- Financial stability
- Understanding of need
- Price or life cycle cost
- Technical expertise
- Quality of past performance
- Ability to complete the work on time

If the organization has a preferred seller list, or a master services agreement with an outside source, that information is also considered when analyzing source selection options.

## Procurement Management Plan

PAGE 475 The procurement management plan documents how procurements will be planned, executed, and controlled. Enterprise environmental factors and organizational process assets will significantly influence this plan. They include the governing approach to procurements for the project, information about how to perform the make-or-buy analysis, and the policies and procedures that will be used in the procurement processes.

The planning portion of the procurement management plan includes standards for selecting the best type of contract to use for each procurement, details of how procurement documents will be created or tailored to meet the needs of the project, and guidelines for establishing selection criteria.

The executing portion of the plan documents how the Conduct Procurements process will flow and outlines the roles and responsibilities of team members as well as the rules for bidder conferences and negotiations.

The control portion of the plan indicates how contract stipulations will be monitored and controlled, and it provides metrics and information on when and how measurements will be taken, guidelines for resolving disputes, the process for accepting deliverables, and the payments to be made.

## Make-or-Buy Decisions

PAGE 479 Make-or-buy decisions are the result of make-or-buy analysis. Any decisions to "buy" will require the team to follow the procurement management process to obtain needed products, equipment, or services. As the planning process continues, make-or-buy decisions may be adjusted, or may necessitate changes to other parts of the project management plan.

## Procurement Strategy

PAGE 476 A procurement strategy is developed for each procurement after the make or-buy-analysis has been completed and the goods or services to be acquired from outside the organization have been identified. The acquisition of these goods or services must be incorporated into an overall procurement strategy for the project. This strategy has three basic elements: how goods or services will be delivered to the buyer (for example, will the procurement include any subcontractors or an

509

outside service provider), what type of contract will be used (for example, fixed-price or cost plus, and will the contract include incentives or award fees), and how the procurement will be carried out throughout each phase. The project manager must manage the procurement to achieve the objectives of each phase, and also manage transitions between the phases.

Remember that organizational process assets include the types of contract approved for use within the organization. The following pages include descriptions of the contract types and exercises to help you understand when each is best to use. Take your time with this section; it includes a lot of information you will need to know for the exam.

## Contract Types[5]    PAGE 471    Many different types of contracts can be used to acquire goods and services on a project. The types of contracts or agreements that are approved for use within an organization are considered organizational process assets. From those contract types, the procurement manager will select the contract type for each procurement based on the following considerations:

- What is being purchased (a product or a service)
- The completeness of the statement of work
- The level of effort and expertise the buyer can devote to managing the seller
- Whether the buyer wants to offer the seller incentives
- The marketplace or economy
- Industry standards for the type of contract used

 Some contract types can be referred to by more than one name. This can make it difficult to learn the contract types. Here is a trick. Start out by understanding the three main categories of contract types, as shown in the following list. Then, when the exam asks a question relating to contract type, first see if knowing which category the contract is in helps you answer the question. In most cases, it does.

The three broad categories of contracts are:
- Fixed-price (FP)
- Time and material (T&M)
- Cost-reimbursable (CR)

You must understand the contract types and be able to recognize the differences between them. Situational questions on the exam may require you to recognize that the project manager's responsibilities and actions will vary depending on the type of contract being used. There may also be questions that require you to pick the most appropriate contract type based on a particular situation. Think through this section carefully!

## Fixed-Price (FP)    A fixed-price contract should be used for acquiring goods, products, or services with well-defined specifications or requirements. In general, with a fixed-price contract, a clearly defined statement of work along with competing bids mean you're likely to get a fair and reasonable price. This is one of the most common types of contract, though it's less likely to be used in something like information technology than in construction. If the costs are more than the agreed-upon amount, the seller must bear the additional costs. Therefore, the buyer has the least cost risk in this type of contract because the scope is well-defined. (Note, however, that when fixed-price contracts are entered into and the statement of work is not sufficiently detailed, claims and disputes over what is in and out of the contract create higher risk of cost overruns or delay.) The seller is most concerned with the procurement statement of work (SOW) in a fixed-price contract. This is going to help them accurately estimate time and cost for the work involved, and allow them to determine a price that includes a fair and reasonable profit. The amount of profit is not disclosed to the buyer in this contract type. Types of fixed-price contracts include firm fixed price, fixed

price incentive fee, fixed price award fee, and fixed price with economic price adjustments. Purchase orders are also a type of fixed-price contract.

For the exam, be aware that even though the buyer may prefer a fixed-price contract as a way to control costs, it is not always the best choice, and in some cases, it may be inappropriate. Sellers in some industries may not have the detailed accounting records of past project activities required to accurately estimate future projects. Buyers may not have the expertise to prepare the clear and complete procurement statement of work required for a fixed-price contract.

Because many buyers are not knowledgeable about contracts, they often ask the seller to provide a fixed price, even when the scope of work is incomplete. In such a case, the procurement statement of work is not really adequate for the seller to make a reasonable estimate of required costs and time. Think for a minute about the following consequences of doing this:

- The seller is forced to accept a high level of risk.
- The seller needs to add a significant amount of reserves to their price to cover their risks; therefore, the buyer pays more than they otherwise might have.
- The seller can more easily try to increase profits by cutting scope or claiming that work the buyer wants is outside the contract and thus requires a change order. The buyer will not be able to state with certainty if something is within the scope of the work or outside of it (and, therefore, needs a change order and additional payment to the seller) if there is not a complete procurement statement of work.

If a fixed-price contract is used when it shouldn't be—and the seller realizes they will not be able to make any profit on the project—the seller might try to take their best people off the project, cut out work that is specifically mentioned in the contract, cut out work that is not mentioned in the contract but is needed, decrease quality, or take other actions to save themselves money.

The following sections discuss some of the most common forms of fixed-price contracts.

**Fixed-Price (FP)** In a FP contract, a fixed total price is set for the project, all requirements have been clearly described, and changes to scope should not occur.

### Example: Fixed-Price Contract

Contract = $1,100,000.

**Fixed Price Incentive Fee (FPIF)** In a FPIF contract, profits (or financial incentives) can be adjusted based on the seller meeting specified performance criteria, such as getting the work done faster, cheaper, or better. The final price is calculated using a formula based on the relationship of final negotiated costs to the total target cost. (See more on incentives later in this section.) A variation on a FPIF is a FPIF Successive Target contract, in which the target for the incentive is changed after the first target is reached.

### Example: Fixed Price Incentive Fee Contract

Contract = $1,100,000. For every month early the project is finished, an additional $10,000 is paid to the seller.

You may need to calculate these incentives for the exam, so make sure you understand the exercises at the end of the contract types discussion in this chapter.

**Fixed Price Award Fee (FPAF)**  In a FPAF contract, the buyer pays a fixed price plus an award amount (a bonus) based on performance. This is similar to the FPIF contract, except the total possible award amount is determined in advance and apportioned based on performance. For example, the buyer might say there is a maximum $50,000 award fee available. It will be apportioned at the rate of $5,000 for every month production exceeds a certain amount. This is a type of incentive contract. In many instances, the award paid is judged subjectively. Therefore, procedures must be in place in advance for determining the award.

The cost to administer the award fee versus the potential benefits must be weighed in the decision to use this type of contract.

### Example: Fixed Price Award Fee Contract

Contract = $1,100,000. For every month that performance exceeds the planned level by more than 15 percent, an additional $5,000 is awarded to the seller, with a maximum award of $50,000.

**Fixed Price with Economic Price Adjustments (FPEPA)[6]**  If a contract will cover a multiyear period, there may be uncertainties about future economic conditions. Future costs of supplies and equipment the seller might be required to provide under contract may not be predictable. In such cases, a buyer might choose a fixed-price contract with economic price adjustments. Think "economy" whenever you see this on the exam, and you should remember it. A similar type of contract is called Fixed Price with Prospective Price Redetermination.

### Example: Fixed Price with Economic Price Adjustments Contract

Contract = $1,100,000, but a price increase will be allowed in year two based on the US Consumer Price Index report for year one.

*Or*

Contract = $1,100,000, but a price increase will be allowed in year two to account for increases in specific material costs.

**Purchase Order**  A purchase order is the simplest type of fixed-price contract. This type of contract is normally unilateral (signed by one party) instead of bilateral (signed by both parties). Most other contract types are bilateral. It is usually used for simple commodity procurements. Purchase orders become contracts when the buyer accepts the terms. The seller then performs or delivers according to those terms (for example, equipment or products). Although unilateral purchase orders are most common, some companies will require the seller's signature on a purchase before the buyer will consider the purchase order official. In that case, it is the signature that forms the acceptance needed to make a contract.

### Example: Purchase Order

Contract = 30 linear meters of wood at $9 per meter.

## Time and Material (T&M)    In this type of contract, the buyer pays on a per-hour or per-item basis. Time and material contracts are frequently used for service efforts in which the level of effort cannot be

defined when the contract is awarded. It has elements of a fixed-price contract (in the fixed price per hour) and a cost-reimbursable contract (in the material costs and the fact that the total cost is unknown). Compared to other types of contracts, time and material contracts typically have terms and conditions that are simpler, to allow for quick negotiations so that work can begin sooner.

If you were going to have to pay someone on a contract basis for every hour they worked, no matter how productive they were and no matter what they were doing, would you want to do this for a long period of time? Remember, the seller's profit is built into the rate, so they have no incentive to get the work done quickly or efficiently. For this reason, a time and material contract is best used for work valued at small dollar amounts and lasting a short amount of time. Knowing when it's best to use time and material contracts can help you get situational questions right on the exam.

To make sure the costs do not become higher than budgeted, the buyer may add a "Not to Exceed" clause to the contract and thus limit the total amount they are required to pay. With a time and material contract, the buyer has a medium amount of cost risk as compared to cost-reimbursable and fixed-price contracts.

### Example: Time and Material Contract

Contract = $100 per hour plus expenses or materials at cost.

*Or*

Contract = $100 per hour plus materials at $5 per linear meter of wood.

**Cost-Reimbursable (CR)**   A cost-reimbursable contract is used when the exact scope of work is uncertain and, therefore, costs cannot be estimated accurately enough to effectively use a fixed-price contract. This type of contract provides for the buyer to pay the seller allowable incurred costs to the extent prescribed in the contract. Such contracts also typically include an additional fee or award amount added to the cost to allow for seller profit. Types of cost-reimbursable contracts include cost, cost plus fixed fee, cost plus incentive fee, cost plus award fee, cost plus fee, and cost plus percentage of costs.

A cost-reimbursable contract requires the seller to have an accounting system that can track costs by project. With a cost-reimbursable contract, the buyer has the most cost risk because the total costs are unknown. The seller provides an estimate to the buyer; the buyer can use the estimate for planning and cost management purposes, but it is not binding. What is binding is the buyer's responsibility to compensate the seller for legitimate costs for work and materials as described in the contract. Research and development or information technology projects in which the scope is unknown are typical examples of cost-reimbursable contracts.

The following sections discuss some of the most common forms of cost-reimbursable contracts.

**Cost Contract**   A cost contract is one in which the seller receives no fee (profit). It is appropriate for work performed by nonprofit organizations.

### Example: Cost Contract

Contract = Cost for work and materials.

There is no profit. With this type of contract, the seller is reimbursed but does not make a profit. Cost contracts are typically used by nonprofit organizations.

513

**Cost Plus Fixed Fee (CPFF)** A cost plus fixed fee contract provides for payment to the seller of actual costs plus a negotiated fee (the seller's profit, usually a percentage of the estimated cost of the project) that is fixed before the work begins. The fee does not vary with actual costs; thus, the seller does not have an incentive to increase or inflate costs. The fee may be adjusted as a result of changes to the procurement statement of work.

### Example: Cost Plus Fixed Fee Contract

Contract = Cost plus a fee of $100,000.

**Cost Plus Incentive Fee (CPIF)** A cost plus incentive fee contract provides for the seller to be paid for actual costs plus a fee that will be adjusted based on whether specific performance objectives stated in the contract are met. In this type of contract, an original estimate of the total cost is made (the target cost) and a fee for the work is determined (a target fee). The seller gets a percentage of the savings if the actual costs are less than the target costs, or shares the cost overrun with the buyer. The ratio is often 80 percent to the buyer and 20 percent to the seller. See more on incentives later in this section.

### Example: Cost Plus Incentive Fee Contract

Contract = $500,000 target cost plus $50,000 target fee. The buyer and seller share any cost savings or overruns at 80% to the buyer and 20% to the seller.

You will need to know how to calculate the total payment or profit on a CPIF contract for the exam. See the exercise at the end of this discussion.

**Cost Plus Award Fee (CPAF)** In a cost plus award fee contract, the buyer pays all costs and a base fee plus an award amount (a bonus) based on performance. This is similar to the CPIF contract, except the incentive is a potential award, and there is no possibility of a penalty. The award amount in a CPAF contract is determined in advance and apportioned depending on performance. This is a type of incentive contract. In some instances, the award paid out is judged subjectively. Therefore, procedures must be in place in advance for determining the award.

As with a FPAF contract, the cost to administer an award fee contract must be weighed against the potential benefits when deciding whether to use this type of contract.

### Example: Cost Plus Award Fee Contract

Contract = Cost plus a base fee plus award for meeting buyer-specified performance criteria. Maximum award available is $50,000.

**Cost Plus Fee (CPF) or Cost Plus Percentage of Costs (CPPC)** A CPF or CPPC contract requires the buyer to pay for all costs plus a percentage of costs as a fee. In the United States, this type of cost-reimbursable contract is generally not allowed for federal acquisitions or procurements under federal acquisition regulations, and it is bad for buyers everywhere. Can you figure out why? If seller profit is based on a percentage of everything billed to the buyer for the project, what incentive is there to control costs? Say a seller has to purchase materials from one of two suppliers. Although the materials from both suppliers meet the quality requirements, one supplier charges $4 per unit and the other charges $40 per unit. A seller might be tempted to choose the $40 per unit charge because they will make more profit. It is possible for the buyer to construct the contract so that the seller will need to prove they pursued the least expensive path in completion of the procurement statement of work when, for example, selecting materials or subcontracting portions of work. This contract type requires the buyer to carefully monitor and control all invoices.

---

### Example: Cost Plus Fee or Cost Plus Percentage of Costs Contract

Contract = Cost plus 10 percent of costs as fee.

---

This brings us to the end of the contract types discussion. Keep in mind that although the buyer initially proposes the contract type, the final contract type is subject to negotiation with the seller. The best contract type meets the needs of the particular procurement, results in reasonable seller risk, and provides the seller with the greatest incentive for efficient performance.

Do you understand what you just read? Can you answer the following questions?

- You do not have a finalized scope. Which contract type is best?
- You do not have a complete scope of work, but you have a fixed-price contract. What problems can you expect to run into?

The exam tests whether you know what to do in different situations, not just if you know definitions.

## Incentives
Sellers are usually focused on the profits to be made on a project. The buyer may be focused on total cost, performance, schedule, or a combination of these concerns. Incentives are used to bring the seller's objectives in line with the buyer's. The buyer will provide an additional fee if the seller meets some cost, performance, or schedule objectives. Incentives, therefore, are designed to motivate the seller's efforts and to discourage seller inefficiency and waste in the areas in which the incentives are designated. Think of an incentive as a bonus for the seller.

Can you see how incentives can change the focus of the seller's work on the project? If there is an incentive for cost savings, then the work is to complete the project *and* to look for cost savings. If the incentive is for some increased level of performance (the system can handle more capacity than contracted for, for example), then the work is to complete the project *and* to look for ways to increase performance. The seller gains profit from both activities.

## Payments
Each contract, no matter the type, will state when payments are to be made to the seller. Payments may be made as work is completed and accepted, as costs are incurred, according to a payment schedule, or only after the successful completion of all the work required in the contract. The project manager needs to know when payments must be made in order to plan for the time required to review and make these payments. The project manager must also ensure the funds will be available to make the payments as scheduled.

## TRICKS OF THE TRADE® Advantages and Disadvantages of Each Contract Type
A trick for the exam is to realize that buyers must select the appropriate type of contract for what they are buying. The following exercise will test whether you really understand the different types of contracts and will help you select the appropriate type of contract.

515

**Exercise** In the following table, write the advantages and disadvantages of each form of contract from the perspective of the buyer.

## Fixed-Price Contract

| Advantages | Disadvantages |
|---|---|
|  |  |
|  |  |
|  |  |

## Time and Material Contract

| Advantages | Disadvantages |
|---|---|
|  |  |
|  |  |
|  |  |

## Cost-Reimbursable Contract

| Advantages | Disadvantages |
|---|---|
|  |  |
|  |  |
|  |  |

**Answer**  There can be more answers than listed here. Did you identify and understand these?

### Fixed-Price Contract

| Advantages | Disadvantages |
| --- | --- |
| This type of contract requires less work for the buyer to manage. | If the seller underprices the work, they may try to make up profits by charging more than is necessary on change orders. |
| The seller has a strong incentive to control costs. | The seller may try to not complete some of the procurement statement of work if they begin to lose money. |
| Companies usually have experience with this type of contract. | This contract type requires more work for the buyer to write the procurement statement of work. |
| The buyer knows the total price before the work begins. | A fixed-price contract can be more expensive than a cost-reimbursable contract if the procurement statement of work is incomplete. In addition, the seller needs to add to the price of a fixed-price contract to account for the increased risk. |

### Time and Material Contract

| Advantages | Disadvantages |
| --- | --- |
| This type of contract can be created quickly, because the statement of work may be less detailed. | There is profit for the seller in every hour or unit billed. |
| The contract duration is brief. | The seller has no incentive to control costs. |
| This is a good choice when you are hiring "bodies," or people to augment your staff. | This contract type is appropriate only for work involving a small level of effort. |
|  | This contract type requires a great deal of day-to-day oversight from the buyer. |

### Cost-Reimbursable Contract

| Advantages | Disadvantages |
| --- | --- |
| This contract type allows for a simpler procurement statement of work. | This contract type requires auditing the seller's invoices. |
| It usually requires less work to define the scope for a cost-reimbursable contract than for a fixed-price contract. | This contract type requires more work for the buyer to manage. |
| A cost-reimbursable contract is generally less costly than a fixed-price contract because the seller does not have to add as much for risk. | The seller has only a moderate incentive to control costs. |
|  | The total price is unknown. |

517

**Exercise**  Name the most appropriate contract type to use in the situation described. Your choices are FP, FPIF, FPAF, FPEPA, purchase order, T&M, CR, CPF or CPPC, CPFF, CPIF, or CPAF contracts. Read each situation carefully to determine whether the information is sufficient to indicate only that some type of cost-reimbursable (CR) or fixed-price (FP) contract would apply, or whether the details of the situation suggest a more specific type of cost-reimbursable (CPF or CPPC, CPFF, CPIF) or fixed-price contract (FPIF, FPAF, FPEPA) should be used.

| | Situation | Type of Contract |
|---|---|---|
| 1 | You need work to begin right away. | |
| 2 | You want to buy expertise in determining what needs to be done. | |
| 3 | You know exactly what needs to be done. | |
| 4 | You are buying a programmer's services to augment your staff for a short period. | |
| 5 | You need work done, but you don't have time to audit invoices. | |
| 6 | You need to rebuild a bridge as soon as possible after a storm. | |
| 7 | The project requires a high level of expertise to complete, and you want to have the best performance possible in the finished product. | |
| 8 | You need to hire a contractor to perform research and development. | |
| 9 | The scope of work is complete, but the economy is currently unpredictable. | |
| 10 | You are buying standard commodities. | |

**Answer**  The answers are below. Also try to think of other situations in which you would use each type of contract.

| | Situation | Type of Contract |
|---|---|---|
| 1 | You need work to begin right away. | T&M |
| 2 | You want to buy expertise in determining what needs to be done. | CR |
| 3 | You know exactly what needs to be done. | FP |
| 4 | You are buying a programmer's services to augment your staff for a short period. | T&M |
| 5 | You need work done, but you don't have time to audit invoices. | FP |
| 6 | You need to rebuild a bridge as soon as possible after a storm. | FPIF |
| 7 | The project requires a high level of expertise to complete, and you want to have the best performance possible in the finished product. | CPIF or CPAF |
| 8 | You need to hire a contractor to perform research and development. | CR |
| 9 | The scope of work is complete, but the economy is currently unpredictable. | FPEPA |
| 10 | You are buying standard commodities. | Purchase order |

## Risk and Contract Type

The exam may ask questions that correlate risk with the different types of contracts. Figure 12.1 shows the amount of cost risk the buyer and seller have with each contract type. Use this diagram to better understand the different contract types and to help answer questions such as:

*Question*   Who has the risk in a cost-reimbursable contract—the buyer or seller?

*Answer*   The buyer. If the costs increase, the buyer pays the added costs.

*Question*   Who has the cost risk in a fixed-price contract—the buyer or seller?

*Answer*   The seller. If costs increase, the seller pays the costs and makes less profit.

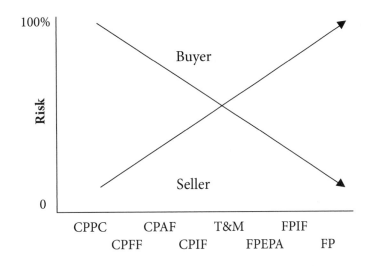

FIGURE 12.1   *Risk to buyer and seller according to contract type*

## Other Terms to Know

Remember, profit and cost are different. Profit is the amount of money the seller has left over after costs are paid. Be careful on the exam to read questions carefully. Also consider the perspective. Are the questions referring to the buyer's cost or the seller's cost? The following list provides definitions of terms you should understand for the exam:

- **Price**   This is the amount the seller charges the buyer.
- **Profit (fee)**   In a fixed-price or time and materials contract, a seller builds a profit margin into the amount they charge the buyer. In cost-plus contracts, the "plus" represents the profit, and that amount is typically negotiated by the buyer and seller.
- **Cost**   This is how much an item costs the seller to create, develop, or purchase. A buyer's costs include a seller's costs and profits.
- **Target price**[7]   This term is often used to compare the end result (final price) with what was expected (the target price). Target price is a measure of success. Watch for similar terms. Target cost plus target fee equals target price. (Remember, we are thinking about procurements from the buyer's point of view!)
- **Sharing ratio**[8]   Incentives are usually expressed as a ratio, such as 90/10. This sharing ratio describes how the cost savings or cost overrun will be shared; the first number represents the buyer portion of the ratio and the second number represents the seller portion (buyer/seller).

519

- **Ceiling price**[9] This is the highest price the buyer will pay; setting a ceiling price is a way for the buyer to encourage the seller to control costs. The ceiling price is a condition of the contract that must be agreed to by both parties before signing. Keep in mind that answers to calculations on the exam can change when a ceiling price is mentioned.
- **Point of total assumption (PTA)**[10] This only relates to fixed price incentive fee contracts, and it refers to the amount above which the seller bears all the loss of a cost overrun. Costs over the PTA are assumed to be due to mismanagement: a design statement of work should have been created to allow for fair and reasonable contract negotiations for the required work, suggesting the seller either did not estimate correctly or did not manage the work well. Sellers will sometimes monitor their actual costs against the PTA to make sure they are still receiving a profit for completing the project.

### Formula: Point of Total Assumption

$$\text{PTA} = \frac{\text{Ceiling price} - \text{Target price}}{\text{Buyer's share ratio}} + \text{Target cost}$$

## Incentives Calculations

Now that you understand the concepts, it is time to work through some examples. You may see up to three questions on the exam requiring you to use these types of calculations. As you do the following exercises, notice the terms "cost," "fee," and "price." These terms all have different meanings, as defined previously.

### Exercise   Cost Plus Incentive Fee Calculation

In this cost plus incentive fee contract, the cost is estimated at $210,000, and the target fee is set at $25,000. The project is complete, and the buyer has agreed that the costs were, in fact, $200,000. Because the seller's costs came in lower than the estimated costs, the seller shares in the savings: 80 percent to the buyer and 20 percent to the seller. Calculate the final fee and final price.

| | |
|---|---|
| Target cost | $210,000 |
| Target fee | $25,000 |
| Target price | $235,000 |
| Sharing ratio | 80/20 |
| Actual cost | $200,000 |

| | |
|---|---|
| Final Fee | |
| Final Price | |

**Answer** Remember that for the exam you may have to calculate both the final fee and the final price.

| | |
|---|---|
| Final Fee | $210,000 − $200,000 = $10,000<br>$10,000 × 20% = $2,000<br>$25,000 target fee + $2,000 = $27,000 fee |
| Final Price | $200,000 + $25,000 + $2,000 = $227,000 |

**Exercise** **Fixed Price Incentive Fee Calculation** Now try the following exercise from the seller's perspective. In this fixed price incentive fee contract, the target cost is estimated at $150,000, and the target fee is $30,000. The project is over, and the buyer has agreed that the costs were, in fact, $210,000. Because the seller's costs came in higher than the target cost, the seller shares in the added cost: 60 percent to the buyer and 40 percent to the seller. Calculate the final fee, the final price, and the point of total assumption. Note the ceiling price.

| | |
|---|---|
| Target cost | $150,000 |
| Target fee | $30,000 |
| Target price | $180,000 |
| Sharing ratio | 60/40 |
| Ceiling price | $200,000 |
| Actual cost | $210,000 |

| | |
|---|---|
| Final Fee | |
| Final Price | |
| Point of Total Assumption | |

**Answer** In this case, the actual cost is higher than the target cost, so the seller receives less fee, or profit. Instead of receiving $30,000 in fee, the seller is due only $6,000. (Note that in the answer table, the parentheses in the cell where this final fee is calculated are a common accounting convention indicating negative numbers.) The actual cost plus fee comes to $216,000, but this is higher than the ceiling price (the maximum amount the buyer will pay). The result is that the seller is paid $200,000 when the costs were $210,000. The seller made no profit, and in fact actually lost $10,000.

© 2018 RMC Publications, Inc.™ • 952.846.4484 • info@rmcls.com • www.rmcls.com

The point of total assumption (the amount above which the seller bears all the loss of a cost over-run) was $183,333. The seller should have calculated the point of total assumption and used it to manage the work and costs to ensure that their costs did not exceed this amount, since the seller suffers the effects of the inability to control the project and loses money on it.

| | |
|---|---|
| Final Fee | $150,000 – $210,000 = ($60,000) overage<br>($60,000) × 40% = ($24,000)<br>$30,000 + ($24,000) = $6,000 |
| Final Price | $210,000 + $6,000 = $216,000<br>However, this amount is above the ceiling price of $200,000. Therefore, the final price (what the buyer will pay) is $200,000. |
| Point of Total Assumption | [($200,000 – $180,000)/60%] + $150,000<br>($20,000/0.6) + $150,000<br>$33,333 + $150,000 = $183,333 |

Imagine that a question on the exam describes a scenario with a fixed price incentive fee contract where actual costs of the work to date are nearing the PTA, and there's still work left to complete. What should the seller do? What would happen if the seller did nothing? The seller's project manager should take the proactive approach of planning and performing cost and schedule management activities on the contract to determine how to address the situation. This should help the project manager anticipate possible problems and find solutions before the seller loses all the profit on the work.

## Exercise  Fixed Price Incentive Fee Calculation
Try this one. For this exercise, you are again the seller in the procurement. In this fixed price incentive fee contract, the target cost is $9,000,000, and the target fee is $850,000. The project is done, and the buyer has agreed that the costs were, in fact, $8,000,000. Because the seller's costs came in lower than the estimated costs, the seller shares in the savings: 70 percent to the buyer and 30 percent to the seller. Calculate the final fee and final price.

| | |
|---|---|
| Target cost | $9,000,000 |
| Target fee | $850,000 |
| Target price | $9,850,000 |
| | |
| Sharing ratio | 70/30 |
| Ceiling price | $12,500,000 |
| Actual cost | $8,000,000 |

| | |
|---|---|
| Final Fee | |
| Final Price | |

**Answer**  In this case, the actual cost is lower than the target cost, so the seller receives more fee, or profit. Instead of receiving just $850,000 in fee, the seller receives that fee plus an additional $300,000—for a total of $1,150,000. The fee added to the cost totals $9,150,000. Because that is less than the ceiling price, the seller gets paid that amount. Therefore, the seller gains because of their ability to control the project.

| | |
|---|---|
| Final Fee | $9,000,000 − $8,000,000 = $1,000,000<br>$1,000,000 × 30% = $300,000<br>Original fee of $850,000 + $300,000 = $1,150,000 |
| Final Price | $8,000,000 + $1,150,000 fee = $9,150,000 |

## Putting It All Together

After going through all these pages, you should start to feel like you understand the different types of contracts. Try the next exercise to help you put it all together.

We've heard people say they love the exercises in this book, but they always jump straight to the answers. We strongly advise against this. The exercises are designed to increase your knowledge as you do them, so don't skip ahead!

You can also use the questions in PM FASTrack® to test your knowledge of contract types.

**Exercise**  Answer the questions in the following table for each contract type. (This is the most challenging exercise in this chapter. The questions are meant to be very difficult in order to further test your knowledge.)

| | Question | Cost-Reimbursable | Time and Material | Fixed-Price |
|---|---|---|---|---|
| 1 | Generally, what is being bought? (Product or service) | | | |
| 2 | How might the costs to the buyer be stated in the contract? | | | |
| 3 | How might the profit be stated in the contract? | | | |
| 4 | What is the cost risk to the buyer? (High, medium, low, none) | | | |
| 5 | How important is a detailed procurement statement of work? (High, medium, low, none) | | | |

523

| | Question | Cost-Reimbursable | Time and Material | Fixed-Price |
|---|---|---|---|---|
| 6 | What industry uses this contract type most frequently? | | | |
| 7 | How much negotiation is usually required to sign the contract after receipt of the seller's price? (High, medium, low, none) | | | |
| 8 | What level of effort and expertise will the buyer need to devote to managing the seller? (High, medium, low, none) | | | |
| 9 | How are costs billed to the buyer? | | | |
| 10 | How much auditing of the seller's costs will the buyer need to do? (High, medium, low, none) | | | |

## Answer

To make sense of this exercise, review the answers in the following table.

| | Question | Cost-Reimbursable | Time and Material | Fixed-Price |
|---|---|---|---|---|
| 1 | Generally, what is being bought? (Product or service) | Service (some products may be included) | Service | Product |
| 2 | How might the costs to the buyer be stated in the contract? | Costs are variable, but the fee/profit is fixed (as a set amount or a percentage) | Hourly rate or price per unit | As a set currency amount (e.g., $1 million) |
| 3 | How might the profit be stated in the contract? | Listed separately, and known to the buyer | Included in the hourly rate, and may be unknown to the buyer | Included in the price, and unknown to the buyer |

| | Question | Cost-Reimbursable | Time and Material | Fixed-Price |
|---|---|---|---|---|
| 4 | What is the cost risk to the buyer? (High, medium, low, none) | High; increases in costs are reimbursed by the buyer | Medium; although the costs are not fixed, they are known per unit, and this contract type is used for small purchases for a limited time | Low; increases in costs are borne by the seller |
| 5 | How important is a detailed procurement statement of work? (High, medium, low, none) | Low; the procurement statement of work only needs to describe the performance or functional requirements, since the seller provides the expertise on how to do the work; the buyer pays all costs, so there is less need to finalize the scope | Low; this type traditionally has very little scope, and may only describe skill sets required | High; the procurement statement of work must be complete so the seller knows exactly what work needs to be done in order to come up with an accurate price to complete the work |
| 6 | What industry uses this contract type most frequently? | IT, research and development, and knowledge work; when the work has never been done before (as is often the case in these industries), the seller cannot fix a price; therefore, this is the best form to use | When hiring people for an hourly rate, you are usually hiring services, such as legal, plumbing, or programming | Complete scope of work is most common in the construction industry |
| 7 | How much negotiation is usually required to sign the contract after receipt of the seller's price? (High, medium, low, none) | High; all estimated costs are looked at to calculate the fee to be paid | Low or none | None |
| 8 | What level of effort and expertise will the buyer need to devote to managing the seller? (High, medium, low, none) | High | Medium | Low |

525

| | Question | Cost-Reimbursable | Time and Material | Fixed-Price |
|---|---|---|---|---|
| 9 | How are costs billed to the buyer? | Actual costs as incurred; profit at project completion, or apportioned as allowed in the contract | Hourly or per unit rate (which includes all costs and profit) | Fixed price (which includes profit) according to a payment schedule as work is completed and as allowed in the contract |
| 10 | How much auditing of the seller's costs will the buyer need to do? (High, medium, low, none) | High; all costs must be audited, and there will be a large number of invoices | None; there may be an audit of work hours completed against those billed, but that will take little effort | Low; since the overall contract costs are fixed, auditing usually focuses on making sure work is completed, not looking at detailed costs and receipts |

## Procurement Statement of Work (SOW)[11]    PAGE 477    The project manager facilitates the creation of a scope of work to be done on each procurement. This is done by breaking down the project scope baseline into the work the project team will do and the work that will be purchased from a seller(s). The work to be done on each procurement is described in a procurement statement of work.

Each statement of work must be as clear, complete, and concise as possible, and it must describe all the work and activities the seller is required to complete. This includes all meetings, reports, and communications. It must also detail the acceptance criteria and the process of gaining acceptance. The cost of adding activities later is typically more than the cost of adding them at the beginning of the procurement. Does this make you think about the amount of work required to create a complete procurement statement of work?

What does the word "complete" mean? It depends on what you are buying. If you are buying expertise (such as software design or legal services), your procurement statement of work will include a detailed description of functional and/or performance requirements, a completion timeline, and evaluation criteria, in addition to required meetings, reports, and communications.

If you are buying the construction of a building, your requirements will be extremely specific, outlining things such as the materials to be used, the process that must be followed, and even a work schedule. If you are hiring staff that you will direct (for example, a programmer to be added to the team), your procurement statement of work will likely contain more details of what you want the person to create or achieve. Ask yourself, "If I were the seller, how comfortable would I be signing a legally binding contract to complete this work for a certain price?" Put yourself in the seller's shoes, and make sure the scope of work is as descriptive and as complete as possible. The level of detail required will influence the selection of the contract type and the creation of the bid documents.

The procurement statement of work may be revised during contract negotiation, but it should be finalized by the time the contract is signed. A procurement statement of work can include drawings, specifications, and technical and descriptive wording. No matter what it contains, however, the procurement statement of work becomes part of the contract. Remember that a contract is a document used to manage a procurement activity. It does not just sit in a drawer. Therefore, both parties to the contract should always be asking, "What does the contract say?" If the procurement statement of work is not complete, the seller may frequently need to request clarification or ask for change orders, which can get expensive, and the project manager and/or the procurement manager may find themselves constantly dealing with questions about whether a specific piece of work is included in the original cost or time estimates submitted by the seller.

Think about change orders in the context of the procurement strategy and the project plan. In general, contract change orders cost money or cause delay. Bad procurement SOWs can result in overspending and delayed or failed projects. Simply put, the procurement SOW should describe what you want, when you want it and how good it should be.

Although they are not specified in the *PMBOK® Guide*, there are several types of procurement statements of work with which you should be familiar. Your choice will depend on the nature of the work, the industry, and the amount of detail that can be provided about the work. The following are types of procurement statements of work:

- **Performance**  This type conveys what the final product should accomplish, rather than how it should be built or what its design characteristics should be. For example, "I want a car that will go from zero to 120 kilometers per hour in 4.2 seconds."

- **Functional**  This type conveys the end purpose or result, rather than the specific procedures or approach. Functional procurement statements of work may include a statement of the minimum essential characteristics of the product. For example, "I want a car with 10 cup holders."

- **Design**  This type conveys precisely what work is to be done. It includes the materials to be used and an explanation of how the work should be completed. Design procurement statements of work are most commonly used for construction and equipment purchases. For example, "Build a garage exactly as shown in these drawings."

- **Terms of reference (TOR)**  If the procurement is for services rather than products, the procurement statement of work may be referred to as terms of reference. It includes the work the seller will perform, standards the seller is expected to achieve, and the data and services that will be provided to the buyer.

## Source Selection Criteria[12]   PAGE 478   

Source selection analysis results in finalized source selection criteria. Often, the criteria are assigned numerical percentage values (weighted) to enable evaluation of proposals based on each criterion. The criteria are included in the bid documents to give the seller an understanding of the buyer's needs and to help the seller decide whether to bid or make a proposal on the work. When the buyer receives the sellers' responses during the Conduct Procurements process, source selection criteria such as cost, quality, and expertise become the basis for the evaluation of the bids or proposals.

## Independent Cost Estimates   PAGE 479   

The buyer may prepare an internal estimate, or use the input of experts, to come up with a benchmark against which to validate the bids provided by outside sellers during Conduct Procurements.

## Bid Documents   PAGE 477   

After the contract type is selected and the procurement statement of work has been created, the buyer can put together the bid document, which describes the buyer's needs to sellers. The following are some types of bid documents.

- **Request for proposal (RFP)**  An RFP (sometimes called a request for tender) requests a detailed proposal that includes information on price, how the work will be accomplished, who will do it (along with résumés, in some cases), and company experience.

- **Invitation for bid (IFB)**  An IFB, sometimes called a request for bid (RFB), usually requests a total price to do all the work. Think of an IFB as a form of RFP where the work described in the procurement statement of work is detailed enough for bidders to determine a total price.
- **Request for quotation (RFQ)**  RFQs request a price quote per item, hour, meter, or other unit of measure.
- **Request for information (RFI)**  An RFI might be used before bid documents are created. Responses to the RFI help the buyer identify which companies are qualified to handle the procurement. Buyers can also use RFIs to collect information on what work is possible, for later inclusion in RFPs or IFBs. Remember that the purpose of an RFI is to get information, whereas the purpose of an RFP or RFQ is to buy something.

To provide the seller with as clear a picture as possible of what needs to be done to win the work and what the work involves, bid documents may include the following information for sellers:

- Background information about why the buyer wants the work done
- Procedures for trying to win the work (such as whether there will be a bidder conference, when the responses are due, and how the winner will be selected)
- Guidelines for preparing the response (such as maximum length and topics to address in the response)
- The exact format the response should be in (such as which forms must be filled out and whether email submissions are allowed)
- Source selection criteria—the criteria the buyer will use to evaluate responses from the sellers (such as number of years in business, quality of the response, or price)
- Pricing forms (forms to adequately describe the price to the buyer)
- Procurement statement of work
- Proposed terms and conditions of the contract (legal and business)

Note that the proposed contract is included in the procurement documents. Do you know why? The terms and conditions of the contract are also work that needs to be done, and there are costs associated with that work, including such things as warranties, ownership, indemnification, and insurance requirements. The seller must be aware of all the work that needs to be completed to adequately understand and price the project.

Well-designed bid documents can have the following effects on a project:

- Easier comparison of sellers' responses
- More complete responses
- More accurate pricing
- Decreased number of changes to the project

Sellers may make suggestions for changes to the procurement documents, including the procurement statement of work and the project management requirements included in the documents, before the contract is signed. When approved, these changes are issued by the buyer as addenda to the bid documents and will ultimately become part of the final contract.

The following sections discuss some additional terms a project manager should know when working with procurements.

## Nondisclosure Agreement
For many procurements, there is a great need for confidentiality. Perhaps the buyer does not want the general public or their competitors to know they are pursuing the procurement. Perhaps the seller will need to send the buyer information they want to keep confidential.

In these and many other cases, there may be a confidentiality or nondisclosure agreement signed before procurement information is released or at any other time when it may be appropriate to protect those interests. Such an agreement between the buyer and prospective sellers identifies the information or documents they will control and hold confidential; it also details who in the organization will have access to the confidential information. With a nondisclosure agreement in place, the buyer can talk more openly about their needs without fear that the public or one of the buyer's competitors will gain access to the information. Like any agreement, a nondisclosure agreement has consequences if violated.

## Standard Contract
The contract terms and conditions are most commonly created by the buyer, who may have even put their terms and conditions into a standard format that is used over and over on similar procurements. Standard contracts are usually drafted—or at least reviewed—by lawyers and generally do not require additional review if used for the purpose for which they were intended. You should understand standard contracts, but also realize the project manager's role in special provisions (described next).

## Special Provisions (Special Conditions)
The project manager must be able to not only read and understand standard terms and conditions but also to determine when additions, changes, or deletions from the standard provisions are required. By facilitating necessary adjustments, the project manager can make sure the resulting contract addresses the particular needs of the project. The project manager (remember when taking the exam that you are the buyer's project manager, unless a question states otherwise) meets with the procurement manager (if there is one) to discuss the needs of the project and to determine the final contract terms and conditions.

Additions, changes, or deletions are sometimes called special provisions and can be a result of any of the following:

- Risk analysis
- The requirements of the project
- The type of project
- Administrative, legal, or business requirements

## Terms and Conditions
Let's start out with a story. A project manager needed his team members to be trained to use some equipment. He contacted a seller to do the work and then proceeded to have his procurement department send the seller a contract. Meanwhile, he arranged for team members to fly in from around the world for the training. In the contract, the project manager's procurement department sent, there were terms and conditions that said the project manager's company would have the rights to create derivative works and make copies of any handouts from class. Those handouts were proprietary and already copyrighted. The seller could not and would not sign such a contract.

The class had to be cancelled at the last minute, after many people were already on planes to attend the training. Whose fault was this? It was the project manager's fault. He should have made sure the procurement department understood what they were buying and also should have taken a look at the contract before it was sent to make sure any inappropriate language was removed. Creating a contract requires the involvement of both the project manager and the procurement manager. Do you work with a procurement manager to review contracts on your projects?

Another reason it is important to understand contract language is to be able to enforce it. Remember, if it is in the contract, it must be done unless both sides agree and a change is issued!

Here's another story. One day, the director of a company called the project manager to ask where the seller's reports were. The project manager did not know what reports the director was asking about; she had not confirmed they were received from the seller. It turned out that those reports, which seemed minor to the project manager when she finally read the contract, had major legal significance to the company. Not receiving them cost the buyer's company an extra $50,000. The lesson? Know what is in your contracts and why.

In another situation, a seller didn't submit testing information required in the contract to the buyer, and the buyer's project manager did not notice it was not received. After four weeks, the company head asked for the testing information. The project manager then asked the seller to send the information. The seller argued, "You did not receive the testing reports for four weeks, and you did not say anything. You have therefore waived your rights to ever get them." They refused to give the reports without a change to the contract and additional payment. This issue went to a court of law to resolve. The court found in favor of the seller. The lesson? Read the contract, and enforce all that is there.

Terms and conditions (either standard or special) in a contract differ depending on what you are buying. If you are buying work that includes equipment, you will need terms that describe when ownership of the equipment will be transferred to the buyer as well as terms that require insurance for damages in transit. If you are buying professional services, you will need terms requiring professional liability insurance or errors and omissions insurance. The required terms are usually determined by the procurement manager. However, the project manager should be generally familiar with most common terms.

The following are some general categories of the terms and conditions that can make up standard or special provisions. You do not need to know specific examples. Instead, you should be generally familiar with what all these concepts mean and what impact they would have on you as the project manager. The exam will often simply use these terms in sentences such as, "There was a force majeure," and you'll need to understand what that means. Conversely, the exam could state, "There was a huge flood that caused the seller to not be able to perform," and you will have to know that this is a force majeure. You need to understand the situation and be able to determine what the appropriate action is.

- **Acceptance**  How will you specifically know if the work is acceptable?
- **Agent**  Who is an authorized representative of each party?
- **Arbitration**  This method to resolve disputes uses private third parties to render a decision on the dispute. Arbitration is paid for by the parties and is used because it is usually faster and cheaper than the courts.
- **Assignment**  This refers to the circumstances under which one party can assign its rights or obligations under the contract to another.
- **Authority**  Who has the power to do what?
- **Bonds**  These are the payment or performance bonds, if any, that must be purchased. For example, a payment bond would protect the buyer from claims of nonpayment by the seller.
- **Breach/default**  This occurs when any obligation of the contract is not met. Watch out—a breach on the seller's part cannot be fixed by a breach on the buyer's part. For example, failure to complete an item in the procurement statement of work (seller's breach) cannot be handled by the buyer stopping all payments (buyer's breach).

  A breach is an extremely serious event. The exam may present situations in which seemingly little things in the contract are not done. The response to a breach must always be to issue a letter formally notifying the other party of the breach. The project manager must understand the legal implications of their actions. If they do not watch out for and send an official notice of breach, the project manager's company could lose its right to claim breach later.
- **Changes**  How will changes be made? What forms will be used? What are the timeframes for notice and turnaround?

- **Confidentiality/nondisclosure** What information must not be made known or given to third parties?

- **Dispute resolution** How will any disputes regarding the contract be settled? Some options for dispute resolution are to use the courts or an arbitrator.

- **Force majeure** This refers to a situation that could be considered an "act of nature," such as a fire or freak electrical storm, and it is an allowable excuse for either party not meeting contract requirements. If a force majeure occurs, it is considered to be neither party's fault. It is usually resolved by the seller receiving an extension of time on the project. Who pays for the cost of the items destroyed in a fire or other force majeure? Usually the risk of loss is borne by the seller and is hopefully covered by insurance. (See also "Risk of loss" below.)

- **Incentives** These are benefits the seller may receive for achieving the buyer's objectives of schedule, cost, quality, risk, and performance.

- **Indemnification (liability)** Who is liable for personal injury, damage, or accidents?

- **Independent contractor** This term means the seller is not an employee of the buyer.

- **Inspection** Does anyone have a right to inspect the work during execution of the project? Under what circumstances?

- **Intellectual property** Who owns the intellectual property (for example: patents, trademarks, copyrights, processes, source code, or books) used in connection with or developed as part of the contract? This may include warranties of the right to use certain intellectual property in performance of the contract.

- **Invoicing** When will invoices be sent? What supporting documents are required? To whom are they sent?

- **Liquidated damages** These are estimated damages for specific defaults, described in advance.

- **Management requirements** Examples of management requirements include attendance at meetings and approval of staff assigned to the project.

- **Material breach** This breach is so large that it may not be possible to complete the work under the contract.

- **Notice** To whom should certain correspondence be sent?

- **Ownership** Who will own the tangible items (such as materials, buildings, or equipment) used in connection with or developed as part of the contract?

- **Payments** When will payments be made? What are the late payment fees? What are reasons for nonpayment? Watch out for questions regarding payment management. For example, as a response to inaccurate invoices, the buyer cannot stop all payments; this would be a breach. They can, however, stop payments on disputed amounts.

- **Procurement statement of work** If it is not a separate document, this will be included as part of the contract.

- **Reporting** What reports are required? At what frequency? To and from whom?

- **Retainage** This is an amount of money, usually 5 percent or 10 percent, withheld from each payment. This money is paid when the final work is complete. It helps ensure completion.

- **Risk of loss** This allocates the risk between the parties to a contract in the event goods or services are lost or destroyed during the performance of a contract.

- **Site access** This describes any requirements for access to the site where the work will be performed.

- **Termination** Termination is stopping the work before it is completed.

- **Time is of the essence** Delivery dates are strictly binding. The seller is on notice that time is important and that any delay is a material breach.

- **Waivers** These are statements saying that rights under the contract may not be waived or modified other than by express agreement of the parties. A project manager must realize that they can intentionally or unintentionally give up a right in the contract through conduct, inadvertent failure to enforce, or lack of oversight. Therefore, a project manager must understand and enforce all aspects of the contract, even if a procurement manager is involved in administering the contract.

- **Warranties** These are promises of quality for the goods or services delivered under the contract, usually restricted to a certain time period.

- **Work for hire** The work provided under the contract will be owned by the buyer.

## Letter of Intent

Negotiating a contract and getting final signatures can take time. In some instances, the seller may need to start hiring people or ordering equipment and materials before the contract is signed in order to meet the contract requirements. If the contract is not signed in time, the seller may ask the buyer to provide a letter of intent. Correctly defined, a letter of intent is not a contract, but simply a letter stating that the buyer intends to hire the seller. It is intended to give the seller confidence that the contract will be signed soon and to make them comfortable with taking the risk of ordering the equipment or hiring the staff that will eventually be needed.

## Privity

Sometimes the exam includes terms that only procurement experts use. This is one of them. Privity simply means a contractual relationship. The following explains privity and shows how questions on this topic may be asked.

*Question*    Company A hires company B to do some work. Company B subcontracts to company C. The project manager for company A is at the job site and tells company C to stop work. Generally, does company C have to listen?

*Answer*    No. Companies C and A have no contractual relationship. Company A needs to talk to company B, who needs to talk to company C.

You may not be familiar with the term, but you might be familiar with the situation just described. Can you see how this would be an important issue for a project manager to understand? Any directive that the project manager from company A may give to company C can cause huge liability for company A. For example, company A may have to pay delay claims to company B, plus the costs of delay to company C if company C stopped work at company A's direction.

## Noncompetitive Forms of Procurement

In many cases, procurement is competitive. There may be multiple sellers who can do the work and who are invited to submit a response to the bid documents. As stated earlier, public organizations are generally required by law to follow certain practices regarding competitive procurements and to make a selection from the prospective sellers in a certain way. For private companies, competitive bidding is not required by law, although they might have internal policies that must be followed regarding procurement practices. Often, a private company may bypass competitive procurement by using master service agreements or preferred seller lists, in which case they could simply issue a purchase order to obtain goods or services from a previously approved or preferred seller.

If there is only one seller who can do the work or an unregulated entity wants to work with a company they have worked with before, they may avoid the competitive procurement process. Regardless of whether the procurement is competitive, however, they must still have a procurement statement of work.

When would you award work to a company without competition?

- The project is under extreme schedule pressure.
- A seller has unique qualifications.

- There is only one seller who can provide the goods or service.
- A seller holds a patent for the item you need.
- Other mechanisms exist to ensure the seller's prices are reasonable.
- The procurement is for a small amount of money.

If you do not use a competitive process, you enter into one of the following types of noncompetitive procurements:

- **Single source** In this type of procurement, you contract directly with your preferred seller without going through the full procurement process. You may have worked with this company before, and, for various reasons, you do not want to look for another seller. In some cases, there may be a master service agreement in place between an organization and a particular seller: this is an established, ongoing contract between the organization and a seller for a particular type of service the organization may require regularly.
- **Sole source** In this type of procurement, there is only one seller. This might be a company that owns a particular patent.

If you are using one of these noncompetitive forms of procurement, you may save time compared with competitive forms by not having to go through the procurement process before bids or proposals are received, but you will still have to spend time in negotiations after the proposal or bid is received to finalize the contract.

 Tricky situational questions on the exam may address procurement concepts you have not dealt with before, such as describing the work that would need to be done to negotiate a contract when there is no competition. The following exercise will help.

**Exercise**  Test yourself! What types of issues might occur in a noncompetitive procurement that would not be as significant in a competitive environment?

| Single Source—There Is a Preferred Seller |
|---|
|  |
|  |
|  |
|  |
|  |
|  |
|  |
|  |

533

| Sole Source—There Is Only One Seller |
| --- |

_____

_____

_____

_____

_____

_____

_____

_____

_____

## Answer

### Single Source—There Is a Preferred Seller

- **Scope**  More work will be needed to document items received without cost in the past to make sure you get them now. Only what is in the contract will be received.

- **Scope**  There could be a tendency for the buyer's organization to say, "The seller knows us, and we know them; we do not have to spend so much time determining our requirements and completing a procurement statement of work. They know what we want."

- **Quality**  The seller may never be asked to prove they have the experience, cash flow, and manpower to complete the new work. Also, the quality of work may not consistently meet stated requirements because the seller knows they are not competing and may not complete work at the quality levels expected.

- **Cost**  It will be necessary to spend time comparing the previous cost to the new cost to check if it is reasonable.

- **Schedule**  Now that the seller knows they have you as a longer-term customer, they may not be as responsive to your schedule requirements.

- **Customer satisfaction**  Now that the seller knows they have you as a longer-term customer, they may not be as responsive to your concerns.

- **Risk**  The risk can be weighted more toward the buyer unless the previous issues are investigated and addressed.

### Sole Source—There Is Only One Seller

- **Risk**  What if the seller owns a patent and goes out of business? What if the seller takes on too much business and can't complete all the work on time?

- **Risk**  If the seller owns a patent and goes bankrupt, who owns the patent? How will you get what you need from the seller?

- **Quality**  You may have to take what you get rather than being able to request a certain quality level.

- **Cost** Multiyear agreements may be required for the purchase of items to prevent a price increase in the future.
- **Schedule** The seller has little incentive to agree to a schedule.
- **Customer satisfaction** The seller has little incentive to be concerned with the buyer's needs and desires.
- **Scope** You may have to change the work specified in the project to "take what you can get," rather than "ask for what you want."
- **Risk** The overall risk may be weighted more toward the buyer unless the previous issues are investigated and resolved.

Make sure you read questions on the exam carefully. They might ask what to watch out for or what needs to be negotiated in noncompetitive procurements. They may simply ask about the procurement process. Do you understand how your efforts during the procurement process are different when there are not multiple companies to go to for the goods or services?

## Change Requests

Keep in mind that many procurements may not begin for months or years after initial project planning is completed. Therefore, the procurement management plan is likely to be iterated, and possibly changed through integrated change control, as each procurement is needed. This is often accomplished through change requests.

The results of procurement management planning may impact existing components of the project management plan. For example, it may be determined in procurement planning that the current budget is not adequate to cover the cost of a procurement, requiring a change request to the cost management plan and baseline. As another example, clarifying needs for physical resources (materials or equipment) may require changes to elements of the project management plan, such as the resource management plan and schedule and cost baselines.

## Conduct Procurements   PAGE 482

> **Process** Conduct Procurements
> **Process Group** Executing
> **Knowledge Area** Procurement Management

This process involves getting the bid documents, including the procurement statement of work and other documents created in the Plan Procurement Management process to prospective sellers, answering the sellers' questions, and receiving and evaluating sellers' responses. You will select a seller using the source selection criteria specified in the procurement management plan, and then negotiate a contract.

The project manager and team will utilize many important inputs in this process. For instance, the procurement management plan gives direction on the work that will be done during this process. Other management plans provide information on how project work will be done, including the work that will be performed by outside sellers. Also note that the cost baseline provides direction regarding the approved budget for costs related to procurements. The schedule indicates dates within which procurements must be completed.

Because the process to finalize procurements is ongoing throughout the project, the project manager and team may be able to make use of lessons learned from prior procurements on the current project. Lessons learned documentation may provide insight into the organization's previous experiences with potential sellers. This information might enable the team to select a seller based on the seller's past performance, eliminating the need for additional evaluation, and making the process more efficient and effective.

535

Of course, the procurement documentation created in planning is also a key input. But before you can send bid documents to prospective sellers, you need to know who those sellers are. A buyer may use techniques such as advertising to find possible sellers or may send the bid documents to a select list of sellers preapproved by the organization (an organizational process asset). The organization may already have an existing agreement with a particular seller. In this case, they could work with that seller to negotiate terms to add new work to the contract.

## Advertising   PAGE 487

To attract sellers, an advertisement may be placed in newspapers, magazines, online, or in other types of media. Not all advertising costs money: the need for sellers could be announced on the company's website, through media releases or professional associations, or through free online advertising. NOTE: The US government and many state and local agencies are required to advertise most of their procurements.

## Bidder Conferences[13]   PAGE 487

Once the prospective sellers have been identified and have received the bid documents, the buyer controls who can talk to the sellers and what can be discussed. This control allows the buyer to maintain the integrity of the procurement process and to make sure all sellers are bidding or proposing on the same work.

To make sure all the sellers' questions are answered, the buyer may invite the sellers to attend a meeting—called a bidder conference, contractor conference, vendor conference or pre-bid conference—in which they can tour the buyer's facilities (if relevant to the project) or attend an online forum and ask questions about the procurement. The questions asked during the bidder conference, along with the buyer's responses, are documented and sent to all prospective bidders to make sure they all have the same information. The questions and answers asked during the bidder conference are also added to the bid documents as addenda.

Getting answers to questions can be important because many bid documents will include a provision saying that by submitting a bid or proposal, the seller warrants that the bid covers all the work. The bidder conference is also an opportunity for the buyer to discover anything missing in the bid documents.

A bidder conference can be key to making sure the pricing in the seller's response matches the work that needs to be done and is, therefore, the lowest price. Bidder conferences benefit both the buyer and seller. It is a good practice for the project manager to attend the bidder conference. The exam often asks what things the project manager must watch out for in a bidder conference. The answers include:

- Collusion
- Sellers not asking questions in front of the competition
- Making sure all questions and answers are put in writing and issued to all potential sellers by the buyer as addenda to the bid documents (ensuring that all sellers are responding to the same procurement statement of work)

## Seller Proposal (or Price Quote or Bid)   PAGE 486

This is a seller's response to the bid documents. A proposal is usually the response to a request for proposal (RFP), a price quote is usually the response to a request for quote (RFQ), and a bid is usually the response to an invitation for bid (IFB). The proposal (or price quote or bid) represents an official offer from the seller. RFP and RFQ responses describe how the seller will meet the buyer's request. A potential seller's response to an RFI provides information to help the buyer better define their procurement need. Responses to a request for information may trigger the buyer's creation of an RFP or RFQ.

Keep in mind that sellers may have many RFPs, RFQs, and IFBs sent to them. They need time to review them and determine which they are interested in responding to. To ensure the best sellers will be interested, the bid documents should be as complete and straightforward as possible.

When a seller decides to respond, they need to form a team, evaluate the buyer's needs, attend the bidder conference, and create a response. This can sometimes take a month or more. The buyer's project manager should allow for this time—and the time required for the rest of the procurement process—in the project schedule.

## Proposal Evaluation   PAGE 487   After receiving the proposals, the buyer (represented by an evaluation committee) may first use a screening system to eliminate sellers who do not meet the minimum requirements of the source selection criteria. Then, the buyers uses the source selection criteria identified in the Plan Procurement Management process to assess the ability and willingness to provide the requested products or services. This data analysis technique provides a basis to quantitatively evaluate proposals and minimize the influence of personal prejudices.

To select a seller:
- The buyer may simply select a seller and ask them to sign a standard contract.
- The buyer may ask a seller to make a presentation, and then, if all goes well, move on to negotiations.
- The buyer may narrow down ("short-list") the list of sellers to a few.
- The buyer may ask the short-listed sellers to make presentations, and then ask the selected seller(s) to go on to negotiations.
- The buyer may negotiate with more than one seller.
- The buyer may use some combination of presentations and negotiations.

The choice of methods depends on the importance of the procurement, the number of interested sellers, and the type of work to be performed. The sellers' proposals are usually reviewed and compared by the evaluation committee using one or a combination of the formal, structured processes discussed next.

## Weighting System[14]   When the responses from sellers have been received, the buyer's evaluation committee will analyze the responses and select a seller to award the contract to or to negotiate with. If the buyer is a public entity and the response is to an invitation to bid, the answer is simple. The work goes to the lowest responsive, responsible bidder. In the case of a proposal, the selection decision is more complicated. The buyer will apply the selection criteria chosen in planning. But which is more important? Price? Competence? Availability? Selection criteria are assigned values based on their relative importance to the procurement. For example, if price is more important, it will be given a higher rating and weight. The buyer's evaluation committee then analyzes seller responses using the weighted source selection criteria.

There are no calculations on the exam regarding weighting systems, but the following example should help you better understand the concept.

| Seller A | | | |
|---|---|---|---|
| | A | B | C |
| Criteria | Weight | Rating for this category (1 to 100) | Category score (column A times B) |
| Number of years in business | 5 percent | 50 | 2.5 |
| Understanding of need | 25 percent | 80 | 20 |
| Price or life cycle cost (see definition in the Cost Management chapter) | 10 percent | 90 | 9 |
| Technical ability | 25 percent | 40 | 10 |
| Ability to complete the work on time | 20 percent | 30 | 6 |
| Project management ability | 15 percent | 30 | 4.5 |
| Total score for this seller | | | 52 |

## Past Performance History

The buyer may consider both their history with the prospective sellers and feedback from other organizations who have done business with the sellers when determining which seller to award the procurement to.

## Independent Cost Estimates

The buyer should compare the seller's proposed cost with an estimate created in-house or with outside assistance during procurement planning efforts. This allows the buyer to discover significant differences between what the buyer and seller intend in the procurement statement of work. The buyer must have their own estimates to check reasonableness and cannot rely solely on the seller's cost estimates. Responses that are significantly different from what is expected may indicate an issue with the sellers' understanding of the procurement statement of work.

## Presentations

In many cases, some of the sellers will be asked to make presentations of their proposals. This is often a formal meeting of the buyer's and seller's teams. It provides the seller with an opportunity to present their proposal, team, and approach to completing the work. The buyer has an opportunity to see the team they may hire and to ask questions to assess the team's competency. Presentations are used most often for procurements that have cost-reimbursable contracts, but they can be used whenever there is a lot to assess.

## Negotiations

PAGE 488 Don't get worried about this topic. You do not have to be an expert negotiator to pass the exam. But, as you have seen in other chapters of this book, the ability to negotiate is an important interpersonal skill for a project manager. The exam assumes the project manager is involved in contract negotiations, although the procurement manager generally leads the negotiations.

Negotiations are not usually needed in a fixed-price contract because the scope is complete and the lowest bidder is selected based on price. If negotiations are needed, they cover only parts of the proposed contract.

If a cost-reimbursable or time and material contract is used, there will likely be negotiations to finalize the contract price and other issues. After the contract is signed, however, there will be negotiations in all contract types whenever there are proposed changes to any part of the contract.

The buyer's and seller's project managers must be involved in negotiations, because they are responsible for facilitating project management and resolution of technical issues on the project. The project managers must be involved in negotiating any issues that affect the key objectives of the project or how the project will be managed. Without the project managers' involvement in negotiations, it is common for a contract to be signed that the project managers later discover cannot be completed.

The exam typically has only one or two questions about contract negotiations, and one of these questions usually deals with the reasons the project manager must be involved.

### Objectives of Negotiations
It is important for everyone involved in negotiations to understand that the objectives of the negotiations are to:

- Obtain a fair and reasonable price.
- Develop a good relationship between the buyer and the seller.

The second item surprises most people, because they think of negotiations as win-lose. In a win-win situation, the buyer gets the work completed and the seller makes a reasonable profit. What is wrong with that? If negotiations turn from a win-win situation (preferable) to a win-lose situation, the seller will be less concerned with completing the work than with recovering what was lost in the negotiations. If negotiations are win-lose (in favor of the buyer), the buyer's project manager will have to spend time making sure the seller does not add extra costs, propose unnecessary work, or initiate other activities through claims or changes to "win" back what the seller lost during the negotiations. Many projects go bad because of the way negotiations were handled, not because of project problems themselves.

### Negotiation Tactics
This topic is often represented within the situational questions on the exam, though it is not covered in the *PMBOK® Guide*. You should be aware that buyers and sellers may use negotiation tactics such as delaying or withdrawal to get what they want. As a project manager, you should have the skills to overcome these tactics.

### Main Items to Negotiate
The main items to address while negotiating a contract can be vastly different, depending on what is being purchased. To achieve a signed contract, the following are usually negotiated in order (see if the order makes sense to you):

- Scope
- Schedule
- Price

Other items to be negotiated include the following:

- Risk
- Responsibilities
- Authority
- Applicable law: if you are working with a seller from a different state, country, or region, you need to agree upon whose law will apply to the contract
- Project management process to be used
- Payment schedule
- Quality

The clearer the scope definition, the easier it will be for the buyer and seller to come to a realistic agreement on the other items.

539

Many people new to procurement management do not realize that price may not be the primary selection criteria nor the major concern while negotiating. Often, price is not a factor at all. Schedule may be more important than budget, and a buyer might sacrifice cost to gain speed. Perhaps the procurement is to solve a problem rather than to complete specific work activities. In that case, the negotiations might involve detailed discussions of the feasibility of the proposed solution.

When negotiations are complete, the procurement contract is awarded to the selected seller. Note that the *PMBOK® Guide* refers to this output using the broader term "agreement," but we'll continue to use the more specific term, "contract," as the most appropriate term for the document describing the legal relationship entered into by the buyer and seller.

## What Is a Contract?   When you think of the word "contract," what comes to mind? If you are like many others, you think of all the legal words, such as indemnification, intellectual property, and other legal fine print. People often think of only the preprinted or standard contracts (boilerplate contracts) supplied to them from the contracting or legal departments. They are only partially correct.

The word "contract" actually refers to the entire agreement between both parties. Therefore, it includes boilerplate language (with the terms and conditions previously described), but it also includes business terms regarding payments, reporting requirements, marketing literature, the proposal, and the procurement statement of work—all the requirements of the project.

What is the purpose of a contract?

- To define roles and responsibilities
- To make things legally binding
- To mitigate or allocate risk

Many project managers and business professionals think the only relevant part of a contract is the procurement statement of work because they are most familiar with that aspect of the contract. However, the procurement statement of work does not include all the requirements. In fact, some of the boilerplate language can be more important. For example, think of a project to develop new software. Who owns the resulting program? Who owns the resulting program if it contains modules or pieces of programs previously used and planned for future reuse? How does the buyer protect their rights and ensure all source code is delivered? The ownership clause in a contract for such services might be more important than the procurement statement of work itself.

A contract is a legally binding document. Therefore, all terms and conditions in the contract must be met. A change process is negotiated and documented as part of the contract, so neither the buyer nor the seller can choose not to conform—or not to do something required in the contract. Changes to the contract must be made formally in writing, and submitted to integrated change control.

### What Do You Need to Have a Legal Contract?

- An offer
- Acceptance
- Consideration (a transfer of something of value, but not necessarily money)
- Legal capacity (separate legal parties that are all legally competent)
- Legal purpose (you cannot have a legal, enforceable contract for the sale of illegal goods or services)

A contract, offer, or acceptance may be verbal or written, though written is preferred.

Imagine that you need plumbing work done on your home. You contact a plumber who sends you a price with a notice that says, "If you want me to do the work on your home, send me a copy of the design drawings." Three weeks later, that plumber shows up at your home to start work. You are surprised, as you signed a contract with another plumber. The plumber says you also have a contract with him because you sent the drawings. Is the plumber right? Yes; acceptance can be an action, or it can be verbal. You have a difficult situation on your hands, and you will likely have to pay this plumber something. The trick is to avoid these situations by understanding contracts.

The key outputs of the Conduct Procurements process are discussed in the following sections.

## Selected Sellers  PAGE 488  After all the work of evaluating responses and negotiating with one
or more prospective sellers is complete, a seller is chosen for each procurement. This means that the buyer and seller have agreed and signed off on all terms and conditions of the contract, and they will move forward to create the product or service during the Control Procurements process.

## Change Requests  PAGE 489  Sometimes during project executing, problems that arise related
to the procurement process (for example, a seller who isn't performing) or to other areas of the project (such as risk, quality, schedule, or scope management) require reevaluation of the procurement management plan and make-or-buy decisions. So, it may be necessary to revisit the work previously done in Plan Procurement Management, which can lead to a decision to contract for resources or goods and make other changes to the project management plan or other aspects of the project. Such changes need to be submitted through integrated change control, where they are evaluated against the entire project, and approved, rejected, or deferred.

It is important enough to state again that contracts may be finalized after other project plans are completed and approved. This could trigger the need for changes to any part of the overall project, potentially including the schedule or cost baselines (to address availability or cost of procured resources), or other components of the project management plan or project documents.

## Project Management Plan and Project Documents Updates  PAGE 490  The
finalized agreement may also necessitate changes to planned approaches to quality or communications management, as agreed upon in the contract between the buyer and seller.

Resource calendars and the requirements traceability matrix may be updated to reflect the responsibilities of new sellers for specific project requirements. The risk register may need to be updated with information regarding risks associated with particular sellers. The preapproved seller list may also be updated based on work done in Conduct Procurements.

## Control Procurements  PAGE 492

| | |
|---|---|
| **Process** | Control Procurements |
| **Process Group** | Monitoring & Controlling |
| **Knowledge Area** | Procurement Management |

The Control Procurements process involves managing the legal relationship between the buyer and seller, and ensuring that both parties perform as required by the contract and that each contract is closed when completed or terminated. Throughout this process, the seller is focused on completing the work while the buyer is focused on measuring the performance of the seller and comparing actual performance to the contract, other procurement documents, and management plans. The exam tends to ask situational questions focusing on what happens after the contract is signed, so the Control Procurements process is an important area on the exam.

You should understand the following about the Control Procurements process (these points are described in more detail later in this chapter).

- What the project manager should be doing at any point in time
- What problems and issues that might affect the management of the project to watch out for under each contract type
- That all work and legal requirements in the contract must be accomplished, however small and seemingly unimportant
- That the project manager must help uphold all parts of the contract, not just the procurement statement of work

## Inputs to Control Procurements   PAGE 495   The procurement management plan includes the actions the project manager and team will take to oversee the procurements and ensure they are completed in accordance with the contract. The project manager may also review lessons learned to avoid the recurrence of issues experienced in the past. Also note that approved change requests from integrated change control are implemented in this process.

The project manager will use the milestone list and schedule, scope, and cost baselines to confirm that the project is progressing as planned. Requirements documentation describes technical and other requirements the procurement is expected to meet. Quality reports indicate whether the work of the procurement is within the established quality metrics. Work performance data from the Direct and Manage Project Work process gives the project manager information on costs and the status of project activities, and is used to evaluate seller performance.

Remember that monitoring and controlling is ongoing throughout the project. The project manager is continually measuring and assessing project progress, as compared to the contract and procurement documentation and management plans. The tools and techniques described later in this section include many ways in which this is accomplished. When variances are identified, they are analyzed and may need to be managed using the integrated change control system. Approved changes will be integrated into the management plans or the contract. Contract changes are handled using the organization's contract change control system,[15] which is an enterprise environmental factor. This system includes change procedures, forms, dispute resolution processes, and tracking systems, and is described in the contract. These procedures must be followed, and all changes should be made formally.

 Sometimes exam questions ask how project control is different in a procurement environment. These types of questions can be particularly difficult for those with little procurement experience. Some possible answers include:

- The seller's organization has a different culture and different procedures than the buyer's organization.
- The buyer and seller have different objectives. The seller's objective is to generate revenue, and the buyer's objective is to complete the work.
- It is not as easy to see problems on the project when the contracted work is being done in a different location.
- There is a greater reliance on reports to determine if a problem exists.
- There is a greater reliance on the relationship between the buyer's project manager and the seller's project manager in terms of resolving issues not covered in the wording of the contract.

Now let's go into detail with the following exercise. What specific work actions do you think must be done during the Control Procurements process? (Do not just look at the answers! Do the exercise once, and you will not have to do it again. Only look at the answers, and you will have to spend three times as long to learn this information.)

**Exercise** Describe the specific actions involved in the Control Procurements process.

_____

_____

_____

_____

_____

_____

_____

_____

_____

_____

_____

_____

_____

_____

_____

_____

_____

_____

_____

_____

_____

**Answer** Be careful while reading over the following list. Do you understand what each of these actions is and how long it might take? Go slowly, and imagine what it would take to handle each one for a multimillion-dollar construction project. (The items in the list are in no particular order.)

Imagine that you are building an office building, and you are the project manager for the building's owner. During this process you may do the following:

- Review invoices. Were they correctly submitted? Do they have all the required supporting information? Are the charges allowable under the contract?
- Evaluate whether a change is needed and is within the approved scope of the project.
- Submit changes through integrated change control as necessary.
- Document and record _everything_. This includes phone calls with the seller, emails, requested changes, and approved changes.
- Manage and integrate approved changes.

543

- Authorize payments to the seller.
- Interpret what is and what is not in the contract.
- Interpret what the contract means.
- Resolve disputes.
- Make sure only authorized people are communicating with the seller.
- Work with the procurement manager on requested and approved changes and contract compliance.
- Hold procurement performance review meetings with your team and the seller.
- Report on performance—this means your own performance as well as the seller's performance.
- Monitor cost, schedule, and technical performance against the contract, including all of its components, such as terms and conditions and the procurement statement of work.
- Understand the legal implications of actions taken.
- Control quality according to what is required in the contract.
- Issue claims and review claims submitted by the seller.
- Authorize the seller's work to start at the appropriate time, coordinating the seller's work with the work of the project as a whole.
- Communicate with the seller and with others.
- Manage interfaces among all the sellers on the project.
- Send copies of changes to the appropriate parties.
- Accept verified deliverables.
- Validate that the correct scope is being done.
- Validate that changes are giving the intended results.
- Perform inspections and audits.
- Identify risks to the completion of future work.
- Reestimate risks, costs, and schedule.
- Monitor and control risk.
- Perform contract closure for each contract as it is complete or terminated.
- Analyze the procurement process for lessons learned, and make recommendations to the organization for improvement.
- Accept final deliverables from the seller, and make final payments.

Now the hard part. The exam will require you to know that management efforts, issues, and potential trouble spots are different under each type of contract, meaning there will be different things you will need to do depending on the type of contract you have. It is critical to be able to apply this concept on your own projects, and there could be up to seven questions on the exam that require you to understand it. So let's try an exercise.

544

**Exercise** Hopefully, you have built a strong working relationship with the seller. But what if the seller has financial troubles, changes owners, or did not include major pieces of the work in their estimate? A good relationship can go bad in an instant. Describe the specific things you must watch out for and spend your time managing during the Control Procurements process for each of the three main types of contracts, regardless of what the relationship is like between the buyer and seller.

**Fixed-Price Contract**

**Time and Material Contract**

**Cost-Reimbursable Contract**

545

**Answer**  This is not a complete list! Think of what other actions may be taken.

### Fixed-Price Contract

Look for the seller cutting scope.

Watch for the seller cutting quality.

When the contract requires the seller's costs to be transparent, make sure the costs are real costs that have been incurred (not future costs)—unless there is an agreement stating otherwise.

Be alert for overpriced change orders.

Check for scope misunderstandings.

### Time and Material Contract

Provide day-to-day direction to the seller.

Attempt to get concrete deliverables.

Make sure the project length is not extended.

Confirm that the number of hours spent on work is reasonable.

Watch for situations in which switching to a different form of contract makes sense (for example, you determine a design statement of work under a T&M contract and then switch to a fixed-price contract for completion of the work).

### Cost-Reimbursable Contract

Audit every invoice.

Make sure all the costs are applicable and chargeable to your project.

Monitor to confirm the seller's work is progressing efficiently.

Watch for the seller adding resources to your project that do not add value or perform real work.

Look for resources being shifted from what was promised in the original proposal.

Disallow seller charges that were not part of the original plan.

Reestimate the cost of the project.

The following tools and techniques can be used during the Control Procurements process.

## Performance Reviews  PAGE 498  During the Control Procurements process, the buyer's project manager analyzes all available data to verify that the seller is performing as they should. This is called a performance review. Often, the seller is present to review the data and, more importantly, to discuss what the buyer can do differently to help advance the work. The purpose of this review is to determine if changes are needed to improve the buyer-seller relationship, what processes are being used, and how the work is progressing compared to the plan. Formal changes to the management plans or the contract may be requested as a result of this meeting.

## Inspection  PAGE 498  Inspections may involve walkthroughs of the project work site or reviews of deliverables produced to verify compliance with the procurement statement of work. Do deliverables meet specifications? Variances or deviations may trigger change requests.

## Audits

PAGE 498   An audit is performed by a team that includes representatives of both the buyer and the seller in a procurement. The purpose of the audit is to confirm that the seller's activities are in compliance with approved procurement policies and processes. Variances are identified, and adjustments are made accordingly. The results of such an audit can be used to improve the procurement process and to capture lessons learned.

## Earned Value Analysis

PAGE 498   Earned value analysis measurements identify scope, schedule, or cost variances from the performance measurement baseline. Variances are analyzed to determine their impact on the project. The results may be used to generate reports, forecast future performance, and predict actual completion dates and costs. Change requests may be requested based on the results of this analysis.

## Trend Analysis

PAGE 498   Trend analysis determines whether performance is getting better or worse, and it can be used to develop forecast estimates and estimate at completion.

## Conflict

Conflict is an important topic that may be addressed in tricky procurement questions on the exam. As we have discussed, in most projects that use a contract, someone other than the project manager controls the contract. In many cases, this person, who may be the procurement manager or contract administrator, is the only one with authority to change the contract. We have also said that the contract includes the procurement statement of work. Can you see the potential for conflict between the procurement manager and the project manager? The buyer's project manager may want to initiate a change to the scope or sequence of work identified in the procurement statement of work (an area seemingly under the project manager's control), but cannot do so without the procurement manager's approval. This adds another layer to the project manager's management activities that you may not have seen if you do not work with procurements.

## Claims Administration

PAGE 498   Conflict can also occur between the buyer and the seller, and may result in the seller submitting a claim against the buyer. A claim is an assertion that the buyer did something that has hurt the seller, and the seller is now asking for compensation. Another way of looking at claims is that they are a type of seller-initiated change requests. Claims can get nasty. Imagine a seller that is not making as much profit as they had hoped, issuing claims for every action taken by the buyer. Imagine the number of claims that can arise if you are working with a fixed-price contract and an incomplete procurement statement of work.

Claims are usually addressed through the contract change control system. The best way to settle them is through negotiation or the use of the dispute-resolution process specified in the contract. Many claims are not resolved until after the work is completed.

## Contract Interpretation

Contract interpretation is never easy and frequently requires a lawyer's assistance. However, the exam may describe a simple situation about a conflict over interpretation of a contract and then ask you to determine the correct answer.

**TRICKS OF THE TRADE®**  Contract interpretation is based on an analysis of the intent of the parties, as reflected in the language of the contract, along with a few guidelines for interpreting that language. One such guideline is that the contract supersedes any memos, conversations, or discussions that may have occurred prior to the contract signing. Therefore, if a requirement is not in the contract, it does not have to be met, even if it was agreed upon prior to signing the contract. The following is an exercise on intent.

547

## Exercise
In each row, circle the item on the left or right side that would "win" in a dispute over contract interpretation.

| | | |
|---|---|---|
| Contract language | Or | A memo drafted by one of the parties describing proposed changes after the contract is signed |
| Contract language | Or | A memo signed by both parties before the contract is signed that describes what was agreed to during negotiations |
| Contract terms and conditions | Or | Procurement statement of work |
| Common definition | Or | The intended meaning (without supplying a definition) |
| Industry use of the term | Or | Common use of the term |
| Special provisions | Or | General provisions |
| Typed-over wording on the contract | Or | A handwritten comment on the contract that is also initialed |
| Numbers | Or | Words |
| Detailed terms | Or | General terms |

## Answer
The correct answers (in bold) show more clearly the intent of the parties to the contract.

| | | |
|---|---|---|
| **Contract language** | Or | A memo drafted by one of the parties describing proposed changes after the contract is signed |
| **Contract language** | Or | A memo signed by both parties before the contract is signed that describes what was agreed to during negotiations |
| **Contract terms and conditions** | Or | **Procurement statement of work** |

*The answer here depends on the Order of Precedence Clause in the contract that describes which terms and conditions take precedence over the others in the event of a conflict between them.*

| | | |
|---|---|---|
| **Common definition** | Or | The intended meaning (without supplying a definition) |
| **Industry use of the term** | Or | Common use of the term |
| **Special provisions** | Or | General provisions |
| Typed-over wording on the contract | Or | **A handwritten comment on the contract that is also initialed** |
| Numbers | Or | **Words** |
| **Detailed terms** | Or | General terms |

The following sections outline the primary outputs of the Control Procurements process.

## Change Requests   PAGE 499   While the work is underway, the buyer's needs may change, and, as a result, the buyer may issue a change order to the contract. The impacts of the contract changes are then negotiated by the two parties. Changes to the contract may be requested throughout the procurement process, and are handled as part of the project's integrated change control efforts, along with all other project changes. Any changes need to be analyzed for their impacts on the rest of the project.

If you do not have experience working with contracts, you should be aware of the concept of constructive changes, which do not result from formal change requests. Rather, constructive changes occur when the buyer, through actions or inactions, limits the seller's ability to perform the work according to the contract. This can include over-inspection or failure to cooperate. The buyer can also cause the seller to file a claim for damages if the buyer fails to uphold their end of the contract (for example, failing to review documents or deliverables on time). Project managers need to be particularly sensitive to constructive changes. Such changes often happen during the course of managing a procurement. A simple direction to the contractor to perform certain work that may seem minor can result in a constructive change that costs the company a lot of money if that change is outside the scope of the contract.

## Procurement Documentation Updates   PAGE 499   Throughout the Control Procurements process, data on the contract and contract performance by both the buyer and the seller is gathered and analyzed. This information needs to be updated and archived.

Because a contract is a formal, legal document, thorough records relating to the contract must be kept. A records management system may need to be used to keep procurement documentation complete, organized, and accessible. Record keeping can be critical if actions taken during a procurement are ever questioned after the procurement is completed, such as in the case of unresolved claims or legal actions. Records may also be necessary to satisfy insurance requirements. For many projects, every email, every payment, and every written and verbal communication must be recorded and stored. On other projects, information about the weather and the number of people on the buyer's property each day may be recorded. Whatever information is appropriate for the particular industry and project is saved.

On large or complex projects, a records management system can be quite extensive, with one person assigned just to manage these records. A records management system can include indexing systems, archiving systems, and information retrieval systems.

## Closed Procurements   PAGE 499   Closing procurements consists of tying up all the loose ends, verifying that all work and deliverables are accepted, finalizing open claims, and paying withheld retainage for each of the procurements on the project. The buyer will provide the seller with formal notice that the contract has been completed. There may be some obligations, such as warranties, that will continue after the procurement is closed.

Procurements are closed:

- When a contract is completed
- When a contract is terminated before the work is completed

Many people who are new to procurement do not realize a contract can be terminated before the work is complete. The contract should have provisions for termination, which can be done for cause or for convenience.

549

When many changes to a procurement are required, it may be best to terminate the contract and start fresh by negotiating a new contract with the existing seller or by finding a new seller. This is a drastic step that should be taken only when the existing contract no longer serves the purposes of defining all the work, roles, and responsibilities.

The buyer may terminate a contract for cause if the seller breaches the contract (does not perform according to the contract). This illustrates another reason the contract should clearly identify all the work required by the buyer. The buyer can also terminate the contract before the work is complete if they no longer want the work done (termination for convenience). Sellers need to realize this can happen.

A seller is rarely allowed to terminate a contract, but it could be appropriate on some projects. In any case, termination can result in extensive negotiations on what costs the buyer will pay. This is controlled by the language of the contract. In a termination for convenience, the seller is usually paid for work completed and work in process. If the contract is terminated for cause due to a default, the seller is generally paid for completed work but not for work in process. The seller may also be subject to claims from the buyer for damages. In any case, termination is a serious issue, and one that has lasting effects on the project. Termination negotiations can be drawn out long after the work has stopped—highlighting yet another reason why details of the project must be documented on an ongoing basis.

All procurements must be closed out, no matter the circumstances under which they stop, are terminated, or are completed. Closure is a way to accumulate some added benefits, such as lessons learned. It provides value to both the buyer and the seller and should not be omitted under any circumstances.

 Some people find the difference between the Close Project or Phase process and procurement closure confusing. This often seems to come up as a question on the exam. The answer is easy, though, if you think of project closure as closing out a project or phase and procurement closure as closing out a procurement. Depending on what choices the exam gives you, the answer could be:

- There may be many procurements in one project, so there can be many procurement closures, but Close Project or Phase only happens at the end of the project or phase. All procurements must be closed as part of monitoring and controlling, before final project closure.

- Upon completion of the contract for each procurement, the project manager performs a review of the procurement process on the contract and the performance of the seller before closing out the procurement. When the project as a whole is completed later, the project manager performs the final administrative and financial closure along with other processes required to close out the project.

- To make it a little more confusing, there may be questions that ask about the frequency of project closure and procurement closure. Read these questions carefully, as the way the questions are written will help you select the right answer. For projects that are managed in phases, such as a design phase, testing phase, and installation phase, the Close Project or Phase process occurs at the end of each project phase as well as at the end of the project as a whole. Make sure you understand this for the exam. In contrast, procurement closure is done at the completion of each contract.

- To protect the legal interests of both parties, procurement closure requires detailed record keeping and must be done more formally than is generally required for project closure.

Make sure you remember these points for the exam.

Now let's think about the real world. What do you think needs to be done at the end of the procurement in order to say the procurement is indeed finished? Wouldn't it be substantially similar to what needs to be done when you close out a project in the Close Project or Phase process?

550

**Exercise**   Describe what work must be done during procurement closure.

 

**Answer**   As you read the answer, think about how similar closing procurements is to the Close Project or Phase process. Procurement closure includes all the following:

- **Product validation**   This involves checking to see if all the work was completed correctly and satisfactorily. The product of the procurement should be the same as what was requested. The product of the procurement should also meet the buyer's needs.

- **Procurement negotiation**   The final settlement of all claims, invoices, and other issues may be handled through negotiations or through the dispute resolution process established in the contract.

- **Financial closure**   Financial closure includes making final payments and completing cost records.

- **Audit of the procurement process**   This is a structured review of only the procurement process. Do not think of this as auditing costs, but rather as capturing lessons learned from the procurement process that can help improve other procurements. Normally this is done by the procurement manager and project manager, but companies that want to improve their processes may also involve the seller. Remember, this is talking about how the whole procurement process went.

- **Updates to records**   This involves making sure all records of the procurement are complete and accessible. This information could include whatever has been recorded to date on the project. These records will become part of the procurement file (described later in this discussion).

- **Final contract performance reporting**   Think of this as creating a final report. First, you need to analyze and document the success and effectiveness of the procurement and the seller, and then turn that into a final report.

- **Lessons learned** Procurement lessons learned are received from everyone involved in the project, even the seller, and become part of the lessons learned for the project. They often include a discussion of what went right, what went wrong, and what can be done better next time. Lessons learned are created as a result of the audit. They then become part of the organizational process assets. Lessons learned are documented and shared throughout the organization.

- **Procurement file** Creating the procurement file involves putting all emails, letters, conversation records, payment receipts, reports, and anything else related to the procurement into an organized file. This file will be stored for use as historical records and will help protect the project in case of arguments or legal action regarding what was done and not done according to the contract. The project manager, with the help of the procurement manager, decides what documents need to be kept.

- **Other** Procurement closure could also include arranging for storage of procurement records and drawings, creating and delivering legal documents, or returning property used for the procurement to its owner.

When closure is completed and the seller has received formal sign-off from the buyer that the products of the procurement are acceptable, the procurement is closed. Expect questions on the exam that describe a situation and require you to determine whether the procurement is closed. In gaining formal acceptance, the seller is also working to measure customer satisfaction. Often, a formal customer satisfaction survey may be included in a seller's closure records. The Close Project or Phase process includes confirmation that contract closure has been done satisfactorily.

**Exercise** **The Procurement Process** Now that you know so much about procurement, test your knowledge by completing the following charts. Notice the word "Actions." For the exam, you need to know what needs to be done during each step as well as what you have when you are done with a process (outputs). Because of the number of questions on the exam that ask about the procurement process, this is one of the most important exercises in this chapter.

Recreate the procurement management process, including the outputs, in the tables on the following two pages. Even with one reading of this chapter, you should get most of the key actions and outputs correct. After you have read the chapter two or three times, you should be almost 100 percent accurate. This exercise is about understanding the most important actions of procurement management, not memorization. Create the chart three times, and you should know it well enough for the exam.

552

| Plan Procurement Management | Conduct Procurements | Control Procurements |
|---|---|---|
| | Key Actions | |
| | | |

| Plan Procurement Management | Conduct Procurements | Control Procurements |
|---|---|---|
| | Key Outputs | |
| | | |

**TRICKS OF THE TRADE®** Here is a trick for understanding the process without memorizing the whole thing—know only the outputs! If a question describes some activity and that activity occurs after the procurement documents are created and before the contract is signed, then it must be taking place as part of the Conduct Procurements process. If it is taking place during the time after the contract is signed through when the work is substantially done, it must be occurring during the Control Procurements process.

554

**Answer**  The following actions and outputs are the ones you should give the most attention to when preparing for the exam.

| Plan Procurement Management | Conduct Procurements | Control Procurements |
| --- | --- | --- |
| | Key Actions | |

**Plan Procurement Management**

- Perform make-or-buy analysis.
- Create a procurement management plan.
- Create a procurement strategy for each procurement.
- Create a procurement statement of work for each procurement.
- Select the appropriate contract type.
- Create terms and conditions, including standard and special conditions.
- Create bid documents.
- Determine source selection criteria.
- Gather and analyze data on prospective sellers, the market, and market price.
- Estimate time and cost for contract and work.

**Conduct Procurements**

- Find potential sellers through advertising, a preapproved seller list, or other means.
- Send procurement documents.
- Hold a bidder conference.
- Answer sellers' questions.
- Receive the seller responses.
- Compare the proposals to the source selection criteria using a weighting or screening system to pick/shortlist the sellers.
- Receive presentations from seller(s).
- Compare to independent estimates.
- Hold negotiations.
- Use interpersonal and team skills, such as negotiation.
- Allocate risk to sellers when appropriate.

**Control Procurements**

- Understand the legal implications of your actions.
- Hold procurement performance reviews.
- Request changes.
- Administer claims.
- Manage interfaces among sellers.
- Monitor, analyze, and report on performance against the contract.
- Review cost submittals, and make payments.
- Perform inspections and audits.
- Maintain records of everything.
- Manage relationships.
- Accept verified deliverables.
- Perform procurement audits.
- Negotiate settlements.
- Create lessons learned.
- Complete final contract performance reporting.
- Validate the product.
- Issue formal acceptance.
- Update records.
- Create a procurement file.
- Perform financial closure.

|  Plan Procurement Management | Conduct Procurements | Control Procurements  |
| --- | --- | --- |
|  | Key Outputs | |
| • Make-or-buy decisions | • Selected sellers | • Substantial completion of contract requirements and deliverables |
| • Procurement management plan | • Signed contracts | • Work performance information |
| • Procurement statements of work | • Resource calendars | |
| • Procurement strategies | • Change requests | • Change requests |
| • Bid documents | • Project management plan updates | • Project management plan updates |
| • Selected contract type | • Project documents updates | • Project documents updates (including updates to procurement documents) |
| • Source selection criteria | • Recommendations and updates to the processes and procedures for organizational procurement practices | • Organizational process assets updates |
| • Change requests | | • Formal acceptance |
| • Independent contract estimates | • Organizational process assets updates | • Closed procurements |
| | | • Lessons learned and records updates |

**Exercise** Here is another exercise to review what we discussed in this chapter. To pass the exam, you must understand the project manager's role in procurements. After reading this chapter, how would you describe the project manager's role?

_____

_____

_____

_____

_____

_____

_____

_____

_____

_____

_____

_____

_____

**Answer** As the project manager, you should:

- Know the procurement process so you integrate all procurements into your project.
- Understand what contract terms and conditions mean so you can read and understand contracts.
- Make sure the contract contains all the scope of work and all the project management requirements, such as attendance at meetings, reports, actions, and communications deemed necessary to minimize problems and miscommunications with the seller(s).
- Identify risks, and incorporate mitigation and allocation of risks into the contracts to decrease project risk.
- Help tailor the contract to the unique needs of the project while it is being written.
- Include adequate time in the project schedule to complete the procurement process.
- Be involved during contract negotiations to protect the relationship with the seller.
- Protect the integrity of the project and the ability to get the work done by making sure the procurement process goes as smoothly as possible.
- Help make sure all the work in the contract is done—including reporting, inspections, and legal deliverables, such as the release of liens and ownership of materials—not just the technical scope.
- Do not ask for something that is not in the contract without making a corresponding change to the contract.
- Work with the procurement manager to manage changes to the contract.

That is the procurement process! Was a lot of this new to you? If you are inexperienced in working with procurements, reread this chapter, and try to visualize how the different topics apply to a large project. The visualization will help you understand the process in a real way, so you know what proper project management is and what your involvement in the procurement process should be.

## Practice Exam

1. Once signed, a contract is legally binding unless:
    A. One party is unable to perform.
    B. One party is unable to finance its part of the work.
    C. It is in violation of applicable law.
    D. It is declared null and void by either party's legal counsel.

2. With a clear procurement statement of work, a seller completes work as specified, but the buyer is not pleased with the results. The contract is considered to be:
    A. Null and void
    B. Incomplete
    C. Complete
    D. Waived

3. You are preparing procurement documents for the building of a community center. There will be government standards, guidelines, and possibly regulations involved. You need to structure the procurement documentation in order to get proposals from qualified prospective sellers interested in doing business on a particular project. All the following statements concerning procurement documents are incorrect except:
    A. Well-designed procurement documents can simplify comparison of responses.
    B. Procurement documents must be rigorous with little flexibility to allow consideration of seller suggestions.
    C. In general, procurement documents should not include selection criteria.
    D. Well-designed procurement documents do not include a procurement statement of work.

4. A project manager for the seller is told by her management that the project team should do whatever possible to be awarded incentive money. The primary objective of incentive clauses in a contract is to:
    A. Reduce costs for the buyer.
    B. Help the seller control costs.
    C. Synchronize objectives.
    D. Reduce risk for the seller by shifting risk to the buyer.

5. All the following statements about change control are incorrect except:
    A. A fixed-price contract will minimize the need for change control.
    B. Changes seldom provide real benefits to the project.
    C. Contracts should include procedures to accommodate changes.
    D. More detailed specifications eliminate the causes of changes.

6. A routine audit of a cost-reimbursable (CR) contract determines that overcharges are being made. If the contract does not specify corrective action, the buyer should:
    A. Continue to make project payments.
    B. Halt payments until the problem is corrected.
    C. Void the contract and start legal action to recover overpayments.
    D. Change the contract to require more frequent audits.

7. Buyers and sellers have many common goals, but some goals of the buyer will not benefit the seller. Likewise, the seller will sometimes have goals that conflict with those of the buyer. These could negatively affect the project if contracts are not negotiated appropriately. The primary objective of contract negotiations is to:

    A. Get the most from the other side.
    B. Protect the relationship.
    C. Get the highest monetary return.
    D. Define objectives and stick to them

8. A seller is working on a cost-reimbursable (CR) contract when the buyer decides he would like to expand the scope of services and change to a fixed-price (FP) contract. All the following are the seller's options except:

    A. Completing the original work on a cost-reimbursable basis and then negotiating a fixed price for the additional work
    B. Completing the original work and rejecting the additional work
    C. Negotiating a fixed-price contract that includes all the work
    D. Starting over with a new contract

9. You have narrowed down the prospective sellers, and conducted a bidder conference. You are prepared to enter into a contract with the desired seller, and are checking that everything is in order for final contract negotiations and contract finalization. You have only a couple of points to clarify with the seller. All the following must be present to have a contract except:

    A. A procurement statement of work
    B. Acceptance
    C. The address of the seller
    D. Buyers' signatures

10. You are the project manager working on a complex structural engineering project. Not an engineer yourself, you will require the assistance of several subject matter experts during the procurement process. In addition to the subject matter experts, the organization has a procurement department that will provide resources for the procurement process on this project. Which of the following best describes the project manager's role in the procurement process?

    A. The project manager has only minor involvement.
    B. The project manager should be the negotiator.
    C. The project manager should provide an understanding of the risks of the project.
    D. The project manager should tell the contract manager how the contracting process should be handled.

11. You are working to plan procurements for a project that will develop a prototype cruise ship. The prototype will be tested, perfected, and then used to create a small fleet. In addition to creating a procurement management plan, you must put together bid documents describing the project needs and the criteria that will be used to select a seller. Which of the following will occur during this project's Plan Procurement Management process?

    A. Make-or-buy decisions
    B. Answering sellers' questions about the bid documents
    C. Advertising
    D. Proposal evaluation

12. Which of the following is the best thing for a project manager to do in the Conduct Procurements process?

    A. Evaluate risks.
    B. Select a contract type.
    C. Perform market research.
    D. Answer sellers' questions about the procurement documents.

13. The sponsor is worried about the seller deriving extra profit on the cost plus fixed fee (CPFF) contract. Each month he requires the project manager to submit CPI calculations and an analysis of the cost to complete. The project manager explains to the sponsor that extra profits should not be a worry on this project because:

    A. The team is making sure the seller does not cut scope.
    B. All costs invoiced are being audited.
    C. There can only be a maximum 10 percent increase if there is an unexpected cost overrun.
    D. The fee is only received by the seller when the project is completed.

14. You are considering using a fixed-price (FP) contract, because you have well-defined requirements for your construction project. With your requirements and your understanding of the seller's competition, you are confident you will be able to establish a complete statement of work. The fee or profit in this type of contract is:

    A. Unknown
    B. Part of the negotiation involved in paying every invoice
    C. Applied as a line item to every invoice
    D. Determined with the other party at the end of the project

15. As part of closing a cost-reimbursable contract on a project, what must the buyer remember to do?

    A. Decrease the risk rating of the project.
    B. Audit seller's cost submittals.
    C. Evaluate the fee she is paying.
    D. Make sure the seller is not adding resources.

16. The sponsor and the project manager are discussing what type of contract the project manager plans to use on the project. The sponsor points out that the performing organization paid a design team a lot of money to come up with the design. The project manager is concerned that the risk for the buyer be as small as possible, and recommends a fixed-price contract. An advantage of a fixed-price contract for the buyer is:

    A. Cost risk is lower.
    B. Cost risk is higher.
    C. There is little risk.
    D. Risk is shared by all parties.

17. You are trying to make sure all records from the procurement are documented and indexed. Which of the following do you not have to worry about?

    A. Proposal
    B. Procurement statement of work
    C. Terms and conditions
    D. Negotiation process

18. A project has a tight budget when you begin negotiating with a seller for a piece of equipment. The seller has told you the equipment price is fixed. Your manager has told you to negotiate the cost with the seller. Your assessment is that the piece of equipment has been offered at inflated pricing. What is your best course of action?
    A. Make a good faith effort to find a way to decrease the cost.
    B. Postpone negotiations until you can convince your manager to change his mind.
    C. Hold the negotiations, but only negotiate other aspects of the project.
    D. Cancel the negotiations.

19. Which of the following is an advantage of centralized contracting?
    A. Increased expertise
    B. Easier access
    C. The project manager doesn't have to be involved
    D. More loyalty to the project

20. With which type of contract is the seller most concerned about project scope?
    A. Fixed-price
    B. Cost plus fixed fee
    C. Time and material
    D. Purchase order

21. Your company has an emergency and needs contracted work done as soon as possible. Under these circumstances, which of the following would be the most helpful to add to the contract?
    A. A clear procurement statement of work
    B. Requirements as to which subcontractors can be used
    C. Incentives
    D. A force majeure clause

22. You are the project manager of a relatively small project to build out improvements to a small shop in a pedestrian mall. The project is using a time and material contract, and you know you must be involved in negotiations. Which of the following is an advantage of a time and material contract?
    A. A time and material contract is less work for the buyer to manage.
    B. The seller has a strong incentive to control costs.
    C. The total price is known.
    D. Negotiations are less extensive.

23. The project team is assessing the responses of prospective sellers who have submitted proposals. One team member argues for a certain seller while another team member wants the project to be awarded to a different seller. What part of the procurement process is the team in?
    A. Plan Procurement Management
    B. Control Procurements
    C. Negotiate Contracts
    D. Conduct Procurements

24. A project manager is in the middle of creating a request for proposal (RFP). What part of the procurement process is he in?
    A. Conduct Procurements
    B. Plan Procurement Management
    C. Administer Procurements
    D. Make-or-Buy Analysis

© 2018 RMC Publications, Inc.™ • 952.846.4484 • info@rmcls.com • www.rmcls.com

25. Your program manager has advised that you need to protect the organization from financial risk. In planning a new project, you realize there is limited scope definition related to the work needed to fulfill the contract. What is the best type of contract to choose?

    A. Fixed-price (FP)
    B. Cost plus percentage of cost (CPPC)
    C. Time and material (T&M)
    D. Cost plus fixed fee (CPFF)

26. Negotiations between two parties are becoming complex, so Party A makes some notes that both parties sign. However, when the work is being done, Party B claims they are not required to provide an item they both agreed to during negotiations, because it was not included in the subsequent contract. In this case, Party B is:

    A. Incorrect, because both parties must comply with what they agreed on
    B. Correct, because there was an offer
    C. Generally correct, because both parties are only required to perform what is in the contract
    D. Generally incorrect, because all agreements must be upheld

27. Your project has just been fast tracked, and you are looking to quickly bring in a subcontractor to complete networking. There is no time to issue a request for proposal (RFP), so you choose to use a company you have used many times before for software development. A primary concern in this situation is:

    A. Collusion between subcontractors
    B. The subcontractor's qualifications
    C. The subcontractor's evaluation criteria
    D. Holding a bidder conference

28. The project manager, the procurement manager, and the project sponsor are discussing the project costs and whether it is better to have their own company do some of the project work or hire another company to do all the work. Generally, it would be better for the organization to do the work internally if:

    A. There is a lot of proprietary data.
    B. You have the expertise, but you do not have the available manpower.
    C. You do not need control over the work.
    D. Your company resources are limited.

29. After much hard work, the procurement statement of work for the project is completed. However, even after gaining agreement that the procurement statement of work is complete, the project manager is unsure of whether it actually addresses all the buyer's needs. The project manager is about to attend the bidder conference. He asks you for advice on what to do during the session. Which of the following is the best advice you can give him?

    A. You do not need to attend this session; the procurement manager will hold it.
    B. Make sure you negotiate project scope.
    C. Make sure you give all the sellers the opportunity to ask questions.
    D. Let the project sponsor handle the meeting so you can be the good guy in the negotiation session.

30. A seller is awarded a contract to build a pipeline. The contract terms and conditions require a work plan to be issued for the buyer's approval prior to commencing work, but the seller fails to provide one. Which of the following is the best thing for the buyer's project manager to do?

    A. File a letter of intent.
    B. Develop the work plan and issue it to the seller to move things along.
    C. Issue a default letter.
    D. Issue a stop work order to the seller until a work plan is prepared.

31. Procurement closure is different from the Close Project or Phase process in that procurement closure:

    A. Occurs before Close Project or Phase
    B. Is the only one to involve the customer
    C. Includes the return of property
    D. May be done more than once for each contract

32. You have just started work on a procurement when management decides to terminate the contract. What should you do?

    A. Go back to the Plan Procurement Management process.
    B. Go back to the Conduct Procurements process.
    C. Complete the Control Procurements process.
    D. Stop working, and consider the procurement finished.

33. The project team is considering the prospective sellers who have submitted proposals. One team member supports a certain seller while another team member wants the project to be awarded to a different seller. The project manager should remind the team that the best thing to focus on in order to make a selection is the:

    A. Procurement documents
    B. Procurement audits
    C. Source selection criteria
    D. Procurement management plan

34. The $800,000 contract specifies that the seller will bill the buyer at $10,000 per month. However, the seller is able to complete the project work faster than planned. Therefore, they bill the buyer for $15,000 for the work performed in the past month. The buyer should:

    A. Send a breach of contract notice.
    B. Pay the invoice, as they will save on future payments.
    C. Meet with the seller to discuss the overcharge.
    D. Adjust the contract to allow for variations in monthly billings.

35. You are the project manager at a software development company, leading a project to develop an innovative application for a client. The project has followed a strict software engineering process. The requirements have been specified in detail, resulting in extensive functional and technical specification documents. Your project team member delivers an interim project deliverable to the buyer. However, the buyer refuses the deliverable, stating it does not meet the requirement on page 300 of the technical specifications. You review the document and find that you agree. What is the best thing to do?

    A. Explain that the contract is wrong and should be changed.
    B. Issue a change order.
    C. Review the requirements, and meet with the responsible team member to review the WBS dictionary.
    D. Call a meeting of the team to review the requirement on page 300.

36. Your organization has recently been informed that several of the regulations related to how your products are manufactured will change in six months. In planning for work to change certain design and production processes, you determine you will need to work with several external organizations to do the work. Which type of contract do you not want to use if you do not have enough help to audit invoices?

    A. Cost plus fixed fee (CPFF)
    B. Time & material (T&M)
    C. Fixed-price (FP)
    D. Fixed price incentive fee (FPIF)

37. A new project manager is about to begin creating the procurement statement of work. One stakeholder wants to add many items to the procurement statement of work. Another stakeholder only wants to describe the functional requirements. The project is important for the project manager's company, but a seller will do the work. How would you advise the project manager?

    A. The procurement statement of work should be general, to allow the seller to make their own decisions.
    B. The procurement statement of work should be general, to allow for clarification later.
    C. The procurement statement of work should be detailed, to allow for clarification later.
    D. The procurement statement of work should be as detailed as necessary for the type of project.

# Answers

1. **Answer** C

   **Explanation** Once signed, a contract is binding to both sides. Contracts typically state that either side can choose to terminate the agreement by negotiating a settlement based on work already performed. Generally, the inability to perform or get financing, or one party's belief that the contract is null and void does not change the fact that the contract is binding. If, however, both sides agree to terminate the contract, the contract can move into closure. An illegal contract is not enforceable.

2. **Answer** C

   **Explanation** If the seller completes the work specified in the procurement statement of work, the contract is considered complete. That does not mean the same thing as the procurement being closed. Procurement closure must still occur. However, in this situation, the contract work is completed.

3. **Answer** A

   **Explanation** Often, the seller is required to inform the buyer of anything that is missing or unclear in the procurement documents. It is in the buyer's best interest to discover missing items, since it will save the buyer money and trouble to correct the problem early. Procurement documents must include terms and conditions and selection criteria, as well as documentation of all the work that is to be done (which includes the procurement statement of work). This is so the seller can price the project and know what is most important to the buyer. Well-designed procurement documents can simplify comparison of responses. This is an important point and is the best answer.

4. **Answer** C

   **Explanation** Incentives are meant to bring the objectives of the seller in line with those of the buyer, so both are working toward the same objective.

5. **Answer** C

   **Explanation** There are always good ideas (changes) that can add benefit to the project, regardless of the contract type. Although detailed specifications may reduce the need for changes, they do not eliminate all the causes. Contracts should include procedures to accommodate changes.

6. **Answer** A

   **Explanation** Halting all payments would be a breach of contract on the buyer's part. Voiding the contract and beginning legal action is too severe and cannot be done unilaterally. Changing the contract to require more frequent audits does not solve the problem presented. A choice that said, "Halt payments on the disputed amount" would probably be the best answer, but it is not offered. The best choice available is to continue to make the payments while working to resolve the issue.

7. **Answer** B

   **Explanation** As a project manager, you want to develop a good relationship during negotiations that will last throughout the project. Negotiations are not about getting the most from the other side (win-lose), as such actions will not create a good relationship. That doesn't mean, however, the buyer sacrifices what is best for the organization.

8. **Answer** D

   **Explanation** The seller can try to negotiate changes or simply continue the original contract and refuse requests to complete additional work, but the seller cannot unilaterally decide to start over with a new contract. Both parties have to agree to this option through negotiations.

565

9. **Answer** C

**Explanation** Many people miss the fact that a contract includes a procurement statement of work. To have a contract, you must also have acceptance. One set of signatures is not enough; you must have sign-off (acceptance) from both parties, not just from the buyer. The address of the seller is not required, and therefore is the exception.

10. **Answer** C

**Explanation** The project manager knows the project risks. They need to make sure provisions are included in the contract to address these risks.

11. **Answer** A

**Explanation** Answering sellers' questions, advertising, and proposal evaluation occur during the Conduct Procurements process. Make-or-buy decisions are made earlier—in the Plan Procurement Management process.

12. **Answer** D

**Explanation** Risk analysis is done before the Conduct Procurements process begins, as procurement is a risk mitigation and transference tool. Selecting a contract type is part of Plan Procurement Management. Market research is also performed in the Plan Procurement Management process, to enable selection of the appropriate sellers for the needs of the project. During the Conduct Procurements process, the project manager answers questions submitted by prospective sellers.

13. **Answer** B

**Explanation** Cutting scope decreases profits on this type of contract, so that would not be a way for the seller to generate extra profits. CPFF contracts generally do not limit fee increases. The fee in a CPFF contract is usually paid out on a continuous basis during the life of the project. One of the ways to change the profit in a cost plus fixed fee contract is to invoice for items not chargeable to the project. This would not be ethical by the seller but does not mean that a seller may not try it. Therefore, all invoiced costs should be audited.

14. **Answer** A

**Explanation** The fee or profit is known to the seller, but this question is asked from the buyer's perspective. The buyer does not know what profit the seller included in the response to the bid document and, therefore, will not know the profit in the fixed-price contract.

15. **Answer** B

**Explanation** Although a reserve might be decreased for the overall project when one of its procurements enters closure, the risk rating of the project is generally not affected. Evaluation of the fee should have been done during the Conduct Procurements process. Making sure the seller does not add resources should not be necessary, as the contracted work has been completed. Auditing the seller's cost submittals is a required aspect of the Control Procurements process.

16. **Answer** A

**Explanation** If you had trouble with this one, you need to remember that the questions are asked from the buyer's perspective unless otherwise noted. The seller has the most cost risk in a fixed-price contract, and the buyer's risk is lower because the buyer will not pay more if the seller does not control costs. The seller has the risk; if they do not control the costs, they could erode the profit margin and even lose money.

17. **Answer** D

**Explanation** The negotiation process is not a document. The proposal, procurement statement of work, and the contract terms and conditions are all records that need to be documented and indexed.

18. **Answer**  A

     **Explanation**  The best choice is to attempt to find a way to decrease the cost.

19. **Answer**  A

     **Explanation**  Centralized contracting refers to a situation in which a procurement department exists to oversee procurements across the entire organization. Because there may be many procurements going on simultaneously, it may be difficult to get access to the procurement manager. As their attention is divided between multiple contracts, the procurement manager has less loyalty to any one project. Even with the procurement department leading a procurement, the project manager must participate in the process, so that is not an advantage. Increased expertise of the procurement manager is an advantage of centralized contracting.

20. **Answer**  A

     **Explanation**  In a fixed-price contract, the seller has the cost risk and therefore wants to completely understand the procurement statement of work before bidding.

21. **Answer**  C

     **Explanation**  If you follow the proper project management process, you always have good definition of scope (in this case, the procurement statement of work). In this situation, both good scope definition and incentives are required. Along with good scope definition, you need the seller to share your need for speed. Incentives bring the seller's objectives in line with the buyer's and thus would be the most helpful. Good scope definition alone does not ensure speed.

22. **Answer**  D

     **Explanation**  Negotiation of a time and material contract is generally less extensive than negotiation of other contract types. The other choices are advantages of a fixed-price contract.

23. **Answer**  D

     **Explanation**  Selected sellers are an output of the Conduct Procurements process.

24. **Answer**  B

     **Explanation**  Bid documents are created during the Plan Procurement Management process. The request for proposal is one of those documents, so the project manager is in the Plan Procurement Management process.

25. **Answer**  D

     **Explanation**  Of the options given, the only contract that limits fees for large projects with limited scope definition is cost plus fixed fee.

26. **Answer**  C

     **Explanation**  Party B is only required to deliver what is defined in the contract.

27. **Answer**  B

     **Explanation**  Although you have used this contractor before, how can you be sure the company is qualified to do the new work, since it is not exactly like the previous work? This is the risk you are taking.

28. **Answer**  A

     **Explanation**  It is generally better to do the work yourself if using an outside company means you have to lose control or ownership of proprietary data to the other company.

567

29. **Answer** C

    **Explanation** The project manager should attend the bidder conference, although the procurement manager may lead it. Did you select negotiating scope? Sellers may ask questions about scope during the conference, but negotiations occur after the bidder conference, when the buyer selects one or more sellers with whom to negotiate. Allowing ample opportunity for all the prospective sellers to ask questions is one of the many challenges of a bidder conference. They may not want to ask questions while their competitors are present.

30. **Answer** C

    **Explanation** When a seller does not perform according to the contract terms and conditions, they have defaulted and the project manager must take action. You might prefer a choice to investigate the default by contacting the seller and asking what is going on, but that choice is not available here. You must send the formal written notice as soon as you become aware of the default so that you do not give up any right to receive the work plan in the future. You can contact the seller for a discussion as the second thing you do. Therefore, the best choice is to let the seller know they are in default. The default notification letter will instruct the seller to meet the performance requirement.

31. **Answer** A

    **Explanation** The customer may be involved in lessons learned and procurement audits, and would certainly be involved in formal acceptance. Both procurement closure and the Close Project or Phase process involve the return of property. Procurement closure is done once for each procurement, at the end of the contract. All procurements are closed before the project is closed.

32. **Answer** C

    **Explanation** Even if the contract is terminated before completion, the procurement needs be closed out. The results of the procurement and its documentation are archived as historical records in the Control Procurements process.

33. **Answer** C

    **Explanation** The source selection criteria are the primary tool for evaluating potential sellers and should be used by the team in order to make a selection.

34. **Answer** A

    **Explanation** By paying the additional amount of this month's invoice, the buyer may waive the right to limit monthly costs to $10,000. The project has allocated $10,000 per month for this seller, and the buyer may not have the capacity to pay more each month. By agreeing to the terms of the contract, the seller is contractually obligated not to exceed that amount. A breach of contract notice from the buyer to the seller is the best way to handle this situation.

35. **Answer** C

    **Explanation** This question is written from the perspective of the seller. The contract could be wrong or the customer could be wrong, but this should have been discovered earlier if proper project management was followed. A seller cannot issue a change order (although they could request one). Did you select calling a meeting of the team? If so, remember that proper project management does not mean making every decision with all the team members. The best choice involves reviewing the requirements documentation and meeting with the appropriate team member. If such a problem has arisen, it could mean something was wrong in the WBS dictionary or in how the team member completed the work.

36. **Answer**  A

    **Explanation**  If you got this question wrong, reread it. You need to audit invoices in all contract types, so how do you choose? Look for the answer that is best. In this case, it would be the choice that requires the greatest effort. A T&M contract should be used for low dollar and short duration contracts (remember that a T&M contract has no incentive to finish), so it does not have a high level of risk. FP and FPIF contracts cannot be best, because the risk to the buyer is limited. The buyer is still only going to pay the contracted price. In a CPFF contract, the buyer pays all costs. The seller could be charging the buyer for costs that should not be allocated to the buyer. Because of the size and dollar amount of this type of contract, and because the risk to the buyer is great, a CPFF contract requires the most auditing. In this case, you would not want to use a CPFF contract.

37. **Answer**  D

    **Explanation**  When the seller has more expertise than the buyer, the procurement statement of work should describe performance or function rather than a complete description of work. In any case, the procurement statement of work should be as detailed as possible.

# Stakeholder Management

## THIRTEEN

Some topics on the exam might seem easy to you—so much so that you might be inclined to skip studying them. Does the topic of stakeholders fall into this category for you? Before you dismiss the importance of this knowledge area, take note of an example of one person who failed the exam because he did not understand proper project management. His method of managing projects was simply to tell people what to do. And because he always worked with the same four people, he didn't think in terms of large projects (those that include hundreds or thousands of stakeholders) and how having so many stakeholders involved would significantly impact a project. In his job, he acted as both a project manager and a subject matter expert, assigning work to a small group of people as well as to himself. During the exam, he thought only in terms of his personal experience, rather than the best practices of project management.

## QUICKTEST

- Stakeholder definition
- Stakeholder management process
- Stakeholder involvement
- Stakeholder analysis
- Stakeholder register
- Stakeholder expectations
- Stakeholder engagement
- Stakeholder engagement plan
- Stakeholder engagement assessment matrix
- Stakes

In reality, the project manager needs to be the expert in project management, while relying on certain stakeholders to serve as experts in what needs to be done and how it should be accomplished. A project manager is much like an orchestra conductor in that regard. As the leader of the orchestra, the conductor doesn't play any of the instruments, but rather provides the sheet music and the guidance to help the musicians put on a great performance. Similarly, a project manager does not do all the work activities within a project—that is the job of the project team. The project manager facilitates, motivates, coordinates, and integrates all of those work activities into a successful outcome. Because he didn't think in this way, the person described in the previous paragraph answered questions incorrectly across all knowledge areas on the exam. His failure to understand the importance of planning, managing, and continuously evaluating stakeholder engagement had a huge impact on his understanding of project management.

What about you? Do you properly involve stakeholders on your projects? Have you had any complaints from key stakeholders about your projects? Have you ever delivered a product, only to discover the stakeholders are not using it? Your projects won't be successful without significant, continuous interactions with stakeholders. Your team can build a great product or service, but if you are not in close contact with the stakeholders who will use it, you may not realize you have missed the mark until it is too late.

Let's think about another scenario. Imagine you are assigned as the project manager for a new project. The director of your department provides you with a 200-page scope of work and a charter, and tells you to get started. What do you do next?

571

# Stakeholder Management

| INITIATING | PLANNING (This is the only process group with a set order.) | EXECUTING | MONITORING & CONTROLLING | CLOSING |
|---|---|---|---|---|
| Select project manager | **Determine development approach, life cycle, and how you will plan for each knowledge area** | Execute work according to the project management plan | **Take action to monitor and control the project** | Confirm work is done to requirements |
| Determine company culture and existing systems | Define and prioritize requirements | Produce product deliverables (product scope) | Measure performance against performance measurement baseline | Complete final procurement closure |
| Collect processes, procedures, and historical information | Create project scope statement | Gather work performance data | **Measure performance against other metrics in the project management plan** | Gain final acceptance of product |
| Divide large projects into phases or smaller projects | Assess what to purchase and create procurement documents | **Request changes** | **Analyze and evaluate data and performance** | Complete financial closure |
| Understand business case and benefits management plan | Determine planning team | Implement only approved changes | **Determine if variances warrant a corrective action or other change request(s)** | Hand off completed product |
| Uncover initial requirements, assumptions, risks, constraints, and existing agreements | Create WBS and WBS dictionary | Continuously improve; perform progressive elaboration | **Influence factors that cause change** | Solicit customer's feedback about the project |
| Assess project and product feasibility within the given constraints | Create activity list | Follow processes | **Request changes** | Complete final performance reporting |
| Create measurable objectives and success criteria | Create network diagram | Determine whether quality plan and processes are correct and effective | Perform integrated change control | Index and archive records |
| Develop project charter | Estimate resource requirements | Perform quality audits and issue quality reports | Approve or reject changes | Gather final lessons learned and update knowledge bases |
| **Identify stakeholders and determine their expectations, interest, influence, and impact** | Estimate activity durations and costs | Acquire final team and physical resources | **Update project management plan and project documents** | |
| **Request changes** | Determine critical path | Manage people | **Inform stakeholders of all change request results** | |
| Develop assumption log | Develop schedule | Evaluate team and individual performance; provide training | **Monitor stakeholder engagement** | |
| **Develop stakeholder register** | Develop budget | Hold team-building activities | Confirm configuration compliance | |
| | Determine quality standards, processes, and metrics | Give recognition and rewards | Create forecasts | |
| | **Determine team charter and all roles and responsibilities** | **Use issue logs** | Gain customer's acceptance of interim deliverables | |
| | **Plan communications and stakeholder engagement** | **Facilitate conflict resolution** | Perform quality control | |
| | Perform risk identification, qualitative and quantitative risk analysis, and risk response planning | Release resources as work is completed | Perform risk reviews, reassessments, and audits | |
| | **Go back—iterations** | Send and receive information, and solicit feedback | Manage reserves | |
| | Finalize procurement strategy and documents | Report on project performance | Manage, evaluate, and close procurements | |
| | Create change and configuration management plans | **Facilitate stakeholder engagement and manage expectations** | Evaluate use of physical resources | |
| | **Finalize all management plans** | Hold meetings | | |
| | **Develop realistic and sufficient project management plan and baselines** | Evaluate sellers; negotiate and contract with sellers | | |
| | Gain formal approval of the plan | **Use and share project knowledge** | | |
| | Hold kickoff meeting | Execute contingency plans | | |
| | Request changes | **Update project management plan and project documents** | | |

## Rita's Process Chart™
## Stakeholder Management
Where are we in the project management process?

Before you answer that question—and before you take the exam—you need to make sure you understand a simple concept: proper project management requires you to identify all stakeholders, analyze their power, interest, and level of engagement, elicit their requirements and expectations (for product, project, project management, quality, communications, etc.), and then evaluate and incorporate all of that information into the product and project scope as needed. You cannot simply accept a scope of work or project charter without considering the project's stakeholders and their requirements. And stakeholder involvement doesn't end there: engaging stakeholders should take place throughout the life of the project. This means you need to build and maintain positive relationships with stakeholders, and make sure they continue to be involved in the project at the level necessary to make it a success.

 If you have access to the *PMBOK® Guide*, review it for the word "stakeholders," and you will see just how many references occur. Think about whether the requisite involvement of stakeholders is different from what happens on your projects, and make note of your gaps.

The following should help you understand how each part of stakeholder management fits into the overall project management process:

| The Stakeholder Management Process | Done During |
| --- | --- |
| Identify Stakeholders | Initiating process group |
| Plan Stakeholder Engagement | Planning process group |
| Manage Stakeholder Engagement | Executing process group |
| Monitor Stakeholder Engagement | Monitoring and controlling process group |

## Stakeholder Involvement in Projects

Let's look at how you should involve stakeholders throughout the life of a project. Some of this discussion touches on processes that fall outside the stakeholder management process, such as Collect Requirements, Plan Communications Management, Manage Communications, and Plan Resource Management. This demonstrates the important role stakeholders play in all aspects of projects.

So, what should you do with stakeholders throughout a project?

- **Identify all of them.** The first step in working with stakeholders is identifying all of them as early as possible. Stakeholders discovered later in the project will likely request changes, which can impact the project and lead to delays.

- **Determine their requirements.** This is neither easy nor fast, but the project manager must make every effort to obtain as many requirements as possible before work begins. This applies to plan-driven projects as well as change-driven ones. The level of detail of the requirements may differ between plan-driven and change-driven projects, but it's still essential to determine as many requirements as possible up front for both. Do you try to do this? Many project managers do not even attempt it.

To understand why this is important, think about the effects of starting a project without all the requirements. Those effects would likely include changes, delays, and possible failure. How would it look if you had to say to your sponsor, "I did not know about that stakeholder's requirement. Now that I know, I need to extend the schedule to accommodate their needs or cut another stakeholder's needs out of the project." This is just bad project management, and it can be avoided with proper stakeholder management.

There are many ways to make sure you have the requirements—from just asking if you do, to conducting requirements reviews, to explaining to people what the negative consequences to the company and the project will be if a requirement is found later.

573

- **Determine their expectations.** What are expectations? They are beliefs about (or mental pictures of) the future. These expectations include what stakeholders think will happen to them, their department, and the company as a whole as a result of the project. Expectations tend to be much more ambiguous than stated requirements, or they may be undefined requirements. They may be intentionally or unintentionally hidden. For example, expectations that your project will not interrupt other work, or that your project will produce dramatic improvements could affect project success. Naturally, expectations that go unidentified will have major impacts across all constraints. Once captured, expectations are analyzed and may be converted to requirements and become part of the project.

  A difference between what a stakeholder thinks will happen and what actually happens might cause conflicts, rework, and changes. Why wait for a change? Why not prevent as many changes as possible by asking stakeholders what they expect and clarifying any expectations that are not accurate or that are poorly defined? This might involve walking stakeholders through what will occur to make sure there are no undiscovered expectations or requirements that could be unrealistic.

- **Determine their interest.** It's important to determine the level of interest each stakeholder has in the project. Does the stakeholder care about the project? Are they likely to be engaged? Once you gather and analyze that information, you can use it to plan out a strategy for maintaining or increasing that stakeholder's interest and level of engagement. You may also find that certain stakeholders are especially interested in working on a particular part of the project—to learn new skills or prove their skills—or that you need attention and support from a key stakeholder for deliverable reviews and acceptance. A great project manager will determine each stakeholder's interests and engagement related to the project, and will structure the work, roles, and responsibilities to maximize engagement.

- **Determine their level of influence.** To some degree, each stakeholder will be able to negatively or positively affect a project. This is their level of influence, and it should be identified and managed.

- **Determine their level of authority** Each stakeholder's level of authority will impact their effect on the work and outcome of the project.

- **Plan to engage stakeholders.** Project management focuses on planning before taking action. You need to plan ahead! How will you keep stakeholders involved in the project? How will you engage with them about their interests, influence, and expectations? How will you include them in project decision-making?

- **Plan how you will communicate with them.** Planning communications with your stakeholders is critical and is related to stakeholder engagement. How can you keep stakeholders involved and get them to communicate their thoughts and concerns if you haven't planned out how information will be shared on the project? Remember that poor communications are the most frequent cause of problems on projects, so careful communication planning can help prevent problems.

- **Manage their expectations, influence, and engagement.** Involving stakeholders doesn't end during initiating or planning. You need to work with them and manage relationships throughout the life of the project.

- **Communicate with them.** Stakeholders are included in project presentations and receive project information, including progress reports, updates, changes to the project management plan, and changes to the project documents, when appropriate.

- **Monitor communications and stakeholder engagement.** Good communication and relationships with stakeholders are critical to success, so it's essential to monitor these two areas on the project. You need to determine if and where communication and/or relationships are breaking down, and then adjust your approach as necessary.

**TRICKS OF THE TRADE®** A key to your success as a project manager is how you handle stakeholder relationships. Stakeholders must be involved, and their involvement must be managed by the project manager. That involvement may range from minor to extensive, depending on the needs of the project and the performing organization. In preparing for the exam, use the following list to help you evaluate your understanding of stakeholder involvement and identify any gaps that may impact how you answer questions. If you are unable to check two or more of the following items, you should spend more time researching this topic.

| How the Project Manager Should Involve Stakeholders on the Project | Place ✓ Here If You Do It; Study Areas Unchecked |
|---|---|
| 1  List all stakeholders by name; this can include individuals as well as groups. | ✓ |
| 2  Determine all the stakeholders' requirements. | ✓ |
| 3  Determine stakeholders' interest in being involved in the project and in the outcomes of the project. | ✓ |
| 4  Determine stakeholders' level of influence on the project. | ✓ |
| 5  Determine stakeholders' expectations, and turn them into requirements as appropriate. | ✓ |
| 6  Determine when stakeholders will be involved in the project and to what extent. | ✓ |
| 7  Get stakeholders to sign off that the requirements are finalized. | ✓ |
| 8  Assess stakeholders' knowledge and skills. | ✗ |
| 9  Analyze the project to evaluate whether stakeholders' needs will be met. | ✓ |
| 10  Let stakeholders know which requirements will be met, which requirements and expectations will not be met, and why. | ✓ |
| 11  Get and keep stakeholders involved in the project by assigning them project work or responsibilities, such as the role of risk response owner. | ✗ |
| 12  Manage and influence the stakeholders' involvement, engagement, and expectations. | ✓ |
| 13  Make the best use of stakeholders' expertise. | ✗ |
| 14  Communicate to stakeholders what they need to know (when they need to know it). | ✓ |
| 15  Make sure stakeholders know what they need to communicate to the project manager and other stakeholders. | ✗ |
| 16  Involve stakeholders, as necessary, in change management and approval. | ✓ |
| 17  Involve stakeholders in the creation of lessons learned. | ✗ |
| 18  Get stakeholders' sign-off and formal acceptance of interim deliverables during the project and at project or phase closing. | ✓ |
| 19  Reassess stakeholders' involvement, and make changes throughout the project as needed. | ✓ |
| 20  Ensure a common understanding of the project objectives, deliverables, work, and acceptance criteria. | ✓ |
| 21  Ask stakeholders to let you know about problems in project communications and relationships. | ✓ |

575

## Identify Stakeholders   PAGE 507

> **Process** Identify Stakeholders
> **Process Group** Initiating
> **Knowledge Area** Stakeholder Management

The first stakeholders are likely those who identify a problem or need. They may be involved in developing business documents for a project to provide a solution. The business case and benefits management plan, created before project initiating, may include lists of stakeholders who will benefit from or be affected by the project. An ongoing, focused effort to identify stakeholders should continue from this point throughout the project.

Why is it so essential to identify all stakeholders? (If you get the answer right, you could answer two more questions correctly on the exam.) Any stakeholders who are missed will likely be found later. When they are discovered, they will probably request changes, which may cause delays. Changes made later in the project are much more costly and harder to integrate than those made earlier. Identifying all stakeholders helps to create a project that considers all the interests, influence, and interdependencies of stakeholders. That said, changes within a project or organization may introduce new stakeholders, or a project manager may simply miss stakeholders in the initial identification. It's important, therefore, to reassess the list of stakeholders throughout the project to determine whether new ones should be added and, if so, what that will mean for the project.

Many project managers fail to consider the broad range of potential stakeholders. Remember, stakeholders are any people or organizations whose interests may be positively or negatively impacted by the project or its product, as well as anyone who can exert positive or negative influence over the project. This diverse group can include the sponsor, team members, senior management, subject matter experts, end users of the product or service, other departments or groups within the organization, functional or operational managers, vendors, consultants, regulatory agencies, customers, financial institutions, and many more. If the project includes procurements, the parties to the contract(s) are also stakeholders.

Keep in mind that you don't need to do the work of identifying stakeholders alone! The project team should be involved in this process. You can also consult subject matter experts, project managers in the organization who have worked on similar projects, and professional associations. And as new stakeholders are identified, they may be able to suggest other stakeholders to add to the list.

The following tools and techniques can be used during the Identify Stakeholders process.

## Questionnaires and Surveys   PAGE 511   Stakeholders, team members, and subject matter experts may be asked to name other potential stakeholders and to provide input regarding management of particular stakeholders or stakeholder groups.

## Brainstorming and Brain Writing[1]   PAGE 511   Participants may take part in brainstorming sessions to help identify additional stakeholders. Brain writing is an individual effort, while brainstorming involves a group of people interacting and working together.

## Stakeholder Analysis   PAGE 512   There are many factors to consider when analyzing stakeholders. Consider their roles and responsibilities on the project, as well as their level of authority and influence within the organization. Every stakeholder has expectations and attitudes toward the project that must be uncovered. You must also determine how interested they are in the project. What is at stake for them?

Examples of stakes include the following:

- **Ownership**  The stakeholder may have to sell property for the new freeway expansion that is proposed.
- **Knowledge**  The stakeholder may be the expert who designed a legacy inventory management system that is being replaced.
- **Rights**  The stakeholder may be concerned that the new development will endanger the community by destroying the watershed.
- **Rights**  A government official may be responsible for ensuring that the safety practices on the construction site comply with state and federal laws.
- **Interest**  The community may be concerned that additional traffic will come into their residential neighborhood if the new commuter rail stop does not have adequate parking facilities.
- **Contribution**  The resource manager may be concerned that team members they must provide to the project will not be able to complete their normal operational work with the addition of project work.

## Document Analysis
PAGE 512  Using this technique involves assessing all project documents and reviewing any lessons learned as well as other historical information (organizational process assets) from past projects. This analysis can be used to identify stakeholders and to collect information about the stakeholders and their stakes in the project.

## Stakeholder Mapping
PAGE 512  In addition to analyzing each stakeholder's potential impact and influence, you need to identify ways to manage them effectively. Stakeholder mapping, which groups stakeholders into categories, is a data representation technique that project managers use to analyze and plan how the project team will build relationships with stakeholders. Creating a stakeholder map with categories and classifications can help you determine how to prioritize your efforts to engage stakeholders on the project.

The following are examples of stakeholder mapping:

- **Power/interest grid**[2]  This grid is used to group stakeholders based on their level of power and their interest in the project's outcome. Variations of this tool emphasize other stakeholder attributes, such as power/influence or impact/influence.
- **Stakeholder cube**[3]  This three-dimensional model is used to represent aspects or dimensions of a stakeholder group.
- **Salience model**[4]  This model is used to group stakeholders based on need for attention, authority level, or level of involvement.

Stakeholders can also be grouped by directions of influence (upward, downward, outward, and sideward).

## Outputs of Identify Stakeholders
PAGE 514  The Identify Stakeholders process results in a stakeholder register, change requests, and updates to the project management plan and project documents such as the assumption log, issue log, and the risk register. These outputs are outlined in the following sections.

## Stakeholder Register
Information about stakeholders is compiled in the stakeholder register, a key output of the Identify Stakeholders process. The stakeholder register may include each stakeholder's name, title, supervisor, project role, contact information, major requirements and expectations, assessment information, impact and influence, attitude about the project, stakeholder classification, and other relevant information. Figure 13.1 shows an example of a stakeholder register.

**Stakeholder Register**

Project Title: ______________________ Project Number: __________

| | | | | | | | Assessment Data Results | | | |
|---|---|---|---|---|---|---|---|---|---|---|
| ID | Name | Title | Contact Information | Major Requirements | Main Expectations | Roles/ Responsibilities | Influence (1 to 5) | Power (1 to 5) | Interest (1 to 5) | Classifications |
| 1 | | | | | | | | | | |
| 2 | | | | | | | | | | |
| 3 | | | | | | | | | | |
| 4 | | | | | | | | | | |

FIGURE 13.1 *Sample stakeholder register*

The stakeholder register is an important input to the Plan Stakeholder Engagement process, as well as to several other planning processes, including Plan Communications Management. Remember that the register will be added to and updated throughout the life of the project.

**Change Requests** As additional stakeholders are identified after the first iteration of stakeholder identification, changes to the project management plan and/or project documents may be required to reflect plans to manage their involvement and meet their needs. Project plans that may be impacted include the requirements, communications, risk, and stakeholder engagement plans.

**Project Management Plan Updates** The identification of new stakeholders, or new information about known stakeholders, may prompt changes in the project's approach to stakeholder engagement, or risk, requirements, or communications management.

**Project Documents Updates** Assumptions about stakeholders may be updated in the assumption log. The issue log and risk register may also be updated to include issues or risks associated with project stakeholders.

## Plan Stakeholder Engagement PAGE 516

**Process** Plan Stakeholder Engagement
**Process Group** Planning
**Knowledge Area** Stakeholder Management

Managing the impact, relationships, and engagement of the stakeholders identified and analyzed during the previous process is essential to project success, but it can take a lot of time. That's why it's so important, as is the case with much of project management, to think and plan ahead before taking action.

Stakeholders can be an asset or a problem on the project, depending on how well the project is planned. To effectively manage relationships with this many people, you need to develop a stakeholder engagement plan. You need to think ahead about how the project will impact stakeholders, how you and the project team will interact with stakeholders, how you will involve stakeholders in making decisions, how you will manage their expectations, and how you can keep them satisfied—to ensure they are an asset on the project.

Planning stakeholder engagement requires you to strategize about your approach to stakeholder involvement, and develop actionable plans. This means you should schedule time to get to know your stakeholders and to check in with them throughout the project. If you know your stakeholders well, you'll have more success managing their engagement and will be better able to predict what engagement will look like throughout the project.

Now you may be thinking, "I have hundreds of stakeholders on my project, located all over the world. How can I possibly build and maintain relationships with them?" This is exactly why you need a plan. You may not be able to have a close relationship with every stakeholder, but you can't afford not to have relationships with key stakeholders and as many project team members as you are able. It's also important for you to plan ways in which you and your team members can develop relationships with stakeholders who are not a part of the project team.

Keep in mind, the closer you are to stakeholders, the more comfortable they will be coming to you with problems and concerns, and the easier it will be for you to pick up on verbal and nonverbal cues that can tell you when something might be wrong. This can be an early warning system for problems on your project. How do you build positive and powerful relationships with your stakeholders? The same way you have built them with your friends and family: by spending time getting to know them and allowing them to get to know you. The more time you spend with someone, the better you'll be able to ascertain their impressions and concerns.

**Exercise**  What are the characteristics that define a good relationship? Take a few minutes to think about this. Draw on your experience with your family, friends, coworkers, and others.

| Characteristics of a Good Relationship | |
|---|---|
| | |
| | |
| | |
| | |
| | |

**Answer**  Some possible answers are listed here. You may have come up with different or additional characteristics.

| Characteristics of a Good Relationship | |
|---|---|
| Trust | Sincerity |
| Honesty | Respect |
| Good communication | Concern |
| Interest | Empathy |

As you plan how you will get to know your stakeholders, remember that these are the qualities you want to nurture in your relationships with them.

579

During planning, you need to determine which stakeholders will require most of your time and effort. These decisions require you to think about the role of each stakeholder, the environment within which they operate, and the specific needs of your project. If there are any procurements in place, you will need to coordinate with the procurement department to plan stakeholder engagement efforts related to parties of the contract.

To plan stakeholder engagement, you will need the details of what has already been planned and documented in plans including resource and communications management, information from the stakeholder register, and any relevant information from past similar projects.

Let's consider an example. Imagine you are managing a project to replace the online application process for open positions in your company. Your sponsor is the human resources director, who wants to streamline the process and encourage candidates with advanced technical experience to apply for jobs. Even though your stakeholders include anyone who is a potential job candidate (possibly millions of people), there are a few key stakeholders with whom you will plan to spend most of your time: your sponsor and the managers in the company who evaluate candidates. As the project team is designing and building the new website to satisfy stakeholder requirements, you will want to receive frequent feedback from your key stakeholders about how the design meets their expectations. You might also identify a few newly hired employees who could help the team understand problems with the existing application process. Your stakeholder engagement plan might include formal review meetings where you discuss progress and get feedback on the progress of the website development.

Your experience on other projects and historical records of similar projects can help you anticipate and plan to meet stakeholder needs on the project. However, you should make use of the expertise of others as well. If you'll be working with a stakeholder for the first time, talk to another project manager or team member who knows this person. Meet with professional organizations, consultants, and subject matter experts to hear valuable insight on working with various stakeholders and stakeholder groups. Ask questions about how best to work with the stakeholders, and then meet with them as soon as possible to initiate these important relationships. Make sure the stakeholders themselves understand how important it is for you to meet their needs, and encourage them to communicate frequently as the planning and project work proceed. These preliminary meetings and conversations are critical for you to get an impression of how best to work with each stakeholder.

Not every stakeholder will be as engaged in the project as you might like, and some might be more engaged than you would wish. Stakeholder engagement can range from unaware of or resistant to the project to neutral to supportive or even interested in taking a leading role on the project. Think about each stakeholder's attitude and interest in the project, as this will help you determine the level of engagement required to make the project successful. You should also consider how much engagement you require from stakeholders during each phase of the project. You may require some stakeholders to be more involved during planning, for example, while others will take on a more prominent role during executing. Identify and analyze variances between the current and desired level of engagement, and work with the team to identify ways to achieve the right engagement level.

The project manager will need to choose tools and techniques to plan stakeholder engagement that are appropriate for the project.

## Stakeholder Engagement Assessment Matrix[5]   PAGE 521   A stakeholder engagement assessment matrix is a data representation tool used to compare stakeholders' current and desired level of engagement (see fig. 13.2). The stakeholder engagement plan documents how adjustments to stakeholders' level of engagement will be achieved. This matrix is revisited as the project progresses, to evaluate ongoing stakeholder engagement. Analysis of updates to this matrix may indicate the need to further plan or alter the stakeholder engagement strategy.

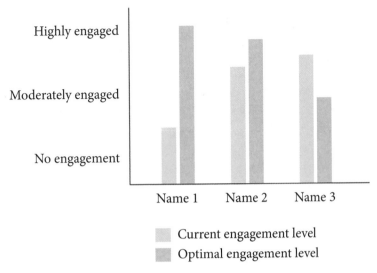

FIGURE 13.2   *Stakeholder engagement assessment matrix*

## Assumption and Constraint Analysis and Root Cause Analysis   PAGE 521   Evaluating assumptions about stakeholders' attitudes toward the project enables the team to determine actions necessary to adjust stakeholders' levels of engagement to benefit the project. Analysis of project constraints can provide insight into determining strategies to adjust stakeholders' levels of engagement.

Root cause analysis is a way for the project manager and team to analyze the cause of the current level of stakeholder support and engagement. Doing so will help them determine how best to facilitate a change to bring the stakeholders' engagement level to what is desired.

**Exercise**   If you've never planned stakeholder involvement on a project before, it can be difficult to imagine how you would go about doing this on an individual level. Think about the various stakeholders involved on a large project. How would you plan to manage the involvement of the stakeholders listed here?

| Stakeholder Description | Options for Managing Stakeholder Involvement |
|---|---|
| High interest in the project, low influence, highly knowledgeable expert on high-risk areas | |
| Low interest, the source of major requirements on the project (high influence), not easy to work with | |
| High interest, high influence, not a supporter of the project | |
| High interest, high influence, a supporter of the project | |
| Moderate interest, high influence, completing many activities on the project, a supporter of the project | |

| Stakeholder Description | Options for Managing Stakeholder Involvement |
| --- | --- |
| Moderate interest, high influence because the stakeholder has identified a large number of potential risks for the project, a supporter of the project | |
| Moderate interest, nervous about completing assigned activities | |

## Answer

Listed here are some suggestions for how you might plan to manage the involvement of these stakeholders. These are generalized descriptions and answers, but if you do not work on large projects in your real world, reviewing the following information will help you better understand the work that needs to be done for large projects.

| Stakeholder Description | Options for Managing Stakeholder Involvement |
| --- | --- |
| High interest in the project, low influence, highly knowledgeable expert on high-risk areas | Invite the stakeholder to participate in analyzing the risks on the project. |
| Low interest, the source of major requirements on the project (high influence), not easy to work with | Determine why the interest is low. Ask the stakeholder about their engagement preferences and how they would like to be involved with the project.<br><br>Identify ways to elicit requirements as efficiently as possible.<br><br>Make sure requirements are clearly captured and approved by the stakeholder as accurate.<br><br>Send reports. |
| High interest, high influence, not a supporter of the project | Ask why the stakeholder is not a supporter. Use your understanding to base your plan for engaging this stakeholder on dealing with those reasons. |
| High interest, high influence, a supporter of the project | Ask the stakeholder what is most important to them, involve the stakeholder in team meetings, report project performance to this person, and include information as the stakeholder requests. |
| Moderate interest, high influence, completing many activities on the project, a supporter of the project | Invite the stakeholder to officially join the project management team. Identify the stakeholder's preferred level of involvement; use this information to continue to get their support throughout the life of the project. |

| Stakeholder Description | Options for Managing Stakeholder Involvement |
| --- | --- |
| Moderate interest, high influence because the stakeholder has identified a large number of potential risks for the project, a supporter of the project | Plan to meet with the stakeholder periodically throughout the project to potentially identify any other risks. Keep the stakeholder informed about the effectiveness of risk efforts, and involve the stakeholder in risk reviews and audits. |
| Moderate interest, nervous about completing assigned activities | Plan to find and forward relevant literature to help the stakeholder, and arrange for training if necessary. |

## Stakeholder Engagement Plan  PAGE 522  The result, or output, of this process is the
stakeholder engagement plan. The plan documents the existing and desired levels of engagement for all stakeholders, including plans to achieve the desired levels. It also provides details about ways in which stakeholders will be involved in the project, and it includes guidelines and metrics for monitoring and evaluating how well the plan is meeting the needs of stakeholders and the project.

 Stakeholder engagement plans generally have a component that addresses how communication will be used on the project to help manage stakeholder engagement and expectations. This means that the stakeholder engagement plan and the communications management plan can be repositories of some similar information about stakeholder communication requirements and who needs to receive what information on a project. But the two plans each have a different focus. The communications management plan emphasizes the details about the technology, methods, and models of communication—the what, when, and how of communication. The stakeholder engagement plan, on the other hand, explains the why of communications—why stakeholders need to receive certain information, and how the sharing of that information will help in managing stakeholder engagement and expectations. As you might expect, portions of these two plans are often created together.

Keep in mind that the stakeholder engagement plan will likely require adjustment throughout the project. We've already discussed how you'll need to reevaluate your list of stakeholders during the project. The discovery of new stakeholders may require changes to the plan, and there may be changes on the project that require less or more involvement from various stakeholders.

Be careful with information about stakeholders! Think carefully before you share the stakeholder engagement plan, your stakeholder register, or other verbal and written communication about stakeholders. Consider all the potentially sensitive information you might be documenting about stakeholders' attitudes and personalities, or obstacles or challenges related to working with a stakeholder. Given how important it is to maintain good relationships with stakeholders, consider how damaging it would be to your project for someone to find a list of stakeholders along with negative comments about some (particularly if the person looking at the list is *on* that list). As the project manager, you always want to maintain a positive attitude toward your stakeholders, even those who are resistant or difficult to work with. A good leader is encouraging and supportive of everyone involved with the project. This means that when you discover an obstacle or challenge associated with a stakeholder, you may decide not to share it with others and not to write it down: so, small portions of your stakeholder engagement plan may reside only in your mind.

583

## Manage Stakeholder Engagement  PAGE 523

To meet stakeholder needs, resolve their issues, and make sure they remain interested and active in the project, it's essential to encourage stakeholder engagement and manage their expectations. Although this is an executing process, managing stakeholder engagement is ongoing throughout the life of the project. When was the last time you did something like the following scenario?

> A project manager knows a particular stakeholder is dissatisfied because one of his requests was not included in the scope of the project. The rest of the stakeholders agreed upon the scope, but the project manager anticipates this person will continue pressing to add his request. The project manager schedules a meeting with the stakeholder to talk about why this request was not a high priority for the other stakeholders and to suggest this stakeholder build a business case for it being included in another project.

How about this situation?

> During requirements gathering, a stakeholder expressed concern about how much the project would impact her department's other work. The project manager contacts her to say, "I have kept your concern in mind while planning the project. You know there is little probability we could do this project without impacting your department, but because of your concerns, I have put together a report telling you when we will impact your department's regular work." As the project moves forward, the project manager continues to check in with the stakeholder to discuss any unforeseen impacts.

Or this one?

> A project manager notices that a stakeholder who used to provide helpful input regularly has become less involved in the project lately. The project manager touches base with the stakeholder to say, "I've really missed getting your feedback on the status reports. I've always appreciated your comments. Is there a reason you've been holding back lately? Is there anything I can do to get you more involved again?"

Why bother doing such work? Such actions are proactive, and let the stakeholders know that their input is important and that their needs and concerns are being considered, even if they are not agreed to. These efforts are much more likely to encourage stakeholder support of the project, and also serve the valuable role of keeping open communication channels with the stakeholders so they can inform the project manager of potential changes, newly discovered risks, and other information.

Do you think you don't have time in your real world to do these things? As with many other areas of project management, such efforts can actually help you be more efficient by reducing the amount of time you are forced to spend dealing with problems. When taking the exam, assume, unless stated otherwise, that the project manager has followed the best practices of project management. Therefore, the project manager has time to continuously encourage stakeholder engagement and manage expectations.

The project manager reviews the stakeholder engagement plan, other management plans, and project documents, such as the stakeholder register, issue log, and change log, to find and address any issues that could be impacting stakeholder engagement. This review may identify sources of confusion or misunderstanding. For example, a deferred or rejected change request could decrease the engagement level of stakeholders who supported the change.

Given how important good communication is to stakeholder management, it's also critical to follow the communications management plan. How can you keep people involved and informed if you're not communicating with them? Managing stakeholder engagement also requires attention to stakeholders' needs while work is being done. And it's essential for the project manager to maintain trust, help resolve conflicts, prevent problems, foster agreement among stakeholders to meet the needs of the project, and generally encourage stakeholder support of the project and the outcome of the project. This requires the use of interpersonal and team skills such as political and cultural awareness, negotiating, and conflict management.

The Manage Stakeholder Engagement process can result in requested changes to the project or product scope as well as updates to the stakeholder engagement plan and communications management plan. It can also lead to updates to project documents, such as the change log and stakeholder register. The issue log may need to be updated to document stakeholders' concerns and their final resolution. Lessons learned may be documented to reflect the results of efforts to engage stakeholders.

## Monitor Stakeholder Engagement  PAGE 530

> **Process**  Monitor Stakeholder Engagement
> **Process Group**  Monitoring & Controlling
> **Knowledge Area**  Stakeholder Management

Maintaining stakeholder relationships and monitoring stakeholder engagement are ongoing responsibilities of the project manager. Monitoring stakeholder engagement will help you understand stakeholder perceptions of project progress. This will allow you to make minor adjustments to ensure continuous stakeholder engagement and support. In addition to evaluating stakeholder engagement and improving and refining strategies for engagement, this process also involves reassessing the stakeholder register, updating stakeholder information, adding stakeholders as appropriate, and noting when a particular stakeholder's involvement is no longer necessary.

Components of the project management plan that are inputs to this process include the resource management plan (remember that all team members are also stakeholders), the communications management plan, and the stakeholder engagement plan. In addition to these plans, the issue log tracks any concerns, disagreements, confusion, or unresolved questions that arise during the project. This log can provide direct or indirect information about stakeholder engagement. Other project documents include the lessons learned register and the risk register. Note the inclusion of the risk register as an input here. It is important to realize that a lack of stakeholder engagement adds risk to the successful completion of the project. Such risks must be identified and managed.

It is important to know that monitoring stakeholder engagement requires you to collect and analyze data. For example, work performance data from the Direct and Manage Project Work process in integration includes measurements of project performance and the engagement levels of specific stakeholders. That data is then used to compare actual engagement efforts against the project management plan to look for variances. Any variances may indicate a potential problem with stakeholder engagement. The stakeholder management plan specifies how this work of analysis and evaluation will be accomplished, who should be involved, how the results should be documented and presented, and how changes will be handled.

How do you analyze the work performance data related to relationships? You should have established in your stakeholder engagement plan some measurable performance metrics regarding stakeholder engagement. You might, for example, use a data analysis technique, such as root cause or alternatives analysis, to assess stakeholder engagement. You could also use the stakeholder engagement assessment matrix to further analyze stakeholder engagement levels. These types of tools will help you figure out if adjustments or changes need to be made to maintain stakeholder engagement.

Work performance data and metrics are useful in giving you information about the quality of relationships, but keep in mind that some of your assessment will also be subjective. For example, if an activity is behind schedule because a stakeholder hasn't provided needed information, the percent complete data will reflect the delay. This might point to a lack of stakeholder engagement or a problem with a relationship on the project. These indicators require the project manager to clarify and analyze the problem, and then work to correct or improve the situation. If the stakeholder in this example is not returning phone calls, the project manager will want to find out why. If the stakeholder is engaged, but having difficulty providing the information or getting the work done, the project manager may need to revise the strategy for engaging this stakeholder and reevaluate the work assignment or the time estimate. This type of assessment can be immensely helpful in monitoring stakeholder engagement.

Communication plays a large part in helping you discover and correct relationship problems. To maintain strong relationships, you need to spend time talking with the stakeholders and develop ways to listen and gather information on their ongoing (and evolving) feelings about the project and other stakeholders. To get feedback, you can of course ask direct questions like, "How do you think things are going?" But assessing success and the strength of relationships often requires a more complex and subtle form of communication. This is when interpersonal skills can really make a difference. To further understand how stakeholders feel, use techniques such as active listening, perception of body language, leadership, facilitation, and emotional intelligence. These skills will help identify issues or concerns that need your attention.

To experience this for yourself, spend a day or two really paying attention to the responses you get to the question, "How are you?" Ask the cashier at your local coffee shop, a virtual team member, the person sitting next to you at work, your sponsor, and people on your project team. Most of the time, people will probably give you a positive response: "I'm doing fine, thanks." Then, try asking follow-up questions such as, "How are sales this week?" or "Are you keeping busy?" You may hear a less positive, but more honest answer: "Well, things are a little tough this week," or "I am so overwhelmed with work I don't think I'll ever get a day off." To get a more detailed (and, often, more accurate) answer, you'll need to spend more time, ask a series of questions, and pay attention to nonverbal cues where possible. This is where all the effort you have put into building stakeholder relationships will come into play: the better your relationship, the more likely the person will tell you the truth. Even so, you may have to probe to get honest status updates and learn what people really think about the project. Sometimes people are reluctant to share bad or difficult news, especially if it is bad news about the project you are managing. It will help if you make it clear to everyone on the project that you want them to come to you with their concerns.

As you learn about problems or issues from individual stakeholders, consolidate the information, look for patterns, and make adjustments as necessary. Your conversations may also reveal the need for a change request. These changes could be recommendations for solving a problem, risk mitigation suggestions to prevent future potential problems, or ways to improve engagement of various stakeholders. The Monitor Stakeholder Engagement process results in work performance information (an analysis of the work performance data gathered through your stakeholder engagement efforts) and possibly updates to the project management plan and project documents, such as the issue log and the stakeholder, risk, and lessons learned registers.

This brings us to the end of the Stakeholder Management chapter. For the exam, keep in mind that stakeholders are important throughout the life of the project. You need to identify all of them as early as possible, and periodically reevaluate the stakeholder list. You also need to plan how to manage their expectations, engagement, and influence, and then follow that plan and adapt it throughout the life of the project.

## Practice Exam

1. The product of your project is a human resource application that will help the company with hiring and onboarding new employees. The team will be working on requirements affecting the needs of some of the stakeholders throughout the project. The requirements of other stakeholders will only come into play during a small part of toward the end of the project. When do stakeholders have the most influence on a project?

    A. At the beginning of the project
    B. In the middle of the project
    C. At the end of the project
    D. Throughout the project

2. The project has been going well, except for the number of changes being made. The product of the project is being installed into seven different departments within the company and will greatly improve departmental performance when operational. The team has selected the appropriate processes for use on the project. The project manager is a technical expert and has been trained in communications and managing people. Which of the following is the most likely cause of the project changes?

    A. The project manager was not trained in understanding the company environment.
    B. The project should have more management oversight since it will result in such great benefits to the company.
    C. The project should have used more of the project management processes.
    D. Some stakeholders were not identified.

3. You have been tentatively assigned to a project that has not yet received final approval. Several stakeholders who will likely be involved or impacted by the project have already been identified. Stakeholders can be identified during which project management process groups?

    A. Initiating, planning, executing, and monitoring and controlling
    B. Initiating and planning
    C. Planning and monitoring and controlling
    D. Monitoring and controlling and closing

4. A particular stakeholder has a reputation for requesting many changes on projects. You'll be working with this stakeholder, as you've just been assigned as project manager of a project with which he'll also be involved. The newly approved project will create a website that has a couple of features the stakeholder's clients will use. However, the clients in this business unit will use the site only occasionally. What is the best approach you can take at the beginning of the project to manage this situation?

    A. Say no to the stakeholder a few times to dissuade him from submitting more changes.
    B. Get the stakeholder involved in the project as early as possible.
    C. Talk to the stakeholder's manager to find ways of directing the stakeholder's activities to another project.
    D. Ask that the stakeholder be changed to one who will better represent those using the core functionality of the new website.

5. Which of the following statements best describes how stakeholders are involved on a project?

    A. They help to determine the project schedule, deliverables, and requirements.
    B. They help to determine the project constraints and product deliverables.
    C. They help to determine the resource needs and resource constraints on the project.
    D. They approve the project charter, help provide assumptions, and create the management plans.

6. You know that some groups within your organization are going to provide input to requirements that may impact your ability to develop a realistic schedule. Managing stakeholder expectations is always important, but achieving stakeholder satisfaction will be more critical with some groups than with others. All the following are parts of the team's stakeholder management effort except:

    A. Determining stakeholders' needs
    B. Identifying stakeholders
    C. Giving stakeholders added value
    D. Managing stakeholders' expectations

7. You are managing a project to develop an organization's new website. The site will be highly complex and interactive, and neither your project team nor the client has much experience with this type of website development.

    The timeline is extremely aggressive. Any delay will be costly for both your firm and the client. You and the project sponsor have achieved agreement and sign-off on both the project charter and the project management plan. Client personnel have been kept fully informed of the project's progress through status reports and regular meetings. The project is on schedule and within budget, and a final perfunctory review has been scheduled.

    Suddenly you hear that the entire effort may be cancelled because the product being developed is totally unacceptable. What is the most likely cause of this situation?

    A. A key stakeholder was not adequately engaged in the project.
    B. The project charter and project management plan were not thoroughly explained to or adequately reviewed by the client.
    C. Communications arrangements were inadequate and did not provide the required information to interested parties.
    D. The project sponsor failed to provide adequate support for the project.

8. A project manager wants to more extensively involve the stakeholders on the project. The project team is colocated, so face-to-face communication with these stakeholders is usually possible, although not all external stakeholders are available to meet in person. Which of the following would be the best way for the project manager to involve the stakeholders more extensively?

    A. Have the stakeholders periodically review the list of project requirements.
    B. Invite the stakeholders to attend project status meetings.
    C. Send status reports to the stakeholders.
    D. Update the stakeholders on the status of all project changes.

9. You are working on a project that requires the use of a stakeholder engagement assessment matrix. This tool can be used to identify:

    A. Additional stakeholders
    B. Variances from anticipated stakeholder involvement
    C. Key relationships between stakeholders
    D. Skill levels of stakeholders

10. A primary goal of your project is to decrease the amount of time it takes for service technicians to help customers resolve issues via an online chat function. The current process includes correctly verifying client authentication information, assessing the problem, and then solving it. The team thinks a technical fix is needed to improve the chat functionality to support the goal of decreasing the time required to resolve customer problems. The customer service representatives think the process is at fault. A few team members have also expressed concern that the customer service representatives are interfering with their work by trying to take on a larger role than is appropriate for the project. The tension among stakeholders is escalating, and leadership is concerned. There has been discussion about who should assign roles for the project. The role of each stakeholder is determined by:

    A. The stakeholder and the sponsor
    B. The project manager and the sponsor
    C. The team and the project manager
    D. The project manager and the stakeholder

11. You are managing a project to update an existing payroll application. You have identified and analyzed your stakeholders and taken measures to ensure positive stakeholder engagement and to ensure that requirements will meet project objectives. The stakeholder register has been an important part of much of this effort. What is a stakeholder register?

    A. A process of systematically gathering and analyzing quantitative and qualitative information to determine whose interests must be taken into account throughout the project
    B. A project document containing assessment and classification information regarding identified stakeholders
    C. An approach to increase the support and minimize negative impacts of stakeholders
    D. A table that links requirements to project objectives

12. The team is working on the development of a new product that is designed to appeal to individuals of all ages throughout the world. Because of the diversity of the stakeholder base, the team has decided to group stakeholders by category, in order to plan effective stakeholder engagement strategies. Which of the following tools will be most beneficial in this effort?

    A. Resource breakdown structure, prioritization, multicriteria decision analysis
    B. Salience model, traceability matrix, prioritization
    C. Power/interest grid, stakeholder cube, salience model
    D. Benefits management plan, focus group, power/interest grid

13. The project manager is trying to recall a stakeholder's preferred communication method. Where can she find that information?

    A. RACI chart
    B. Stakeholder engagement assessment matrix
    C. Stakeholder engagement plan
    D. Resource management plan

14. You are planning a project to develop a website for a large medical center. The site will be used by patients, medical professionals, support staff, and insurance company representatives. Which tools will best help you determine the current attitudes of stakeholders toward the project and the level of engagement you will need from each of these groups?

    A. Stakeholder register and stakeholder engagement assessment matrix
    B. Trend analysis and requirements traceability matrix
    C. Data analysis and resource management plan
    D. Assumption and constraint analysis

15. The key objective of stakeholder management is:
    A. Communication
    B. Coordination
    C. Satisfaction
    D. Relationships

16. As project manager, you are unable to allocate as much time as you would like to interact with your stakeholders. Which of the following stakeholders will you make it a priority to get to know?
    A. The stakeholder who is an expert on the product of the project, but is not interested in implementing it in his department
    B. The manager of the department that will use the product of the project, who is known to be resistant to change
    C. The project sponsor, with whom you have successfully worked on many projects
    D. The department employee who is unfamiliar with the product of the project, but open to the positive impacts he believes the product will have on his work environment

17. A stakeholder's belief about or mental picture of the future is a(n):
    A. Requirement
    B. Heuristic
    C. Expectation
    D. Constraint

18. The degree to which a particular stakeholder may be able to positively or negatively affect a project is their:
    A. Level of engagement
    B. Level of interest
    C. Level of commitment
    D. Level of influence

19. In an effort to identify stakeholders who may be affected by your project, you're looking over the organizational structure of your client's company. As you identify stakeholders on the organizational chart, you request meetings with each stakeholder. You'll document the information you learn about each stakeholder in the stakeholder register. This register can then be used as an input to which of the following processes?
    A. Plan Risk Management and Collect Requirements
    B. Perform Integrated Change Control and Plan Communications Management
    C. Plan Quality Management and Manage Quality
    D. Identify Risks and Develop Project Charter

20. A project manager on a multinational website implementation project is at a party and talks to friends who will be heavy users of this new website when the project is complete and the site is rolled out. They describe some annoying aspects of the current website. The project manager takes this feedback to the sponsor, and encourages design and scope changes. Which of the following best describes what the project manager has done?
    A. Scope validation
    B. Integrated change control
    C. Stakeholder analysis
    D. Scope planning

## Answers

1. **Answer** A

   **Explanation** Stakeholders have an impact throughout the project, but they must be identified and involved at the beginning of the project in order to determine their requirements and expectations. This means that even stakeholders who play a smaller role or whose requirements are addressed later in the project are included early. If this effort is not done early, the results may be expensive changes and/or dissatisfaction later in the project.

2. **Answer** D

   **Explanation** It is important to look for the choice that would solve the real problem. The most likely root cause is that stakeholders were missed and, as a result, their requirements were not identified. Those stakeholders are now requesting changes to accommodate their needs. There is no reason to think that training, management oversight, or a need for more processes are factors contributing to the number of changes.

3. **Answer** A

   **Explanation** Stakeholders can be identified throughout the project. However, the earlier stakeholders are identified, the better for the project. If all the stakeholders' needs and requirements are taken into account before plans are finalized and project work is begun, fewer changes will be needed later in the project, when they will be more costly.

4. **Answer** B

   **Explanation** By definition, stakeholders can impact or be impacted by the project. The project manager may not choose who to recognize as a stakeholder. Although this particular individual may be difficult, the project manager cannot avoid him, because he has a stake in the project. The project manager can say no, but this does not solve the root cause of the problem. There may be some good ideas within those change requests.

   The only choice that deals with the problem is getting the stakeholder involved in the project as soon as possible. Changes generally arise due to lack of input at the beginning of the project. If the project manager begins effective communication with this stakeholder early, there is a much better chance his changes will be discovered during the planning process, when they will have less of an impact on the project.

5. **Answer** B

   **Explanation** The project manager determines the project schedule through schedule development. The team and other stakeholders provide the inputs. Since it is also the project manager's role to determine resource needs and create management plans, the choices including those roles cannot be best. The project sponsor approves the project charter, not the stakeholders. Stakeholders do, however, help determine project constraints and product deliverables. Notice how tricky questions can be if you do not read them correctly! Watch for this in other questions, and pay close attention to the wording.

6. **Answer** C

   **Explanation** Identifying all the stakeholders, determining their needs, and managing their expectations are all parts of good stakeholder management. Giving stakeholders added value (including extras not documented in the requirements) is known as gold plating. This is not effective stakeholder or quality management.

7. **Answer** A

   **Explanation** A single high-level executive can end an entire project if they are not satisfied with the results, even if that person has, by choice, been only tangentially involved in the project. It is critical to ensure that all the final decision makers are identified and engaged early in a project in order to ensure that their concerns are addressed.

8. **Answer** A

   **Explanation** It seems like all of these are good ideas, but having the stakeholders review the list of project requirements helps discover errors and changes, and would therefore be considered the best choice.

9. **Answer** B

   **Explanation** The stakeholder engagement assessment matrix can be used to compare the actual engagement levels (involvement) of individual stakeholders versus the desired levels of engagement needed to optimize the plan. Any discrepancies can be analyzed, and efforts to adjust the engagement levels can be implemented.

10. **Answer** D

    **Explanation** The role of each stakeholder is determined by the project manager and the stakeholder. It is important that stakeholders have input into what they will be contributing to the project. The role of the project manager is not to tell people what to do!

11. **Answer** B

    **Explanation** Gathering and analyzing information to determine whose interests must be considered is part of stakeholder identification and analysis. Increasing support and minimizing negative impacts of stakeholders is a part of stakeholder management. Linking requirements to project objectives is included in a requirement traceability matrix. A stakeholder register is a document that includes assessment and classification information related to identified stakeholders.

12. **Answer** C

    **Explanation** The power/interest grid, stakeholder cube, and salience model are ways of representing data about stakeholder groups, enabling the team to plan how to engage and manage all of the stakeholders effectively.

13. **Answer** C

    **Explanation** Stakeholders' individual communication requirements are documented in the stakeholder engagement plan.

14. **Answer** A

    **Explanation** The stakeholder register contains information including the stakeholders' requirements and expectations, as well as their levels of interest and influence. The stakeholder engagement assessment matrix graphically illustrates the current and desired levels of stakeholder engagement. This information can be used to determine actions required to close gaps between those levels.

15. **Answer** C

    **Explanation** While communication, coordination, and development of relationships are parts of stakeholder management, collectively they contribute to the main objective of this process—stakeholder satisfaction.

16. **Answer** B

    **Explanation** As the department manager, this person is a key stakeholder, and wields a lot of influence over other stakeholders in her department. The fact that she is resistant to change indicates she will need some personal reassurance from the project manager, or she may exert her influence to derail the project.

17. **Answer** C

    **Explanation** Expectations are not as direct or straightforward as requirements. Nonetheless, they are important to recognize and address to ensure stakeholder satisfaction with the project. Therefore, the project manager must do additional work to uncover the expectations of stakeholders.

18. **Answer** D

    **Explanation** This question is referring to levels of influence. Each stakeholder's level of influence may be based on status within the organization, seniority, or other factors. The level of influence of each stakeholder should be identified and managed throughout the project.

19. **Answer** A

    **Explanation** Of the choices listed, the stakeholder register is an input to Collect Requirements, Plan Quality Management, Plan Communications Management, Plan Risk Management, and Identify Risks. Be sure you understand why it is important in each of these processes.

20. **Answer** C

    **Explanation** The project manager has performed stakeholder analysis by learning stakeholder requirements, and making recommendations to fulfill those requirements. Scope validation is a control function related to gaining customer acceptance of deliverables. Integrated change control relates to looking for multiple impacts of changes. Scope planning creates a scope management plan.

593

# Professional & Social Responsibility

## FOURTEEN

Although the *PMBOK® Guide* does not include a chapter dedicated to professional and social responsibility, it is an important aspect of a project manager's job. Project managers are responsible for upholding the standards of the profession as their actions can have positive impacts on the project and the organization, as well as on the profession as a whole. If someone with a PMP certification does not act professionally and ethically, the credibility of the certification and the practice of project management is diminished. For this reason, concepts related to professional and social responsibility are tested throughout the exam. Be aware that professional and social responsibility should be part of everything a project manager does, from project initiating to closing.

To study this topic, read and make sure you understand the concepts discussed in this chapter. Be honest with yourself about what you know and do not know, and identify gaps in your knowledge. It's important to know that these gaps do not make you an unethical project manager. We all have gaps we need to fill.

In addition, you should review and understand PMI's Code of Ethics and Professional Conduct (pmi.org/codeofethics) since many questions on the exam relate directly to that code. The Code of Ethics and Professional Conduct breaks down professional and social responsibility into the following categories:

- Responsibility
- Respect
- Fairness
- Honesty

Do these four categories seem difficult? If asked if we are responsible, respectful, fair, and honest, most of us would, of course, say yes. But can you think of a time when you did not complete all your responsibilities? How many times have you been disrespectful or unfair? Hopefully we do the right thing most of the time, but none of us are perfect. This chapter discusses some important points about these categories, and it will also address two other important topics not specifically covered in the Code of Ethics and Professional Conduct that can help you on the exam: the ethical application of project management, and PMI-isms related to professional and social responsibility.

# Professional & Social Responsibility FOURTEEN

| INITIATING | PLANNING (This is the only process group with a set order.) | EXECUTING | MONITORING & CONTROLLING | CLOSING |
|---|---|---|---|---|
| Select project manager | Determine development approach, life cycle, and how you will plan for each knowledge area | Execute work according to the project management plan | Take action to monitor and control the project | Confirm work is done to requirements |
| Determine company culture and existing systems | Define and prioritize requirements | Produce product deliverables (product scope) | Measure performance against performance measurement baseline | Complete final procurement closure |
| Collect processes, procedures, and historical information | Create project scope statement | Gather work performance data | Measure performance against other metrics in the project management plan | Gain final acceptance of product |
| Divide large projects into phases or smaller projects | Assess what to purchase and create procurement documents | Request changes | Analyze and evaluate data and performance | Complete financial closure |
| Understand business case and benefits management plan | Determine planning team | Implement only approved changes | Determine if variances warrant a corrective action or other change request(s) | Hand off completed product |
| Uncover initial requirements, assumptions, risks, constraints, and existing agreements | Create WBS and WBS dictionary | Continuously improve; perform progressive elaboration | Influence factors that cause change | Solicit customer's feedback about the project |
| Assess project and product feasibility within the given constraints | Create activity list | Follow processes | Request changes | Complete final performance reporting |
| Create measurable objectives and success criteria | Create network diagram | Determine whether quality plan and processes are correct and effective | Perform integrated change control | Index and archive records |
| Develop project charter | Estimate resource requirements | Perform quality audits and issue quality reports | Approve or reject changes | Gather final lessons learned and update knowledge bases |
| Identify stakeholders and determine their expectations, interest, influence, and impact | Estimate activity durations and costs | Acquire final team and physical resources | Update project management plan and project documents | |
| Request changes | Determine critical path | Manage people | Inform stakeholders of all change request results | |
| Develop assumption log | Develop schedule | Evaluate team and individual performance; provide training | Monitor stakeholder engagement | |
| Develop stakeholder register | Develop budget | Hold team-building activities | Confirm configuration compliance | |
| | Determine quality standards, processes, and metrics | Give recognition and rewards | Create forecasts | |
| | Determine team charter and all roles and responsibilities | Use issue logs | Gain customer's acceptance of interim deliverables | |
| | Plan communications and stakeholder engagement | Facilitate conflict resolution | Perform quality control | |
| | Perform risk identification, qualitative and quantitative risk analysis, and risk response planning | Release resources as work is completed | Perform risk reviews, reassessments, and audits | |
| | Go back—iterations | Send and receive information, and solicit feedback | Manage reserves | |
| | Finalize procurement strategy and documents | Report on project performance | Manage, evaluate, and close procurements | |
| | Create change and configuration management plans | Facilitate stakeholder engagement and manage expectations | Evaluate use of physical resources | |
| | Finalize all management plans | Hold meetings | | |
| | Develop realistic and sufficient project management plan and baselines | Evaluate sellers; negotiate and contract with sellers | | |
| | Gain formal approval of the plan | Use and share project knowledge | | |
| | Hold kickoff meeting | Execute contingency plans | | |
| | Request changes | Update project management plan and project documents | | |

**Rita's Process Chart™
Professional &
Social Responsibility**
Where are we in the project management process?

## The Ethical Application of Project Management

Are you honest? Most people are essentially honest, but we all have our moments. For example, have you ever agreed to and started work on a project without being reasonably sure the end date could be met? Is that honest? Is it ethical? People often do this without ever labeling it as being dishonest or unethical. For the exam, however, you need to understand that part of professional and social responsibility is the ethical application of project management in the real world.

Did you know it is unethical to provide a project schedule that you do not believe to be accurate? It is also unethical to waste company resources because you have not properly planned a project. And it is unethical to manage a project without a project charter or a WBS. These are serious issues in the real world, and they are serious for the exam.

So why is the lack of such project management activities unethical? Think about the impact project management tools, such as a charter or WBS, have on a project. Not having a project charter affects your project and, at the very least, causes increased costs and wasted time. Not having a WBS means that some of the scope will likely be missed. When it is discovered later, that work will cost more to complete than if it had been included in the project from the beginning. Does this sound realistic? If not, you may not fully understand the benefits of these tools and should review them again in this book. Practice using these tools on your projects to experience the advantages for yourself. To correctly answer exam questions about ethics, compare what you should be doing on your projects with what you are currently doing, and note any discrepancies.

Project managers must understand the project management process in order to do the right thing.

Some organizations do not give their project managers the authority needed to get projects done. For example, is it ethical to skip identifying an approach (plan-driven versus change-driven) to a project management plan? Imagine a situation in which the project manager only has the authority to write reports and transmit them to others. This lack of authority means no one is directing the integration of the work. As a result, the project will likely be late and people working on the project will waste valuable time in rework. To uphold the standards of the project management profession, project managers have a professional responsibility to obtain the authority necessary to manage the project.

Now let's think about unrealistic project completion deadlines or milestones. Have you experienced an unrealistic schedule constraint? Many project managers with unrealistic deadlines just implement the project the best they can and wait to see what happens regarding the timeline. Some will move forward with the project and force resources to make the deadline by working overtime. Many studies have shown this is not an ethical solution to the problem for several reasons. For example, the more overtime team members work, the less productive they will be and the lower the quality of their work will be. This impact to quality will mean higher costs, diminished stakeholder engagement, more rework, and extra time. Does this scenario meet the expectations of professional and social responsibility for our projects?

Professional and social responsibility requires project managers to handle unrealistic schedule problems up front. This may mean saying, "You have requested that the project be completed within six months. Our analysis makes us certain that we can meet that due date only if we adjust the scope, cost, or quality on this project. If we cannot make any changes, the project will be completed in eight months." Or it may mean telling the project sponsor to assign the project to someone else.

Professional and social responsibility may also mean saying, "I am sorry you do not want to support my efforts in planning the project and want me to start producing work right away. As part of my PMP certification, however, I am ethically bound to do project management for the best interests of the project and the company. This means I must have a project charter and, at the very least, a high-level work breakdown structure." Project managers are required to stand up for the right process.

597

© 2018 RMC Publications, Inc.™ • 952.846.4484 • info@rmcls.com • www.rmcls.com

Consider this scenario from another perspective: tailoring your project management. Not all projects require the same level of application, use, and detailed approach to project management. Have you been in a situation in which strictly adhering to all project management best practices wasn't the most appropriate or efficient approach? Perhaps the project was short in duration, the size or the importance of the project did not make it critical, or the best approach to planning and managing the work was a change-driven approach. To meet the expectations of professional and social responsibility, tailoring project management efforts to fit the needs of a project and its team members is necessary. By tailoring the approach and work of project management to fit a project, the best solution is created within the structure of how you plan and manage the project, which can prevent issues such as delayed delivery of business value, rework, overspending, missed schedules, and miscommunication. It is the project manager's responsibility to analyze each project they are given to determine the best approach, and to tailor their work to determine the best combination of inputs, tools and techniques, outputs, and processes to manage a project based on the best interests of the project and its organization.

Did you notice the attitude illustrated in the statements in the scenario described on the previous page? Do you have such an attitude? A project manager is required to be assertive and in control. For the exam, make sure you understand this assertive, proactive attitude as well as what it means for what a project manager should and should not be doing. Attitude is extremely important, and the expectation for project managers to be assertive and in control applies to project managers in every country and culture.

## PMI-isms Related to Professional and Social Responsibility    We discussed PMI-isms and their impact on the exam in the first chapter of this book. You need to be aware of PMI-isms related to professional and social responsibility as well. You may encounter a question on the exam that talks about the relationship of a PMP certification holder to PMI and how that person should not only encourage others to practice good project management as outlined by PMI but also invite their organization to see the benefits of a PMP certification. The exam may also include a question that assumes you are involved with PMI as a chapter member or chapter officer. These types of questions are relatively easy if you maintain the PMI focus described in the following points:

- You will not get involved with PMI to promote your own business.
- You have a duty of loyalty to PMI. When acting on behalf of a PMI chapter, you will keep the best interest of PMI in mind—not your own best interests.
- When contracting for services for the chapter, you will provide equal access for all to submit proposals and not keep the work for your own company or your friends. You will also practice ethical contract management in relation to all contracts and contract reviews.
- You will not let anyone cheat on the application for the PMP exam.
- You will not let anyone copy PMP exam prep materials or perform other illegal behavior.
- You will not disclose PMP exam questions.

## Categories of Professional and Social Responsibility    Now that we've discussed the ethical application of project management as well as PMI-isms related to professional and social responsibility, let's look at the four categories in PMI's Code of Ethics and Professional Conduct. Read the following list, and make a note in the right-hand column of any areas where you have had problems in the past. The topics you have had difficulty with are the ones you should think about a little more.

Remember that ethics is a messy topic, and no one is perfect. This simple exercise will help shorten your study time and keep you more focused on what you need to know for the exam.

| Responsibility—Ownership of Decisions and Actions | Areas Where I Have Had a Problem |
|---|---|
| Make decisions based on the best interests of the company and the team, as well as society, rather than your own best interests. | |
| Only accept assignments you are qualified to complete. | |
| If you are given a project to manage that is beyond your qualifications or experience, make sure the sponsor knows of any gaps in your qualifications before accepting the assignment. | |
| Use tools, techniques, and processes to efficiently plan a project in order to use organizational resources (people, materials, equipment, facilities, money, etc.) as best you can. | |
| Do what you say you will do—including completing projects on time. | |
| Acknowledge your own errors. | |
| Respect confidentiality requirements and protect proprietary information—including obeying copyright laws. | |
| Uphold laws. | |
| If you witness or are aware of unethical decisions and/or actions, or even potentially unethical behavior, report it to management and to those the behavior affects. | |
| Report violations of PMI's Code of Ethics and Professional Conduct when you have factual proof of the violation. | |

| Respect—The Appropriate Treatment of People and Resources | Areas Where I Have Had a Problem |
|---|---|
| Maintain an attitude of mutual cooperation. | |
| Facilitate distributed teams; engage and invite ideas and best practices to be shared among team members to better the project. | |
| Respect cultural differences. | |
| Do not gossip or say things that could damage another person's reputation. | |
| Engage in good faith negotiations. | |
| Avoid approval of overtime as a way to solve scheduling problems as people deserve an appropriate work life balance. | |
| Respect others. | |
| Be direct in dealing with conflict. | |
| Do not use your power or position to influence others for your own benefit. | |

599

| Fairness—Being Objective and Making Impartial Decisions | Areas Where I Have Had a Problem |
|---|---|
| Act impartially without favoritism, nepotism, bribery, or prejudice, and frequently stop to reexamine your actions to make sure you are being impartial. | |
| Continuously look for conflicts of interest and disclose them. | |
| Do not discriminate against others. | |
| Honor your duty of loyalty to those companies and organizations with whom you are affiliated. | |
| Do not use your position for personal or business gain. | |

| Honesty—Understanding the Truth and Taking Action Based on Truth | Areas Where I Have Had a Problem |
|---|---|
| Try to understand the truth. | |
| Be truthful in all communications, including making sure the information you are using or sending out is truthful. | |
| Work to create an environment in which others tell the truth. | |
| Do not deceive others. | |

Now let's take a more detailed look at some of the points in each category.

## Responsibility—Ownership of Decisions and Actions

- **Make decisions based on the best interests of the company, rather than your own best interests.** This one sounds simple, doesn't it? But be careful. If the exam were to pose a direct question on this topic, everyone would get it right. But most questions on the exam are not so direct. For example, what about a situation in which you discover the project is suffering because you have not created a project management plan, and you worry that if you tell management about the problem, you will look bad or lose your job? In such situations, the correct answer is to deal with the issue hurting the project and put the project's needs before your own. This is an easy rule to remember, but it can be difficult to apply.

- **Only accept assignments you are qualified to complete.** Can you imagine telling your manager that you cannot take an assignment because it requires the control of cost on a project and that you're not qualified to manage costs? It is smart to make sure you can handle a job before it is assigned to you, but situations in the real world may be much more complex than those described on the exam.

- **Ensure proper project planning.** The ethical application of project management includes upholding your responsibilities to legal and/or regulatory compliance to ensure a project is properly planned, and using all the organization's resources (both physical resources and team members) efficiently. It also includes having a reasonable scope definition on which to base a project management plan. Use project management best practices to plan the project and determine the appropriate life cycle and approach (plan-driven or change-driven, for example) using tools such as the project charter, WBS, and network diagram.

600

- **Protect proprietary information.** Do you know someone who made a copy of something that was marked "not to be reproduced" and then gave that copy to someone else? Do you know that such materials are considered proprietary items and copying them could be a violation of copyright laws? Such actions are also likely violations of PMI's Code of Ethics and Professional Conduct. Because this is an area many people have misconceptions about—and because it is a concept frequently tested on the exam—we'll explain it in more detail. Make sure you understand the concept of protecting proprietary information.

  International copyright laws give the owner of a copyright the exclusive rights to make copies of the relevant work and to create derivative works. It is illegal to infringe upon these rights—that is, to use the copyrighted work in certain ways without the owner's permission. For example, without the copyright owner's permission, no one may copy or reproduce any part of a book, create new material based on or incorporating any part of a book, or sell or distribute copies of a book except in limited instances covered by the Fair Use Doctrine.[1] A copyright notice is not required on the document for something to be considered copyrighted.

  Copyright laws are international, which means that people can be prosecuted for copying works by authors outside their country. Know that the exam may test to see if you understand what actions are ethical in terms of the use of copyrighted materials.

  Assume all documents, software, applications, articles, books, training materials, and every other work created by someone else are considered proprietary information and copyrighted. The general rule is to not copy without written permission from the author.

  When you are working with copyrighted materials, you should be mindful of the following issues:

  - If you need another copy of software, does the software license give you permission to simply make a copy, or does it require you to purchase another copy?
  - If you are a contractor asked to create a copyrightable work, who owns the copyright—you or the company that hired you to create it?
  - If you are an employee and create a work, do you own the copyright or does your employer?

  These are some basic issues confronting project managers who deal with copyrighted works. Before taking any action that could result in copyright infringement, a project manager should ask questions to make sure they understand the situation, and possibly seek legal counsel or approval.

- **Report unethical behavior and violations.** What would you do if someone in your company told you that they do not follow a certain company procedure? The correct answer is to report the person to those responsible for the policy.

  Do you agree with this answer? Many people find questions like this challenging, so let's look at why the ethical choice is to report the violation. You are probably not the one who created the policy and are therefore not the best person to explain the reasons behind the policy. If you attempt to explain it to the person, you could misrepresent the policy and cost the company time and money. It is best to leave such things to those responsible for them. Does your role and responsibility seem simple or clearer now? Questions on the exam may discuss situations in which the project manager must immediately report violations of policies, laws, or ethics to a manager or supervisor.

  The easier questions on this topic typically involve a situation in which someone violates PMI's Code of Ethics and Professional Conduct. Review questions related to reporting unethical behavior carefully before answering them. Also, know that you're expected to help create an environment in which project team members can report ethics violations without fear of repercussion.

## Respect—The Appropriate Treatment of People and Resources

- **Maintain an attitude of mutual cooperation.** For example, think about your interactions with resource managers. They are responsible for managing team members as well as physical resources; they must also balance the competing demands of projects (yours and others) and ongoing business

601

operations. Are you in the habit of going to them and asking for the immediate assignment of the resources you need for your project? This action is contrary to the concepts of respect and maintaining an attitude of mutual cooperation.

Put yourself in the shoes of a resource manager for a moment. Resource managers are usually evaluated based on how well they do their own work, not how well they support projects. They have their own needs and responsibilities. A project manager has an ethical responsibility to provide resource managers with advance notice regarding what resources a project needs and what the impacts to the project will be if those resources are not available. The project manager must also provide a realistic schedule, so the resource managers know when their resources will be used. That information enables the resource managers to better manage project work with their other work. This scenario is an example of both mutual cooperation and the ethical application of project management in the real world. For exam questions related to this concept, you will need to know the proper use of project management tools, techniques, and practices, all of which allow you to request resources and communicate accurately regarding resources.

Now let's look at the team. Do you consider the reputation of each of your team members to be in your hands? How well the project goes will reflect on their careers. If a team member believes the project will be unsuccessful, the individual will more than likely remove themselves from as much work on the project as possible so it does not tarnish their reputation. The project manager has a duty to team members that includes making sure there is a realistic schedule so they know when they really need to complete work on the project, providing a reward system, seeking out their opinions, asking them to contribute to the development of the project management plan, and providing formal and informal training as needed so they can effectively work on the project. Team members also need to help control the project. This is another example of the ethical application of project management in the real world.

How you choose to communicate with others also falls under this topic. Would your team members or stakeholders be surprised if you asked them about the best way to communicate with them about various topics? Such actions should be commonplace. Asking these types of questions not only shows respect for the other person, it also helps you effectively plan communications.

- **Respect cultural differences.** Another part of respect as it relates to professional and social responsibility has to do with cultural differences. Cultural differences can mean differences in language, values, nonverbal actions, and cultural practices. If you do not plan how to handle these differences and do not monitor and control their impacts, they can easily impede the project.

  One major cause of cultural differences is ethnocentrism,[2] which is the tendency for people to look at the world primarily from the perspective of their own culture. Ethnocentric individuals take the viewpoint that their own group is the center of everything.

  It's not just people from different countries that can have cultural differences; individuals from different regions of the same country may have cultural differences as well. Even organizations can have cultural differences around issues such as roles and responsibilities, divisions or work areas, and expectations of employees.

  Project managers need to take actions to diminish the negative impacts and enhance the positive impacts of cultural differences. Such actions include:

  - Embrace diversity. Cultural differences can make a project more fun.

  - Prevent culture shock[3] (the disorientation that occurs when you find yourself working with other cultures in a different environment). Thorough research and training about different cultures will help prevent culture shock.

  - Expect cultural differences to surface on a project. Have a plan in place to help the team and project grow and move forward during these times. This might involve educating the team about inclusion and respect, and giving them a process to follow to get help or answers if necessary.

602

- Use clear communication to the appropriate people and in the right format, as outlined in the Communications Management chapter, to prevent cultural differences from becoming a problem.
- Uncover cultural differences when identifying stakeholders, including differences in work ethics and practices.
- Ask for clarification whenever a cultural difference arises.
- Discuss the topic of cultural differences at team meetings as needed.
- Follow practices in use in other countries when appropriate—as long as they do not violate laws.

- **Engage in good faith negotiations.** Think about your experiences in the real world. Have you ever witnessed someone negotiating with another party when you know they have no intention of entering into a contract? Or have you watched someone negotiate a provision in a contract they have no intention of honoring? What about someone presenting information as a fact when the person knows the information is untrue? How about someone trying to strip out all of a seller's profit during contract negotiations? These are all examples of people not negotiating in good faith. Negotiations can and will impact the buyer/seller relationship; acting in an unethical way can have more than one negative affect.

- **Be direct in dealing with conflict.** The topic of conflict is discussed throughout this book and is primarily covered in the Resource Management chapter, but an important aspect of professional and social responsibility involves dealing with conflict. As a project manager dealing with conflict, it is inappropriate and unproductive to complain or talk about a conflict or about others involved in a conflict behind their backs. Do you see this happening in the real world? Although such behavior is common, a project manager has a professional responsibility to deal directly and openly with the other party and say to the person, "What you have done has caused a problem. Can we discuss it?" This can be easier said than done. Imagine that the person causing the problem is powerful or uninterested, or that the person is your manager. Regardless of the situation, questions on the exam expect you to address conflict directly and openly.

- **Do not use your power or position to influence others for your own benefit.** Have you ever said to yourself, "How do I get this person to do what I want?" This could be a violation of professional and social responsibility if you are trying to influence others to do what you want, rather than what is right or most appropriate in a given situation. Project managers cannot use their power or position to pressure others for their own benefit.

## Fairness—Being Objective and Making Impartial Decisions

- **Act impartially without bribery.** So, what is bribery? Is it bribery if someone asks you to pay a fee in order to bring machinery through a city? How about if someone requests a payment for police protection?

  In many countries, fees for services such as protection and bringing machinery through a town, or fees for issuing permits and other official documents, are allowable and are not considered bribes. Payments to convince a government official to select your company for a project are bribes, however. Many companies have policies or codes of business conduct to help prevent bribes and other illegal activity.

  Consider what you should do about other types of payments. Would it be appropriate to accept a car or vacation as a form of payment? These forms of payment are probably not allowable. Thomas Donaldson, in *The Ethics of International Business* (Oxford University Press, 1991), suggests a practice is permissible if you can answer no to both of the following questions:

  1. Is it permissible to conduct business successfully in the host country without undertaking the practice?

© 2018 RMC Publications, Inc.™ • 952.846.4484 • info@rmcls.com • www.rmcls.com

2.  Is the practice a clear violation of a fundamental international right?

Fundamental rights include the right to food, a fair trial, nondiscriminating treatment, minimal education, physical safety, and freedom of speech.

There may be a few exam questions on this topic. If you think you need help to understand it more fully, see the exercise later in this chapter.

- **Continuously look for conflicts of interest and disclose them.** A conflict of interest occurs when a person must make a decision or take action that could help one person or organization while hurting another person or organization to which they have a duty of loyalty. For example, "If I help my friend, I hurt my company," or "If I help this organization, I hurt my own company." Because the exam does not always ask questions that are direct and clear, you might see a question that provides a detailed description of a situation even though all you really need to understand is that there is a conflict of interest. So, what do you do when there is a conflict of interest? You should disclose it to those affected, and let them decide how to proceed. If something appears to be a conflict of interest, it should be handled as if it actually is a conflict of interest.

  What does it mean to continuously look for conflicts of interest? This practice involves more effort than simply noticing conflicts of interest when they arise. It involves frequently sitting down and reviewing the project for areas that have the potential to create such conflicts, and identifying how to avert or reduce the number of conflicts. You need to be proactive in this effort.

- **Do not discriminate against others.** Discrimination seems to be all around us. People discriminate against those from different economic backgrounds (rich and poor), against those from a different area of the country or world, and against others based on race, religion, gender, age, disability, or sexual orientation, etc. Professional and social responsibility requires us to treat others fairly and not discriminate.

- **Do not use your position for personal or business gain.** Most people realize that someone working for the government should not use their position to obtain wealth. But what about people who join organizations (such as PMI) not to help promote the organization's mission, but to gain business from other members of the organization? It is a violation of professional and social responsibility to use your position for personal or business gain.

## Honesty—Understanding the Truth and Taking Action Based on Truth

- **Try to understand the truth.** The truth is not always easy to find, especially when you are running around managing projects. Someone may tell you something that they perceive to be the truth, but there might be more to what is really going on. We often simply accept what people tell us and do not spend time seeking the whole truth. When you think of the many activities on a project and the different people involved, you can see how important it is to accurately understand a situation.

- **Be truthful in all communications, and create an environment in which others tell the truth.** Do you ever hide the fact that a project is in trouble? Do you say that you can accomplish some piece of work or a whole project when you are not really sure if you can? If so, you might have some issues with scenarios on the exam that test or require truthful communication. If we stretch the truth or outright lie, our team members will start to do it, too, and we will not have fostered an environment in which others tell the truth. As a result, the project and those involved in it, including the project manager, will suffer.

  If everyone starts being untruthful, how will you know what information you can trust? Imagine you provide a schedule to the team that you know to be unreasonable or unrealistic and do not inform the team. They quickly realize the schedule is unreasonable and, as a result, do not cooperate with you or tell you what is really going on. When you take the exam, you need to understand the consequences of such actions. The consequences of being untruthful include poor cooperation and less accurate information from others.

**Exercise** Let's try to put it all together. Look at the following situations and determine what to do.

1. Your management has told you that you will receive part of the incentive fee from the customer if you can bring the project in early. While finalizing a major deliverable, your team informs you that the deliverable meets the requirements in the contract, but will not provide the functionality the customer needs. If the deliverable is late, you know the project will not be completed early. What action should you take?

2. You are asked to make a copy of a magazine article and include it in the internal training and support materials for the new software being created as part of your project. You see the article has a copyright notice. What is the best thing to do?

3. Your company is in competition to win a major project for the government of country X. You are told you must make a large payment to the foreign minister in order to be considered for the project. What is the best thing to do?

4. You provide a cost estimate for the project to the project sponsor. He is unhappy with the estimate, because he thinks the cost should be lower. He asks you to cut 15 percent off the project estimate. What should you do?

5. In reviewing the draft of the monthly project update report published by the project management office, you notice another project manager is exaggerating his project's status. You know this project manager is being untruthful because a deliverable due to your project is estimated to be delivered in two weeks. He is reporting the delivery has already taken place. What do you do?

6. You have three sellers bidding on some of your project work. You have worked with one of the sellers (X) before and know they do excellent work. The project manager from company X calls to ask for clarification on the RFP you sent out last week so they can better address your needs. What do you do?

7. As stated in situation 5, a project manager is exaggerating his project's status. You notified him of the inaccuracy, but he still did not change his monthly update. What do you do now?

8. You and a friend from college regularly attend your alma mater's sports games together. Your company has hired the firm your friend works for to do some work on your project. Your friend is not in the division that is working on your project, nor is she involved with any of the work. Your friend calls excitedly and says that due to her efforts this year, she has gotten two tickets to the division football game from her manager. She wants you to go with her. Should you go?

9. You have been asked to give a presentation about your project's status to senior management in your company and to the external customer. The day before the meeting, you realize a delay in delivery of some critical materials will cause a two-month delay in the critical path. You do not have time to work out a plan to get the project back on track before the presentation. You are sure the delay can be made up and don't want to scare the customer unnecessarily, nor do you want the extra work that will be required if you present the information now. What should you do?

10. You have successfully guided your project team through four of five phases of your project. Testing went especially well due to a subject matter expert's earlier input, which helped avoid a critical threat from occurring. At the quarterly senior management review, they specifically comment about how well you are doing with the project so far, especially with testing, and congratulate you. How do you respond?

**Answers**  The answers depend on the exact wording of the choices, but generally:

1.  Review the situation with the customer; review what is required in the contract.

2.  Ask the copyright owner for permission.

3.  Refuse to make the payment; it appears to be a bribe. If the exam has an answer that suggests you consult with your legal department to get a recommendation for the best course of action, that could be the best answer unless the scenario implies you have already done this.

4.  Look for options such as compressing the schedule, reestimating, or changing scope.

5.  Hold the project manager accountable by notifying him of the discrepancy and reporting accurately on your own project.

6.  Either provide all sellers the additional information or do not provide the information to the project manager from company X.

7.  Report the other project manager's dishonesty to both your manager and his.

8.  Most likely no, because this could be perceived as a conflict of interest, which must be avoided. If a similar question appears on the exam, look carefully at the answers, however. It's possible an alternative correct answer might be to disclose the situation to your manager and the sponsor and ask for permission.

9.  You should present the current status of the project, without downplaying or minimizing the effect of the delay. You cannot bury the bad news in an effort to avoid conflict. You need to present the information, along with your planned approach for developing possible solutions to the problem, and provide the customer with a timeline for when they can expect an update.

10. You need to give credit to the subject matter expert and let senior management know the expert's input helped ensure the testing process went smoothly. You cannot take credit for the good work of others, nor can you pass blame down to others.

Professional and social responsibility can seem easy at first, but it can quickly get complicated. This is an important topic to understand, not just for the exam but also in the real world. Unethical and unprofessional behavior hurts the project, the organization, and the profession. As project managers, and especially as PMP certification holders, we have a responsibility to uphold the standards of the profession and prove the value project management brings to all who benefit from successful project results.

## Practice Exam

1. A project manager is being considered for a particular project that will deal exclusively with global virtual teams. He only has experience with local teams. What should he do when discussing the opportunity with the sponsor?

    A. Since the project manager has managed many projects and teams, it does not make any difference that the new project involves global virtual teams. He should tell the sponsor he has the relevant experience.

    B. The project manager should avoid any conversation regarding the types of teams involved so the sponsor does not know he lacks experience in this area.

    C. The project manager should point out to the sponsor that he has not had experience with global virtual teams, and then explain why he thinks he is a good fit for the project anyway.

    D. The project manager should point out to the sponsor that he has not had experience with global virtual teams and therefore must decline the assignment.

2. A project manager gathered data to perform earned value calculations on his project. He used the results to report to management that the project is under budget and on schedule. After reporting this information, he discovered the base figures he used in the calculations were incorrect, as they came from an old copy of the project file that had not been updated. What should he do now?

    A. He should contact management and tell them to expect some changes in the next reporting period as things are starting to look gloomy.

    B. He should contact management to make them aware of the error, provide the correct information, and explain how he made the mistake.

    C. He should use the correct figures to calculate the information when it is time for the next report and ignore the fact that he reported incorrect information.

    D. He should tell management that he received incorrect data from team members, resulting in an inaccurate report.

3. A project manager is working with a seller on a project that is time-sensitive due to government regulations requiring it to be completed by a certain date. She learns one of the sellers has bribed a subcontractor to work on this project instead of fulfilling previous commitments to other projects. What should she do?

    A. She should report the offense to management and to the project managers of the affected projects.

    B. She should not do anything because this is the seller's problem. The project manager herself didn't do anything wrong.

    C. She should report this to other subcontractors.

    D. She should resign from the project so as to remove herself from this type of activity, but keep her discovery to herself rather than cause problems.

4. You are in the middle of a new product development project that has an NPV of $10.5 million. The schedule performance index (SPI) is 0.99. There are strict rules in your publicly traded company regarding risk, quality, and procurement. You discover the previous project manager made a $3 million payment that was not approved in accordance with your company policies. Your relationship with the sponsor is strained, as you've had to request changes because the previous project manager didn't have a complete project management plan. The sponsor and the previous project manager are good friends outside of work and coach your daughter's sports team together. Luckily, the project cost performance index (CPI) is 1.2. What should you do?

   A. Contact your manager.
   B. Put the payment in an escrow account.
   C. Bury the cost in the largest cost center available.
   D. Ignore the payment.

5. You are staffing a project in another country, and the project leader from that country has recommended a project team that consists of members of the project leader's family. Your first course of action should be to:

   A. Inquire if hiring through family lines is common practice in the project leader's country.
   B. Review the résumés of the individuals to see if they are qualified.
   C. Ask the project leader to provide additional names of people unrelated to them.
   D. Use a different project leader to prevent problems later in the project.

6. When checking the calendar of a team member to schedule a meeting, you see she has scheduled a meeting with a key stakeholder that you were not informed of. This stakeholder has been vocal in her concern that her requirements for the project have been ignored and that she doesn't think you are a good project manager. You know that the stakeholder and the team member are friends outside of the organization and that their children are in school together. Your organization's PMO has a policy stating that the project manager is to be informed of, and invited to, all project-related meetings. This is a functional organization that has struggled with communications and stakeholder participation. You have heard that the team member thinks the PMO policy regarding notifying and inviting the project manager to all meetings is intrusive and gets in the way of effective communications with stakeholders; she has also complained that project managers are not available because of multiple projects and too many meetings. She doesn't feel trusted, and is frustrated. Her complaints have been reported to other departmental leaders, and the PMO has been asked to review the policy. The best approach would be to:

   A. Avoid mentioning it to the team member but continue to watch her activities.
   B. Notify the PMO about the problem.
   C. Address the concern with the team member's manager.
   D. Address the concern with the team member.

7. Your team member is three days late with a report. Five minutes before the meeting where the topic of the report is to be discussed, she hands you the report. You notice some serious errors in it. What should you do?

   A. Cancel the meeting and reschedule when the report is fixed.
   B. Go to the meeting and tell the other attendees there are errors in the report.
   C. Allow the team member to do the presentation and remain silent as the other attendees find the errors.
   D. Cancel the meeting and rewrite the report yourself.

609

8. A manager has responsibility for a project that has the support of senior leadership as it will fulfill a strategic organizational objective. From the beginning, you (the project manager) have disagreed with the manager as to how the project should proceed and what the deliverables should be. You and she have disagreed over many issues in the past. Your department has been tasked with providing some key work packages for the project. What should you do?

    A. Provide the manager with what she needs.

    B. Inform your manager of your concerns to get her support.

    C. Sit down with the manager at the beginning of the project, attempt to describe why you object to the project, and discover a way to solve the problem.

    D. Ask to be removed from the project.

9. A large, complex construction project in a foreign country requires the movement of heavy equipment through crowded city streets. The officials in the city know that you have a large, complicated project and that staying on schedule and within budget is important to your company. You have coordinated moving equipment in other countries for other projects without problems. To ensure the equipment is transported successfully, your contact in the country informs you that you will have to pay the local police a fee for coordinating traffic. What should you do?

    A. Do not pay the fee because it is a bribe.

    B. Eliminate the work.

    C. Pay the fee.

    D. Do not pay the fee if it is not part of the project estimate.

10. You are responsible for negotiations with all potential government subcontractors, of which there are many, on an important highway project. A major negotiation with a potential subcontractor is scheduled for tomorrow. Theirs was the lowest starting bid, and included a new approach that could make this project less expensive than other similar projects already completed. You have serious reservations as to whether they will be able to deliver as promised—for the cost and in the period of time agreed upon. You have now discovered there is a good chance the project will be cancelled. What should you do?

    A. Do not spend too much time preparing for the negotiations.

    B. Keep the negotiations short.

    C. Only negotiate major items.

    D. Postpone the negotiations.

11. You've been assigned to take over managing a project that should be half complete according to the schedule. After an extensive evaluation, you discover the project is running far behind schedule, and will probably take twice the time originally estimated by the previous project manager. However, the sponsor has been told the project is on schedule. What is the best course of action?

    A. Try to restructure the schedule to meet the project deadline.

    B. Report your assessment to the sponsor.

    C. Turn the project back to the previous project manager.

    D. Move forward with the schedule as planned by the previous project manager, and report at the first missed milestone.

12. You are halfway through a major network rollout. There are 300 locations in the United States, with another 20 in England. A software seller has just released a major software upgrade for some of the equipment being installed. The upgrade would provide the customer with functionality they requested, which was not available at the time the project began. What is the best course of action under these circumstances?

    A. Continue as planned; your customer has not requested a change.
    B. Inform the customer of the available upgrade, and explain the impacts to the project's timeline and functionality if the upgrade is implemented.
    C. Implement the change and adjust the schedule as necessary because this supports the customer's original request.
    D. Implement the change on the remaining sites and continue with the schedule.

13. You are a project manager for one of many projects in a large and important program. At a high-level status meeting, you note that another project manager has reported her project on schedule. Looking back on your project over the last few weeks, you remember many deliverables from the other project that arrived late. What should you do?

    A. Meet with the program manager.
    B. Develop a risk control plan.
    C. Discuss the issue with your manager.
    D. Meet with the other project manager.

14. You have always been asked by your management to cut your project cost estimates by 10 percent after you have submitted them. The scope of your new project is unclear, and there are over 30 stakeholders. Management expects a 25 percent reduction in downtime as a result of the project. Which of the following is the best course of action in this situation?

    A. Replan to achieve a 35 percent improvement in downtime.
    B. Reduce the estimate, and note the change in the risk response plan.
    C. Provide an accurate estimate of the actual costs, and be able to support it.
    D. Meet with the team to identify where you can find 10 percent savings.

15. You are in the middle of a project when you discover that a software seller for your project is having major difficulty keeping employees due to a labor dispute. Many other projects in your company are also using the company's services. What should you do?

    A. Attempt to keep the required people on your project.
    B. Tell the other project managers in your company about the labor problem.
    C. Contact the company and advise that you will cancel the company's work on your project unless the labor dispute is settled.
    D. Cease doing business with the company.

16. You have been assigned a second project with your new company. This project is a construction project. You have received positive feedback on your performance so far, but are unfamiliar with construction. All the following are your responsibilities as a project manager except:

    A. Maintain the confidentiality of the customer's confidential information.
    B. Determine the legality of company procedures.
    C. Ensure that a conflict of interest does not compromise the legitimate interest of the customer.
    D. Provide accurate and truthful representations in cost estimates.

17. Although your company is not the lowest bidder for a project, the client has come to expect good performance from your company and wants to award the contract to you. To be awarded the contract, the client asks you to eliminate your project management costs. The client says your company has good project processes, and project controls unnecessarily inflate your costs. What should you do under these circumstances?

    A. Eliminate your project management costs, and rely on experience.
    B. Remove costs associated with project team communications, meetings, and customer reviews.
    C. Remove meeting costs but not the project manager's salary.
    D. Describe the costs incurred on past projects that did not use project management.

18. You are the project manager for one part of a new program in your organization. Four months into a three-year project, your project team has already made some significant discoveries that have led to vastly improved performance and efficiencies on your project. What is the best thing to do?

    A. Make certain the discoveries are included in the final project lessons learned.
    B. Make certain the discoveries are reported in the monthly status report.
    C. Make certain you mention the discoveries at the senior management meeting in two months.
    D. Make certain you tell the other project managers involved in this program about the discoveries at the weekly meeting.

19. You just discovered an error in the implementation plan that will prevent you from meeting a milestone date. Up to this point, your project has been running true to its baselines, and you will be delivering a routine status report tomorrow. The milestone in question is not on the critical path, but it is on a near-critical path. What is the best thing you can do?

    A. Develop options to meet the milestone date.
    B. Change the milestone date.
    C. Remove any discussion about dates in the project status report.
    D. Educate the team about the need to meet milestones.

20. While testing the strength of concrete poured on your project, you discover that over 35 percent of the concrete does not meet your company's quality standards. You are certain, however, that the concrete will function as it is, and you don't think the concrete needs to meet the quality level specified. What should you do?

    A. Change the quality standards to meet the level achieved.
    B. State in your reports that the concrete simply "meets our quality needs."
    C. Ensure the remaining concrete meets the standard.
    D. Report the lower quality level, and try to find a solution.

21. You are the project manager for a new international project, and your project team includes people from four countries. Most of the team members have not worked on similar projects before, but the project has strong support from senior management. What is the best thing to do to ensure that cultural differences do not interfere with the project?

    A. Spend a little more time creating the work breakdown structure and making sure it is complete.
    B. Make sure you choose your words carefully whenever you communicate.
    C. Ask one person at each team meeting to describe something unique about their culture.
    D. Keep communication short and to the point.

612

22. You are negotiating with a seller for a piece of equipment on a project with a tight budget. The seller has told you the equipment price is fixed. Your manager has told you to negotiate the cost with the seller. Your assessment is that the piece of equipment has been offered at inflated pricing. What is your best course of action?

    A. Make a good faith effort to find a way to decrease the cost.
    B. Postpone negotiations until you can convince your manager to change his mind.
    C. Hold the negotiations, but only negotiate other aspects of the project.
    D. Cancel the negotiations.

23. A PMP-certified project manager is contacted by PMI and asked to provide information regarding a team member, who is also a personal friend. The PMP-certified project manager cannot think of a reason he would be contacted by PMI about this individual unless someone had reported that this team member has been involved in unethical activities. The PMP-certified project manager has information that would likely support the accusations. He is thinking that the best thing to do is to not respond to avoid the risk that what he says could hurt his friend. This way he is not responsible for confirming or denying the accusations. Is this the right thing to do?

    A. Yes. It is acceptable to just ignore the request and stay out of it.
    B. No. He is required by PMI's Code of Ethics and Professional Conduct to cooperate.
    C. No. It would be better to deny the charges against his friend to maintain the relationship.
    D. Yes. It is best if project managers support each other in the field.

24. A project manager discovers a defect in a deliverable that is due to the customer under contract today. The project manager knows the customer does not have the technical understanding to notice the defect. The deliverable meets the contract requirements, but it does not meet the project manager's quality standard. What should the project manager do in this situation?

    A. Issue the deliverable, and get formal acceptance from the customer.
    B. Note the problem in the lessons learned so future projects do not encounter the same problem.
    C. Discuss the issue with the customer.
    D. Inform the customer that the deliverable will be late.

25. Your company wants to open a plant in a country where the law stipulates that women can earn only 50 percent of what men earn. Under these circumstances, what should you recommend to your company?

    A. Do not open the plant.
    B. Meet with government officials and try to get a waiver that equalizes the pay rate between men and women.
    C. Do not hire women.
    D. Provide the women you hire with extra work to increase their salary.

© 2018 RMC Publications, Inc.™ • 952.846.4484 • info@rmcls.com • www.rmcls.com

26. Three students from another country are working as interns on a project. The project manager has arranged for some games to be played as team-building activities to help develop a stronger sense of team with the group members. At the event where the activities are taking place, the three students refuse to participate, claiming the behavior involved is unacceptable in their country and that they would be very uncomfortable participating. What should the project manager do?

   A. He should tell the students they need to become familiar with how things are done in this country and they must participate.

   B. He should excuse the students from participating and arrange to discuss with them alternative team-building activities they would be more comfortable with.

   C. He should report the students to their functional manager and request they be removed from the project since their attitude will have a negative impact on the project.

   D. He should tell the students they are excused from the activities and to not attend any team-building activities in the future.

27. You are finalizing the monthly project status report due now to your manager when you discover that several project team members are not reporting actual hours spent on project activities. This results in skewed project statistics. What is the most appropriate action to take?

   A. Discuss the impacts of these actions with team members.

   B. Report the team members' actions to their functional managers.

   C. Continue reporting information as presented to you.

   D. Provide accurate and truthful representations in all project reports.

© 2018 RMC Publications, Inc.™ • 952.846.4484 • info@rmcls.com • www.rmcls.com

## Answers

1. **Answer** C

   **Explanation** This project will likely involve many issues that the project manager has not had experience with. It is unethical to overtly or indirectly mislead the sponsor about his qualifications. On the other hand, the project manager may have so many skills that would benefit the project that his lack of experience with global teams might not be a major problem. The project manager must make sure the sponsor is aware of his skills, as well as the gaps in his qualifications, so the sponsor has the correct information on which to base a decision.

2. **Answer** B

   **Explanation** Although things may be gloomy, this is not a new development, since the report was based on old data. It is unethical for the project manager not to admit his mistake, or to blame someone else for his error. The ethical thing to do is to acknowledge and take responsibility for the error.

3. **Answer** A

   **Explanation** It is the responsibility of the project manager to report unethical behavior to management and the affected project managers. Not reporting this knowledge to the appropriate people is unethical.

4. **Answer** A

   **Explanation** Putting the payment in an escrow account or burying the cost hides it. Ignoring the payment is not an option. Project managers must deal with potentially unethical situations like the situation described. This payment must be brought to the attention of the project manager's manager.

5. **Answer** A

   **Explanation** Ask yourself, what is the root problem? Your first action should be to find out whether working with family members is a common practice in that country, as there is nothing inherently illegal in this activity. Then, review qualifications. You may find it is not necessary to ask the project leader to provide additional names, or to consider using a different project leader.

6. **Answer** D

   **Explanation** Not mentioning the issue to the team member is withdrawal. Notifying the PMO or the team member's manager would not be appropriate until you learn the root cause of the problem. Always look for the choice that deals with and solves the problem. In this case, the best course of action is to address your concern with the team member directly.

7. **Answer** A

   **Explanation** Allowing the team member to deliver the inaccurate report would penalize and embarrass her. The only choice that does not involve hurting the team member's morale or wasting the time of the other attendees is to cancel the meeting and reschedule when you and the team member have identified and addressed the root cause of the problem with the report.

8. **Answer** A

   **Explanation** We assume that proper project management was followed and your opinion was considered during project initiating and planning. Therefore, you need to provide the work as approved by management.

9. **Answer** C

   **Explanation** This is a legitimate fee for special accommodations. It is therefore not a bribe.

10. **Answer** D

    **Explanation** Postponing the negotiations is the most ethical choice and demonstrates good faith. Why spend time in negotiations if it may be wasted time?

615

11. **Answer** B

    **Explanation**  It is not possible to turn the project back to the previous project manager—the previous project manager may have left the company or she may be busy with new projects. That is a form of withdrawal. Moving ahead without addressing the situation also withdraws from the problem, and withdrawal is not the best choice. There are two problems described here: the project is behind schedule, and the sponsor does not know it. There seem to be two possible right answers: restructuring the schedule, and reporting the situation to the sponsor. You should work to get the project on schedule. However, looking only at restructuring the schedule excludes other possibilities, such as cutting scope, which might more effectively deal with the schedule problem. You do not know if the project completion date is critical. What if the sponsor would agree to change the due date? The best choice in this situation is to inform the sponsor of the revised completion time estimate, and discuss options.

12. **Answer** B

    **Explanation**  Professional and social responsibility includes looking after the customer's best interests. Therefore, ignoring the newly available upgrade cannot be best. In this case, the schedule and scope are already approved, and all changes must go through the integrated change control process. Implementing the change on any of the sites without following the process is not acceptable. The best option is to inform the customer of the available upgrade, and explain the impacts to the project's timeline and functionality if the upgrade is implemented.

13. **Answer** D

    **Explanation**  You should deal with the problem by discussing it with the other project manager. You can then find out if the other project really is on schedule and thereby confirm or deny your information. Meeting with the program manager or with your manager would be the next step if meeting with the other project manager does not satisfactorily resolve the issue. You might also develop a risk response plan to deal with the risk to your project. First, though, you need to meet with the other project manager regarding those late deliverables.

14. **Answer** C

    **Explanation**  This is a common problem on projects. If your estimates are accurate, you are ethically bound to stand by them. Management's only option to cut cost is to support the project manager in looking for alternatives related to all project constraints.

15. **Answer** B

    **Explanation**  Attempting to keep the required people on your project puts your interests over those of your company, so it cannot be the best choice. There is no indication the labor dispute has caused any problems, so there is no need to cancel this work or to cease doing business with the company. The best choice would be to inform others in your company about the labor dispute.

16. **Answer** B

    **Explanation**  The project manager is neither empowered nor competent to determine the legality of company procedures. The other choices all represent responsibilities of the project manager.

17. **Answer** D

    **Explanation**  Describing the costs incurred due to project management processes not being used on past projects addresses the real problem by giving the client information they may not have. An alternate choice is to explain that project management and its associated costs are reasons for the company's past performance and success. Project management activities are not optional.

18. **Answer** D

    **Explanation** The sooner such discoveries are made known to other project managers, the sooner you can improve the capabilities of colleagues in your company. It is part of a project manager's professional and social responsibility to build such capabilities. After you've updated the other project managers, you can then document the discoveries in the project lessons learned and the status report, especially if that report has a wider distribution.

19. **Answer** A

    **Explanation** Educating the team on the importance of milestones is not addressing the real problem. Changing the milestone date is unethical. Avoiding mention of the due date in the status report violates the rule to report honestly. Only developing and reporting options to meet the milestone date solves the problem.

20. **Answer** D

    **Explanation** Changing the quality standards or stating that the concrete "meets our quality needs" would be unethical. Ensuring that the remaining concrete meets the existing quality standards withdraws from the problem and is therefore not the best solution. The only possible choice is to report the lower quality level. That choice would involve quality and other experts to find a resolution.

21. **Answer** C

    **Explanation** Since this is an issue involving everyone, everyone should be involved in the solution. Spending extra time with the team on creating the WBS is generally a good idea, but it does not specifically address cultural issues. The best choice is to ask one person at each team meeting to describe something unique about their culture. This will lead to better understanding among people of different cultures, and help to avoid potential culture-related problems.

22. **Answer** A

    **Explanation** The best choice is to attempt to find a way to decrease the cost.

23. **Answer** B

    **Explanation** Ignoring the request from PMI and lying for the project manager do not support PMI's request for information and are unethical actions. PMI's Code of Ethics and Professional Conduct requires PMP-certified project managers to report unethical behavior and violations of the code. The PMP-certified project manager is obligated to cooperate with PMI in collecting information.

24. **Answer** C

    **Explanation** Issuing the deliverable with the defect does not protect the best interests of the customer. Simply noting the issue in lessons learned does not solve the problem. Informing the customer that the deliverable will be late will cause a default of contract. Although the deliverable meets the contractual requirements, it is best to bring the problem to the customer's attention so an option that does no harm can be found.

25. **Answer** A

    **Explanation** Working under these rules would be a clear violation of the fundamental right to nondiscriminating treatment. You should recommend that your company not open the plant in that location.

617

26. **Answer** B

    **Explanation** Insisting that the team members participate is forcing them to do something that is unacceptable in their culture. Requesting their removal from the project penalizes the team members for expressing their cultural preferences, which is not a valid reason to remove them. Excluding them from all future team building does not show respect for their culture, and would have a negative impact on the project. Excusing them from playing, and discussing alternative activities for the whole team with which they would be more comfortable is best because it demonstrates respect for cultural differences.

27. **Answer** D

    **Explanation** The project manager's responsibility is to provide truthful project information. You should then discuss the impacts of the team members' actions with the team members. If that does not work, the next step is to report the team members' behavior to their functional managers. In the meantime, the project manager must report the status as accurately as possible.

© 2018 RMC Publications, Inc.™ • 952.846.4484 • info@rmcls.com • www.rmcls.com

# Tips for Passing the PMP Exam the First Time

FIFTEEN

Are you worried you might fail the exam? It is natural to be worried, but here is something that may help increase your confidence: RMC has spent years counseling people who have failed the exam, and in this book, we have addressed all the reasons they failed. This chapter serves as a review of some of the key things you need to understand as you prepare for the exam. Take this opportunity to find any remaining gaps in your knowledge so you are prepared to pass the exam on your first try.

## Putting It All Together

Many people preparing for the exam study each topic individually and never put it all together. Rita's Process Chart™ is one trick designed to help you connect the concepts in this book. If you worked through the exercises in chapter 3, you should understand the overall project management process, including all the efforts involved in it. If you skimmed over these exercises, go back and spend time on them. In this chapter, we provide some additional information and exercises to help you put all the concepts together.

Certain themes appear throughout the *PMBOK® Guide*. There are also some terms that are repeated throughout most of the knowledge areas. We covered many of these in chapter 2. These are not necessarily the most important topics to know, but understanding them will help you see how each concept relates to the overall project management process. And because these concepts appear so often in the *PMBOK® Guide*, they may also frequently appear on the exam. Hopefully you also use them regularly as you manage projects in the real world.

Over the next several pages, we discuss some of the frequently occurring terms you need to understand for the exam.

**Organizational Process Assets**   How many times have you seen the term "organizational process assets" in this book? Do you understand what it really means? Organizational process assets are an organization's existing processes, procedures, and historical data that influence the way a project is managed. With this definition in mind, can you see why organizational process assets are inputs to many of the individual project management processes from initiating to closing?

Remember that "organizational process assets" is a PMI-ism, and they can be considered inputs to most processes even when they are not specifically listed in this book or in the *PMBOK® Guide*. Similarly, updates to the historical databases are outputs of many processes. These updates can provide valuable records, lessons learned, and other information for future projects.

619

### Enterprise Environmental Factors
Enterprise environmental factors are also frequent inputs to project management processes. Think of enterprise environmental factors as a company's culture and existing systems that the project will have to deal with or can make use of. Enterprise environmental factors are outside the control of the team and may originate from within the organization or from external sources. Enterprise environmental factors could include the culture, mission, and values of the organization, as well as governance factors external to the organization.

Remember that "enterprise environmental factors" is a PMI-ism. Like organizational process assets, enterprise environmental factors can be considered inputs even when they are not specifically listed in this book or in the *PMBOK® Guide*. Updates to enterprise environmental factors are outputs of many processes as well—providing valuable historical data regarding the company's culture or systems for the benefit of future projects.

### Management Plans for Each Knowledge Area
Planning is a key step in addressing the knowledge areas of scope, schedule, cost, quality, resource, communications, risk, procurement, and stakeholder management. Creating a management plan for each of these knowledge areas, plus plans for change, configuration, and requirements, is a crucial part of a project manager's job. These plans become part of the project management plan. They are vital tools that empower team members to take responsibility for their actions, work, and participation. In creating these plans, the project manager proactively thinks through not just how the project should be planned, but also how the work of executing, monitoring and controlling, and closing should be carried out. These plans provide direction for the project manager and team. And because the plans will address the majority of questions and concerns that might come up, they allow the project manager and team to spend more of their time completing the work of the project and less time dealing with problems. Unless stated otherwise, assume on the exam that the project manager has created a management plan for each knowledge area.

### Project Management Plan
The project management plan is described in the Integration Management chapter and discussed throughout this book. This plan contains the blueprint for the project. It is an input to many planning, executing, and monitoring and controlling processes, as well as the Close Project or Phase process. Work is compared against the plan to ensure that the correct work is being accomplished. Because the plan is the blueprint for the project, it is maintained throughout the project, and it is updated when there are changes. Therefore, project management plan updates are an output of most of the executing and monitoring and controlling processes, as well as some planning processes. (See the "Project Management Plan Updates and Project Documents Updates" section later in this chapter for more on this topic).

### Baselines
Baselines help the project manager control the project. This is an important concept for the exam. The knowledge areas of scope, schedule, and cost have baselines, which combine to create the performance measurement baseline for the project. How well the project is performing in terms of scope, schedule, and cost is determined by comparing performance measurements against these baselines. Change requests that affect the baselines must be approved in the Perform Integrated Change Control process before the baselines can be changed.

### Work Performance Data, Information, and Reports
The terms work performance data, work performance information, and work performance reports differentiate the various stages of project data and information. Work performance data is made up of the initial measurements and details gathered during project work (executing). When work performance data has been analyzed for conformance to the project management plan during the controlling processes, it becomes work performance

information. This information can then be organized into work performance reports, which are distributed to the various stakeholders who need to receive and possibly act on the information.

## Expert Judgment

Expert judgment, a frequently used tool of project management, refers to the knowledge and experience of someone who has done the types of things necessary to complete the work for the project. Although it is not often discussed in this book, expert judgment is used throughout the project in every process group, including every integration management process. Expert judgment is particularly valuable in planning a project and is a tool and technique for most of the individual planning processes.

## Project Management Plan Updates and Project Documents Updates

Updates to the project management plan and project documents are frequent outputs of the project management processes across planning, executing, and monitoring and controlling. Updates to the project management plan may include updates to any of the plan's components.

Project documentation is updated to reflect adjustments, actions, and changes. In planning, updates include iterations of the plan and knowledge gained as planning processes are followed. In executing and monitoring and controlling, project documents are updated with work performance data and information. These updates ensure everyone has a common understanding of the project as it progresses. They also allow the project manager to reliably use documentation to measure and control the project.

Project documents, including the requirements traceability matrix, stakeholder register, activity list, quality checklists, risk register, change log, resource calendars, and issue log, are updated throughout the project.

## Change Requests

Change requests include recommended corrective and preventive actions and defect repair. They are outputs of some planning processes, most of the executing processes, and all the monitoring and controlling processes except Perform Integrated Change Control. Change requests are inputs to Perform Integrated Change Control, where they are reviewed. The approved change requests (outputs of Perform Integrated Change Control) are inputs to Direct and Manage Project Work and Control Procurements, where the changes are implemented. In Control Quality, the approved changes are verified to make sure that they return the intended results.

## Understanding Inputs and Outputs

What about other inputs and outputs? Many people who have not had good project management training stress over memorizing the inputs and outputs.

First, let's review the definitions of inputs and outputs.

An input means:

> *"What do I need before I can . . ."*

An output means:

> *"What will I have when I am done with . . ."*

> Or,

> *"What am I trying to achieve when I am doing . . ."*

Do you realize how many inputs and outputs there are, and how much time you could spend focusing on memorization? Since the exam will test your ability to apply knowledge, such memorization would waste your valuable time, and it will not benefit you in the real world. If you know Rita's Process Chart™ and understand project management and the actions that occur in each of the knowledge area processes, you

621

can use logic to identify most of the key inputs and outputs that appear on the exam, rather than relying on memorization. For example, if you know what a WBS is, you should understand that you need information about scope and requirements to create the WBS. Therefore, the project scope statement and requirements documentation are key inputs. If you understand the integrated change control process, you should know that it results in changes to project documents and components of the project management plan affected by approved changes.

The following exercises will give you some additional help with inputs and outputs.

**Exercise**   The following are some of the project management processes for which you should know the inputs and outputs. Use logic and your understanding of the process to complete the following. Enter the inputs and outputs for each process, including any real-world inputs and outputs that you can think of that are not in the *PMBOK® Guide*. When you are finished, check your answers with the *PMBOK® Guide* and the rest of this book.

| Project Management Process | Key Inputs | Key Outputs |
|---|---|---|
| Close Project or Phase | | |
| Sequence Activities | | |
| Develop Project Management Plan | | |
| Plan Procurement Management | | |
| Collect Requirements | | |

| Project Management Process | Key Inputs | Key Outputs |
|---|---|---|
| Define Activities | | |
| Estimate Activity Resources | | |
| Direct and Manage Project Work | | |
| Define Scope | | |
| Identify Stakeholders | | |
| Develop Schedule | | |
| Validate Scope | | |
| Monitor Risks | | |

| Project Management Process | Key Inputs | Key Outputs |
|---|---|---|
| Manage Stakeholder Engagement | | |
| Conduct Procurements | | |

If you found this exercise helpful, you may want to continue to test yourself on other processes not listed here.

## Exercise
Here is another way to get more familiar with the project management processes. For each process listed, fill in the appropriate information in the columns that follow. Note that the last two columns are asking which process comes before or after *within* the knowledge area.

| Project Management Process | Knowledge Area | Process Group | What Does It Include? | What Knowledge Area Process Comes Before? | What Knowledge Area Process Comes After? |
|---|---|---|---|---|---|
| Define Activities | | | | | |
| Plan Procurement Management | | | | | |
| Monitor and Control Project Work | | | | | |

| Project Management Process | Knowledge Area | Process Group | What Does It Include? | What Knowledge Area Process Comes Before? | What Knowledge Area Process Comes After? |
|---|---|---|---|---|---|
| Sequence Activities | | | | | |
| Collect Requirements | | | | | |
| Direct and Manage Project Work | | | | | |
| Develop Project Management Plan | | | | | |
| Develop Schedule | | | | | |
| Validate Scope | | | | | |
| Perform Qualitative Risk Analysis | | | | | |
| Identify Stakeholders | | | | | |

| Project Management Process | Knowledge Area | Process Group | What Does It Include? | What Knowledge Area Process Comes Before? | What Knowledge Area Process Comes After? |
|---|---|---|---|---|---|
| Conduct Procurements | | | | | |
| Define Scope | | | | | |
| Perform Integrated Change Control | | | | | |

**Answer**  The answers to this exercise provide the essence of the actions required, but note that you could add the words "Whatever needs to be done as part of" to the start of each answer in the "What Does It Include?" column. These descriptions are meant to hint at all the soft, interpersonal skills activity required, as well as the project management and technical activity needed.

| Project Management Process | Knowledge Area | Process Group | What Does It Include? | What Knowledge Area Process Comes Before? | What Knowledge Area Process Comes After? |
|---|---|---|---|---|---|
| Define Activities | Schedule management | Planning | Creating an activity list from each work package | Plan Schedule Management | Sequence Activities |
| Plan Procurement Management | Procurement management | Planning | Creating the procurement statements of work, bid documents, and the procurement management plan | None | Conduct Procurements |
| Monitor and Control Project Work | Integration management | Monitoring and controlling | Measuring and analyzing performance against the project management plan and baselines | Manage Project Knowledge | Perform Integrated Change Control |

626

| Project Management Process | Knowledge Area | Process Group | What Does It Include? | What Knowledge Area Process Comes Before? | What Knowledge Area Process Comes After? |
|---|---|---|---|---|---|
| Sequence Activities | Schedule management | Planning | Creating a network diagram | Define Activities | Estimate Activity Durations |
| Collect Requirements | Scope management | Planning | Documenting detailed requirements and creating the requirements traceability matrix | Plan Scope Management | Define Scope |
| Direct and Manage Project Work | Integration management | Executing | Facilitating and producing work according to the project management plan | Develop Project Management Plan | Manage Project Knowledge |
| Develop Project Management Plan | Integration management | Planning | Integrating all the individual management plans and baselines, and creating a project management plan that is bought into, approved, realistic, and formal | Develop Project Charter | Direct and Manage Project Work |
| Develop Schedule | Schedule management | Planning | Creating a bought into, approved, realistic, and formal schedule and schedule baseline | Estimate Activity Durations | Control Schedule |
| Validate Scope | Scope management | Monitoring and controlling | Meeting with the customer to gain formal acceptance of interim deliverables | Create WBS | Control Scope |
| Perform Qualitative Risk Analysis | Risk management | Planning | Analyzing the probability and impact of potential risks to determine which risks might warrant a response or further analysis | Identify Risks | Perform Quantitative Risk Analysis (don't forget, however, that some projects, or individual project risks, may skip this process and go straight to Plan Risk Responses) |

627

© 2018 RMC Publications, Inc.™ • 952.846.4484 • info@rmcls.com • www.rmcls.com

| Project Management Process | Knowledge Area | Process Group | What Does It Include? | What Knowledge Area Process Comes Before? | What Knowledge Area Process Comes After? |
|---|---|---|---|---|---|
| Identify Stakeholders | Stakeholder management | Initiating | Identifying, documenting, and analyzing information about stakeholders on the project | None | Plan Stakeholder Engagement |
| Conduct Procurements | Procurement management | Executing | Selecting a seller and obtaining a signed contract | Plan Procurement Management | Control Procurements |
| Define Scope | Scope management | Planning | Creating the project scope statement | Collect Requirements | Create WBS |
| Perform Integrated Change Control | Integration management | Monitoring and controlling | Evaluating the impact of requested changes to the project and approving or rejecting change requests | Monitor and Control Project Work | Close Project or Phase |

If you found this exercise helpful, you may want to continue to test yourself on other processes not listed here, and review your answers against the process descriptions in this book.

## Formulas to Know for the Exam

Although we do not suggest you memorize a lot of information to prepare for the exam, the following formulas are ones you do need to memorize, as well as understand. The exam will not include a lot of questions involving formulas, but knowing these formulas will enable you to apply them at a moment's notice. If you are not comfortable with math, you will be happy to hear that you can know none of these formulas and still pass the exam! The most important formulas are those relating to earned value because earned value is a key component of monitoring and controlling.

### Formulas to Know for the Exam

| Name | Formula | PMP® Exam Prep Chapter Reference |
|---|---|---|
| Present value (PV) | $\dfrac{FV}{(1 + r)^n}$ | Integration Management |
| Expected activity duration (triangular distribution)* | $\dfrac{P + M + O}{3}$ | Schedule Management |
| Expected activity duration (beta distribution)* | $\dfrac{P + 4M + O}{6}$ | Schedule Management |
| Total float | LS − ES or LF − EF | Schedule Management |
| Cost variance (CV) | EV − AC | Cost Management |
| Schedule variance (SV) | EV − PV | Cost Management |
| Cost performance index (CPI) | $\dfrac{EV}{AC}$ | Cost Management |
| Schedule performance index (SPI) | $\dfrac{EV}{PV}$ | Cost Management |
| Estimate at completion (EAC) | AC + Bottom-up ETC | Cost Management |
| Estimate at completion (EAC) | $\dfrac{BAC}{CPI^C}$ | Cost Management |
| Estimate at completion (EAC) | AC + (BAC − EV) | Cost Management |
| Estimate at completion (EAC) | $AC + \dfrac{(BAC - EV)}{(CPI^C \times SPI^C)}$ | Cost Management |
| To-complete performance index (TCPI) | $\dfrac{(BAC - EV)}{(BAC - AC)}$ | Cost Management |
| Estimate to complete (ETC) | EAC − AC | Cost Management |
| Variance at completion (VAC) | BAC − EAC | Cost Management |
| Communication channels | $\dfrac{n(n - 1)}{2}$ | Communications Management |
| Expected monetary value (EMV—Cost) | P × I | Risk Management |
| Expected value (EV—Schedule) | P × I | Risk Management |

*Remember that these formulas can be used for costs as well as activity durations.*

629

**TRICKS OF THE TRADE®** In the Cost Management chapter, we also highlighted some reverse formulas to help you calculate earned value (EV). With so many other formulas listed here, you may not want to memorize these (particularly if you understand the process for reversing the formulas), but they can be useful. They are EV = CV + AC, EV = SV + PV, EV = CPI × AC, and EV = SPI × PV.

## **TRICKS OF THE TRADE®** Before You Take the Exam

> If you purchased this book directly from RMC, you should have received tips about how to use the *PMBOK® Guide* along with this book to help you prepare for the exam.

Many people fail the exam because they did not properly prepare. You can avoid that mistake. Read the following tips slowly, and honestly assess how each item applies to you:

- Know the material thoroughly, but do not approach the exam assuming it simply tests facts that you must memorize. The exam tests knowledge, application, and analysis. You must understand how to use all concepts and processes in the real world, including how they work in combination with each other in the context of a large project.

- Have real-world experience using major project management tools and techniques. If you do not have this experience now, try to get it. If you cannot get this experience before you take the exam, make sure you can visualize how tools and processes would be used on real projects. This visualization will help you understand the benefits of using project management tools and techniques in the real world, and help you prepare for situational questions on the exam.

- As noted throughout this book, make sure you are thinking in terms of large, plan-driven projects when studying for and taking the actual exam. This will help you remember the importance of processes, tools, and techniques that you may not be using in your real-world project management.

- Understand the areas that PMI emphasizes (PMI-isms, explained in chapter 1 and throughout this book).

- Be familiar with the types of questions you can expect on the exam, but do not be alarmed if you see new types of questions when you take the exam.

- Be prepared to see situations on the exam that may be ambiguous and wordy—requiring you to read multiple paragraphs. Practice interpreting these types of questions using the practice exams or PM FASTrack® if you have it.

- If you have PM FASTrack®, practice using analysis to select the best answer from what appears to be two or more "right" answers. (See the next section for more information.)

- Decide in advance what notes you will write down at the beginning of your exam. This may include formulas or gaps in your project management knowledge. Practice creating this "download sheet" before taking the exam. (See the next section for more information.)

- Deal with stress before you take the exam. If you are a nervous test taker, using PM FASTrack® can give you an opportunity to practice stress control.

- Plan and use a strategy for taking the exam. This may mean you will take a five- to ten-minute break after every 50 questions, or that you will answer all exam questions as quickly as possible and then take a break before you review, and potentially adjust, your answers.

- Expect that there will be questions you cannot answer or even understand. This happens to everyone. Be prepared so you do not get anxious or doubt your abilities during the exam.

- Visit the exam site before your exam date to determine how long it will take to get there, see what the testing room looks like, and learn how you will access any food or beverages that you may bring to the testing center. This is particularly helpful if you are a nervous test taker.

- Do not expect the exam site to be quiet. A student from one of RMC's PMP® Exam Prep courses had to deal with a band playing outside the testing center for three hours. Others have had someone taking an exam that required intensive typing, and thus more noise, right next to them. Many testing sites will have earplugs or headphones available. If you have PM FASTrack®, practice answering questions in an environment that is not 100 percent quiet.

- Do not overstudy. Getting completely comfortable with all the material in this book is just not possible. It is not worth studying for hundreds of hours. It is a waste of time and will not guarantee you'll pass the exam.

- Do not study the night before you're scheduled to take the exam. Instead, do something relaxing and get extra sleep. You want to be fresh and well rested.

## TRICKS OF THE TRADE® Tricks for Taking and Passing the PMP Exam

This book has presented what you should do and know before you take the exam. Now, let's prepare you for the big day. The following are some tips for taking—and passing—the exam.

1. You must bring your authorization (email or letter) from PMI to the test site, as well as two forms of ID with exactly the same name you entered on the exam application.

2. Make sure you are comfortable during the exam. Wear layered clothing so you can remove outer layers if you become too warm. (Note, however, that some testing centers may require you to store any layers of clothing removed during the exam outside the exam room.)

3. Bring something to eat and drink in case you need either during the exam. You will not be able to take food or beverages into the exam room, but you will be able to access your things outside the exam room. You do not want to be distracted by being hungry.

4. You will be given paper and pencils to make notes during the exam. The type, size, and amount of paper varies based on each testing center. Some locations may instead provide a marker and erasable board or laminated paper. Note that the testing center will require you to exchange your used paper if you need more during the exam.

5. After you start your exam, consider taking no more than five to seven minutes of your test time to create your "download sheet," which is where you write down anything you have trouble remembering. It will free up your mind to handle exam questions once the information you are most concerned about is written down.

6. After you are shown to your assigned space in the testing center, you'll typically have two computer tutorials (general testing center and PMP test–specific) to complete prior to the start of the exam. This will help you become familiar with the computer-based test functionality. You need to start and complete those tutorials within their allotted time. Then you can start your four-hour exam.

7. You will have access to a calculator during the exam. With computer-based testing, the computer will have a calculator function and the tutorial will show you how to use it, or you may be given a physical calculator. Contact the testing center ahead of time if you have a question about this.

8. The exam does not adapt to your answers. This means 200 questions are selected when your exam starts, and those 200 questions will not change.

9. Use deep-breathing techniques to help you relax and focus. This is particularly helpful if you are very nervous before or during the exam and when you notice yourself reading the same question two or three times. Breathing techniques can be as simple as breathing deeply five times, to provide more oxygen to your brain.

10. Smile when taking the exam. This may sound hard to do when you are stressed and taking an exam for four hours, but studies show that smiling relieves stress and makes you feel more confident.

631

11. Use all the exam time. Do not submit your exam early unless you have reviewed every question you skipped or marked for review.

12. Everyone has their own unique test-taking quirks and style. If you have PM FASTrack®, pay attention to your quirks while you work through the exam simulations. You may have to create a plan to ensure your style will not negatively impact you while taking the exam.

13. Control the exam; do not let it control you. How would you feel if you read the first question and didn't know the answer? And then the same thing happened after you read the second and third questions as well? This can happen because you are just not ready to answer questions and your level of stress is not allowing you to think. So what do you do? If you do not immediately know the answer to a question, leave it blank, or use the Mark for Review function and come back to it later.

14. Control frustration, and maintain focus on each question. You might dislike or disagree with some of the questions on this exam. You might also be surprised at how many questions you mark for review. Make sure you stay focused on the current question. If you are still thinking about question 20 when you reach question 120, there will have been 100 questions that you have not looked at closely enough.

15. Answer each question using your knowledge of project management good practices, not the perspective you have acquired from your real-world or life experiences. Many people who failed the exam tried to answer questions from their real-world experience. Since these people did not use good practices of project management on their projects, they got many questions wrong on the exam. If approaching it from the perspective of project management good practices does not give you an answer, rely on your training. If this still does not help you answer the question, only then should you rely on your real-world experience.

16. Computer-based testing allows you to highlight information that you think is relevant to answering the question and strike through things that are distractors, or less important, to solving the problem or situation. If you use these features as you read the situation and the answers, you are more likely to have to read a question only once.

17. First, identify the actual question in the words provided (it is often the last sentence), and then read the rest of the text. Note the topics discussed in the question and in the descriptors. This should help you understand what the question is asking and reduce the need to reread questions.

18. Carefully consider each answer choice listed, and choose the best one of the choices given. Don't read into the answers.

19. One common reason people answer questions incorrectly is they do not read all four answer choices. Do not make this mistake. Make sure you read the question and all four choices. This will help you select the best answer. If you find yourself forgetting to read all answer options, start reading the choices backwards (choice D first, then C, etc.).

20. There may be more than one "correct" answer to each question, but only one "best" answer. Make sure you are looking for the best answer.

21. Be alert to the fact that the answer to one question is sometimes given away in another question. Write down things you do not understand as you take the exam (also note the question number so you can easily go back to it). Use any extra time at the end of the exam to go back to these questions.

22. Almost all the answer choices will be the same length for each question. Therefore, do not follow the old "rule" that the longest answer is likely to be the right one.

23. There will be answer choices that are meant to distract you from the correct answer. These are plausible choices that less knowledgeable people will pick. Such choices make it appear as though some questions have two or more right answers. To many people, it seems as though there are only shades of difference between the choices. As noted earlier, make sure you look for the best answer for such questions, and think about the situation in terms of project management good practices.

24. Be aware that questions may also include irrelevant information, to distract you from the real problem in the situation being described.

632

25. Look for words and phrases such as "still," "yet," "first", "last," "next," "except," "not," "most likely," "less likely," "primary," "initial," and "most." Make certain you clearly read the question, and take note of these words so you will answer the question correctly.

26. Watch for choices that are true statements but do not answer the question.

27. Watch for choices that contain common project management errors. They are intentionally there to determine if you really know project management. You can combat this by looking for errors in your knowledge and correcting those errors as you go through this book. (See the "Common Project Management Errors and Pitfalls" section at the end of this chapter.)

28. Options that represent broad, sweeping generalizations tend to be incorrect, so be alert for words such as "always," "never," "must," "completely," "all," and so forth. Alternatively, choices that represent carefully qualified statements tend to be correct, so be alert for words such as "often," "sometimes," "perhaps," "may," and "generally."

29. You may see some poorly worded or grammatically incorrect questions or answer choices on the exam; don't let this distract you.

30. Look for answers that support the value of project management with underlying messages such as, "Hooray for project management!"; "The project manager is so important"; or "The WBS is so useful." They are generally the correct choice.

The exam will not be scored until you indicate you are ready, or four hours are up. You will also be asked if you are certain you want to score your exam after you submit it. You will receive a printed summary of your test results. If you pass, the testing center will print out a certificate, and you will officially be certified. If you do not pass, PMI will send you information on retaking the exam. You will have to pay an additional fee to retake the exam.

## Tricks to Keep in Mind

Are you ready for some very important tricks to keep in mind when you take the exam? Pay careful attention.

A major reason people get questions wrong on the exam is that they do not do or realize the following:

- Recognize that "rules" (what we think should be best) are meant to be broken. Rules, such as what to do when there is a conflict, can change depending on the situation. This drives some people crazy—especially those who expect the exam to just test facts. You need to be able to read and understand the situations on the exam and then be able to figure out the best thing to do *in that situation*. Most of the questions are situational.

- Unless stated otherwise, assume proper project management was done. For example, assume there is a charter, a WBS, and management plans on the projects described on the exam, even if the question does not say so. If you answer a question thinking about real-world projects that do not use proper project management, you might miss the correct answer. If the question makes it clear that proper project management has not been done, you'll likely need to think about what is missing, how to solve the root cause of the problem, and how to make sure proper project management is carried out going forward on the project.

- When reading a scenario question, notice which part of the project it is occurring in. If the situation described in the question is taking place during project planning, your answer may be different than if it was occurring during project executing.

- Be prepared for questions with multiple problems. A question may describe a situation with various problems and ask you to determine which one to address first. Here is an example:

  *Two stakeholders are disagreeing via a series of emails as to whether a deliverable meets the acceptance criteria. The cost-benefit analysis done in planning did not support delivering a higher level of performance, and the stakeholders agreed. A team member has just informed you that a problem with his work has occurred. The deliverable he is working on must be shipped today or there will be a project breach. One of the stakeholders having the email disagreement comes to you to complain about the other. What should you do?*

The following tips will help you focus on the most important problem in order to select the best answer. It is important to note that all these tips will not apply all the time, and they do not have an order of importance.

- Determine the immediate problem to address.
- Deal with the root cause first.
- Deal with the problem with the greatest negative impact first.
- Solve the problem that occurred the earliest.
- Look for a proactive solution.

## Common Project Management Errors and Pitfalls

As mentioned at other points in this book, the exam often includes common errors in project management as possible answers. Read the following summary of some of the major errors even highly experienced project managers make, and make sure you understand why these are errors.

Common project management errors include the following:

- Focusing primarily on asking for percent complete
- Holding "go around the room" status meetings
- Spending most of your time micromanaging team members by constantly checking on them
- Asking team members to cut 10 percent off their estimates
- Thinking a bar (Gantt) chart from scheduling software is a project management plan
- Not attempting to obtain finalized requirements
- Not getting real resource commitments
- Not having a rewards and recognition system
- Not focusing on quality
- Not having a change control system
- Not having management plans
- Not measuring against the project management plan
- Not creating metrics to measure and evaluate performance
- Not spending time finding and eliminating root causes of problems or deviations
- Not implementing corrective actions to keep the project in line with the project management plan
- Not reevaluating the effectiveness of the project management plan
- Not reevaluating the accuracy or completeness of scope, schedule, or cost
- Not keeping the project management plan and project documents updated to reflect changes and revised information about the project
- Ignoring resource managers' responsibilities to manage ongoing business operations in addition to responding to project needs (team and physical resources).
- Not realizing the project can affect the reputation of team members

- Not realizing the project manager has resource responsibilities; these can include responsibilities to the project team (such as creating project job descriptions, evaluating individual and team performance on the project, and adding letters of recommendation to team members' human resource files) as well as responsibilities related to physical resources
- Blaming unrealistic schedules on management instead of realizing that developing a realistic schedule is the project manager's responsibility

## A Day-in-the-Life Exercise

The following exercise provides one last opportunity to test yourself to see if you really understand what a project manager does.

**Exercise** Many people do not practice the breadth of project management good practices described in the *PMBOK® Guide* on their real-world projects. This may be because they have not received the training needed or because they do not understand the project management process or its value. A lack of experience in using these practices to properly manage large projects can have a significant impact on how you perform on the exam. This exercise is designed to help you uncover what you might be doing incorrectly on your projects so differences between your real-world experience and the world of project management good practices do not get in your way on the exam. In the following table, list which activities a project manager should spend the most, medium, and least amount of time on during a typical day after planning is complete and the team has begun working on the project.

| Most | Medium | Least |
|------|--------|-------|
|      |        |       |
|      |        |       |
|      |        |       |
|      |        |       |
|      |        |       |
|      |        |       |
|      |        |       |
|      |        |       |
|      |        |       |

© 2018 RMC Publications, Inc.™ • 952.846.4484 • info@rmcls.com • www.rmcls.com

**Answer**   There are a number of correct answers to this question. Let's first review what should not be on your "Most" list, and then we will look at what efforts a project manager should focus on during the course of a day. Think through the items listed here, and identify whether you have any misconceptions about what you should be doing as a project manager. If you do, you need to clarify and fix these misconceptions before you take the exam.

Items that should not be on your "Most" list:

- Dealing with problems and unexpected changes (rather than preventing them)
- Schedule and other items related to schedule management
- Meetings
- Micromanaging
- Completing work activities

The following items should have been included in your "Most" list:

- Using project management tools, such as a charter, WBS, and project management plan
- Measuring
- Recommending and taking corrective and preventive actions
- Doing risk management and implementing risk responses
- Coaching, mentoring, and team building
- Communicating and using active listening
- Managing by exception to the plan
- Interacting with stakeholders to maintain and improve stakeholder engagement
- Looking for possible changes

# Conclusion

You have reached the end of this book! Congratulations!

As noted in chapter 1, we recommend that you review the information in this book several times to really retain what you learned. So read through this book again, focusing on the areas where you have identified gaps in your knowledge. In a second pass through this book you will find that you understand some topics differently than you did the first time, and other concepts will stand out to you that you previously missed. In particular, make sure you review the PMI-isms in chapter 1, the most commonly used tools and techniques in chapter 2, and Rita's Process Chart™ and the project management process exercises in chapter 3. Having a solid understanding of the project management process and the material presented in this book will not only help you pass the exam (you can use logic instead of having to memorize information), it will also enable you to apply what you have learned to your real-world projects.

Thank you for taking this journey with us. We hope you will come back to RMC Learning Solutions after you have earned your PMP. We can help you continue your training and earn PDUs to maintain your certification through our advanced instructor-led and eLearning courses and products. So good luck, and we look forward to seeing you after you pass the exam!

# Endnotes

The following notes provide the historical background of many of the terms in this book. You do not need to know this information for the exam. It is simply provided for your interest and reference.

## CHAPTER TWO

1. **Business case**  This term has been in wide use for decades; business cases were being written and studied in the 1920s as part of the scientific management movement. They became popular in the 1950s after the Harvard Business School began using them as a teaching method. [Michael Davis, *Ethics and the University* (New York: Routledge, 1999), 145.]

2. **Benefits management plan**  The benefits management plan was introduced in the 1990s in the United Kingdom. The concept spread to the United States in the early 2000s. [Roland Munro and Jan Mouritsen, *Accountability: Power, Ethos and the Technologies of Managing* (Stamford, CT: International Thomson Business Press, 1996), 133.]

3. **Project management office**  The development of departments within organizations to manage projects dates back to the beginning of project management as a discipline. [Frank Parth, Cynthia Snyder, and Cynthia Stackpole, *Introduction to IT Project Management* (Vienna, VA: Management Concepts, 2007), 22.]

4. **Organizational project management**  The concept of organizational project management began in the information technology sector in the 1980s; within a decade it had become widely popular throughout management science. [British Standards Institution, *Use of Network Techniques in Project Management: Guide to the Use of Graphical and Estimating Techniques* (London: British Standards Institution, 1984), 1.]

5. **Matrix**  These categories were defined in 1971 by Jay R. Galbraith to help organizations improve their management efficiency. [Jay R. Galbraith, "Matrix Organization Designs: How to Combine Functional and Project Forms," *Business Horizons* 14, no. 1 (1971): 29–40.]

6. **Project expediter**  The concept of the project expediter was developed in the Soviet Union to help projects get through the tangle of Soviet bureaucracy. [Karl W. Ryavec, *Soviet Society and the Communist Party* (Amherst: University of Massachusetts Press, 1978), 54.]

7. **Organizational knowledge repository**  The concept of the organizational knowledge repository was created by J. M. An and fellow researchers in 1992, as they began work on early search engines. The idea was quickly adopted and was common in knowledge management research by the end of the decade. [J.M. An, R.G. Hung, and G.L. Sanders, "The Role of Domain Coverage and Consensus in a Network of Learning and Problem Solving Systems," in *Proceedings of the Twenty-Fifth Hawaii International Conference on System Sciences* (Los Alamitos, CA: IEEE Computer Society Press, 1992), 443.]

8. **Lessons learned repository**  The organization of formal systems to integrate experience into corporate management is a fairly recent development. J. G. March and J. P. Olsen published a paper in 1975 that became the basis for "organizational learning." The concept of the lessons learned repository was developed by the US military to build on this as part of its 1985 overhaul of contracting standards; it was disseminated into wider management practice in the 1990s. [Department of Defense, *Military Standard Specification Practices* (Washington, DC: U.S. Department of Defense, 1985).]

# Endnotes

9. **Constraints** Dr. Martin Barnes was the first to describe what he called the "iron triangle" of time, cost, and output in his course "Time and Money in Contract Control" in 1969, laying the foundations for what has become known as the "triple constraint" (schedule, cost, and scope constraints). [Patrick Weaver, "The Origins of Modern Project Management" (lecture, Fourth Annual PMI College of Scheduling Conference, Vancouver, Canada, April 15–17, 2007).]

10. **Stakeholder** The first use of the word "stakeholder" in management literature was in 1963 in an international memorandum at the Stanford Research Institute. [Robert Y. Cavana and Arun A. Elias, "Stakeholder Analysis for Systems Thinking and Modelling." Paper presented at ORSNZ, Wellington, New Zealand, December 2000.]

11. **Stakeholder management** The concept of stakeholders became central to management in 1984, when R. Edward Freeman published his book *Strategic Management: A Stakeholder Approach*. [Robert Y. Cavana and Arun A. Elias, "Stakeholder Analysis for Systems Thinking and Modelling." Paper presented at ORSNZ, Wellington, New Zealand, December 2000.]

## CHAPTER THREE

1. **Project life cycle** Dr. Russell Archibald, a founder of PMI, was one of the theorists who refined the concept of the project life cycle. [R. Max Wideman, *The Role of the Project Life Cycle (Life Span) in Project Management* (Vancouver: AEW Services, 2004), 2.]

2. **Development life cycle** The concept of the development life cycle originated in US military contracting during the Vietnam War, influenced by the lessons learned by NASA during the space race of the 1950s and 1960s. It spread quickly into IT and general management in the 1970s. [Gerald R. Holsclaw, "Integrated Logistic Support—The Life-Cycle Task of Support Management," *Defense Industry Bulletin* 4, no. 2 (June 1968): 11.]

3. **Phase gate** The phase gate concept is derived from the "stage gate" system developed by Robert G. Cooper in the late 1980s, which underlies most modern waterfall deployment models. [Robert G. Cooper, "Stage-Gate Systems: A New Tool for Managing New Products," *Business Horizons* 33, no. 3 (May–June 1990): 44.]

4. **Progressive elaboration** The term "progressive elaboration" has been present in medical science since the nineteenth century, and was widely popularized during the twentieth century in a variety of contexts. Its use in management science dates to the 1980s, when it evolved from the iterative nature of computer science. [D.K. Hitchins, "Managing System Creation," *IEE Proceedings-A* 133, no. 6 (September 1986): 343.]

5. **Rolling wave planning** This process was refined by Gregory Githens and J. Rodney Turner in the 1990s to improve the balance of flexibility and structured process in project management. [J. Rodney Turner, *The Handbook of Project-Based Management*, 3rd ed. (New York: McGraw-Hill, 2008), 56.]

## CHAPTER FOUR

1. **Integration management** The concept of "systems integration management" arose from the highly technical management requirements of post–World War Two engineering projects. By the end of the 1960s, integration management was a common term in project management. [Society of Automotive Engineers, "Jet Plane Costs Need Not Skyrocket with Performance," *SAE Journal*, August 1953: 66.]

2. **Benefit measurement methods** Benefit measurement first evolved as a cost-benefit analysis method. After a series of studies on productivity improvements and information technology in the 1990s, it became an important project management tool. [Sonia Mountain, "New Corporate Systems: Adding Value or Keeping with the Times?" Paper presented at the ATEM NZ Conference, Wellington, New Zealand, 1994, 9.]

3. **Murder board**   The idea of a "murder board" came out of US military staff planning during World War II when major actions, ideas, and strategies were relentlessly grilled by a murder board. After the war, the concept moved out of military colleges and into corporate management. [Earl Burton, *By Sea and by Land: The Story of Our Amphibious Forces* (New York: McGraw-Hill, 1944), 47.]

4. **Constrained optimization methods**   Constrained optimization as a pure mathematical technique dates back to the eighteenth-century French mathematician Lagrange. In the 1920s, students of the economist Alfred Marshall began applying optimization techniques to economic planning. The use of constrained optimization in project management has evolved from these techniques. [William Lazonick, *Business Organization and the Myth of the Market Economy* (Cambridge, MA: Cambridge University Press, 1991), 292.]

5. **Present value, net present value, internal rate of return, payback period, cost-benefit analysis, opportunity cost, sunk costs, depreciation**   These key terms are borrowed from accounting and economics. The investment of time and money in a project should be reviewed as carefully as the investment of time or money in any business venture. [Colin Haslam and Alan Neale, *Economics in a Business Context* (London: Thomson, 2000).]

6. **Economic value added (EVA)**   This term was coined by Thomas B. McMullen in 1997 as a new label for earlier work by Eliyahu M. Goldratt. [Thomas B. McMullen, *Introduction to the Theory of Constraints (ToC) Management System* (Boca Raton, FL: CRC Press, 1998).]

7. **Law of diminishing returns**   This is one of the fundamental principles of modern economics, developed by David Ricardo and Thomas Malthus in 1815. It has been applied to many fields of social science in the two centuries since its discovery. [Mark Skousen, *The Making of Modern Economics: The Lives and Ideas of the Great Thinkers* (Armonk, NY: M.E. Sharpe, 2001), 100.]

8. **Project charter**   While the concept of the project charter is very old, it was refined as part of the Six Sigma methodology. [Penelope Przekop, *Six Sigma for Business Excellence* (New York: McGraw-Hill, 2003), 61.]

9. **Assumption log**   The assumption log is a new practice in project management. [John Murdoch et al, "Measuring Safety: Applying PSM to the System Safety Domain," *Proceedings of the 8th Australian Workshop on Safety Critical Systems* 33 (2003): 50.]

10. **Project management plan**   The integration of various project management techniques into a formal process began in the 1950s with projects coordinated for the US Department of Defense by the RAND Corporation and Booz Allen Hamilton. [Lauren Keller Johnson, Richard Luecke, and Robert Daniel Austin, *The Essentials of Project Management* (Boston: Harvard Business School, 2006), xv.]

11. **Baseline**   The use of the baseline as a statistical tool dates to the nineteenth century. The word has been redefined in the context of management science, although it still generally refers to measurement using numerical or statistical methods. [Harold Kerzner, *Project Management: A Systems Approach to Planning, Scheduling and Controlling* (Hoboken, NJ: Wiley, 2001), 1014.]

12. **Configuration management system**   Configuration management was first developed in the 1950s by NASA. The technique was then borrowed by the US Department of Defense, before it was refined by private corporations in the 1960s. It was originally intended to manage large, complex projects, such as the design and launch of rockets. [Frank B. Watts, *Engineering Documentation Control Handbook* (Norwich, NY: William Andrew, 2000), 10.]

13. **Work authorization system**   The concept of a refined work authorization system evolved from the PERT methodology of the 1960s and quickly spread from the US federal government to private corporations. [Gregory A. Garrett and Rene G. Rendon, *U.S. Military Program Management: Lessons Learned and Best Practices* (Vienna, VA: Management Concepts, 2007), 133.]

# Endnotes

14. **Defect repair**  Defect repair has been a management term for decades. [Barbara M. Bouldin, *Agents of Change: Managing the Introduction of Automated Tools* (Old Tappan, NJ: Pearson Education, 1988).]

15. **Integrated change control processes**  The concept of integrated change control was refined at NASA, where an Integrated Change Control Board was organized in the late 1970s. [Gale Research Company, *Acronyms, Initialisms and Abbreviations Dictionary* (Farmington Hills, MI: Gale Research Company, 1980), 1512.]

16. **Change control board**  The change control board was an important part of the change control process from its earliest days in the 1970s. [John A. Burgess, *Design Assurance for Engineers and Managers* (Boca Raton, FL: CRC Press, 1984), 96.]

## CHAPTER FIVE

1. **Requirements elicitation**  This term became widely popular in the field of information science during the 1980s and quickly assumed an important role in project management. [Rudy A. Hirschheim, *Information Systems Development as Social Action: Theory and Practice* (Oxford: Oxford Institute of Information Management, 1987), 2.]

2. **Work breakdown structure (WBS)**  The work breakdown structure was developed as part of the PERT methodology, although it was not mentioned by name in the 1959 paper that introduced PERT. The term was in widespread use by 1961. [Gregory T. Haugan, *The Work Breakdown Structure in Government Contracting* (Vienna, VA: Management Concepts, 2003), 8.]

3. **Multicriteria decision analysis**  This was popularized as a management concept in the 1980s. [Milan Zeleny, *MCDM: Past Decade and Future Trends: A Source Book of Multiple Criteria Decision Making* (Greenwich, CT: JAI Press, 1984).]

4. **Affinity diagrams**  Affinity diagrams were devised as part of the total quality management method in the 1970s. [Shigeru Mizuno, *Management for Quality Improvement: The Seven New QC Tools* (New York: Productivity Press, 1988).]

5. **Mind maps**  While similar techniques have been used for centuries, the modern mind-mapping technique was developed by British consultant Tony Buzan. Buzan first conceived of the mind map in the 1970s and has continually refined the technique. [Tony Buzan, *How to Mind Map* (New York: Thorsons, 2002).]

6. **Nominal group technique**  This technique was invented by researchers Andre Delbecq and Andrew Van de Ven in 1971 to overcome the hesitation some participants might feel in a face-to-face meeting. [Charles M. Judd and Harry T. Reis, *Handbook of Research Methods in Social and Personality Psychology* (Cambridge, MA: Cambridge University Press, 2000), 181.]

7. **Context diagrams**  Context diagrams began as a tool for structured analysis management in the 1970s. [Tom DeMarco, *Structured Analysis and System Specification* (New York: Yourdon, 1978).]

8. **Requirements traceability matrix**  The requirements traceability matrix was developed in the software industry and was adopted as standard procedure by the US Department of Defense in 1988. [Deborah A. Cerino, Judith A. Clapp, and Wendy W. Peng, *Software Quality Control, Error Analysis, and Testing* (Park Ridge, NJ: Noyes Data Corporation, 1995), 45.]

9. **Project scope statement**  The concept of the project scope statement is very old, but the term itself originated in IT projects of the 1970s. [Maurice Blackman, *The Design of Real Time Applications* (Hoboken, NJ: Wiley, 1975), 236.]

10. **Control account**  This concept was developed as part of the work breakdown structure; it has been part of the PERT methodology since 1959. [Gregory T. Haugan, *The Work Breakdown Structure in Government Contracting* (Vienna, VA: Management Concepts, 2003).]

11. **Scope creep**    This term was coined by the military during the Vietnam War, but it did not become widely popular until the 1990s. [U.S. House of Representatives, *Military Construction Appropriations for 1973* (Washington, D.C.: U.S. Government Printing Office, 1973), 315.]

12. **Decomposition, deconstruction**    These terms were developed as part of the work breakdown structure; they have been part of the PERT methodology since 1959. [Gregory T. Haugan, *The Work Breakdown Structure in Government Contracting* (Vienna, VA: Management Concepts, 2003).]

## CHAPTER SIX

1. **Rolling wave planning**    See note 1 for chapter 3.

2. **Network diagrams**    The network diagram was developed in the 1950s as part of the PERT methodology. [Robert T. Futrell, Donald F. Shafer, and Linda Shafer, *Quality Software Project Management* (Upper Saddle River, NJ: Prentice Hall PTR, 2002), 501.]

3. **Arrow diagramming method (ADM)**    James E. Kelley and Morgan Walker began devising the algorithms that became the Activity-on-Arrow scheduling method in 1956 and 1957 for E. I. du Pont de Nemours. [Patrick Weaver, "A Brief History of Scheduling: Back to the Future" (lecture, Canberra, Australia, April 4–6, 2006).]

4. **GERT**    The GERT method was developed by Alan Pritzker in 1966 for the RAND Corporation to improve the scheduling of work. [Peter W. G. Morris, *The Management of Projects* (London: Telford, 1994), 79.]

5. **Precedence diagramming method**    The precedence diagramming method was developed in 1961 by Dr. John Fondahl as an alternative to the critical path method. [Patrick Weaver, "The Origins of Modern Project Management" (lecture, Fourth Annual PMI College of Scheduling Conference, Vancouver, Canada, April 15–17, 2007).]

6. **Mandatory, discretionary, external dependency**    The use of these terms in project management dates to the 1980s, when they were popularized as part of the Six Sigma methodology. [Mathematical Sciences Education Board and National Research Council, *Reshaping School Mathematics: A Philosophy and Framework for Curriculum* (Washington, DC: National Academies Press, 1990), 34.]

7. **Lessons learned register**    While the general concept of "lessons learned" is centuries old, the lessons learned register is a recent innovation that did not begin appearing regularly in management literature until the first decade of the twenty-first century. [Jonathan Paul Scopes, "London 2012: A New Approach to CDM Coordination," *Proceedings of the Institution of Civil Engineering* 162, no. 2 (May 2009).]

8. **Resource breakdown structure**    This concept is related to the work breakdown structure; like that concept, it was also developed as part of the PERT methodology. [Gregory T. Haugan, *The Work Breakdown Structure in Government Contracting* (Vienna, VA: Management Concepts, 2003), 8.]

9. **Analogous estimating**    This type of top-down estimation is ancient. The term itself derives from mathematical theory, and its use in project management dates to the 1990s. [American Mathematical Society, *20 Lectures Delivered at the International Congress of Mathematicians* (Providence, RI: American Mathematical Society, 1974), 111.]

10. **Regression analysis**    Regression analysis was first developed by the British scientist Sir Francis Galton as part of his research into human heredity in 1886. [Michael Patrick Allen, *Understanding Regression Analysis* (New York: Plenum Press, 1997), 2.]

11. **Heuristics**    Heuristics are as old as human language. Modern computer-assisted heuristics can be traced to the work of information theorist Claude Shannon in the 1950s. [Bruce Abramson, *Digital Phoenix: Why the Information Economy Collapsed and How It Will Rise Again* (Cambridge, MA: MIT Press, 2005), 86.]

# Endnotes

12. **Three-point estimating**  Three-point estimating is part of the PERT methodology. [Christopher D. McKenna, *The World's Newest Profession: Management Consulting in the Twentieth Century* (New York: Cambridge University Press, 2006), 294.]

13. **Beta distribution**  This is a statistical term associated with the PERT process. [Rodney D. Stewart, Richard M. Wyskida, and James D. Johannes, *Cost Estimator's Reference Manual* (New York: Wiley, 1995).]

14. **PERT**  The concept of PERT was developed in 1957 by a team from the US Navy Special Projects Office, Bureau of Ordinance, and the consulting firm Booz Allen Hamilton. [Patrick Weaver, "A Brief History of Scheduling: Back to the Future" (lecture, myPrimavera06, Canberra, Australia, April 4–6, 2006).]

15. **Standard deviation (SD)**  The term "standard deviation" was invented in 1893 by the mathematician Karl Pearson, although the technique had been used by earlier mathematicians, such as Gauss. [Theodore M. Porter, *Karl Pearson: The Scientific Life in a Statistical Age* (Princeton, NJ: Princeton University Press, 2004), 237.]

16. **Contingency reserve and management reserve**  These concepts have been part of financial planning for decades; Samuel Paul suggested integrating reserve analysis techniques into project management in 1982. [Peter W. G. Morris, *The Management of Projects* (London: Telford, 1994), 18.]

17. **Schedule model**  This concept was developed by the RAND Corporation in the 1960s and popularized in management theory over the next few years. [William J. Abernathy et al., *A Three-Stage Manpower Planning and Schedule Model* (Stanford, CA: Stanford University Press, 1972).]

18. **Critical path method**  The critical path method was developed in 1956 when E. I. du Pont de Nemours was trying to find a use for its UNIVAC computer. James E. Kelley and Morgan Walker presented the critical path method to the public at a conference in 1959. [Patrick Weaver, "A Brief History of Scheduling: Back to the Future" (lecture, myPrimavera06, Canberra, Australia, April 4–6, 2006).]

19. **Near-critical path**  This concept was developed as part of the critical path method. [Patrick Weaver, "A Brief History of Scheduling: Back to the Future" (lecture, myPrimavera06, Canberra, Australia, April 4–6, 2006).]

20. **Float**  The concept of float is part of the critical path methodology. [Rocco Martino, *Project Management* (Springfield, MO: Management Development Institute, 1968), xiii.]

21. **Schedule compression**  Schedule compression and the terms "fast tracking" and "crashing" are part of the critical path methodology. [Charles Heath and James L. Riggs, *Guide to Cost Reduction Through Critical Path Scheduling* (Englewood Cliffs, NJ: Prentice Hall, 1966), 118.]

22. **Crashing**  This informal engineering term was popularized in management theory in the 1980s. [American Society of Civil Engineers, *Proceedings of the Second Conference on Computing in Civil Engineering* (Reston, VA: American Society of Civil Engineers), 1980.]

23. **Monte Carlo analysis**  The Monte Carlo method was first used in 1930 by Enrico Fermi to calculate the properties of the neutron. It was also used by scientists working on the Manhattan Project during World War II; the development of the electronic computer allowed the Monte Carlo method to be refined in the 1950s. [Jeffrey Seth Rosenthal, *Struck By Lightning: The Curious World of Probabilities* (Washington, DC: Joseph Henry Press, 2006), 186.]

24. **Resource optimization**  This is an engineering term that entered management theory in the early twentieth century. [Frank K. Schenck, *Application of Time Study to Foundry Operations* (Flemington, NJ: Foran Foundry, 1955).]

25. **Resource leveling**   This concept was first used in the construction industry; it rapidly spread to other areas of management science in the 1980s. [Thomas J. Driscoll, Stephen B. Hurlbut, and Jon M. Wickwire, *Construction Scheduling: Preparation, Liabilities, and Claims* (New York: Aspen Publishers, 2003), 423.]

26. **Resource smoothing**   This concept is taken from the critical path management method. [Paul Barnetson, *Critical Path Planning: Present and Future Techniques* (London: Newnes Books, 1968).]

27. **Milestone charts**   Milestone charts were developed in the 1940s. [Patrick Weaver, "The Origins of Modern Project Management" (lecture, Fourth Annual PMI College of Scheduling Conference, Vancouver, Canada, April 15–17, 2007).]

28. **Bar charts**   The bar chart was first developed by Karol Adamiecki in 1896; it was popularized and refined during the 1910s by management consultant Henry Gantt. [Peter W. G. Morris, *The Management of Projects* (London: Telford, 1994), 18.]

## CHAPTER SEVEN

1. **Life cycle costing**   The modern conception of life cycle costing can be traced to 1965, when the Logistics Management Institute published a document outlining the basics of the concept. [B. S. Dhillon, *Medical Device Reliability and Associated Areas* (Boca Raton, FL: CRC Press, 2000), 172.]

2. **Value analysis**   Value analysis was first developed by L. D. Miles, a researcher for General Electric, in 1947. He was trying to develop a new method to scientifically predict the best way to reduce costs while improving the value of projects. [D. H. Stamatis, *TQM Engineering Handbook* (Boca Raton, FL: CRC Press, 1997), 306.]

3. **Cost risk**   First developed in the 1970s, cost-risk analysis seeks to estimate exact cost figures for risks, mainly by using Monte Carlo simulations. [John Bartlett et al., *Project Risk Analysis and Management Guide* (High Wycombe, UK: APM, 2004), 163.]

4. **Bottom-up estimating**   This is an old practice, but time-consuming. Parametric estimating was developed to solve some of the difficulties with bottom-up estimating. [John C. Goodpasture, *Quantitative Methods in Project Management* (Boca Raton, FL: J. Ross, 2004), 89.]

5. **Rough order of magnitude (ROM) estimate**   This type of estimating has been around for a long time, although the title is fairly new. The RAND Corporation developed parametric estimating to refine their ROM estimates. [RAND Corporation, *The Rand Paper Series* (Santa Monica, CA: RAND Corporation, 1988), 17.]

6. **Funding limit reconciliation**   This term was recently invented. However, the process it describes—checking costs against the project's budget—has been a part of project management since its beginning. [U.S. Department of Defense, *Financial Management in the Department of Defense* (Washington, DC: U.S. Department of Defense, 1954), 21.]

7. **S-curve**   The application of the S-curve to corporate planning can be traced to B. Ryan and N. C. Gross at Iowa State University, who were projecting the adoption of corn varieties by farmers in 1943. [Hendrik Van den Berg and Joshua J. Lewer, *International Trade and Economic Growth* (Armonk, NY: M. E. Sharpe, 2007), 118.]

8. **Earned value measurement**   The earned value technique was developed by the US Department of Defense in the 1960s as an alternative to the PERT methodology. It began to spread into the corporate world in the 1980s. [Wayne F. Abba, "Earned Value Management: Reconciling Government and Commercial Practices," *PM Magazine*, January/February 1997, 58–63.]

9. **Cost performance index (CPI)**   This is a standard accounting term. Its use in project management is derived from US Department of Defense contracts of the 1950s. [Cecil Hamilton Chilton, ed., *Cost Engineering in the Process Industries* (New York: McGraw-Hill, 1960), 337.]

# Endnotes

## CHAPTER EIGHT

1. **Gold plating**   This term is commonplace in contracting; it was already the subject of criticism in a 1962 paper analyzing US defense contracts. [Peter W. G. Morris, *The Management of Projects* (London: Thomas Telford, 1997), 58.]

2. **Kaizen**   Masaaki Imai made the term *kaizen* famous in his 1986 book, *Kaizen: The Key to Japan's Competitive Success*. [Masaaki Imai, *Kaizen: The Key to Japan's Competitive Success* (New York: McGraw-Hill, 1986).]

3. **Total quality management (TQM)**   Ways to implement total quality management can be traced to quality gurus such as Philip B. Crosby, W. Edwards Deming, Armand V. Feigenbaum, Kaoru Ishikawa, and Joseph M. Juran. ["Total quality management (TQM)," ASQ Quality Glossary, s.v., accessed October 14, 2008, http://www.asq.org/glossary/t.html.]

4. **Six Sigma**   In the late 1980s, Mikel Harry, an engineer at Motorola, developed the concept of Six Sigma, which became a key method for doing business at Motorola. [George Eckes, *The Six Sigma Revolution: How General Electric and Others Turned Process Into Profits* (New York: Wiley, 2001), 5.]

5. **Just in time (JIT)**   JIT systems were refined by Japanese corporations during the 1980s, although the process may have originated from the observations of Taiicho Ohno, who studied the stocking systems of US supermarkets during the 1950s. [Ian Inkster, *The Japanese Industrial Economy: Late Development and Cultural Causation* (New York: Routledge, 2001), 106.]

6. **CISG**   This acronym stands for the United Nations Convention on Contracts for the International Sale of Goods, which is a treaty governing international trade. The CISG is in constant change, and the courts of many nations interpret it in different ways. Periodically, conventions have met to reconcile the differing interpretations. [Joseph M. Lookovsky, *Understanding the CISG in the USA.* (The Hague, Netherlands: Kluwer Law International, 2004), 34.]

7. **ISO 9000**   The ISO (International Organization for Standardization) introduced the ISO 9000 standards in 1987, just as the European Union (EU) was being formed. The adoption of ISO 9000 standards by the EU led to their widespread adoption throughout the world. [Paul A. Nee, *ISO 9000 in Construction* (Hoboken, NJ: Wiley, 1996), 5.]

8. **Benchmarking**   The modern benchmarking process originated at Xerox in the 1980s. Dr. Robert Camp was instrumental in developing and popularizing the benchmarking process. [James L. Heskett, W. Earl Sasser, and Leonard A. Schlesinger, *The Value Profit Chain: Treat Employees Like Customers and Customers Like Employees* (New York: Free Press, 2003), 103.]

9. **Cost-benefit analysis**   Cost-benefit analysis was fully developed as a technique by the US Army Corps of Engineers in the 1930s. The technique spread throughout the US federal government, and was integrated into corporate planning after World War II. [Michael Power, *Accounting and Science: Natural Inquiry and Commercial Reason* (Cambridge, MA: Cambridge University Press, 1996), 41.]

10. **Cost of quality (COQ)**   This concept was developed and refined in the 1980s as part of the Six Sigma methodology. [William Truscott, *Six Sigma: Continual Improvement for Businesses: A Practical Guide* (Boston, MA: Butterworth-Heinemann, 2003), 26.]

11. **Costs of conformance and noncomformance**   These concepts—like other concepts in this chapter, such as the cost of quality—were refined in the 1980s as part of the Six Sigma methodology. [William Truscott, *Six Sigma: Continual Improvement for Businesses: A Practical Guide* (Boston, MA: Butterworth-Heinemann, 2003), 26.]

12. **Marginal analysis**   Marginal analysis was used by early economists, such as David Ricardo, and revived as a theory in 1934 by economist Joan Robinson. [Kenneth Ewart Boulding and W. Allen Spivey, *Linear Programming and the Theory of the Firm* (New York: Macmillan, 1960), 2.]

13. **Matrix diagram**   This tool was popularized in the 1980s after decades of use. [Jack Stone, "Long-Range Planning: One Formula for Success," *Computerworld*, Oct. 20, 1980, 35.]

14. **Cause-and-effect diagram (fishbone diagram, Ishikawa diagram)**   The cause-and-effect diagram is sometimes referred to as the "Ishikawa diagram" because it was developed by Kaoru Ishikawa. ["Cause and Effect Diagram," ASQ Quality Glossary, s.v., accessed October 14, 2008, http://www.asq.org/glossary/c.html.]

15. **Histogram**   Although the word "histogram" was first coined in 1892, the earliest known histogram appeared in 1786. These tools were well-known and used throughout the nineteenth century. [Yannis Ioannidis, The *History of Histograms (abridged)* (Athens, Greece: University of Athens, 2003), 1.]

16. **Scatter diagram**   The scatter diagram, or scatter plot, was invented by Sir Francis Galton in 1908 as part of his research on human heredity. [A. Reza Hoshmand, *Design of Experiments for Agriculture and the Natural Sciences* (Boca Raton, FL: CRC Press, 2006), 269.]

17. **Design of experiments (DOE)**   Experimental design has been a central concern of scientists for centuries. The application of scientific methods to management problems was an important part of the revolution in management science after World War II. [Jiju Antony, *Design of Experiments for Engineers and Scientists* (Oxford: Butterworth-Heinemann, 2003), 29.]

18. **Process analysis**   While process analysis is an old concept, it has been refined as part of the Six Sigma methodology. [George Eckes, *Six Sigma for Everyone* (Hoboken, NJ: Wiley, 2003), 49.]

19. **Flowchart**   The flowchart was first invented by Frank Gilbreth in 1921 to better document processes and was quickly adopted throughout the management industry. It was refined during the 1940s by researchers at Procter & Gamble, as well as by Princeton's John von Neumann. [Mark R. Lehto and James R. Buck, *Introduction to Human Factors and Ergonomics for Engineers* (New York: Lawrence Erlbaum, 2008), 100.]

20. **Control chart**   Walter Shewhart came up with the idea of a production control chart in 1924. [Stuart Crainer, *The Management Century: A Critical Review of 20th Century Thought and Practice* (San Francisco: Jossey-Bass, 2000), 82.]

21. **Control limits**   Control limits are part of the control chart, invented by Walter Shewhart at Bell Labs in the 1920s. [W. Edwards Deming, *Out of the Crisis: Quality, Productivity, and Competitive Position* (Cambridge, MA: Cambridge University Press, 1986).]

22. **Specification limits**   Specification limits have been a standard statistical term for decades. [Society of Quality Control Engineers, *Industrial Quality Control*, vol. 17 (Buffalo, NY: Society of Quality Control Engineers, 1960).]

23. **Rule of seven**   This is a statistical rule of thumb—if seven runs of data produce results on the same side of the target value, then the mean is assumed to have changed. [Christopher Chatfield, *Statistics for Technology: A Course in Applied Statistics* (New York: Chapman and Hall, 1983), 301.]

24. **Assignable cause/special cause variation**   This concept was first developed in 1924 by the researcher Walter Shewhart. It was later refined in total quality management and Six Sigma. [William C. Johnson and Richard J. Chvala, *Total Quality in Marketing* (Delray Beach, FL: St. Lucie Press, 1996), 43.]

25. **Pareto chart**   The Pareto chart or diagram was defined in 1950 by Joseph M. Juran. It is based on the Pareto principle, which was named after the nineteenth-century economist Vilfredo Pareto. ["Pareto Chart," ASQ Quality Glossary, s.v., accessed October 14, 2008, http://www.asq.org/glossary/p.html.]

# Endnotes

## CHAPTER NINE

1. **Responsibility assignment matrix (RAM)**   The RAM was first developed by IT project managers in the 1970s; it spread into wider use over the next decade. [M. D. Wadsworth, *Electronic Data Processing Project Management Controls* (New York: Prentice Hall, 1972), 43.]

2. **RACI chart**   The RACI chart was invented and popularized in the 1990s. [Jeff R. Greenberg and J. R. Lakeland, *A Methodology for Developing and Deploying Internet and Intranet Solutions* (Upper Saddle River, NJ: Prentice Hall, 1998).]

3. **Organizational breakdown structure**   After the work breakdown structure became a common tool in industry during the 1980s, the organizational breakdown structure also became widespread. [Peter W. G. Morris, *The Management of Projects* (London: Telford, 1994), 264.]

4. **Resource breakdown structure**   See note 8 for chapter 6.

5. **Recognition and reward systems**   This term derives from the total quality management method. [Michael B. Weinstein, *Total Quality Safety Management and Auditing* (West Hartford, CT: CRC Press, 1997).]

6. **Halo effect**   This effect was first demonstrated with objective data in 1920 by Edward Thorndike, who was studying the ratings of officers in the US Army. Thorndike's findings were quickly applied to business. [Neil J. Salkind and Kristin Rasmussen, *Encyclopedia of Educational Psychology* (Thousand Oaks, CA: Sage, 2008), 458–59.]

7. **Motivation theory**   Modern motivation theory has its roots in the work of pioneering economists such as Adam Smith, who asserted that money was the root of all motivation. Twentieth-century psychologists began developing new concepts as part of modern management theory. [Patrick J. Montana and Bruce H. Charnov, *Management* (Happauge, NY: Barron's, 2000), 238.]

8. **McGregor's theory of X and Y**   Douglas McGregor introduced this theory in 1960. He hoped to persuade managers to trust their employees, and, therefore, to act according to Theory Y. [Donald Clark, "A Time Capsule of Training and Learning," accessed October 14, 2008, http://www.skagit-watershed.org/~donclark/hrd/history/xy.html.]

9. **Maslow's hierarchy of needs**   Abraham Maslow introduced this theory in his 1943 article "A Theory of Human Motivation." While later researchers have questioned Maslow's results, the hierarchy of needs has become accepted wisdom. [Christopher D. Green, "Classics in the History of Psychology," accessed April 16, 2013, http://psychclassics.yorku.ca/Maslow/motivation.htm.]

10. **McClelland's theory of needs**   David McClelland first developed this theory at Harvard in the 1960s as part of his research into political power and motivation theory. [Ellen Weisbord, Bruce H. Charnov, and Jonathan Lindsey, *Managing People in Today's Law Firm* (Westport, CT: Quorum Books, 1995), 35.]

11. **Herzberg's two-factor theory of motivation**   Frederick Herzberg refined this theory in a series of papers between 1959 and 1968. He hoped to help create a new kind of workplace based on employee satisfaction. [Robert B. Denhardt, Janet Vinzant Denhardt, and Maria Pilar Aristgueta, *Managing Human Behavior in Public and Nonprofit Organizations* (Thousand Oaks, CA: Sage, 2001), 150.]

12. **Forming, storming, norming, performing**   Psychologist Bruce Tuckman described the phases of team development as forming, storming, norming, and performing in 1965. He later added a final stage of adjourning, also referred to as mourning. ["Forming, Storming, Norming, and Performing: Helping New Teams Perform Effectively, Quickly," accessed April 16, 2013, http://www.mindtools.com/pages/article/newLDR_86.htm.]

13. **Colocation**   In this context, the term dates from the 1990s and the rise of telecommuting. [Donald Reinertsen, *Managing the Design Factory* (New York: Simon & Schuster, 1997).]

14. **Expectancy theory**  Expectancy theory was developed in 1964 by Victor Vroom of the Yale School of Management to explain the motivations of employees. [Ronald R. Sims, *Managing Organizational Behavior* (Westport, CT: Greenwood Press, 2002), 62.]

15. **Fringe benefits**  In 1942, the US War Labor Board approved employee benefits such as health insurance to allow employers to attract new employees. The term "fringe benefit," first used around this time, took several years to gain wide acceptance. [Nelson Lichtenstein, *Labor's War at Home: The CIO in World War II* (Cambridge, MA: Cambridge University Press, 1982), 240.]

## CHAPTER TEN

1. **Interactive, push, pull communication**  These categories have been used in communication theory for decades. More recently they have been popularized by the explosion of the internet and the replacement of early "pull" technologies, such as websites, with "push" technologies, such as RSS feeds and email updates. [National Association of Women Deans, Administrators and Counselors, *Journal of the National Association of Women Deans, Administrators and Counselors* (1958): 61.]

2. **Communication channels**  The literal meaning of this term quickly gave rise to a metaphorical use in psychological theory. By the end of the 1960s, this new usage was widespread. [Wiener, Morton, and Mehrabian, Albert. *Language Within Language: Immediacy, a Channel in Verbal Communication.* (New York: Appleton-Century-Crofts, 1968).]

3. **Communication blockers**  The term "communication blocker" first appeared in the 1990s in the therapeutic community. It was introduced to project management theory in the early 2000s. [Cornell Cooperative Extension, *Parent-Caregiver Partnerships: Communication Workshops for Parents and Child Care Providers.* (Ithaca, NY: Cornell University, 1992).]

4. **Trend report**  The concept of the trend report arose in the scientific management movement of the 1920s; it gained wide popularity in the 1930s because of the planning documents of the New Deal. [National Opinion Research Center, *Do Americans Support Gasoline Rationing? Trend Report Based on Eight Nation-wide Surveys.* (Denver, CO: University of Denver, 1943).]

5. **Forecasting report**  The concept of forecasting arose in the nineteenth century in the field of meteorology. It was applied to management by the scientific management movement of the 1920s. [*The Problems of Business Forecasting*, William Persons, ed. (Boston: Houghton Mifflin, 1924).]

6. **Variance report**  This is an accounting term; its use in project management dates to the 1970s. [Harold Kerzner, *Project Management: A Systems Approach to Planning, Scheduling, and Controlling* (New York: Van Nostrand Reinhold, 1979), 447.]

7. **Earned value report**  Earned value management techniques were first developed and used by the US government in the 1960s. [David I. Cleland and Lewis R. Ireland, *Project Manager's Portable Handbook* (New York: McGraw-Hill, 2004), 389.]

## CHAPTER ELEVEN

1. **Risk management**  The concept of risk management exploded out of the insurance industry to become nearly universal in management theory during the 1960s. [U.S. Department of Agriculture, *Farmers' Bulletin No. 2137: Insurance Facts for Farmers* (Washington, D.C.: U.S. Government Printing Office, 1967), 3.]

2. **Risk response**  This idea came into widespread use as the discipline of risk management moved from insurance to general management. [Lindon J. Robison and Garth Carman. "Aggregate Risk Response Models and Market Equilibrium," in *Risk Management in Agriculture: Behavioral, Managerial and Policy Issues* (Champaign, Ill.: University of Illinois Press, 1979), 139.]

# Endnotes

3. **Root cause analysis**   Root cause analysis was first developed in the 1950s by the US Department of Energy to investigate industrial (and specifically nuclear) accidents. The methodology was refined by the health-care field, and became popular in management science in the 1980s. [B. S. Dhillon, *Reliability Technology, Human Error, and Quality in Health Care* (Boca Raton, FL: CRC Press, 2008), 45.]

4. **Strengths, weaknesses, opportunities, and threats (SWOT) analysis**   SWOT analysis was developed by Albert Humphrey of Stanford University to improve long-range planning techniques. Humphrey and his colleagues introduced SWOT in 1964, and the first prototype project using SWOT was completed in 1973. [Regina Fazio Maruca, *The Way We Work: An Encyclopedia of Business Culture* (Westport, CT: Greenwood Press, 2008), 244.]

5. **Risk register**   The concept of the risk register began in the United Kingdom as a medical tool in the 1960s; it was later adopted as a project management tool. [Fred Grundy, *The New Public Health: An Introduction to Personal Health and the Welfare Services for Health Visitors, Social Workers and Midwives* (London: H. K. Lewis, 1968), 63.]

6. **Qualitative risk analysis**   In its simplest form—thinking carefully about the risks of any project—qualitative risk analysis is as old as civilization. In its modern sense, qualitative risk analysis and the related terms in this chapter have been developed over the last few decades; the term itself first appeared in the 1970s. [Tom Kendrick, *Identifying and Managing Project Risk: Essential Tools for Failure-Proofing Your Project* (New York: AMACOM, 2003), 165.]

7. **Probability and impact matrix**   This tool was devised by researcher D. C. Hague in 1984. [Sui Pheng Low, *Marketing Research in the Global Construction Industry* (Singapore: Singapore University Press, 1993).]

8. **Quantitative risk analysis**   As the concept of risk management moved from insurance to general management, the idea of quantitative risk management moved with it. [Mohammed Gahin, *A Theory of Pure Risk Management in the Business Firm.* (Madison, WI: University of Wisconsin Press, 1966), 214.]

9. **Sensitivity analysis**   Originally an engineering term, sensitivity analysis entered management theory in the 1960s. [Rajko Tomovic, *Sensitivity Analysis of Dynamic Systems* (New York: McGraw-Hill, 1963).]

10. **Tornado diagram**   Introduced in the 1980s, the tornado diagram became a popular management tool in the 1990s. [Robert M. Oliver and J. Q. Smith, *Influence Diagrams, Belief Nets, and Decision Analysis* (New York: Wiley, 1990).]

11. **Decision tree**   This concept is very old—an excellent early example is the system invented by Carl Linnaeus in the 1730s to classify species by kingdom, phylum, and class. [Michael J. A. Berry and Gordon Linoff, *Data Mining Techniques for Marketing, Sales, and Customer Relationship Management*, 2nd ed. (Indianapolis, IN: Wiley, 2004), 166.]

12. **Pure (insurable) risk**   This term was invented in Britain in the nineteenth century, as the first modern insurance companies were taking shape. [J. M. Ross, ed., *The Globe Encyclopaedia of Universal Information* (Edinburgh, UK: Grange, 1877), 507.]

13. **Residual risks**   Residual risk was defined as a business term during the scientific management movement after World War I. By 1922, it was familiar to many managers and business owners. [Fred Emerson Clark, *Principles of Marketing* (New York: Macmillan, 1922), 361.]

14. **Risk trigger**   This term was in general use by 1980. [United States House of Representatives, *Oversight Hearing on the Child Labor Provisions of the Fair Labor Standards Act* (Washington, DC: US General Printing Office, 1980).]

15. **Reserves (contingency)**   The concept of contingency reserve has been used in creating business and government budgets for over a century. It was popularized during the scientific management movement of the 1920s. [Actuarial Society of America, *Transactions* (New York: Actuarial Society of America, 1907), 109.]

16. **Risk thresholds**   The concept of a risk threshold became widely popular as a business term in the 1960s. It originated as a medical term and spread into business through engineering. [Max H. O'Connell, *Aircraft Noise* (Brooks City, TX: US Air Force School of Aerospace Medicine, 1960), 2.]

17. **Risk audits**   This concept was first used for managing serious problems such as epidemics and disasters. The concept spread in the 1990s to apply to project management. [Alan E. Boyle, *Environmental Regulation and Economic Growth* (Oxford: Oxford University Press, 1994), 42.]

## CHAPTER TWELVE

1. **Procurement management**   Procurement management as a discipline dates to the 1930s, when the federal government massively increased spending and began organizing a number of large, long-term projects. [Michael C. Loulakis, ed., *Design-Build for the Public Sector* (New York: Aspen, 2003), 61.]

2. **Bid and procurement documents**   These terms have been in general use since the 1930s, having originated in federal government contracts. The massive expansion of the federal government in the 1930s due to the Great Depression and the outbreak of World War II required the creation of new terms and processes to manage large contracts. [U.S. Interior Department, *Interior Department Appropriation Bill for 1940* (Washington, D.C.: U.S. Government Printing Office, 1940), 125.]

3. **RFP, IFB, RFQ**   These terms were first used in the nineteenth century. The US government pioneered procurement law, with the first such law in 1795. Corporations adopted many later refinements of procurement by the US federal government. [Margaret M. Worthington, Louis P. Goldsman, and Frank M. Alston, *Contracting with the Federal Government* (New York: Wiley, 1998), 1.]

4. **Make-or-buy analysis**   This process relies heavily on the research of consultant Michael Porter, who introduced analytical tools for make-or-buy analysis in the 1980s. [Chris Argyris, Derek F. Channon, and Cary L. Cooper, *The Concise Blackwell Encyclopedia of Management* (Malden, MA: Blackwell Business, 1998), 681.]

5. **Fixed-price, time and material, cost-reimbursable contracts**   Contract law has distinguished between these types of contracts for a long time—the term "fixed-price contract" appears in legal documents from 1845. These contract types were defined by the US government in the late nineteenth century to streamline military procurement. [US Office of the Federal Register, *Code of Federal Regulations* (Washington, DC: US National Archives, 1901), 15.]

6. **Fixed-price with economic price adjustment (FPEPA)**   Introduced in government contracting in the late 1980s, this term quickly entered use in private procurement in the 1990s. [John J. Marciniak, *Encyclopedia of Software Engineering*, vol. 1, *Acquisitions–Outsourcing* (New York: Wiley, 1994).]

7. **Target price, sharing ratio, ceiling price**   The use of these standard terms was popularized by the RFPs issued by the US government after World War II. [A. Michael Agapos, *Government-Industry and Defense: Economics and Administration* (Tuscaloosa, AL: University of Alabama Press, 1975), 164.]

8. **Sharing ratio**   See note 7.

9. **Ceiling price**   See note 7.

10. **Point of total assumption (PTA)**   The term "total assumption" has a long history, having been used in government contracts and debates since the nineteenth century. "Point of total assumption" is a newer term that was introduced by the US government. [John W. Langford, *Logistics: Principles and Applications* (New York: McGraw-Hill, 2007), 207.]

11. **Statement of work**  The first clearly defined statement of work in the modern sense was published in 1908 by the US government, which issued requirements for an airplane prototype to be purchased by the US Army. [Michael G. Martin, *Delivering Product Excellence with the Statement of Work* (Vienna, VA: Management Concepts, 2003), 4.]

12. **Source selection criteria**  This term entered government contracts in the 1960s and spread into private sector procurement in the 1970s. [Frederick M. Scherer, *The Weapons Acquisition Process: Economic Incentives* (Boston: Harvard University Press, 1964).]

13. **Bidder conferences**  These conferences became common after the concept was introduced at the 1959 conference of the American Society for Quality Control. [American Society for Quality Control, *National Convention Transactions, 1959* (Milwaukee, WI: American Society for Quality Control, 1959), 438.]

14. **Weighting system**  The concept of a weighting system has a long history in economics. The application of this term to project management, and specifically to contracting, is fairly recent. [Michael Greer, *The Project Manager's Partner: A Step-by-Step Guide to Project Management* (Amherst, MA: Human Resource Development Press, 2001), 108.]

15. **Contract change control system**  When the concept of change control was introduced in the 1970s, it was quickly adapted for use with contracts, since many of the companies that used change control for IT projects were also government contractors. [Philip A. Metzger, *Managing a Programming Project* (New York: Prentice-Hall, 1973), 84.]

## CHAPTER THIRTEEN

1. **Brainstorming/brain writing**  The term "brainstorm" was coined in the nineteenth century and first used as a verb in the 1920s. An ad agency in the 1930s was the first to hold a "brainstorming session," and the idea became a standard part of business management in the mid-1950s. [Metcalf, Allan and Barnhart, David K., *America in So Many Words: Words That Have Shaped America* (New York: Houghton Mifflin Harcourt, 1997), 221.]

2. **Power/interest grid**  Researchers Kevan Scholes and Gerry Johnson created the power/interest grid to help managers assess the engagement and strength of project stakeholders. [Gerry Johnson and Kevan Scholes, *Exploring Corporate Strategy*, 3rd ed. (New York: Prentice Hall, 1993), 184.]

3. **Stakeholder cube**  The concept of the power/interest grid quickly took hold in the 1990s and was expanded into the stakeholder cube to take into account a third variable, attitude. [*GIS Applications in Natural Resources 2* (New York: GIS World Books, 1996), 52.]

4. **Salience model**  Although the salience model has been used in the social sciences since the 1970s, the application of this model to project stakeholders was developed in 1997 by Mitchell, Agle, and Wood. [Ronald K. Mitchell, Bradley R. Agle and Donna J. Woo, "Toward a Theory of Stakeholder Identification and Salience: Defining the Principle of Who and What Really Counts," *The Academy of Management Review* 22, no. 4 (Oct. 1997): 853–86.]

5. **Stakeholder engagement assessment matrix**  The stakeholder engagement matrix was developed in 1991 by a team of researchers at the Academy of Management. [Grant T. Savage, Timothy W. Nix, Carlton J. Whitehead, and John D. Blair, "Strategies for Assessing and Managing Organizational Stakeholders," *The Executive* 5, no. 2 (May 1991): 61–75.]

## CHAPTER FOURTEEN

1. **Fair use doctrine**  This is a doctrine in US law that allows limited use of copyrighted materials. For more information, see the Fair Use web page maintained by the US Copyright Office: http://www.copyright.gov/fls/fl102.html.

2.  **Ethnocentricism**    The term was coined in 1906 by the American anthropologist William Graham Sumner. He argued that scientists had to recognize and see past ethnocentrism to effectively observe the world. Over the last century, the concept has been explored intensively. [James William Neuliep, *Intercultural Communication: A Contextual Approach* (Los Angeles: Sage, 2009), 183.]

3.  **Culture shock**    This term was coined by the anthropologist Kalervo Oberg to describe the disorientation of young anthropologists thrust into the new and often radically different cultures they studied. He first presented the term in a speech in 1954, and it became widely known after its re-publication in 1960. [Kalervo Oberg, "Cultural Shock: Adjustment to New Cultural Environments," *Practical Anthropology* 7 (1960): 177–82.]

# Index

# Index

# Index

# Index

© 2018 RMC Publications, Inc.™ • 952.846.4484 • info@rmcls.com • www.rmcls.com

# Index

# Index

# Index

# Index

# Notes

# Notes

670

# Notes

# Notes

# Notes